D0958217

WOMEN'S RIGHTS
IN THE MIDDLE EAST
AND NORTH AFRICA

WOMEN'S RIGHTS IN THE MIDDLE EAST AND NORTH AFRICA

❖

PROGRESS AMID RESISTANCE

Sanja Kelly
Julia Breslin
EDITORS

FREEDOM HOUSE
NEW YORK • WASHINGTON, D.C.

ROWMAN AND LITTLEFIELD PUBLISHERS, INC.
LANHAM • BOULDER • NEW YORK • TORONTO • PLYMOUTH, UK

Published by Rowman & Littlefield Publishers, Inc.
A wholly owned subsidiary of The Rowman & Littlefield Publishing Group, Inc.
4501 Forbes Boulevard, Suite 200, Lanham, Maryland 20706
http://www.rowmanlittlefield.com

Estover Road, Plymouth PL6 7PY, United Kingdom

Copyright © 2010 by Freedom House

All rights reserved. No part of this book may be reproduced in any form or by any
electronic or mechanical means, including information storage and retrieval systems,
without written permission from the publisher, except by a reviewer who may quote
passages in a review.

British Library Cataloguing in Publication Information Available

Library of Congress Cataloging-in-Publication Data

Women's rights in the Middle East and North Africa progress amid resistance / Sanja
    Kelly, Julia Breslin, editors.—2010 ed.
        p. cm.
    ISBN 978-1-4422-0395-2 (cloth : alk. paper)—ISBN 978-1-4422-0396-9 (pbk. : alk.
paper)— ISBN 978-1-4422-0397-6 (electronic)
    1. Women's rights—Middle East. 2. Women's rights—Africa, North. I. Kelly, Sanja.
II. Breslin, Julia, 1980-
HQ1236.5.M65W66 2010
305.4209172'4—dc22

                                                                2010014925

∞™ The paper used in this publication meets the minimum requirements of American
National Standard for Information Sciences—Permanence of Paper for Printed Library
Materials, ANSI/NISO Z39.48-1992.

Printed in the United States of America

CONTENTS

ACKNOWLEDGEMENTS

Completion of the *Women's Rights in the Middle East and North Africa* publication would not have been possible without the tireless efforts of the following people.

As managing editor, Sanja Kelly directed the research, editorial, and administrative operations for the survey. Together, she and Julia Breslin provided essential analysis, edited the country reports, and conducted field research in Bahrain, Egypt, Kuwait, Jordan, and the United Arab Emirates. Tyler Roylance copyedited the volume and provided critical editorial and analytical insight throughout.

General oversight was provided by Christopher Walker, Arch Puddington, and Jennifer Windsor. Helpful contributions and insights were made by the Middle East and North Africa team in Washington, D.C., including Katie Zoglin, Richard Eisendorf, Sherif Mansour, Marwan Maalouf, and Susan Kemp. Lama Khries, program director of the Freedom House Jordan office, Mohamed Abdel Aziz, Freedom House's country coordinator in Egypt, Ola Zoubi, a member of the Freedom House field team in Bahrain, and Nancy Sharp Nti Asare, director of the Freedom House Kuwait office, provided guidance and logistical aid while field research was conducted in Amman, Cairo, Manama, and Kuwait City, respectively. Special thanks go to our Kuwaiti partner, the Women's Cultural and Social Society, whose members provided useful feedback on the Kuwait chapter.

Outside consultants also contributed to the publication's completion. Beverly Butterfield typeset and Joanne Farness proofread the entire volume. Graphic designer Amanda Clark created the artwork for this project. Chapters were translated into Arabic by Ashraf Rady, Ahmed al-Baddawy, Rafiah al-Talei, Rana Husseini, Mona Khalaf, Miriam Ahmed Ahmed, and Fatima Sadiqi. Translations from French into English were provided by Renee Schwarz.

This project was funded, in part, through the Department of State, Bureau of Near Eastern Affairs, Office of Middle East Partnership Initiative (MEPI) under Cooperative Agreement Number S-NEAPI-05-CA157.

The opinions, findings, and conclusions or recommendations expressed in this volume are those of the authors and do not necessarily reflect those of the Department of State. MEPI supports efforts to expand political participation, strengthen civil society and the rule of law, empower women and youth, create educational opportunities, and foster economic reform throughout the Middle East and North Africa. In support of these goals, MEPI works with nongovernmental organizations, the private sector, and academic institutions, as well as governments. More information about MEPI can be found at: www.mepi.state.gov.

This study was also supported through grants by the United Nations Development Fund for Women (UNIFEM) and the United States Agency for International Development (USAID).

SURVEY CONTRIBUTORS

Freedom House Staff
  Sanja Kelly, Project Director
  Julia Breslin, Research and Editorial Associate
  Tyler Roylance, Staff Editor

Contributing Authors
  Algeria
    Nadia Marzouki, Postdoctoral Associate and Lecturer, Council on Middle East Studies, Yale University
  Bahrain
    Dunya Ahmed Abdulla Ahmed, Assistant Professor and Lecturer, Department of Social Sciences, University of Bahrain
  Egypt
    Mariz Tadros, Research Fellow, Institute of Development Studies, University of Sussex
  Iran
    Nayereh Tohidi, Professor and Chair, Department of Gender and Women's Studies, California State University, Northridge
  Iraq
    Huda Ahmed, journalist, former special correspondent and translator for the *Washington Post* and McClatchy Newspapers in Iraq
  Jordan
    Rana Husseini, journalist, *Jordan Times*; women's rights activist
  Kuwait
    Haya al-Mughni, sociologist and independent researcher
  Lebanon
    Mona Chemali Khalaf, economist and independent consultant; former director of the Institute for Women's Studies in the Arab World, Lebanese American University

Libya

Alison Pargeter, Senior Research Associate, Department of Politics and International Studies, University of Cambridge

Morocco

Fatima Sadiqi, Senior Professor of Linguistics and Gender Studies, University of Fes; Director, Isis Centre for Women and Development

Oman

Rafiah al-Talei, journalist; freelance columnist, *Alshabiba*, Muscat

Palestine

Suheir Azzouni, independent expert on gender and human rights; former General Director, Women's Affairs Technical Committee, Palestinian Territories

Qatar

Julia Breslin, Research and Editorial Associate, Freedom House

Toby Jones, Assistant Professor, Department of History, Rutgers University

Saudi Arabia

Eleanor Abdella Doumato, Visiting Fellow, Watson Institute for International Studies, Brown University

Tunisia

Lilia Ben Salem, Professor, Faculty of Social Sciences, University of Tunis

United Arab Emirates

Serra Kirdar, Founder and Director, Muthabara Foundation, Dubai

Yemen

Elham Manea, Lecturer, Political Science Institute, University of Zurich

Regional Advisory Committee

Algeria

Boutheina Cheriet, Professor of Comparative Education, University of Algiers

Bahrain

Munira Fakhro, Associate Professor, University of Bahrain

Egypt
   Nehad Abul Komsan, Director, Egyptian Center for Women's
   Rights, Cairo
Iraq
   Sundus Abass, Director, Women in Leadership Institute, Erbil
Jordan
   Ibtesam al-Atiyat, Professor, Department of Anthropology and
   Sociology, St. Olaf College
Kuwait
   Lubna al-Kazi, Professor, Department of Sociology,
   Kuwait University
Lebanon
   Lina Abou-Habib, Director, Collective for Research and Training
   on Development Action, Beirut

   Marie-Rose Zalzal, human rights lawyer
Morocco
   Souad Eddouada, Professor, Cultural and Gender Studies,
   Iben Tofail University, Kenitra
Oman
   Ebtisam al-Kitbi, Professor, Faculty of Human and Social Sciences,
   United Arab Emirates University

   Dawn Chatty, Deputy Director, Refugee Studies Centre;
   University Reader in Anthropology and Forced Migration,
   University of Oxford
Palestine
   Soraida Hussein, Director of Research, Centre for Legal Aid and
   Counseling, Ramallah
Qatar
   Mona al-Mutawa, attorney, Al-Mutawa Law Firm; founding
   member, Qatari Bar Association
Saudi Arabia
   May al-Dabbagh, Research Fellow and Lecturer, Director of the
   Gender and Public Policy Program, Dubai School of Government
Tunisia
   Mounira Charrad, Professor, Department of Sociology and Middle
   Eastern Studies, University of Texas at Austin

United Arab Emirates

Rima Sabban, Assistant Professor of Sociology, Zayed University, Dubai

Yemen

Wameedh Shakir, Gender Program Officer, Legal Protection and Advocacy Program, OXFAM, Sana'a

Legal Advisor

Badria al-Awadhi, attorney; former Dean of the Faculty of Law, Kuwait University

HARD-WON PROGRESS AND A LONG ROAD AHEAD: WOMEN'S RIGHTS IN THE MIDDLE EAST AND NORTH AFRICA

by Sanja Kelly

As the governments of the Middle East and North Africa (MENA) undertake the difficult process of enacting social and political change, the unequal status of women presents a particularly formidable challenge. In Iraq, deliberations over women's legal status have been as contentious as negotiations over how to structure the government. In Jordan, measures to increase penalties for so-called honor crimes faced strong resistance by ultraconservative parliamentarians and ordinary citizens who believe that tradition and religion afford them the right to severely punish and even murder female relatives for behavior they deem immoral. These debates are not just legal and philosophical struggles among elites. They are emotionally charged political battles that touch upon fundamental notions of morality and social order.

In order to provide a detailed look at the conditions faced by women in the Middle East and understand the complex environment surrounding efforts to improve their status, Freedom House conducted a comprehensive study of women's rights in the region. The first edition of this project was published in 2005. The present edition offers an updated examination of the issue, with a special focus on changes that have occurred over the last five years. Although the study indicates that a substantial deficit in women's rights persists in every country in the MENA region, the findings also include notable progress, particularly in terms of economic opportunities, educational attainment, and political participation.

The Middle East is not the only region of the world where women experience inequality. In Asia, Africa, Latin America, Europe, and North America, women continue to face gender-based obstacles to the full realization of their rights. In the United States, women have come a long way since the Equal Pay Act of 1963 and the Civil Rights Act of 1964, but even today they earn roughly 23 percent less than men and make up only 3 percent of the Fortune 500 chief executives. It is, however, in the MENA region that the gap between the rights of men and those of women has been the most visible and severe.

The country reports presented in this edition detail how women throughout the Middle East continue to face systematic discrimination in both laws and social customs. Deeply entrenched societal norms, combined with conservative interpretations of Shari'a (Islamic law), continue to relegate women to a subordinate status. Women in the region are significantly underrepresented in senior positions in politics and the private sector, and in some countries they are completely absent from the judiciary. Perhaps most visibly, women face gender-based discrimination in personal-status laws, which regulate marriage, divorce, child guardianship, inheritance, and other aspects of family life. Laws in most of the region declare that the husband is the head of the family, give the husband power over his wife's right to work, and in some instances specifically require the wife to obey her husband. Gender-based violence also remains a significant problem.

Nevertheless, important steps have been made to improve the status of women over the last five years, and 14 out of 17 countries have recorded some gains.* The member states of the Gulf Cooperation Council (GCC or Gulf)—which scored the worst among 17 countries in the 2005 edition—have demonstrated the greatest degree of improvement, shrinking the gap between them and the rest of the region on some issues. The most significant achievement occurred in Kuwait, where women received the same political rights as men in 2005, enabling them to vote and run for office, and paving the way for the election of the country's first female members of parliament in 2009. In Bahrain and the United Arab Emirates (UAE), the first women judges were appointed in 2006 and 2008, respectively. Women have also become more visible participants in public life, education, and business throughout the region, including Saudi Arabia. They have gained more freedom to travel independently, as laws requiring a guardian's permission for a woman to obtain a passport have been rescinded in Bahrain, Kuwait, and Qatar during this report's coverage period.

Outside the Gulf, the most notable reforms occurred in Algeria and Jordan. Following the Moroccan example from the year before, Algeria made sweeping amendments to its personal status code in 2005, vastly

---

* The 2010 edition covers 18 countries. Iran was not evaluated in 2005.

improving women's power and autonomy within the family. The new law prohibits proxy marriages, limits the role of a woman's guardian during marriage proceedings, recognizes the parental authority of custodial mothers, and removes the requirement that a wife obey her husband. In Jordan, after years of lobbying by women's organizations for protections against gender-based violence, the government enacted the Family Protection Law (FPL) in 2008 and established a specialized court in 2009 that handles cases involving honor crimes. The FPL specifies the procedures that police, the courts, and medical authorities must follow when dealing with victims of domestic abuse, and prescribes penalties for the perpetrators. Jordan is only the second country in the region—after Tunisia—to pass such legislation, although parts of the law are not yet enforced.

In nearly all of the countries examined, however, progress is stymied by the lack of democratic institutions, an independent judiciary, and freedoms of association and assembly. Excessively restrictive rules on the formation of civil society organizations make it more difficult for women's advocates to effectively organize and lobby the government for expanded rights. The scarcity of research and data on women's status further impedes the advocacy efforts of nongovernmental organizations (NGOs) and activists. And ultimately, the passage of new laws that guarantee equal rights for women means little if those guarantees are not fully enforced by state authorities. Throughout the region, persistent patriarchal attitudes, prejudices, and the traditionalist inclinations of male judges threaten to undermine new legal protections.

Overall conditions for women have worsened in only three places: Iraq, Yemen, and Palestine (West Bank and Gaza Strip). In all of these cases the negative trend is partly related to an uncertain security situation. For example, while the lives of citizens of both genders are affected by the war in Iraq, the conflict's effect on women has been particularly severe. The instances of gender-based violence in Iraq—including honor killings, rapes, and kidnappings—increased significantly during the last five years. This forced women to stay home, thereby hindering most aspects of their lives, including employment and education. Despite these conditions, progress has been achieved on some issues. Women currently hold 25 percent of the seats in the parliament thanks to a new quota system, a new nationality law allows women to transfer citizenship to their children and foreign-born husbands, and women's rights NGOs have grown stronger and more effective.

Similarly, in Palestine (West Bank and the Israeli Occupied Territories), internal political tensions between Fatah and Hamas—coupled with Israeli restrictions on the movement of civilians and military incursions—have seriously affected the health, employment opportunities, access to education, and political and civil liberties of Palestinian women. In particular, due to the increased number of checkpoints and the construction of the West Bank separation wall, women now experience further separation from their families, farmlands, water resources, schools, and hospitals. Moreover, the new, more conservative social order imposed by Hamas has led to greater restrictions on women's rights in Gaza, and women's labor force participation remains the lowest in the region as the local economy has all but collapsed.

While it is possible to identify net gains or losses for women's rights in a given country, the situation is rarely as simple as that, and the course of events often reflects a great deal of contestation. In many states where significant progress has been achieved, elements of the society have tried, sometimes successfully, to introduce measures that are detrimental to women's rights. For example, in Syria, where women have made notable improvements in terms of educational and employment opportunities, the government considered amendments to the family law that would have increased the discretionary power of religious judges in family matters, until the public outcry and activism of women's rights organizations prompted lawmakers to cancel the proposed legislation. In Libya, after it was leaked that the government had imposed a regulation prohibiting women under the age of 40 from leaving the country without a male relative, even the state-owned newspaper was critical, leading the authorities to deny that such a rule had been instituted. In Kuwait, just three years after women got the right to vote and a year before the election of first female lawmakers, the parliamentary committee on education issued a directive instructing the government to start enforcing a law on gender segregation at private universities by 2013.

Among other important findings and developments are the following:

❖ As measured by this study, Tunisian women enjoy the greatest degree of freedom in the MENA region, followed by women in Morocco, Algeria, Lebanon, Egypt, Jordan, Palestine, Kuwait, Bahrain, Syria, Libya, the UAE, Iraq, Qatar, Oman, and Iran. Yemen and Saudi Arabia lag significantly behind.

❖ The greatest gains were achieved in the areas of employment, education, and political representation. More women today hold jobs, are literate, and enroll in areas of study previously deemed inappropriate for them. Women's rights organizations are becoming more vocal and better organized, and women are increasing their representation in elected government bodies, albeit with the help of quota systems.

❖ Gender-based violence remains one of the most serious obstacles in women's lives. Laws that would protect women from spousal abuse are absent in most countries, spousal rape is not criminalized, and honor killings still occur and are on the rise in Iraq and Palestine.

❖ Women's access to justice remains poor due to their low degree of legal literacy, cultural requirements that women first seek mediation through the family before turning to courts, the patriarchal leanings of many male judges, and the fact that in most countries a woman's testimony is worth only half that of a man in certain areas of the law.

MAIN FINDINGS

The 2010 edition of *Women's Rights in the Middle East and North Africa* identifies a complex set of obstacles that prevent women from enjoying the full range of political, civil, economic, and legal rights. However, the study and the accompanying data also indicate that certain gains have been made in recent years, providing grounds for cautious optimism.

Economic Opportunities Grow Despite Persistent Challenges

On average, only 28 percent of the adult female population in the Middle East is economically active, the lowest rate in the world. In nearly all MENA countries, however, women today are better represented in the labor force and play a more prominent role in the workplace than was the case earlier this decade. In Qatar, for example, the proportion of adult women with jobs has increased from roughly 36 percent in 2000 to 42 percent in 2007. Similarly, the proportion of working women has grown by 6 percent in Algeria (to 38 percent) and nearly 4 percent in Libya (to 27 percent). Compared with male employment, these figures remain glaringly low; depending on the country, the share of adult men with jobs ranges from 60 to 90 percent. But male employment has remained static and in some instances decreased since 2000.

The growing number of working women appears to be the result of increased literacy and educational opportunities, slowly changing cultural attitudes, and in some countries, government policies aimed at reducing dependence on foreign labor. Although society as a whole tends to view formal employment and business as male activities, parents and husbands alike are starting to rely more on the financial support provided by their daughters and wives. In Egypt and Bahrain, several women interviewed for this study said that their marriage prospects improve if they hold a solid job, as "young men nowadays look for a wife that can help with family expenses."

Employment also gives women a degree of financial independence from families and husbands, something they lacked in the past. Divorced or widowed women increasingly seek employment to support themselves, instead of relying on their extended families. And with divorce rates on the rise—approximately 46 percent in the UAE, 40 percent in Egypt, 38 percent in Qatar, and 30 percent in Tunisia—married women increasingly see a separate income as vital insurance against future trouble in their relationships. Whether married or not, working women say that they have started to earn greater respect and have a greater voice within their families.

Women in the Gulf generally have higher labor-force participation rates than their counterparts elsewhere in the MENA region. This can be explained by lower unemployment rates overall, meaning women do not have to compete with men for jobs, and by comparatively higher levels of literacy and education. In addition, Gulf women have benefited from government policies designed to reduce dependence on foreign labor, as companies have aggressively recruited female workers to fill newly established quotas for citizen employees. In the UAE, for example, the Ministry of Labor no longer allows foreigners to work as secretaries, public-relations officers, or human resources personnel; consequently, most of the new hires for those positions are Emirati women. In Oman, a policy of "Omanization" has had a particularly positive effect on poor, less-educated women, allowing them to obtain jobs as cleaners, hospital orderlies, and kitchen help, and thus to support themselves in the face of economic hardship and secure a new role in the community.

Although such policies have increased the overall number of working women, they have also highlighted the cultural limits placed on female professionals. Many women complain of difficulty in advancing beyond entry-level positions despite their qualifications and job performance, leading to a popular perception that they were hired only to satisfy the government quotas. In other words, as noted in the UAE report, these policies have resulted in a "sticky floor" for young and ambitious women. Indeed, across the Middle East, very few women are found in upper management and executive positions, arguably due to cultural perceptions that women are less capable, more irrational, and better suited for domestic responsibilities than men.

Women throughout the region earn less than men despite labor laws that mandate equal pay for the same type of work and equal opportunities for training and promotion. While such laws are essential, they are frequently violated in terms of salary and employment perks like housing allowances or loans for senior officials. Women in most countries can file discrimination complaints with government agencies, but these bodies often lack the capacity to investigate discrimination cases or impose penalties for violations by employers, rendering their work largely ineffective. Sexual harassment is also a problem due to the lack of laws that clearly prohibit the practice and punish the perpetrators. Jordan's new 2008 labor law prohibits "sexual assault," but its protections for victims are extremely weak, and it lacks clear definitions and strong punishments for offenders.

In addition, women face significant discrimination in laws regulating pension and similar benefits. In many countries, gender plays an important role in determining the length of employment necessary to qualify, the eligible beneficiaries, and the conditions under which benefits are provided. Upon death, a female employee generally cannot pass her pension to her surviving spouse or children, whereas a male employee can, although female workers give up the same share of their salaries for such benefits as men. Moreover, men employed in the public sector are often eligible for special family and cost-of-living allowances, which are only available to a woman if her husband is dead or disabled.

Several long-standing cultural mores regarding proper professions for women remain cemented into the law. In virtually every country in the region, labor laws prohibit women from undertaking dangerous or arduous work, or work that could be deemed detrimental to their health or morals. In 12 of the 18 countries, women are prohibited from working late at night, with the exception of those employed in medicine and certain other fields. While these provisions are seen locally as a means of protecting women, in effect they treat women as minors who are unable to make decisions regarding their own safety, and they hold women's guardians responsible if the rules are violated. Since most women opt to work in the public sector due to its shorter workdays and better pay, these restrictions generally affect only a limited number of female employees.

Academic Achievement Expands Women's Prospects as New Threats Emerge

Education has been a prime area of progress for women in the region, and it is an important avenue for their advancement toward broader equality. Since the 1990s, women in all 18 MENA countries have made gains in access to education, literacy, university enrollment, and the variety of academic fields available to them. That trend has continued, for the most part, over the past five years. The female literacy rate has grown by 5.3 percent in Algeria, 6.8 percent in Iran, 3.6 percent in Morocco, and 5.8 percent in Yemen. In most countries, women outnumber men at the tertiary education level, and Qatar and the UAE have the highest female-to-male university enrollment ratio worldwide.

Although women are generally encouraged to study in traditionally female disciplines such as teaching and health care, they have started entering new fields, including engineering and science. For example, in Qatar, women were accepted for the first time in 2008 in the fields of architecture and electrical and chemical engineering. In Saudi Arabia, three educational institutions began to permit women to study law in 2007, although the graduates are only allowed to act as legal consultants to other women and remain prohibited from serving as judges and advocates in court. In countries such as Tunisia, Algeria, and Egypt, where women have long been able to enroll in any course of study, educators report increasing numbers of female students in their traditionally male classes, such as math and science.

Despite these improvements, many barriers to true gender equality in education persist, while new measures intended to cap surging female enrollment threaten to undermine the progress to date. In Kuwait and Oman, women are required to achieve higher grade-point averages (GPAs) than men to enroll in certain disciplines at the university level. For example, female students in Kuwait must obtain a 3.3 GPA to be admitted to the engineering department, while male students need a GPA of just 2.8. As women make up almost two-thirds of the student body at Kuwait University, the disparity in admission requirements is explained by university officials as "reverse discrimination," intended to increase the percentage of male students in certain fields. Similarly, Iran has recently implemented a rule requiring an equal number of male and female students in select fields like medicine.

In a handful of countries, universities largely remain segregated by gender. It is unclear to what extent the segregation affects the quality of education, but in at least some countries, including Saudi Arabia, the number and diversity of classes offered to men are much greater than those available to women. As noted above, Kuwaiti legislators in 2008 called for an existing law mandating segregation at private universities to be implemented within five years, despite concerns at the Ministry of Education that it would be extremely difficult to create adequate facilities before that deadline.

Protection from Domestic Abuse Remains Minimal

While no part of the world is free from the stain of domestic abuse, the countries of the Middle East are exceptional in their array of laws, practices, and customs that pose major obstacles to the protection of women and the punishment of abusers. Physical abuse is generally prohibited, but among the 18 countries examined, only Tunisia and Jordan offer specific protections against domestic violence, and none prohibit spousal rape. Other contributing factors include a lack of government accountability, a lack of official protection of individual rights inside the home, and social stigmas that pertain to female victims rather than the perpetrators.

Very few comprehensive studies on the nature and extent of domestic violence have been conducted in the Middle East. Nonetheless, domestic abuse is thought to be widespread in every country in the region, with its existence typically covered up by and kept within the family. Many women feel that they cannot discuss their personal situation without damaging their family honor and their own reputation. Consequently, abused women rarely attempt to file complaints with the police. When they do choose to seek police protection, they frequently encounter officers who are reluctant to get involved in what is perceived as a family matter, and who encourage reconciliation rather than legal action. In Saudi Arabia in particular, guardianship laws make it very difficult for battered women to find a safe haven. For example, this study cites the case of a girl who sought police protection after being sexually molested by her father, only to be turned away and told to bring her father in to file the complaint.

Honor killing, in which a woman is murdered by a relative for suspected extramarital sex or some other behavior that is considered a slight to the family's honor, represents the most extreme form of domestic violence. Such murders have been reported in Jordan, Syria, Palestine, Egypt, Iraq, Iran, and Yemen, but are not exclusive to the Middle East; they also occur in South and Central Asia, and to a lesser extent elsewhere. Generally, the perpetrators of honor killings serve minimal time in prison due to judicial discretion and laws that prescribe leniency for murders committed in the heat of passion. While Jordan and Syria have recently instituted stiffer penalties to deal with these crimes, honor killings are reportedly on the rise in other countries, such as Palestine and Iraq.

Over the last five years, nearly all countries in the region have taken some steps to combat spousal abuse. In Jordan, the parliament enacted the Family Protection Law in January 2008 after years of lobbying by governmental and civil society actors. As noted above, the law prescribes prison time and financial penalties for abusers, and specifies procedures that the police, the courts, and medical authorities must follow when handling cases of domestic violence, although several important provisions of the law have not yet been implemented. In Tunisia and Algeria, the authorities have joined women's groups in campaigns against domestic violence, holding workshops and engaging police, judges, and social workers. Draft legislation that would prohibit domestic violence was considered by the Lebanese government in June 2009, but it was referred to a ministerial committee for further review.

In Bahrain, Lebanon, Morocco, and Jordan, the network of NGOs that support victims of domestic violence is steadily growing, and an increasing number of women seem to be aware of such organizations and the services they provide. Several new shelters have opened over the last five years, and civil society has become more active in its advocacy efforts. The issue of domestic violence has also garnered more attention in Qatar and Saudi Arabia, although it is unclear what practical steps those governments intend to take to combat the problem. In Iran, Kuwait, and Yemen, there is not one shelter or support center for victims of domestic abuse.

Political Rights Improve Amid Low Regional Standards

Throughout the MENA region, both male and female citizens lack the power to change their governments democratically and have only limited rights to peaceful assembly and freedom of speech. According to *Freedom in the World*, the global assessment of political rights and civil liberties issued annually by Freedom House, none of the countries examined here earn the rating of Free, and none qualify as electoral democracies.

In all 18 countries, gender-based obstacles to women's participation in public life remain deeply rooted. Politics is viewed as the domain of men, and female leaders must contend with cultural attitudes that resist the idea of being politically represented by a woman. In Yemen, for example, a group of Salafist clerics recently issued a handbook that argues against gender-based quotas in political life, claiming that "opening the door for women to leave their houses and mix with men will lead to sexual chaos." Even in Egypt, one of the more liberal countries in terms of women's rights, a former grand mufti issued a fatwa (religious opinion) in 2005 that prohibited women from assuming the position of president. Although the sitting grand mufti later clarified that a woman could lead a modern Muslim state, the disagreement among religious scholars, and their influence on such an overtly political and constitutional issue, are indicative of the challenges faced by women in their struggle to assume leadership positions.

Despite these obstacles, women in 11 of the 18 countries have made gains over the last five years in their ability to vote and run for elected office, hold high-level government positions, and lobby the government for expanded rights. Reforms have been particularly visible in the GCC countries, where women's participation in politics has traditionally lagged behind the rest of the region. In Kuwait, women received the same political rights as men in 2005 and four women were elected to the parliament in May 2009, for the first time in the country's history. In the UAE, eight women were appointed and one secured election to the 40-member Federal National Council (FNC), an advisory body to the hereditary rulers of the seven emirates. Previously, no women had served on the FNC, which until 2006 was fully appointed by the seven rulers. In other countries, such as Oman and Bahrain, the government has appointed an increasing number of women to unelected positions, including cabinet and diplomatic posts. Saudi Arabia remains the only country in which women are not permitted to vote or run for elected office.

Outside of the Gulf, the positive change has been more subtle. In Iraq, women's rights activists mounted a successful campaign of rallies and lobbying to secure a 25 percent quota in the parliament and incorporate that rule into the constitution. Still, electoral laws have been formulated in a way that allows female representation to fall below 25 percent in provincial councils. The implementation of quota systems, either on state or local levels, has increased women's participation in electoral politics in other countries as well. Jordan's government, responding to an initiative by women's organizations, introduced a 20 percent quota for the July 2007 municipal elections, leading to significantly more women on local councils. Nonetheless, very few women are able to achieve electoral success in their own right. The typical female lawmaker is a close relative of a prominent male leader or a member of a traditional political family.

Working from outside the government, women's advocates in several countries have been able to lobby more effectively for expanded rights in recent years, despite persistent restrictions on freedom of association. In Morocco, Algeria, and Egypt, women's rights activists have been particularly successful in lobbying their governments to reform family laws and implement new protections for women. However, throughout the region, restrictions on civic organizations and human rights advocacy represent one of the main impediments to the expansion of women's rights, since activists are unable to organize and voice their demands without fear of persecution.

Women Are Still Denied Equality Before the Law

Apart from Saudi Arabia, all countries in the MENA region have clauses in their constitutions that guarantee the equality of all citizens. Specific provisions calling for equality between the sexes have been adopted in Algeria, Bahrain, Iraq, Libya, Oman, Palestine, Qatar, Syria, and Tunisia. While the constitutions of Egypt, Jordan, Lebanon, Kuwait, Morocco, the UAE, and Yemen do not include gender-based nondiscrimination clauses, they do declare that "all citizens are equal under the law."

Regardless of constitutional guarantees, women throughout the region face legal forms of discrimination that are systematic and pervade every aspect of life. For example, in most of the 18 countries, women do not enjoy the same citizenship and nationality rights as men, which can carry serious repercussions for the choice of a marriage partner. Under these laws, a man is able to marry a foreign woman with the understanding that his spouse can become a citizen and receive the associated benefits. By contrast, a woman who marries a foreigner cannot pass her citizenship to her spouse or their children. Children from such marriages must acquire special residency permits, renewed annually, to attend public school, qualify for university scholarships, or find employment.

Over the last five years, several countries have made it possible for foreign husbands or children of female citizens to obtain citizenship. In Algeria, Iraq, and Tunisia, a woman can now pass her citizenship to her husband and children, pending approval from the relevant ministries (male citizens need no such approval). In Egypt, the parliament amended the nationality law in 2004, allowing the children of Egyptian mothers and foreign fathers to obtain Egyptian citizenship, but the law still prohibits such children from joining the army, the police, and some government posts. Similarly, the new Moroccan nationality law, which came into force in April 2008, enables women married to noncitizen men to pass their nationality to their children, provided that the marriage took place in accordance with Moroccan personal status law. These reforms, although incomplete, are seen as significant steps forward.

As described above, women also face gender-based restrictions in labor laws, can legally be denied employment in certain occupations, and are discriminated against in labor benefits and pension laws. However, gender inequality is most evident in personal status codes, which relegate women to an inferior position within marriage and the family, designate the husband as the head of household, and in many cases explicitly require the wife to obey her husband. Under the family codes of most Middle Eastern countries, a husband is allowed to divorce his wife at any time without a stated reason, but a wife seeking divorce must either meet very specific and onerous conditions or return her dowry through a practice known as *khula*. Furthermore, with the exceptions of Tunisia and Morocco, women need a guardian's signature or at least his presence to complete marriage proceedings, limiting their free choice of a marriage partner. In Saudi Arabia, there is no codified personal status law, allowing judges to make decisions regarding family matters based on their own interpretations of Shari'a. In Bahrain, the 2009 personal status code is applicable only to Sunni Muslims.

Following years of lobbying by women's rights organizations, Algeria's personal status code was amended in 2005 to prohibit proxy marriages, set the minimum legal age for marriage at 19 for both sexes, impose several conditions on the practice of polygamy, and remove the provision that required a wife's obedience to her husband. Several other countries, including Tunisia and Bahrain, made lesser amendments, mainly to prevent the marriage of underage girls. In the UAE and Qatar, personal status laws were codified for the first time in 2005 and 2006, respectively. Although the new laws contain provisions granting women additional rights and are viewed as a positive development, many clauses simply codify preexisting inequalities.

A number of other legal changes over the last five years, if properly implemented, have the potential to improve women's rights. For example, laws requiring women to obtain permission from their guardians in order to travel were rescinded in Bahrain, Kuwait, and Qatar. In Oman, the government introduced a law in 2008 to stipulate that men's and women's court testimony would be considered equal, although it is unclear to what extent this will apply to personal status cases.

Throughout the region, however, the prevailing patriarchal attitudes, prejudices, and traditionalism of male judges, lawyers, and court officials— as well as the lack of an independent judiciary that is capable of upholding basic legal rights despite political or societal pressure—threaten to undermine these new legal protections. Unless effective complaint mechanisms are in place and the appropriate court personnel are trained to apply justice in an impartial manner, the new laws will not achieve the desired effect. Moreover, unless the judicial system of each country becomes more independent, rigorous, and professional, women of high social standing will continue to have better access to justice than poor women and domestic workers.

AUTHOR

Sanja Kelly is a senior researcher and managing editor at Freedom House. She presently serves as the project director for the survey of women's rights in the Middle East and North Africa. In that capacity, she manages a team of over 40 international consultants based in the MENA region. In recent years, Ms. Kelly has conducted extensive field research and consulted with over 200 leading women's rights activists, public figures, and scholars in the Middle East. She is the author and editor of several articles and books examining democratic governance and women's rights.

APPENDIX
SUMMARY OF FINDINGS BY COUNTRY

Algeria: Legislative changes adopted in recent years have the potential to improve women's rights considerably. The 2005 nationality law allows women to transfer their citizenship to their children and foreign husbands, subject to certain conditions. Sweeping amendments to the personal status code, also enacted in 2005, improve women's autonomy within the family. Most recently, a new law against trafficking in persons was approved in January 2009. However, women generally lack an understanding of their legal rights, which threatens to negate the positive impact of these reforms. The political environment remains restrictive, and freedom of expression is curtailed for all.

Bahrain: The autonomy and personal security of Bahraini women improved over the past decade with the adoption of the National Action Charter, the ratification of the new constitution, and, in May 2009, the adoption of a personal status code for Sunnis. Bahrain appointed its first female judge in 2006 and rescinded a law requiring women to gain a male guardian's approval to obtain a passport. In 2007, the minimum age for marriage—previously unspecified—was set at 15 for girls and 18 for boys. However, women's access to justice remains poor. There is no personal status law for Shiite Muslims, so related judgments are handled by religious courts and based on individual judges' interpretations of Shari'a. Over the last five years, Bahraini women's rights NGOs have become more active, and both they and the government are increasingly taking steps to address domestic violence.

Egypt: Women in Egypt have made small gains in all categories under study, with the exception of political rights. The nationality law was amended in 2004 to permit the children of Egyptian mothers and foreign fathers (except Palestinians) to obtain Egyptian citizenship. Steps have been taken to combat gender-based violence and sexual harassment, and a law banning female genital mutilation was adopted in 2008, although it is unclear how effective it will be against what is a widespread and socially accepted tradition. In addition, women are taking on a larger role in society; the first female marriage registrar and the first female mayor were appointed in 2008, and in 2009 the first female university president took office. However, the emergency law remains in effect, curtailing a range of civil liberties, and women's political participation has been on the decline. To increase women's representation in the legislature, a gender-based quota system for the lower house of parliament was passed in 2009 and is scheduled to be implemented in 2010.

Iran: Iran has undergone political and social upheaval in recent years, most recently following the disputed 2009 presidential election. Women were visible participants in the postelection demonstrations, marching alongside men to protest voting irregularities and human rights violations. However, Iranian women are unable to pass their nationality to their children or foreign husbands, must secure their guardians' permission before undergoing serious surgical procedures, and are subject to a discriminatory penal code. For instance, to avoid being punished for adultery, a rape victim must prove that she was under duress and did not do anything to invite an attack. Since the election of President Mahmoud Ahmadinejad in 2005, restrictions regarding modest attire and gender segregation in public places have been more strictly enforced. Restrictions on free speech have led to the closure of prominent women's rights publications, and participants in peaceful women's rights demonstrations have been routinely jailed. Indeed, while resourceful women's rights defenders have launched significant campaigns, such as those that aim to eliminate discriminatory legal provisions and ban executions by stoning, they also face severe persecution and are regularly threatened with heavy fines and long jail sentences.

Iraq: The status of women in Iraq has fluctuated over the past five years, in large part due to changing security conditions. Violence against women—particularly honor killings, rapes, and abductions—significantly escalated during the coverage period. This forced women to stay at home, and has negatively affected their opportunities for employment and education. Nevertheless, some progress toward gender equity has been achieved. For instance, women currently hold 25.5 percent of the seats in the parliament, and a new nationality law allows women to transfer citizenship to their children and foreign-born husbands. It remains unclear whether women will be adequately protected by laws that are currently under consideration. It is also uncertain whether existing discriminatory provisions, such as a rule that permits lenient sentences for perpetrators of honor crimes, will be amended. Consistent vigilance by state and nongovernmental actors both within Iraq and abroad will help to ensure that the rights women have gained to date survive on paper as well as in practice.

Jordan: Jordanian civil society actors remain outspoken proponents of women's rights, even as the government has enacted a restrictive law that limits the freedom of NGOs. Lobbying efforts by women's rights activists helped to secure the Family Protection Law in 2008, providing key safeguards against domestic abuse, although some of the law's most important provisions remain unenforced. The government also established a specialized court in July 2009 to hear cases involving honor crimes, and the court issued several convictions by year's end. There are only seven female members of parliament out of 110, and men continue to dominate the national political scene. But at the subnational level, women have made political headway: the first female governor was appointed in January 2007, and a 20 percent quota was introduced for the municipal elections the same year.

Kuwait: Women voted and ran for office for the first time in municipal and national elections in 2006. In 2009, they reached another milestone when four women were elected to the parliament. Women in Kuwait enjoy higher levels of economic participation than most of their counterparts in the region, but they remain barred from serving as judges or in the military. And as is the case elsewhere in the Gulf, they face unequal rights within the family and cannot transfer their nationality to children or foreign-born husbands. Domestic violence, although a problem, remains largely unaddressed by the government and women's rights organizations.

Lebanon: Women continue to face gender-based injustices, such as the inability to pass citizenship to their children and a penal code provision that offers reduced sentences for perpetrators of honor crimes. However, women's rights organizations have been increasing their efforts to combat these inequities. The issue of violence against women has gained prominence in recent years. A well-known religious cleric issue a fatwa against honor killings in 2008, the government is reviewing legislation that would ban domestic violence, and the number of hotlines available to victims of abuse has increased. Although more women now head economic enterprises than before, few are participating in national or local politics.

Libya: Some positive changes for women's rights have occurred in the last five years, including a growing female role in the labor force and the state's attempts to promote a greater awareness of domestic violence. However, women's rights have also been threatened, as when the government briefly barred women from leaving the country without a male guardian, a decision that was withdrawn only a week later after a public outcry. Restrictions placed on civil society organizations are extreme, meaning there are few entities that can help bridge the gap between the regime's favorable rhetoric on women's rights and the reality on the ground, and there has been no fundamental shift in societal attitudes or behavior toward women.

Morocco: The sweeping changes engrained in the 2004 family law have been unevenly enforced, and many women—particularly those who live in rural areas or are uneducated—continue to face discrimination in practice. However, access to justice has improved in recent years. Women may now travel without a guardian's approval, are leading business ventures and advancing to higher levels of education in greater numbers, and are better able to negotiate their marriage rights. In addition, the new nationality law enables Moroccan women married to noncitizen men to pass their nationality to their children if certain conditions are met. Some progress has also been made in protecting women from domestic violence, and support networks for victims are getting stronger. Women continue to make gains politically, and a 12 percent quota was implemented for the June 2009 local elections, substantially increasing female political representation on this level. While women's rights groups and individual activists have collaborated with the government to improve the rights of all women, true equality remains a distant goal.

Oman: Women in Oman are being appointed to more senior government positions, registering to vote in larger numbers, and increasingly running as parliamentary candidates. However, no women were elected in 2007, and in any case the parliament serves only in an advisory capacity. The overall level of political and civic participation remains patently low. The testimony of men and women in Omani courts is now equal in most situations under a new law on evidence. If properly implemented, this law would set an important precedent in the Gulf region. In 2008, the country's first major law against human trafficking was enacted, and the land entitlement system was amended to ensure equality between male and female applicants. Despite these advances, women continue to face significant legal and social obstacles, and are required to obtain the written consent of a male relative before undergoing any kind of surgery.

Palestine: Internal political tensions between Fatah and Hamas—coupled with Israeli military incursions and restrictions on the movement of civilians—have seriously affected the health, employment opportunities, access to education, and political and civil liberties of Palestinian women. The conservative social order imposed by Hamas in Gaza has led to greater restrictions on women's rights there, and women's labor-force participation rate remains one of the lowest in the region, as the local economy has all but collapsed. Electoral laws were amended in 2005 to ensure greater political participation for women, and women are extremely active in their communities and in civil society. But while they continue to push for gender equality, political and economic issues, as well as the Israeli occupation, consistently draw attention away from such campaigns.

Qatar: In recent years, the government has taken several steps to promote equality and address discrimination, including adopting the country's first codified family law and enacting a new constitution in 2004 that specifically prohibits gender-based discrimination. Since 2007, women have been allowed to apply for their own passports, and in late 2008 they were accepted into the electrical and chemical engineering program at Qatar University for the first time. Nevertheless, women continue to be treated unequally in most aspects of life and face cultural and social norms that prevent them from making a full contribution to society.

Saudi Arabia: This country performs well below its neighbors in all categories, and Saudi women are segregated, disenfranchised, and unable to travel or obtain certain types of medical care without male approval. Gender inequality is built into Saudi Arabia's governmental and social structures, and it is integral to the state-supported interpretation of Islam. Still, women's status improved slightly over the last five years, as they are now allowed to study law, obtain their own identification cards, check into hotels alone, and register businesses without first proving that they have hired a male manager. In addition, two new universities provide a limited form of coeducational experience.

Syria: The Syrian government strictly limits civil society activity, meaning much-needed legal reforms to ensure gender equality must generally originate in and be supported by the regime. Activists are not free to lobby the government or generate grassroots support, without which long-term change is difficult, and existing legal protections are weakened by the lack of mechanisms for women to challenge enforcement and implementation. Women enjoy reasonably high levels of literacy and labor-force participation, and their presence in the parliament is larger than in most neighboring countries. However, the parliament has little power in practice, and women's lack of representation in the executive and judiciary prevents them from developing, implementing, and enforcing policy decisions. Honor killings remain a problem in Syria, with an estimated 200 women murdered each year, although the government instituted stiffer penalties in 2009.

Tunisia: Tunisian women have long enjoyed rights for which other women in the region continue to struggle. The practices of polygamy and divorce by repudiation were banned years ago, girls have had access to free education on par with boys since 1958, and women earned the right to vote in 1957. After the most recent parliamentary elections, women made up 15.2 percent of the upper house and 27.6 percent of the lower house, and both houses have a female vice president, although the country's president holds nearly all political power in practice. Yet even as women continue to pursue a positive trajectory, particularly in terms of academic and economic achievement, inequity persists. Women in rural areas are often unaware of their rights, and women remain underrepresented in community and political life. Restrictions on free speech affect both men and women, although the authorities do not consider the issue of women's rights to be a particularly sensitive subject.

United Arab Emirates: The status of women is improving as the UAE seeks to transform itself into a modern state. Emirati women are entering new professional fields, serving as judges and prosecutors, and being appointed to high-profile positions within the government and private sector. More women are joining the workforce, and the UAE's female labor-force participation and female literacy rates are among the highest in the MENA region. The codification of the family law in 2005 is also seen as a step forward, although the law contains many discriminatory provisions based on conservative interpretations of Shari'a. Women's limited ability to access justice through the courts and combat discrimination remains a significant concern.

Yemen: In Yemen, where the tribal structure plays an influential role and the government is increasingly controlled by a single leader and political party, women are subjected to various forms of violence and discrimination. These include domestic abuse, deprivation of education, early or forced marriage, restrictions on freedom of movement, exclusion from decision-making roles and processes, denial of inheritance, deprivation of health services, and female genital mutilation. In recent years, security forces have implemented heavy-handed policies toward opposition groups and critical journalists, hampering the ability of women's rights activists to advocate for greater equality. In a positive development, some educational and executive institutions have allowed women to join their ranks for the first time, and the Islamist opposition party Islah undertook internal changes that led to the election of the first women to its higher decision-making bodies. However, Yemeni laws still discriminate against women, treating them as inferiors or minors who need perpetual guardianship, and women's representation in the executive and legislative bodies remains very poor.

TABLES & GRAPHS

COUNTRY RATINGS

	Nondiscrimination and Access to Justice	Autonomy, Security, and Freedom of the Person	Economic Rights and Equal Opportunity	Political Rights and Civic Voice	Social and Cultural Rights
Algeria	3.1	3.0	3.0	3.0	3.0
Bahrain	2.2	2.6	3.1	2.3	2.9
Egypt	3.0	2.9	2.9	2.7	2.6
Iran	1.9	2.1	2.7	2.1	2.5
Iraq	2.7	1.9	2.6	2.6	2.3
Jordan	2.7	2.7	2.9	2.9	2.8
Kuwait	2.2	2.4	3.1	2.4	2.9
Lebanon	2.9	3.0	3.0	2.9	3.1
Libya	2.4	2.6	2.8	1.8	2.5
Morocco	3.1	3.2	2.8	3.1	2.9
Oman	2.1	2.1	2.9	1.8	2.5
Palestine	2.6	2.4	2.9	2.7	2.6
Qatar	2.1	2.3	2.9	1.8	2.5
Saudi Arabia	1.4	1.3	1.7	1.2	1.6
Syria	2.7	2.3	2.9	2.2	2.5
Tunisia	3.6	3.4	3.2	3.1	3.3
UAE	2.0	2.3	3.1	2.0	2.5
Yemen	1.9	1.9	1.9	2.0	2.0

NONDISCRIMINATION AND ACCESS TO JUSTICE

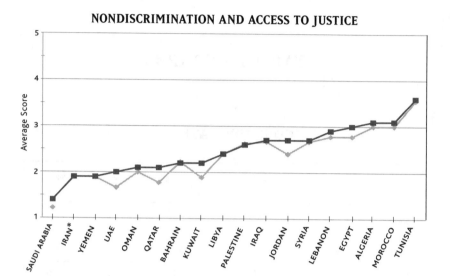

*Iran was not reviewed in 2004   2004   2009

AUTONOMY, SECURITY, AND FREEDOM OF THE PERSON

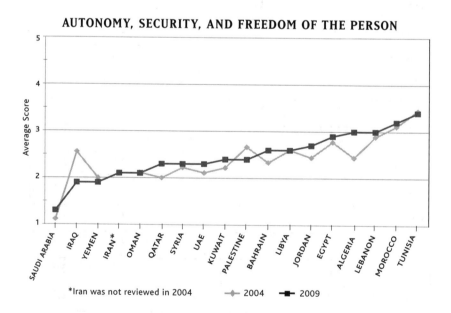

*Iran was not reviewed in 2004   2004   2009

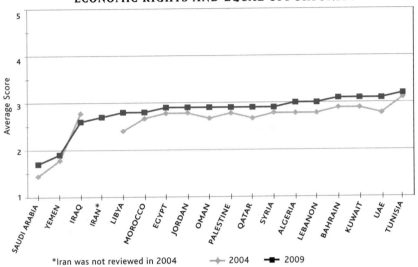

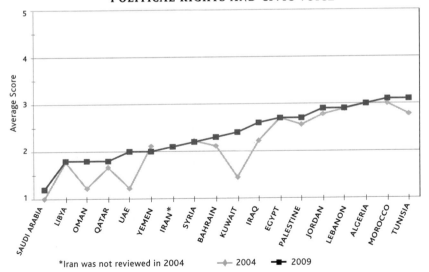

SOCIAL AND CULTURAL RIGHTS

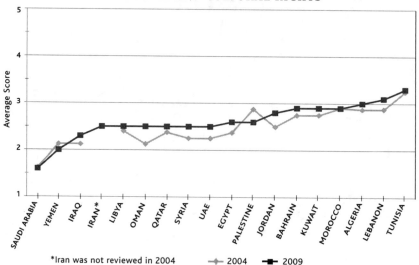

*Iran was not reviewed in 2004 ── 2004 ── 2009

INTRODUCTION TO COUNTRY REPORTS

The 2010 edition of *Women's Rights in the Middle East and North Africa* contains reports on 17 countries and one territory. Each report begins with a section containing basic data in the following categories: population and gross national income (GNI) per capita. The figures for population were obtained from the Population Reference Bureau and reflect mid-2009 estimates. Data on GNI were taken from the United Nations World Statistics Pocketbook and reflect the Atlas-method GNI for 2007.

In addition, numerical ratings are provided for the five thematic categories reviewed in the survey including: Nondiscrimination and Access to Justice; Autonomy, Security, and Freedom of the Person; Economic Rights and Equal Opportunity; Political Rights and Civic Voice; and Social and Cultural Rights. A rating of 1 represents the lowest level and 5 the highest level of freedom women have to exercise their rights. For a full description of the methods used to determine the survey's ratings, please see the chapters on "Survey Methodology" and "Ratings and Scoring System." The Iran chapter was not included in the first edition and represents an increase in the scope of the project.

Following the header information, each country report is divided into six parts. An introductory overview is provided at the outset that discusses the current status of women, often highlighting the historical growth of the women's rights movement. This section of the report also provides a basic understanding of the major improvements or setbacks made to women's rights since 2004, when the coverage of the 2005 edition ended. Each of the five thematic sections contains a set of recommendations highlighting the specific areas of most immediate need for reform.

ALGERIA

by Nadia Marzouki

POPULATION:	35,370,000		
GNI PER CAPITA:	US$3,729		

COUNTRY RATINGS	2004	2009
NONDISCRIMINATION AND ACCESS TO JUSTICE:	3.0	3.1
AUTONOMY, SECURITY, AND FREEDOM OF THE PERSON:	2.4	3.0
ECONOMIC RIGHTS AND EQUAL OPPORTUNITY:	2.8	3.0
POLITICAL RIGHTS AND CIVIC VOICE:	3.0	3.0
SOCIAL AND CULTURAL RIGHTS:	2.9	3.0

(COUNTRY RATINGS ARE BASED ON A SCALE OF 1 TO 5, WITH 1 REPRESENTING THE LOWEST AND 5 THE HIGHEST LEVEL OF FREEDOM WOMEN HAVE TO EXERCISE THEIR RIGHTS)

INTRODUCTION

Although Algerian women played a key role in the war for independence from France, which lasted from 1954 to 1962, the battle for gender equality has long been overshadowed by the nationalist struggle. Since 1962, government officials have formally acknowledged women's central role in the construction of an independent nation. However, very few grassroots feminist organizations developed in the 1960s and 1970s. Even former female combatants in the independence struggle often argued that nationalist objectives were more pressing than the elimination of gender discrimination.

The National Liberation Front (FLN), which led the independence movement and remains the ruling party in Algeria, was largely ambivalent on gender issues. The socialist aspects of its ideology advocated women's equality, but more conservative strains within the movement viewed women as the vessels of Islamic and traditional values. In the two decades following independence, groups that supported divergent political projects clashed over personal status issues, and their failure to reach a consensus thwarted various attempts to codify family law. In 1981, an extremely conservative draft family law was vehemently rejected by a grassroots movement of women from different professional backgrounds, including

29

university professors, schoolteachers, medical doctors, and laborers. They came together to organize petitions and demonstrate against the proposed legislation. Under this pressure, the government retracted the 1981 draft, but on June 9, 1984, a very similar code was passed without public debate.[1]

The 1984 family code established the concept of an agnatic family structure characterized by patriarchal authority. Under this code, which was designed to appeal to Islamic fundamentalists by meeting a few of their basic priorities, women were primarily recognized as guardians of kin and tradition rather than as autonomous individuals.[2] In 2005, partly under the pressure of women's organizations, the family code was finally amended by the government of President Abdelaziz Bouteflika, who has been in power since 1999.

The new code has brought a number of positive changes. It grants women more rights in terms of divorce and housing, reduces the role of a woman's male guardian to a largely symbolic status, and ensures Algerian women's right to transmit citizenship to their children. However, most women's rights groups continue to regard the amended code as far too hesitant to create true gender equality.

While the 2005 revision of the family code represents the most important change for women's rights over the last five years, there were several other positive developments. The Algerian constitution, amended in 2008, now officially recognizes women's political role (Article 31 bis). Since a new article was added to the penal code (Article 341 bis) in 2004 to penalize sexual harassment, some victims have stood up and decided to file suits. Women's security in the public space has continued to improve, and even though the threat of attacks by radical groups remains real, the memory of the "Black Decade" of political and civil violence is slowly fading away. The fighting, triggered by the cancellation of democratic election results in 1991, had pitted Islamist groups against the FLN and caused around 100,000 deaths, with terrible consequences for women's security.

However, some existing freedoms for both men and women have been recently challenged, including religious freedom. The ordinance 06-03, passed in February 2006, criminalized attempts by groups or individuals to convert Muslims to another religion, intimidating a number of Muslim women who had converted to Christianity. The broader political conditions have also helped to obstruct progress on women's rights. A 2008 constitutional amendment suppressing presidential term limits has further reduced the chances of political change, and despite the repeated objections of human rights activists, the government maintains the state of emergency that was first declared in February 1992 and allows the authorities to circumvent the rule of law in the name of national security. The state of emergency is increasingly seen as a way for the government to monitor associations and prevent the formation of a democratic public sphere. Similarly, the 2005 National Charter on Peace and Reconciliation criminalizes the activities of organizations that investigate the disappearance of civilians at the hands of the military or Islamist groups during the civil conflict.

A number of features of Algerian society continue to play against women's emancipation and have not changed substantially over the last five years. Except in a few cities such as Algiers and Oran, divisions between secularists and advocates of a more religiously oriented way of life remain important. While these divisions do not prevent the hybridization of practices, they are a significant barrier to the emergence of productive public debates. Most discussions on gender and women adhere to this antagonistic structure. Conditions for women are also greatly affected by the clientelist dimension of social relations. Algerian society is organized around competing networks of influence (clienteles), and each may take up or drop the defense of women's rights to suit their interests at any given time. Finally, the housing crisis that has developed since the early 1990s is a major obstacle to women's emancipation, particularly for divorced or single women. Despite several programs launched by the government, housing remains insufficient, rents are too high, the housing infrastructure is extremely precarious,[3] and rental transactions are subject to clientelist practices.

The present situation for Algerian women is complex and often ambiguous. Some believe that the family code, even with the recent revisions, is discriminatory and should be replaced by secular civil laws. This view has been continuously defended, notably, by Louisa Hanoune, a secular feminist and the only female leader of a political party, the Party of Workers ("Parti des Travailleurs"). However, women's empowerment is also inhibited by other factors, including gender-based prejudices, the lack of legal awareness among women, and broader government restrictions on civil liberties and political rights. Despite these constraints, the number of women's rights organizations has grown since 2004. Analysts praise the energy of these organizations as well as the interest that Algerian women display in learning about their rights whenever they are given the opportunity to do so. Scholars and activists emphasize the fact that the actual practices of Algerian society are often more progressive than official discourse or formal laws may suggest.

The burgeoning number of women's rights groups over the last five years showcases growing activism and civic involvement among women. However, the feminist movement continues to face challenges. Women's rights organizations are increasingly fragmented along ideological lines, and activists do not necessarily agree on what constitutes the best strategy for achieving further advances. While some emphasize the need for change at the legal level, particularly within the family code, others contend that establishing and enforcing the rule of law and extending civil liberties at all levels are more pressing objectives. However, it is clear that none of these approaches can be entirely successful as long as the government continues to exercise tight controls on the use of the public sphere and within political parties, and women remain unaware of their existing or potential rights.

NONDISCRIMINATION AND ACCESS TO JUSTICE

Women's rights are generally acknowledged and protected under the constitution, civil laws, and penal code, although discriminatory provisions on topics including rape and witness testimony continue to exist. Reforms of the family code and nationality code in 2005 were seen as positive even if incomplete, and amendments made to the constitution in 2008 illustrate the government's more active commitment to promoting women's political role. However, factors such as the irregular enforcement of laws and women's lack of knowledge about their rights hinder equal access to justice.

First adopted in 1963, the constitution was most recently amended in November 2008. In addition to suppressing presidential term limits, the amendments formally acknowledged "women's political role" under Article 31 bis. Article 29, which existed prior to the 2008 changes, enshrines the general principle of equality before the law and nondiscrimination on the basis of gender. Some women's rights advocates question the relevance of officially endorsing women's political role in the amended constitution when nondiscrimination was already guaranteed. They argue that the primary motivation behind the amendment was to win the female vote. Other activists believe the amendment was a positive measure and are convinced that the government's commitment is necessary to advance women's rights.

Civil laws and policies apply to men and women equally, but Article 1 of the civil code stipulates that "in the absence of any legal disposition, the judge pronounces himself according to the principle of Islamic law and, if necessary, according to customary law."[4] It is primarily for crimes against women, such as rape or abduction, that such legal dispositions are missing. Consequently, women are the main victims of this legal dualism. In the private sphere and in all matters concerning the family, the 1984 family code applies. This code—which is based on Shari'a, customary law, and French law—severely restricts women's liberties and opportunities. Amendments in 2005 removed some of its gender-based inequities, but many discriminatory provisions remain.

Since 2005, the amended nationality code has recognized Algerian women's ability to transmit citizenship to their children when the father is a foreigner. Article 6 of the new code stipulates that a child is considered Algerian when born to a father *or a mother* of Algerian citizenship. However, Article 26 subjects this provision to the approval of the Ministry of Justice.[5] In light of the change to the code, the Algerian government recently withdrew its reservation to Article 9(2) of the Convention on the Elimination of All Forms of Discrimination against Women (CEDAW). Article 9 bis of the code also recognizes the ability of a man to acquire Algerian citizenship when he marries an Algerian woman and the couple lives in Algeria.

All citizens are entitled to equal access to justice regardless of their gender, and women are fairly well represented in the judiciary as judges and lawyers. However, in practice, women typically either do not know their legal rights or refrain from asserting them through formal legal channels. This is particularly true regarding claims involving domestic violence, sexual harassment, and rape. The reluctance to pursue these claims can be attributed to several factors, including the real and perceived biases in the law and the ongoing prevalence of patriarchal attitudes in society. Laws concerning women's rights are sometimes implemented in an arbitrary manner, especially in cases that pertain to the family code. In addition, the significant financial cost associated with pursuing legal cases is a major obstacle for women, who are often economically dependent on their husbands or fathers.

Except in cases of adultery and rape, men and women are generally treated equally within the penal code. According to Article 339, both married men and married women who commit adultery are punished by one to two years of imprisonment. However, men face this penalty only when they act with the knowledge that the woman is married, whereas women are punished even if they act without such knowledge. Article 279 excuses both men and women if they commit assault or murder upon discovering a spouse in the act of adultery, although women rarely commit such crimes.

Article 336 of the penal code does not specifically define the crime of rape. The French version of the code uses the word *viol* (rape).[6] However, the Arabic text uses the phrase *hatk al-'ardh* (attack on the honor) rather than the more explicit *ightisab* (rape). This alters the character of the crime from a violent sexual offense against an autonomous individual to an offense that primarily affects family honor. Consequently, if the victim is not married, the rapist may avoid punishment by marrying her and expunging the dishonor. In keeping with this view of women's autonomy, spousal rape is not outlawed.

Algerian men and women are protected against arbitrary arrest and detention under Articles 45–48 of the constitution. Articles 107–111 of the penal code punish all civil servants, persons representing state authority, law enforcement agents, judges, policemen, and prison guards who abuse their authority and arbitrarily limit individuals' freedom. The National Consultative Commission for the Promotion and Protection of Human Rights, appointed by the government in 2001, also promotes individuals' protection against arbitrary detention and arrest, though many human rights activists remain skeptical about its effectiveness and argue that it mainly serves the government's goal of maintaining the approval of the international community. In this context, most citizens do not feel that they are safe from arbitrary detention and arrest, particularly when they attempt to exercise freedom of speech. Several journalists were charged with or convicted of defamation in 2008 for criticizing the regime in their writings.[7]

The courts consider male and female plaintiffs and defendants to be equal before the law, but the Ministry of Justice considers the testimony of two female witnesses to be equal to that of one male witness in criminal cases. Female defendants can receive different sentences based on their gender in certain circumstances. For instance, Article 16 of the code of penitentiary organization stipulates that the punishment of a woman can be suspended if she is pregnant or has a child less than two years old (the breastfeeding period is defined as 24 months).[8] In addition, when both the father and the mother of dependent children are sentenced to time in prison, the mother's sentence is delayed until the father has been released from prison. Of the estimated 54,000 prisoners in Algeria, only 1.1 percent were women as of 2006,[9] so these rules affect relatively few sentences. While they are intended to be beneficial, the special provisions for women are based primarily on their role as mothers, reinforcing patriarchal values in society.

Algeria ratified CEDAW in 1996, but cited the family code in attaching reservations regarding Article 2, which addresses the general goal of eliminating discrimination against women; Article 15(4), on freedom of movement and residence; and Article 16, on marital and family rights. On July 15, 2009, the government reported that it was lifting its reservation to Article 9(2) on transferring nationality to children, as noted above.[10]

Women's rights associations and civil society actors are limited in their ability to effect change. The Ministry of Interior tightly regulates most associations, and women's rights groups are extremely fragmented along class lines and between secular and religiously oriented ideologies. In addition, organizations such as the Wassila Network, which struggles against domestic violence, lack the funding necessary to carry out their work. Despite the efforts of associations like the Children of Fadhma n'Soumer to educate women about their rights and inform them of the constraints imposed by the family code, women are generally unaware of the rights they already have.[11] Finally, the divergence between rights granted by the constitution and the restrictions imposed by the family code remains a major obstacle for women's emancipation.

Recommendations

+ The government and women's advocacy groups should actively educate women and men about women's constitutional rights regarding health, employment, security, and citizenship, as well as the full array of their existing rights under the law.
+ Rape should be clearly defined in the penal code as a physical attack against an individual and punished as such. The code should specifically outlaw spousal rape.
+ In order to ensure the adequate enforcement of existing laws that offer equal protection to men and women, the government should establish mechanisms to identify and punish judges who abuse their authority and fail to adhere to the law. The 2006 law (06-01) on the prevention

and struggle against corruption should be fully implemented in the judicial sphere, and projects similar to Italy's *Mani pulite* (clean hands) investigation into judicial corruption should be launched in Algeria.

✤ Women's organizations should educate the public about the government's remaining reservations to CEDAW and encourage debate on the areas where existing laws, particularly the family code, clash with the treaty's provisions.

AUTONOMY, SECURITY, AND FREEDOM OF THE PERSON

Algerians have begun to enjoy an improved sense of personal security in recent years as the Black Decade recedes in their memories, but most remain preoccupied about their safety. Women are able to travel freely in most places, though freedom of movement is sometimes restricted for women as a practical matter. While the 2005 amendments to the family code granted new rights to women and more assertively acknowledged their autonomy, the code retains restrictions that present major obstacles to the realization of gender equality. Consequently, many women continue to call for the abolition of the family code as a whole.

Islam is established as the state religion in the constitution, which also prohibits discrimination against religious minorities (Article 2). Religious minorities, primarily Christians and Jews, have been relatively free to practice their faiths since independence in 1962, although they must adhere to the family code, which is derived from Islamic schools of jurisprudence. Muslim women may only marry Muslim men for their marriages to be legally recognized, whereas Muslim men are free to marry Muslim, Christian, or Jewish women.

The government and members of the Association of Ulama (Islamic scholars) have expressed some concern over what they view as a worrying rise in evangelical Christian missionary activities. In this context, officials have reportedly closed dozens of churches, although the government denies closing any authorized churches.[12] In February 2006, ordinance 06-03 was promulgated to criminalize attempts by groups or individuals to convert Muslims to another religion. This ordinance also subjects the exercise of religions other than Islam to special authorization by the provincial governor. Habiba Kouider, a Muslim convert to Christianity, was arrested in March 2008 and charged with practicing a faith other than Islam without authorization after several copies of the Bible were found in her purse.[13]

Women are permitted to travel freely, and freedom of movement for all Algerians has appreciably improved in the past 10 years. Algerian women are able to obtain their own passports and leave the country without their husbands' permission, but a woman cannot leave with her children without authorization from the husband. Moreover, female workers who migrate within the country to find a job or women who travel alone sometimes face condemnation, particularly in the rural areas.

The 1984 family code was amended on February 22, 2005, to improve several key provisions. For instance, under Article 7 of the amended code, the legal age of capacity for marriage changed from 21 for men and 18 for women to 19 for both sexes. In addition, proxy marriages are now prohibited. This practice, in which a prospective spouse could be represented by a proxy during a marriage ceremony, facilitated forced marriages and was especially common in rural areas. In some cases a bride might not even be aware of her marriage—agreed upon by her family and the groom—until after the fact.

Despite these amendments, many believe that the family code remains too ambiguous on several central issues and retains a number of discriminatory provisions. For instance, a bride's *wali* (marriage guardian, usually her closest male relative) must be present when she concludes her marital contract, though he is now reduced to an honorary role and defined as her father, a relative, or "any other person of her choice." A wali cannot force a woman to marry someone against her will or oppose the marriage.[14] Given this reduced authority, some women's rights advocates defend the decision to retain the wali institution because it acts mainly as a tribute to Islamic culture without obstructing women's autonomy. Others feel that the practice contradicts the amendment raising the marriage age to 19 for women and does not fully recognize women's autonomy. They note the inconsistency of a code that retains the requirement that wali be present while simultaneously allowing women to freely choose their wali.

Polygamy remains legal under Article 8 of the family code, although it is now subject to several conditions. The court must certify that there is "justified motivation" behind the decision to take more than one wife, that the man is able to take care of an additional spouse, and that all of the spouses involved consent to the marriage. Currently, only 3 percent of Algerian households are polygamous. However, single and divorced women are increasingly marginalized by society. A 2006 nationwide survey showed that 55 percent of the sample of women (whose average age was 33) were single, 36 percent were married, 6 percent were widows, and 3 percent were divorced.[15] Consequently, becoming someone's second wife is an increasingly attractive option when the alternative is to remain single. The supporters of polygamy argue that because most people who disappeared during the Black Decade were men, there are more women than men of marrying age.

Retaining polygamy while attempting to accommodate the concerns of women's rights activists may create more problems than it solves. Now that the consent of the first spouse is required, the husband often chooses to divorce the first spouse if she rejects his request for a second wife. If he and the first wife were childless or if their children are adults, the divorced wife has no right to the marital home or alimony. Consequently, women over the age of 60 increasingly find themselves divorced and homeless as their ex-husbands take new wives. This illustrates the difficult task of reconciling civil law and Islamic law, under which polygamy is conditioned not on the consent of the first wife, but on the ability of the husband to care, materially and morally, for all of his spouses. Some maintain that these are more sensible conditions than those included in the new law, but most women's rights activists argue that polygamy should be banned altogether.

Although these conservative provisions regarding polygamy and the necessity of a wali have been widely criticized, it seems that the government is reluctant to change them further due to pressure from conservative Islamist groups and their constituents.[16] Since President Bouteflika's election in 1999, the government and these Islamist groups have operated under a tacit agreement whereby the former refrains from enacting reforms on sensitive social issues and the latter withhold criticism on other matters.

Article 19 of the amended family code legally entitles both spouses to make stipulations, either within the marital contract or in another instrument, that guarantee them certain rights within the marriage. The article specifically mentions the right to set conditions regarding polygamy and the right to work.[17] The marital rights and duties of men and women differ, although the duty of a wife to obey her husband has been removed from the new code.[18] Article 78 requires men to provide financial maintenance for their wives. For their part, wives must breastfeed and rear the children, and have only supplemental and poorly defined authority within the family. Upon divorce, however, the parental authority of a mother with custody of her children is fully acknowledged under Article 87. Despite this change, many administrative agents still refuse to let such women travel abroad with their children without the father's authorization. The new code allows paternity to be established through DNA testing, and if a couple was married at the time of the child's conception, the husband is obliged to acknowledge paternity. Article 64 grants the mother custody of male children only until age 10 and of female children until they reach marriage age.

While men may initiate divorce without explanation, women filing for divorce must generally cite one or more of 10 specific reasons, such as abandonment for a year without justification.[19] Should a woman wish to initiate a divorce for other reasons, her only option is *khula*, the traditional Islamic practice that permits a woman to unilaterally initiate divorce if she pays the husband a sum of money.[20] Under Article 37 of the family code, each spouse retains his or her own property upon marriage, and they can agree to hold their new property in common or determine their respective shares through stipulations in the marriage contract or a separate document. Household properties in dispute upon divorce are divided according to rules specified under Article 73. The law entitles husbands to keep property that is "for exclusive male use," and wives to keep exclusively "female" items, without specifying how such items are to be defined. While men are automatically granted the "male" objects, in practice judges may arbitrarily require women to prove that they bought the "female" items over which they claim ownership.

Article 72 of the family code guarantees that, upon divorce, women who retain primary custody over their children will receive proper housing. This is a major improvement from the 1984 code, under which men kept the marital home upon divorce, often forcing divorced women and their children onto the streets. However, because of the current housing crisis, many judges allow divorced men to keep the house if they offer equivalent funding to their ex-wives and children. Consequently, unemployed men or those with low incomes provide too little money to allow their ex-wives and children to find decent housing. Some argue that this new rule encourages divorced men to more vehemently invoke their custody rights, because divorced women who do not retain custody of their children (and those without children) are not entitled to alimony or housing. Women who remarry after divorce lose custody of their existing children.

Women's rights groups have indicated that the 2005 amendments to the family code have not been properly implemented. For instance, because women tend to be unaware of the new code and judges are often reluctant to implement it, some judges still require that a bride's father act as wali or permit marriages by proxy. Article 7 bis, which requires prospective spouses to present health certificates to prevent the spread of disease, has been interpreted by some officials as an obligation for women to present a virginity certificate. And although the new code prevents imams from conducting religious marriage ceremonies unless the spouses submit a civil contract first, some couples try to avoid this requirement. When such marriages end in divorce, women lack the protections of a marital contract.

Article 34 of the constitution prohibits all violations of human dignity, while Articles 342 and 343 of the penal code criminalize most forms of sex trafficking and exploitation of minors. Little data exists on the extent of domestic slavery and human trafficking in Algeria. From the government's perspective, the issue of human trafficking is secondary to the more pressing question of illegal immigration from sub-Saharan Africa. According to a report published in 2007 by the U.S. State Department, of the 15,000 illegal sub-Saharan African immigrants residing in Algeria, about 9,000 were victims of trafficking, sexual exploitation, or involuntary forms of servitude.[21] The report also found that the government did not adequately distinguish between human trafficking and illegal immigration, though it is possible that this will change under a new antitrafficking law approved in January 2009.

The government must protect all persons under Article 24 of the constitution, and security has significantly improved in the past 10 years. Nonetheless, women remain vulnerable to different forms of violence. Domestic abuse is not specifically prohibited by law, and because society considers it a private matter, it remains difficult to combat. As one women's rights activist put it, within the private sphere of the home, "women escape the protection of the law and men escape the sentence of the law."[22] A national survey commissioned in 2006 by the Ministry in Charge of the Family and Women's Affairs found that some 10 percent of the female respondents were exposed "daily" or "often" to physical abuse, while 31.4 percent were regularly exposed to threats of violence.[23] However, these figures are generally considered to be much lower than the actual incidences of domestic violence and threats. Women tend to avoid reporting abuse or going to court for fear that they will incur further violence or face hostile judges. According to one lawyer, a specialist in domestic violence, victims "are attacked twice, one time by their husband and another time by the judge."[24]

International organizations including Amnesty International have also raised concerns about the treatment of irregular immigrants in "waiting centers,"[25] and the condition of male and female refugees from Western Sahara.[26] While no policies specifically discriminate against women within these groups, the violence and other harsh living conditions of waiting centers and refugee camps often affect women more severely than men.

Civil society actors have fiercely and openly taken up issues related to women's autonomy and security. The debate regarding the family code has continued after 2005, and organizations such as the Children of Fadhma n'Soumer Association, which advocates the abolition of the family code, have published booklets detailing the contradictions and drawbacks of the code. Associations of this type complain about the government-imposed limitations on the scope of their message and audience, as well as their financial constraints and failure to coordinate with one another. The family code debate has developed a hostile tone, marked by a divide between conservatives who claim to defend Islamic tradition and the secular or Islamic progressive groups.

Because domestic violence is no longer considered a taboo subject, the government has launched a national strategy aimed at combating the problem and consolidating initiatives taken by various domestic civil society organizations. The Ministry of National Solidarity and Family operates the National Shelter, a home for female victims of domestic violence located in Bou Ismail. Nongovernmental organizations (NGOs) such as SOS Women in Distress and RACHDA also operate shelters in Algiers, but they rely mostly on international and private donations for funding, and their capacity is limited. The Wassila Network provides assistance to victims of domestic violence by offering judicial and psychological counseling.[27] Women's rights groups emphasize the importance of defining psychological and verbal violence in addition to physical abuse, in conformity with the Arab Human Rights Charter.

Civil society actors are also working to bring closure to the families of those who disappeared during the Black Decade, although recent developments have hindered their work. The Collective of the Families of the Disappeared in Algeria (CFDA), an NGO led by Nassera Dutour, has long advocated the formation of a commission that would fully investigate each disappearance. In 2003, an ad hoc commission appointed by the government found 6,146 cases in which state agents were allegedly responsible for the disappearance of an individual. The 2005 Charter for Peace and National Reconciliation came as a major disappointment to victims' families. Indeed, Articles 45 and 46 of the charter, and the subsequent 2006 decree implementing it (Law 06-01), grant full immunity to security forces and effectively criminalize those refuse to put the matter behind them. Since the charter's adoption, the work of organizations such as the CFDA has been fiercely restricted. Several demonstrations and reunions have been banned, and mothers of the victims have been beaten by the police during protests.[28]

Recommendations

❖ The government, in conjunction with related civil society actors, should launch an awareness campaign regarding the rights granted to women under the 2005 amendments to the family code. This information initiative should focus on local and personal stories, which have been described as more persuasive to the public than the mere presentation of legal norms.

❖ All parties and groups, despite their sometimes opposing ideologies, should work together to resolve the remaining contradictions of the new code, notably those involving divorce, polygamy, and the need for a wali.[29]

❖ National and international human rights groups should continue to advocate for a thorough investigation into the thousands of alleged forced disappearances during the Black Decade.

❖ Domestic violence should be criminalized, and prosecution should continue even if the victim forgives her abuser. A 2003 Spanish law, which contains such a provision and also calls for judges to respond to domestic violence complaints within 72 hours, has often been cited as a model.

ECONOMIC RIGHTS AND EQUAL OPPORTUNITY

In the last five years, women's economic rights and opportunities have improved in some respects. The amended family code gave women the ability to establish the separation of goods in their marriage contracts. Although the inheritance law is still governed by Shari'a, practices and opinions related to inheritance are changing. Women's literacy, enrollment in universities, and employment are steadily increasing. And since 2004, the penal code has criminalized sexual harassment. However, the effects of negative stereotypes and habits remain a major obstacle to women's economic empowerment.

The constitution and the family code protect the right of Algerian women to own and independently use land and property, although social norms encourage women to let men make ownership decisions. An article of the family code that required women to obey their husbands was amended in 2005, but upon divorce a woman must bring evidence that she participated in the funding of items she wants to keep. Article 37 of the amended family code permits the prospective bride and groom to add a provision in their marriage contract establishing the separation of their goods.

Algeria's inheritance law is based on the Maliki school of Islamic jurisprudence, under which a daughter is entitled to the equivalent of half her brother's share of inheritance. When a woman has no brother, the share that would have gone to a brother is divided among other male relatives. Most women's rights activists oppose the current inheritance scheme, but those in favor of it argue that men are responsible for the material well-being of their wives and daughters under Islamic law and therefore need an extra share of inheritance. Many families circumvent the inequities of the inheritance law by giving portions of estates to daughters while the owner is still alive, a practice that some government officials have criticized as a form of tax evasion. If the government regulates these lifetime donations more rigidly without making a corresponding amendment to the inheritance law, families could have greater difficulty ensuring that their daughters receive equal shares. Some women are pressured by male relatives to give up their legal share of inheritance to keep land and other property in the male line of the family, but the situation is improving slowly, and there is considerable variation from place to place. A recent survey by the Center for Information and Documentation on Children's and Women's Rights (CIDDEF) showed that 76 percent of teenagers (ages 14–17) and 59 percent of adults (aged 18 and over) are in favor of equal inheritance rights. Among the male population, 38 percent of adults and 50 percent of teenagers share this opinion.[30]

Children between the ages of 6 and 16 must attend school, which is free under Article 53 of the constitution. A 2006 national education survey found that 96.3 percent of girls and 96.9 percent of boys received primary education.[31] However, the study showed that more girls than boys obtain secondary and postsecondary education. Fifty-seven percent of girls between ages 16 and 19 enrolled in secondary education, compared with only 43 percent of boys of the same age; the figures for higher education were 25.4 percent and 18.4 percent, respectively. Enrollment statistics collected by the World Bank show an overall improvement for both girls and boys between 2000 and 2007, although the gains for girls appeared somewhat larger, and primary enrollment for both declined slightly from 2004 to 2007.[32]

Despite gains in education, illiteracy rates among women remain high in certain areas of the country.[33] According to the 2006 national education survey, 31.6 percent of 10-year-old girls and 16.5 percent of 10-year-old boys were illiterate, while 34 percent of women living in rural areas had never been to school. The literacy rate for adult women (aged 15 and above) has improved from 60.1 percent in 2004 to 66.4 percent in 2007, compared with 79.6 percent and 84.3 percent for adult males, according to the World Bank. In 2009, the government launched a national strategy to eliminate illiteracy by 2015. The Ministry of Education requires employers to educate their illiterate employees, although this rule is only sporadically enforced. Several women's organizations close to the government, such as Horizons for Algerian Women (HFA), have made eradicating illiteracy their priority. HFA has launched literacy programs in several of the country's 48 provinces (*wilayat*), and women who have received a certificate of literacy from one of their programs are able to secure jobs more easily.

In an effort to promote gender sensitivity from a young age, women's rights organizations have drawn attention to the persistence of negative or patriarchal stereotypes in textbooks and the views of both male and female teachers. They have had little success in ameliorating this problem, however.

The significant representation of women at the university level has not produced a corresponding representation in the labor market. According to a 2006 national survey, only 18.7 percent of women were employed, with 60 percent working in the public sector and 40 percent in the private sector.[34] The latter consisted of 18.5 percent working in the formal sector and 21.5 percent in the informal sector, where women earn low wages and have no benefits. Urban women tend to be more economically active and represented over 70 percent of employed women in the survey.[35] Statistics compiled by the World Bank, based on International Labor Organization estimates, show a female labor force participation rate of 38.1 percent for 2007, up from 35.5 percent in 2004. The rate for men was 80.7 percent for 2007 and 81.6 percent in 2004.[36]

Algerian women are free to enter into and negotiate business contracts, but according to the 2006 survey, women represent only 4 percent of all business owners.[37] This can be attributed to a lack of incentives, education, and opportunities. Some organizations that work closely with the government, such as the Association of Algerian Female Executives (AFCARE), promote the advancement of women within all sectors of employment. They provide women with information regarding their economic rights and offer project management training. Other organizations launch profit-generating projects at the local level to help women start their own business. The Children of Fadhma n'Soumer Association, for example, has encouraged the creation of small rural cooperatives.

In theory, women may freely choose their profession. Article 55 of the constitution guarantees the right to work for all Algerian citizens, and as discussed in the previous section, women may stipulate the right to work as a precondition in their marriage contracts under Article 19 of the family code. However, women's rights activists argue that Article 19 could be used to undermine the constitutional guarantee, since husbands could argue that their wives gave up the right to work by failing to include it in the marriage contract. Women are present in all sectors of employment, and some even work as taxi drivers, policewomen, or members of the military. However, most employed women work in health care, education, or the legal field. As of 2006, women reportedly represented 50 percent of teachers, 53 percent of medical doctors, and 37 percent of magistrates (prosecutors and judges).[38]

Women also tend to limit their employment options to those located near their parents or husband. It is socially acceptable for female civil servants to move within Algeria for work-related reasons because the government is considered a reliable guardian.[39] However, divorced or single women who migrate inside the country to work in the private sector often suffer from patriarchal prejudices, which label them as immoral. These stereotypes, combined with the resentment toward female employment that comes with the high rate of unemployment among men, limits the actual freedom of movement of women in search of economic opportunity. When individuals in power stoke such negative attitudes, it can lead to incidents like the attack on female migrant workers in Hassi Messaoud.

Article 84 of the employment code of 1990 guarantees equal pay for men and women who have equal qualifications and perform equal tasks.[40] The code outlaws all forms of gender-based discrimination in employment contracts. Employers in both the private and public sectors are bound to provide three months of paid maternity leave, two hours per day for breastfeeding, and retirement benefits. Women are eligible for retirement at age 55, compared with 60 for men. Women can also receive one year of early retirement for each child (up to three children) that she raised for nine years.[41] Despite these employment benefits, many women choose to stop working when they get married. According to the 2006 national survey, 49 percent of women with private-sector jobs stopped working when they got married, and 16.3 percent of those in the public sector did the same. Less than 30 percent of women interviewed opposed the idea of working, suggesting that most women would be interested in employment if they had the opportunity. The women surveyed identified several factors that deterred them from pursuing or maintaining employment, including transportation problems, family pressure, wages, child care obstacles, discrimination, and sexual harassment.[42]

In 2004, the penal code was amended to criminalize sexual harassment under Article 341 bis. However, this amendment disappointed women's organizations in that it only criminalized sexual harassment based on abuse of authority, apparently leaving many forms of abuse, including harassment by peers, unaddressed. It is likely that most cases of harassment go unreported, but 4,500 complaints of violence and harassment were filed with the police between January and June 2008.[43] Single women, whether divorced, widowed, or never married, are the most common victims of harassment. Most women refrain from going to court, either for fear of being ostracized by their family and colleagues or because they are not informed of their rights. Complainants must present evidence of the harassment, but their colleagues are usually afraid to testify on their behalf for fear of reprisal firings or countersuits accusing them of defamation. In November 2008, two female employees at the Bank of Algeria spoke to the newspaper *Djazair News* about their claim to have been harassed on the job. Their employer countersued, and the court handed them a two-month suspended jail sentence, in addition to fines and damages, for defamation.[44]

Recommendations

✤ The government should fund cooperative projects at the local level and facilitate the provision of credit to women who want to start or expand their own businesses. These could include agricultural projects such as those promoted by the Children of Fadhma n'Soumer Association, but the effort should address the full range of economic activities in which employed urban women are already involved.

❖ The government should enact legislation extending the ban on sexual harassment to all relevant behavior that creates a hostile working environment for women. The law should include specific protections barring retaliation against complainants and witnesses. Meanwhile, both civil society actors and the government should launch an awareness-raising campaign on the existing ban, and judges should receive training on how to properly adjudicate cases.

❖ The government should foster a public debate and discussions among experts on how to make inheritance law fair for women while respecting religious norms.

❖ The government should offer special financial incentives for poor families to send both male and female children to school through completion of the secondary level. Officials should also consult with local women's NGOs on how to eliminate negative gender stereotypes from school curriculums in a manner that is respectful of Algerian culture and in accord with Islamic traditions.

❖ The government should launch an initiative that encourages both job seekers and employers to raise women's representation in decision-making positions to a level that matches their substantial educational achievements.

POLITICAL RIGHTS AND CIVIC VOICE

Restrictions on the political and civil rights of women are just one aspect of the broader limitations affecting the public sphere in Algeria. The freedoms of expression and association are restricted by a government that is heavily influenced by the military and the ruling FLN party. If a woman belongs to an influential group, she may wield more power than men belonging to a less important group. Thus the activism of privileged women belonging to powerful clans tends to overshadow more discreet forms of activism by civil society. Whatever their affiliations, women remain severely underrepresented in the executive branch, the parliament, and local government bodies.

Algerian women were granted the right to vote and run for office in 1962. A multiparty system was established by the 1989 constitution, and since then women and men have actively participated in politics within the limits imposed by the state of emergency and the constraints defined by the Ministry of Interior.

The most recent parliamentary elections took place in May 2007, and female candidates won 30 of the 389 seats in the National People's Assembly, the lower house of parliament. Most of the women elected are members of the FLN, which led the voting with 136 seats overall, and the Workers' Party, which is led by a woman, Louisa Hanoune, and took 26 seats overall. This representation of just 7.7 percent is a slight improvement over the previous elections in 2002, in which women secured little more than 6 percent of the chamber. As of the end of 2008, women held only 4 of the 144 seats in the Council of the Nation, the upper house; this chamber is one-third appointed by the president and two-thirds indirectly elected by local and provincial officials.[45] Women hold only about 5 percent of the seats in the country's local popular assemblies.

Women are fairly well represented in the judiciary, making up over a third of the country's prosecutors and judges. However, few women work in the top ranks of the executive branch, and only 3 of 35 cabinet members are women: Khalida Toumi is the minister of culture, Nouara Saâdia Djaafar is a delegate minister at the Ministry of National Solidarity and Family, and Souad Bendjaballah is a delegate minister at the Ministry of Higher Education and Research. Hanoune, the Workers' Party leader, was the only woman to run for president in 2004 and April 2009, taking roughly 1 percent and 4 percent of the vote, respectively. She notably finished second in the 2009 election, as the incumbent, President Bouteflika, was credited with over 90 percent of the vote amid fraud allegations from the opposition.[46] Although she does not define herself as the "candidate of women," Hanoune advocates the abolition of the family code, a position generally endorsed by women's rights activists.

Women may participate in political parties at all levels, but they generally constitute no more than 10 percent of most parties' membership. In April 2009, the Ministry of Justice appointed a commission to consider a law that would mandate a quota of 30 to 40 percent for women in all political parties. However, many politically active women are ambivalent about this plan, arguing that the number of women within political parties should not be the sole indicator of women's political empowerment, and that the agenda of each party should be taken into account. For example, Islamist parties generally have more female members than secular parties, but these women often adopt a very conservative stance on gender equality.

Few women hold leadership positions that would allow them to influence policymaking. This is explained by the combined effect of conservative prejudices, the failure of the educational system to steer women toward such careers, and restrictions on the civil liberties of all citizens. The ability of Algerian citizens to participate in political and civic life varies between regions. For example, men and women in Kabylia have often resisted government repression more vehemently than those living in other areas, and the government has consequently responded more harshly there to signs of opposition or criticism from student groups and civil society leaders.

As individuals, Algerian women and men are, in theory, guaranteed freedom of assembly and expression. However, aspects of association law, the precarious security in certain areas of the country, and the fragmentation of women's groups are major obstacles to the development of women's civic and political voice. The 1992 decree establishing the state of emergency requires associations to obtain the governor's permission before holding public demonstrations, which is almost always refused to independent organizations. A law passed on June 18, 2001, also prohibits peaceful marches or public demonstrations in Algiers. Women's issues are increasingly addressed in the media, but often in the form of a sensationalist and polemical discussion that does not necessarily help women's empowerment. Journalists are able to cover these topics so long as they do not criticize the government.

Under Article 7 of association law 90-31, associations, political parties, and labor unions require special authorization (*agrément*) from the Ministry of Interior to legally exist. The government justifies this procedure by citing the state of emergency, and uses it to monitor and restrict the activities of civil liberties advocates. Most legally established women's rights organizations are not rooted deeply in Algerian society, however sincere they might be in their commitments to achieving gender equality. Many are instead incorporated into the clientelist system, catering to the needs of their respective interest groups rather than the collective needs of Algerian women. Because these relatively small and fragmented groups do not present a serious threat to the prevailing system, they encounter little government hostility. The effort to defend the families of victims of forced disappearances is one of the few movements that is connected to society and transcends class or clientelist divides. While it is not defined specifically as a women's movement, its ranks are composed mostly of women.

However, the efforts of organizations like the CFDA are now limited by the 2005 Charter for Peace and National Reconciliation, which effectively outlaws all criticism of the charter by victims' families and human rights activists.

Women's access to information has improved as the number of privately owned and independent French or Arabic newspapers has increased significantly over the past 10 years, and as more households are equipped with Internet access, televisions, and radios. However, most Algerian women, particularly the youth, are not aware of their ability and right to participate in civic and political activities. This is due in part to a high degree of illiteracy in certain areas, as well as social biases against politically and publicly powerful women that are perpetuated through the school system. The residual sense of insecurity due to the Black Decade is also a contributing factor. Many women may be too preoccupied with personal safety and daily needs to seek out information on civic and political affairs, or feel that political involvement could expose them to personal threats. Some activists dismiss these arguments, claiming instead that restrictions imposed by the government and the clientelist social structure are the main factors limiting women's empowerment and restricting their access to information. For example, while Internet access has expanded in recent years, the government actively monitors e-mail and other online content, and service providers can be held criminally responsible for material on websites they host.

Recommendations

* The government and human rights groups should create common platforms for open discussion where secular nationalists, progressive Islamists, and conservative Islamists can find common ground on women's rights and other important civic issues.
* The government should officially end the state of emergency and lift the associated restrictions on civil liberties.
* The need to secure an *agrément*, the main obstacle to the establishment of independent associations, should be abolished.
* Existing women's rights groups and female members of political parties should form broad coalitions to carry out projects of mutual interest, such as a campaign to encourage young women to vote and run for office, or joint events at which women can consider membership in a variety of organizations.

SOCIAL AND CULTURAL RIGHTS

Women in Algeria have benefited in recent decades from steady improvements in health care in certain areas, including childbirth and contraception. Early marriages are less common, and fertility rates have declined. However, the delivery of health services is uneven, often depending on the patient's wealth, personal connections, or place of residence. Prevailing cultural attitudes continue to cause serious difficulties for single mothers, who face poverty and a lack of housing. And while the reasons are complex, more women have begun wearing the veil in recent years. Women are well represented in the media, but they face discrimination in promotions and salary, and their ability to influence public perceptions of gender may be limited.

Algerian women are generally able to make independent decisions regarding their health care and reproductive rights. Married women may receive free contraceptives in public hospitals, and, due to the increased use of contraceptives and the rise in the average age of marriage, fertility rates have dropped from 2.7 births per woman in 2000 to 2.4 in 2007.[47] Abortion is illegal under Articles 304–313 of the penal code, but public health legislation provides exceptions for cases where the mother's physical or mental health is seriously jeopardized.[48] Separately, a 1998 *fatwa* (religious opinion) by the High Islamic Council, an official advisory body, allowed women who had been raped by armed groups to resort to abortion. According to gynecologists and women's rights groups, who would prefer that the issue of abortion be addressed publicly, many women undergo illegal, clandestine abortions. This is due to the limited circumstances under which abortion is legal as well as the shame attached to abortion and pregnancy out of wedlock.

Algerians have enjoyed free, universal health care since 1974, and the rate of births attended by skilled medical professionals increased from 77 percent in 1992 to 95 percent in 2006.[49] In spite of this, the rate of maternal mortality remains high in certain areas, especially in the southern provinces. According to a 2006 survey, only 30.6 percent of mothers benefit from postnatal care.[50] Mothers who have children out of wedlock are vulnerable to poverty and social prejudices. In most cases they are rejected by their families, and they do not benefit from any preferential access to subsidized housing. The few organizations that offer single mothers material help and legal counseling often treat them as "sinners" who must be morally reeducated.

Article 54 of the constitution enshrines the right to health care for all citizens. The implementation of this right is complicated less by gender disparity than by inequality among economic classes and social groups. Although health care is free, those with wealth and family or social connections to powerful groups have better access to the health system's limited resources than those without such advantages. This inequality can take on a regional character, as some areas are more impoverished and neglected by the state than others.

Harmful practices such as female genital mutilation hardly exist in Algeria. The number of women who are veiled has increased over the past decade, and this is sometimes interpreted as a sign that society is becoming more conservative. However, it is a complex phenomenon that includes an element of personal piety or social activism. Most women, veiled and unveiled, reject the notion that the practice of veiling is incompatible with women's autonomy. The types of veil worn by Algerian women range from those that cover the entire body to the *hijab*, a scarf that covers the head and neck. The most enveloping forms of veil, such as the *burqa*, are rarely worn, and Algerian women view such garments as foreign traditions.

As noted above, the amended family code requires a father to provide housing for his children and divorced wife so long as she retains custody. Women are legally able to obtain their own housing, but it is very difficult in practice. Given the limited housing infrastructure, high rents, and high unemployment rates, women are more vulnerable to poverty than men. This is particularly true for female victims of violence and the wives and children of those who disappeared during the Black Decade. No government program provides psychological help to the latter group, and the financial compensation now offered to them is a source of significant moral and psychological distress for most. As a precondition to receiving benefits, families must sign the death certificate, thereby renouncing the right to investigate the disappearance.

Women are very active at the community level, especially in schools and mosque-related associations. They are also active members of the media, but it is unclear whether they are able to influence media content. Women make up more than 50 percent of employees at public and private media outlets, 74 percent of journalists on television channels, and 88 percent on national radio channels. More than 50 percent of the female journalists interviewed in a 2006 survey had been journalists for over 15 years. Seventy-four percent of female journalists work for daily periodicals, while

16 percent work for weekly magazines. Despite being heavily represented in the workforce, female journalists are discriminated against in terms of salary. At least half work as freelancers and therefore do not receive retirement or health care benefits. Eighty-four percent of female journalists are not affiliated with a union.[51] Women are also less likely to be promoted due to the persistence of prejudices against female leaders and the negative effects of a clientelist social structure on the promotion system.

Scholars and journalists are ambivalent about the ability of women to influence perceptions of gender in media. For instance, domestic violence is increasingly addressed on the front pages of newspapers. Some women's rights advocates consider such coverage to be a positive step toward breaking the taboo against open discussion of the issue, and believe that it is a necessary method of informing the public about the plight of victims. However, other commentators are concerned that increased coverage of this sensational topic is primarily used to sell more newspapers and does not contribute to an improved image of women.[52]

Women's rights associations that concentrate on the advancement of social and cultural rights are able to operate with slightly more freedom than groups advocating for political and civil rights. However, it is difficult to disconnect the agenda of the former from the objectives of the latter. Organizations working to promote women's social and cultural rights complain about the restriction of their freedom of expression, insufficient funding, and fragmentation among groups with similar goals, which prevents the launching of any awareness campaign on a large scale.

Recommendations

+ The media and civil rights activists should propagate narratives about women's emancipation that circumvent the constraints of the typical antagonism between Islamism and secularism. Rather than drawing on experiences from Europe or North America, they could cite the achievements of women in countries with large Muslim populations, such as India or Indonesia.

+ The government should increase spending on health care infrastructure for neglected populations and enlist independent auditors to regularly and publicly assess the delivery of health services nationwide.

+ The government should establish and implement a plan that would address the housing crisis, the effects of which are felt more acutely by women than men. Such measures may encourage victims of violence to assert their rights more freely, as many currently remain silent for fear of being forced to live on the streets.

❖ The government should provide single mothers with adequate housing subsidies and assistance in accessing health care.

AUTHOR

Nadia Marzouki is a political scientist who works on religious pluralism in Europe and North Africa. She holds a PhD from Institut d'Etudes Politiques de Paris and is currently a postdoctoral associate and lecturer at the Council on Middle East Studies at Yale University. She conducted the fieldwork for this report during the summer of 2009.

NOTES

[1] However, very lively and noisy debates took place within the National People's Assembly in 1982 and 1984 between opposing political factions. See Boutheina Cheriet, "Islamism and Feminism: Algeria's Rites of Passage to Democracy," in *State and Society in Algeria,* ed. John P. Entelis and Phillip C. Naylor (Boulder: Westview Press, 1992), 171–216.

[2] Mounira M. Charrad, *State and Women's Rights: The Making of Postcolonial Tunisia, Algeria and Morocco* (Berkeley: University of California Press, 2001), 199.

[3] Craig S. Smith, "Quake Demolishes Confidence in Algerian Rulers," *New York Times,* May 30, 2003, http://www.nytimes.com/2003/05/30/world/quake-demolishes-confidence-in-algerian-rulers.html.

[4] Order No. 75-58 of September 26, 1975, of the Civil Code (Ministry of Justice), Article 1: "La loi régit toutes les matières auxquelles se rapporte la lettre ou l'esprit de l'une de ses dispositions. En l'absence d'une disposition légale, le juge se prononce selon les principes du droit musulmane et, à défaut, selon la coutume. Le cas échéant, il a recours au droit naturel et aux règles de l'équité."

[5] A copy of the nationality code, in French and Arabic, is available at http://www.droit.mjustice.dz/code_nation_alger.pdf.

[6] *Viol* is based on the same root as the English word *violence.*

[7] Amnesty International, "Algeria," in *Amnesty International Report 2009* (London: Amnesty International, 2009), http://report2009.amnesty.org/en/regions/middle-east-north-africa/algeria.

[8] A copy of the code is available at http://www.droit.mjustice.dz/SOFF.htm.

[9] International Centre for Prison Studies, "World Prison Brief," King's College (London), http://www.kcl.ac.uk/depsta/law/research/icps/worldbrief/wpb_country.php?country=1 (accessed September 16, 2009).

[10] See Multilateral Treaties Deposited with the Secretary-General, Status of Treaties, Chapter IV, CEDAW, Endnote 2, http://treaties.un.org/Pages/ViewDetails.aspx?src=TREATY&mtdsg_no=IV-8&chapter=4&lang=en#2 (accessed September 16, 2009).

11 The group is named after Lalla Fadhma n'Soumer, a female leader of the Kabylian anti-colonial struggle who lived from 1830 to 1863.

12 Amnesty International, "Algeria."

13 Kouider faces up to three years in prison, but the final verdict was postponed indefinitely in May 2008. Prominent Algerian intellectuals launched a petition in March 2009 to defend Kouider and religious freedom generally. The petition, entitled "SOS Libertés," was signed by more than 2,800 persons and published by the Francophone newspaper *El-Watan*.

14 The judge will act as wali for any bride who has none.

15 *Synthése de l'enquête nationale sur l'intégration socio-économique de la Femme* [Synthesis of the National Survey on Socio-Economic Integration of Women] (Algiers: Ministry Delegate for the Family and the Status of Women, 2006), http://www.ministere-famille.gov.dz/?page=Synthese.

16 Florence Beaugé, "En Algérie, le code de la famille maintient la femme sous tutelle" [In Algeria, the Family Code Keeps the Woman Under Guardianship], *Le Monde*, February 25, 2005.

17 Under Article 35, if the marriage contract contains stipulations that contradict the contract, the stipulation is void and the contract is valid. Moreover, stipulations may not contradict the law.

18 Prior to the 2005 amendments, the duty to obey was found in Article 39 of the family code.

19 A woman can initiate a divorce for the following reasons: the husband fails to pay financial maintenance during the three-month period before a divorce initiated by him is finalized; the husband cannot have children; the husband refuses to sleep with his wife for more than four months; the husband has been convicted of a crime; the husband has been absent for one year without giving any reason or without giving any money to the family; any form of "moral mistake"; a continuing disagreement between the spouses; the provisions stipulated in the marriage contract are broken; Article 8 of the family code, which sets the rules for polygamy, is violated; any form of legally acknowledged prejudice.

20 Article 54 of the family code allows for khula but leaves the parties to decide the sum owed by the wife to her husband. If they are unable to agree to a sum, the judge will order payment that does not exceed the worth of the proper dowry.

21 Office to Monitor and Combat Trafficking in Persons, *Trafficking in Persons Report 2007* (Washington, DC: U.S. Department of State, June 2007), http://www.state.gov/g/tip/rls/tiprpt/2007/82805.htm.

22 Private interview, Algiers, June 29, 2009.

23 Cited in *Report of the Special Rapporteur on Violence Against Women, Its Causes and Consequences, Mission to Algeria* (Geneva: UN Human Rights Council, February 13, 2008), 15, available at http://www2.ohchr.org/english/issues/women/rapporteur/visits.htm.

24 Private interview, Algiers, June 30, 2009.

25 The law 08-11, passed on June 25, 2009, allows for the creation of waiting centers where irregular immigrants can be detained for an indefinite time.

[26] United States Committee for Refugees and Immigrants, "Algeria," in *World Refugee Survey 2008* (Arlington, VA: U.S. Committee for Refugees and Immigrants, June 2008), http://www.refugees.org/countryreports.aspx?id=2116. Algeria has officially renounced all territorial claims in Western Sahara, but it continues to host roughly 100,000 Sahraoui refugees in camps at Tindouf. The Western Sahara issue remains a point of contention between Algeria and Morocco, which controls the territory.

[27] The activists of the Wassila Network use the phrase "marital violence" rather than "domestic violence" to emphasize the fact that the violence often takes place between spouses, and to avoid confusing this problem with other issues, such as the use of violence by parents against children. They attribute the high rate of "marital violence" in Algeria to the effects of the terrorist violence that wounded Algerian society during the 1990s, rather than to the prejudices against women that are traditionally cited.

[28] For example, a workshop scheduled to take place on February 7 and 8, 2008, was banned at the last minute, and several guests from abroad were denied visas. See "17 ans après le putsch : Le combat pour la Vérité et la Justice continue" [17 Years After the Putsch, the Struggle for Truth and Justice Continues], *Algeria Watch*, January 11, 2009, http://www.algeria-watch.org/fr/aw/combat_verite_justice.htm; Amnesty International, "Algeria."

[29] See for example Global Rights, *Conditions Bien Pensées, Conflits Evités: Promouvoir les Droits Humains des Femmes au Maghreb à travers l'Utilisation Stratégique du Contrat de Mariage* [Terms of Thinking, Conflict Avoided: Promoting Women's Human Rights in the Maghreb Through the Strategic Use of the Marriage Contract] (Rabat: Global Rights, 2009), http://globalrightsmaghreb.files.wordpress.com/2009/03/livret-de-discussion-maroc-francais.pdf.

[30] "Oui pour l'héritage égalitaire, l'abolition de la polygamie et le hidjab" [Yes to Equal Inheritance, Abolition of Polygamy and Hijab], *El-Watan*, March 2, 2009, http://www.elwatan.com/Oui-pour-l-heritage-egalitaire-l.

[31] Cited in *Report of the Special Rapporteur*, 10.

[32] World Bank, "Genderstats—Education," http://go.worldbank.org/RHEGN4QHU0.

[33] High rates of illiteracy are reported in the provinces of Djelfa, Relizane, Ain Delfa, and Tamanrasset.

[34] *Synthèse de l'enquête nationale sur l'intégration socio-économique de la Femme*. In 2004, women made up only 14.6 percent of the employed population.

[35] *Synthèse de l'enquête nationale sur l'intégration socio-économique de la Femme*.

[36] World Bank, "Genderstats—Labor Force," http://go.worldbank.org/4PIIORQMS0.

[37] *Report of the Special Rapporteur*, 11.

[38] *Rapport National sur le Developpement Humain: Algerie 2006* [National Human Development Report: Algeria 2006] (Algiers: National Economic and Social Council, 2007), 50, http://hdr.undp.org/en/reports/nationalreports/arabstates/algeria/nhdr_2006_algeria-fr.pdf.

[39] Dalila Iamarène-Djerbal, "Affaire de Hassi Messaoud," *NAQD, Femmes et Citoyenneté*, Fall/Winter 2006, 21.

[40] "All employers must guarantee, for any work of equal value, equality of salary among workers without discrimination." A copy of this article is available at http://lexalgeria.free.fr/titre_ivtravail.htm (in French).

[41] See Algerian National Center for Retirement, http://www.cnr-dz.com/vos_droits/retraite _normale.php.

[42] *Synthése de l'enquête nationale sur l'intégration socio-économique de la Femme.*

[43] Amnesty International, "Algeria."

[44] Salima Tlemçani, "Victimes de harcèlement sexuel: 2 mois de prison avec sursis pour avoir brisé le silence" [Victims of Sexual Harassment: 2 Months Suspended Imprisonment for Breaking Silence], *El-Watan*, November 4, 2008, http://www.elwatan.com/Victimes-de-harcelement-sexuel-2.

[45] Inter-Parliamentary Union, "Women in National Parliaments," http://www.ipu.org/wmn-e/world.htm.

[46] "Landslide Win for Algeria Leader," British Broadcasting Corporation (BBC), April 10, 2009, http://news.bbc.co.uk/2/hi/africa/7993671.stm.

[47] World Bank, "Genderstats—Health," http://go.worldbank.org/UJ0Q1KQKX0.

[48] UN Population Division, *Abortion Policies: A Global Review* (New York: Department of Economic and Social Affairs, 2002), http://www.un.org/esa/population/publications/abortion/index.htm.

[49] World Bank, "Genderstats—Create Your Own Table," http://go.worldbank.org/MRER20PME0.

[50] *Report of the Special Rapporteur,* 13.

[51] Jamal Eddine Naji, "La Journaliste Algérienne," in *Profession: Journalism Maghrébin au Feminine* (Rabat: UNESCO, December 2006), http://rabat.unesco.org/article.php 3?id_article=1004.

[52] Ghania Mouffok, "Violences et images de femmes dans la presse écrite algérienne" [Violence and Images of Women in the Algerian Press], *NAQD, Femmes et Citoyenneté,* Fall/Winter 2006, 91–102.

BAHRAIN

by Dunya Ahmed Abdulla Ahmed

POPULATION: 1,217,000
GNI PER CAPITA: US$24,984

COUNTRY RATINGS	2004	2009
NONDISCRIMINATION AND ACCESS TO JUSTICE:	2.2	2.2
AUTONOMY, SECURITY, AND FREEDOM OF THE PERSON:	2.3	2.6
ECONOMIC RIGHTS AND EQUAL OPPORTUNITY:	2.9	3.1
POLITICAL RIGHTS AND CIVIC VOICE:	2.1	2.3
SOCIAL AND CULTURAL RIGHTS:	2.8	2.9

(COUNTRY RATINGS ARE BASED ON A SCALE OF 1 TO 5, WITH 1 REPRESENTING THE LOWEST AND 5 THE HIGHEST LEVEL OF FREEDOM WOMEN HAVE TO EXERCISE THEIR RIGHTS)

INTRODUCTION

The Kingdom of Bahrain, a small island nation off the Arabian Peninsula, is generally considered more liberal in its interpretation and application of Islam than adjacent countries. Spurred by the political and economic reforms of hereditary ruler Hamad bin Isa al-Khalifa, women's rights have steadily improved since he took the throne in 1999. Shari'a (Islamic law) is the main source of legislation, and the rights, duties, and gender roles of women in Bahrain are strongly influenced by the country's culture and religion. Bahraini citizens make up approximately one half of the resident population, which is believed to have reached one million.[1]

Bahrain is for the most part a peaceful nation, but friction between the Sunni-led government and the largely Shiite opposition persists. Although they constitute the majority of the population, Shiites face discrimination in employment, government services, and the education system. While the ongoing ethnic and sectarian tensions are deeply troubling, they have acted as a catalyst for increased women's participation in political movements and demonstrations calling for social equality and the promotion of democratic rights.[2]

With pressure and encouragement from local nongovernmental organizations (NGOs), unions, and international bodies, the government has taken steps toward improving the standing of women in Bahrain in recent years. The quasi-governmental Supreme Council for Women (SCW) has played an important role in this process, and NGOs—including the Women's Union umbrella group—also promote women's rights. In particular, these entities have worked toward the promulgation of a personal status code, in part to mitigate injustices in the arbitrary application of Shari'a in family-related matters, as well as toward amending the nationality law, which currently allows only men to pass citizenship to their children and foreign-born spouse.

After years of lobbying by civil society actors, in May 2009 the government adopted the country's first personal status law—which regulates family matters such as marriage, divorce, child custody, and inheritance—but the code is only applicable to the Sunni population. The originally drafted legislation was conceived to be applicable to both the Sunnis and the Shiites, and it contained separate chapters for the two sects. However, the Shiite portion was excluded from the draft in February, after hard-line Shiite scholars and legislators, who perceive the codification of family law as the first step toward secularization, threatened to set off country-wide protests.

Women have long been subjected to severe forms of discrimination in Shari'a courts by judges who issued rulings based on their personal interpretations of Islamic texts instead of codified law. The process has been so arbitrary that in some instances women's petitions were turned down even before the plaintiffs had an opportunity to present their case. The new law, although encompassing many traditional Shari'a provisions deemed unfair to women under international conventions, institutionalizes important protections such as the woman's consent for marriage, woman's ability to include conditions in the marriage contract, and the right for separate residence if her husband takes another wife. Women's rights organizations, nonetheless, protested the adoption of a divisive law that does not apply to over a half of the population, preferring instead to wait until parliament passes a law applicable to the both sects.

Bahrain ratified the Convention on the Elimination of All Forms of Discrimination against Women (CEDAW) in 2002 but made reservations to many important provisions, including those regarding family law, the granting of citizenship, and housing rights. Implementation of CEDAW has been slow, though a personal status code for Sunnis has been formed and women have been able to pass Bahraini citizenship to their children under certain, extremely limited circumstances. Although they now have access to adequate health care, academic opportunities, and employment, women need continued support in these areas to achieve equality with men. Their participation in the workplace and in business has increased, and several Bahrainis are now listed among the most powerful business-women in the Arab world.[3]

Women have also achieved modest gains in terms of their political participation. One woman won a seat in the popularly elected Council of Representatives in 2006 after running uncontested, becoming the first elected female member of parliament in any Gulf Cooperation Council (GCC) member state. Several women have also entered the judiciary in recent years, and two are now government ministers. However, women continue to be underrepresented in decision-making positions in both the public and private sectors. Their representation in the government, judicial system, and political parties also remains insufficient.

NONDISCRIMINATION AND ACCESS TO JUSTICE

Gender-based discrimination continues to be evident throughout Bahrain's legal system, although the kingdom's recent election to the UN Human Rights Council has instilled hope among activists that the government will continue to expand women's rights. Over the last five years, local NGOs have continuously lobbied for the creation of a codified personal status law, as well as amendments to a law that would allow women to pass their citizenship to their spouse and children. The adoption of a personal status code for Sunnis in May 2009 constitutes a partial victory, but the success of other efforts has so far been limited.

Bahrain's 2002 constitution guarantees equality between men and women "in political, social, cultural, and economic spheres, without breach-ing the provisions of Islamic canon law."[4] According to Article 2, Shari'a is considered the main source of legislation. The constitution also provides citizens the right to education, health care, property, housing, work, the right to defend the country, and the right to engage in economic activities. Although the constitution does not discriminate between people based on their gender, there are no laws that directly ban discrimination either. The Penal Code (No. 15 of 1976) does not contain any provisions that would punish individuals found guilty of discrimination against women at the workplace or in other facets of society.

Bahraini women are unable to pass their citizenship to their non-Bahraini spouses, even though Article 7 of the Bahraini Citizenship Law of 1963 permits male Bahraini citizens to do so. Moreover, the law stipulates that children may only receive Bahraini citizenship from their father, and the child of a Bahraini mother and a foreign father may not receive his mother's nationality.[5] In September 2006, over 370 children of Bahraini mothers and noncitizen fathers were granted Bahraini citizenship, but this was an ad hoc decision made at the discretion of the king, and there is no guarantee that such an act will be repeated again.[6] In November 2008, in efforts to provide consistency and a legal foundation in such cases, the SCW recommended amendments to the citizenship law that would permit children from these unions to receive Bahraini citizenship after certain requirements are met.

Momentum for a change to the nationality law continued to build throughout 2009, spurring hope for government's action. In May, a Bahraini woman and her foreign husband filed a petition in court challenging the constitutionality of the law.[7] In June, the government extended a waiver for government fees—such as those related to health care, education, and visas—to all stateless children and children with Bahraini mothers who are nationals of their father's country.[8] Although this eases some of the day-to-day difficulties experienced by these children, legal inequality persists. By July 2009, the SCW officially announced the launch of a major lobbying campaign to amend the nationality law.[9]

The legal system in Bahrain is composed of civil law courts and Shari'a courts. The civil courts have jurisdiction over cases related to civil, commercial, and criminal matters, as well as those related to family issues of non-Muslims. The Shari'a courts—which are separated into Sunni and Shiite courts—adjudicate disputes over personal status issues, including marriage, divorce, child custody, and inheritance involving the Muslim population. The judges in these courts are often conservative religious scholars with little or no formal legal training, who make judgments according to their own interpretations and readings of Islamic law. Because they may implement Shari'a in an arbitrary manner, rulings are commonly detrimental to women's rights.

After years of lobbying efforts by women's rights activists and organizations, Bahrain adopted its first personal status code in May 2009. The new code, however, will only apply to Sunnis, whereas personal status issues for the Shiites will still be left to the discretion of individual judges in Shiite courts.

Women's rights NGOs began advocating for a codified personal status law as early as 1982, and the movement has been publicly supported by SCW since late 2005. The strongest opposition has been from religious groups who demand that Shiites and Sunnis have their own divorce and inheritance laws, as well as conservative segments of the population who seek to return to traditional values. In November 2005, the Islamic political group Al-Wefaq organized a demonstration against the introduction of the personal status law that grew to include 120,000 people. By contrast, an alliance of women's rights organizations held a rally in support of the law on the same day that attracted only 500 supporters. In a successful bid to exclude Shiites from the scope of the 2009 draft law, Al-Wefaq threatened to provoke demonstrations similar to those organized in 2005 and derail the passage of the bill entirely.[10]

A woman's testimony before a Shari'a court is worth half that of a man's, and women's legal claims are treated unequally by the Shari'a judiciary. On the other hand, the testimony of both sexes are weighted equally in civil and criminal courts, and women are able to bring charges in court without permission from male family members. Civil and criminal laws apply equally to both men and women, but fewer women than men go to prison because this is viewed as a punishment more appropriate for men.

No laws or government policies specifically address the issue of gender-based violence, and enforcement mechanisms are lacking for the existing legal provisions that may apply. The penal code generally addresses violence against citizens, but this is not adequate to protect against sexual harassment and domestic abuse. Wives, daughters, and female foreign workers rarely seek legal redress for violence committed against them, and when they do, the perpetrators often avoid punishment, thereby exposing victims to additional maltreatment. If a man commits a violent offense against a female relative, he may face a few days in jail, then sign a pledge and pay a fine.

The punishment for rape is life in prison, but spousal rape is not considered a crime.[11] Additionally, under Article 353 of the penal code, a rapist may avoid punishment if he agrees to marry his victim.[12] Although this is viewed by some as protecting women from shame, the psychological effects of this policy are grave and divorces after such unions are likely. Additionally, the rapist may later initiate a unilateral divorce, thereby avoiding both a rapist's punishment and a husband's responsibilities. These considerations make women less likely to report rape. Honor killings are punishable under Bahraini law, but Article 334 of the penal code permits a reduced penalty for one who surprises his or her spouse in the act of adultery and immediately assaults or kills the spouse or the spouse's accomplice.[13]

Women are normally protected from discriminatory or arbitrary detention and exile, but they are vulnerable to these abuses in relation to prohibited sexual activities such as prostitution and *zina* (sexual relations outside marriage). The penal code prohibits adultery, sex outside of marriage, and homosexuality, all of which are also religiously and culturally forbidden. However, extramarital sexual activities by men are far more culturally acceptable than those of women. Articles 324 through 332 of the penal code prohibit prostitution for citizens and noncitizens of both sexes, but noncitizens—particularly women—are more likely to be prosecuted for such offenses. For instance, in May 2008, an Indian woman staying at a hotel in Bahrain with her husband and children was arrested during a "vice raid" on suspicion of being a prostitute, although there was no evidence to support this claim.[14]

Having ratified CEDAW in 2002, Bahrain is required to institute a number of measures to prevent gender-based discrimination in law and in practice. However, reservations were placed on several CEDAW provisions in so far as they conflict with Shari'a, including the Article 2 prohibition against discrimination within government policies, particularly in the area of inheritance; the right of a woman to pass her citizenship to her husband and children under Article 9, paragraph 2; a woman's freedom of movement and choice regarding residence and housing under Article 15, paragraph 4; and equality in marriage and family life under Article 16.[15]

The reservations are the result of religious, cultural, and societal obstacles that will likely take time to overcome. Reservations to Article 2 are based on the Shari'a mandate that men receive greater inheritance than women in certain situations. The reservation to Article 9(2) regarding nationality reflects the tradition that children take the citizenship of their father to avoid dual citizenship. Full realization of Article 15 is hindered by social customs that prevent women from taking a full role in public life, and reservations were placed on Article 15(4) because it is still unacceptable for unmarried women to live outside their family homes. Finally, a reservation was placed on Article 16 in the belief that it conflicts with the Shari'a provisions that control marriage rights.

In October 2008, the SCW and Bahraini NGOs met before the CEDAW Committee at the United Nations offices in Geneva to discuss Bahrain's implementation of CEDAW. The SCW submitted a report on behalf of the government, defending its choice not to remove certain reservations and explaining efforts that have been made to empower Bahraini women. Simultaneously, "shadow reports" were also submitted by Bahraini NGOs that asked the government to remove its reservations to CEDAW and improve women's rights in Bahrain.

The main government-sponsored entity that promotes and protects women's rights is the SCW, which was created by royal decree in 2001 for the purpose of helping the government formulate policies on women's issues. The council's relative power and state support, however, has somewhat diminished the role of women's rights NGOs. In addition to publishing studies, promoting political participation of women, organizing workshops, and advocating for gender equality, the SCW has supported the codification of Bahrain's family law and equal citizenship rights. Its approach, however, is tempered due to its association with the government. Within the state structure, the head of SCW has a rank equivalent to minister without portfolio.

Recommendations

❖ The government should treat women as full persons before the law by recognizing their equality in courtroom settings, whether as litigants or jurists.

❖ The government should amend the nationality law to allow women to confer their Bahraini nationality to their children and foreign-born spouses.

❖ In consultation with the SCW, the Women's Union and other NGOs, and liberal religious scholars and judges, the government should enact a codified personal status law that extends to both the Sunni and the Shiites.

❖ The Women's Union, with the support of international and domestic NGOs, should establish a specialized committee dedicated to CEDAW that will monitor its implementation and work to remove reservations to provisions that do not conflict with Islamic law.

❖ The government should immediately remove its reservations to CEDAW and bring Bahraini law into compliance by providing women with equal citizenship, residence, marital, and custody rights as men.

AUTONOMY, SECURITY, AND FREEDOM OF THE PERSON

Despite the protections offered by the 2001 National Action Charter, improvements to women's personal freedoms and security have been hampered by insufficient legal literacy, unequal marriage and divorce rights, and the lack of legal prohibitions against domestic abuse. In efforts to combat some of these problems, the government and women's rights organizations have stepped up their training and advocacy efforts, opened new facilities for the victims, and implemented steps to combat human trafficking. However, additional measures are essential in order to ensure that Bahraini women are sufficiently protected from violence and discrimination in family life.

Bahraini law ensures freedom of worship under Chapter 1, section 3 of the National Action Charter.[16] According to the 2001 census, 81.2 percent of the population are Muslim (the majority of which are Shiites), 9 percent are Christian, and the remaining 9.8 percent belong to other religions.[17] The king's family is Sunni, and it is widely acknowledged that Sunnis hold more influential positions in government and the economy.

Religion is inherited primarily from one's extended family. In a marriage between a Sunni and a Shiite, each person is generally permitted to retain his or her own beliefs, although marriage between persons from different sects is increasingly uncommon. Moreover, all Muslims are encouraged to marry within the faith, but unlike women, Muslim men may take Christian or Jewish spouses.[18] Apostasy is punishable by death under Shari'a, although Bahrain does not enforce this punishment. Regardless, many nonpracticing Muslims of both genders are fairly quiet about their lack of faith out of concern for cultural demands.

Despite the country's relative liberalism, some Bahrainis continue to hold a more conservative interpretation of Islam, especially Salafi Sunnis and inhabitants of Shiite villages. Bahrain has been influenced by the regimes of nearby Iran and Saudi Arabia, which have strict Islamic ideas and practices, and recent increases in sectarian violence in Iraq and Lebanon have stoked sectarianism in Bahrain. Since the 1980s, the resurgence of Islamic conservatism led to the return of traditional dress and social codes for women, although the *hijab* (veil) is not compulsory.[19]

The rules governing marriage and family life in Bahrain are deeply rooted in Shari'a (see "Nondiscrimination and Access to Justice"), and they grant men and women with unequal rights with certain distinctions based on the sectarian affiliation. Unlike her groom, a Sunni bride is required to have a *wali* (marriage guardian) who will represent her during the marriage proceedings. A wali is most often a father, grandfather, or uncle. If a woman does not have a wali, the judge will represent her in completing the marriage formalities. Conversely, most Shiite women sign their own marriage contracts, although practically this does not give them more independence in selecting their marriage partner. In all cases, the agreement of the family is important, and it is not socially acceptable to marry without the family's permission.

Most prospective brides are sought out and selected by the man's family. A suitable wife is considered to be a woman from the same social class, religious sect, ethnicity, and educational level; both she and her family must have a good reputation in terms of *sharaf* (honor). Only men can solicit their own marriage partners if a match is not arranged for them. Dating has become more common, but romantic relationships are not generally made public because of a constant concern about *kalām al-nās* (gossip) and sexual relations outside of marriage are criminalized.

Young people in Bahrain are becoming increasingly independent when choosing their future life partners, but families remain influential in the final decision. Women may make whatever stipulations they wish in a marriage contract, but very few women practice this right. Instead, the contract concentrates predominantly on the details of the woman's *mahr* (dowry). In 2007, the minister of justice and Islamic affairs established 15 and 18 as the minimum age of marriage for women and men, respectively. Previously, no minimum age existed. Conservative lawmakers argue that setting a minimum age for marriage violates Shari'a, which is silent on the matter, while women's rights advocates argue that the minimum age should be the same for both sexes.[20]

Women do not face any legal restraints in terms of their freedom of movement, although some cultural boundaries still exist. Regardless of her age or marital status, a woman's behavior traditionally reflects not only upon herself but also upon the honor of her family and tribe, while men's honor depends on their ability to protect the women in their family. In July 2004, Article 13 of the passport law was amended to permit married women to apply for passports without permission from their husbands. Women are also not required to seek permission from their guardians before traveling abroad, and citizens of the GCC countries do not require visas or passports to travel between the member states, making movement within the region easier for both men and women.

On a practical level, unmarried women are less able to move freely and their whereabouts are indirectly monitored by their families and community. They generally live with their families until marriage and are required to adhere to rules that are intended to protect their reputation and virginity. Single women that are beyond the traditional age of marriage may have greater freedom of movement within cultural limits because they are viewed as being more sexually neutral than their younger counterparts. Married women have additional freedoms because society believes that the responsibility for their husbands and children makes them more "reasonable" than single women. However, a married woman is traditionally expected to be obedient to her husband; as such, he may forbid her from traveling or visiting her friends and family.

Unlike men, women face significant legal, financial, and societal hurdles if they want to obtain a divorce. Men have the right to divorce that is effective immediately—Sunni men need only orally announce their intent to divorce while Shiite men must record their intent. On the other hand, women must either seek out a judicial divorce based on extremely narrow reasons, such as desertion or impotency, or else initiate *khula*. Khula is the Islamic practice of divorce initiated by a woman, but it requires the woman to return her dowry. Some men abuse khula—in certain instances requesting that the wife pays the approximate amount the husband spent on her during the entire marriage—taking advantage of the fact that women use this form of divorce because it is faster than the alternative. A judicial divorce may take years, during which time women may not be financially supported, and is not guaranteed to end in a divorce.

Divorced Shiite women retain physical custody of their sons until they are seven and their daughters until they are nine. The new personal status law allows Sunni mothers to retain custody of their daughters until they are 17 or married (whichever comes first) and sons until they are 15. When the children reach the specified age, they may choose their custodian. Despite the regulations that award women with physical custody, the father retains parental authority and guardianship over his children, effectively being in a position to prevent his former wife from traveling with their children or moving away.

Bahrain has consistently been listed in the U.S. State Department's *Trafficking in Persons Report* as a known destination for trafficked persons, including women trafficked for sexual purposes.[21] In November 2007, the government created a special unit within the Ministry of the Interior for the purpose of investigating sex trafficking in particular, but only one conviction and three investigations have been reported as of October 2009. Between April 2007 and February 2008, 45 foreign workers, many of whom claimed to have been physically abused by their employers, received help from a government shelter, and the international community has recognized these efforts.[22] Although the government has enacted many of the laws necessary to combat trafficking, they continue to be inadequately enforced.

Slavery is forbidden in Bahrain under the tenets of Islam, yet slavery-like conditions continue to exist for some laborers, especially female foreign domestic workers. Bahraini labor law forbids the withholding of salaries and travel documents from foreign workers, while excluding them from the broader labor protections afforded to citizen workers.[23] Nevertheless, many cases have been reported in which passports are taken and wages are withheld from employees, restricting their freedom of movement and leaving them vulnerable to other abuses.[24] If abused workers are fortunate they will be sent home by their sponsors, but generally without any compensation for suffering.[25] Female domestic workers commonly report physical (often sexual), psychological, and verbal abuse by their male employers, who are also often their visa sponsors.[26] Informal shelters for abused workers run by local NGOs receive no funding from the government. The Indian Ladies Association has provided one year's rent for a government-approved shelter, paid through the Migrant Workers Protection Society, but such individualized efforts, while helpful, are far from sufficient.[27]

Domestic violence in Bahrain is thought to be widespread, but its existence is usually covered up and kept within the family. Studies carried out by the Information Center for Women and Children, a regional research organization, indicate that 30 percent of Bahraini women face some sort of domestic abuse.[28] Although laws generally prohibit assault and battery, domestic violence is not specifically prohibited under Bahraini law or addressed by any government policy.

Accusations of domestic violence are rarely taken into account in divorce cases and abused women seldom seek any form of legal recourse.[29] Recent statistics released by the Batelco Anti-Domestic Violence Center indicate that the number of women seeking protection from violence in the first half of 2008 doubled as compared to 2007.[30] Such a surge may indicate women's growing awareness and comfort with such centers rather than any general increase in violence against women.

The number of NGOs that support victims of domestic violence is steadily increasing in Bahrain, a marked improvement for a society that did not condone speaking of such matters until recently. The Awal Women's Society has provided free legal advice to abused women since the late 1990s and also offers a telephone hotline for anonymous emotional support. The Bahraini Young Ladies' Association established the Aisha Yateem Family Coaching Center, which offers consultancy services and residential facilities. Established in March 2007, this is the only private shelter in the kingdom, but it lacks staff with adequate experience.

The Batelco Anti-Domestic Violence Center, a nonprofit organization that was created in 2006 to rehabilitate victims of domestic violence, is the only successful partnership between the private sector and civil society in the field of domestic violence. Another partnership was formed in 2007 between the U.S.-based NGO Vital Voices, the Bahraini company Smart Coaching and Research Center, and the U.S. State Department's Middle East Partnership Initiative. Together, these entities work to advance civil society activity regarding domestic violence. The program also attempts to provide training in advocacy, volunteerism, and other areas.

Victims of gender-based violence had only recently begun to receive support from the government when the Dar al-Aman Care Center for battered women was established in 2006. In May of that year, control over the shelter was transferred to the Sociologist Association; however, the center has since been publicly criticized for restricting the victims' freedom of movement and for an absence of qualified personnel. The government has also initiated training for judges who deal with domestic abuse, increased the number of policewomen, and amended Law No. 26 of 1986 to streamline Shari'a court procedures, especially with respect to alimony and child custody.[31] Furthermore, the SCW has established a hotline that offers free legal advice and support to victims, and it has conducted a number of conferences and training sessions for different groups, including judges, on the issue of gender-based violence.

Although commendable, the improvements made by both NGOs and the government are insufficient to protect women from domestic abuse, particularly those who need a safe place to stay. Both the Dar al-Aman and Aisha Yateem shelters are only available to battered women for a limited period of time, and victims must seek approval by the police in order to become residents. Until suitable alternative residences exist, financial and social pressures may force many battered women to remain in abusive homes.

Political, religious, and cultural barriers continue to restrict the free and effective work of both the government and NGOs with regard to gender-based violence and marital rights. Efforts to protect other rights for women, such as freedom of movement, have been more successful as the civil and public entities have fought to increase awareness of existing rights and advocate for their expansion. However, Bahraini activists generally remain less engaged in the fight again human trafficking and slavery-like practices, which are considered by many to be an issue reserved for international organizations.

Recommendations

❖ The government should enact legislation that specifically outlaws domestic violence and prescribes substantial penalties that will have a deterrent effect on offenders. Subsequently, the police and prosecutors should be trained to enforce such legislation effectively.

❖ Abused women should no longer be required to seek approval from the police before they may access domestic abuse shelters. Moreover, the funding should be increased for NGO programs aimed at expanding shelter capacities for abused women and monitoring vulnerable populations, including foreign workers.

❖ The government should provide specialized law enforcement units with the legislative and budgetary tools they need to carry out successful investigations and prosecutions of human trafficking offenses.

❖ Victims of trafficking should be guaranteed immunity from prosecution for prostitution, illegal migration, and related offenses, granted protective and rehabilitation services, and encouraged to testify against those who confined or abused them.

❖ Domestic NGOs, in conjunction with international bodies with experience in data collection, should conduct research that quantifies the existence of gender-based violence. This data can then be used to raise awareness and to help train the police, social workers, psychologists, and medical staff who deal directly with abused women.

ECONOMIC RIGHTS AND EQUAL OPPORTUNITY

True economic equality between men and women has been difficult to achieve in Arab countries, including Bahrain, where society tends to view formal employment and business as issues for men. Islamic history, nevertheless, supports the idea of economic rights for women, and some point to Sayeda Khadijah, the Prophet Mohammad's first wife, as an example of a successful, economically independent businesswoman.

According to certain Islamic scholars, a woman's duty is to care for her home, husband, and children, while a man's duty is to treat women fairly and shoulder his family's financial responsibilities.[32] These expectations have resulted in corresponding gender roles for many households, but some adopt less traditional arrangements, and women are increasingly becoming financially independent through employment.[33] Women's responsibilities in the home have also been reduced through the widespread use of cheap domestic help, even among lower middle-class families.

Bahraini women are free to own land and property, subject to their individual financial constraints.[34] In the 1970s, the government established the Productive Family Project to encourage families to run small businesses from home. Following in this tradition, the government—particularly the SCW—has initiated several programs intended to increase women's economic participation. It has financed small and medium-sized enterprises and established the Family Bank to improve the living standards of low-income families and create jobs.[35] In addition, many NGOs, some with help of the United Nations Development Programme (UNDP), provide microcredit programs in an effort to encourage women to participate in small business ventures. The Bahrain Development Bank also offers both microcredit and larger loans, and 73 percent of its beneficiaries are now women.

Previously, women found it difficult to run their own businesses because cultural norms required that they hire men to authorize their work or manage all government documents, such as customs forms and work permits. However, since 2000, women have begun to provide such document-clearance services. Consequently, liberal, educated, middle-class women have begun to run businesses independently or hire document-clearance services operated by both sexes, which saves time and energy.

Although rules differ slightly between Sunnis and Shiites, inheritance law is governed by Shari'a. Women inherit less than men in a number of situations, including where the man and woman are similarly related to the deceased. For example, a sister inherits half of her brother's share. This disparity is generally justified by the fact that men have greater financial responsibilities under the Koran and, unlike women, inherit the debts of the deceased.[36] Problems arise when executors, usually a male family member, do not follow the law and refuse to give women the inheritance to which they are legally entitled. Consequently, women often face injustice during the actual division of estates.

In 2007, Bahraini women constituted 72 percent of students enrolled at the Arabian Gulf University and 67 percent of those enrolled at the University of Bahrain, the two largest postsecondary education institutions in Bahrain.[37] As educated members of society, graduates tend to be more conscious of their rights and more forthright in demanding that they be respected. However, some fields remain segregated based on gender. For instance, certain technical subjects in high schools are restricted to boys, while textile classes are limited only to girls. This segregation affects future job opportunities and reflects government support for societal biases. Although no other subjects are actually restricted, women remain underrepresented in areas such as engineering and overrepresented in education and health care. From a practical standpoint, this limits women's freedom to choose their university courses and leads them to study subjects in low demand in the labor market, increasing their unemployment rate.

Article 12 of the constitution provides equal rights and opportunities to all laborers. However, according to a recent study, men, as a group, earn more than women. The average monthly salary for women employed in the public sector is 643 dinars (US$1,705) and for men is 706 dinars (US$1,872). The gender gap in private sector wages is even more evident: women earn an average monthly salary of 307 dinars (US$814) while men earn 454 dinars (US$1,204).[38] Moreover, women—mainly domestic workers—tend to face harsher treatment and poorer working conditions than men in similar positions.[39]

Although most women are free to choose their professions, certain restrictions in this domain still exist. Under Article 301 of the Private Labor Law (No. 63 of 1976), women are prohibited from working between 8:00 p.m. and 4 a.m., with certain exceptions such as jobs in health care. Law No. 5 of 1977, issued by the Ministry of Health, prohibits women from doing hazardous work, which includes predominantly heavy industrial jobs.[40] Traditionally, women are required to seek their husband's permission to get a job, a rule that has been cemented under the 2009 Sunni personal status law.

Women constituted approximately 21 percent of the country's labor force and approximately 34 percent of adult women were employed in 2007.[41] Although many obstacles to women's full and equal economic participation persist, most commonly those involving traditional social attitudes, there is a growing awareness that such mindset must change if Bahrain is to achieve its full economic potential. Exemplifying this increased awareness, a female government employee named S. Ahmed brought the first discrimination court case in 2005 after she was denied a promotion because of her gender. The case is still pending.[42]

In an effort to decrease Bahrain's dependence on foreign labor, companies are restricted as to the number of foreign employees they may hire in comparison to the number of Bahraini employees they have. Law No. 56 of 2008 encourages private companies to hire Bahraini women by counting each female employee as two Bahraini citizens, thereby permitting the company to hire more foreigners, who are generally cheaper to employ than citizens.

The labor law offers gender-based protections by prohibiting employers from firing women during maternity leave or because they get married.[43] Several improvements have been made to gender-based workplace benefits in recent years. In 2005, maternity leave increased from 35 to 60 working days, breaks for breast-feeding increased from one to two hours a day for a six-month period, and mothers can now obtain unpaid leave for a maximum of two years at a time on three separate occasions during their working lives.[44] Women tend to work longer hours than most nurseries are open, creating friction between the obligations of work and motherhood. They also generally lack support as they attempt to balance their jobs with their other home duties, which continue to include most domestic chores.[45]

Economic support provided for women by the state is a new concept for Bahraini society, which has traditionally considered it a man's duty to care for his female relatives. The SCW is doing its part by promoting laws that reward companies that employ and promote women. In addition, the MSD and the Ministry of Justice administer funds created by the government to assist divorced women and their children.[46]

Meanwhile, the Bahrain Businesswomen's Society has provided women with training opportunities in cooperation with other entities, such as the government and the UNDP. Although women represent a significant portion of the workforce and are members of the General Federation of Bahraini Trade Unions, women's issues are not on the federation's agenda to any substantial degree.[47] Despite the continuing existence of cultural barriers, concrete advances have been made in upholding women's economic rights in recent years.[48]

Recommendations

✤ The government, in cooperation with local NGOs, should create special programs to encourage women to study subjects in which they are currently underrepresented. For example, they could initiate public campaigns that highlight female engineers and scientists, create public-private partnerships that bring highly accomplished women to classrooms to act as role models, or create girls' science clubs.

✤ The working hours of nurseries should be expanded to fully accommodate employed women, and the government should provide incentives for public and private companies to maintain on-site childcare.

✤ The General Federation of Bahrain Trade Unions should make gender discrimination in the workplace one of its main issues.

✤ The government should scrutinize inheritance proceedings to ensure that women receive their share, provide efficient mechanisms for filing and adjudicating complaints, and publicize penalties for deliberate abuses by executors and guardians.

POLITICAL RIGHTS AND CIVIC VOICE

In 2002, Bahrain became the first GCC member to grant universal women's suffrage. Chapter 1, section 2(1) of the National Action Charter provides equal rights and opportunities for all citizens of Bahrain.[49] Furthermore, Article 1(e) of the constitution states, "all citizens, both men and women, are entitled to vote and to stand for election, in accordance with this constitution and in the conditions and principles laid down by law. No citizen can be deprived of the right to vote or to nominate oneself for elections except by law." In spite of these broad reforms, women have remained underrepresented in the legislature, the government, the judicial system, and political parties.

The constitution grants the king with the power over the executive, legislative, and judicial authorities. He appoints cabinet ministers and members of the 40-seat Consultative Council, the upper house of the National Assembly. The lower house, or Council of Representatives, consists of 40 elected members serving four-year terms.

In 2002, six women ran unsuccessfully as candidates for the Council of Representatives. After losing that year's election by a small margin, Latifa al-Gaoud ran again in 2006, this time unopposed, and became Bahrain's first and only female parliamentarian. Generally, women face unique obstacles while campaigning, in part because they have fewer opportunities to address large groups and mixed-gender groups than men, who have wider access to mosques and other community gatherings. In all, 16 female candidates ran in the 2006 elections, and women constituted 50.2 percent of the voters, a vast improvement over the 2002 elections.

One female candidate, Munira Fakhro, a former Harvard academic and member of Wa'ad, the largest liberal political society, ran against the incumbent candidate Salah Ali, a member of the Al-Menbar Sunni Islamic Society. Fakhro had only limited support from the Al-Wefaq National Islamic Society, but the majority of women from her own region supported her in the 2006 electoral contest. She lost by only a few votes and, believing that voting irregularities had taken place, she took the case to court to ask for a repeat vote. Her request was denied. None of the liberal parties such as Wa'ad won, suggesting that her defeat was not only due to her gender but also due to her party affiliation. None of the female candidates were members of the male-dominated Islamist parties, which won the majority of the available seats.

The first Consultative Council under the current charter, appointed in 2001, started with four female members, and that figure rose to six by 2002. Eleven female members were appointed in 2006, but Houda Nonoo, a Jewish council member, has left her position to act as the Bahraini ambassador to the United States. This leaves only 10 women, or 25 percent of the council's members.

Participation by women in the national government and decision-making positions also remains low. Bahrain has had female ambassadors since the 1990s and became the first Arab country to have a female minister of health when Nada Haffadh was appointed in 2004. Fatima al-Baloshi of the Al-Eslah Sunni Society was later appointed minister of social development in January 2005.[50] Moreover, in November 2008 Sheikha May bint Mohammed al-Kalifa became the first woman in Bahrain to be appointed as minister of culture and information. In addition to cabinet posts, women have also been appointed as undersecretaries, college deans, and even as a university president.

Freedom of assembly in Bahrain is equally restricted for both men and women. It is regulated by Law No. 32 of 2006, which requires persons organizing a public meeting to notify the Department of Public Security. In recent years, women have freely participated in a number of demonstrations and political and social gatherings. However, in a December 2007 demonstration by families of detained political activists, both the Special Security Force and the Women's Police, Bahrain's all-female police force, were accused of dispersing the crowd in a violent and humiliating manner. Journalists were not permitted to take photographs, and some of the women who took part in the demonstration were hospitalized. When one of these women saw her mother faint inside the prison, she was allegedly forced to kiss an officer's foot before she was permitted to help her mother.[51] This type of treatment is not common, especially after the adoption of the National Action Charter, but when it does happen, it is not widely publicized in the media.

All NGOs in Bahrain, including women's rights organizations, are supervised by the MSD. Because NGOs are forbidden from engaging in vaguely defined "political activity," the MSD can effectively ban work on a variety of controversial topics. Any NGO whose annual budget is over 10,000 dinars (US$26,522) must use an external auditor to monitor its finances. Moreover, all funds and donations from foreign entities are scrutinized by the government, limiting the assistance that NGOs may receive from outside sources and subjecting NGOs to additional government supervision and control.

According to Article 134 of the penal code, citizens may not attend unauthorized meetings, conferences, or symposiums held abroad or contact foreign ministers, representatives, or organizations for the purpose of discussing Bahrain's economic, political, or social issues that may harm the country's reputation. Such actions are punishable by a minimum of three months in prison and/or a fine of not less than 100 dinars (US$265). Although this law existed prior to the sweeping 2001 reforms, it was not strictly enforced until Minister of the Interior Shaikh Rashid al-Khalifa threatened to do so in November 2008. It is unclear what kind of impact the law's enforcement will have on activists' ability to openly discuss women's rights in Bahrain with various entities outside of the country.

Legal restrictions on press freedoms are also not gender based—the rights of both male and female members of the media are limited. The Press Law (No. 47 of 2002) continues to be used to restrict the coverage of sensitive issues, particularly corruption.[52] In 2007, 15 journalists were referred to the public prosecutor, mainly for alleged defamation of a government official or department. According to the Bahrain Center for Human Rights, state-owned Batelco, Bahrain's only Internet provider, blocked 23 discussion forums in 2007.[53] Although the number of female journalists has steadily risen in recent years, only a few broadcast programs engage in open discussions about women's issues including women's political rights and domestic violence.

Thirty-one percent of Bahraini lawyers were women in 2001, and according to the University of Bahrain's records, most of the graduating and current law students since have been women. These numbers are strong compared with those in neighboring countries, in part because women have been able to act as lawyers in Bahrain since 1976. In 2003, three Bahraini women were appointed as prosecutors, two of whom have since been promoted and replaced by women, and a woman was appointed director of public prosecutions in 2007. In June 2006, Mona al-Kawari was appointed to the High Civil Court as Bahrain's first female judge. A second, Dhouha al-Zayani, was appointed to the Constitutional Court in 2007, and Fatima Hubail was appointed in 2008 as a Lower Criminal Court judge. In total, there are only seven women in the judiciary and none in the Shari'a courts, which hear the cases that most often and most directly affect women.[54] Although a variety of views exist on the matter, most Islamic scholars in Bahrain believe that women may not act as judges in the Shari'a courts.[55] Some, however, suggest that women could be appointed in cases related to women's issues.

Political organizations such as the Al-Wefaq National Islamic Society and the Al-Menbar Sunni Islamic Society hardly address women's political rights in their agendas. Meanwhile, the Women's Union and other NGOs advocate for women's rights generally, and although they incorporate women's political rights into their work plans, their political work is limited because they are not registered as political societies. Additionally, because most of the political societies are religious, cooperation between them and women's societies is limited at best, and they often conflict.

Recommendations

❖ Local NGOs should provide training for female political candidates on how to run successful political campaigns, mobilize popular support, and effectively engage the media. They should also organize networking events in which successful female candidates from other Arab nations could share their election strategies with female political leaders in Bahrain.

❖ The government should abolish Article 134 of the penal code so that governmental and NGO representatives, including women's rights activists, may take part in meetings and discussions with foreign entities about issues pertaining to Bahrain without fear of persecution.

❖ The government should appoint a larger number of women to the Consultative Council and the judiciary, especially the Shari'a courts, and place more women in decision-making positions.

❖ Secular women's rights organizations should initiate a frank dialogue with religious groups. Such a dialogue would enable discussions about religion, women, and politics, and would provide opportunities for strategic cooperation.

SOCIAL AND CULTURAL RIGHTS

The social and cultural rights of Bahraini women are greatly affected by traditional societal norms, which place higher premiums on the rights and preferences of men. As a result, women tend to be treated unequally in diverse areas of social and community life. Within the last five years, however, modifications have been made to housing and unemployment benefits in order to protect both men and women from poverty. The establishment of the Women's Union and greater participation by women's NGOs has further increased women's influence in society, but their power still remains limited.

Women and men have equal access to health care, which is provided to citizens free of charge and to resident noncitizens for a low fee. The government has placed great importance on health care rights, which have improved significantly in recent years. Life expectancy in 2006 was 76 years for women and 74 years for men, up from 74 years for women and 72 years for men in 2000. According to the World Health Organization, the maternal mortality rate during childbirth is 32 in 100,000, which is significantly lower than the world's average but higher than several other GCC countries including Kuwait, Saudi Arabia, and Qatar.[56]

Although women are legally permitted to make decisions about birth control, they often ask permission from their husbands and may take advice from religious leaders when deciding on the matter. Sterilization is allowed only with the permission of the husband and may only be carried out in a legally and religiously acceptable manner. Ultimately, the decision depends on the health condition of the woman and whether normal birth control methods will work.

A woman must also secure her husband's permission before she may undergo a cesarean section delivery unless the surgery is urgent or if the husband is absent. Abortion is only permitted for the health of the mother and also requires a husband's permission. If an abortion is sought for financial or family planning reasons, it will not be permitted, and even in cases of fetal impairment, it is generally not acceptable. Bahrain is one of the first countries in the GCC region to require premarital health check-ups, which include blood screenings for genetic conditions, partly because of the high rate of marriage between relatives.[57]

A woman's virginity is considered an important part of her family's honor, but brides are no longer required to provide proof of their virginity, and harmful traditional practices such as female genital mutilation are not common in Bahrain.[58] Polygamy is practiced among a diverse minority within the country, including members of different sects and men with varying levels of education. However, the practice is not highly widespread because it requires the husband to have substantial financial resources so that he may support his wives and children. *Muta'a* (short-term marriages) are practiced by some Shiites, and other types of temporary marriages occur within Sunni communities, but people do not generally discuss these practices and they are not universally accepted.

Unmarried women typically live with their parents or, if their parents are no longer living, with a male relative, and they are expected to look after the old and sick in the family.[59] It is socially unacceptable for a woman to live alone, but it has become more permissible for multiple related women to live together without a male relative. Single women living with their families may be allotted a separate area of the house which they may treat as their own, effectively living alone within the family household.

In Bahrain, housing benefits were established as early as 1975 to provide suitable homes for families who were unable to build their own. Law

No. 12 of 2004 grants divorced women the right to their share of the family home if they can prove that they have contributed to monthly property payments. Families that are unable to afford a house are entitled to benefits if they are: a husband and a wife (polygamy does not give the man the right to more than one house); a single-parent family, whether the lone parent be a man or a woman; or an adult, unmarried son or daughter residing with his or her parents if neither the applicant nor the parents own a suitable home or land that is fit for building a home.[60] Regarding the first category, if only the man pays the premiums, the house must be registered in his name alone. However, if the wife or wives contribute, then the house is registered according to the contributions of each occupant.[61]

Women are better able to participate in and influence community life, policies, and social development at the local level than at the national level. Today, more than 4,000 women constitute over 60 percent of the membership in NGOs, and many have taken leading roles in their organizations.[62] There are 456 NGOs in Bahrain as of May 2008,[63] but only 19 concentrate on women's rights. Twelve of these women's organizations are members of the Bahraini Women's Union, which aims to involve women actively in political life—including decision-making positions in parliament and other government bodies—and fight all forms of gender discrimination. It was officially created in September 2006 after almost five years of political and legal battles surrounding its licensing.

Women's participation in NGOs directly relates to their success in local and national elections because female candidates depend on support from their groups' members. Only five female candidates ran in the 2006 municipal elections as compared to 31 candidates in 2002, perhaps because highly qualified women preferred to run in the parliamentary elections instead.[64]

The media today plays an important role in people's lives, and Bahraini women have always been steady but underrepresented participants in this field. Women constitute 30 percent of employees at the Ministry of Culture and Information, and 13 percent of these play an active role in the functioning of their respective media outlets. Twenty-one percent of Bahrain Radio and Television Corporation employees are women, the majority of whom are broadcasters. In addition, women make up 50 percent of print editors, and there are twice as many female students as male students in the Information Department at the University of Bahrain. However, not many media outlets produce quality programming on women's rights.

Radio, television, print, and Internet media cover traditionally female topics such as family, fashion, beauty, and cooking. For instance, an English-language women's magazine called *Women This Month* focuses on beauty, fashion, and similar issues, while websites and online magazines such as WomenGateway.com cover a variety of subjects including business, legal rights, and news concerning women. Moreover, the SCW issues an Arabic-language magazine that focuses on news from the SCW, conferences, and new royal decrees benefiting Bahraini women.

Although Bahrain has produced only a few movies, several television series are made each year, many of which depict violence toward women as an accepted societal practice rather than raising awareness about women's issues. On the rare occasions when serious issues regarding domestic violence or human trafficking are highlighted, the viewership tends to be low and many complain about the program in the newspapers.

The government attempts to protect both male and female citizens from poverty, and the kingdom ranks third among Arab countries and 41st worldwide in the UNDP's 2008 Human Development Index. Laws and policies have been altered in an effort to raise the standard of living for all citizens, and women in particular have benefited from these changes. Monthly assistance is now offered to orphans and widows, female government workers are granted social allowances,[65] and unskilled labor contracts reserved for Bahraini citizens include workers of both genders.[66]

The National Employment Project was established in 2005 to increase employment opportunities for Bahraini nationals and provide training programs for those seeking jobs. Women account for 74 percent of those who registered for this project. In December 2007 the first eligible Bahraini citizen was paid under the Unemployment Insurance System. Of the 7,810 citizens eligible for this plan, 81 percent were female.[67] Some citizens, including a large number of women, allegedly register for unemployment benefits even though they never intend to apply for a job.

Human rights standards, including women's rights, have the potential to improve in accordance with the commitments that the kingdom made by becoming a member of the UN Human Rights Council. The effectiveness of women's rights NGOs, however, continues to be constrained by the rules of the MSD, which monitors their work and limits their international funding. In particular, NGOs are not permitted to accept funds from or donate money to foreign organizations without permission from the MSD. Some religious scholars also advocate on behalf of women, but their intentions and purposes differ greatly from those of NGO members and other women's rights activists.

Recommendations

❖ Women should be permitted to make all decisions regarding their health independently, including whether to have a cesarean section at childbirth.

❖ The government, national, and international organizations should sponsor television programming and other media content that appropriately addresses—whether directly or indirectly, or in dramatic, documentary, or talk-show formats—problems like domestic violence and human trafficking, as well as subtler social obstacles faced by women. Moreover, the government should withhold all state funding from programming that portrays violence against women as socially acceptable.

❖ The government should extend housing benefits to broader categories of applicants, such as single or separated women, to accommodate individuals escaping abusive households or pursuing economic and social independence.

❖ The Women's Union should establish a website that addresses women's issues in Bahrain and raises awareness about women's rights on all levels. This website should contain links to websites that address women's issues worldwide.

AUTHOR

Dunya Ahmed Abdulla Ahmed is an assistant professor and lecturer in the Department of Social Sciences at the University of Bahrain. She completed her PhD in social work at the University of Warwick, specializing in gender, disability, and Islam. She is the first person to hold a PhD in social work in Bahrain and concentrates mainly on gender equality and the rights of people with disabilities. She is also an active member of several NGOs.

NOTES

1   Cabinet Affairs Minister Sheikh Ahmed bin Ateyetala, as quoted in A. Glass, "Bahrain Accused of Population Cover-Up," in *Arabian Business*, February 6, 2008, http://www .arabianbusiness.com/510464-expatriates-rob-bahrain-nationals-of-jobs?ln=en.

2   I. Glosemeyer, "Political Parties and Participation: Arabian Peninsula," in *Encyclopedia of Women and Islamic Cultures*, 551–553; M. Seikaly, "Women and Religion in Bahrain:

An Emerging Identity," in Y. Haddad Yvonne and J. Esposito, eds., *Islam, Gender, & Social Change* (New York, Oxford: Oxford University Press, 1998), 169–189.

3   "Four Bahrainis Among 50 Most Powerful Arab Businesswomen," *Al-Waqat* (Bahrain), May 23, 2008.

4   Constitution of the Kingdom of Bahrain, Law No. 17 of 2002, Article 5(b), http://www .pogar.org/publications/other/constitutions/bahrain-02e.pdf.

5   Bahraini Citizenship Act (last amended 1981), September 16, 1963, Articles 4 and 5, http://www.unhcr.org/refworld/docid/3fb9f34f4.html.

6   Habib Toumi, "Children of Foreign Fathers Get Bahraini Citizenship," *Gulf News*, September 20, 2006, archive.gulfnews.com/articles/06/09/20/10068736.html.

7   Suad Hamada, "Bahraini Nationality Law Challenged in Court," *Khaleej Times*, May 26, 2009, http://www.khaleejtimes.com/darticlen.asp?xfile=data/middleeast/20 09/May/middleeast_May520.xml&section=middleeast&col.

8   Suad Hamada, "GULF: Gender Discrimination in Nationality Laws," IPS News, September 17, 2009, http://www.ipsnews.net/news.asp?idnews=48473; see also Suad Hamada, "Bahraini Women to Get Equal Nationality Rights," *Khaleej Times*, July 13, 2009, http://www.khaleejtimes.comDisplayArticleNew.asp?section=middleeast&xfile =data/middleeast/2009/july/middleeast_july261.xml.

9   Rose Foran, "Women in Bahrain to Lobby for Equal Nationality Rights," the Media Line (reprinted on the Bahrain Center for Human Rights website), July 13, 2009, http:// www.bahrainrights.org/en/node/2927.

10 "New Personal Status Law for Sunni Women"; see also "Bahrain Parliament Passes Family Law for Sunni Section," *Sahil News*, May 14, 2009, http://www.sahilnews.org/ english/news.php?catID=gulfnews&nid=5370.

11 Bahrain Penal Code, Articles 339, 344-1, 345-1, 346-1, 347, 348, http://www.women gateway.com/arwg, in Arabic.

12 Bahrain Penal Code, Article 353, http://www.womengateway.com/NR/exeres/73F00 D14-DE0A-41E1-86CF-55E18761850D.htm, in Arabic.

13 Bahraini Penal Code, Article 334, http://www.scw.gov.bh/media/pdf/Initial-Second-Periodic-Reports.pdf, in Arabic, and http://www.unhcr.org/refworld/docid/47ea235f 2.html, 104, in English.

14 B. P. Pradeep, "Mum Caught Up in Hotel Vice Raid," *Gulf Daily News* (Manama), 2008.

15 "The Supreme Council for Women in Bahrain Established," *Bahrain Brief* (London: Gulf Centre for Strategic Studies) 3, No. 4 (2002).

16 Bahrain National Action Charter (2001), http://www.pogar.org/publications/other/ constitutions/bahrain-charter-01e.pdf.

17 Embassy of the Kingdom of Bahrain, "About: Religion," http://www.bahrainembassy .org/index.cfm?fuseaction=section.home&id=28.

18 H. Kholoussy, "Marriage Practices: Arab States," in *Encyclopedia of Women & Islamic Cultures*, 250–252.

19 Munira A. Fakhro, *Women at Work in the Gulf* (Abingdon: Taylor & Francis, 1990).

20 Suad Hamada, "Lawmaker in Bahrain Slams Minimum Age for Marriage," *Khaleej Times*, April 24, 2009, http://www.khaleejtimes.com/DisplayArticleNew.asp?col=& section=middleeast&xfile=data/middleeast/2009/April/middleeast_April398.xml;

"Bahrain: Opposition to Minimum Age Marriage Age of 15," *Arab News* (reprinted in Women Under Muslim Law), May 5, 2009, http://www.wluml.org/node/5230.

21 *Trafficking in Persons Report* (U.S. Department of State, June 4, 2008), http://www.state.gov/g/tip/rls/tiprpt/2008/105387.htm.

22 S. S. Grewal, "Bahrain Removed from U.S. State Department Blacklist on Trafficking," All Headline News, June 2008, http://www.allheadlinenews.com/articles/7011168940.

23 Sigma Huda, *Report of the Special Rapporteur on Trafficking in Persons, Especially Women and Children: Mission to Bahrain, Oman and Qatar* (New York: UN General Assembly, Human Rights Council, ed., 2007), http://www.universalhumanrightsindex.org/documents/847/1131/document/en/pdf/text.pdf.

24 G. Bew, "Lanka Clamp on Maids to Bahrain," *Gulf Daily News*, 2008; Sigma Huda, *Report of the Special Rapporteur; Suffering in Silence: Domestic Workers Need Legal Protection* (United for Foreign Domestic Workers' Rights [UFDWR], April 14, 2008 [accessed August 8, 2008]), http://ufdwrs.blogspot.com/2008/04/suffering-in-silence-domestic-workers.html; G.M.-F. Chammartin, *Domestic Workers: Little Protection for the Underpaid,* April 2005 [accessed August 8, 2008], http://www.migrationinformation.org/Feature/display.cfm?id=300.

25 *Suffering in Silence* (UFDWR), http://ufdwrs.blogspot.com/2008/04/suffering-in-silence-domestic-workers.html.

26 Chammartin, *Domestic Workers,* http://www.migrationinformation.org/Feature/display.cfm?id=300.

27 *Bahrain: Domestic Workers' Shelter Seeking Cash Support* (Manila: Scalabrini Migration Center, 2008 [accessed August 8, 2008]), http://www.smc.org.ph/amnews/amn060131/middleast/Bahrain060131.htm; S. Al-Moayyed, "Law Blind to Maids' Agony," *Gulf Daily News,* July 13, 2008.

28 "Domestic Violence," in *Domestic Violence (Causes and Solutions)* (Bahrain: Information Center for Women and Children, 2008).

29 *Human Rights: Bahrain* (U.S. Embassy Bahrain), manama.usembassy.gov/bahrain/hrarabic.html; "Bahrain Human Rights Practices 1994," *Human Rights Report* (U.S. Department of State, February 1995), http://dosfan.lib.uic.edu/ERC/democracy/1994_hrp_report/94hrp_report_nea/Bahrain.html.

30 "Domestic Violence Is Doubled in 2008," *Al-Ayam,* June 21, 2008, Bahrain, 1–2.

31 Law 40 of 2005; "Bahrain Legislation Has Lack of Incrimination Codes on Women Violence," *Al-Waqt,* March 8, 2008, 747.

32 L. Ahmed, *Women and Gender in Islam: Historical Roots of a Modern Debate* (New Haven, CT, London: Yale University Press, 1993); L. Abu-Lughod, "The Marriage of Feminism and Islamism in Egypt: Selection Repudiation as a Dynamic of Postcolonial Cultural Politics," in L. Abu-Lughod, ed., *Remaking Women: Feminism and Modernity in the Middle East* (Princeton, NJ, Chichester: Princeton University Press, 1998).

33 Fakhro, *Women at Work in the Gulf;* I. M. Maclagan, "Food Preparation: Arabian Peninsula," in *Encyclopedia of Women & Islamic Cultures,* 107–108.

34 *Statistics on Bahraini Women* (Bahrain: Supreme Council for Women, 2007), 1–24, http://www.scw.gov.bh/media/pdf/statistics-Bahraini-Women.pdf.

35 "The Role of Rehabilitation and Training in the Empowerment of Women and Employment" (paper presented at the Third Arab Conference for Human Resources Development, Manama, 2008).

36 J. Esposito and N. J. DeLong-Bas, "Women in Muslim Family Law," *Contemporary Issues in the Middle East,* 2nd ed. (Syracuse, NY: Syracuse University Press, 2001); A. Al-Hibri, "Muslim Women's Rights in the Global Village: Challenges and Opportunities," in F. Afzal-Khan and N. El Saadawi, eds., *Shattering the Stereotypes: Muslim Women Speak Out* (New York: Olive Branch Press, 2005), 158–178.

37 *Combined 5th, 6th and 7th Periodic Reports of States Parties: Bahrain* (UN CEDAW, June 6, 2008), 19–20, http://www.unhcr.org/refworld/docid/48bbec292.html.

38 "Study: Bahrain Working Women Are Ill-Treated," Women Gateway, http://www .womengateway.com/enwg/Research+and++Studies/working+women.htm.

39 "Hurdles for Working Women," *Bahrain Tribune,* August11, 2007.

40 H.H. King Hamad Bin Isa Al Khalifa, *Constitution of the Kingdom of Bahrain* (2002), 50; Laws Regulation, *Night Work (Women)* (Kingdom of Bahrain: Civil Service Bureau, ed., 2007); "The Role of Rehabilitation and Training," Third Arab Conference.

41 World Development Indicators, online database (World Bank 2009), http://web.world bank.org/WBSITE/EXTERNAL/DATASTATISTICS/0,,contentMDK:217254 23~pagePK:64133150~piPK:64133175~theSitePK:239419,00.html. Last accessed on December 15, 2009.

42 Author obtained information from a client and member of Bahrain Women Union.

43 "The Role of Rehabilitation and Training," Third Arab Conference.

44 "Will Women Be Election Sure-Bet?" Bahrain News Agency, November 17, 2006 [accessed August 8, 2008], http://english.bna.bh/?ID=53081.

45 "The Role of Rehabilitation and Training," Third Arab Conference.

46 "Social Welfare in Bahrain," *Bahrain Brief* (London: Gulf Centre for Strategic Studies) 6, No. 8 (2005); D. Isa, "Activists: Alimony Fund Bahraini Important Step but the 200 Dinars Inadequate," *Al-Waqt,* January 2, 2007; "Activists Not Happy with the Alimony Fund," Women Gateway, December 2007.

47 "Bahraini Women and Unionism," Women Gateway, 2007, http://www.womengateway .com/NR/exeres/1B893363-8305-4B4A-905B-DF20D7575166.htm.

48 "The Role of Rehabilitation and Training," Third Arab Conference.

49 H.H. King Hamad bin Isa Al-Khalifah, *Bahrain National Action Charter,* 2001.

50 Glosemeyer, "Political Parties and Participation: Arabian Peninsula," in *Encyclopedia of Women and Islamic Cultures,* 551–553; "Pioneer Bahraini Women," *Bahrain Brief* (London: Gulf Centre for Strategic Studies) 7, No. 7 (2006).

51 G. Jamsheer, "Women's Petition Committee Condemns the Attack on Women at the General Prosecutor's," *Bahrain Eve,* January 1, 2008 [accessed June 9, 2008] http:// bahrain-eve.blogspot.com/2008/01/womens-petition-committee-condemns.html.

52 "Reporters Without Borders: Bahrain—Turning Promises into Reality" (Manama: Bahrain Center for Human Rights, 2007 [accessed August 8, 2008]), http://www.bahrain rights.org/en/node/1920.

53 *Bahrain: Country Summary* (New York: Human Rights Watch, 2008), 1–5.

54 W. AlMasry, *A Comparison Between the Kingdom of Bahrain and Human Development Report for the Actual Position of Women* (Bahrain: Supreme Council for Women, round table discussion, 2008).

55 A. A. Khamis, *Report of the United Nations Fact-Finding Mission in Saudi Arabia over the Judiciary and Lawyers* (Saudi Arabia: Saudi Centre for Human Rights, ed., 2002), http://www.saudiaffairs.net/webpage/sa/issue07/article07l/issue07lt03.htm, in Arabic.

56 WHO Statistical Information System (World Health Organization [WHO]), http://www.who.int/whosis/en/.

57 Law 11 (2004); "Electors want more health facilities and adequate training. Developing health services top the priorities of voters who are looking forward to high standard health infrastructure including high tech equipment and qualified staff," Bahrain News Agency, November 14, 2006 [accessed February 14, 2008], http://english.bna.bh/?ID=53078.

58 R. B. Serhan, "Virginity," in *Encyclopedia of Women & Islamic Cultures*, 457–458.

59 M. Poya, *Women, Work and Islamism: Ideology and Resistance in Iran* (London, New York: ZED Books, 1999).

60 Ministerial Decree No. 83 of 2006.

61 *National Report Submitted in Accordance with Paragraph 15(a) of the Annex to Human Rights Council Resolution 5/1: [Universal Periodic Review]: Bahrain* (Geneva: United Nations, 2008), 28.

62 "Bias Against Women Continues," *Bahrain Tribune*, December 15, 2007.

63 "Janahi: NGO Law with MB's," *Al-Waqt*, May 23, 2008, 823.

64 W. AlMasry, *A Comparison Between the Kingdom of Bahrain.*

65 Decree No. 27 (2003).

66 Cabinet Decree No. 1156-01 (October 2001).

67 S. Baby, "Accept All Jobs Plea to Women," *Gulf Daily News*, May 25, 2006, 66.

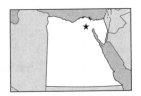

EGYPT

by Mariz Tadros

POPULATION:	78,629,000		
GNI PER CAPITA:	US$1,788		

COUNTRY RATINGS	2004	2009
NONDISCRIMINATION AND ACCESS TO JUSTICE:	2.8	3.0
AUTONOMY, SECURITY, AND FREEDOM OF THE PERSON:	2.8	2.9
ECONOMIC RIGHTS AND EQUAL OPPORTUNITY:	2.8	2.9
POLITICAL RIGHTS AND CIVIC VOICE:	2.7	2.7
SOCIAL AND CULTURAL RIGHTS:	2.4	2.6

(COUNTRY RATINGS ARE BASED ON A SCALE OF I TO 5, WITH I REPRESENTING THE LOWEST AND 5 THE HIGHEST LEVEL OF FREEDOM WOMEN HAVE TO EXERCISE THEIR RIGHTS)

INTRODUCTION

Over the past decade, women in Egypt have made great strides in addressing discriminatory laws. The country's personal status legislation, which had been a source of gender discrimination since its inception in the 1920s, has undergone reform, especially with respect to its procedural elements. Legal prohibitions preventing women's equal access to and representation in the judiciary have been lifted, and social taboos that have restricted their access to certain professions have been broken. At the same time, increasing poverty and hardship have taken their toll on women and their families, limiting their choices and reducing their opportunities to assert their rights. Rising social conservatism with respect to gender roles and increasing deprivation could ultimately undermine women's ability to translate legal rights into lived realities.

Egypt is a republic, led by a president who serves as head of state and a prime minister who is the head of government. The legislative branch consists of the mostly elected People's Assembly (*Majlis al-Sha'b*) and the partially elected Consultative Council (*Majlis al-Shura*). Hosni Mubarak has been the president since the 1981 assassination of his predecessor, Anwar al-Sadat. He has maintained an authoritarian regime, with sweeping powers legitimized through an emergency law that has been in effect since he took office. The president's term has been renewed every six years.[1] Until recently, citizens could only vote for or against a single nominee in a referendum. However, an amendment to Article 76 of the constitution in 2005 allowed for the nomination of alternative candidates.[2] While this represented a step toward democratic competition, it was accompanied by other amendments that, according to the opposition, inhibit political parties' ability to contest the hegemony of the ruling National Democratic Party. And any improvements to the electoral framework continue to be overshadowed by the government's use of authoritarian tactics in practice.[3]

In this deeply contested environment, Egyptians have engaged in a high level of political activism on several fronts. To contest Mubarak's bid for a fifth presidential term and the possibility that he would "bequeath" the office to his son, Gamal Mubarak, a movement of mostly urban, professional women and men known as Kefaya (Enough) staged its first protest in December 2004. Since then the group has led several demonstrations in Cairo and across the country to demand genuine political reform. On another front, female students, mostly belonging to various Islamist movements, have been exceptionally active in student opposition to the encroachment of security forces on their rights and space in the universities. Women and men of all political stripes also took to the streets in large numbers following the Israeli assault on Gaza in January 2009. Moreover, factory workers and civil servants have instigated a number of strikes and demonstrations, in which women have played a leading role, calling upon the government to address the problem of corruption and the failure to provide wages that meet the rising cost of living. Protests related to gender-specific issues have been less common, although female activists have protested against women's molestation on the street.

The years 2004–09 featured continued progress in the removal of gender inequality from the Egyptian legal system. One of the main demands of women's rights groups was finally met in 2004, when the government submitted proposed changes to the nationality law that would enable Egyptian women married to foreign men to pass on their nationality to their children. The new law was approved by the legislature, and it has helped to secure the rights of children whose mothers had non-Egyptian spouses. Two major reforms took place in 2008. First, the Supreme Judicial Council allowed women to become judges and sit on the bench for the first time in the country's history. Second, amendments to the child law included crucial steps toward gender equality, such as an increase in the minimum age of marriage to 18 and the criminalization of female genital mutilation (FGM).

Despite these advances, gender discrimination remains widespread in the legal system. The penal code offers lenient sentences for men convicted of committing honor killings and defines the crime of adultery differently for male and female perpetrators. The personal status law—which regulates issues including marriage, divorce, and child custody—has long been viewed as a major source of discrimination against women. And due to conservative interpretations of Shari'a (Islamic law), the worth of a woman's testimony in family court is considered to be half that of a man's. Even the reforms that have been passed in recent years could be undermined in practice by entrenched societal norms and a lack of effective enforcement mechanisms. For example, FGM is illegal, but it is still widely practiced, particularly in rural areas.

The challenge in the years to come will be to adopt the institutional and policy framework necessary to make the amended child law and other such reforms enforceable. Proper implementation will also require sensitive and consistent awareness-raising and activism at the community level, as only social changes can make beneficial laws a reality in people's lives.

NONDISCRIMINATION AND ACCESS TO JUSTICE

While some discriminatory aspects of Egypt's legal regime have been hotly debated and reformed in recent years, others have gone unaddressed. The nationality law was amended in 2004 to remove a discriminatory provision against a mother's right to pass citizenship on to her children, and social dialogue has increased regarding the unequal worth of women's testimony in family courts. However, practical obstacles to equal access to justice persist, and discriminatory penal code provisions related to honor killings and adultery remain unchanged.

According to Article 40 of the constitution, all citizens are equal, irrespective of race, ethnic origin, language, religion, or creed.[4] Article 40 does not explicitly mention gender, but it is commonly interpreted as protecting women from discrimination. In 2007, Article 62 was amended to call for minimum representation of women in the parliament, opening the door for the establishment of a quota (see "Political Rights and Civic Voice").

While many of the country's policies and laws ensure women's equality in principle, institutionalized forms of gender discrimination founded on patriarchal values regularly deny women's equal rights in practice. This is reflected in Article 11 of the constitution, which obligates the state to harmonize women's duties toward their families with their "work in society," while providing them with equality in political, social, cultural, and economic spheres so long as the rules of Islamic jurisprudence are not violated. This seemingly benevolent article opens the door to the unequal treatment of women because conservative interpretations of Shari'a are often at odds with the principles of gender equality. Poor women are at a particular disadvantage, as they frequently lack the education, resources, and social connections that would enable them to assert their rights.

Despite recent legislative reforms, women do not enjoy the same citizenship rights as men. The parliament amended the nationality law in 2004, allowing the children of Egyptian mothers and foreign fathers to obtain Egyptian citizenship, but the law still prohibits such children from joining the army, the police, and certain government posts.[5] Moreover, those born before the reform's enactment had to apply for citizenship within one year or permanently lose the right to become citizens. The law continues to prohibit citizenship for the children of Egyptian mothers and Palestinian fathers.[6] Prior to the 2004 amendment, Egyptian women married to foreigners could not pass their citizenship to their husbands or children, even if they lived permanently in Egypt. The ban on women passing their citizenship to their foreign spouses has been retained, although no such restriction is placed on Egyptian men married to foreign women.

Sustained efforts to address gender discrimination in access to justice have been met with immense political and social opposition. Cultural attitudes dissuade women from filing complaints in court, which is seen as a public exposure of personal problems. Instead, they are encouraged to deal with problems in a private, nonconfrontational manner, for instance through mediation within the family. Social values regarding women's voice and representation in public, and the patriarchal attitudes of some lawyers and judges, also cast doubt on women's ability to give credible, coherent, and accurate testimony. However, one of the greatest impediments to justice for both women and men is lack of economic resources. The cost of filing a lawsuit and the ongoing expenses of prolonged cases deter many from defending their rights. These factors together make access to justice especially difficult for poor women.

Activists continue to challenge discriminatory provisions of the Egyptian penal code, though their success so far has been limited. Nongovernmental organizations (NGOs) dedicated to women's rights have lobbied against Article 17, which allows judges to hand down lenient sentences to men convicted of so-called honor killings. These crimes typically involve the murder of a woman by a relative for perceived moral or sexual transgressions that supposedly stain the family's honor. Unlike the penal codes of neighboring countries, which require a man to catch his female family member in a compromising act, honor killings in Egypt are excusable even when based on rumors and speculation (see "Autonomy, Security, and Freedom of the Person"). In addition, Article 277 of the penal code defines adultery differently for men and women. While a man is guilty of adultery only if he commits the act in his marital home, a woman is guilty regardless of where the act takes place.[7]

Women's testimony and the evidentiary strength of female witnesses are considered to be equal to those of men, though there are some exceptions, including matters related to the personal status code. Most of the current legal codes do not distinguish between men's and women's testimony. Instead, the judge assesses the worth of testimony based on its credibility, strength, and consistency.[8] Under the personal status law, however, two female witnesses are the equivalent of one male witness in a marital contract, and the testimony of two women is equivalent to that of one man in the family courts, which adjudicate personal status cases.[9] As a practical matter, family court judges require two female witnesses to comply with the legal regulations, but then often take into account only the testimony of the relevant female witness.[10]

Since the personal status law is based primarily on Shari'a, a key to challenging discriminatory personal status provisions lies in the potential for different interpretations of the Koran. In 2008, Zeinab Radwan, a deputy speaker of the lower house of parliament and an expert in Islamic jurisprudence, contested the interpretation of Koranic verses that are often invoked to deny equal weight to the testimony of women. She argued that the verses "related to a specific situation in which women were illiterate at the time, and could also forget the details of the incident since what they were giving was verbal testimony, not written."[11] Important independents and respected scholars, such as Mahmoud Bassiyouny, supported this view, but the ensuing parliamentary discussions were highly antagonistic, with some lawmakers—particularly those from the Islamist camp—arguing that Radwan's views were a distortion of the Muslim faith.[12]

Egypt ratified the Convention on the Elimination of All Forms of Discrimination against Women (CEDAW) in 1981. It placed reservations on Article 9(2), regarding the right of women to pass their nationality to their children; Article 16, related to equality within marriage; Article 29(2), on the resolution of disputes related to the convention; and Article 2, which calls for the implementation of policies designed to eliminate gender discrimination, on the grounds that this could violate Shari'a in some cases. The reservation to Article 9(2) was lifted in 2008 after the nationality law was amended to allow women to transfer citizenship to their children. However, the other reservations remain.[13]

The Egyptian delegation to CEDAW justified the reservations to Article 16 by arguing that Shari'a provides equivalent—rather than equal—rights to women that balance the proper roles of men and women during the course of and in the dissolution of a marriage.[14] In light of the virtual monopoly held by highly conservative and reactionary religious elites over the process of determining what conforms with and what defies Shari'a in the Egyptian context, the push for more progressive interpretations has proven an uphill battle for proponents of reform.

Egyptian institutions and organizations lobbying for changes in the penal code or pressing the government to implement CEDAW are able to operate freely. This is partly because much of the lobbying work for a constitutional amendment that would allow for affirmative action was initiated by the National Council for Women, an official entity headed by the current first lady that reports directly to the president. Nevertheless, nongovernmental women's organizations have been active in lobbying for CEDAW implementation as well.

Recommendations

❖ The government should expand the nationality law to enable the foreign husbands of Egyptian women to obtain Egyptian citizenship.

❖ The penal code must be amended to create a nondiscriminatory definition of adultery and to eliminate leniency for honor killings.

❖ Egypt should remove its reservations to Article 16 of CEDAW and bring domestic legislation into compliance with international standards regarding women's marriage and divorce rights.

❖ The government and NGOs should improve women's access to the courts by providing free legal advice to prospective litigants and subsidizing the court expenses of indigent women.

❖ For existing antidiscrimination laws and policies to be effective, the government must proactively enforce them by prosecuting offenders.

AUTONOMY, SECURITY, AND FREEDOM OF THE PERSON

While national laws guarantee women's personal security and autonomy, the government and private actors undermine these rights in practice. Although amendments to the personal status law made in 2000 instituted some positive changes, women's personal freedoms remain constricted, especially within the marital relationship. In addition, sexual and physical harassment continue in both the private and the public sphere, leaving women vulnerable to abuse in many facets of their lives.

Muslims, nearly all of them Sunni, comprise approximately 90 percent of the population in Egypt, while the remaining 10 percent consists largely of Coptic Christians.[15] Article 46 of the constitution grants all persons the freedom of belief and the right to practice their religious rites, and Article 40 prohibits discrimination on the basis of religion. Despite legal protections, followers of different religions do not enjoy equal privileges and benefits, and people born into the Muslim faith who wish to change their religion face practical difficulties in doing so.[16] Muslim women are prohibited from marrying non-Muslim husbands, whereas Muslim men are permitted to wed Christian or Jewish wives. Within the Coptic Orthodox Church, women who marry men of other faiths are prohibited from partaking of communion, one of the faith's central rites.

As in most other Arab states, Egypt's personal status laws—which govern all matters pertaining to family life, including marriage, the spousal relationship, divorce, and child custody—are widely seen as one of the primary sources of discrimination against women in legislation and practice. Egypt does not have a unified personal status code that applies to citizens of all faiths. Instead, the Personal Status Law (No. 25 of 1925, as amended in 1979, 1985, 2000, and 2004) governs the Muslim majority, while most other faiths apply their own community's religious standards to family matters, assuming all parties to a dispute belong to the same faith. The most recent draft of a personal status law for non-Muslims was submitted to the Ministry of Justice in 1998, but it is still awaiting review.[17] Family issues for Coptic Christians are handled in the same family courts used by Muslims, with judges who are trained in the application of both Muslim and Christian religious laws. The personal status law for Muslims automatically applies in marriages between Muslim husbands and non-Muslim wives, putting the wives at a distinct disadvantage.

While some marriages are still arranged by families, particularly in rural areas, this practice is not believed to be as common as in the past. In all cases, however, there is an increasing societal understanding that women and men should meet and get to know each other before marriage, and that a woman's consent must be secured for a marriage to proceed.

A Muslim woman's right to make stipulations within the marriage contract is guaranteed under law. Such provisions may include the right to pursue one's education, the right to continue working while married, or even the parameters of any future divorce. However, in practice, the legal requirement that a *wali*, or marriage guardian, must negotiate the marriage contract on the bride's behalf limits women's ability to determine the terms of marriage, and social norms strongly discourage the inclusion of stipulations.[18]

Women are also severely disadvantaged under the system of *urfi* (customary) marriages, which have become increasingly common among Egyptian youth. Urfi marriages are informal civil contracts, signed in the presence of two witnesses, that allow couples to live together, often without the knowledge of their family. Some argue that urfi marriages have proliferated because of the high costs of traditional marriage, whereas others argue that their purpose is to legitimize sexual relations. Approximately three million urfi marriages have been documented by notaries in Egypt, although the actual number is thought to be much higher.[19] Urfi marriages are particularly harmful for women because they are not registered as traditional marriage contracts, and the husband is not deemed financially responsible for the wife or held liable for alimony or child support in case of separation. If an urfi husband hides or destroys the marriage document, the wife can neither petition for divorce nor remarry for fear of being accused of bigamy. In addition, paternity suits often arise regarding the children from such unions when the father refuses to acknowledge the urfi marriage and hides the marital document.[20] The parliament is currently considering a law that would outlaw urfi marriages and impose penalties on those who do not comply.[21]

Under the Muslim personal status law, men have the unilateral and un-conditional right to divorce at will (*talaq*) by telling their wives three times that they are divorced and registering the announcement at a religious notary office within 30 days.[22] Conversely, women are required to petition the court and seek either a fault-based or no-fault (*khula*) divorce.

The fault-based divorce is available to women only when the husband has exhibited one of the following four faults: (1) illness, including men-tal illness or impotence; (2) failure to provide maintenance or financial support; (3) absence or imprisonment; and (4) harmful behavior, such as mental or physical abuse. Although the last provision theoretically allows abused women to get out of a marriage, judges have considerable discre-tion in deciding whether to grant a divorce because the necessary degree of injury is not clearly established. For example, they are free to tailor their decisions regarding this threshold based on the socioeconomic class of the woman—the poorer she is, the more harm she is expected to endure and the less likely she is to be granted a divorce.[23]

Until the 2000 amendments to the personal status law, this fault-based system was a woman's only avenue to initiate divorce. Now, Article 20 of the personal status law codifies the traditional Islamic practice of khula, a no-fault mechanism in which women exchange their financial rights—forgoing alimony and returning their dowry—for a divorce. There is a requisite arbitration period of three months, and the entire process should take no more than six months to complete, but reports indicate that stall-ing tactics allow men to delay rulings for years.[24]

According to the 2008 bylaws that govern Coptic Christian marriages, divorce for both men and women is permitted only on the basis of adul-tery or conversion of one spouse to another religion.[25] This differs from regulations issued in 1938 by the Coptic Orthodox Milli Council, which also allowed divorce in cases of domestic violence, male impotence, or male abandonment.

Due to persistent and effective activism by women's rights organiza-tions, Article 20 of the Muslim personal status law was amended in 2005 to permit mothers to have custody of children until they turn 15 years old or until they remarry, whichever comes first.[26] Previously, women's custody rights ended when the boys reached the age of 10 and the girls reached 12. Although this amendment is viewed as a positive step, the law retains an arbitrary limitation to a mother's custody rights rather than allowing the family court to assess each situation in accordance with the best interest of the child. In practice, men rarely petition for custody of their children unless they wish to do so as a form of punishment for their ex-wives: once a woman loses custody, she also loses the right to the marital home or housing support.

Among children resulting from marriages between Muslim husbands and non-Muslim wives, children younger than 15 are by law considered Muslim. Consequently, if the husband in a Christian family decides to convert to Islam, he not only changes the set of laws that regulate the couple's marriage, divorce, and child custody disputes, he also automatically converts his children to Islam. Judges frequently deny child custody to Christian women with Muslim husbands on the premise that they need to protect the Muslim faith of the children. In June 2009, however, the Court of Cassation overturned a decision by the Alexandria Appeals Court and awarded the custody of twin boys to a Christian mother who divorced her Muslim husband, creating a theoretical precedent for considering the best interest of the child in custody decisions.[27] It is not clear to what extent other judges will be influenced by this verdict when ruling on similar cases.

Under amendments to the child law (No. 12 of 1996) made in June 2008, Article 20 now permits illegitimate children to receive birth certificates in the mother's name if the father is unknown. Previously, such children were left without an official identity unless their fathers voluntarily claimed them. If left unclaimed, they were denied all citizenship rights, including the right to vaccinations, education, and Egyptian nationality. The new provision greatly helps children born out of wedlock or resulting from urfi marriages,[28] although on the societal level, such children often remain stigmatized.

The child law amendments also increased the minimum age of marriage to 18 for both sexes.[29] According to one of the legislators speaking in favor of the amendment in the parliament, a poll indicated that 73 percent of Egyptian families would approve of a ban on marriage below the age of 18. However, the Muslim Brotherhood, an Islamist opposition group, objected to the new article, arguing that it defied Shari'a, which sets the age of marriage at 15 for girls and 16 for boys.

Freedom of movement, one of the most basic personal freedoms and a prerequisite to any reasonable level of autonomy, is restricted for women in some respects. In 2000, the Supreme Constitutional Court (Case 243 of the 21st Judicial Year) ruled that women no longer needed the permission of their husbands or fathers to obtain passports and travel. However, a husband or father can still restrict a woman's travel if he obtains a court order to that effect, for example to prevent the woman's flight during a child-custody dispute.[30] Social restrictions regarding appropriate behavior for women inhibit freedom of movement, particularly for those who live in rural areas and belong to socially and religiously conservative families. The notion that a man has the right to prohibit his wife from leaving the house, while still prevalent, is being increasingly contested even in rural contexts. Generally speaking, women of all backgrounds exercise their agency by seeking to negotiate the terms of their mobility, and they often do so successfully, enabling them to pursue greater opportunities for education or employment.

Violence against women is a serious problem in Egypt, and no law specifically prohibits domestic abuse. Family violence can theoretically be prosecuted under the penal code provisions that prohibit bodily injury in general, but this has largely been ineffective, partly because Article 60 of the penal code excuses acts that have been committed in "good faith" pursuant to a right established under Shari'a. Since Shari'a is often deemed to permit the "disciplining" of "disobedient" women, this article has been employed to excuse domestic violence, so long as the beating is not severe and is not directed at the face or other critical areas.[31] Very few mechanisms are currently in place to protect women or provide adequate support for victims of abuse. The state runs seven shelters for abused women, but husbands and family members have access to the facilities, and they are viewed more as centers for rehabilitation and mediation than as true sanctuaries.

One private organization, the Association for the Development and Enhancement of Women, set up its own shelter—Beit Hawa, or the House of Eve—in 2006.[32] It is free of charge and enforces strict security measures to provide abused women and their children with a sense of safety. However, it is constantly threatened with closure due to lack of resources.[33] Women's rights activists have continued to push for increased media attention on the subject of gender-based violence, making it a less taboo topic in recent years, but there is no conclusive evidence that more battered women are seeking redress.

Honor killings, the most extreme form of gender-based violence, still occur in Egypt. Such murders are often based on nothing more than rumors about the woman's behavior. Patriarchal control over women, rising social and religious conservatism, and the tribal system that remains prevalent in rural areas and among urban people of rural origin have all contributed to the problem. The last official statistics on honor killings were released in a 1995 report, which estimated that 52 out of 819 reported murders were honor killings.[34] Due to the penal code's leniency toward men who commit honor killings, judges have often sentenced such individuals to as little as six months in prison.

Widespread sexual harassment on the streets of Egypt undermines women's freedom of movement and their right to be protected against gender-based violence outside the home. A study undertaken by the Egyptian Center for Women's Rights in July 2008 found that 46.1 percent of Egyptian women and 52.3 percent of foreign women are subjected to sexual harassment on a daily basis, including men staring inappropriately at their bodies, inappropriate touching, sexually explicit comments, and stalking.[35]

In 2006 and 2008, two incidents garnered massive attention for their boldness and brutality during the Eid al-Fitr, the holiday marking the end of the holy month of Ramadan. In 2006, dozens of women were harassed by large groups of men on the streets of central Cairo. Women of all ages were targeted, whether alone or accompanied by family members, fully veiled or covered only by the *hijab* (headscarf). Shopkeepers offered the women refuge in their stores as they sought to avoid having their clothes ripped off and being molested in the streets. The police were present but did nothing to intervene. No efforts were made to prosecute the perpetrators, even though the incident was filmed on mobile telephones and the images were widely distributed on the Internet. Officials initially denied that the incident occurred, but local and national news outlets eventually began discussing it and generally questioning women's security on the streets of Egypt.[36]

Women's rights activists reacted by holding demonstrations in Cairo calling for safer streets for women and for the adoption of an appropriate policy to address the problem. When a similar incident occurred in 2008 in the middle-class suburb of Mohandeseen, the official reaction was very different.[37] Again, women's clothes were ripped off and they were physically abused by hordes of men, but this time the police intervened immediately and arrested some of those involved. Under pressure from activist lobbying, sustained press coverage, and wide discussion of the 2006 incident by bloggers, the government attempted to avoid additional political embarrassment for its inability to protect citizens and maintain security. It conducted a broader clampdown,[38] which included the sentencing of one man to a year in prison and another to three years in prison for sexual harassment.[39] However, until this issue is adequately addressed by legislation and other measures like police training, widespread sexual harassment will continue to encourage families to exercise control over women's free movement and limit their presence in public space out of fear for their safety and welfare.

Women's rights organizations regularly tackle issues such as violence against women, sexual harassment, and discrimination in the personal status code. A coalition of nine women's NGOs has called for reforms to the personal status code to address gender inequalities, including a provision requiring the registration of urfi marriages.[40] In addition, the instances of mass sexual harassment that occurred in recent years led to the emergence of new women's groups and a wave of collective action by existing women's rights NGOs. Consequently, sustained campaigns against harassment and in favor of greater accountability for perpetrators have been organized. The Egyptian Center for Women's Rights has long advocated on behalf of harassed women. It launched a campaign called "Making Our Streets Safer for Everyone," and provides the public with relevant information about the issue. A May 2005 incident in which female journalists were harassed and assaulted in an apparently politicized attack ahead of the presidential election (see "Political Rights and Civic Voice") led to an NGO-organized vigil and a conference entitled "The Street Is Ours," in a bid to reclaim public space, freedom of association, and freedom of expression for women. The Egyptian Mothers' Network, formed immediately after the May 2005 attack, organized a demonstration that was attended by over 500 people.[41] These advocacy efforts have helped lift the taboo against discussing such issues, and the media are increasingly covering both the offending events and the reaction of NGOs.

On the individual level, some women have started to courageously break societal norms and fight against gender-based violence. One woman, after being groped on the street, reported the man who harassed her to the authorities. Despite the initial reluctance of the police to open an investigation, the case received wide media attention, and the man was eventually sentenced to three years in prison. According to women's rights activists, it was the first time someone had received a prison sentence for this kind of harassment.[42]

Recommendations

✤ To protect citizens from gender-based violence and harassment in the public space, the government should provide extensive training to create a more sensitized and responsive police force, impose strict accountability mechanisms to deal with officers showing laxity in their work, and invest in improved lighting for poor neighborhoods.

❖ The authorities should vigorously prosecute perpetrators and complicit actors in cases of sexual harassment and molestation, and publicize the verdicts and sentences as a deterrent to future offenders.

❖ Women's civil society organizations should seek to strengthen the voice of Coptic women by engaging those who are socially active in discussions on revisions to Coptic personal status regulations.

❖ The personal status code should be amended to streamline the fault-based divorce process for abused women and reduce the ability of husbands to delay or thwart no-fault (khula) divorce proceedings.

❖ The government and civil society organizations should support the establishment of more women's shelters across the country, with qualified staff and adequate resources.

ECONOMIC RIGHTS AND EQUAL OPPORTUNITY

Women remain significantly underrepresented in the labor force, but more women now hold jobs than ever before, and female unemployment figures have decreased since 2004. The gender gap in education has been closing, with 95 girls for every 100 boys enrolled in primary schools in 2007, a significant improvement over the 66 girls for every 100 boys in 1975.[43] However, these gains risk being undermined by the country's general economic deprivation, which is taking an increasing toll on both the middle class and the already marginalized segments of the population.

Current Egyptian laws do not discriminate on the basis of gender with respect to ownership and use of land and property. Similarly, nothing in the laws restricts women's full and independent use of their income and assets. Nevertheless, women in practice often delegate the responsibility of managing property, land, assets, and businesses to their brothers, fathers, or husbands out of respect for patriarchal norms. Some argue that these norms are justified because it is the legal and social duty of men to assume financial responsibility for women and act as their caretakers throughout life. For example, the failure of a man to provide for his wife and children is one of the legal grounds for a divorce initiated by a woman. However, this patriarchal control of assets is sometimes manipulated to deprive and cheat women of their economic rights. They are left vulnerable and virtually defenseless to such abuses and must depend on the good will of their male relatives for their welfare.

Women in Egypt do not have inheritance rights on par with those of men. According to the Inheritance Law (No. 77 of 1943), which is applied to all citizens regardless of their faith, women are only entitled to half the inheritance of men when both have the same relationship to the deceased. In practice, some women are deprived even of this share and are inhibited by existing social norms from asserting their rights. For example, a recent study conducted in the Upper Egyptian governorate of Assiut suggested that the expropriation of female heirs was still practiced by many families, although it failed to provide statistics. The study also showed that women are most often deprived of inherited agricultural land, which is usually split up among male heirs by mutual consent. Women are sometimes given a compensatory sum of money, although it is generally well below the value of their rightful inheritance. In some rare cases, women and their husbands and children have gone to court to claim the denied inheritance.[44]

Under the current law, a non-Muslim woman married to a Muslim man is not entitled to inheritance upon his death. In March 2008, when she submitted her argument against giving less weight to women's testimony (see "Nondiscrimination and Access to Justice"), Zeinab Radwan also proposed an amendment to the inheritance law that would allow non-Muslims to inherit from Muslims. However, the proposal was turned down by the Islamic Research Council on the grounds that it was in violation of Islamic jurisprudence; as an alternative, the council agreed that mandatory wills could be imposed to ensure non-Muslim widows' welfare.

Under Article 18 of the constitution, education is a right guaranteed by the state and is obligatory through primary school. Female students, like their male counterparts, have free access to public education at all levels but are sometimes unable to take advantage of this right as a practical matter. Cash-strapped parents often send their children to work at extremely early ages, with some as young as four used to peddle goods on the streets, and this contributes to a relatively low (though improving) literacy rate. According to figures for 2006, 87.9 percent of males aged 15 to 24 are literate, compared with only 81.8 percent of females. However, female youths' literacy improved sharply from 2005, when it stood at 78.9 percent, while male youths' literacy dropped from 90.1 percent. The gender gap in literacy widens among older generations, with only 74.6 percent of adult men and 57.8 percent of adult women literate as of 2006.[45]

Government statistics have shown improvements in the gender gap in education level. Girls remain behind boys for all levels except general secondary, where girls had a 7.8 percent advantage as of 2006. At the university level, the government reported an 8.2 percent gender gap at women's expense, but this was less than half that reported for 2001.[46] In a recent positive step, Egypt appointed its first female university president in June 2009.[47]

Women remain grossly underrepresented in the workforce. However, their participation in economic activity has been on the rise. In 2007, an estimated 25.7 percent of women aged 15 to 64 participated in the labor force, slightly up from 24.9 percent in 2004. Government data indicate that the female unemployment rate dropped precipitously from 24.3 percent in 2004 to 18.6 in 2007, while the male unemployment rate rose slightly from 5.9 to 6.0 percent.[48] It is anticipated that the current global economic downturn will drive down women's and men's employment rates in the coming years.

The Labor Law (No. 12 of 2003) protects women from various aspects of gender discrimination, but also imposes certain gender-based restrictions. Article 35 of the law prohibits gender-based wage discrimination, and Article 88 stipulates that all provisions of the labor code apply to female workers. Article 92 prohibits the dismissal of a woman while she is out on maternity leave, and Article 95 requires employers with at least five female employees to post in an obvious place the legal regime related to female workers. However, Article 89 provides that the relevant government ministers may establish conditions under which it is inappropriate for women to work between 7 p.m. and 7 a.m., while Article 90 allows the concerned minister to determine unwholesome or morally harmful areas of work for women, as well as jobs from which women are barred.[49] Like many other countries in the Middle East and North Africa, these discriminatory provisions treat women as if they are unable to make sound decisions regarding their own safety and well-being.

Article 91 of the Labor Law mandates a 90-day paid maternity leave for women who have served for 10 months with the same employer. Such leave is available twice "throughout the female worker's period of service," although it is unclear whether that period refers to service with one employer or her entire working career. Article 93 guarantees women two paid, half-hour nursing breaks each day for two years after the birth of a child, in addition to the paid break enjoyed by all employees. Women working at establishments with at least 50 employees are entitled to two years of unpaid leave, which is available twice during the course of her service period. Establishments that employ at least 100 female workers at one location are required to establish or assign daycare facilities for those with children. Employers sometimes fail to comply with these laws in practice, and there have been instances in which employers deliberately avoid employing more than 99 women so as not to trigger the daycare rule. In cases where women's rights are violated, they may file complaints with the ombudsman's office at the National Council for Women, but it has no legal powers over the employers; at best, it can seek to mediate on behalf of the complainants.

Significantly, the Labor Law's protections largely exclude women working as domestic servants or agricultural laborers, and in many cases these women work in poor conditions and without regular cash compensation. This affects their ability to provide for their families and pay for health care, insurance, and other services. The situation is even worse when such women are disabled or divorced, or when the family lacks any other breadwinner.

An early retirement scheme for female public-sector employees was introduced in 2006, lowering women's retirement age to 45 while keeping men's at 50, provided that they have worked for the same employer for 19 years or more. The sum of money provided to women who opt for early retirement is significantly less than what they would be awarded if they retired later, leaving women even more dependent on their male family members for financial support. Moreover, although the scheme is technically optional, some fear that women will be pushed into retiring early amid waves of privatization of public enterprises, pressures to trim the state payroll, and the global economic crisis. Such provisions also affect the natural arc of a woman's working life, encouraging her to leave the workforce rather than establish a long-term career, thereby reducing women's chances for promotion to managerial positions.[50]

The privatization process was accelerated in the late 1990s and has lacked transparency and accountability. Government mismanagement of state-owned enterprises and high levels of corruption have taken their toll on all workers in Egypt. Many workers have mounted protests against meager wages that do not match galloping inflation rates, months-long delays in dispensing bonuses, and in some instances, cancellation of bonuses altogether. Female workers in Mahalla, a textile-manufacturing town near

Cairo, initiated a major strike in December 2006 in response to the failure of the authorities to deliver long-promised bonuses. The Mahalla strike had a ripple effect on workers and civil servants across the country. Female workers played a central role in mobilizing strikers and sustaining sit-ins, in which they slept on the factory floor overnight.[51] Hundreds of thousands of workers have taken part in protests, seriously affecting manufacturing and the textile industry as well as other economic sectors, including the civil service and railways.

In 2007, civil servants that deal specifically with property-tax accounting protested their wages, believed to be 10 times less than other tax workers.[52] Women comprised a significant proportion of the property-tax workers who participated in the sit-ins, which were staged in tents outside of government buildings. Female protesters brought their entire families with them, including infants and toddlers, as well as food, drink, and blankets to withstand the winter nights. Their goal was to maintain the protest until the government heeded their calls for fairer wages, and their participation changed the face of peaceful protests by drawing in the whole family.

The significance of women's participation and in some cases leadership in organizing protests and sit-ins against the government is manifold. First, it was women who broke the barrier of fear of brutal reprisals by security forces in a highly authoritarian domestic environment, and this "shamed" the men into also becoming active in demanding their rights. Second, the phenomenon challenged conventional ideas about appropriate modes of action and expression for women, gender mixing, and proper "spaces for women." When women were holding public sit-ins, day in and day out, it was difficult to suggest that they live only in the domestic sphere. Finally, women's roles challenged patriarchal notions of masculinity and gender hierarchies. In some cases, women were nominated by both male and female workers to lead protests and communicate their demands to the government. Male workers did not consider this as undermining their masculinity or their male pride.

Recommendations

❖ The government should encourage women's economic participation through measures beyond the offering of microcredit, which— although important—cannot be mainstreamed and applied to women generally.

✤ The most pressing needs of the labor market should be identified, and the government and education system should make a concerted effort to train and educate women so that they obtain the skills necessary to fill these gaps.

✤ The government should proactively address the issues underlying the demands of workers in sectors with large numbers of female employees, rather than merely responding to specific protests. Such underlying issues include lack of financial transparency, lack of opportunities for direct worker-employer negotiations, and an inadequate wage policy.

✤ The ombudsman's office, established by the National Council for Women to receive women's complaints, should be given enhanced powers to investigate and resolve economic grievances.

✤ Civil society organizations and the National Council for Women should play a more active role in monitoring the implementation of existing legislation to ensure that violations are punished and legal loopholes are identified.

POLITICAL RIGHTS AND CIVIC VOICE

Both men and women have been affected by the suppression of protests against the government's undemocratic practices. President Hosni Mubarak, who assumed control of the state after the assassination of President Anwar al-Sadat in 1981, has since maintained a highly authoritarian regime. The Emergency Law (No. 162 of 1958) has been in effect without interruption since Mubarak assumed power, and the state of emergency was extended in May 2008 for an additional two years. Several elections have been held in recent years, but few female candidates or voters participated, and even fewer women were voted into office. However, a ban against female judges was officially lifted in 2007, and in June 2009 the parliament passed legislation establishing a quota system for women in the People's Assembly, the lower house of the legislature.

The upper house of the bicameral legislature, the Consultative Council, acts only in an advisory capacity. It has 176 directly elected members and 88 members appointed by the president, all of whom serve six-year terms; half of the seats come up for renewal every three years. The People's Assembly has 444 directly elected members and 10 appointed by the president, although the total number will increase to 518 after the 2010 elections, to account for the addition of 64 seats reserved for women. Members serve five-year terms.[53]

The 2005 elections for the People's Assembly were marked by one of the lowest female participation rates in decades. There were only 131 women out of 5,165 candidates, of which only four were elected. Subsequently, Mubarak appointed five women to the chamber, bringing the total to nine;[54] one later resigned, reportedly under pressure from her husband, a powerful member of the ruling party.[55] In general, the elections were characterized by vote fraud and violence, as well as a conspicuous lack of security that resulted in the deaths of at least 11 people.[56] The disorder deterred many women from voting and running for office, and in some instances hired thugs molested female candidates and verbally harassed them by making implications about their sexual morality. Female campaign workers and voters were in some cases turned away from polling places due to their support for female candidates.[57]

As of 2009, there were 18 female members in the 264-seat Consultative Council. No women were elected to the body during the 2004 midterm elections, although Mubarak subsequently appointed 11 women. Ten women out of 609 candidates competed for seats in 2007; only one was successful, and nine were subsequently appointed.[58]

The right of women to participate as candidates in elections is hindered by their socioeconomic dependence on men and a patriarchal culture that mistrusts female leaders. Women often lack the financial resources and personal connections that are necessary for a successful campaign. According to a survey conducted by the UN Development Programme (UNDP), fewer Egyptians favor female political empowerment than do those in the three other countries surveyed: Morocco, Lebanon, and Jordan. The study found that just over 60 percent of the Egyptians interviewed believe women should have the right to political participation, and 66.1 percent believe that women should have the right to become a cabinet minister. Worse still, only 45.9 percent believe women should have the right to become prime minister, and a mere 25.7 percent believe women should have the right to become head of state.[59] Reflecting this lack of confidence in female leaders, political parties tend to nominate few female candidates, meaning most run as independents.

Women are poorly represented in local government. In December 2008, lawyer and Coptic Christian Eva Kyrolos became the first female mayor in Egypt, presiding over the village of Komboha in Upper Egypt.[60] Her father was mayor before her, and such positions are often passed on from father to son. However, after her brother's application was rejected for residency reasons, Kyrolos was appointed by the Interior Ministry over five other candidates.

Women are present in Egypt's executive branch, although not in the highest executive positions. One woman, Nawal el-Saadawi, announced that she was considering candidacy in the 2005 presidential election.[61] Although she ultimately decided not to run, a former grand mufti of Egypt responded by issuing a *fatwa* (religious opinion) that prohibited women from assuming the position of president. The sitting grand mufti, Ali Gomaa, initially appeared to endorse the opinion, but he later clarified that a woman could lead a modern Muslim state.[62] This disagreement among religious scholars, and their influence on such an overtly political and constitutional issue, are indicative of the obstacles faced by women in their struggle to assume leadership positions.

Egypt has had female cabinet ministers since 1962, when the first was appointed with a portfolio in social affairs. As of 2009, there are three female ministers: Minister of Manpower and Immigration Aisha Abdel-Hady Abdel-Ghany, Minister of International Cooperation Fayza Abul Naga, and Minister of State for Family and Population Mosheera Mahmoud Khattab. According to official statistics, women held 25.7 percent of management-level civil service positions in 2004, including first undersecretaries, undersecretaries, and directors general.[63]

On March 14, 2007, the long-standing ban on female judges was lifted. Although Tahany el-Gabaly became the first female judge in 2003 when she was appointed to the Supreme Constitutional Court, she was not a trial judge and could not hold hearings. Women's organizations such as the Alliance for Arab Women had lobbied for a repeal of the ban for decades, highlighting the fact that many Muslim countries allowed women to become judges. Workshops and conferences were organized over the last decade regarding the religious and legal dimensions of the prohibition, and studies were released to show the prevalence of female judges in countries including Sudan, Tunisia, and Iran. Female judges from these countries were invited to talk about their experiences and strategies in dealing with opposition, and were instrumental in initiating the 2007 reform. Such campaigning by civil society organizations influenced the media and led to positive coverage of the issue. Crucially, the activists were able to force the matter before the minister of justice by mobilizing support among key policymakers.

A few high-ranking judges opposed the lifting of the ban on religious grounds, and some vowed not to allow the new appointees to become members of the highly influential Judges' Club (JC). The JC provides an important forum for judges to discuss the state of judicial affairs and to represent their interests vis-à-vis the Ministry of Justice. Exclusion of women from such an important body would mean the denial of their right to participate in deliberations over policies and issues that directly affect the judiciary and its individual members. However, with the exception of a handful of judges, no major public outcry against the removal of the ban occurred, and shortly after it was lifted, 30 female judges were appointed. Even after this step forward, women who wish to become judges continue to encounter obstacles. Many of the female judges who were initially appointed had fathers in the judiciary, calling into question the neutrality of the appointments. In addition, the new judges faced stereotypes in their assignments: many were assigned to family courts, and none were sent to criminal courts.

Freedom of opinion and expression in Egypt is protected under Article 47 of the constitution, while freedom of the press is protected under Article 48. However, the Emergency Law, the Press Law, and provisions of the penal code that regulate the press contain significant restrictions. Journalists of both genders may face harassment, imprisonment, and even torture if they convey views or report information that offends the government. Gender-specific attacks on female journalists have become increasingly common. For instance, in May 2005, female journalists taking part in, watching, or reporting on an opposition protest ahead of that year's presidential election were attacked by thugs, who tore their clothes and pushed them to the ground in the hopes of inflicting further abuse. The assaults took place in front of security personnel who did nothing to stop them, and the general prosecutor failed to hold perpetrators accountable after the journalists filed complaints.[64] Some argue that the attackers were hired by the ruling National Democratic Party to discourage anti-Mubarak protests.

Article 54 guarantees the freedom of public and private assembly within the limits of the law. Article 55 permits citizens to establish societies, so long as they are not "hostile to the social system," clandestine, or military in nature. The Emergency Law, however, gives the government sweeping powers to repress activities that it considers threatening to the regime. Moreover, the Law of Associations (No. 84 of 2002) grants the executive branch broad authority to dissolve NGOs, virtually eliminates access to foreign funding, and limits local NGOs' ability to join international associations. The law also prohibits any activism that is "political" in nature, although it is unclear to what degree women's rights activism would be banned under this wording.[65] Finally, the law subjects those who run unregistered NGOs to fines and up to a year in prison.

Although public voices of dissent are suppressed, women have found multiple ways of expressing themselves, participating in civic life, and seeking to influence policy. For example, human rights and political activists made plans to stage a protest on April 6, 2008, against authoritarian rule and deteriorating economic conditions. The state security apparatus announced, unofficially, that stringent measures would be taken against anyone who participated in the planned demonstrations. However, Israa Abdel-Fatah, a young activist, used a social-networking website—as well as e-mail and SMS, or text messaging—to organize a successful general strike in Cairo, in which everyone was encouraged to simply stay home.[66] The unusual emptiness of downtown Cairo sent a strong message of protest against the government. The "Facebook Girl," as Abdel-Fatah came to be known, managed to outmaneuver the government and catalyze a highly effective and memorable form of public mobilization. Surprised by her success, the government detained Abdel-Fatah for two weeks under the Emergency Law.[67]

Access to information is limited for all Egyptians, but this is particularly true for women, in that they are likely to have fewer personal connections and less power and money than men. Various NGOs have sought to empower women with knowledge of their rights, including the Center for Egyptian Women's Legal Assistance, the Egyptian Center for Women's Rights, and the New Woman's Research Foundation. The ombudsman's office of the National Council for Women has also played a role in disseminating information on women's rights. However, outreach by both independent and official bodies has been sporadic.

Recommendations

✤ The Emergency Law, which empowers the state security apparatus to take highly repressive measures against voices of political dissent, should be abolished.

❖ The government should pursue a nondiscriminatory policy for assigning female judges to all courts, including criminal courts.

❖ The government should revise the Law on Associations to remove bureaucratic obstacles and political restrictions that hinder the founding, funding, and daily operations of NGOs.

❖ International donors supporting women's empowerment initiatives should ensure that funding is directed to women who have leadership skills and activist backgrounds but have been marginalized from activism because of their socioeconomic class.

SOCIAL AND CULTURAL RIGHTS

Egyptian women face considerable challenges to their social and cultural rights at both the community and national levels, although recent appointments of officials like the first female mayor and the first female marriage registrar were encouraging developments. Legislation that criminalized FGM was adopted in 2008, but it is unclear how effective it will be against such a widespread and socially accepted tradition. And while women's rights activists have been able to harness the media to address problems such as sexual harassment in recent years, the media continue to portray women in gender-stereotyped roles. To truly affect social and cultural rights, the government and civil society must develop social interventions and processes that can elicit changes in values and beliefs at the grassroots level.

Women do not enjoy the freedom to make independent decisions about their general or reproductive health. Social norms and values often give husbands and other family members the right to interfere in such decisions and coerce women into conforming to certain patterns of behavior. For example, family members, particularly in-laws, often put considerable pressure on women to bear children immediately after marriage, and to continue to have children until they give birth to a boy. Class, not gender, is the main determining factor in access to health care, as soaring poverty rates lead many women to prioritize the health of their children over their own. Women do not have the right to abortion except when the mother's life is in danger, and the prevalence of contraceptive use stands at about 60 percent.[68]

Traditional gender-based practices, such as FGM and defloration, are serious problems in Egypt; they are most common in rural areas and in urban quarters populated by rural migrants. Defloration is the forceful rupture of a woman's hymen by her husband or a midwife on the wedding night. A handkerchief bearing her blood as a sign of virginity is then displayed to the public. This practice seems to be less common than in the past, but there are no available data regarding its prevalence.

FGM, a far more common practice, is the full or partial removal of the clitoris and/or labia minora. Among the mostly African countries where the practice has been documented, Egypt has one of the highest rates of FGM, with approximately 95.8 percent of women aged 15 to 49 having undergone the procedure as of 2005.[69] Activists have worked for decades to eradicate the practice. A 1997 law prohibited FGM except when it was deemed medically necessary, offering a loophole for those who wished to evade the ban. However, after a young girl died in 2007 while undergoing the procedure, the resulting public outcry sparked a ministerial decree banning FGM altogether.[70] Amendments to the child law in 2008 codified this prohibition and criminalized the act of carrying out FGM under Article 61. Practitioners now face a fine of 1,000 to 5,000 Egyptian pounds (US$182 to US$909) and up to two years in prison. The Muslim Brotherhood expressed opposition to the new law, arguing that FGM is not prohibited by Islam and that as an established Egyptian custom, it should not be banned.

FGM remains a deeply rooted social practice, and many have vowed to defy the ban because they believe it ensures that their daughters will be pure, free from sexual desires and sin, and accepted by future husbands.[71] Since the child law amendments were passed, no one has been charged with violating the FGM ban. Hoping to encourage a grassroots acceptance of the prohibition, the National Committee on Children and UNICEF have begun going door-to-door in rural areas to discuss the risks of the procedure with families.[72] Unless culturally sensitive approaches and consistent efforts to promote social awareness are pursued in the long term, such laws will only force FGM to become an underground practice.

Women face discrimination in their right to own and use housing under existing divorce rules and due to their traditional dependence on men. Husbands effectively have sole ownership rights to the marital home upon divorce. Under Article 18 of the personal status law, an ex-wife is entitled to use the marital home or receive substitute accommodations only insofar as she has custody of the children and the father is obliged to provide for them. Because Egypt's public housing service is overcrowded and inefficient, childless women and those who lose custody often become homeless if their families are unable to care for them.[73]

Many women have assumed leadership positions on a local level in recent years, thus increasing their ability to influence gender-based stereotypes, ideas, and values in their communities. In 2008, just two months before Egypt's first female mayor—Eva Kyrolos—was appointed (see "Political Rights and Civic Voice"), Amal Afifi became the country's first *maazouna*, or female marriage registrar, overcoming fierce challenges from conservative Islamic jurists.[74] Afifi, who holds degrees in law, criminal justice, and Shari'a, was ultimately deemed the most qualified candidate to take up the post of marriage registrar in her town, beating out 10 male applicants.[75] Her appointment created a regional domino effect, and another maazouna was appointed shortly thereafter in Dubai, United Arab Emirates. The cases of Afifi and Kyrolos are important in that they rose from within their communities, have continued to live there, and thus have the potential to transform local notions of women's participation, engagement, and leadership by virtue of their daily lives.

Women have gained greater visibility in the media, suggesting that their influence over how women are portrayed has increased. Female broadcasters and journalists have taken advantage of the new Arabic-language satellite television stations, where there are far more employment opportunities than at the state-controlled, overstaffed national television station. Nevertheless, soap operas, other television series, and films generally continue to portray women in a manner that conforms to gender stereotypes, with stock characters such as the submissive housewife, the sexually alluring unmarried woman, and the overbearing matriarch. The images conveyed often reinforce the overarching stereotype of women as emotional beings who lack rationality, and highlight the conservative social climate's creation of two stark options for women: meek, domestic, and maternal, or beautiful, rich, and licentious. Positive images of women in leadership positions remain the exception rather than the norm.

Social class and economic background tend to be the main factors in determining the manner in which poverty affects women. Middle- and upper-class women who are widows or have been abandoned or divorced by their husbands generally have a far better quality of life than married women from poorer households. Their level of education, family support, and social networks allow them to sustain the quality of life they enjoyed prior to the loss of the husband. Moreover, not all poor female-headed households are necessarily in the same disadvantaged situation. Widows, whether Christian or Muslim, are likely to receive sustained financial assistance from religious charities and institutions. Both widowed and divorced women are entitled to monthly government assistance, though the amount is entirely inadequate for survival. By comparison, abandoned women are less likely to receive assistance from their husbands and are more likely to have difficulties obtaining government benefits. In addition, the social stigma associated with abandonment and divorce makes engagement with government welfare agencies particularly traumatic for the women concerned.[76] A new initiative by the government has sought to facilitate divorced women's access to their financial rights by creating a special fund administered by the government-owned Bank Nasser to disburse the money to them. However, the efficacy of the initiative has recently been called into question.[77]

Recommendations

✤ Women's organizations should work more closely with the media sector and universities to expand opportunities for women to begin careers in journalism and other media-related professions.

✤ Civil society organizations should play a more active watchdog role by monitoring the proliferation of negative gender images in the media and immediately responding to harmful material with public campaigns and letters of complaint to the appropriate officials.

✤ Sustained, consistent, and long-term initiatives by the Ministry of Education should be launched to provide opportunities for transformative change in the attitude and practices of the school administration and teachers vis-à-vis gender roles.

✤ The government should respect and protect the rights of all citizens on a more consistent basis so that their motives for improving women's rights and protecting them from, for instance, FGM would appear legitimate rather than another example of cracking down against conservative religious factions.

AUTHOR

Mariz Tadros is a research fellow with the Participation, Power and Social Change Team at the Institute of Development Studies, University of Sussex. Previously, she was an assistant professor in the political science department at the American University in Cairo. She also worked as a journalist for many years at *Al-Ahram Weekly*, where she wrote frequently on the women's movement, gender and development, civil society, and human rights.

NOTES

[1]   Article 77 of the Egyptian constitution, September 11, 1971.

[2]   Mariz Tadros, "Egypt's Election All About Image, Almost," Middle East Report Online, September 6, 2005, http://www.merip.org/mero/mero090605.html.

[3]   For example, the 2005 amendment led to a multicandidate presidential election that year, but Mubarak's strongest challenger, Ayman Nour, head of the recently founded Ghad Party, was imprisoned almost immediately thereafter under the pretext that he had allegedly falsified documents. Nour was released on health grounds in February 2009 after three years of incarceration. Similarly, while parliamentary elections were also held in 2005, they were marred by one of the highest reported incidences of electoral violence in the republic's history, stifling free and fair competition and inhibiting citizen participation.

[4]   An English version of the constitution is available at http://www.egypt.gov.eg/english/laws/Constitution/chp_three/part_one.aspx.

[5]   Law No. 154 of 2004. See also Reem Leila, "Citizens at Last," *Al-Ahram Weekly* no. 697 (July 1–7, 2004), http://weekly.ahram.org.eg/2004/697/eg10.htm.

[6]   Euro-Mediterranean Human Rights Network (EMHRN), *Recommendations on Human Rights in Egypt, in View of the Second EU-Egypt Subcommittee on Political Matters* (Copenhagen: EMHRN, July 2009), http://www.euromedrights.net/usr/00000022/000 00051/00000160/00003077.pdf.

[7]   Fatma Khafagy, *Honour Killing in Egypt* (Cairo: Association of Legal Aid for Women, 2005), 4, http://www.un.org/womenwatch/daw/egm/vaw-gp-2005/docs/experts/khafagy .honorcrimes.pdf.

[8]   Nehad Abul Komsan, "Women's Testimony: A Problem with the Female Mind or the Egyptian Mind," Center for Women's Equality, March 26, 2008, http://www.c-we.org/ eng/show.art.asp?aid=559.

[9]   Amina al-Naqash, "Against the Current," *Al-Wafd*, April 3, 2008 (in Arabic).

[10] Nehad Abul Komsan, "Women's Testimony."

[11] Reem Leila, "In Her Favour," *Al-Ahram Weekly* no. 895 (May 1–7, 2008), http://weekly .ahram.org.eg/2008/895/eg4.htm.

[12] Mohammed Abou Zeid, "Zeinab Radwan Calls for the Testimony of a Woman to Be Equal to That of Man," *Al-Masry al-Youm,* March 11, 2008 (in Arabic).

[13] Convention on the Elimination of All Forms of Discrimination against Women, Reservations by Egypt, endnote 20, http://treaties.un.org/Pages/ViewDetails.aspx?src =TREATY&mtdsg_no=IV-8&chapter=4&lang=en#20.

[14] Convention on the Elimination of All Forms of Discrimination against Women, Reservations by Egypt, http://treaties.un.org/Pages/ViewDetails.aspx?src=TREATY&m tdsg_no=IV-8&chapter=4&lang=en.

15 The religious breakdown of Egypt's population is a politically charged topic. No definitive, accurate estimates exist, as even the official census does not tabulate the population according to religion. The Coptic Orthodox Church, Egypt's largest Christian denomination, claims that its congregation constitutes 12 percent of the population. It argues that the government's estimate of 6 percent deliberately deflates the true figure. Mohammed Heikal, a leading political figure, made a more reasonable estimate of 10 percent. See also the U.S. Central Intelligence Agency's 2009 *World Factbook* at https:// www.cia.gov/library/publications/the-world-factbook/geos/EG.html.

16 "Egypt Court Rejects Ex-Muslim Convert's Case," AlArabiya.net, June 14, 2009, http://www.alarabiya.net/articles/2009/06/14/75916.html.

17 Ali El Bahnasawy, "Holy Defiance," *Egypt Today* (April 2008), http://www.egypttoday .com/article.aspx?ArticleID=7969.

18 Human Rights Watch, *Divorced from Justice: Women's Unequal Access to Divorce in Egypt* (New York: Human Rights Watch, 2004), http://www.hrw.org/en/node/11887.

19 Caroline Wheeler, "Egypt Cracks Down on the £5 'License to Live in Sin,'" *Telegraph* (London), April 27, 2008, http://www.telegraph.co.uk/news/worldnews/africaandindi anocean/egypt/1904329/Egypt-cracks-down-on-the-5-licence-to-live-in-sin.html.

20 "High-Profile Paternity Case Highlights Risks of Common-Law 'Urfi' Marriages," Voice of America, June 7, 2006, http://www.voanews.com/english/archive/2006-06/2006-06 -07-voa19.cfm?moddate=2006-06-07.

21 Caroline Wheeler, "Egypt Cracks Down."

22 Human Rights Watch, *Divorced from Justice*.

23 Human Rights Watch, *Divorced from Justice*.

24 Human Rights Watch, *Divorced from Justice*, 22.

25 Sherif El Dawakhely, "Today Is the Beginning of the Implementation of the Reforms of the Bylaws of Personal Status Affairs for the Coptic Orthodox," *El Destour*, July 3, 2008 (in Arabic).

26 Law No. 4 of 2005, amending Article 20 of Law No. 25 of 1929; see also Reunite International, "Child Abduction and Custody Laws in the Muslim World: Summary Text for Egypt," July 2005, http://www.reunite.org/edit/files/Islamic%20Resource/EGYPT %20text.pdf.

27 Egyptian Initiative for Personal Rights, "Court Decision Grants Long-Awaited Custody of Twins to Christian Mother," news release, June 21, 2009, http://www.eipr.org/en/ press/09/2106.htm.

28 International Network to Analyze, Communicate and Transform the Campaign against Female Genital Mutilation (INTACT), *The 1996 Child Law Amendments: News Articles on the Progress* (Cairo: INTACT, June 2008), 6, 9, http://www.crin.org/docs/Egypt_ Child_Law_Amendments.pdf.

29 Gamal Essam el Din, "Children Accorded Greater Rights," *Al-Ahram Weekly* no. 901 (June 12–18, 2008).

30 Reunite International, "Summary Text for Egypt"; U.S. Department of State, "International Parental Child Abduction: Egypt," http://travel.state.gov/family/abduction/ country/country_490.html.

31 Human Rights Watch, *Divorced from Justice*.

[32] Association for the Development and Enhancement of Women (ADEW), "Violence Elimination Program," http://www.adew.org/en/?action=10003&sub=7.

[33] Jürgen Stryjak, "Beit Hawa Women's Refuge in Egypt: Shelter from Domestic Violence," Qantara.de, 2009, http://www.qantara.de/webcom/show_article.php/_c-478/_nr-889/i.html.

[34] Fatma Khafagy, *Honour Killing in Egypt*.

[35] Aliyaa Shoukry and Rasha Mohammed Hassan, *'Clouds in Egypt's Sky'—Sexual Harassment: From Verbal Harassment to Rape* (Cairo: Egyptian Center for Women's Rights, July 2008), Chapter II, http://ecwronline.org/index.php?option=com_weblinks&catid=52&Itemid=110.

[36] Egyptian Center for Women's Rights, *ECWR Update* (September/October 2006); Nabil Sharaf Din, "Uprising of Predators in Central Cairo," *Al-Masry al-Youm*, October 30, 2006, http://www.almasry-alyoum.com/article2.aspx?ArticleID=35083 (in Arabic).

[37] "Sexual Assaults in Egypt Mar Eid Holiday," AlArabiya.net, October 5, 2008, http://www.alarabiya.net/articles/2008/10/05/57724.html.

[38] Mustafa Suleiman, "550 Egyptian Schoolgirls Harassed in One Day," AlArabiya.net, November 20, 2008, http://www.alarabiya.net/articles/2008/11/20/60477.html; Nadim Audi, "Clampdown on Sexual Harassment in Cairo," *Times Topics* (*New York Times*), December 10, 2008, http://topics.blogs.nytimes.com/2008/12/10/clampdown-on-sexual-harassment-in-cairo/.

[39] Nelly Youssouf, interview with Nihad Abu al-Qumsan, "When Sexual Harassment Becomes an Everyday Occurrence," Qantara.de, 2009, http://en.qantara.de/webcom/show_article.php/_c-478/_nr-856/i.html.

[40] Afaf Hedayat, "Women's Organizations Call for Raising the Age of Marriage to 18 and Registering Urfi Marriages Within 5 Years," *Al-Badeel*, June 5, 2008.

[41] Paul Schemm, "Fired Up by May 25, Egyptian Women Fuel Opposition," *WeNews*, June 17, 2005, http://www.womensenews.org/article.cfm/dyn/aid/2339/context/archive.

[42] "Egyptian Sexual Harasser Jailed," British Broadcasting Corporation (BBC), October 21, 2008, http://news.bbc.co.uk/2/hi/middle_east/7682951.stm.

[43] World Bank, "GenderStats—Create Your Own Table," http://go.worldbank.org/MRER20PME0.

[44] Essam el-Zanaty, *Depriving Women of Inheritance: A Study in the Governorate of Assiut* (Cairo: Center for Egyptian Women's Legal Assistance, 2008), http://www.cewla.org/ (in Arabic).

[45] World Bank, "GenderStats—Create Your Own Table," World Bank, http://go.worldbank.org/MRER20PME0.

[46] *Combined Sixth and Seventh Periodic Reports of States Parties: Egypt* (New York: UN Committee on the Elimination of Discrimination against Women, September 2008), 42, http://www.arabhumanrights.org/publications/countries/egypt/cedaw/cedaw-c-egy7-08e.pdf.

[47] Reem Leila, "Glass Ceilings Shatter," *Al-Ahram Weekly* no. 952 (June 18–24, 2009), http://weekly.ahram.org.eg/2009/952/eg11.htm.

[48] World Bank, "GenderStats—Labor Force," http://go.worldbank.org/4PIIORQMS0.

[49] Labor Law (No. 12 of 2003), http://www.egypt.gov.eg/english/laws/labour/default.aspx.

50   Egyptian Center for Women's Rights, "Removal of Women Employees After Age 45," news release, January 11, 2006, http://ecwronline.org/index.php?option=com_content &task=view&id=268&Itemid=104; "Women Activists Slam Early Retirement Plan," Integrated Regional Information Networks (IRIN), January 17, 2006, http://www.irin news.org/report.aspx?reportid=26056.

51   Ann Alexander and Farah Koubaissy, "Women Were Braver Than a Hundred Men," *Socialist Review* (January 2008), http://www.socialistreview.org.uk/article.php?article number=10227.

52   Serene Assir, "Promises, Promises," *Al-Ahram Weekly* no. 875 (December 13–19, 2007), http://weekly.ahram.org.eg/2007/875/fr2.htm.

53   Adam Morrow and Khaled Moussa Al-Omrani, "Disputes Rise Over Quotas for Women MPs," Inter Press Service, July 27, 2009, http://ipsnews.net/news.asp?idnews=47799.

54   Programme on Governance in the Arab Region (POGAR), "Egypt—Elections," UN Development Programme (UNDP), http://www.pogar.org/countries/theme.aspx?t=3 &cid=5; Inter-Parliamentary Union, "Egypt: Majlis Al-Chaab (People's Assembly)," http://www.ipu.org/parline/reports/2097.htm.

55   Various sources alleged that lawmaker Shahinaz el-Naggar resigned at the request of her new husband, Ahmed Ezz, a business tycoon and chairman of the assembly's budget committee. Gamal Essam El-Din, "Brothers Versus Sorour," *Al-Ahram Weekly* no. 872 (November 22–28, 2007), http://weekly.ahram.org.eg/2007/872/eg2.htm.

56   For excellent coverage of the 2005 elections, see Farid Zahran, ed., *Report on the Egyptian Parliamentary Elections 2005* [in Arabic] (Cairo: Al-Mahrousa Press, 2008); "Not Yet a Democracy," *Economist*, December 8, 2005, http://www.economist.com/ world/mideast-africa/displaystory.cfm?story_id=E1_VNRDJSG.

57   Egyptian Center for Women's Rights, "Relapse or Deterioration in Phase 1 of the Parliamentary Election," news release, November 23, 2005, http://ecwronline.org/index .php?option=com_content&task=view&id=218&Itemid=96.

58   Inter-Parliamentary Union, "Egypt: Majlis Ash-Shura (Shoura Assembly)," http://www .ipu.org/parline/reports/2374_A.htm.

59   UNDP, *The Arab Human Development Report 2005: Towards the Rise of Women in the Arab World* (New York: UNDP, 2006), 94, 261, http://hdr.undp.org/en/reports/ regionalreports/arabstates/RBAS_ahdr2005_EN.pdf.

60   Jeffrey Fleishman, "In Egypt, a Village Boasts the Nation's First Female Mayor," *Los Angeles Times*, March 8, 2009, http://articles.latimes.com/2009/mar/08/world/fg-egypt -mayor8?pg=1; Amany Abdel-Moneim, "Girl Power: First Female Mayor," *Al-Ahram Weekly* no. 928 (January, 1–6, 2009), http://weekly.ahram.org.eg/2009/928/li1.htm.

61   Prior to the 2005 amendment of Article 76, the president was approved by referendum after the People's Assembly had selected a nominee. See POGAR, "Egypt—Elections."

62   UNDP, *The Arab Human Development Report 2005*, 198; Summer Said, "Ex-Mufti's Fatwa Evokes Mixed Reaction," *Arab News*, March 9, 2005, http://www.arabnews.com/? page=4&section=0&article=60159&d=9&m=3&y=2005; Agence France-Presse (AFP), "Islam Not Against Women Presidents, Says Egypt's Cleric," *GulfTimes*, February 5, 2007, http://www.gulf-times.com/site/topics/article.asp?cu_no=2&item_no=131132&ver sion=1&template_id=37&parent_id=17; "Egypt's Grand Mufti Says Women Can Lead

Modern Islamic Nations," Al Bawaba, February 4, 2007, http://www.albawaba.com/en/news/209210.

63 Egypt State Information Service, "Women in the Executive Authority," http://www.sis.gov.eg/En/Story.aspx?sid=2259.

64 Reporters Without Borders, "Call for New Investigation into Attacks on Women Journalists in Cairo," news release, January 5, 2006, http://www.rsf.org/Call-for-new-investigation-of.html.

65 South Asian Human Rights Documentation Centre (SAHRDC), "Mubarak Plays Pharaoh: Egypt's 'New' NGO Law," Human Rights Features, July 25, 2002, http://www.hrdc.net/sahrdc/hrfeatures/HRF61.htm. According to this article, one newspaper quoted a government official as stating that an organization backing the Palestinian cause would not be considered political in nature, and would therefore be acceptable, whereas a group that promoted democracy would be inappropriate.

66 David Wolman, "Cairo Activists Use Facebook to Rattle Regime," Wired Magazine, October 20, 2008, http://www.wired.com/techbiz/startups/magazine/16-11/ff_facebook egypt?currentPage=all; Magdy Samaan, "From Cyber to Reality: New Political Stars Emerge from Facebook," Daily News (Egypt), June 29, 2008, http://www.dailystar egypt.comarticle.aspx?ArticleID=14739.

67 Ahmed Abd el-Gawad, "Release of the Young Woman Israa . . . ," Al-Destour, April 15, 2008 (in Arabic).

68 UNDP, The Arab Human Development Report 2005, 291.

69 UNICEF, Female Genital Mutilation/Cutting: A Statistical Exploration (New York: UNICEF, 2005), 6, http://www.unicef.org/publications/index_29994.html; World Health Organization (WHO), Eliminating Female Genital Mutilation: An Interagency Statement (Geneva: WHO, 2008), 29, http://whqlibdoc.who.int/publications/2008/9789241596442_eng.pdf.

70 UNICEF, "Fresh Progress Toward the Elimination of Female Genital Mutilation and Cutting in Egypt," news release, July 2, 2007, http://www.unicef.org/media/media_40168.html.

71 Liam Stack, "Egypt's Child Protection Law Sparks Controversy," Christian Science Monitor, July 24, 2008, http://www.csmonitor.com/2008/0724/p05s01-wome.html.

72 Iman Azzi, "Egypt Has Yet to Feel Impact of Female Genital Mutilation Ban," Women's E-News, May 5, 2009, http://towardfreedom.com/home/content/view/1580/1/.

73 Human Rights Watch, Divorced from Justice, 22.

74 Amany Abdel-Moneim, "Girl Power: Maazouna for the First Time," Al-Ahram Weekly no. 928 (January 1–6, 2009), http://weekly.ahram.org.eg/2009/928/li2.htm.

75 "Egypt Officially Appoints First Female Marriage Clerk," Islam Today, October 10, 2008, http://www.islamtoday.com/showme2.cfm?cat_id=38&sub_cat_id=1992.

76 For a full discussion of women and welfare rights in Egypt, in theory and in practice, see Iman Bibars, Victims and Heroines: Women, Welfare and the Egyptian State (New York: Zed Books, 2001). See also Mariz Tadros, "Food for Faith: Welfare Provision in a Poor Urban Settlement of Cairo" (doctoral thesis, Oxford University, 2004).

77 Human Rights Watch, Divorced from Justice.

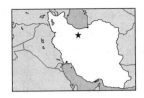

IRAN

by Nayereh Tohidi

POPULATION:	73,244,000		
GNI PER CAPITA:	US$3,998		

COUNTRY RATINGS	2004[1]	2009
NONDISCRIMINATION AND ACCESS TO JUSTICE:	N/A	1.9
AUTONOMY, SECURITY, AND FREEDOM OF THE PERSON:	N/A	2.1
ECONOMIC RIGHTS AND EQUAL OPPORTUNITY:	N/A	2.7
POLITICAL RIGHTS AND CIVIC VOICE:	N/A	2.1
SOCIAL AND CULTURAL RIGHTS:	N/A	2.5

(COUNTRY RATINGS ARE BASED ON A SCALE OF 1 TO 5, WITH 1 REPRESENTING THE LOWEST AND 5 THE HIGHEST LEVEL OF FREEDOM WOMEN HAVE TO EXERCISE THEIR RIGHTS)

INTRODUCTION

A populist revolution in 1978–79 put an end to Iran's long-standing tradition of monarchy, replacing it with a unique Islamic republic, wherein religious clerics assumed political control under a supreme leader, Ayatollah Ruhollah Khomeini. Despite massive participation by women in the revolution and a subsequent increase in the levels and forms of women's social presence and educational achievements, the Islamic Republic brought many negative changes to women's rights and personal freedoms. Sex segregation and compulsory veiling, discrimination in penal and civil codes, and setbacks in personal status and family law further institutionalized patriarchal gender relations and cultural attitudes.

The discriminatory state ideology and policies of the Islamic Republic run against the modern socioeconomic and demographic realities in the country, especially with respect to the growing number of urban, educated, middle-class women. Their quest for equal rights and collective action to improve their status began during the Constitutional Revolution of 1906–11. Continuous pressure from women's groups led to government reforms concerning women's education, employment, suffrage, and family law under the Pahlavi dynasty, which ruled from 1925 until 1979.

The rapid process of uneven and autocratic modernization and Westernization under the Pahlavi shahs alienated many in the traditionalist populace, especially powerful Shiite Muslim clerics, the poor, and the secular intelligentsia—both male and female.[2] At the outset of the revolution, the secular democratic forces were weak and unorganized, in part due to systematic repression by the shah's infamous secret police. The Islamists, meanwhile, were bolstered by the strong organizational structures and financial resources of the clerical establishment, helping them gain an upper hand in the ensuing struggle with other groups and secure control after the shah fled Iran.

Under the Islamic Republic in the 1980s, the few significant progressive reforms of the Pahlavi era, such as those made to the family law in the 1960s and 70s, were repealed, and both the family law and the penal code regressed to match their condition in the 1930s and 40s.[3] Although the shah's Family Protection Law was annulled, women's rights defenders resisted the regression and no replacement legislation was passed, leaving the old law in place as the practical guide for answering questions that were not explicitly addressed by Shari'a (Islamic law).[4]

The "era of construction" under President Ali Akbar Hashemi Rafsanjani (1989–97) ushered in some positive changes to the government's gender policies. These came about as the result of Iranian women's demands from both inside and outside Iran, as well as international pressures, particularly the growing global women's activism sponsored by the United Nations. For example, a woman was appointed as a presidential adviser on women's issues, and the Office of Women's Affairs was established as required by the UN Commission on the Status of Women. There were also more systematic activities, such as preparation of national reports on the status of women in response to the UN-sponsored World Conference on Women in Nairobi (1985) and Beijing (1995).

Iran experienced an era of uneven reform under the presidency of Mohammad Khatami (1997–2005). Women's sociopolitical participation and civic activism increased considerably, while restrictions on personal freedoms and dress were loosened. Women made impressive gains in literacy and educational attainment, and enjoyed improved access to primary health care and birth control. They increasingly contributed to cultural and artistic production, and some of the best-selling films, novels, and paintings were produced by female artists. However, attempts by reform-oriented members of the parliament (the Islamic Consultative

Assembly, or Majlis) to make progressive changes, including ratification of the Convention on the Elimination of All Forms of Discrimination against Women (CEDAW), were blocked by the conservative Guardian Council.[5]

The election of President Mahmoud Ahmadinejad in 2005 marked a return to power for hard-liners and negatively affected almost all areas of women's social life. Violations of human rights generally and women's rights in particular have intensified, and censorship has increased. The overall condition of women in Iran has also suffered from revived sociopolitical restrictions on women's dress, freedom of assembly, social advocacy, cultural creativity, and even academic and economic activity. Attempts at legal reforms in favor of women's rights have been blocked, and a government-backed proposal that would have reinforced polygamy and temporary marriage made women's rights a more urgent concern for a broad spectrum of the female population. Additionally, economic mismanagement that has helped to squander Iran's abundant oil and gas reserves, combined with the global economic downturn, has left the country with a high rate of unemployment that especially affects women and young people.[6]

At the same time, growing globalization, increased access to new communications technology, and recent demographic changes have countered some of these negative trends. Iran has undergone rapid urbanization, and 70 percent of its population is under the age of 30, contributing to a transformation in gender roles. These factors, combined with resistance by women and youth and their collective campaigns for equal rights, have stirred factional conflicts and differences on gender issues among the clerics and other ruling elites. The women's rights movement is reasonably well-organized and surprisingly effective considering the repressive conditions within which it operates. Women's rights defenders have influenced public discourse surrounding discriminatory laws, challenging the regime while pushing for change and often leveraging public opinion to influence policy at high levels.

Conflicts within the leadership came to the fore during and after the June 2009 presidential election, of which Ahmadinejad was declared the winner by a wide margin. Iranian women played a prominent role in the large preelection rallies and in the massive street protests that followed the vote, as opposition candidates and their supporters raised accusations of wholesale fraud in the official results. Women were seen marching in the demonstrations in large numbers and braving the violent response by security forces, dramatically illustrating the clash between a changing society and an increasingly repressive government.

NONDISCRIMINATION AND ACCESS TO JUSTICE

Under the Islamic Republic of Iran, discrimination and segmentation on the basis of religion and gender have been institutionalized in the constitution, government policies, and state ideology. The system explicitly favors men over women, Muslims over non-Muslims, and Shiite Muslims over other Muslim sects.[7] The constitution and the Shari'a-based penal and civil codes, especially those sections pertaining to family and personal status, legalize the subordination of women, treating them as second-class citizens with unequal rights. Women's rights activists have launched widely publicized equal-rights campaigns that have been successful within the parameters established by the theocracy. However, the overall legal framework remains discriminatory, with the state's theocratic underpinnings consistently negating its progressive and democratic elements.

For instance, Article 19 of the constitution states: "The people of Iran regardless of ethnic and tribal origin enjoy equal rights. Color, race, language, and the like will not be cause for privilege."[8] Note that while discrimination on the basis of ethnicity and race is prohibited, neither religion nor sex is mentioned. Other sections of the constitution directly address women's rights. Article 20 states: "All citizens of the nation, whether men or women, are equally protected by the law. They also enjoy human, political, economic, and cultural rights according to Islamic standards." This language carefully avoids a guarantee of equal rights for women, despite the pledge of equal protection, and the qualifier of "Islamic standards" effectively limits women's rights to those available under Shari'a.

The preamble and Article 21 glorify motherhood and the family as "the foundation of society," and obligate the government to offer protective measures in support of the family unit, mothers, orphans, widows, and old or destitute women. The preamble also states that "motherhood is accepted as a most profound responsibility in the Muslim viewpoint and will, therefore, be accorded the highest value and generosity."[9] However, Article 21 calls for the government to grant child custody only to "worthy mothers," and only "in the absence of a lawful guardian."

Under Shari'a, the lawful guardian of children is the father, or in his absence, paternal kin.

Shari'a is the only source of legislation under Article 4 of the constitution. Therefore, any changes or reforms made to women's rights are contingent upon the political influence of the *ulema* (Islamic clerics) and their interpretation of Islam. Shiites adhere to the Ja'fari school of Shari'a, which differs in some respects from the four Sunni schools of Islamic jurisprudence. For instance, women with no brothers are entitled to greater inheritance rights than their Sunni counterparts. Still, women of both sects face discrimination in their inheritance rights, their right to act as a witness in court, and the right to become a judge.

The Ja'fari approach to women and gender relations, much like the Sunni schools of jurisprudence, is frequently at odds with the universalism and egalitarianism of modern international human rights conventions. The reformist Sixth Majlis made several reservations when it ratified CEDAW in 2003, but the move nevertheless caused uproar among conservative clerics in Qum, the largest center of Shiite scholarship. The ratification was therefore vetoed by the Guardian Council. The disputed legislation was then sent to the Expediency Council for a resolution, and it has been awaiting consideration there ever since.

Women cannot pass on nationality and citizenship to their children or their husbands. Children's nationality and citizenship are determined through their fathers only.[10] A Muslim man can marry non-Muslim women with no legal problem or state intervention, as it is assumed that the wife's religion and citizenship are determined through her husband. A Muslim woman can marry a previously non-Muslim man only if it is proved that he has converted to Islam, and even in this case, a non-Iranian man cannot earn citizenship through his Iranian wife.[11] These citizenship restrictions have affected thousands of Iranian women, particularly those married to Afghan or Iraqi refugees, as well as expatriate Iranian women married to non-Iranians. As Iran has pushed millions of such refugees to return to their homelands in recent years, many Iranian women have been forced to choose between their native country and their noncitizen husbands and children.

The penal code is broken down into *hodud* (or *hadd*, singular) punishments, which are prescribed in religious law; *qisas*, or the law of retribution, in which the punishment is equal to the suffering of the victim;

diyeh, or blood money, in which the families of victims receive financial compensation; *ta'zir*, or sentences that are left undefined and open to interpretation by judges; and punishments intended to ensure peace and stability for the community.

Many of these mechanisms are clearly retrograde in nature. The penalty of death by stoning for adulterers, for example, had not existed in Iran for a century, but it is now part of the penal code and is sporadically practiced in the Islamic Republic. Article 630 of the penal code allows a man to murder his wife and her lover if he catches them having consensual sex. If the wife is being raped, he may only murder the man.[12] A married man is legally allowed to engage in affairs under the guise of *sigheh* (temporary marriage) as many times as he wishes, whereas a married woman can be stoned to death or murdered in an "honor killing" for participating in a similar relationship. In addition, the blood money paid for a slain Muslim or non-Muslim woman is half that for a Muslim or non-Muslim man.[13]

Head and body coverings for women are mandatory under Article 638 of the penal code, which stipulates that those who fail to comply with *hijab sharèe* (Shari'a-based veiling) face 10 days to two months in prison or fines between 50,000 and 500,000 rials (US$5 to US$50).[14] The law lacks specificity on what constitutes a violation, but in practice, women have been punished for all of the following: showing part of one's hair, using cosmetics, wearing sunglasses, wearing a tight or short *manteau* (coat or gown), showing skin above the wrist or ankle, showing neckline, and wearing boots over (rather than under) trousers.[15] No private plaintiff is necessary for prosecution, as it is the state's prerogative to monitor and control women's apparel.

Harsher enforcement has increased the number of arbitrary arrests and detentions in recent years. Immediately following the revolution, observance of head coverings and modest dress for women was enforced by a special police service in all public places, and women were harassed, arrested, fined, and detained for violations. During the reform era under President Khatami (1997–2005), this enforcement was relaxed considerably although not eliminated. However, since 2006, male and female officers have stopped, verbally scolded, physically attacked, arrested, or temporarily detained thousands of women and some young men for wearing insufficiently modest clothing, or "bad hijab."

Individual members of women's rights groups are subject to arbitrary arrest and detention as well as smear campaigns in the state-run media, verbal and physical harassment, travel bans, and other forms of suppression.[16] In the last two years alone, 68 women involved in the One Million Signatures Campaign to Change Discriminatory Laws (Change for Equality) have been arrested and imprisoned.[17] Due to domestic and international pressure by human rights activists and organizations, and especially intervention by defense lawyers such as Nobel laureate Shirin Ebadi, most activists have been released on bail after a few days or weeks in prison. The government continues to intimidate some of the released activists by summoning them to court for interrogation under the pretense of due process.[18]

However, authorities have recently broken with the practice of releasing activists on bail. In February 2009, Alieh Eghdamdoust, 57, became the first women's rights activist in the Islamic Republic to have her prison sentence implemented. According to the International Campaign for Human Rights in Iran, the sentence was based solely on her activities promoting women's rights.[19] Eghdamdoust was arrested in June 2006 with 70 others during a peaceful women's rights protest in Tehran's Hafte Tir Square. After a week in prison, she was charged with violation of national security through participation in an illegal protest and disrupting public order. Eghdamdoust was initially sentenced to 20 lashes and three years and four months in prison, but an appeals court reduced the penalty to three years in prison. On February 1, 2009, she was transferred to the Office of Implementation of Sentences at the Revolutionary Courts, and began serving her sentence. Her lawyer, Nasim Ghanavi, argues that her participation in the peaceful protest was authorized by Article 27 of the constitution, which holds protests to be legal as long as the demonstrators do not carry arms or insult Islam.[20]

An adult woman is generally not recognized as a full person in court. Except for civil law cases, in which women's testimony has the same value as that of men, the testimony of two women equals that of one man. Nonetheless, judges retain wide discretion in determining what constitutes acceptable testimony. In cases involving major crimes, such as murder, a woman's testimony is impermissible in court.[21] This rule is obviously detrimental to justice in practice, especially when a murder takes place in an exclusively female gathering.

The customary practices in most parts of Iranian society are often more progressive than the laws, with the exception of some ethnic groups and tribal communities in a few underdeveloped regions of the country. Because of this gap between law and society, women's rights activists have made legal reforms their top priority.

The largest and most influential organized movement for legal reform is the Change for Equality campaign.[22] A smaller but more focused project is the Stop Stoning Forever Campaign.[23] Other small-scale campaigns include the Women for Equal Citizenship Campaign, the Women's Access to Public Stadiums Campaign, the National Women's Charter Campaign, and Mothers for Peace. All of these are lawful movements that operate peacefully and transparently, but human rights defenders involved with them are vulnerable to persecution by the regime.

The government views such activities with utmost suspicion, and women's rights advocates are frequently charged with "endangering national security" and "contributing to the enemy's propaganda against the regime." The authorities have pointed to real or supposed foreign funding as evidence that civic groups are involved in a U.S.-led plan for "regime change."[24] Such claims are patently absurd. As one activist against polygamy argued, "How could my protest against my husband's right to bring a second wife into our home threaten my country's national security?"[25] But because of the government's crackdown, most women's rights organizations are careful not to accept any financial support from international donors.

In an effort to protect their members, many women's nongovernmental organizations (NGOs) are depriving themselves of the resources available to similar groups in other countries. Even international awards that include monetary prizes have become a source of tension and political divisions among the activists.[26] While most groups avoid accepting any financial help or even symbolic awards from "Western" sources, some see this as yielding to government pressure in a manner that is contrary to their practical needs and interests.

Even Ebadi—one of the most prominent human rights defenders in Iran—has not been immune from recent governmental attacks. A smear campaign waged against her by the conservative press took a drastic and violent turn in December 2008.[27] Her organization, the Defenders of Human Rights Center (DHRC), was closed on December 21, and her private law office was raided a week later by men who identified themselves as tax officials. They confiscated her computers and private client files. On January 1, 2009, a group of approximately 150 people demonstrated in front of Ebadi's home, chanting threatening slogans and vandalizing her property. The police arrived after she called for help, but they took no steps to restrain or disperse the protesters. Attacks on Ebadi have likely increased because she has acted as legal counsel for a number of Baha'is; the government does not recognize the Baha'i faith and considers its adherents to be apostates. On January 14, Jinous Sobhani, one of Ebadi's Baha'i colleagues, was arrested without cause. She was released on March 11, with bail set at 700 million rials (US$70,000), pending the determination of her trial date.

The DHRC is the main human rights organization in Iran that provides pro bono services to those accused of political crimes and offers support to families of imprisoned political activists. It publishes regular reports on the situation of human rights in Iran. Hadi Ghaemi, director of the International Campaign for Human Rights in Iran, noted that "the closure of the DHRC signals a shift in the approach of security forces and attests to the lack of tolerance on their part, not only for dissent by political and social activists, but also for any defense, even legal defense in court."[28] If Ebadi, given her international prestige, is not immune from this type of pressure, then other women human rights defenders are at even greater risk. The crackdown was also interpreted as a bid to silence voices of dissent and criticism ahead of the 2009 presidential election.[29]

Recommendations

❖ The government should immediately stop all forms of harassment and attacks against women's groups that are pursuing gender equality through peaceful and transparent means.

❖ The Majlis should pass legislation establishing effective citizen-complaint mechanisms and criminal penalties for security personnel who engage in verbal harassment, physical abuse, or arbitrary arrest, particularly while enforcing rules on personal attire and appearance. NGOs should create telephone hotlines and other programs to provide legal advice and assist victims in pursuing complaints.

❖ The Expediency Council should promptly review and approve the Majlis's ratification of CEDAW, which has been delayed for several years. This will facilitate the legal reform process with respect to polygamy, diyeh, and stoning, among other issues.

❖ Since the women's NGOs cannot simply wait for or rely on the CEDAW ratification, they should both pursue major campaigns like Change for Equality and continue to create smaller movements focused on individual issues, like equality in inheritance and access to justice for victims of domestic violence.

AUTONOMY, SECURITY, AND FREEDOM OF THE PERSON

In Iran, the behavior and sexuality of women, especially younger women, is traditionally viewed as a matter of family honor that must be controlled by a woman's father, brothers, and husband. Since the establishment of the Islamic Republic and the application of Shari'a to all public and private spheres, the state has inserted itself into this role, pledging to "protect the honor of the nation's women" in terms of their public appearance and apparel, sexuality, personal interactions, and spatial mobility. This state intrusion violates the autonomy, security, and freedom of all persons, and women in particular are negatively affected.

Iran is a heterogeneous country combining many ethnic, religious, tribal, and regional crosscurrents. Although the majority of the population are Persian Shiites, ethnic minorities—including Azeris, Gilaki and Mazandarani, Kurds, Arabs, Lurs, Baloch, Turkmens, and others—make up a significant portion of the population. Women belonging to certain groups may face unique constraints imposed by their culture or religious denomination. Some patriarchal practices and gender-related restrictions against women, such as "honor killings" and forced marriage, are more prevalent in the more impoverished and less developed provinces largely populated by ethnic minorities such as Arabs and Kurds.

Article 13 of the constitution recognizes Christians, Jews, and Zoroastrians as religious minorities and grants them limited freedom of religious practice, education, and political representation within the Majlis. However, conversion by Muslims to other religions is considered apostasy, as is being a member of the unrecognized Baha'i faith. Baha'i men and women are routinely denied the fundamental legal protections and state benefits afforded to other Iranians, and even recognized religious minorities are subject to various forms of discrimination. Muslim women are not permitted to marry non-Muslim men, but the non-Muslim wives of Muslim men are presumed to have accepted Islam. The personal status of the members of recognized religious minorities, such as Christians and Jews, are governed by their own sectarian laws. Nonetheless, certain discriminatory rules such as mandatory hijab and sex segregation apply to all citizens regardless of their religious or nonreligious beliefs or values.

Women's freedom of movement is restricted by both cultural traditions and legal restrictions. A woman may not obtain a passport or leave the country without her husband's written permission.[30] In addition, the domicile of a married woman is considered to be that of her husband under Article 1005 of the civil code, and she must reside in the house determined by her husband under Article 1114 unless she reserves the right to live elsewhere in their marriage contract. Certain public spaces are segregated by sex and select services are completely out of reach for women. For example, women are not allowed to attend soccer games, and a woman cannot stay in a hotel unless she is accompanied by a male relative, even though there are no laws specifically barring women from such places.

The laws regulating the personal status and family rights of women, found mostly in Books 7 to 10 of the civil code, are discriminatory in relation to marriage, the right to divorce, and child custody. The government-proposed Family Protection Bill was passed in September 2008, but not before a large and diverse coalition of women's groups, supported by moderate clerics and politicians, was able to secure the removal of two of the most onerous provisions. Under the bill's original version, a man would no longer be required to have his first wife's permission before taking another wife, and women would have been required to pay tax on their *mehriyeh* (dowry) at the outset of marriage.

According to Article 1034 of civil code, marriage is defined as being between a man and woman, and a man may become the suitor of any eligible woman. Implicit in law and reinforced by cultural attitudes is the notion that men, not women, should propose marriage. Article 1070 of the civil code requires the mutual consent of both bride and groom for a marriage contract to be valid. In practice, however, very young or widowed women, particularly those living in provincial and rural areas, may be forced into marriage either out of poverty or based on traditional and tribal customs. Although men may also be forced into marriage by their families, rural girls are far more susceptible to such practices.

The legal age of consent is 13 for girls and 15 for boys, but a permit may be obtained for the marriage of even younger girls or boys upon the request of a father or paternal grandfather to the court. This flexibility, combined with the already-low legal marriage age, increases the likelihood of young girls being married off to older men for financial reasons. More recent sociocultural trends in Iran, however, indicate that such laws are lagging far behind the new realities. At present, the average age of the first marriage for women and men are actually 24 and 27 respectively.

The validity of a woman's first marriage is contingent upon the approval of her father or paternal grandfather, regardless of her age. If she has no father or grandfather, or can argue that they refused her choice without justification, the daughter may appeal to the court and register her marriage with the court's approval. Such restrictions do not apply to men.[31] It is uncommon and largely undesirable for a young woman to marry without parental (especially the father's) approval, as it may ostracize her from her relatives and community.

Only men are permitted to marry multiple spouses. They can take up to four wives and engage in an unlimited number of temporary marriages (*sigheh* or *mutâ*). In reality, polygamy is not a common practice, and most people disapprove of sigheh.[32] However, because sexual relationships outside of marriage are criminalized under Article 63 of the penal code, sigheh is occasionally used by members of the secular and nonconformist youth to avoid punishment for otherwise illicit sexual activity.[33]

While the power of divorce lies principally with the husband, he cannot divorce his wife without going through the family court and its required procedures. The court appoints arbitrators, usually from among the relatives of the couple, in an attempt to secure reconciliation. If the husband insists on divorce, the court will grant its approval.[34] The process is less arduous if the couple files for divorce on mutual basis, but far more difficult when the wife applies for divorce on her own. According to Article 1130 of the civil code, she has the burden of proving that the continuation of the marriage would expose her to "difficult and pressing conditions." These can include the husband's addiction, impotence, adultery, abandonment, and physical abuse. Polygamy cannot be cited as the reason for a divorce unless it violated a condition in the couple's marriage contract. Another option for women is a type of divorce called *khula*. According to the Article 1146 of the civil code, a woman can file for such a divorce, based on her disgust toward the husband, if she forfeits her mehriyeh or pays him an equivalent sum. It should be noted that khula is possible only when the husband concedes.[35]

In a divorce initiated by the husband, it is his prerogative to return to the wife and reconcile the marriage during the course of a waiting period known as *eddeh* (three months or three menstrual cycles), regardless of the wife's wishes. A divorced wife consequently has to remain in the husband's residence for three months after the intent to divorce is stated.

After a divorce, a woman's child custody rights are determined by law based on the child's age. Article 1169 of the civil code originally gave women primary custody rights over their children until boys turn two and girls turn seven, but the age for boys was later raised to seven as well. After children reach the age threshold, custody goes to the father, unless his insanity or some other disqualifying factor is proven in court. According to Article 1170, the mother loses her custody rights to young children "if she becomes insane or marries another man during her period of custody."[36] Article 1174 guarantees access to the child for the noncustodial parent.

Measures intended to improve women's rights under the personal status and family laws have been enacted over the years. To help women secure better marital conditions and divorce terms, the prenuptial "conditions" envisioned under Article 1119 of the civil code have been added to the printed standard marriage contract. This reflects the Islamic tradition that allows a woman to request certain conditions, such as the right to divorce and the right to a residence separate from her husband's relatives. Although the validity of these stipulations is conditional upon the approval of the prospective husband, they nonetheless provide an important potential protection. A prospective bride and her family may feel awkward requesting them during marriage negotiations, and men may simply refuse to accept them. Furthermore, many women are unaware of their legal rights in this area. These factors weaken the potential protection offered by the practice, and unless such conditions become fully integrated into the marriage law, many men will consider them to be "extra rights" or "privileges" to which they may refuse to submit.

Many of the improvements made to women's marital rights center on financial support offered to women during marriage and upon divorce. A woman is entitled to mehriyeh, a sum of money or object of monetary value specified in the marriage contract that a husband is obligated to pay to his wife. Generally, the dowry is paid upon divorce and is intended to deter men from initiating divorce or, failing that, to provide financial support to divorced women. Article 336 of civil code was amended in 2006 to allow a wife to demand monetary compensation from her husband for domestic labor she performed during their marriage, particularly when the man initiates the divorce without a reasonable excuse.[37] Finally, a divorced woman is entitled to her *jahiziyeh*, the items she brought into the home upon marriage.

Although these provisions potentially protect the financial security of women, in practice it is difficult to secure the mehriyeh or compensation for domestic labor. Given other imbalances in the marriage law, especially the fact that the right to divorce lies almost exclusively with men, women often forfeit their mehriyeh and other financial benefits in exchange for a divorce, buying their freedom from unhappy or abusive marriages.

Women's extensive legal vulnerability to divorce, polygamy, sigheh, and loss of child custody, combined with broader economic difficulties in Iran, has led prospective wives and their families to demand extremely large mehriyeh as a protective measure. This in turn adds to prospective husbands' apprehension about marriage, given rising unemployment and housing costs and their obligation to support their new families financially. The resulting delayed or precarious marriages have added to social problems in the country.

Women are legally protected from slavery and gender-based, slavery-like practices. Iran is a member of all major international conventions against slavery and human trafficking for both labor and sexual exploitation. However, academic research and official reports indicate that the number of runaways and the rate of drug addiction and prostitution among girls is rising, adding to the vulnerability of poor or lower-class women.[38]

Women and men are both subject to state-sanctioned torture and cruel, inhuman, or degrading punishments for political activism or sexual transgressions. For example, individuals found guilty of adultery can be sentenced to death by stoning under Article 83 of the penal code, although such convictions are rare due to relatively strict evidentiary requirements. In practice, significantly more women than men are sentenced to stoning. The punishment's legality has important implications and is based on the assumption that sexual relationships are to be punitively controlled by religious authorities rather than governed by the mutual consent of two adults. Moreover, the public ritual surrounding these tortuous killings reinforces violence, cruelty, and misogyny in general.

Iran and the Sudan are the only Muslim-majority countries that have included stoning in their criminal codes.[39] In the 1980s, bowing under domestic and international pressure, Ayatollah Khomeini issued a decree banning the practice, but after his death, some local judges began implementing the punishment again.[40] In 2002, Ayatollah Mahmoud Hashemi Shahroudi, the head of the judiciary, declared a moratorium on stoning, but the practice continued, particularly in small towns. State authorities usually deny that this punishment is carried out, but because it has not been outlawed, some local judges consider it a matter of discretion. Following the stoning of two men in January 2009, a spokesman for the judiciary, Ali Reza Jamshidi, stated that the moratorium was considered only advisory and not binding.[41]

In mid-2006, a group of lawyers, academics, and activists inside and outside Iran formed the Campaign to Stop Stoning Forever, which has been relatively effective in exposing the practice, providing legal assistance, and conducting advocacy work. In the subsequent months, the group identified and provided legal representation for nine women and two men sentenced to death by stoning, which resulted in reduced punishment in several cases. As of July 2009, a bill that would ban stoning was under consideration by the government.[42]

Sexual relationships are only permissible within the construct of a legal, heterosexual marriage. Homosexual acts between men are illegal and punishable by death under Article 109 of the penal code. Proof is established by the testimony of four male witnesses; the testimony of women—even in conjunction with men—may not establish the crime. Homosexual acts between women (*mosaheqeh*) are outlawed under Article 127, and while the standard of proof is the same, the punishment is far less severe. Women convicted of mosaheqeh are subject to as many as 100 lashes under Article 129, unless they repent before witnesses give their testimony. If a woman is convicted for a fourth time, the punishment is death under Article 131.[43]

Violence against women is a frequent topic of discussion in the media and within NGOs, but political and cultural factors have prevented systematic studies on this issue. It can take a number of forms—physical, sexual, psychological, financial, and political—and is not limited to the home or family, as women can encounter violence in the workplace or in the community due to societal prejudices or biases in the law.[44]

During the reform era that lasted from 1997 to 2005, the media were able to conduct investigative reports that uncovered various forms of violence against women throughout Iran. However, coverage has been more limited as media restrictions have increased in recent years. Sporadic reports indicate ongoing "honor killings" and serial killings of women in different regions. Close to 50 women were murdered during 2008 in four reported cases of serial killing in Abadan, Karaj, Varamin, and Gilan. According to one report, even the state-run newspaper *Iran* was pressured to refrain from publishing information related to these murders.[45]

No specific law criminalizes domestic violence, and Iran has no public or private shelters for abused women. Due to legal shortcomings, societal attitudes, and the very nature of such abuse, domestic violence remains a private hardship. Victims who turn to the police are treated no differently from those who are attacked by a stranger. They can be compensated through the diyeh system of the penal code, provided they supply witnesses and medical reports. Victims of bodily injury may also seek out retribution under Article 273 of the penal code. Sexual harassment in public places is outlawed under Article 619 of the penal code, which generally prohibits verbal or physical harassment of women or children in public places. If convicted under this statute, offenders face two to six months in prison and up to 74 lashes.

Certain laws and cultural practices reinforce violence against women. Polygamy and temporary marriages destabilize spousal relations, increasing the likelihood of domestic violence. In addition, rape is not criminalized as a distinct offense. Instead it falls under the penal code's Article 63 definition of adultery, as sexual intercourse between a man and a woman "forbidden to each other." The victim of rape can assert that she committed adultery under duress and escape punishment, but this claim is difficult to establish because judges often look to the clothing and behavior of women—rather than the aggression of the perpetrator—for the "cause" of the rape.[46] Because the satisfaction of the husband's sexual needs is considered a wife's duty, spousal rape is not seen as a crime.

Recommendations

+ Rape, defined as sexual intercourse without mutual consent, should be distinguished from consensual extramarital sex in the penal code.
+ Equal legal rights concerning divorce and child custody should be granted to men and women. This will have the added benefit of reducing the need for an extremely large dowry designed to protect women from divorce and its consequences.
+ The Majlis should draft a law banning domestic violence, with provisions for law enforcement training, complaint collection and adjudication, restraining orders, protection against retaliation, and compensation mechanisms. The government should also provide support for the establishment of women's shelters.
+ Women's rights NGOs should intensify their educational and training efforts and provide legal and psychological counseling with regard to

anger management, domestic violence, and child abuse. The government should support such activities and protect them from harassment by state and societal actors.

✤ NGOs should form task forces to conduct a needs assessment and propose legal reforms concerning serial murder, honor killing, rape, and other forms of violence against women.

ECONOMIC RIGHTS AND EQUAL OPPORTUNITY

Iranian women's economic status does not yet match the remarkable expansion in their literacy rates, educational attainment, and sociopolitical activism. As of 2006, the female labor-force participation (LFP) rates in the formal sector of economy remained very low: 12.6 percent in urban areas and 12.3 percent in rural areas, for an overall female LFP rate of 12.5 percent, compared with 66.1 percent for men. These official statistics may be misleading, as data on women's overall economic activity, especially in the informal and private sectors, have been inconsistent and the subject of debate among economists. Depending on the methods of assessment and criteria used, the estimates have varied widely and they mostly give results much higher than the official rates. For example, the World Bank, whose figures include both the formal and informal sectors, estimated the 2006 LFP rate at 32 percent for women and 75 percent for men.[47]

Women hold a minimal share of executive, administrative, and managerial positions (3.4 percent as of 2006).[48] This is due in part to the bulging youth population and its rising demand for new jobs, combined with cultural and ideological biases that give priority to hiring and promoting men, especially in the private sector.

Trends in women's economic rights reflect the impact of changing state policies, legal reforms, and cultural attitudes. A considerable decline in female LFP and employment in the aftermath of the 1979 Islamic revolution has been attributed to the impact of policies such as compulsory sex segregation, the weakening of the private sector, and disruption in trade and industries that had served as important sources of employment for women in previous years.[49] Unlike many other developing countries, which rely on cheap female labor in manufacturing for exports, female employment in Iran has gradually shifted away from the agricultural and manufacturing sectors, such as the export-oriented carpet industry, and toward the service sector, particularly education, health, and social services.[50] This shift is the result of many different factors, including "particularly large oil revenues, a demographic transition, and rapid expansion of female education."[51]

Article 38 of the 1991 labor law mandates equal pay for equal work and prohibits discrimination on the basis of sex in determining wages. However, this requirement is not always enforced, and women workers do not receive the same retirement and family benefits as men. According to Article 75 of the labor law, women are barred from dangerous jobs and hazardous working conditions, the definition of which is established by the Ministry of Labor and Social Affairs.[52] This law is reinforced by the right of a husband to prevent his wife from taking up employment that is "incompatible with the family interests or the dignity of himself or his wife."[53]

Certain benefits concerning maternity leave and job security are allotted to working mothers. Under legislation passed by the Majlis in 1995, the duration of paid maternity leave for breastfeeding mothers in both the public and private sectors increased to four months. This law requires public employers to provide working mothers with sufficient breaks and proper locations in the workplace to breastfeed their babies.[54] According to a decree issued by one of the agencies of the Ministry of Labor and Social Affairs in 1992, employers are required to provide childcare centers located near the workplace of their female employees, preferably in the same vicinity or building.[55]

Some legal measures intended to protect female employees with regard to their maternal roles and responsibilities have negatively affected women's chances for employment. For instance, a 1983 law that encourages women to become part-time instead of full-time employees was supposedly intended to ease pressure on working mothers. In practice, however, the policy has contributed to the rise in female unemployment, because many employers have preferred full-time male workers.[56] In addition, there are no specific laws against gender-based discrimination or sexual harassment in the workplace or in universities, and no labor unions offer support to victims of such violations. These factors constitute major hurdles for those seeking justice.

A married woman has the right to independently manage her own property under Article 1118 of the civil code, and few legal barriers limit this right. Under Note 2 of Article 987 of the civil code, women who renounce their Iranian citizenship for that of their husband lose the right to own "landed property" where such ownership would give "economic dominance" to a foreigner. Similarly, women have the legal right to independent use of their income and assets. However, many women face de facto discrimination or restrictions due to the normative male control over the material affairs and income of the family. For instance, women's more limited access to spatial mobility, travel, and trade due to sex segregation constrains their ability to enter into business or put their own land and property to economic use.

The civil code's inheritance laws contain many gender-based inequalities, reflecting the traditional duty of men to support the female members of his family. When a couple is childless, a widow may inherit one-quarter of her deceased husband's estate, while a widower may inherit one-half of his deceased wife's estate, with the remainder going to other beneficiaries. If they have children, the widow is entitled to one-eighth and a widower to one-quarter of the deceased spouse's assets.[57] Article 907 mandates that, upon the death of a parent who leaves no surviving mother or father, daughters inherit half the share of their brothers. Small improvements have been made to women's inheritance rights in recent years. As of February 2009, women may inherit immovable property, such as land, from their deceased husbands, whereas previously their inheritance was limited to moveable property. Also as of 2009, insurance companies are obligated to pay equal compensation (diyeh) for the death of a woman and a man.

Women are not always able to exercise the limited inheritance rights they have under the law. Cultural norms encourage women to forgo their inheritance, either to keep property within the family or so that male kin control the selling and division of the inherited assets.

Women's right to education and to enter into business contracts and activities are limited more by traditional societal attitudes than legal barriers. A husband can legally prevent his wife from working outside the home only if he can prove to the court that her occupation is incompatible with the reputation and well-being of the family.[58] The requirement that a married woman lives in her husband's residence can also affect her options for employment. While the wife and family members are expected to move to wherever the husband finds employment, the same is usually not expected when it comes to the wife's career. For example, according to Article 32 of the army law, women can be hired into the army and security forces only to fill certain positions, such as those related to health care or female prisons, and the work sites of such employees are determined on the basis of their husbands' place of residence and employment.[59]

The gender gap in education is closing, as evidenced by literacy rates of 87 percent for men and 77 percent for women as of 2007,[60] and women are actually outperforming men at the tertiary level. While initially the Islamic Republic government prevented women from studying in certain fields at universities, most fields of study and employment have been legally open to women since the late 1990s. The number of female students in nontraditional majors such as engineering, medicine, law, and the natural sciences has been growing, and women have also engaged in many nontraditional occupations.

At the same time, female students are increasingly being denied their choice of university because of sex segregation and new regulations introduced in 2007 and 2009, which impose gender quotas and force students to attend university in their hometowns. Women's rights activists have argued that these measures aim to limit the social and geographic mobility of students, especially female students, and decrease the rising proportion of female students in nontraditional fields such as medicine. Especially in small towns and rural or tribal areas, access to schools and opportunities for higher education are much more limited for female students. Unfair and sex-segregated distribution of university facilities and resources on different campuses, such as dormitories, food courts, and libraries, result in dampened morale and a sense of marginalization among female students.

Despite increasing repression of women activists, a coalition of various women's groups came together in 2006 to study and discuss women's concerns in various areas of life. In May 2009, they issued specific demands in a preliminary draft of the "Iranian Women's Charter," upon which many of the recommendations below are based.[61]

Recommendations

❖ NGOs and the government should work together to improve women's access to employment and education by investing in financial capital allocation, such as credit, loans, and insurance for self-employed women; human capital, such as educational certificates and vocational trainings; and social capital, such as support for women's role in unions, chambers of commerce, and NGOs.

✤ To improve female labor-force participation rates, the government should establish an affirmative action or quota system within the public sector and provide financial incentives (such as reduced tax) to encourage the employment of women in private institutions.

✤ The government should establish a mechanism to allow women to file gender-based discrimination complaints against public or private employers.

✤ To support socially vulnerable women, the government should increase budget allocations and encourage the creation of support networks such as microcredit lenders, women's cooperatives, and vocational training and internships for women in both rural and urban areas.

✤ Special aid programs should be provided to widows, divorcees, single mothers who are their households' sole breadwinners, caregivers in families headed by women, and caregivers to the elderly.

✤ Women's NGOs should create exploratory need-assessment and research projects on practices and laws concerning gender-related discrimination in employment and at universities. Particular attention must be paid to sexual harassment and sexual abuse in universities and workplaces, which remains a taboo subject with no legal recourse for the victims.

POLITICAL RIGHTS AND CIVIC VOICE

Even with sex segregation, discriminatory laws, and state policies stressing women's domestic duties, women in Iran play a considerable and very visible role in the public sphere. Using any available spaces and legal rights, they have demonstrated their activism in both formal and informal political and civil society organizations. A growing women's rights movement, especially in the past 10 years, has been challenging discriminatory laws and policies in various areas of life, including those that prevent women from taking part in high-level decision-making and political power. Women's activities have been constrained by some cultural traditions and state repression, especially under the presidency of Ahmadinejad.

Women in Iran have the right to vote and run for public office but are excluded from holding leadership roles in the main organs of power, such as the office of the supreme leader, the Assembly of Experts, the Guardian

Council, the Expediency Council, the judicial branch, and the presidency. These positions have been reserved exclusively for men, most of whom are also clerics. After the establishment of the Islamic Republic, women were barred from serving as judges, and existing female judges—including Shirin Ebadi, Iran's first female chief judge of a district court—were demoted to administrative positions. Changes made in 2003 allowed women to hold the rank of judge and the right to serve as legal counselors, but they remain prohibited from issuing and signing final verdicts.[62]

There has been very little female representation in the executive branch or the diplomatic corps. President Khatami appointed the first woman as one of Iran's several vice presidents, and she also served as head of the Environmental Protection Organization. Another woman was appointed as Khatami's presidential adviser on women's affairs and led the Center for Women's Participation Affairs within the President's Office.[63] Ahmadinejad also chose a woman for this post but changed its name to the Center for Women and Family Affairs. Marzieh Vahid-Dastjerdi, who had held a seat in parliament twice before, was appointed as the Minister of Health in September 2009, becoming Iran's first female cabinet minister. At the same time, two other female minister candidates nominated by Ahmadinejad were rejected by the conservative parliament.[64]

Women play a significant part in politics at both the formal and informal levels, often pushing against state-imposed boundaries regarding appropriate gender roles. Most recently, women influenced the direction and duration of the protests that followed the June 12, 2009, presidential election. Ahmadinejad was declared the winner with 63 percent of the vote in the first round, finishing far ahead of leading opposition candidate Mir Hossein Mousavi, a former prime minister, as well as two other challengers. The official results ran against widespread expectations that the race would be close, and were greeted with skepticism for a variety of reasons. Many voters, reformist politicians, international observers, and some high-ranking clerics described the results as fraudulent, and criticized the administration for dismissing legitimate doubts.[65] Massive, largely peaceful protests took place in Tehran and other cities in the days after the results were announced, and participants used the Internet and other new media to disseminate videos, photographs, and real-time updates of the demonstrations. This became particularly important to the free flow of information as independent and foreign journalists were arrested or sequestered from the events, ending the comparatively open media environment that prevailed during the presidential campaigns.

The protests turned violent when the regime unleashed the Basij and other security forces on demonstrators, leaving scores dead or injured. The bravery and commitment displayed by female protesters during these clashes became a central theme in coverage of the events by international media outlets.[66] Experts argued that the visibility of women within the protests reflected the frustration and dissatisfaction felt by citizens—particularly young females—prior to the vote combined with the knowledge that women would likely suffer the most if the election's outcome stood.[67] Although the supreme leader's quick and clear endorsement of the official results was supported by the Guardian Council, popular unrest persists and the dispute remains unresolved to date.

Due to the long-standing suppression of secular parties, all 240 registered political parties or organizations in Iran are at least nominally Islamist, and are often broadly classified as either "reformist" or "conservative." Of the registered groups, 18 are women's groups. Some women's rights activists work mainly within these formal and state-recognized political entities, but many others interact with secular or Islamic women who favor oppositional politics. While most feminists have maintained their independence from state-sanctioned bodies and organizations, they still collaborate and build coalitions with women's groups that work within the reformist Islamic camp or lobby the state organs for legislative changes.

Female candidates face a number of gender-specific obstacles while campaigning for office, namely the sex segregation of many public spaces and the difficulty of meeting with male voters or holding mixed-gender assemblies. During the parliamentary elections of 2000, over 500 female candidates competed for available parliamentary seats, more than ever before.[68] The quality and composition of the 10 who won seats in the 290-member Majlis was encouraging, although some, including Fatemeh Haqiqatjou and Elaheh Koolaee, were persecuted by hard-liners due to their outspoken commitment to reform and women's rights issues. A dozen women were elected to the Majlis in 2004, and just eight won races for the Eighth Majlis in 2008. This was the lowest since 1988, when only 30 women ran for office and three were elected.[69] The decline was due in part to the Guardian Council's mass disqualification of reformist candidates and the effects this had on voter confidence in the electoral process. The female

deputies elected in 2004 and 2008 have been overwhelmingly conservative, doing little to support women's rights.

In recent years, conservative, Islamic, and reformist women's groups
have formed coalitions on certain issues, including the goal of establishing a 30 percent quota for women on their respective parties' electoral
lists. While this effort has been so far unsuccessful, allied women's groups
in 2008 were able to force changes to the government-proposed Family
Protection Bill, aimed at facilitating polygamy and temporary marriage.
Moreover, they helped to secure an amendment that allows women to
inherit land from their deceased husbands.

In the run-up to the 2001 presidential election, 47 women nominated
themselves as candidates, and in 2005 that number grew to 100, though it
fell to 40 in 2009. The Guardian Council has disqualified all female candidates, but they do not openly admit that its judgments are based on gender. This is, in part, due to an ambiguous clause in the constitution that
requires the president to be a *rajol,* an Arabic word that can mean either
"someone male" or "a politically experienced and knowledgeable person."
Some reformist women's rights activists, including Azam Taleghani, continue to nominate themselves because they know that there is no consensus
among clerics about the meaning of rajol in this context. This approach
reflects women's determination to take advantage of any possible opening
that could allow them to raise their political profile.

Women have effectively used their involvement in city councils as a
method of influencing community life and policies. In 1999, during the
first municipal elections, women made up 7.3 percent of candidates; 2,564
urban women and 4,688 rural women ran in municipal and village council elections. More important, many actually succeeded in their bids for
office. A total of 1,120 women were elected, winning one-third of the
available seats in major cities. Except in the provinces of Ilam, Sanandaj,
and Yasooj, women won the highest number of votes in the main city of
each province.

Article 24 of the constitution guarantees press freedom, and Articles 26
and 27 protect the freedoms of association and peaceful assembly, but only
insofar as they do not conflict with the "basic tenets of Islam" or "Islamic
standards." In practice, state authorities exploit this language to restrict,
harass, attack, and ban nearly all peaceful assemblies by citizens making
legitimate economic or sociopolitical demands. Women's rights activists
have been detained for taking part in peaceful assemblies, petitioning to

change discriminatory laws, or publishing critical commentaries on the Internet.

Freedom of assembly for women has been curtailed in recent years as officials systematically deny women's rights activists the permits necessary to hold peaceful public demonstrations. Informational meetings and seminars are increasingly disbanded, and even small gatherings in private homes have been broken up.[70] Nine women's rights activists were arrested on charges of disturbing public order on June 12, 2008, as they attempted to convene a seminar in honor of the anniversary of the national day of solidarity of Iranian women.[71] Security officials and police prevented the seminar from taking place, and the arrested women were then released within a few hours on absurdly high bail. Twelve other women's rights activists were arrested in March 2009 on Sohrevardi Avenue in Tehran while meeting to visit families of imprisoned social and political activists on the occasion of the Iranian New Year.[72] Those arrested were eventually taken to Evin Prison and charged with "disruption of public opinion" and "disruption of public order." All were eventually released on bail, which was set at 500 million rials (US$50,000).

Radio, television, and most newspapers are controlled by the state or government allies. The remaining independent newspapers and magazines are subjected to state censorship, and they exercise self-censorship on issues related to human rights and women's rights abuses. The state-controlled media rarely offer programs intended to empower women, educate them about their rights, improve their legal and social status, or openly discuss their daily concerns. When such content does appear, it is typically quashed due to objections by conservatives. For instance, the country's most prominent women's magazine, *Zanan*, circulated widely among educated, professional women of both secular and moderate Islamic backgrounds until it was shut down by the government in January 2008. It had been in operation for 16 years, having survived several previous threats, and had published 140 issues.[73] Because of this tight domestic media control, civic activists, including women's rights activists, often turn to foreign news services such as the British Broadcasting Corporation, Voice of America, U.S.-backed Radio Farda, Deutsche Welle, Radio France International, and Dutch-based Radio Zamaneh.

The ability to access information—particularly through home Internet service, mobile phone text-messaging (or SMS), and other new communications technology—has been instrumental in women's continued reform efforts. It has led to an explosion of online journalism, websites, and blogs on issues of importance to them. Women's sites and feminist online journals such as Change for Equality, Feminist School, and Meydaan have been filtered or blocked dozens of times by the government, and several bloggers have faced arrest and persecution.

Despite living under highly restrictive conditions, Iranian women have been resourceful and determined, as recent bouts of activism have demonstrated. They have used e-mail and SMS to create networks among activists, mobilize mass support, and mount street protests. The best examples are the Campaign for Equality, the coalitions formed to oppose the recent Family Protection Bill, and the political mobilization surrounding the 2009 presidential election, especially the large coalition formed to press the presidential candidates on two specific sets of women's demands.[74] In the vote's aftermath, the authorities censored traditional domestic media outlets and attempted to block foreign broadcasts, but they also cracked down on Internet access and mobile-phone usage as it became clear that such new media were crucial in organizing protests and communicating with the outside world.

Increased repression under the Ahmadinejad administration has hampered the expansion of the women's movement, forcing activists to make even greater sacrifices as they defend women's political and civil rights. Nevertheless, the level of gender consciousness, the extent of demands for women's rights, and the organizational skills in networking and resource mobilization (at both international and domestic levels) that activists currently enjoy is unprecedented in the history of the women's movement in Iran. This is in part a natural response to the extent of the state's gross sexism and discrimination against women. However, it is also a result of the efforts of women from the growing middle class who are highly educated and—thanks to the expanding global feminist movements—acutely aware of the international standards for human and women's rights.

Recommendations

+ The Guardian Council should immediately and unequivocally declare that women as well as men can stand for election to all public governmental positions. The term "rajol" in the constitution should be clarified to mean "qualified person" rather than "man."

❖ All political parties should establish a quota system under which women would account for 30 percent of their candidates.

❖ The government of Iran should uphold women's rights to freedom of assembly and political participation in the process of reform toward nonviolent and egalitarian laws and policies.

❖ Government filtering of the websites of women's rights groups should be stopped.

❖ The government should restore the license and free operation of *Zanan* magazine and other independent media outlets so that women have a balanced, objective, and open platform for dialogue regarding gender issues.

❖ Women's NGOs and women who are active in political parties should offer workshops and training programs—especially for high school girls—on successful debating and public speaking skills, leadership and organizational skills, managing political campaigns, and demand-centered coalition building.

SOCIAL AND CULTURAL RIGHTS

Despite many cultural, political, and legal restrictions, women in Iran have a visible presence in contemporary literature, poetry, art, and cinema. A number of best-selling books and award-winning movies are the creations of female writers and directors. Women's health indicators have also improved considerably. A marked decline in the fertility rate has been associated with gains in women's literacy rates and overall health status. Yet the stresses stemming from economic hardship and increased political repression in the last five years have negatively affected psychological well-being and cultural productivity, including of women activists.

Health care for women has improved over the past few decades, and women activists have played a remarkable role through their voluntary and NGO activism in different parts of Iran.[75] Today, women have reasonable access to family planning methods, which has helped reduce the fertility rate from 6.0 births per woman in 1986 to 2.0 in 2005. There has also been an expansion of primary health care networks, an overall increase in life expectancy, and a more than 50 percent decrease in child mortality rates, which has also reduced the motivation for multiple births. All these seem to correlate with an increase in the literacy rate among women, from 36 percent in 1976 to 80 percent in 2005, and an increase in the average age of first marriage for women, from 20 in 1986 to 24 in 2005.

Although access to birth control and reproductive care has increased in recent years, women have limited control over their own care as written permission from the husband or father is needed for major surgical operations. Abortion remains illegal under the penal code, except where the life of the mother is threatened and "ensoulment"—exhibited by signs of life as established in Islamic law—has not occurred in the fetus.[76] It is unclear whether a pregnancy that threatens a mother's life but has progressed to ensoulment could be legally aborted. Illegal abortion is punishable under the diyeh, or compensatory, section of the penal code, but can also be punished through qisas, or retaliation, if it occurs after ensoulment. The father or paternal grandfather is the guardian of the fetus and is therefore entitled to the blood money and retaliation.

If someone other than the mother causes the abortion, the amount of diyeh depends on the fetus's stage of growth until it gains its "human spirit." After that point, Article 487 of the penal code indicates that a male fetus draws the full diyeh of a male human being, a female fetus draws half that amount, and a fetus of uncertain sex is worth three-quarters of the sum for the male. According to Articles 623 and 624, doctors or any other individuals who play a role in illegal abortion are also punished with prison terms ranging from three months to five years, and payment of diyeh.[77] If the mother aborts her own pregnancy, Article 489 requires her to pay the fetus's full diyeh to the father or his family.

Women are protected by law from harmful traditional practices such as female genital mutilation (FGM) and forced marriage. Article 479 of the penal code establishes qisas for the cutting of women's genitalia; the amount of blood money owed to the woman depends on the extent of the damage done. In practice, however, FGM is sporadically practiced in certain parts of Iran, in particular Iranian Kurdistan. However, research indicates that as awareness regarding the hazards of FGM increases, educated parents are refusing to impose the practice.[78]

During its formative years, the Islamic Republic deliberately presented sex segregation and mandatory *hijab* (veiling) as the hallmarks of its cultural identity. However, there has never been a consensus among the ulema on the meaning and extent of Islamic hijab; some do not consider it to be a mandate under the Koran. Conservative clerics and authorities view *chador* (an all-encompassing black cloak worn over street clothes) as the most desirable hijab, with some considering the garment to be an Islamic mandate. However, the less restrictive *manteau-rusary* (a long overcoat, trousers, and a head-scarf) is increasingly acceptable, and the number of women in chadors is decreasing. Many women in major cities have turned the dull color and form of manteau-rusary into colorful, stylish fashions and are using cosmetics in larger numbers, although they risk punishment for doing so.

Women influence their local communities by engaging in civic activities, often through membership in NGOs. In 1997, there were only 67 NGOs devoted to women's and children's rights; by 2005, encouraged by the Khatami administration, this number had reached 480.[79] Through their participation in NGOs, women are able to advocate for environmental protection and promotion of sustainable development programs. They have established cooperatives, community-based sources of fundraising and loans, local libraries, study groups, and cultural centers. Some are involved in raising awareness about AIDS and the dangers of drug abuse, while others provide antiviolence training, or legal advice and protection for battered women. Still other groups work to improve the living conditions of the poor and working-class women.[80] However, the antireformist backlash under Ahmadinejad's presidency has hampered the ability of some NGOs to effectively advocate for change, and the growth of the nongovernmental sector has slowed since he came to power.

Women participate in print and electronic media as journalists, and some even host regular shows, albeit less frequently than men. The Association of Women Journalists was formed to address gender-specific discrimination and the concerns of female journalists. Despite this female presence, women's rights defenders have little or no access to the conventional media.

Single mothers and women who are the sole breadwinners for their families are among the most vulnerable groups in society, and their numbers are steadily increasing. Official reports indicate that there were 1,641,000 families headed by women in 2006, a 35 percent increase from 1996. This suggests a change in family structure and women's socioeconomic roles, but it also signals that women are increasingly exposed to poverty. The state provides limited protective measures for women who act as heads of their households. Legally, these women should receive government support equal to 40 percent of the minimum monthly salary, or about US$120. In practice, they receive no more than US$60, leaving many destitute. Consequently, some resort to seasonal, unsafe, and exploitative economic activities within the informal economy.[81] Rates of addiction, drug abuse, and prostitution are increasing among the most vulnerable categories of women, and as the number of prostitutes rises, their average age has decreased.[82]

Women's rights activists among the Iranian communities in North America and Europe play a significant role in presenting alternative images and ideas about women and women's rights in Iran. In collaboration or solidarity with women activists inside Iran who are campaigning for equal rights, women overseas contribute to the process of change through their publications, translations into Farsi of feminist literature, media programs, and activism at the international level.[83] In the past 30 years, approximately 162 Iranian women's groups have formed on four continents, in 16 countries, and in 40 cities.[84]

Recommendations

❖ The government should allow women's rights activists to have access to the mainstream media by allocating airtime and special columns in major daily papers to the discussion of women's issues and concerns.

❖ The government should respect the freedom of choice of women, Muslim and non-Muslim alike, in terms of their dress and public appearance. Covering one's hair and wearing a headscarf or chador should not be mandatory.

❖ Women should have access to both male and female doctors and medical staff so as to achieve access to health care on par with men.

❖ Nongovernmental organizations should be established with the purpose of providing services to households headed by women, including subsidized or free food and household items.

AUTHOR

Nayereh Tohidi is Professor and Chair of the Department of Gender and Women's Studies at California State University, Northridge, and a Research Associate at the Center for Near Eastern Studies at the University of California, Los Angeles (UCLA). She earned her doctorate and master's degrees from the University of Illinois at Urbana-Champaign, and a bachelor's degree from the University of Tehran. Dr. Tohidi was the editor or author of publications including *Globalization, Gender and Religion:*

The Politics of Women's Rights in Catholic and Muslim Contexts (2001); *Women in Muslim Societies: Diversity Within Unity* (1998); and *Feminism, Democracy and Islamism in Iran* (1996). In 2001, she ran a weekly radio program, *Women and Society in Iran*, which was broadcast to Iran, Central Asia, and Europe by Radio Free Europe/Radio Liberty.

NOTES

1   Iran was not included in the 2004 edition of *Women's Rights in the Middle East and North Africa.*

2   See Nikki Keddie, "Iranian Women's Status and Struggles Since 1979," *Journal of International Affairs* 60, no. 2, (Spring 2007).

3   See Mehrangiz Kar, "Discrimination Against Women Under Iranian Law," *Gozaar*, December 8, 2008, www.gozaar.org/template1.php?id=1163&language=english.

4   See Ziba Mir-Hosseini, "Negotiating the Politics of Gender in Iran: Ethnography of a Documentary," in *The New Iranian Cinema*, ed. Richard Tapper (2002), 167, 187.

5   The Guardian Council is composed of six clerics appointed by the unelected supreme leader and six jurists selected by the head of the judiciary for approval by the Majlis. The Council has veto power over bills passed by the elected parliament.

6   In patriarchal societies, such as Iran, that treat men as being solely responsible for the family's financial stability, women are far more likely to lose their jobs in times of economic hardship.

7   For discrimination and segmentation on the basis of religion and ethnicity, see Eliz Sanasarian, *Religious Minorities in Iran* (London: Cambridge University Press, 2000); and Nayereh Tohidi, "Ethnicity and Religious Minority Politics in Iran," in *Contemporary Iran: Economy, Society, Politics*, ed. Ali Gheissari (London: Oxford University Press, 2009), 299–323.

8   Rouhollah Ramezani, "Constitution of the Islamic Republic of Iran," *Middle East Journal* 34, no. 2 (Spring 1980): 181–206; a copy of the constitution in English is available at www.salamiran.org/content/index.php?option=com_content&task=view&id=43&Itemid=79.

9   Ramenzani, "Constitution," 186, 191.

10   See Article 976, section 6, and Article 989 of the civil code, as discussed in Shirin Ebadi, *Hoqouq-e Zan dar Qavanin-e Jomhouri Eslami Iran* [Women's Rights in the Laws of the Islamic Republic of Iran] (Tehran: Ganj-e Danesh, 1381/2002), 118.

11   See Articles 976 and 987 as described in Ebadi, *Hoqouq-e Zan*, 118.

12   For more discussion on this law, see Ebadi, *Hoqouq-e Zan*, 85–87.

13   Because of this difference in value, if the family of a murdered woman insists on retribution (qisas) against a male culprit, the law requires them to hand over half of the blood money that would otherwise pertain to his death. The sum must be paid either to the murderer himself or to his family before the qisas punishment can be implemented. See Articles 209, 213, and 300 of the penal code.

[14]   The code refers to the covering of the whole body except for the face, hands, and feet up to the ankle. It does not specify the color, fabric, or model of the covering. See Ebadi, *Hoqouq-e Zan*, 83–84.

[15]   See Kar, "Discrimination Against Women."

[16]   For a report on recent smear campaigns against Shirin Ebadi and other women activists, see Nayereh Tohidi, "Iran's Women's Rights Activists Are Being Smeared," Women's eNews, September 17, 2008, www.womensenews.org/article.cfm/dyn/aid/3743.

[17]   See Feminist School, "Iranian Women's Movement Detainees," http://femschool.info/english/spip.php?rubrique5.

[18]   See Feminist School, "Summoning Five Members of the One Million Signatures Campaign," news release, April 9, 2009, www.feministschool.com/english/spip.php?article274.

[19]   See International Campaign for Human Rights in Iran, "Report on the Status of Women Human Rights Defenders," April 2009, www.iranhumanrights.org/2009/04/whrdreport/print/#sec2.

[20]   See Change for Equality, "Alieh Eghdam Doust to Serve Three Year Prison Term," news release, February 1, 2009, www.campaignforequality.info/english/spip.php?article455; see also "Hope for Judicial Review: Interview with the Lawyer of Alieh Eghdamdoust," *Roozonline*, February 18, 2009, www.roozonline.com/archives/2009/02/post_11643.php.

[21]   See Articles 74–76, 119, 153, 170, 189, 199, 237 (Section B), and 248 of the penal code, and Article 230 of the civil code, as discussed in Ebadi, *Hoqouq-e Zan*, 77–81.

[22]   Sussan Tahmasebi, "Answers to Your Most Frequently Asked Questions About the Campaign," Change for Equality, February 24, 2008, www.changeforequality.info/english/spip.php?article226. For a detailed analysis of the birth of this campaign and related issues, see Noushin Ahmadi Khorasani, *Jonbesh yek million emza: Ravayati az daroun* [The One Million Signatures Movement: A Narrative From Inside] (Summer 1386/2007), available at www.femschool.info/campaign/spip.php?article86.

[23]   See the website Meydaan that frequently reports on the activities of the campaign against stoning: www.meydaan.org/petition.aspx?cid=46&pid=9.

[24]   For example, in 2007 the office of Rahi (a center that offered legal advice to abused and violated women) was shut down in Tehran, apparently for receiving grants from the Netherlands-based organization Hivos (Humanist Institute for Development Cooperation).

[25]   Quote from Shirin Ebadi, who made this point during one of her media appearances in May 2007.

[26]   The latest case in point is the Simon de Beauvoir prize, worth 30,000 euros, which a French foundation awarded to the Change for Equality campaign (One Million Signatures Campaign to Change Discriminatory Laws) in 2008. The honor caused a heated debate among the activists involved, and they ultimately decided to accept the prize, but not the money.

[27]   On the latest attacks on Shirin Ebadi's office, see Change for Equality, "Campaign to Defend the Defenders of Human Rights Center Launched," news release, January 3, 2009, www.changeforequality.info/english/spip.php?article432.

28 See International Campaign for Human Rights in Iran, "Report on the Status of Women Human Rights Defenders."

29 International Campaign for Human Rights in Iran, "Report on the Status of Women Human Rights Defenders," 4.

30 See the Immigration and Passport Regulation of Iran (1971), cited in Kar, "Discrimination Against Women." Also note that under urgent conditions, a married woman can obtain passport without her husband's permission by appealing to the court. See Shirin Ebadi, *Hoqouq-e Zan*, 121.

31 See Articles 1043 and 1044 of the civil code.

32 Sigheh is a provision within Shi'a Islam that gives legitimacy to sexual relationships of any duration and to their offspring. It is a contract between a man and a woman based on a specified sum of money paid to the woman. The majority of the world's Muslims (Sunnis) and even many Shiites do not approve of this practice. On sigheh practice in Iran, see Shahla Haeri, *Law of Desire: Temporary Marriage in Shi'i Iran* (Syracuse University Press, 1989).

33 For more information on sigheh in Iran, see Shahla Haeri, *Law of Desire: Temporary Marriage in Shi'i Iran* (Syracuse University Press, 1989).

34 See Shirin Ebadi, *History and Documentation of Human Rights in Iran* (New York: Bibliotheca Persica Press, 2000), 119.

35 See Ebadi, *Hoqouq-e Zan*, 142–158.

36 Ebadi, *History and Documentation*, 114.

37 This measure was initially passed by the reform-oriented Majlis in 2002 (1381), but because of the Guardian Council's objection, it was referred to the Expediency Council. It took until 2006 (1385) for the Expediency Council to declare it "compatible with the expediency of the regime," thus effective as a law. See www.dadkhahi.net/modules.php?name=News&file=print&sid=470.

38 For a research report on changing trends in prostitution in Iran, see www.irwomen.info/spip.php?article6557.

39 For an extensive documentation of the campaign against stoning, see Rochelle Terman, "The Contemporary Iranian Women's Rights Movement," *Women Living Under Muslim Laws*, 2009 (forthcoming).

40 See Hossein Zahedi, "Qesseh por ghosseh sangsar," Iran-Emrooz, March 30, 2009, www.iran-emrooz.net/index.php?/hright/more/17706/.

41 Thomas Erdbrink, "Iran Stones 2 Men to Death; 3rd Flees," *Washington Post*, January 14, 2009, http://www.washingtonpost.com/wp-dyn/content/article/2009/01/13/AR2009011302174.html.

42 "Stoning to Be Omitted from Iran Penal Laws," Press TV, June 23, 2009, www.presstv.ir/detail.aspx?id=98845&sectionid=351020101.

43 See also Article 131 of penal code as discussed by Ebadi, *Hoqouq-e Zan*, 73.

44 For an extensive study on this subject, see Mehrangiz Kar, *Pazhouheshi dar bareh-ye khoshounat aleyhe Zanan dar Iran* [Research About Violence Against Women in Iran] (Tehran: Roshangaran Publications, 1379/2000).

45 See Shahram Rafizadeh, "Rosvayi qazayi dar parvandeh zan konshi-ha-ye Abadan" [Judicial Scandal in the Case of Serial Killing of Women in Abadan], *Rooz*, 17 Farvardin 1388/April 6, 2009. www.roozonline.com/archives/2009/04/post_12133.php.

[46] Article 67 of the penal code; see also Shadi Sadr, "Women in Iran Deem Rape Law Unfair," Women's eNews, December 12, 2003, www.womensenews.org/article.cfm/dyn/aid/1650/.

[47] *World Development Indicators,* Online Database (Washington, DC: World Bank, 2008), http://web.worldbank.org/WBSITE/EXTERNAL/DATASTATISTICS/0,,content MDK:20523397~isCURL:Y~pagePK:64133150~piPK:64133175~theSitePK:23 9419,00.html (subscription required).

[48] For more reports and analyses on women's employment, see Roksana Bahramitash and Hadi Salehi Esfahani, "Nimble Fingers No Longer: Women's Employment in Iran," in *Contemporary Iran,* edited by Ali Gheissari (London: Oxford University Press, 2009), 85; Fatemeh E. Moghadam, "Women and Labour in the Islamic Republic of Iran," in *Women in Iran from 1800 to the Islamic Republic,* ed. Lois Beck and Guity Nashat (Chicago: University of Illinois Press, 2004), 163–181; Valentine Moghadam, "Women's Socioeconomic Participation and Iran's Changing Political Economy," in *The Economy of Iran: The Dilemmas of an Islamic State,* ed. Parvin Alizadeh (London: I. B. Tauris, 2000), 233–260; Maryam Poya, *Women, Work & Islamism* (London: Zed Books, 1999).

[49] Bahramitash and Salehi Esfahani, "Nimble Fingers," 119.

[50] Bahramitash and Salehi Esfahani, "Nimble Fingers," 118.

[51] Bahramitash and Salehi Esfahani, "Nimble Fingers," 119.

[52] Ebadi, *Hoqouq-e Zan,* 57.

[53] Iranian civil code, article 1117.

[54] Ebadi, *Hoqouq-e Zan,* 65.

[55] This decree contains many positive requirements in favor of women workers. See Ebadi, *Hoqouq-e Zan,* 59–61.

[56] See Ebadi, *Hoqouq-e Zan,* 62–64, 68.

[57] See Article 913 of the civil code.

[58] See Ebadi, *Hoqouq-e Zan,* 120.

[59] See Ebadi, *Hoqouq-e Zan,* 67.

[60] World Bank, "GenderStats: Education," http://go.worldbank.org/RHEGN4QHU0.

[61] See the preliminary draft of the "Manshur-e Zanan-e Iran" [Iranian Women's Charter] by the Women's Charter Coordinating Group, May 2009, www.manshour.net.

[62] The Law Governing the Appointment of Judges, ratified in 1982, as discussed in Kar, "Discrimination Against Women," 5.

[63] This center was originally established under President Rafsanjani as the Office of Women's Affairs; it was headed by the only woman member in his cabinet.

[64] "Iran Backs First Female Minister," BBC News, September 2, 2009, http://news.bbc.co.uk/2/hi/8235264.stm.

[65] See, for example, Paul Reynolds, "Iran: Where Did All the Votes Go?" BBC News, June 23, 2009, http://news.bbc.co.uk/2/hi/middle_east/8113885.stm.

[66] "Iranian Women Stand Up in Defiance, Flout Rules," CNN, June 23, 2009, www.cnn.com/2009/WORLD/meast/06/23/iran.women/; Emily Bazaar, "Iranian Women Play Key Role in Protests," *USA Today,* June 24, 2009, www.usatoday.com/news/world/2009-06-24-iranianwomen_N.htm.

67 Rebecca Santana, "Women in Iran's Protests: Headscarves and Rocks," Associated Press, June 24, 2009, www.google.com/hostednews/ap/article/ALeqM5hkzosTgK3ner6Hky GtGYXjNNo9vQD9918E0G0.

68 See Zhila Baniyaghoob, "Zanan der dowran-e riyasat jomhouri-ye Mohammad Khatami" [Women During the Presidency of Mohammad Khatami], *Gooya News*, 3 Shahrivar 1384/2005.

69 Inter Parliamentary Union, 1988 Majlis election, Islamic Republic of Iran, www.ipu .org/parline-e/reports/arc/IRAN_1988_E.PDF.

70 See International Campaign for Human Rights in Iran, "Report on the Status of Women Human Rights Defenders."

71 The women were Nahid Mirhaj, Aida Saadat, Nafiseh Azad, Nasrin Sotoudeh, Jelve Javaheri, Jila Baniyagoub, Sarah Loghmani, Farideh Ghaeb, and Alieh Motalebzadeh.

72 The women arrested were Delaram Ali, Khadijeh Moghadam, Leila Nazari, Farkhondeh Ehtesabian, Mahboubeh Karami, Bahara Behravan, Ali Abdi, Amir Rashidi, Mohammad Shoorab, Arash Nasiri Eghbali, Soraya Yousefi, and Shahla Forouzanfar.

73 For more on *Zanan*, see Nayereh Tohidi, *Encyclopedia of the Modern Middle East and North Africa*, 2nd edition, ed. Philip Matter (Detroit: Macmillan Reference USA, 2004), vol. 4, 2423–24.

74 For information on this particular coalition see: http://www.feministschool.com/spip .php?article2461

75 See Homa Hoodfar, "Activism Under the Radar: Volunteer Women Health Workers in Iran," *Middle East Research and Information Project (MERIP)* 39, no. 250 (Spring 2009): 56–60.

76 Farokhzad Jahani, *Iran Daily* 9, no. 2698 (January 15, 2004): 13, www.parstimes.com/ law/abortion_law.html; United Nations, "Abortion Policies—A Global Review, Iran (Islamic Republic of)," (New York: United Nations, 2002), www.un.org/esa/population/ publications/abortion/profiles.htm.

77 See Article 489 of the penal code; Ebadi, *Hoqouq-e Zan*, 134.

78 Golnaz Esfandiari, "Female Genital Mutilation Said to Be Widespread in Iraq's, Iran's Kurdistan," Radio Free Europe/Radio Liberty, March 10, 2009, www.rferl .org/content/Female_Genital_Mutilation_Said_To_Be_Widespread_In_Iraqs_Irans_ Kurdistan/1507621.html.

79 Amnesty International, *Women's Rights Defenders Defy Repression* (London: Amnesty International, 2007), 2, www.amnesty.org/en/library/asset/MDE13/018/2008/63dd89 33-e16d-11dc-9135-058f98b1fb80/mde130182008eng.pdf.

80 Examples include the Women's Cultural Center, led by Noushin Ahmadi Khorasani, Mansoureh Shojaee, and others; the Training Center for Women's NGOs, led by Mahboubeh Abbasqoli-zadeh; the Rahi Center, led by Shadi Sadr; and the Association of Health Advocates, led by Rezvan Moghadam.

81 See Farideh Ghaeb, "Zanani ke az faqr ranj mibarand" [Women Who Suffer from Poverty], *Kanoon Zanan Irani*, (Esfand 1387/February 2008), www.irwomen.info/spip .php?article7067.

82 See Mehdi Afrouzmanesh, "Roshd zanan khod-foroush . . ." [The Growing Prostitution Among Educated and Married Women], Azar 1387/November 2008, www.irwomen .info/spip.php?article6557.

[83] See Nayereh Tohidi, "The International Connections of the Women's Movement in Iran: 1979–2000," in *Iran and the Surrounding World: Interaction in Culture and Cultural Politics*, ed. Nikki Keddie and Rudi Matthee (Seattle: University of Washington Press, 2002), 205–231.

[84] See Shahin Navaeei, *Avaye Zan* no. 38/39 (Winter 1999): 18, and *Arash* no. 100 (October 2007): 161.

IRAQ

by Huda Ahmed

POPULATION: 30,047,000
GNI PER CAPITA: US$2,406

COUNTRY RATINGS	2004	2009
NONDISCRIMINATION AND ACCESS TO JUSTICE:	2.7	2.7
AUTONOMY, SECURITY, AND FREEDOM OF THE PERSON:	2.6	1.9
ECONOMIC RIGHTS AND EQUAL OPPORTUNITY:	2.8	2.6
POLITICAL RIGHTS AND CIVIC VOICE:	2.2	2.6
SOCIAL AND CULTURAL RIGHTS:	2.1	2.3

(COUNTRY RATINGS ARE BASED ON A SCALE OF I TO 5, WITH I REPRESENTING THE LOWEST AND 5 THE HIGHEST LEVEL OF FREEDOM WOMEN HAVE TO EXERCISE THEIR RIGHTS)

INTRODUCTION

Iraqi women's rights advocates, men and women alike, began their struggle for equality at the beginning of the last century. They formed organizations and mounted rallies and demonstrations to demand political, social, and economic rights from the turbulent country's successive regimes. Women managed to secure some of these rights after General Abdel-Karim Qassim seized power in 1958 and passed a new personal status law in 1959.[1]

The new law gave Iraqi women what were considered progressive rights regarding marriage, inheritance, polygamy, and child custody. However, any legal guarantees remained tenuous given Iraq's unstable political situation. In 1963, Qassim was overthrown and killed by his erstwhile comrade, Abdel-Salam Arif, with the help of the Ba'ath Party. Arif later reversed Qassim's personal status code and reintroduced rules based on Shari'a (Islamic law). He also turned against the Ba'ath Party, leading to a feud that ended with his death in a helicopter crash. He was succeeded by his brother, Abdel-Rahman Arif, until the Ba'ath Party took power in 1968.

The constitution implemented by the Ba'ath Party in 1970 barred gender discrimination and provided women with additional rights in the areas of education and employment, among others. To strengthen secularism and gain the support of women, the Ba'ath Party established the General

Federation of Iraqi Women (GFIW) on March 4, 1969. It was the only official women's organization and became a model for the Arab world. The federation was financed and supported by the regime, serving as a tool to promote the party's revolutionary and socialist principles, as well as Arab national unity against Zionism and imperialism. It had branches in every neighborhood, province, and rural area in the country. Besides promoting the regime's agenda, the GFIW opened literacy centers, held driving workshops, and offered classes in art, music, sewing, cooking, and crafts to help women become more independent and capable of supporting their families. Meanwhile, successful government-sponsored literacy campaigns helped Iraq to achieve one of the region's lowest illiteracy rates.[2] Finally, under the Ba'athist regime's new leader, Saddam Hussein, Iraqi women received the right to vote in 1980.

The Iran-Iraq war of 1980–88 had a huge impact on the women and children of Iraq, leaving many of them widows and orphans. Between 160,000 and 240,000 Iraqi soldiers died, though the figure could be higher, as many went missing. Also uncertain is the number of civilian victims executed or "disappeared" by the Ba'athist regime because of suspected connections to Iran or differing political ideologies. The government tried in the first years of the war to compensate soldiers' widows with a sum of money or the continued salary of the husband, and paid for the school supplies of orphans through college. The government also built modern villages for the slain soldiers' families and for disabled soldiers and officers, and distributed land to many officers. However, these efforts decreased dramatically toward the end of the war in light of Iraq's huge debts and devastated economy.

The trauma of war, isolation from the world due to a government ban on travel for most Iraqis, and the changing policies of the regime strongly influenced Iraqi morals and ethics, creating a more conservative society. In the early 1980s, the regime used financial incentives and maternity leave policies to encourage increased birth rates and make up for the significant loss of life on the battlefield. The authorities also cracked down on liberal styles of dress, first painting the legs of women found on the streets wearing short skirts, then banning such skirts, attacking women who wore them, and questioning the relationship of their male escorts. By contrast, until the mid-1970s, intellectual women had regularly attended mixed-gender cultural events or social gatherings without a related male escort.

At the same time, due to the war-related manpower shortage, the regime urged women to fill empty positions in the government, schools, universities, farms, and factories. It pushed women to seek education in every field considered helpful to the country, even traditional male domains like the military and various mechanical, electrical, and other technical fields, although once they had worked for 15 years they were encouraged to retire. Despite all the progress women achieved because of the war, many suffered greatly. Those suspected of disloyalty—and often their extended families and associates—were imprisoned, exposed to torture, raped in front of male relatives, or executed. Others were released from prison with chronic illnesses.

A new constitution in 1990 retained the previous charter's nondiscrimination clause, but in the subsequent years the government made a number of legal changes that disadvantaged women, including the repeal of certain provisions from the 1959 personal status code.[3] Among other things, these changes allowed men to practice polygamy without the first wife's consent and afforded leniency to men who committed so-called "honor crimes," allowing them to receive as little as six months in prison for killing female relatives suspected of sexual transgressions. The government also established and encouraged students to study at colleges for Islamic studies. This assortment of reactionary changes were part of Saddam's attempt to gain the support of tribal and religious leaders after the 1991 Shiite uprising, which led to the deaths of thousands of Iraqi men, women, and children and shook the regime after its defeat in the Persian Gulf War.

The UN sanctions imposed on Iraq following that war had a corrosive effect on Iraqi society and contributed to the deterioration of women's rights, health, and nutrition. There was increased discrimination against women in government offices as well in the private sector. Women, including female students, endured sexual exploitation and harassment to provide food and clothing for themselves or their families. Many families were forced to marry off or effectively sell their young daughters for money. Inflation exacerbated the economic and social breakdown, as did corruption that infected every government entity.

After the U.S.-led invasion of Iraq in 2003, the Coalition Provisional Authority (CPA) dismantled the Iraqi military and carried out a rigorous "de-Ba'athification" policy to purge the ruling party from the state apparatus. The invasion and its aftermath caused chaos in the country, leaving ordinary Iraqis as well as the courts and other official bodies unsure as to which laws they should follow. These conditions, combined with deep-rooted patriarchal attitudes that deem women unequal to men, dramatically exacerbated the challenges facing women. Nonetheless, women's rights advocates were able to achieve some success in pushing for reforms and lobbying against measures that would further institutionalize gender discrimination.

In 2004, as the CPA-backed Iraqi Governing Council (IGC) was drafting a Transitional Administrative Law for the country, women's rights advocates demanded a female quota of 40 percent in the Iraqi parliament and the abolition of the proposed Resolution 137, which would rely exclusively on Shari'a for personal status issues. The CPA ultimately granted women a 25 percent parliamentary quota that year, which was considered a good start. However, many of the women who have gained seats in the parliament are conservative and have not attempted to push for change. Instead, they follow instructions from their party leaders and tend to vote against the expansion of women's rights.

On October 15, 2005, Iraqis voted in a referendum to approve a new constitution to replace the transitional law. Some groups objected to certain articles, including Article 41,[4] which covered personal status law. The provision allows each religious group to govern its own personal status matters, potentially strengthening the roots of Iraq's sectarian strife and giving male religious authorities an opportunity to infringe on women's rights. For example, the article could legalize and encourage *mut'ah* marriage, a form of temporary union that grants women no legal protections. The work of a constitutional amendment committee has been very slow, and there is little time left for the parliament to review its proposals before elections that are scheduled for January 2010. In the meantime, some Sunni and Shiite religious authorities have been vocal in calling for compulsory veiling for women, facing strong resistance by women's rights activists.

The sectarian violence that escalated from 2005 to mid-2007 claimed the lives of many families, and women, as well as men, were killed for political, ethnic, sectarian, and economic reasons. There is no accurate number of casualties, since the government in 2005 barred the Health Ministry from releasing this information to the press.[5] Estimates of the death toll from violence since 2003 range from 100,000 to one million people, and there are an estimated 740,000 widows in the country.[6] Amid volatile security situation, violence against women has increased—particularly the instances of honor killings, rapes, and kidnapping—forcing women to stay at home and limiting their employment and educational opportunities.

It is difficult to predict when or whether the Iraqi parliament will be able to finish and approve the many disputed articles of the constitution, but the outcome of the effort will determine the country's adherence to the rule of law and to basic women's rights principles in particular. It is similarly unclear what will happen to existing women's rights after U.S. troops leave Iraq. Only consistent vigilance by state and nongovernmental actors both within Iraq and abroad will ensure that the rights women have gained to date survive on paper as well as in practice.

NONDISCRIMINATION AND ACCESS TO JUSTICE

Despite enacting the nondiscriminatory 1970 constitution and signing major international conventions that protect human rights, the Ba'athist regime (1968–2003) invested little effort to create an institutional framework that would make these obligations enforceable. In fact, divergence from their principles actually increased under Saddam Hussein. The post-Saddam leadership has attempted to create an equitable democratic system, but there are many obstacles in the way, especially with respect to women's rights. For instance, most of the lawmakers who participated in drafting the 2005 constitution are members of Islamic fundamentalist political parties, whether Sunni or Shiite. As a result, the charter prohibits any laws that contradict Islam, which is designated as the official religion and the foundation of legislation, opening door to discriminatory treatment of women rooted in conservative interpretations of Shari'a. Another major barrier to progress has been the ongoing violence in the country, which hampers the operation of the legal system in general and raises the risks involved in any open political disagreement, including the subject of women in the society.

Article 14 of the 2005 constitution states that Iraqis are equal before the law and bars discrimination based on "gender, race, ethnicity, nationality, color, origin, sect, belief or opinion, or economic or social status." Unfortunately, there is no practical enforcement of this principle at present. The various parties of the government and parliament hold different views on women's rights, and many are firmly attached to traditional views that oppose the empowerment of women. Even if some factions support women's rights to a certain degree, they are often unable or unwilling to assert their views and antagonize those who differ.

The Ba'athist-era labor code of 1987 and penal code of 1969 remain in effect, and the parliament has amended only a few of their provisions. These laws ostensibly protect women from gender-based discrimination at work, in the courts, and in public, though not in their private or family lives. The previous regime did not properly enforce the laws, and the current government does little to implement what protections they provide. In some cases, the new constitution contradicts itself or other laws that are in force. For example, the personal status provision in Article 41 of the constitution emphasizes the role of religion and sect in establishing rules on marriage rights, divorce, child custody, inheritance, and other issues. This effectively conflicts with Article 14's call for equality before the law. Article 41, which has not been put into effect pending possible revisions, raised significant concerns among women's advocates as it threatens to strip women of many of their previous legal rights and place them under the control of religious authorities and tribal customs.

Iraq now has one of the most progressive laws regarding citizenship rights in the Arab world, although the law falls short from guaranteeing full gender equality. Article 18 of the constitution guarantees that every child born to an Iraqi father or mother has the right to Iraqi nationality, and Article 3(a) of the Nationality Law (No. 26 of 2006) reflects this principle. The subsequent provisions, however, place some gender-based limitations on conferral of nationality from mother to child. For example, according to Article 4, persons born outside Iraq to an Iraqi mother and unknown father—or a father with no nationality—can obtain Iraqi nationality upon petitioning the Ministry of Interior, provided that they fulfill certain residency and age requirements. No such conditions are placed on children born to Iraqi fathers.

The new Nationality Law provides for the naturalization of the husband of an Iraqi woman as well as the wife of an Iraqi man; in the past this right was restricted to an Iraqi man married to a foreign woman. In addition, an Iraqi woman can now confer her property on her non-Iraqi husband and children after they become Iraqis. However, foreign husbands of Iraqi women need to reside at least 10 years in Iraq before they may apply for citizenship (Article 6), whereas foreign wives of Iraqi men qualify after five years (Article 11).

Iraqi women are rarely familiar with their right to access justice, unless their work brings them into contact with the judicial system or they have a case in court. Media outlets broadcast talk shows and other programs with lawmakers, judges, and lawyers to explain the legal system to the people, including personal status law. These programs existed during the former regime and continue to air, but poverty, violence, and a lack of electricity has isolated many citizens from such information sources. The situation is worse in rural areas, where women live within patriarchal families and communities and have little contact with outsiders. Nongovernmental organizations (NGOs) traveled among the villages to help raise awareness of the laws and women's rights after 2003, but the insurgency seriously restricted the movements of aid workers after 2004. Women are legally permitted to file lawsuits in court without the permission of their husbands or male guardians. In more conservative rural areas, however, men typically carry out all such functions, and the courts sometimes ask female litigants to appoint male relatives to pursue the case on their behalf.

The justice system does not always treat women and men equally, notably in the issues related to honor killings, rape, and personal status law. Article 409 of the penal code offers leniency in honor killing cases, setting a maximum penalty of three years in prison for a man who kills his wife or close female relative and her partner after catching them in an act of adultery. It also deprives the victims of the legal right to self-defense in such situations. Article 130 of the penal code allows penalties of as little as six months in prison for the killing of a wife or female relative for honor-related reasons. Revolutionary Command Council (RCC) Order No. 6 of 2001 extended the application of such mitigated sentences to those who kill third parties for "making reference" to the dishonorable act by the slain woman, and prohibited acts of revenge against the killer.[7]

After 2003, the instances of gender-based violence, including honor killings, soared throughout Iraq. In the southern city of Basra, authorities had recorded a 70 percent increase in such murders in 2008, with 81 reported by late November, resulting in only five convictions.[8] Lawyers who represent the victims of rape and other violence against women receive death threats. Most honor crimes go unreported by the family members, who bury the victims themselves and attribute the deaths to militia violence or other causes. Such families often receive sympathy and tolerance from the police, if not encouragement for doing what they see as the right thing. Perpetrators are released without investigation or charges, and the government remains silent, treating the cases as private matters. This response leaves women paralyzed with fear and vulnerable to daily domestic violence, sexual harassment, and killings. A deep feeling of injustice and powerlessness sometimes leads women to believe that the only escape is suicide.

In 2000, the Kurdish regional government revoked the laws on mitigated sentences for honor crimes and, a year later, made them punishable by up to 15 years in prison. These measures, however, did not apply in the rest of Iraq. In 2008, Narmin Othman, the current Minister of Environment and one-time acting minister of state for women's affairs, led a campaign to make honor killings throughout the country punishable by life imprisonment or death. Although many parliamentarians supported the proposal, they faced opposition from the Shiite-led United Iraqi Alliance and the Sunni-led Iraqi Accord Front. Party members claimed that such killings of women are permitted under Shari'a.[9]

Articles 19 and 37 of the constitution prohibit arbitrary arrest and unlawful detention, as well as all forms of torture or inhumane acts. But many Iraqi women, as well as men, have been unlawfully arrested and detained in crowded prisons for months or years without trial or access to a lawyer. Prisons allow women to keep their children with them if there is no extended family, especially if the child is an infant, and childcare supplies are provided. There are separate prisons for males, juveniles, and females. Still, some female inmates allege that they are sexually assaulted, tortured, beaten, and raped by Ministry of Interior guards and police investigators seeking confessions. According to one report, the women's prison of Kadhamiya in Baghdad was infiltrated by Jaish al-Mahdi (JAM), the Shiite militia, and operated as a brothel at night. Its 174 female inmates and 17 children were later relocated to a new women's prison.[10]

Iraqi law considers women to be adults at age 18. However, the courts draw many of their rules from Shari'a, which requires two female witnesses for their testimony to be considered, whereas a man can stand as a sole witness. The uncorroborated testimony of a woman is acceptable for certain documents like marital contracts, although in the Kurdish region a woman needs a supporting witness for her testimony to be acceptable in these cases. Iraqi courts treat women as equal to men in compensation for wrongful death. Sometimes the court allows the two parties to agree on the compensation, but in other cases the court will decide the appropriate amount.

Iraq acceded to the international Convention on the Elimination of All Forms of Discrimination against Women (CEDAW) in 1986, but with reservations exempting it from conformity to Article 2 (f) and (g), which call on states to modify or abolish existing laws and penal codes that discriminate against women; Article 9, which requires equal rights regarding changes and transfers of nationality; and Article 16, which concerns the elimination of discrimination in marriage and family relations. Iraq also filed a reservation on Article 29, paragraph 1, with regard to the principle of international arbitration on the interpretation or application of the convention.[11] In practice, the former regime disregarded CEDAW at will. The current government has not discussed ratifying CEDAW or revoking the existing reservations.

The work of Iraqi women's NGOs had been assisted by foreign and international organizations like the U.S. Agency for International Development (USAID), the UN Development Programme (UNDP), the UN Assistance Mission for Iraq (UNAMI), the UN Development Fund for Women, WADI, Women for Women International, the UN High Commissioner for Refugees (UNHCR), and the U.S. military. However, most foreign civilian aid workers left Iraq after violence began to soar, and at least 94 aid workers were killed between 2003 and late 2007.[12] Only local NGOs remained active in most areas outside the relatively peaceful Kurdish region, and these lack support and protection from the government despite a constitutional provision seeking to strengthen, support, develop, and preserve the independence of civil society (Article 45).

Recommendations

* The parliament should expedite the process of reforming and replacing Ba'athist-era labor and penal codes, drawing on the advice of international experts and the experience of foreign legal systems to develop laws that will best serve the Iraqi people. Particular attention should be paid to eliminating penal code provisions that provide leniency in honor-related cases.

* The parliament should revise Article 41 of the constitution to ensure that personal status issues will be governed by a unified legal code and will not be left in the hands of unaccountable religious authorities and tribal leaders. Lawmakers should consult with scholars and experts to develop a personal status code that draws on the best elements of different religious traditions, meets international standards, and protects women's rights.

* The government, in cooperation with international bodies, should develop mechanisms to protect local women's rights activists who work in conflict zones.

❖ The government must ratify CEDAW without reservations, implement its provisions in practice, and raise public awareness about the legal rights its entails. International organizations should establish training programs for lawyers and judges focusing on the mechanisms of dealing with international conventions such as CEDAW.

AUTONOMY, SECURITY, AND FREEDOM OF THE PERSON

Although some of the laws enacted by Iraq's successive 20th-century governments were relatively ambitious and progressive with respect to women's rights, the prevailing instability and frequent policy reversals—particularly under Saddam Hussein—often put women in severe danger. Iraqi women seized the opportunity after 2003 to form NGOs and demand protection from the violence, tribal traditions, and social norms that constrained their lives and prevented them from contributing to their country's development. Women have succeeded in blocking implementation of a potentially harmful constitutional provision on personal status issues, but the last five years have largely been characterized by a stark contrast between constitutional guarantees and women's inability to exercise these rights in the face of widespread violence. Under the pressures of displacement and poverty, women have increasingly fallen victim to human trafficking, sexual exploitation, and a controversial form of temporary marriage.

Iraq has long been home to a variety of religious groups, including Sunni and Shiite Muslims, Christians, Jews, Mandaeans, and Yazidis. The current and previous Iraqi constitutions granted the right of religious freedom, and Articles 37 and 43 of the 2005 charter also prohibit religious coercion and protect religious sites, respectively. To convert from one religion to another, however, is very difficult if not impossible in practice, because each religion enforces its own restrictions or prohibition on conversion. Both Muslim and Christian women are subject to social ostracism or even murder if they convert to another faith. Moreover, the law does not allow Muslim women to marry non-Muslim men, but Muslim men can marry Christian or Jewish women.[13]

From 2004 to 2007, Iraq's sectarian civil war stoked religious extremism and brought serious hardships to women. Various Islamist militias and gangs harassed, threatened, mutilated, or killed women if they did not adhere to a harsh interpretation of Islamic behavior. Those living in an area dominated by another sect were forced to flee their homes in large numbers. Non-Muslim minorities were targeted for selling alcohol or refusing to convert to Islam, and mass emigration has reduced the Christian population to well under one million, from almost 2.5 million in 2003. The Kurdish region was the only relatively safe haven for all religions within Iraq.

In Islam, children traditionally follow the father's religion. But because the country is home to two major Islamic sects—Shiite and Sunni—and a significant number of mixed marriages, parents try not to allow sectarian differences to divide the family. During the past five years of violence, however, some mixed couples were forced to separate under family pressure, and many parents gave their babies neutral names to avoid identification with any particular sect in the future. There were some signs that mixed marriages were becoming more common and open after security improved in 2008.[14]

Article 44 of the constitution guarantees freedom of movement, travel, and residence inside and outside of Iraq, but certain laws contradict this constitutional provision. Following the Gulf war, in an effort to gain tribal and religious support, the Ba'athist regime restricted women's movement outside the country, generally refusing to issue passports to women under 45 unless they would be traveling with a male guardian. After 2003, the CPA issued a law guaranteeing all Iraqis age seven and older the right to obtain passports (through a guardian for children) and all adult women the right to travel without a male guardian. However, the Iraqi government changed the law in 2004; as a result, women are now again required a guardian's approval to obtain a passport. The poor security situation has also impacted the ability of citizens to move freely and dissuaded many women from traveling by land without a male escort for protection.

The original version of the 1959 personal status code granted Iraqi women progressive rights that were advanced for the Arab region at the time. It provided women with inheritance rights equal to those of men; restricted polygamy; and protected divorced wives, giving them custody over their children, child support payments from the father, and related housing rights. Women's rights in these areas shifted over the subsequent years, as the code was altered, eclipsed by executive decrees, or poorly enforced under different governments.

In December 2003, the governing council established by the CPA proposed Resolution 137, which would have fully repealed the 1959 code and placed decisions about family matters in hands of religious authorities.

Though this measure was canceled after women's rights advocates raised objections, a similar provision appeared in the 2005 constitution as Article 41, which gives Iraqis the right to choose what personal status rules they want to follow based on their "religions, sects, beliefs, or choices." Article 41, however, is currently suspended after women's advocates, NGOs, members of parliament, legal professionals, and the judiciary protested against the provision, viewing it as a way to increase sectarian divisions and impose undue restrictions on women. Until the dispute over Article 41 is resolved, the unified system based on the 1959 code remains in effect. In practice, a woman's ability to defend her rights often depends on decisions by her family, tribal authorities, or the officials of her religious sect, as personal status disputes are commonly settled without recourse to a civil court.

The law sets the minimum marriage age for both sexes at 18, though courts can permit juveniles as young as 15 to marry with a guardian's approval or as a matter of urgent necessity. Unauthorized, underage marriages are potentially punishable by imprisonment, but such marriages do take place, conducted by religious leaders with little regard to women's well being.

During marriage, a husband is legally obliged to support his wife financially, and there is an implied obligation for the wife to obey her husband, so long as it does not conflict with Islam. Shari'a, as commonly interpreted in Iraq, holds that a husband is free to have sex with his wife unless she is ill or has a compelling reason to refuse. There is no law against spousal rape, as it is considered a private matter. Paragraph 41 of the 1969 penal code considers a husband's punishment of his wife to be a legitimate private right. While this is consistent with prevailing interpretations of Shari'a, it contradicts Article 29 of the constitution, which prohibits all forms of violence and abuse in the family.

Polygamy is permitted under the law if a court finds that the husband can financially support more than one wife and treat them equally, but Ba'athist-era amendments allow men to evade even these restrictions if the new wife is a widow or if the husband initiates a divorce, marries, and then reconciles with his first wife. Previously, a valid polygamous marriage required the consent of the first wife, but this restriction was also removed over time. Polygamy is relatively common in practice and rarely faces obstacles in the courts.[15]

After 2003, the Shiite practice of mut'ah marriage grew more popular, having been banned under Saddam Hussein.[16] Women's NGOs reported in 2006 that there were some 300 temporary marriages occurring daily in the major cities of the Shiite-dominated south.[17] In mut'ah marriages, an unmarried woman can temporarily marry a man whether or not he is already married, often for a fixed amount of time and in exchange for a certain amount of money. The time period can range from an hour to years, and only the man has the right to dissolve the marriage, unless there was a prior agreement between them. Women have no right to support if they become pregnant. Most of these marriages are carried out secretly without the knowledge of the participants' families, and women who resort to them often do so out of poverty. Shiite clerics who encourage the practice argue that it prevents fornication and adultery while helping widows and other impoverished women, but critics view it as a form of prostitution.[18]

A legal marriage entails a freely entered contract between the bride and groom, and the law allows a wife to revoke the contract if the husband fails to fulfill its conditions. However, divorce procedures greatly favor the husband.[19] The law allows men to unilaterally divorce their wives, though a court can award damages worth up to two years of financial maintenance if it finds that the repudiation was unjust. Either spouse can also file for divorce based on one of several causes, including an unspecified "conflict" between them, and the wife can file based on various forms of neglect or infirmity on the husband's part. If the wife is deemed responsible for a conflict, she can be required to return all or part of her dowry. Another option available to women is *khula*, a form of divorce in which she compensates the husband financially in exchange for ending the marriage. In practice, many women are not aware of their legal options regarding divorce. Those who would assert their rights face obstacles including family or social pressure, domestic violence, and sometimes inefficient or unsympathetic courts.

Article 57 of the personal status code grants divorced women custody of their children up to age 10, during which time the father must pay child support. Custody can be extended by the court to age 15 if it is in the child's interest; after that point the child can choose his custodian. If the divorced mother remarries, her custody is not revoked unless it is in the child's interest.

Article 37 of the 2005 constitution prohibits "forced labor, slavery, the slave trade, trafficking in women or children, and the sex trade," but the law offers little protection in practice. Instead, women are seen as responsible for their circumstances and may be punished or ignored rather than granted the right to seek punishment for their exploiters' abuses. Iraq became a country of origin for women and girls trafficked to nearby countries for the purposes of sexual and labor exploitation during the Iran-Iraq war, and the pace of this trade increased amid the sanctions and economic difficulties of the 1990s. The trafficking often took the form of false marriages, in which perpetrators effectively bought the women from their impoverished families, while others were lured with promises of legitimate work. Internal and cross-border sex trafficking continued after 2003, and the displacement of millions of people due to sectarian warfare exacerbated the situation.[20] Thousands of Iraqi women have been forced to work as prostitutes in countries like Syria, Jordan, and the United Arab Emirates.[21] However, due to the security circumstances in Iraq, it is difficult to accurately gauge the scope of human trafficking, and the government has done little to monitor or address the problem.

Although Article 29 of the constitution bars violence in the family, schools, and society, in a contradictory manner, Paragraph 41 of the penal code allows husbands to punish their wives. Domestic violence is a growing problem, and it is generally considered a private matter, to be dealt with through the intervention of relatives or tribal sheikhs. In these cases, even if the decision is in the woman's favor, reconciliation does not stop men from repeating their crimes. A woman is punished and resented if she tries to defend herself. Moreover, in the context of Iraq's ongoing insurgency, women have suffered torture, mutilation, rape, and other forms of inhuman treatment at the hands of Iraqi and American forces, sectarian militias, terrorists, and their own tribes and families. There are no exact statistics on any of these forms of abuse, as the victims risk further harm if they speak out or seek justice. Depending on the nature of the crime, victims may even face honor killings by their families.

The Kurdish authorities have said that they are trying to identify the best means of educating people about the wrongful nature of violence against women, and that the effort had produced a certain amount of backlash. They have helped to open shelters and support NGOs dedicated to women at risk of violence, honor killing, or rape in the Kurdish region. In addition, they have created special family protection units within the police through which women may file complaints and seek protection. Nonetheless, these units are not always effective and often fail to protect women. In one recent case, a girl seeking police protection after eloping with her boyfriend was turned over to her father, after the father allegedly bribed the police officer. Soon after her release, the girl was stoned to death by her family, while the local authorities reportedly refused to intervene in what they perceived as a "tribal issue."[22] Moreover, a report by the region's Human Rights Ministry said that the number of women who committed suicide by burning themselves—an act that is often ordered by the family or otherwise associated with family pressure—increased from 36 in 2005 to 133 in 2006.[23]

Rape is treated as a private offense under the penal code, meaning the state cannot take action in a given case without the consent of the complainant or her legal guardian. The minimum penalty for various rape and sexual assault offenses is five years in prison, and the maximum ranges from 7 to 15 years depending on the nature of the crime and the age of the victim.[24] One of the most controversial provisions in the penal code is Paragraph 398, according to which a defendant is excused in cases of rape and sexual assault if he marries his victim. The law provides that the sentence will be reinstated or the prosecution will resume if the defendant divorces the victim without legal justification within three years. This law effectively sentences the victim to a minimum of three years with her rapist.

Women continue to be harassed or attacked by insurgents, militias, and Iraqi security forces for not wearing *hijab* (head covering) or otherwise failing to observe the perpetrators' interpretation of proper Muslim attire. Women have also been victimized for driving and for walking or talking with unrelated males.[25] Iraqi police forces, who receive no training on these issues, have been at best indifferent and sometimes hostile to the victims. Even the few female members of the security forces are subject to sexual harassment from their colleagues. In a disturbing trend, Iraqi women have been increasingly used as suicide bombers. Some are desperate women seeking vengeance for a slain loved one or escape from poverty and abuse, while others—reportedly including women suffering from mental illness—are abducted by insurgents, raped, and then forced to become suicide bombers to save their honor. Between 2003 and mid-2008, 43 women carried out suicide bombings in Iraq, including 20 in the first half of 2008.[26]

Since the fall of the Ba'athist regime in 2003, dozens of NGOs have been active in spreading awareness of women's personal status rights and the problem of gender-based violence, and in providing assistance to female victims. Local activists have received training and support from international NGOs, the World Bank, USAID, and the United Nations.

However, security problems have forced many NGOs to close down. In Basra, 9 of 12 volunteer organizations helping women have closed down since the U.S.-led invasion.[27] Death threats against NGOs that work on behalf of women have spread through the country. In Baghdad, female NGO workers have had to go undercover and chain their office doors.

Women's organizations also face bureaucratic hurdles. Those seeking to establish shelters for female victims of domestic violence, rape, and other abuse must obtain approval from four ministries and from the police. Among the NGOs that have continued to work on these issues are ASUDA Organization for Combating Violence against Women, the Amal Association, OWFI, the German charity WADI, and the Iraq Foundation, led by Rend al-Rahim, a former Iraqi ambassador to the United States. Currently, five women's shelters operate in Iraqi Kurdistan, including one run by ASUDA. Few shelters, if any, operate in Baghdad or Basra.

Recommendations

* ❖ The government should reverse the 2004 change in passport rules and grant adult women the unrestricted right to obtain and use passports autonomously.

* ❖ The parliament should update the penal code to eliminate leniency for rape and sexual assault defendants who agree to marry their victims.

* ❖ The parliament should ban the practice of mut'ah marriage, imposing fines for violations and harsher penalties if coercion or fraud is involved. Indigent women involved in such arrangements should be treated as victims by the law, and should be referred to social welfare agencies for financial and other assistance. Women who become pregnant through mut'ah marriages should be entitled to child support.

* ❖ The government should provide extensive training programs for all security personnel on the international human rights standards. The police should also receive clear guidelines on how to deal with the instances of gender-based violence in an effective and sensitive manner.

* ❖ The government should remove unnecessary bureaucratic barriers to the establishment of shelters for abused women, and actively encourage the formation of such facilities in cooperation with local and international NGOs.

* ❖ The Iraqi government should investigate the commercial sexual exploitation of women and children within the country, and carefully distinguish between victims and perpetrators in their handling of these cases.

ECONOMIC RIGHTS AND EQUAL OPPORTUNITY

Despite its enormous economic potential, Iraq has suffered from decades of Ba'athist misrule, warfare, and economic sanctions, and women have often borne the brunt of the consequences in terms of employment, property rights, and education. After the U.S.-led invasion in 2003, women's living conditions worsened on a variety of levels, particularly because the daily violence left many women widowed, displaced, or unemployed. The security situation has interrupted many girls' schooling, adding to the gender gap in educational attainment, and the distribution of government ministries to Islamist parties has made it more difficult for women to obtain public-sector jobs.

The constitution of 1970 encouraged women to enter diverse professions, and Article 22 of the 2005 constitution guarantees the right of work for all Iraqis. However, women have long been seen by the government as an auxiliary force that could meet the country's labor needs during crises and return to their homes when the need had passed. The 1970s and 80s featured a large increase in women working in the public sector, especially during the Iran-Iraq war, when Saddam Hussein urged women to fill men's places in schools, universities, hospitals, factories, the army, and the police. But women's employment subsequently decreased as they were encouraged to make way for returning soldiers in the late 1980s and the 1990s. After 2003, women hoped to secure equal opportunities to obtain employment in their chosen professions. However, the various government ministries were divided among political and sectarian groups, which in most cases favored male employees and would not employ women unless they belonged to the right party and sect and wore hijab. This screening process led to massive unemployment among women of all ranks and ages.

Iraqi women were early pioneers in the competitive and male-dominated world of commerce, but the country's long isolation from international trade and innovation severely limited the opportunities available to such entrepreneurs. After the fall of the Ba'athist regime, U.S. and international organizations launched extensive programs to support small and medium-sized businesses run by women, including water treatment facilities, textile factories, and construction businesses.[28] While some businesses have succeeded, others have failed or stalled due to escalating violence against the women who run them, and these women will face even greater risks once American forces withdraw from Iraq.

The lack of security has had a profoundly negative impact on women's economic participation, as many female professionals including doctors, engineers, politicians, teachers, and civil servants were exposed to violence. Growing killings and kidnappings have been orchestrated by extreme religious militias in an effort to dissuade women from working. In some instances, women were allegedly attacked out of envy or hatred by their male counterparts, who would hire gangs to carry out the crimes.[29] The more general violence in the streets caused many people, both men and women, to flee to safer areas at the cost of their livelihoods.

According to the UN, only 17 percent of women were participating in the labor market in 2007. Of those, 23 percent were unemployed and looking for work. Workforce participation was strongly associated with education levels; about 80 percent of women with a university education were seeking work or employed, compared with 30 percent of those with a secondary-level education and just 10 percent of those with only a primary-level education. The report noted the outsized role of the state in the economy, with public-sector workers almost doubling in number since 2005 and accounting for 43 percent of employed Iraqis (and nearly 60 percent of full-time employment). At the same time, full-time private-sector employment fell from 25 percent in 2003 to 17 percent in 2008. Iraq was consequently hit hard in 2008 when oil prices dropped sharply, causing a similar decline in the government's oil-dependent income.[30]

Iraqi female employees are allowed to work nightshifts in a small number of settings—such as public hospitals or university dorms—but not in factories or government offices, limiting their ability to compete in the job market. After 2003, at the urging of U.S.-led coalition forces, some Iraqi women enlisted in the military, joining their male colleagues in combat and raids on insurgents and criminal gangs. From 2004 to 2008, when attacks by female suicide bombers increased, the Iraqi government recruited women for the police force to search female civilians at checkpoints. In that respect, women's entry into the security field was essentially an accommodation of existing cultural sensitivities rather than an acceptance of gender equality.

Though Article 22 of the 2005 constitution stipulates that labor regulations would observe "the rules of social justice," no new labor rules have been enacted, and both male and female employees are vulnerable to summary dismissal. The constitution's Article 14 and the 1987 labor code's Article 2 prohibit gender discrimination, and the code's Article 4 calls for equal pay and benefits. However, under the 1969 Worker's Social Security and Retirement Law, women can receive retirement benefits five years earlier than men, encouraging them to leave the workforce sooner. Women also face discrimination in promotions, and working women must adapt themselves to what are sometimes hostile, male-dominated working environments.

Under the Maternal Law of 1971, women in the public sector receive six months' paid maternity leave and may take a further six months of leave at half-pay. Private-sector workers are entitled to 72 days of paid maternity leave, and medical officials can extend that to a maximum of nine months if necessary, in which case the mother would receive social security payments rather than salary. The 1987 labor code states that pregnant women may not be assigned extra work that may cause harm to them or their pregnancy (Article 82), but these protections do not apply to women working informally in the agricultural sector. The code also grants nursing women one hour per day to feed their children (Article 87). Working women with children under six years old are allowed three days of unpaid leave at a time to care for a sick child. Women working in the private sector are generally more vulnerable than state employees, as they are not as well protected by the law and most private employers can violate their rights with impunity.

The labor code of 1987 and the penal code of 1969 protect working women from sexual harassment in the workplace, but in practice these laws are not enforced, and most women lack any knowledge of their labor rights. They are reluctant to come forward with complaints or charges, fearing humiliation, threats of violence, or social consequences. The country's fragile security situation exposes women to attacks or murder by the men they have accused of harassment, since the crimes can be attributed to the insurgency.

Article 23 of the 2005 constitution guarantees the protection of private property without distinction based on gender, stating that the owner "shall have the right to benefit, exploit and dispose" of it within the limits of the law. Consequently, Iraqi women are legally permitted to buy and hold property under their own names, although due to the current social and political situation, fewer women are able to exercise that right. Women also have full legal freedom to use their income and assets. They can open bank accounts in their name and receive bank loans or mortgages without the involvement of their husbands or male relatives. In practice, however, women are socially obligated to give up some or all of their income to help support their unemployed husbands and relatives. Women are also legally able to bid for and sign contracts without male involvement, and they can enter into business partnerships with men without major social restrictions. Still, they face obstacles including the societal perception that men are better at running businesses, making critical decisions under pressure, and taking on the risk necessary to succeed.

The 1959 personal status code guaranteed equal inheritance rights to men and women in most cases, but subsequent amendments restored Shari'a-based rules by which daughters and wives typically receive half the share of sons and husbands. Women frequently face pressure to give up their inheritance to brothers or other family members, and in some cases male relatives will forge a woman's signature or otherwise deceive the court to obtain her share. Even in cases where women are aware of their legal rights, they are often reluctant to bring the matter to the courts rather than resolving the dispute privately.

Education is free for both girls and boys at all levels, and Article 34 of the 2005 constitution identifies it as a right guaranteed by the state. Primary schooling is compulsory. Education boomed after the Ba'ath Party took power in 1968 and announced free education and a literacy campaign across Iraq. However, conditions deteriorated in the 1980s and 90s, in part because war and economic sanctions compelled many women to leave school and either obtain low-paying jobs or get married to ease the economic burden on their families. After the U.S.-led invasion in 2003, many schools and universities were looted and burned. The U.S. government, NGOs, and international organizations including the World Bank helped to shore up the educational infrastructure, but the daily violence between 2003 and 2008 kept some schools closed for weeks at a time, and parents were often hesitant to send their daughters to school. There was a huge drop in female enrollment due to the fear of violence or abduction.

Schools for younger children and most universities are mixed gender, but schools for children at the middle and secondary stages are segregated. Male and female students study the same materials with a few exceptions; for example, biology books for female students are slightly different, especially on sexual subjects. Female students also have little access to vocational schools or technical universities, due in part to social and cultural changes and the rise of Islamist political parties after 2003. Some families have a substantial influence over whether, what, and where their daughters will study. They may send their girls to an all-female college, determine their field, or compel them to marry rather than pursue higher education. In rural areas, most girls attend school only through the primary level, after which they stay home to help in the fields or marry.

Educational attainment for girls has consistently lagged behind that of boys. According to the 2006–07 WHO survey, 26.8 percent of women in all age groups had never attended primary school, compared with 14.6 percent of men; similarly, 13.7 percent of women had completed secondary school, compared with 21.9 percent of men. The survey also found that 17.3 percent of women aged 15 to 49 had no education; the remainder had attended at least primary school, with 22.5 percent reaching the secondary level and 11.7 percent attending higher education. Overall, 65.7 percent of women in this age group were literate.[31] Another household survey conducted by Iraqi and Kurdish statistics agencies in cooperation with the World Bank found that 88.4 percent of men and 73.6 percent of women over age 10 were literate.[32]

After 2003, women's rights groups—with the help of international actors—worked effectively under very difficult circumstances to educate women about their economic rights and encourage female participation in the economy. For example, the U.S. Army's Project and Contracting Office promoted the use of female-owned businesses in the reconstruction effort. As of February 2006, over 250 contracts worth a total of more than $250 million had gone to such businesses.[33] By about the same time, USAID had awarded nearly 60 percent of its small-business grants to women.[34] Many women remain unfamiliar with their economic rights, but there are some signs that NGO education and advice programs, along with television and radio campaigns, are reaching growing numbers of women.

Recommendations

❖ The parliament should enact new laws regulating employment and business activity, with specific language emphasizing women's rights as workers, managers, entrepreneurs, and retirees. These protections should include effective complaint and enforcement mechanisms, particularly for the neglected private sector.

❖ The parliament should restore equality in inheritance rights for men and women, and establish more rigorous court procedures to ensure that women receive their fair share in practice.

❖ The government should offer financial incentives that encourage poor families to keep their daughters in primary and secondary school, and special stipends to help women pursue higher education.

❖ The government, state banks, and private banks should adopt measures designed to provide women with business loans, and NGOs should help educate female business owners on the means of marketing and profiting from their skills and products.

❖ The government should actively pursue the hiring and promotion of women in all fields of the public sector. Instances of political, religious, or gender bias against women in personnel decisions should be methodically investigated and punished.

❖ The parliament must draft and enact laws to regulate the activities of foreign companies and provide basic labor protections for foreign workers in Iraq.

POLITICAL RIGHTS AND CIVIC VOICE

Iraqi women were actively involved in the movement against British occupation in the early 20th century, and they organized political and cultural organizations to fight for women's rights in the 1940s and 50s. After the Ba'ath Party came to power and eliminated all independent groups, women's participation in politics was limited. Beginning in 2003, however, they gathered spontaneously and organized themselves to renew their involvement in political life. In 2004 and 2005, they mounted a successful campaign of rallies and lobbying to secure a 25 percent quota in the parliament and incorporate that rule into the new constitution. Still, electoral laws have been formulated in a way that allows female representation to fall below 25 percent in provincial councils, and women remain underrepresented in national government and the judiciary. Insurgent and other violence in recent years has prevented women from exercising their rights to free assembly and expression.

Article 20 of the 2005 constitution specifically grants the right to vote and run for office to both men and women. However, many female candidates who ran in elections over the past four years, beginning with January 2005 elections for a Transitional National Assembly (TNA), have faced significant obstacles, including having their campaign posters torn down. They also received threats or warnings not to campaign in conservative districts of Baghdad and other cities. Some female candidates decided not to place their posters on the streets because of the lack of security. Female politicians generally face more barriers and dangers than their male counterparts, as they usually have less experience and need to counter the widespread belief that women are less capable in politics than men. They also tend to enjoy less financial independence and have fewer social or professional contacts than male candidates.

Voting patterns of Iraqi women often vary according to educational levels; social, tribal, and sectarian pressures; and support from male family members. During the January 2005 TNA and provincial council elections and the December 2005 elections for a permanent Council of Representatives (parliament), many men demanded that their wives, sisters, and mothers vote as they instructed. Even in the Kurdish region, women frequently followed their male family members' orders. When a group of women were asked for whom they would vote in the July 2009 Kurdish elections, they said they would support "the political entity which their husbands or parents vote for." Very few expressed personal interest in political party platforms, while most said that they only voted because of family pressure.[35] In part due to these cultural attitudes, important women's issues, such as unemployment, assistance for unmarried women over 30, and domestic violence are rarely addressed in election campaigns.

Article 49 of the 2005 constitution states that electoral laws should "aim to achieve" a 25 percent minimum quota for women in the parliament. That year's elections law called for women to occupy one out of every three names on a party's candidate list, and the rules ultimately succeeded in meeting the quota. However, women's numbers in the legislature declined from 87 of 275 after the January 2005 TNA elections to the current 70 of 275, partly because of party fragmentation.[36] As of the end of 2008, women chaired two of the parliament's 24 standing committees.

There are no women among the country's 18 governors. Although the constitution does not call for it, the electoral laws governing provincial elections have included provisions—similar to those for the national parliament but staying shy from the actual quota—to encourage female representation in provincial councils. In practice, however, the results have varied from place to place, often falling below 25 percent.[37]

Women are also underrepresented in the national government structures. They occupy only 4 of 36 posts in the cabinet: Environment, Housing and Construction, Minister of State for Women's Affairs, and Human Rights. In 2004, they held 6 of 28 posts. Women also head two of the eight ministries of state, Women's Affairs and Tourism and Antiquities. The Ministry of Women's Affairs (MSWA) was established in 2003, but has been severely underfunded and has not implemented any major reform efforts. There are a handful of female ambassadors serving in Iraqi embassies around the world, an encouraging sign considering that high level diplomatic posts were previously assigned almost exclusively to men.

Women can organize and participate in political parties and processes at all levels, but due to societal attitudes, not many do so. After the fall of the Ba'athist regime, numerous political parties began to emerge or return from exile, all run entirely by men. To meet the election quotas, they deliberately chose obedient or conservative women as candidates on party lists. In general, many male party leaders view their female colleagues as too mentally and physically weak to handle high-level roles. In 2005, female intellectuals and advocates for women's rights attempted to establish their own parties, but they failed because they did not get the necessary financial support or encountered open hostility. Women have made somewhat more political progress in Iraqi Kurdistan, but they still face many obstacles.

The United Iraqi Alliance (UIA), an electoral bloc representing the main Shiite Islamist parties, secured a plurality of 41 percent in the December 2005 parliamentary elections and sent the largest number of women to the legislature. Women who joined the UIA had to abide by the Islamic clothing code and represent the conservative vision of their respective parties, applying their interpretations of Shari'a to all women's issues. Generally, male members of parliament hesitate to discuss any issue related to women, because power rests in the hands of hard-line Islamist leaders. Women's issues are seen as less of a priority than concerns about the country's devastated infrastructure, soaring unemployment, the insurgency, daily violence, and reforming the Ba'athist-era laws. Women in Kurdish parties, secular Arabs, and independent members of parliament have made a greater effort to push for women's rights.

Since the 1920s, women have participated in the judicial system as lawyers, legal advisers, criminal investigators, prosecutors, social workers, clerks, and crime lab assistants. Zakkiya Haqqi became Iraq's first female judge in 1959, a major advance in the Arab world at the time; she is now a member of the Iraqi parliament. In 1976, women were admitted to the Judicial Institute in Baghdad and were appointed as judges and prosecutors. Saddam Hussein forbade women from entering the Judicial Institute in 1984, and retained only those who had been judges before the decree. He did not bar women from being lawyers, prosecutors, and clerks in the courts.

Since 2003, the Iraqi Higher Judicial Council has appointed former graduates of the Judicial Training Institute to the bench. Still, only 4 of 79 new judicial appointees in 2006 were women. As of late 2006, just 13 of the 738 judges outside Iraqi Kurdistan were female, while the Kurdish region itself had only three female judges, all in the juvenile courts. However, this number appears to have increased. The UNDP announced that 57 female judges received training regarding women's rights, international and Iraqi standards for the right to fair trial, and modern legal research tools during a workshop held in February 2009.[38]

Despite this training and other similar initiatives, the few women who have secured positions as judges have a limited role and reduced means of gaining judicial experience. They are excluded from the personal status courts and criminal courts, and are found only in the juvenile courts and the civil courts of first instance. There are no female judges in the Court of Cassation, the 18 provincial appellate courts, or the Federal Supreme Court appointed in 2004. Also as of late 2006, women comprised 16 of the 205 prosecutors in the central and southern regions of Iraq; roughly 150 were employed by the Office of the Prosecutor General in Iraqi Kurdistan.[39] Some female lawyers run private offices. Female lawyers are generally hired to address personal status cases involving divorce, marriage, and inheritance, as well as some business contracts and criminal cases.

Some conservative provinces strongly resist admitting women into the judicial system. In mid-2003, a U.S. military administrator in Najaf abandoned his attempt to appoint the city's first female judge after Shiite religious authorities—including Grand Ayatollah Ali al-Sistani—issued edicts that tacitly or openly opposed the move.[40] With the exceptions of Baghdad and Kurdistan, female lawyers face discrimination from their colleagues and sit in separate waiting chambers in courts. Many of them have been urged by their brothers, spouses, or fathers to stay home because of family obligations or to avoid conflict with males that could endanger their security. Female lawyers have also received death threats urging them to stay home, and some have been killed by their clients' opponents, though the death toll in recent years remains unclear.

Article 38 of the 2005 constitution guarantees the freedoms of expression, the press, and peaceful assembly, provided they do not violate public order or morality. But women took to the streets to defend their interests as early as 2004, demonstrating against the proposed Resolution 137 of the Transitional Administrative Law, which would have repealed the 1959 personal status code and placed decisions over family matters in the hands of religious authorities. At the same time, women demanded a firm quota for representation in the parliament. After a series of peaceful rallies and related media coverage, Resolution 137 was withdrawn and women were granted the 25 percent parliamentary quota. Many Iraqi women considered that victory a first step in demanding more rights. Since no women were included on the committee drafting the 2005 constitution, activists and NGOs organized lectures, workshops, and meetings across the country to raise awareness of the importance of women's rights.

When Resolution 137 returned in the new constitution in the form of Article 41, women went to the streets again, successfully demanding the article's suspension. The deterioration of Iraq's security situation—particularly after the February 2006 bombing of the Golden Dome, an important Shiite shrine in Samarra, triggered an escalation in sectarian violence—prevented further peaceful demonstrations on behalf of women's rights. Yet activists and NGOs have continued to arrange meetings and workshops inside and outside the country, training women in leadership, debating, and organizational skills.

Women similarly used media outlets to promote their interests after the fall of the Ba'athist regime in 2003, only to face violence and regression as security worsened. Many members of NGOs were threatened or killed for appearing on television or radio, or for criticizing Islamist rules imposed on women. In the autonomous Kurdish region, journalists who wrote unfavorable articles about the government and security forces were arrested, and some were killed. In other parts of Iraq, both male and female journalists were beaten, arrested, and killed for their writing on insurgents, the government, or political parties. The authorities did very little to investigate such cases, and to make matters worse, the government proposed new laws that would tighten its control over political parties, NGOs, and the media. The government also put media outlets under close scrutiny to encourage self-censorship, and at one point barred journalists from covering sessions of the parliament.

In February 2004, Yanar Mohamed, a prominent women's rights activist and founder of OWFI, received death threats for campaigning to repeal Resolution 137; she went into hiding but kept working. Another leading activist was not so lucky. Nahla Hussein, leader of the Kurdish Communist Party's women's league, was found beheaded in her home in the northern city of Kirkuk in December 2008.[41] Most cases of threats and attacks on activists, including those with male victims, go unreported and are not investigated by the authorities.

All Iraqis, including women, have unrestricted access to online information, but this access has been hampered by the country's weak infrastructure and the lack of basic services like electricity. Many women cannot afford computers or face other financial barriers. Though women's NGOs and international partners such as USAID and UNDP have provided computer training centers, the priority has been to get women involved in politics, the economy, health care, and human rights issues. Iraqi women's NGOs are trying their best to organize workshops for that purpose, but the hardships of life in Iraq, and the inability of the government to protect women from kidnapping, rape, and murder, has led many women to stay at home.

In general, the daily need to secure electricity, water, food, and health has made most women in the suburbs and provinces indifferent to political participation—even if they have acquired political knowledge through the broadcast media or discussions with male family members. Most have lost faith in their female representatives and the government, which has failed to fulfill its promises to improve their lives. Women in rural areas are more isolated and unaware of their civil and political rights, living in closed, conservative communities dominated by family and tribe.

Recommendations

- ✤ The government should take concrete steps to systematically train and recruit female judges for service at all levels of the judiciary and in all parts of the country.
- ✤ The government should elevate the MWSA to a full ministry with an independent budget and a clear mandate developed in consultation with women's NGOs. Its functions should include monitoring other state entities and vetting proposed laws and constitutional amendments for possible violations of women's rights.
- ✤ The government, in cooperation with local and international NGOs, should integrate the idea of women's participation in politics through awareness campaigns and provide capacity-building training for emerging female leaders.

✤ The Iraqi government and the Kurdish regional government must lift all restrictions on free expression and the media. Journalists and other media workers must be given wide latitude to do their jobs in accordance with their constitutional rights.

✤ The government should create standing task forces—including police, prosecutors, and representatives of other security agencies—to investigate and punish crimes against journalists and civil society activists.

SOCIAL AND CULTURAL RIGHTS

The dire security situation that prevailed in the years after the U.S.-led invasion severely hampered women's full and equal access to health care. Civilians attempting to travel to hospitals—particularly in Baghdad—had to avoid false checkpoints erected by insurgents and sectarian death squads, who targeted individuals based on their apparent ethnic or religious affiliations. Several sick and pregnant women were killed by U.S. soldiers looking to ward off insurgent attacks, or by the attacks and bombings themselves. Because of these hazards, women are often forced to wait until they face a real health emergency before seeking professional care, and summoning an ambulance has become nearly impossible in some areas, as the vehicles risk being ambushed by insurgents or militias. Even if patients are able to reach a hospital, they could encounter armed groups inside, and medical staff are often swamped by the victims of bombings and shootings. Many women choose to give birth at home despite the lack of sanitation and medical expertise, leading to reports of death in childbirth.

Women are legally free to make independent decisions about their health and reproductive rights, but they are less able to exercise this freedom outside large cities. In rural areas and smaller, more conservative towns, contraceptives are not as readily available, and a woman's family members are more likely to control her health care choices. The custom in rural districts is to have many children to help support the family's farming efforts. Furthermore, greater poverty and ignorance about women's health issues leads many families in these areas to resort to folk remedies and informally trained midwives.

In small towns and villages, women generally cannot seek medical advice without the permission of their husbands or male guardians, and unmarried women especially are escorted to doctor's visits by male guardians. This is less of a problem in urban areas, but it is still considerable. According to the 2006–07 WHO household survey, 72.4 percent of women in rural areas and 64.1 percent of those in cities reported having to ask permission to visit a health facility.[42] The breakdown in security after 2003 added to the difficulty of obtaining medical care. A male escort was seen as more of a necessity, and men were more likely to demand to be informed of women's whereabouts.

Abortion is generally allowed only in cases of rape, fatal defects in the fetus, or when continuing the pregnancy would endanger the mother's life. Illegal abortions are punishable by up to one year in prison under the 1969 penal code, which also states that shame as a motive is considered a mitigating factor when unmarried women or their family members induce miscarriages. Those who induce a miscarriage without the woman's consent face up to 10 years in prison.

Some Iraqi women continue to be subjected to harmful traditional practices like genital mutilation, as well as honor killings and forced marriages. Female genital mutilation (FGM) occurs almost exclusively in the Kurdistan region, where more than 60 percent of women have undergone the procedure, according to a study conducted in 2008 by the German charity WADI.[43] Legislation aimed at outlawing FGM has stalled in the Kurdish regional parliament, as government officials do not consider it a priority. However, women's rights groups in Kurdistan work relentlessly to change the perception that the practice is harmless and required by Islam.

Social norms generally prevent women from living without a husband or male relatives, as they would be considered vulnerable to robbery, rape, or assault, and the authorities would regard them as partly responsible for any such occurrence. In divorce cases, the disposition of the marital home is decided by the court based on the law and the husband's financial condition. If the divorced woman has custody of the children, the court will grant her the marital home for up to three years. Aside from child support, she is not entitled to any alimony from her former husband once the divorce is finalized, contributing to rising poverty among female-headed households. The Ministry of Labor and Social Services provides small monthly payments to divorced, widowed, disabled, and elderly women who prove that they have no male supporter or are very poor. However, many such women were displaced by the sectarian violence, disrupting their access to state benefits. Only about one in six widows, many of whom are homeless, are believed to receive state aid.[44]

Iraqi women have long been pioneers in social and community services. After the 2003 invasion, many female retirees and those who had been forced to leave their jobs for political or economic reasons began to participate in school boards, parent-teacher associations, and neighborhood associations, exercising a positive influence on life in their communities. However, the subsequent rise in violence forced many to return to their homes. Schools and other civic buildings became regular targets or sites for armed encampments; in 2006 alone, more than 300 teachers and Education Ministry employees were killed.[45]

There are no accurate statistics on how many women work in the numerous local media outlets that were opened after 2003 by the government, various political parties, and other interests. Most outlets are directed by men, but women manage to participate as broadcasters, talk-show hosts, announcers, print journalists, and even newspaper owners. Iraqi women journalists have proven that they can handle one of the most difficult professions in one of the most dangerous places in the world. Many have dared to criticize government dysfunction, official corruption, and abuses by both security forces and illegal armed groups, all despite death threats, harassment, abductions, and murders. According to the Committee to Protect Journalists, more than 130 journalists have been killed in Iraq since March 2003, and 11 of the victims were women.[46]

Depending on their political affiliations, media outlets either fight for women's rights, claim to espouse women's interests for political ends, or denounce the core concepts of women's rights as foreign and un-Islamic. Some women's issues like honor killings, FGM, and domestic abuse have been addressed—at least on the surface—by the Iraqi media. However, these and other such topics are still considered to be minor or prohibitively complicated problems, and the government has subordinated them to its broader security interests. In 2007, after a woman appeared on the satellite television station Al-Jazeera and claimed that she had been raped by police officers, Prime Minister Nuri al-Maliki quickly denounced the account as a fabrication designed to discredit the security forces. The accused officers were promised promotions, and the woman was ultimately arrested.[47]

Iraqi and Arab periodicals deal with general subjects involving women, including beauty, cooking, home management, and family health care, but there are few articles on more sensitive subjects. Stories on domestic abuse sometimes excuse men's behavior as a result of trauma and harsh economic conditions, and advise women to be patient and defer to their husbands to protect the family union. This is consistent with the stereotypical view that Muslim women should obey their husbands except when doing so would contradict Islam. Despite such counterproductive content, periodicals also include articles calling for tolerance, understanding, and promotion of women's interests.

Iraqi women's rights activists and NGOs continued to work while maintaining a low profile during the worst of the violence in the country. Many NGOs workers were targeted by security forces, militias, insurgents, and gangs, either because of their progressive ideas or clothing, or for simple criminal reasons. Few cases were investigated, and the government did not provide any protection or support for these NGOs. Although the violence has abated considerably in the last two years, attacks on female activists continue, and the affected NGOs have maintained their security precautions. Even so, they have managed to remain active, creating shelters for victims of violence and setting up training centers to combat illiteracy, provide handicraft and computer skills, offer civil rights instruction, disseminate health information, and help women open small businesses.

Recommendations

❖ The government should encourage or sponsor independent media outlets and programs dedicated to educating women about their own worth as well as the skills of debate and constructive criticism, human rights, legal and religious rights, and free expression—all within the context of the positive values of Iraqi society and religion. This will help to confirm that these values are not imported from abroad, making it easier to confront the opponents of women's rights using their own language and terms.

❖ The government should reopen community recreational and educational centers where men and women of all ages can pursue their interests in sports, science, literature, and social development.

❖ The Kurdish regional parliament should decisively outlaw FGM and authorize an information campaign designed to discourage the practice. The regional government should work with NGOs to monitor the incidence of FGM in Iraqi Kurdistan over time.

❖ The government should set the levels of state aid to widows and other vulnerable women so as to match the cost of living in the country, and reduce bureaucratic hurdles that prevent potential recipients from benefiting. The government should sponsor shelters for homeless women and children that provide rehabilitation services and assistance in locating permanent housing.

✤ International and domestic NGOs should organize training workshops for the media on how to report on events in a gender-sensitive manner, without perpetuating stereotypes against women.

AUTHOR

Huda Ahmed, an Iraqi journalist, served in Baghdad as a special correspondent and translator for the *Washington Post* from 2003 to 2004, and for McClatchy Newspapers from 2004 to 2006. She has reported on and provided translation for a wide range of breaking news and feature stories, and was recognized by Knight Ridder's Washington bureau for "extraordinary" bravery in covering combat during the siege of Najaf in 2004. Ahmed received the International Women's Media Foundation Courage in Journalism Award for 2007, as well as the foundation's Elizabeth Neuffer Fellowship. Also in 2007, she received a joint fellowship at the Center for International Security and Cooperation and the Center for Democracy, Development, and the Rule of Law—both parts of the Freeman Spogli Institute for International Studies at Stanford University. Currently, Ahmed is a graduate student at the University of California at Berkeley, studying both journalism and international and area studies. She hopes to return to the Middle East to continue her work as a journalist.

NOTES

[1] An English translation of the law, with subsequent amendments, is available on the American Bar Association's website at http://www.abanet.org/rol/publications/iraq_personal_status_law_1959_english_translation.pdf.

[2] Judith Colp Rubin, "Women in the New Iraq," *Middle East Review of International Affairs* 12, no. 3 (September 2008), http://www.meriajournal.com/en/asp/journal/2008/september/rubin/3.pdf.

[3] Iraq Legal Development Project, *The Status of Women in Iraq: Update to the Assessment of Iraq's De Jure and De Facto Compliance with International Legal Standards* (Washington, DC: American Bar Association, December 2006), http://www.abanet.org/rol/publications/iraq_status_of_women_update_2006.pdf.

[4] The article states: "Iraqis are free in their commitment to their personal status according to their religions, sects, beliefs, or choices, and this shall be regulated by law." An English version of the constitution can be found at http://www.uniraq.org/documents/iraqi_constitution.pdf.

5   In 2006, Prime Minister Nuri al-Maliki instructed the ministry to stop providing mortality figures to the United Nations as well. See Colum Lynch, "Iraq Aims to Limit Mortality Data," *Washington Post*, October 20, 2006.

6   Timothy Williams, "Iraq's War Widows Face Dire Need with Little Aid," *New York Times*, February 22, 2009.

7   Iraq Legal Development Project, *The Status of Women in Iraq*, 62.

8   Afif Sarhan, "Hitmen Charge $100 a Victim," *The Observer*, November 30, 2008.

9   Basim al-Shara, "Honor Killings Remain Above the Law in Iraq," *Kuwait Times*, April 9, 2008, http://www.kuwaittimes.net/read_news.php?newsid=MTIyNzM4ODE3Ng==.

10 Bureau of Democracy, Human Rights, and Labor, *2008 Human Rights Report: Iraq* (Washington, DC: U.S. Department of State, February 25, 2009).

11 Division for the Advancement of Women, "Declarations, Reservations and Objections to CEDAW," UN Department of Economic and Social Affairs, http://www.un.org/womenwatch/daw/cedaw/reservations-country.htm.

12 Missy Ryan, "War-Weary Aid Groups Weigh Risk, Need in Iraq," Reuters, November 21, 2007, http://www.reuters.com/article/middleeastCrisis/idUSRYA739414; Inter-Agency Information and Analysis Unit, "The Humanitarian Situation in Iraq: Inter-Agency Fact Sheet," UN Office for the Coordination of Humanitarian Affairs, August 2009, http://www.uniraq.org/documents/Factsheet-EnglishR190809.pdf.

13 Article 17 of the 1959 personal status code.

14 Alexandra Zavis, "Iraq Marriages Are a Casualty of War," *Los Angeles Times*, April 13, 2008; Hazim al-Shara, "Mixed Marriages Survive Conflict," Institute for War and Peace Reporting, September 24, 2008.

15 Iraq Legal Development Project, *The Status of Women in Iraq*, 96–97, 108.

16 Mut'ah marriages are not specifically addressed in the 1959 personal status code.

17 Judith Colp Rubin, "Women in the New Iraq," 44; "Iraq: Women's Groups Blast 'Temporary' Marriages," IRIN, January 23, 2006, http://www.irinnews.org/report.aspx?reportid=26074; Isobel Coleman, "Women, Islam, and the New Iraq," *Foreign Affairs* (January/February 2006).

18 Judith Colp Rubin, "Women in the New Iraq," 44.

19 Divorce procedures are covered in Articles 34–50 of the 1959 personal status code.

20 "Iraq-Syria: Sex Traffickers Target Women in War-Torn Iraq," IRIN, October 26, 2006.

21 Rania Abouzeid "Iraq's Unspeakable Crime: Mothers Pimping Their Daughters," *Time*, March 7, 2009, http://www.time.com/time/world/article/0,8599,1883696,00.html?xid=rss-world#ixzz0WVVBISIA.

22 "Kurdistan Aziz: Another Victim of Stoning," IKWRO, June 6, 2008, http://www.ikwro.org.uk/index.php?option=com_content&task=view&id=298&Itemid=26.

23 "Iraq: 'Honour Killings' Persist in Kurdish North," Integrated Regional Information Networks (IRIN), December 6, 2007, http://www.irinnews.org/Report.aspx?ReportId=75714.

24 Revolutionary Command Council Decision No. 488 of 1978 introduced the death penalty for certain cases of incest. Such offenses would now result in a penalty of life imprisonment under subsequent revisions to the laws pertaining to the death penalty.

[25] Silvia Spring and Larry Kaplow, "Sacrificed to the Surge," *Newsweek*, April 14, 2008, http://www.newsweek.com/id/130602/page/1.

[26] Alissa J. Rubin, "Despair Drives Suicide Attacks by Iraqi Women," *New York Times*, July 5, 2008, http://www.nytimes.com/2008/07/05/world/middleeast/05diyala.html?_r=1.

[27] Afif Sarhan, "Hitmen Charge $100 a Victim."

[28] See, for example, "Capacity Building for Women in Business: The Example of Iraq," *PSD Gender Notes* 1, no. 1 (May 2004), http://www.ifc.org/ifcext/economics.nsf/AttachmentsByTitle/GI-PSDGenderNotes11.pdf/$FILE/GI-PSDGenderNotes11.pdf; "Women-Run Iraqi Firms Worry About US Departure" by Deborah Amos, National Public Radio, August 28, 2009, http://www.npr.org/templates/storystoryphp?storyId=112304714.

[29] Deborah Amos, "Women-Run Iraqi Firms Worry About US Departure."

[30] Inter-Agency Information and Analysis Unit, "Iraq Labour Force Analysis 2003–2008," UN Office for the Coordination of Humanitarian Affairs, January 2009, http://www.iauiraq.org/reports/Iraq_Labour_Force_Analysis.pdf.

[31] World Health Organization (WHO), *Iraq Family Health Survey 2006/7* (Amman: WHO, 2008), 13, 17, http://www.emro.who.int/iraq/pdf/ifhs_report_en.pdf.

[32] World Bank, Central Organization for Statistics and Information Technology (COSIT), and Kurdistan Region Statistics Organization (KRSO), *Iraq Household Socio-Economic Survey (IHSES)—2007* (Amman: National Press, 2008), http://go.worldbank.org/CBZHBK9N00.

[33] Ylli Bajraktari, "Economic Empowerment of Women in Iraq: The Way Forward," United States Institute of Peace Briefing, May 2006, http://www.usip.org/resources/economic-empowerment-women-iraq-way-forward.

[34] USAID, "USAID Support to Iraqi Women," fact sheet, March 2006, http://www.usaid.gov/iraq/updates/mar06/iraq_fs19_031006.pdf.

[35] Qassimk Khidhir Hamad, "Kurdish Women Political Voice Unheard," Iraq Oil Report, July 8, 2009, http://www.iraqoilreport.com/life/kurdish-women-political-voice-unheard-1929.

[36] A proliferation of smaller parties can lead to lower female representation. If each party secures seats only for its top one or two candidates, the women occupying the third position on the party lists will be excluded.

[37] Alissa J. Rubin and Sam Dagher, "Changes in Iraq Election Law Weaken Quota for Women," *New York Times*, January 13, 2009, http://www.nytimes.com/2009/01/14/world/middleeast/14iraq.html.

[38] "Footprints," UNDP Iraq Quarterly E-Magazine, no. 5 (October 2009), http://www.uniraq.org/documents/Footprint5_211009.pdf.

[39] Iraq Legal Development Project, *The Status of Women in Iraq*, 24–25, 163.

[40] Neil MacFarquhar, "In Najaf, Justice Can Be Blind but Not Female," *New York Times*, July 31, 2003.

[41] "Women's Rights Activist Beheaded in Iraq," CNN, December 18, 2008, http://edition.cnn.com/2008/WORLD/meast/12/18/iraq.arrests/index.html.

[42] WHO, *Iraq Family Health Survey 2006/7*, 24.

43 Amit R. Paley, "For Kurdish Girls, a Painful Ancient Ritual," *Washington Post*, December 29, 2008.

44 Timothy Williams, "Iraq's War Widows."

45 Nancy Trejos, "Women Lose Ground in the New Iraq," *Washington Post*, December 16, 2006.

46 Committee to Protect Journalists, "Iraq: Journalists in Danger," http://cpj.org/reports/2008/07/journalists-killed-in-iraq.php (accessed September 3, 2009).

47 Ned Parker, "Woman Arrested Over Police Rape Claims," *Times* (of London), March 13, 2007.

JORDAN

by Rana Husseini

POPULATION:	5,915,000		
GNI PER CAPITA:	US$2,708		
COUNTRY RATINGS		**2004**	**2009**
NONDISCRIMINATION AND ACCESS TO JUSTICE:		2.4	2.7
AUTONOMY, SECURITY, AND FREEDOM OF THE PERSON:		2.4	2.7
ECONOMIC RIGHTS AND EQUAL OPPORTUNITY:		2.8	2.9
POLITICAL RIGHTS AND CIVIC VOICE:		2.8	2.9
SOCIAL AND CULTURAL RIGHTS:		2.5	2.8

(COUNTRY RATINGS ARE BASED ON A SCALE OF 1 TO 5, WITH 1 REPRESENTING THE LOWEST AND 5 THE HIGHEST LEVEL OF FREEDOM WOMEN HAVE TO EXERCISE THEIR RIGHTS)

INTRODUCTION

The women's rights movement in Jordan began in the early 20th century in the form of voluntary social and charitable activities. The Jordanian Women's Union was established in January 1945, and after the kingdom gained independence from Britain in May 1946, the movement became more active in demanding greater political, social, legal, and economic rights.[1] Educated women were granted suffrage in 1955, but it was not until 1974 that all women received the right to vote and run as candidates in parliamentary elections. In 1993, the first female candidate was elected to the lower house of parliament and the first woman was appointed to the upper house, as women increasingly occupied leadership positions and stepped up their involvement in the political and social spheres.[2]

From 2004 until the end of 2009, the women's movement made a number of important gains, including the publication of the Convention on the Elimination of All Forms of Discrimination against Women (CEDAW) in the official gazette, which gave it the force of law. Additionally, the government has taken steps to address the problem of domestic abuse, including the February 2007 opening of the country's first major women's shelter, the Family Reconciliation House, and the March 2008 promulgation of the Family Protection Law, designed to regulate the handling of domestic abuse cases by medical workers and law enforcement bodies. Gender-based violence, nonetheless, remains a serious concern, and women may be severely beaten, or even murdered, if they disobey their male family members or commit an act deemed "dishonorable," such as socializing with an unrelated man.

While Jordanian women now largely enjoy legal equality on issues such as their freedom of movement, health care, education, political participation, and employment, they still suffer from discriminatory statutes like the nationality and citizenship law, which bars them from passing Jordanian citizenship to their spouses or children. Women also face gender-based discrimination in family laws, in the provision of pensions and social security benefits, and on the societal level due to deeply entrenched patriarchal norms. These legal obstacles, combined with domestic violence and traditional societal restrictions on the scope of female employment and property ownership, have prevented many women from fully participating in the economy or achieving financial independence. Divorced women, the elderly, and widows are most likely to experience poverty and deprivation, and they are often forced to depend on relatives, friends, or welfare support.

Women have continued to be politically active over the past five years, exercising their civic voice in a variety of ways. They have assumed high-level governmental positions in greater numbers, gaining appointments as ministers and lawmakers with increasing frequency. An average of three ministerial portfolios has been assigned to women in each cabinet since 2004, and a gender-based quota system, first introduced for the lower house of parliament in 2003, was expanded to municipal councils in 2007.

General political environment and legal restrictions on freedom of assembly and association have had an impact on the activities of women's groups and their ability to advocate for reform. The Public Gathering Law, though amended in 2008 to allow groups to hold internal meetings without prior approval, still requires government approval for demonstrations and "public meetings," including workshops and trainings. Additionally, the new Societies Law enacted in September 2008 places restrictions on civil society funding sources and permits the government, rather than the judiciary, to try local nongovernmental organizations (NGOs) for alleged violations of the law. The measure sparked fierce debate throughout Jordan, with women's rights activists complaining that it would allow the authorities to closely monitor and interfere with their activities, including by placing government officials on their boards.[3] Activists convened a number of press conferences and meetings with state representatives to voice their objections, and by the end of 2008, the government was engaged in a dialogue with civil society groups on possible changes to the law.

Despite the new regulations, the number of registered NGOs stood at 3,000 by end of 2008, and women's rights groups continued to enjoy a fair amount of freedom to pursue their mission. They have called for the elimination of laws that discriminate against women, and have kept women's rights on the national agenda. Their continued success and ability to win government cooperation will be crucial in ensuring women's well-being and equality in practice, which in turn form key components of any plan for sustainable development in Jordan.

NONDISCRIMINATION AND ACCESS TO JUSTICE

The Jordanian government has held open dialogues with the women's rights movement over the past five years to discuss amending laws that discriminate against women, including statutes that prevent Jordanian women from passing their citizenship to their spouses and children, and laws that offer leniency to the perpetrators of so-called "honor crimes." While these laws remain in place, criminal courts have begun to issue stricter sentences for honor killings and a new specialized tribunal for cases involving honor crimes was created in 2009. Meanwhile, social norms often deter women from seeking justice and protection through the legal system on the premise that they are disobeying their family. Many women have internalized such cultural attitudes and believe that discrimination and abuse are unavoidable parts of their existence.

Jordanian laws are derived from the Napoleonic code (inherited from the Ottoman and Egyptian legal systems) and Shari'a (Islamic law), and have been influenced by tribal traditions. The highest court in Jordan is the Court of Cassation, followed by the Courts of Appeal. The lower courts are divided into civil courts and religious courts. In the civil court system, the Courts of First Instance have general jurisdiction over criminal and civil cases, and the Magistrate Courts largely handle smaller claims. The Shari'a Courts have jurisdiction over personal status for Muslims, including issues related to marriage, divorce, and inheritance; parallel tribunals handle such matters for non-Muslim minorities.[4] The rulings of religious courts can be appealed to the Courts of Appeal. Separately, the semi-military State Security Court hears cases on offenses against the state as well as drug-related crimes, and other special panels are empowered to interpret the constitution and laws at the request of political leaders.

Article 6(1) of Jordan's 1952 constitution states that all Jordanians are equal before the law, and discrimination is prohibited on the basis of race, language, or religion. Article 6(2) of the constitution requires the government to ensure, "within the limits of its possibilities," work, education, tranquility, and equal opportunity for all Jordanians. While the constitution's repeated reference to the rights of "every Jordanian" is generally understood to include both men and women, the document fails to specifically prohibit gender discrimination. Many laws governing women's lives are not consistent with the concept of equality among Jordanian citizens, including those related to retirement and social security. However, the absence of a constitutional court makes it difficult for women to contest the constitutionality of discriminatory laws, and Jordanian NGOs that offer support or legal advice to victimized women lack the standing to file cases in higher courts on their behalf.

Under the Nationality Law (No. 6 of 1954), all children of Jordanian fathers are Jordanian nationals, regardless of where the children are born, and Jordanian men can transfer their citizenship to foreign spouses. By contrast, Jordanian women married to non-Jordanian men cannot pass their citizenship to their children or husbands, although they may retain their own Jordanian citizenship. The government maintains that allowing women to transfer their citizenship to their husbands and children would encourage the immigration and assimilation of non-Jordanians, particularly Palestinians, which in turn would undermine the effort to secure Palestinian statehood and the right of return for Palestinian refugees.

Lack of Jordanian citizenship creates obstacles for children, including a requirement that they pay fees to attend government schools, whereas the primary education is free for citizens. The alternative—enrollment in private schools—entails high tuition payments. Noncitizen children and spouses require a yearly residency permit to access government health services, and under the Law of Residency and Foreigners' Affairs (No. 24 of 1973), they must each pay 400 dinars (US$564) in annual residency fees.

In civil courts, women have the right to be plaintiffs and defendants. They can testify as witnesses or experts, and their testimony is considered equal to that of men. Women can serve as translators in courts, and are free to appear before the police and the public prosecutor. However, access to justice for women is limited in a variety of ways. In Shari'a courts, for instance, the testimony of two women is equal to that of one man, and female expert witnesses and translators are not accepted. Additionally, women often fear social retribution if they were to testify against family members, and the prohibitive costs of court proceedings prevent women who are not financially independent from pursuing justice without securing support from their families. Further restricting women's ability to defend their legal rights is the fact that the actual implementation of Jordan's laws is often influenced by factors such as a lack of training of police and court officials and inefficiency in the judicial sector.

The Jordanian penal code (No. 16 of 1960) contains certain provisions that discriminate against women. For example, Article 308 allows rape charges to be dropped if the perpetrator agrees to marry the victim. He is prohibited from divorcing the woman for a period of three years. Another provision, Article 98, prescribes sentences of three months to two years in prison for murders committed in a fit of rage that stems from an unlawful or dangerous act by the victim. In practice this provision is applied to "honor killings" in which a woman is murdered by a relative for suspected extramarital sex or some other behavior that is deemed a slight to the family's honor. There are an estimated 20 such murders each year.

Sentences in these cases can also be reduced if the victim's family drops the charges, which often happens when victim and perpetrator belong to the same family. In one recent case in November 2008, a man faced a 15-year prison sentence for killing his married sister, whose only fault was to temporarily leave her family's house to stay with friends after experiencing marital problems. Although the court rejected the defendant's plea that he committed the murder in a moment of rage, his sentence was cut in half after the family dropped the charges.[5] The government has pledged to amend Article 98 on various occasions, either during workshops or in private meetings with lawyers, activists, and diplomats. However, the pledges remain unfulfilled to date. A few cases have been appealed by prosecutors, leading to stiffer sentences of up to 10 years in prison. Additionally, the Ministry of Justice established a special tribunal in July 2009 to hear cases involving honor crimes in the hopes that such a body would create coherence in related jurisprudence and speed up efforts to bring perpetrators to justice.[6]

The prevalence of honor killings has given rise to a unique form of gender-based arbitrary arrest and detention. Anyone who constitutes a danger to the community or whose life is under threat may be incarcerated by the regional governor under the Crime Prevention Law (No. 7 of 1954). Consequently, women whose lives are deemed to be threatened by their families, predominantly for reasons related to family honor, are often protected by being incarcerated. There are approximately 25 women "protected" in Jordanian prisons at any given time. Unable to petition for their own release, some have remained incarcerated for over 10 years. Their freedom turns on whether a male guardian signs a 5,000 dinar (US$7,052) guarantee that he will not harm his female relative. Despite such pledges, these women are almost always killed shortly after their release. Prison officials can refuse to release a woman to her male guardian if they feel her life is still in danger.

A coalition of NGO representatives and government officials was formed in 2006 to find safe alternative solutions for women in protective custody, and has succeeded in helping several women to reconcile with their families or otherwise live in security beyond the prison walls. However, the widespread patriarchal attitudes and practices lead many women to believe that discrimination and violence are acceptable parts of their daily lives. Women's NGOs continue to operate a range of programs designed to minimize the effect of these cultural forces and prevent them from hindering women's advancement.

Jordan signed CEDAW in 1980 and ratified it in 1992, although the country included reservations concerning Article 9(2), on nationality; Article 15(4), on freedom of housing and movement; and Article 16(1), paragraphs (C), (D), and (G), related to marital, custody, and personal status issues.[7] In May 2009, Jordan formally reported that it was lifting its reservation on Article 15(4), leaving just two reservations in effect. The convention's publication in the official gazette on August 1, 2007, represented a key step toward its full implementation. The move was the result of persistent efforts by the majority of women's organizations, and had the effect of giving CEDAW the force of law. Any violations of the convention can now be challenged in court through lawsuits, although it remains to be seen whether this will be an effective mechanism in practice.

Jordan's compliance with CEDAW is also monitored by the Jordanian National Commission for Women (JNCW), a semi-governmental body established in 1992 to craft policies and legislation concerning women's issues. Women's rights groups have continued to press the government to lift its reservations to CEDAW, and officials regularly discuss the matter in dialogues with the women's movement. A group of women's rights organizations prepared and submitted Jordan's first CEDAW "shadow report" in August 2007 detailing the government's areas of noncompliance and recommending policies to improve protection of women's legal rights.

Recommendations

✤ The nationality and residency laws should be amended to ensure that men and women have equal rights to pass on their citizenship and related privileges to their spouses and children.

✤ The government and civil society organizations should expand legal aid services for women to educate them about their rights and help those who cannot afford an attorney on their own. Outreach to rural areas is particularly important.

✤ The government should amend Article 98 of the penal code to eliminate leniency for murders committed in the name of family honor, and introduce new laws to increase the penalties for such murders.

✤ The government should remove the remaining reservations to CEDAW regarding citizenship rights and personal status law, and additional steps should be taken to implement and enforce the convention domestically. International bodies should provide training to local NGOs on how to practically utilize the government's obligations under CEDAW to defend women's rights.

AUTONOMY, SECURITY, AND FREEDOM OF THE PERSON

The Jordanian government has taken a number of steps over the last five years to improve women's personal security. It established the country's first well-resourced shelter for victims of domestic abuse in 2007, and new laws passed in 2008 overhauled the way law enforcement bodies handle domestic abuse cases and extended labor protections to domestic workers. However, widespread patriarchal attitudes within the society and court system routinely prevent women from taking full advantage of their legal rights and stigmatize victims of abuse. Jordanian women also continue to suffer from legal inequality with respect to marriage, divorce, and child custody.

Article 14 of the constitution guarantees freedom of religion, provided that religious practices are consistent with "public order and morality." Islam, Christianity, and Judaism are the only state-recognized religions, although the unrecognized Druze and Baha'i faiths are not prohibited. More than 95 percent of Jordanians are Sunni Muslims, and approximately

4 percent are Christians. Shiite Muslims, Druze, and Baha'is make up the remainder. Matters of personal status—such as marriage, divorce, child custody, and inheritance—fall within the exclusive jurisdiction of Shari'a courts for Muslims, Druze, and Baha'is, and are regulated by the Personal Status Law (No. 61 of 1976). State-recognized religious minorities have tribunals that apply their own personal status laws, which are not published in the official gazette. Shari'a does apply to the inheritance matters of non-Muslims, but Christian institutions often do not enforce this in practice.

Jordanian law upholds citizens' rights to move freely within the country and abroad, except in designated military areas. Under the current Provisional Passport Law (No. 5 of 2003), women are no longer required to seek permission from their male guardians or husbands before obtaining or renewing their passports. Nevertheless, the Personal Status Law allows fathers to prevent their children from traveling, and in several recent cases handled by women's rights groups, mothers involved in divorces were barred from traveling abroad with their children due to a travel ban imposed by their husbands. Social norms continue to play a major role in restraining women's freedom of movement in other ways, particularly in rural areas. For example, some families withdraw their girls from school at age 16 or refuse to allow them to attend universities, particularly if that involves moving to another place of residence.

Welaya (guardianship) is a system in Jordanian law whereby a male relative is appointed to act on behalf of and in the interests of a minor or any other person of limited legal capacity. Any single woman under the age of 40—whether divorced, widowed, or never married—is considered a dependent of her guardian. Should such a woman rebel against her guardian's decisions, she will no longer be entitled to her financial maintenance. Although Islamic legal principles allow women to be the legal guardians of their children, the Personal Status Law in Jordan only allows men to act in this capacity.

Jordanian Muslims are required to marry according to Islamic marriage law. Muslim women are prohibited from marrying men of other religions unless the spouse agrees to convert to Islam, while Muslim men are permitted to wed Christian and Jewish wives. A marital contract is concluded between the prospective husband and the guardian of the prospective wife, although a woman marrying for the second time can do so without her family's approval. Under Article 19 of the Personal Status Law, a woman is entitled to make stipulations in the marriage contract, such as the right to obtain an education or work, provided that the conditions are not unlawful and do not affect the rights of any other person. In practice, however, this right is rarely exercised because many women are either unaware that it exists or reluctant to risk their marriage by invoking it. Women's rights groups including the Jordanian Women's Union have suggested attaching a list of the possible conditions to the actual marriage contract in order to inform women of their available rights.

Amendments made to the Personal Status Law in 2001 raised the minimum age of marriage to 18 years, but the chief justice retains the discretion to permit the marriage of anyone who is at least 15 years old if it is deemed to be in his or her interest.[8] Women's groups have reported several cases in which teenage girls aged 15 and above were still being married to older men, a practice that results in social problems and in some cases psychological, sexual, and physical violence, including murders.

While the Hanafi school of Islamic law, which is dominant in Jordan, does not require a male guardian to conclude a marriage contract on behalf of an adult Muslim woman, the government elected to adopt the position of the Maliki school in this matter. The consent of a Shari'a judge is required to conclude the marriage if the woman's guardian opposes it without lawful justification—in the absence, for instance, of any financial impediments that would prevent the prospective husband from supporting the woman. Article 66 of the Personal Status Law obliges a husband to provide for the financial maintenance of his wife, including food, clothing, housing, and medical care.

Polygamy is allowed for Muslim men, but a judge must verify that they have the means to financially maintain a new wife.[9] In addition, the 2001 amendments to the Personal Status Law require the courts to inform each wife of the others' existence. If a man can satisfy all financial and legal requirements, he may be legally married to up to four wives at one time. Polygamy is reportedly uncommon in practice, with just one wife in 93.2 percent of Jordanian households. There are two wives in 5.9 percent of households, three in 0.9 percent, and four in 0.03 percent. The figures for rural areas are somewhat higher, with two wives in 8.1 percent of households and three in 1.4 percent as of 2002.[10]

The Personal Status Law also protect an employed woman's right to financial maintenance as long as her husband views her work as legitimate and has agreed to it. Once a husband has accepted the wife's work, he cannot negate her right to maintenance by subsequently withdrawing his approval. Similarly, the husband cannot object to his wife's work if she was already employed before they married. The concept that approval is necessary to legitimize a wife's choice of profession stems from the injunction in Shari'a that a wife should obey her husband, which some Jordanian jurists have interpreted as the husband's right to confine a woman to the home. In practice, the legal and social hardships that some women encounter while pursuing their right to financial maintenance diminishes the positive aspects of this right.

Men and women in Jordan have access to different forms of divorce. The most common form, available only to men, is *talaq* (arbitrary divorce), which permits a husband to divorce his wife without providing any legal reason. This can be initiated either orally or in writing, but it must eventually be registered by a court. Women who have been divorced by this method have the right to compensation equivalent to her maintenance for no less than one year and no more than three years; the amount is determined by the court based on the husband's financial status. Following talaq, the wife also has the right to keep her dowry and the maintenance she accumulates during the *iddat*, a compulsory three-month waiting period after the initial separation before the divorce takes full effect. The iddat, covered under Article 135 of the Personal Status Law, is designed primarily to ensure that the wife is not pregnant by the husband who is divorcing her. Although there is increasing social resistance to arbitrary divorce, there are no legal restrictions on this practice.

A woman seeking a divorce in Jordan has two options. She may file for a judicial divorce at the Shari'a court, but only if she can cite one of a limited number of valid reasons, which require strong evidence and witness testimony. While domestic abuse is a valid reason for initiating such a divorce, it is often very difficult for a woman to prove her case, because Shari'a courts require the testimony of two male witnesses. The testimony of the wife alone is not accepted as sufficient evidence. Other acceptable reasons include the husband's failure to provide a home or financial maintenance, and his unjustified absence for more than one year. Divorce cases initiated through these means often last for years, and in the end the woman's petition is most often denied.

The second option available to women—added to the Personal Status Law in 2001—is *khula*, a form of divorce permitted by Shari'a in which the wife can unilaterally end the marriage by returning her dowry and giving up all rights to future financial maintenance. She is not obliged to provide a reason or justification for her decision, other than stating that she detests living with the husband. The court will ask her to reconsider, but if she insists, the divorce will be granted. The khula provision remains on the books despite the lower house of parliament's attempts to ban the practice in 2003 and 2004. Khula eases the procedural and evidentiary burden on women seeking a divorce, but it is not a viable option for those who cannot afford to give up financial maintenance or return their dowry.

After a divorce, the woman has the right of custody of her children until they reach the age of puberty; at that point the children decide who they will live with. If the mother remarries, she loses custody and the children return to their father, his mother, or the wife's mother, as decided by a judge. Even when the mother holds the custody rights, the father is almost always considered to be the legal guardian of his children, permitting him the final say over decisions such as the place of residence and education.

Jordan remains a destination and transit point for men and women trafficked into forced labor from South and Southeast Asia, as well as a destination for women trafficked into prostitution from Eastern Europe and Morocco. Most domestic workers come from the Philippines, Sri Lanka, and Indonesia. Typically they are poor and uneducated, do not speak Arabic or English, and live essentially at the mercy of their employers and the recruitment agencies that brought them to Jordan. Approximately 40,000 registered migrant domestic workers live in Jordan, along with an estimated 30,000 more who are unregistered.[11]

The parliament in January 2009 approved legislation designed to combat human trafficking, calling for penalties of up to 10 years in prison for forced prostitution and other serious crimes, and permanent closure for companies involved in illegal trafficking. The law also envisioned the establishment of shelters for trafficking victims awaiting repatriation. However, the authorities have not worked effectively to identify or protect victims, and its enforcement policies have reportedly encouraged victims to return home rather than remain in Jordan to pursue legal cases against their traffickers.[12] Several local NGOs such as the Jordanian Women's Union and foreign embassies offer limited protection services for abused domestic workers.

Gender-based violence—including spousal abuse, honor killings, and sexual violence—remains significant problem in Jordan (see more about honor killings in "Nondiscrimination and Access to Justice"). The attitudes of police officers, judges, and prosecutors regarding the treatment of victims of domestic violence and honor crimes have undergone a positive shift in recent years, although many problems remain, particularly in the rural areas. Investigations into the murders of women have been expanded and handled more seriously, and prosecutors consequently offer stronger evidence against alleged perpetrators of gender-based crimes. The media have also played a major role by highlighting the issue in general and reporting on individual cases.

Numerous projects and training efforts have helped raise the level of services provided to abused women. One major program was the Jordanian Family Protection Project, which ran from 2000 to 2005, focused on training judges, prosecutors, police, investigators, government physicians, religious leaders, and other experts working in this field. Many cases of domestic violence are now handled by the Family Protection Department, a specialized police center. The National Council for Family Affairs (NCFA) in September 2007 launched a five-year project targeting violence against women by using media campaigns, public events, private counseling sessions, and training for medical staff.[13] Additionally, the JNCW opened the Women's Complaint Office in early 2009, which offers legal aid to women who are victims of violence or who need advice regarding labor disputes, the citizenship law, or other issues that directly affect women.[14]

In another sign of progress, the parliament enacted the Family Protection Law (FPL) in January 2008 after years of lobbying by governmental and civil society actors. The FPL alters the way in which the police, the courts, and medical authorities deal with victims of domestic violence, specifying the procedures each institution must follow as it handles such cases. It gives greater authority and jurisdiction to the police, allowing them to detain suspected abusers for 24 hours. Although a key goal of the legislation is to prevent the destruction of families, the FPL prescribes penalties of up to six months in prison and 100 to 200 dinars (US$141 to US$282) in damages for physical or psychological abuse. The most serious cases of violence may still be adjudicated in criminal courts under the ordinary penal code. The law also calls for the creation of mediation committees to manage problems that occur within families and reconcile the parties involved so that the case does not have to proceed to court, although none had been formed as of October 2009.

While the FPL includes many improvements, police are not required to enforce the law until the mediation committees are formed. Gender-based crimes continue to occur, and further efforts must be made to protect victims, prosecute offenders, and prevent future assaults from occurring. Activists have noted gaps in the law, including the fact that it only applies to families living together in the same house, and restricts its definition of domestic violence to acts committed in the home of the victim. Critics of the FPL also argue that it should have created a specialized family court to handle cases of domestic violence, and that a provision requiring follow-up meetings between government and social workers and the perpetrator has not been adequately enforced. If a suspected abuser apologizes to the victim and they agree to reconcile, he can return home.

Long-standing cultural attitudes stymie the effectiveness of laws like the FPL and other such efforts. Female victims continue to be blamed for the abuse they face. The social stigma and shame associated with crimes such as rape and molestation often discourage victims from turning to the authorities, and battered women are sometimes pressured by their families to drop the charges. In fact, in most cases, a perpetrator of rape or molestation can avoid punishment if he marries his victim in accordance with Article 308 of the penal code. Lawmakers justify this provision by stating that it protects the victim from social ostracism. There are no clear procedures to ensure that the victim approves of this solution, which is usually arranged through her male guardian.

The Family Reconciliation House (FRH) in Amman was created by the Ministry of Social Development in 2007 to provide shelter for domestic violence victims. Women's organizations run a few temporary shelters in the country, but their capabilities are quite limited compared to those of the FRH. In addition to providing housing, it employs social and legal experts who attempt to mediate conflicts between the victims and their abusers. Women can stay at the FRH for roughly six months, although the limit is reportedly more flexible. The FRH was originally intended to provide victims with rehabilitation and a long-term solution to their problems. However, government officials feared that it would be attacked by conservatives in society as a refuge for "bad women." As a result, women facing enduring threats from their families continue to be imprisoned for their own safety.

Women's rights NGOs have worked independently and in cooperation with the government, UNIFEM, USAID, and other donor agencies to address issues of gender-based and domestic violence. Hotlines, social and legal consultations, and other forms of assistance were offered by women's organizations including the Sisterhood Is Global Institute (SIGI) and the

Jordanian Women's Union. The union has also consulted with the JNCW on possible amendments to the Personal Status Law.

Recommendations

✤ The government and parliament, in consultation with women's rights activists, should amend the Personal Status Law to remove provisions that infringe on women's equality within marriage, including the requirement that husbands approve of their choice of work or profession. Exceptions that allow underage marriages should be more tightly restricted or eliminated entirely.

✤ NGOs should make a concerted effort to raise women's awareness of their legal rights regarding marriage, and the government should work with legal experts and civil society groups to develop a list of sample stipulations that can be attached to marriage contracts. Officials should read these aloud to prospective spouses to accommodate individuals who may be illiterate.

✤ The government should take additional steps to protect the rights of migrant domestic workers and victims of human trafficking. Temporary shelters should be established by the government or NGOs to house victims of abuse or those with pending legal cases until their situations are resolved.

✤ To aid larger numbers of domestic abuse victims, the government should open branches of the Family Reconciliation House in governorates outside the capital, and its mandate should be expanded to provide rehabilitation and long-term housing solutions to its clients.

✤ The government should criminalize domestic violence and work with civil society organizations to raise public awareness of the problem and the need to support victims through media outreach and visits to rural areas.

✤ The government should revise the Family Protection Law to expand its narrow definitions of domestic violence and create a specialized family court to adjudicate domestic disputes.

ECONOMIC RIGHTS AND EQUAL OPPORTUNITY

The economic transformation in Jordan over the past two decades did not benefit all sectors of society equally, and women continue to suffer from a number of crucial disadvantages.[15] According to a report presented by a group of activists in 2007, gender-based violence plays a role in undermining a woman's ability to participate in the economy.[16] Women's economic competitiveness is also hindered by a legal framework that reinforces their traditional financial dependence on male relatives, affecting areas including inheritance, salary, and retirement benefits. While the laws and social norms place certain restrictions on women's working hours and job types, they have been slowly expanding into new categories of employment and increasing their overall presence in the workforce over the last several years.

Jordanian women have the right to own property and enter into business contracts, and do not require their husband's or guardian's approval for such activities. Nevertheless, according to a 2008 government report, only 15.1 of women own land and 19.4 percent of women over the age of 15 own apartments.[17] Patriarchal attitudes, especially in rural areas, hinder women's ability to obtain economic resources, particularly for land ownership and finance.

There are no legal restrictions on the rights of women to enjoy their income and assets independently. However, it is the accepted norm for single working women, who represent the highest percentage of economically active women, to contribute to the family income by giving their salaries to their families. Working wives, on the other hand, often use their salaries to pay for family expenses directly.

Women are guaranteed the right to inheritance under Shari'a as applied in Jordan, but in many situations the woman is entitled to half the share of a male heir. This reflects the Shari'a requirement that, while a woman may use her inheritance for her sole benefit, a man also must use his inheritance to support all dependent members of his family. In addition, real assets are often transferred to male family members prior to the owner's death so as to circumvent inheritance rules. This is justified in part by the perceived need to keep property within the family and prevent women from taking their portions to other families when they marry. If a father dies before making such a legal transfer, no laws can prevent a daughter from receiving her share as calculated under Shari'a, but even in these cases women are pressured to waive their portions in favor of their brothers or other male family members. There are no legal procedures in place to protect women from such pressure, and many women in rural areas may not be aware that they can refuse to waive their inheritance or know how to defend their rights in court.

Education up to age 16 is compulsory and free in government schools for all Jordanians under Article 20 of the constitution, though students are required to pay nominal "donations" ranging from 3 to 6 dinars (US$4 to US$8).[18] Societal norms generally encourage families to enroll their children in schools and universities. Although the educational system does not contain policies that pro-actively discriminate against women and girls, the curriculum is conservative and lacks gender-sensitive language and concepts. The illiteracy rate among Jordanian women in 2007 was 11.6 percent, down from 16.5 percent in 2000, according to government figures.[19] Meanwhile, 55 percent of university graduates over the past decade were females. Many of these graduates, however, do not contribute to the labor market, in part because they have acquired skills that are not in high demand.[20]

Article 23 of the constitution protects the right to work and the principle of equal opportunity for all citizens. Workers and employees are defined in gender-neutral terms in both Article 2 of the Labor Law (No. 8 of 1996), which defines the worker as "each person, male or female, who performs a job in return for wages," and in the Civil Service Ordinance (No. 30 of 2007), which regulates public-sector employment. Nonetheless, no provisions specifically prohibit gender discrimination in employment or stress equal salaries for men and women who hold the same positions. Social discrimination against women is common and many Jordanians believe that women who enter the job market are doing so to supplement their family income rather than to become economically independent or to achieve meaningful career.

Women contributed 8 percent of the gross domestic product in 2007, and female employees constituted 37 percent of the workforce in the public sector and 12 percent in the private sector.[21] Women's participation in the labor market reached 14.7 percent in 2007, up from only 2.6 percent in 1990.[22] These gains are partly attributable to increases in the number of educated women and social acceptance of women in new economic roles. However, unemployment continues to affect women more severely than men. In 2008, for example, while the unemployment rate among men was 10.1 percent, the rate among women was 24.4 percent. Women's career paths are negatively affected by the continuing duty to perform traditional household chores, especially after marriage, as well as the expectation that they work near their family home, preferably in the government sector.

Women's freedom to choose their profession is influenced by legal regulations and cultural attitudes dictating what kind of jobs are appropriate for women. According to Article 23 of the constitution and Article 69 of the labor code, the minister of labor issues decisions specifying the industries and economic activities that are off limits for female workers, as well as the hours during which women are prohibited from working. Women are barred from working in mines and quarries and are not allowed to work between 8:00 p.m. and 6:00 a.m., except in places like hotels, theaters, restaurants, airports, offices of tourism, hospitals, clinics, and some transportation industries. Exceptions are also made for special conditions like annual inventories and preparations for seasonal retail sales, as well as jobs that involve a fear of financial loss. Evening work for women is limited to 30 days per year, and there is also a maximum of 10 working hours a day. Although these restrictions limit women's ability to compete with men in the job market, they are seen among many Jordanians as legitimate means of protecting women from harmful working conditions.

Over 60 percent of working Jordanian women are employed in "social" professions such as education (41 percent), health and social work (15.1 percent), and personal, social, and service activities (5.7 percent).[23] The salaries in these professions tend to be low. Women have also begun to challenge social norms by assuming jobs in male-dominated fields. They have become plumbers, garbage-truck drivers, demining technicians, power-line workers, pilots, and traffic police, among other professions. The percentage of women entrepreneurs in 2008 reached 6 percent in the formal sector. Similarly, the share of administrative and managerial positions held by women rose from 2 percent in 1998 to 11 percent in 2005.[24]

Although gender-based discrimination in employment is not officially permissible, it is widespread in practice. According to Article 41(c) of the 2007 Civil Service Ordinance, public-sector employment is determined solely by the results of exams and personal interviews. Nevertheless, the ordinance favors men in the distribution of benefits like family and cost-of-living allowances. For example, a married man with children under 18 receives a monthly allowance of 15 dinars (US$21), and a married man with no children receives 10, while a woman may receive this benefit only if she is a widow or her husband is disabled. This disparity is premised upon that fact that within the Jordanian legal, cultural, and religious value system, women technically have the right to be financially supported by husbands.

Gender also plays an important role in determining the length of employment necessary to qualify for retirement benefits, eligible beneficiaries, and the conditions under which benefits are provided in the event of the death of an employee. For example, under the Social Security Law, which largely regulates the private sector, the widow and dependents of a deceased male employee automatically qualify for the survivor benefits (pension). By contrast, the husband of a deceased female employee qualifies for such benefits only if he is completely disabled, has no other source of income, or his income is lower than his wife's pension.[25] In recent years, debates have raged regarding the need to amend related portions of the Civil Retirement Law and the Social Security Law that discriminate against retired women and their families, particularly because female workers pay the same share for such benefits as men. By the end of 2008 no such amendments had been made.

Among the provisions under discussion are also Article 14 of the Civil Retirement Law and Articles 44/45 of the Social Security Law. Both allow women to resign and withdraw their retirement fund after working for a certain period, giving them an incentive to quit jobs should their families encounter financial trouble. In a bid to encourage women's enrollment and long-term participation in the labor market, the government in 2003 increased the years of service required before women are eligible for such early retirement from 15 to 20. The regular retirement age for women is 55 and for men 60. While these policies were created to help women, they effectively prevent them from accumulating more years of service thereby leading to smaller pensions.

Women enjoy specific benefits in the workplace intended to help them balance their family demands with work. Article 105 of the Civil Service Ordinance provides for a 90-day maternity leave for women who work in the government sector, of which six weeks must be allowed immediately following the birth of the child. Women in the private sector are granted 70 days of maternity leave under Article 70 of the Labor Law. A private employer with 20 or more female workers must provide an onsite childcare facility for their children under the age of four if at least 10 children need such care. Furthermore, a working mother may take a year-long leave of absence without pay to raise her children under Article 67 of the Labor Law, and a mother is entitled to paid breaks to breastfeed her child during the first year after birth under Article 171 of the Labor Law. However, female workers often avoid taking advantage of the various maternity benefits out of fear of losing their jobs. Some employers are also reluctant to hire women because of the high cost associated with these benefits.

Sexual harassment in the workplace is not explicitly defined or prohibited by law, although under amendments made in July 2008, the Labor Law now addresses sexual assault. Specifically, Article 29 of the amended law allows victims to prematurely end their employment contract while retaining their end-of-service rights and the right to compensation for damages, but most women are unaware of this provision or the channels through which they can file complaints.

Foreign female workers, who are employed primarily as domestic helpers, receive few legal protections from gender-based discrimination. They often suffer cruel and inhuman treatment at the hands of their employers. Some are forced to work long hours without days off, are locked in their employers' homes, and suffer from physical and sexual abuse. They are often not paid the salary promised to them, if they are paid at all, and many have their passports confiscated by employers to prevent them from leaving the country. Women who escape or ask the authorities for help are often detained because their employers have not properly registered them or have filed retaliatory complaints against them, such as theft. Out of desperation, some female domestic workers have attempted to escape their employers' homes by jumping from windows or balconies, and some have committed suicide.[26]

Before July 2008, the protections of the Labor Law had not extended to domestic workers, farm workers, and cooks, the majority of whom are women. Although the amended law now covers these particularly vulnerable categories of employees and imposes a 1,000 dinar (US$1,410) fine on employers who coerce a person to work, including by withholding passports,[27] it is unclear to what extent these measures have been enforced in practice.

Women's groups continue to advocate for greater economic participation by women and are lobbying for amendments to the Civil Service Ordinance and the Social Security Laws that would guarantee greater rights for retired women and their families. Women's organizations and other community development programs also run income-generation projects that are aimed at women. The Jordanian Forum for Business and Professional Women, for example, encourages female entrepreneurship through training and the provision of enterprise incubators. In the public sector, the JNCW has worked with the Civil Service Commission to move toward gender equality among state employees.

Recommendations

✤ The government and parliament should pass legislation banning gender-based discrimination in all stages of employment and within employment benefits. Enforcement mechanisms should be put in place that allow women to file labor discrimination complaints and receive justice.

✤ The government and parliament should pass legislation that clearly defines sexual harassment in the workplace and establish procedures for filing and adjudicating complaints. NGOs should initiate public awareness campaigns aimed at working women to educate them about the issue and provide practical advice on what steps to make to remedy the problem.

✤ NGOs and the government should collect and analyze data regarding the prevalence of sexual harassment and the various forms that it takes in the workplace. These statistics should be used in part to educate the public about the phenomenon.

✤ The government should amend the Civil Retirement and Social Security laws by revising provisions that are unfair to women, including the definitions and eligibility requirements for families of deceased female employees.

✤ NGOs should expand their efforts to actively educate women on their inheritance and property rights under the law, and the government should regulate large property transfers within families to ensure that potential heiresses are not unduly expropriated.

POLITICAL RIGHTS AND CIVIC VOICE

Women remain underrepresented in political parties, professional organizations, and positions of power in the government and legislature, but they have been increasing their political and civic participation in recent years. In 2007, the government added a quota for female members of municipal councils to an existing rule that reserved a small number of seats in the lower house of parliament for women. During that year's elections, female candidates won more seats than were set aside for them at both the national and municipal levels. Meanwhile, media coverage of women's issues has been growing despite certain restrictions on other topics deemed politically sensitive.

King Abdullah II is the ruler of the country, with powers ranging from dissolving the 110-seat Chamber of Deputies, the lower house of parliament, to appointing the prime minister and the 55-member upper house, the Senate. The central government appoints the 12 regional governors, and the entire Chamber of Deputies is elected by the people every four years. The king serves as the head of the judiciary. Municipal councils were half elected and half appointed in 2003, but in 2007 this was true only for the Amman council, with the rest fully elected.

Women have had the right to vote and run as candidates under successive election laws since 1974. They face no legal barriers in their participation in politics and government bodies at various levels, but social barriers can sometimes limit their role. Most families expect women to focus more on their household and children than on civic affairs. The state has taken some steps to encourage women's participation in the public sphere, and there are currently four female ministers, 215 elected municipal council members, one mayor, one governor, seven members of each house of parliament, and two ambassadors.

Legislation passed in 2003 (No. 42 of 2003) reserved 6 out of 110 seats in the Chamber of Deputies for women. Previously, only one woman, in 1993, had won a seat in direct elections, although dozens ran as candidates before and after that year. The quota system was deemed necessary in part because of Jordan's single, nontransferable vote system, in which voters select only one candidate in their multimember district, and those with the most votes win seats. A female candidate did win a seat beyond the quota in the November 2007 parliamentary elections, and some observers attributed the achievement to society's growing acceptance of female lawmakers since the quota was introduced. The winner of the seventh seat had in fact served one term under the quota system already, and voters were apparently pleased with her performance. However, women's groups have argued that the single, nontransferable voting system continues to limit women's chances to win additional seats. Individuals generally cast their one vote based on tribal and family affiliations, and female candidates are less likely to become the chief representatives of such traditional social structures.

Women can also run and vote in municipal council elections, although they have generally shown less interest in races at this level. Responding to an initiative by women's organizations including the JNCW and the Jordanian National Forum for Women, the government introduced a

20 percent quota for the July 2007 municipal elections, which resulted in women winning a total of 215 seats across 93 municipalities (195 through the quota and 20 through direct competition). In addition, a female mayor was voted into office through direct competition with male candidates, although an earlier female mayor had been elected in 1995. Separately, in January 2007, the government appointed the first female governor in the country's history.

Women account for about 40 of more than 600 judges in Jordan's court system, although hundreds of women hold administrative jobs in the judiciary. In May 2007, Judge Ihsan Barakat was appointed as chief justice of West Amman Court of First Instance, but no female judges currently serve in the Court of Cassation or the Shari'a courts. In the same year, the Ministry of Justice set a 15 percent quota for women's membership in the Judicial Institute of Jordan, which is a prerequisite to becoming a judge; the previous female membership had been much lower, threatening the continuity of women's presence in the body.

Article 4 of the Political Parties Law (No. 32 of 1992) grants Jordanians the right to form and join political parties. Conditions for membership, as listed in Article 5, do not discriminate against women. Under a recent overhaul of the law (No. 19 of 2007), Article 5(a) requires each political party to have a minimum of 500 founding members representing at least five governorates, with at least 10 percent in each governorate. The measure consequently decreased the number of registered political parties from 36 to 12. A study prepared in 2008 indicated that women's participation in Islamist parties and organizations is on the rise, and that these entities are depending more on women to expand their membership base and address certain issues such as education and the right to work.[28] It remains unclear whether female members will have significant influence over the policies and proposals of such groups, however. According to a 2007 UNIFEM study, the percentage of leading positions in political parties held by women was 5.3.[29]

Under the Public Gathering Law (No. 40 of 2008), political parties and NGOs can hold internal meetings without prior approval from the regional governor, but demonstrations do require the governor's permit. If the governor fails to reply to a request for a demonstration within 48 hours, it can legally go forward. In practice, such requests are often denied without detailed explanation. A coalition of groups advocating reforms to the Personal Status Law was reportedly denied permission, without explanation, to hold a march in Amman in June 2008. NGOs have also been affected by the Societies Law enacted in September 2008, which restricts their funding sources, increases government monitoring of their internal activities and decision making, and allows government bodies rather than the courts to adjudicate alleged violations of the law.

Freedom of speech and freedom of the press are guaranteed in Article 15 of the constitution, and women, as well as men, are free to express their opinions in public and in the media within the confines of Jordanian law. A 2007 press law abolished imprisonment of journalists for ideological offenses; however, there were limited incidents of detention and imprisonment of journalists for defamation and slander. All publications must be licensed by the government, which has the discretion to issue fines, withdraw licenses, and order media shutdowns, enabling the state to control the editorial content of newspapers. Journalists writing on women's rights issues are generally not subjected to government interference, although they sometimes receive threats from within the society, including accusations of being "agents of the West." The number of media articles on gender topics—including domestic violence, honor killings, family laws, and working women—has been on the rise in recent years.

Women are increasingly participating in civic life through professional organizations, which frequently engage in political activity. Women currently constitute almost 21,000 of the 100,000 members of professional organizations in Jordan, including those for engineers, journalists, physicians, and lawyers.[30] However, they remain underrepresented in these associations and their governing bodies.

Women have relatively free access to information that can empower them in their civic and political lives. A growing number of women are taking advantage of Internet resources or attending lectures and other activities that will strengthen their knowledge and experience. More women are also beginning to use the latest online media platforms, including blogging, social-networking sites, and video-sharing sites like YouTube.

Recommendations

✤ The government should appoint more women as ministers, senators, and governors, and as senior officials in Jordan's diplomatic corps and civil service.

✤ The government should appoint female judges to the Court of Cassation and other high courts, as well as to the Shari'a courts.

✣ Professional associations and political parties should take steps to ensure that women have full and equal opportunities to participate as members and leaders in their organizations.

✣ The government and parliament should reform the voting system for Chamber of Deputies elections to improve the odds of success for female candidates, and consult with women's NGOs and other experts to devise the best possible model. The potential benefits of a single transferable vote system should be examined as part of this process.

✣ NGOs should organize lectures and training activities, including leadership institutes and debate classes, to encourage women to join and lead political parties.

✣ Domestic and international NGOs should initiate programs to train female campaign managers on how to effectively run political campaigns for women candidates. They should focus on campaign strategies that have proven successful for women in other Arab countries.

SOCIAL AND CULTURAL RIGHTS

Social tension between women's rights and family obligations continues to impede the advancement of the status of women. Some within the conservative establishment fear that calls made by women's groups for equality, independence, and the right to work might lead to the destruction of the family unit. As a result of these dominant cultural attitudes and the divide between public and private life, Jordanian women face particular challenges in obtaining full social rights.

Women are legally free to choose their own physicians, visit health clinics, and make decisions about most aspects of their health care. However, they face a number of social and financial restrictions on their independence. According to customs prevalent in rural areas, many women do not visit the doctor alone, especially if they are unmarried. Moreover, a majority of women are financially dependent on their husbands or fathers, who must pay for their medication. Most women, particularly those who do not work, are beneficiaries of their husband's or father's employment-based health insurance, though working women enjoy full health coverage if their employer provides it.

Female civil servants are eligible for health insurance for themselves and their dependents if their husbands are not also public employees.[31]

Women working in the private sector may also extend their coverage to their children if they are not already covered by the husband's insurance, although benefits for private-sector workers vary in practice. The prevailing female dependence on a husband's financial support and health insurance means that medical expenses are a particular problem for divorced and widowed women.[32]

Under legislation covering family planning matters (Law No. 5 of 2004), a woman is not required to inform her husband or obtain his approval concerning her choice of contraception. However, contraceptive service providers seek the husband's approval in practice, and a husband's written consent is needed before a wife may undergo tubal ligation.[33] Forty-two percent of women were using contraceptives in 2007, while 40 percent discontinued the use of contraceptives after one year. Consequently, approximately 30 percent had unplanned pregnancies.[34]

Abortion is illegal in Jordan except in special circumstances to preserve the life or health of the mother.[35] Article 321 of the penal code prescribes penalties of six months to three years in prison for women who perform abortions on themselves, and Article 322 assigns one to three years in prison to those who perform abortions on others, including doctors. If an abortion leads to the death of the mother, the culprit faces a minimum sentence of five years in prison. Under Article 323, those who perform an abortion on a woman against her will can be sentenced to a maximum of 10 years in prison, or a minimum of 10 years if the woman dies. Article 324 provides for reduced sentences—ranging from three months to two years—if a woman performs her own abortion to protect her family's honor, or if the individual carrying out the abortion does so to protect the honor of a female relative.

The government is currently promoting family planning in an effort to reduce the fertility rate, which stood at 3.6 children per woman in 2007.[36] A survey released in July 2008 indicated that 94 percent of married women and 90 percent of married men believe smaller families lead to a better quality of life. However, only 44 percent of married women and 50 percent of married men practice family planning due to social pressures that include cultural preference for boys and the desire to have larger families. The survey also revealed that, regardless of educational background, married women continue to prefer to give birth to boys. The survey indicated that for uneducated women, the ideal number of boys would be 2.2, compared with 1.9 girls, while those with a higher degree preferred 2.1 boys, compared with 1.7 girls.[37]

A woman's right to housing is connected to her status as a wife or a daughter. According to Article 36 of the Personal Status Law, "the husband prepares a residence which includes the living necessities in accordance with his abilities." In the event of divorce, a woman only has a right to housing if she is nursing or has been given custody of the children. In general, social traditions discourage women from living alone, particularly when they are single. However, anecdotal evidence suggests that more single, widowed, or divorced women, mainly in the upper middle class, are now defying these norms by choosing to live alone. The Law of Owners and Lessees (No. 11 of 1994) declares that property intended for purposes other than residence should be transferred to the heirs of the deceased and to his wife. The wife and children in an arbitrary divorce or an ecclesiastical separation (whereby the husband abandons them along with the leased property) have the right to continue to occupy the property as original lessees, provided that a final judgment is issued from a competent court.

The populations most affected by poverty in Jordan are the elderly, the sick, widowed women, the disabled, and those without family support. These groups are often uneducated, have poor-quality housing, and are dependent on cash assistance and welfare services. Government welfare payments typically amount to about 36 dinars (US$51) a month per person for a family of five. The assistance varies based on the family's access to other income. Some are unable to gain access to welfare assistance and must depend on relatives, friends, or charity groups.

Widows, divorcees, abandoned women, and girls over age 18 with no provider are categorized as eligible for aid under the Law of the National Aid Fund (No. 36 of 1986). Jordanian women married to non-Jordanians are also eligible, but on an individual basis and subject to review by fund officials. In addition, emergency aid is provided to families if their financial provider has died, was imprisoned, or is ill, or if the family home was destroyed or affected by a natural disaster. Article 14 of the Regulation for Financial Assistance (No. 1 of 2008) states that this aid should not exceed 200 dinars (US$282).

Women are able to advocate openly for the promotion and protection of women's human rights in Jordan. The country's legal restrictions on freedoms of speech, assembly, and association are not typically applied to women's issues. While advocacy on topics such as honor crimes, women's reproductive rights, and sexual harassment is often met with skepticism in society, activists continue to lobby for advances in these areas. Women's overall participation in NGOs is on the rise, and women's groups are engaging in debates over domestic violence and women's political participation. However, the percentage of women working in NGOs outside of Amman and other urban areas remains relatively low, meaning rural women still have difficulty accessing the services and information provided by these groups.

Women remain poorly represented in Jordan's media sector, particularly in senior, decision-making positions, although they participate in multiple media, including radio, television, and Internet blogging. According to the former president of the Jordan Press Association, Tareq Momani, the group's 800 members include about 150 female journalists. No woman has ever served as editor in chief or assumed a high position in the leading Arabic dailies. Women have been appointed as editors in chief of several local magazines, but these have usually dealt with women's issues. Even so, more often than not, the image of women portrayed in the media often works against harmful traditional views and supports improvements in women's status.

Recommendations

❖ The government should enact health care regulations that ensure the confidentiality of women's decisions regarding contraception.

❖ The parliament should pass legislation granting men and women equal opportunities to extend employer-provided health insurance to their spouses and children.

❖ The government and media leaders should provide additional training to journalists on women's rights issues, including investigative reporting, and facilitate the research capabilities of more women in order to encourage gender-related analysis of social policies.

❖ The government should ensure that all women, and particularly those who have been divorced, abandoned, or widowed, have full access to a basic level of health care and housing, in part through the designation of special clinics and housing units for vulnerable populations.

❖ Women's rights organizations and governmental bodies should actively engage men in their grassroots outreach and educational campaigns to combat gender discrimination.

AUTHOR

Rana Husseini is a journalist, author, consultant, and women's rights activist based in Jordan. While writing for the *Jordan Times*, the country's leading English-language daily, she focused on social issues, with a special emphasis on so-called honor crimes and other forms of violence against women. She has worked on these topics with domestic NGOs as well as international organizations including UNIFEM, Equality Now, and Freedom House. She is the author of *Murder in the Name of Honor*, a new book on the effort to combat honor crimes.

NOTES

1   Samar Haddadin, "Jordanian Women Contributed in Achieving and Strengthening Independence," *Al-Rai*, June 5, 2009, http://www.alrai.com/pages.php?news_id=273 982.

2   Haddadin, "Jordanian Women."

3   The possible penalties for violations of the Societies Law include fines ranging from US$1,400 to US$14,000, up to six months' imprisonment, and seizure of the organization's finances. Women's rights activists said the law would leave them at the mercy of the government, which would be free to meddle in their decisions. The government defended the measure by stressing that it replaced a 42-year-old statute and was meant only to regulate the work of these organizations. Although officials yielded to local and international pressure and promised to study the activists' complaints, the government had taken no action by year's end to amend the law or draft a new version.

4   Shari'a Courts also handle issues pertaining to the Islamic *waqfs*. Regular courts have jurisdiction in cases involving parties of different religions.

5   Rana Husseini, "Man Receives Reduced Sentence for Killing Sister," *Jordan Times*, December 1, 2008, http://www.jordantimes.com/index.php?news=12512.

6   "Special Tribunal to Hear Honour Crimes in Jordan," *Gulf News*, July 29, 2009, http://gulfnews.com/news/region/jordan/special-tribunal-to-hear-honour-crimes-in-jordan-1.503127.

7   For the text of CEDAW, see http://www.un.org/womenwatch/daw/cedaw/text/econven tion.htm; for Jordan's reservations, see http://daccessdds.un.org/doc/UNDOC/GEN/N06/309/97/PDF/N0630997.pdf?OpenElement.

8   Law No. 82 of 2001, amending the Personal Status Law (No. 61 of 1976).

9   Article 6/A of the Personal Status Law.

10 *Combined Third and Fourth Reports of States Parties: Jordan* (New York: UN Committee on the Elimination of Discrimination against Women, March 10, 2006), 89, http://www.un.org/womenwatch/daw/cedaw/reports.htm#j.

11 Amnesty International, *Isolated and Abused: Women Migrant Domestic Workers in Jordan Denied Their Rights* (London: Amnesty International, October 30, 2008), 2–3, http://www.amnesty.org/en/library/info/MDE16/002/2008/en.

12 "Jordan: Government Adopts Anti–Human Trafficking Law," Integrated Regional Information Networks (IRIN), January 27, 2009, http://www.irinnews.org/report.aspx ?ReportId=82587; Office to Monitor and Combat Trafficking in Persons, *Trafficking in Persons Report 2009* (Washington, DC: U.S. Department of State, 2009), http://www.state .gov/g/tip/rls/tiprpt/2009/index.htm.

13 "Jordan: Project Launched to Fight Violence Against Women," IRIN, September 12, 2007, http://www.irinnews.org/Report.aspx?ReportId=74255.

14 Rana Husseini, "52 Women Seeking Legal Guidance Contact Complaint Office," *Jordan Times*, February 12, 2009, http://www.jordantimes.com/?news=14230.

15 Musa Shtwei, *Economic Marginalization of the Jordanian Woman* (UNIFEM, 2008), 16, http://www.unifem.org.jo/Attachments/1358/5b8a9df3-0fb9-4606-a938-9bc1ef673 55d.pdf (in Arabic).

16 According to the report, "Rather than contributing to the family economy and national economic growth, an abused woman is more likely to be less productive and will have needs that require greater social spending on hospitals, police, courts, and crisis response systems." See Layla Naffa, Fatima al-Dabbas, Afaf Jabiri, and Nour al-Emam, *Shadow NGO Report to CEDAW Committee Jordan: Evaluation of National Policy, Measures and Actual Facts on Violence Against Women* (Karama Network of Jordan, July 2007), http:// www.iwraw-ap.org/resources/pdf/39_shadow_reports/Jordanian_SR_2.pdf.

17 Jordan Department of Statistics, *Jordanian Woman in Numbers* (Amman: Department of Statistics, March 2009), http://www.dos.gov.jo/sdb_pop/sdb_pop_e/ehsaat/alsokan/ wom_in/home_w4.htm.

18 Noncitizens must pay higher fees to access government schools, particularly at the university level.

19 Jordan Department of Statistics, *Jordanian Woman in Numbers*. See also http://www .dos.gov.jo/dos_home_e/king.htm.

20 Hani Hazaimeh, "Women Contribute 8 Percent of GDP," *Jordan Times*, March 10, 2008, http://www.jordantimes.com/index.php?news=6308.

21 Hani Hazaimeh, "Women Contribute 8 Percent of GDP."

22 Jordan Department of Statistics, *Jordanian Woman in Numbers*.

23 Musa Shtwei, *Economic Marginalization*, 16.

24 World Bank, "GenderStats—Create Your Own Table," http://go.worldbank.org/MRER 20PME0.

25 Article 56, Social Security Law (Law No. 19 of 2001), http://www.ssc.gov.jo/english.

26 Amnesty International, *Isolated and Abused*, 2–3.

27 Bureau of Democracy, Human Rights, and Labor, "Jordan," in *2008 Country Reports on Human Rights Practices* (Washington, DC: U.S. Department of State, 2009), http:// www.state.gov/g/drl/rls/hrrpt/2008/nea/119118.htm .

28 Taylor Luck, "Women's Participation in Islamist Parties on the Rise—Study," *Jordan Times*, February 18, 2009, http://www.jordantimes.com/index.php?news=14384.

29 UNIFEM, "Table 9," in *Jordanian Women's Participation in Political Life: An Analytical Study of the Performance of Female Deputies in the 14th Parliament of 2003* (UNIFEM, 2007), 45, http://unifem.org.jo/Attachments/1124/5cb902a9-8653-430d-8859-9f6b 86cb8c3d.pdf.

30 Taylor Luck, "Women's Participation."

31 *Combined Third and Fourth Reports of States Parties: Jordan*, 61.

32 Layla Naffa, *Shadow NGO Report*, 13.

33 Layla Naffa, *Shadow NGO Report*, 13.

34 Dalya Dajani, "Focus on Family Planning Essential to Further Reduce Fertility Rates," *Jordan Times*, November 19, 2008, http://www.jordantimes.com/?news=12232.

35 Health Law No. 20 of 1971, Section 62[a]. Prior approval by two physicians is necessary, as is the signed consent of the pregnant women unless she is incapacitated, at which point her husband or guardian must consent in her place.

36 See World Bank, "GenderStats—Create Your Own Table."

37 Dalya Dajani, "Social Norms, Gender Preference Hindering Family Planning," *Jordan Times*, July 21, 2008, http://www.jordantimes.com/?news=9451.

KUWAIT

by Haya al-Mughni

| POPULATION: | 2,985,000 | | |
| GNI PER CAPITA: | US$43,063 | | |

COUNTRY RATINGS	2004	2009
NONDISCRIMINATION AND ACCESS TO JUSTICE:	1.9	2.2
AUTONOMY, SECURITY, AND FREEDOM OF THE PERSON:	2.2	2.4
ECONOMIC RIGHTS AND EQUAL OPPORTUNITY:	2.9	3.1
POLITICAL RIGHTS AND CIVIC VOICE:	1.4	2.4
SOCIAL AND CULTURAL RIGHTS:	2.8	2.9

(COUNTRY RATINGS ARE BASED ON A SCALE OF 1 TO 5, WITH 1 REPRESENTING THE LOWEST AND 5 THE HIGHEST LEVEL OF FREEDOM WOMEN HAVE TO EXERCISE THEIR RIGHTS)

INTRODUCTION

Since the 1960s, Kuwaiti women have enjoyed access to higher education and relative freedom to advocate for improved economic and cultural rights, particularly as compared to women in neighboring countries. Kuwait's first women's organizations actively lobbied for the broader involvement of women in the labor market, equal political rights, and greater cultural and educational opportunities. It was the 1990–91 Iraqi occupation of Kuwait, however, that arguably served as a catalyst for the eventual liberalization of women's political and social rights. During that period, many women assumed important social responsibilities and were instrumental in the survival of their besieged community. Some volunteered in hospitals to compensate for the lack of medical staff; others smuggled food, money, and weapons across military checkpoints.

The ousted government made several public promises that after Kuwait was liberated, women would "play a greater role and make more noble contributions" to the country that they had valiantly helped to defend, an apparent nod toward granting them rights on par with men.[1] After the occupation ended, women did assume new and influential titles including university rector, vice-president of the Kuwait Oil Company, and even ambassador when, in 1993, Nabila al-Mulla became the first female ambassador in the Gulf region.[2] True political equality, however, remained elusive as the Election Law (No. 35 of 1962) continued to ban political rights for women for another decade.

In May 1999, during an interregnum between parliaments, the emir of Kuwait promulgated a decree granting women the right to vote and run for office in parliamentary and municipal elections. However, the decree was overturned by the parliament several months later. In protest, civic activists organized a series of demonstrations, during which hundreds of women stormed registration offices in an attempt to vote and enter their names on the ballots. After being turned away, they challenged this in courts in hopes that the judiciary would hold the election law unconstitutional.[3] However, the cases were dismissed on technicalities, sparking mass demonstrations and bringing the issue to the international forefront.[4] Another government-sponsored bill that would give women the right to vote and run in municipal councils was rejected by the parliament in 2003.

Because of the combined efforts of activists, lawyers, politicians, and everyday citizens, women were finally granted full political rights in May 2005. Kuwaiti women voted and ran for office in the 2006 and 2008 municipal and national elections, although no female candidates were successful in their bids for office. The May 2009 national elections, however, saw the election of four women, Kuwait's first female parliamentarians.[5] Considering that the National Assembly has the power to overturn decrees issued by the emir, women now have the unprecedented potential to directly influence Kuwaiti society.[6] The government has also integrated women into the national decision-making process by assigning ministerial portfolios to three women since 2005 and appointing two others to the Municipal Council, which controls the administration of public services.

Despite these significant developments, Kuwaiti women still face discrimination in many areas of life. They remain prohibited from serving as judges and joining the military, have unequal marital rights, and are not allowed to pass their nationality on to their children and foreign-born husbands. They also lack equal rights in laws regulating social security, pensions, and inheritance. Provisions regarding inheritance, however, are mandated in the Koran and take into consideration that men, legally and socially, bear the burden of financial responsibility for all female family members. As a result there is little, if any, political or popular will to change this practice.

Advocacy for women's rights in Kuwait has been strong and visible in recent years, particularly with respect to political participation. Although the women's movement achieved a monumental milestone with the election of female candidates to the parliament in 2009, activists today still face challenges as turnout among female voters has been consistently low. Furthermore, the amended election law requires all voters and candidates, regardless of their gender or religion, to adhere to the principles and rules of Shari'a (Islamic law). This ambiguous requirement has led conservative Islamist parliamentarians to exert mounting pressure on the government to compel women ministers to wear the veil, with the National Assembly's legal and legislative committee in 2008 going so far as to find female ministers who refused to wear the *hijab* (headscarf) while being sworn in guilty of having violated the constitution and the elections law.[7]

Islamists have dominated Kuwait's parliament since the first postwar national elections in 1992. Their rise to power is partly the result of their strong grassroots organizations and community-outreach programs. Their message of social justice, anticorruption, and religious authenticity has had a great appeal among the electorate, including women. While the Islamists' call to make Shari'a the main source of legislation has been a contentious issue in national politics, they have succeeded in passing a number of laws with conservative overtones. These efforts include a women's early retirement bill intended to enable mothers to devote their time to child rearing, a measure imposing gender segregation in postsecondary schools, and a law that criminalizes cross-dressing.[8]

Government restrictions on nongovernmental organizations (NGOs) and freedom of assembly present additional challenges to women's rights activists. Formal political parties are banned, but numerous informal political groups are active both inside and outside the parliament. Kuwait's NGOs, which have had a wider impact on society than many political groups, are controlled and funded by the state. The government has, however, made some institutional efforts to address human rights issues directly. The Kuwait Human Rights Society was finally licensed in 2004 after much struggle, and the following year, the Ministry of Justice established a Human Rights Committee to review and address human rights violations in accordance with national laws. In addition, the parliament's Human Rights Defense Committee set up an Expatriate Workers Affairs Committee to deal with individual complaints from foreigners living in the country. Despite an apparent interest among the political elite in minimizing abuse and discrimination on a wider societal level, the issue of women's rights is more complex due to the country's patriarchal culture and conservative interpretation of Islam.

This prompts the question of what women's rights NGOs should do to preserve the gains to date and advance citizenship rights in the future. There is no single solution to this challenge. One possible strategy is to engage in an open dialogue with the Islamist groups and their supporters, with the goal of reaching a consensus on what constitutes women's civil rights. Women's groups may also need to influence the representation of women in the media to highlight the social realities of women's lives, as well as reenergize their campaign message with new ideas, such as the notion of social justice, to appeal to a larger segment of society. Finally, they should reach out to other local NGOs both to galvanize support for female political candidates and to encourage greater coordination among such candidates during national and local elections.

NONDISCRIMINATION AND ACCESS TO JUSTICE

Over the past five years, Kuwait has made limited progress in bringing national laws in line with international standards for nondiscrimination. Until recently, the country lacked an institution devoted specifically to the enforcement of human rights, instead relying on several independent committees within different governmental bodies. In 2005, the Ministry of Justice set up a Human Rights Committee to review and address human rights violations. Little information is available, however, on the committee's work or its effectiveness.

Although Kuwait's constitution recognizes the principle of equality among its citizens regardless of "race, origin, language, or religion," it contains no specific protections against gender-based discrimination, and national laws continue to discriminate against women. In a few glaring instances, such as the Social Security Law (No. 22 of 1987) and the Housing Assistance Law (No. 47 of 1993), Kuwait's laws and policies still treat women as dependents of men rather than individuals with equal rights and responsibilities.

Female Kuwaiti citizens remain unable to confer their nationality on their children or foreign-born spouses, while Kuwaiti men are permitted to exercise this right. A Kuwaiti woman married to a foreign national can transfer her nationality to her children only if the father is unknown or has died, or if there has been an "irrevocable" divorce. Conversely, the foreign-born wife of a Kuwaiti man may become a Kuwaiti national after 10 years or less of marriage.

The noncitizen husbands of Kuwaiti women, like temporary foreign workers, are treated as guest workers under the Residency Law (No. 17 of 1959). To remain in the country, both populations must have valid work permits, pay residency fees, and renew their residency permits every three years or less. The same conditions apply to the mature children of Kuwaiti women married to noncitizens. On the other hand, the foreign wife of a Kuwaiti man is granted immediate residency upon marriage.[9]

Kuwait has a three-tiered judicial system consisting of the courts of first instance, the appeals court, and the Court of Cassation. Additional specialized courts exist for administrative, military, and constitutional cases. Personal matters, including marriage, divorce, and inheritance, are governed by Shari'a but handled in the state's court system. For these matters, Sunni and Shiite Muslims have recourse to courts that adhere to their respective schools of Islam. Family law courts value the testimony of a woman as half that of a man, but all other courts consider the testimony of men and women to be equal.

The criminal procedures code provides all residents, regardless of their gender or nationality, with equal access to courts and entitles them to a court-assigned lawyer and an interpreter. All victims have the right to seek recompense through the courts, but enforcement mechanisms to ensure the implementation of judicial decisions remain weak.[10] Most foreign-born domestic workers are unaware of their legal rights and are often reluctant to bring charges if they have suffered a serious offense or violence at the hands of their employers.

Kuwait's penal code is generally nondiscriminatory, although it still permits reduced sentences for men who commit honor killings. In principle, all perpetrators of murder, rape, kidnapping, or violence against women are subject to penalties ranging from lengthy prison sentences to the death penalty. According to Article 153 of the Penal Code (No. 16 of 1960), however, if a husband kills his wife or her illicit partner during an adulterous act, his sentence is capped at three years in prison. The same penalty applies for anyone who, in the heat of the moment, kills his daughter, sister, or mother for their involvement in acts of *zina* (unlawful sexual relations) carried out before him. Honor killings in Kuwait are rare, and in the past five years only one was reported: the murder of a young woman by her brothers in 2006. More recently, a young girl was given police protection after reporting that her family intended to kill her over an affair with an unrelated man in 2008. The male members of her family were arrested, detained for questioning, and later released on bail.[11]

Kuwait continues to implement the death penalty, but mothers of dependent children are not executed, and the penal code prohibits the execution of pregnant women. Women are housed in a separate prison from men, and those who are pregnant are exempted from prison work and receive special treatment in terms of food and rest.[12] In 2008, the emir responded to a direct appeal by the president of the Philippines and reduced the death sentence of a Filipina domestic worker to life imprisonment for the murder of her Kuwaiti employer. Another Filipina maid is on death row for killing her employers' two children. The Court of Cassation has submitted the death sentence in that case to the emir for final approval.[13]

Sexual relations outside marriage are considered moral crimes, and those engaging in such activities run the risk of arrest, imprisonment, and deportation. Prostitution is illegal. Under Article 194 of the penal code, consensual sexual relationships between adults who are not married to each other are punishable by up to three years' imprisonment. Article 195 mandates an even harsher punishment for adultery: any married person who has consensual sexual relations with a person other than his or her spouse can be punished by up to five years' imprisonment.

Kuwait ratified the UN Convention on the Elimination of All Forms of Discrimination against Women (CEDAW) in 1994 with reservations on Article 9, paragraph 2 concerning citizenship rights and Article 7 regarding equal voting rights. Reservations were also appended to Article 16, paragraph 1(f), which calls for equal rights on guardianship and the adoption of children, on the grounds that they were incompatible with Shari'a. In December 2005, Kuwait lifted its reservation related to women's political participation and subsequently took steps to integrate women into the political sphere as government ministers.

Women's rights activists are generally free to advocate openly against discriminatory laws and women's unequal access to justice. Although activists and organizations, in particular the Women's Cultural and Social Society (WCSS), have lobbied for laws that would permit women to pass their Kuwaiti citizenship to their noncitizen children, the government has not taken any measures to address gender inequality in nationality laws.

Recommendations

❖ The government should amend the Kuwait Nationality Act of 1959 to ensure that Kuwaiti women have the same rights as Kuwaiti men to transfer citizenship to their children and foreign-born spouses.

❖ The government and NGOs should create and promote legal resource guides, community seminars, and public awareness campaigns that educate women, particularly domestic workers, about their legal rights and steps to enforce them.

❖ The government should amend the penal code to eliminate leniency for honor killings.

❖ The government should remove all reservations to CEDAW and take steps to bring national laws into conformity with the convention; Kuwaiti NGOs should jointly produce a shadow report that monitors the government's implementation of CEDAW.

AUTONOMY, SECURITY, AND FREEDOM OF THE PERSON

The state religion of Kuwait is Islam, and the majority of Kuwaiti nationals are Muslim; roughly 70 percent of those are Sunni and 30 percent are Shiite. Foreign nationals, however, make up 68 percent of Kuwait's resident population and include Muslims, Christians, Hindus, and Sikhs. The government has actively promoted religious tolerance and interfaith dialogue in recent years.

Muslim women have the freedom to practice their religion. A growing number of Kuwaiti women are choosing to adhere to an Islamic lifestyle by wearing the hijab, attending Islamic schools, and performing the *hajj* (pilgrimage to Mecca). They see Islam as an intrinsic part of their cultural identity and many reach out to teach others the values and principles of Islam, reflecting the long-held practice of Kuwaiti women serving as religious teachers. Non-Muslim women also enjoy religious freedom. Kuwait has officially recognized seven Christian denominations: Roman Catholic, Anglican, Greek Orthodox, Armenian Orthodox, Coptic Orthodox, Greek Catholic, and National Evangelical. Minority groups such as Sikhs, Hindus, Buddhists, and others are allowed to practice their religions but are limited to private homes or the premises of the recognized churches.

Kuwaiti women enjoy relatively uninhibited freedom of movement and may travel abroad without a *muharam* (male relative). Many companies send their female employees abroad for business trips or conferences, and it is uncommon for women to face problems in their employment due to gender-related travel restrictions. Article 15 of the Passport Law (No. 11 of 1962), which prohibited a married Kuwaiti woman from applying for a passport without the consent of her husband, was overturned in October 2009. Now all women over 21 years old may obtain a passport without permission from their husbands or guardians. Social norms, rather than law, require Kuwaiti women to notify or, depending on the strictness of their family, get permission from their parents to travel abroad or visit friends at night. Police generally do not arrest and return a woman to her family if she is found to be traveling alone.

Depending on their sect, Muslim women are affected by one of two sets of active family laws in Kuwait. Personal life for Sunnis is regulated by the Personal Status Law (No. 51 of 1984), based on the Maliki school of Sunni Islam, while Shiite family law is based on the Jaafari school of interpretation. The treatment of women differs slightly under the two schools, particularly in areas of marriage, child custody, and inheritance. For instance, Sunni family law is more restrictive toward women's marital rights, while Shiite family law is more restrictive toward women's custody rights. Furthermore, while Sunni family law allows women to inherit a physical piece of property, under Shiite law a woman can inherit only the value of the property.[14]

The personal status law legitimizes male dominance over women. While it requires husbands to support their wives and children, the law nevertheless does not endow the husband with the absolute right to expect *ta'a* (obedience). Article 89 specifies that a husband should not forbid his wife from working outside the home unless the work negatively affects "family interests," but the phrase is ambiguous and can be interpreted as referring to the stability of the marriage or the upbringing of the children.

Kuwaiti society continues to uphold the notion that the role of women should be primarily limited to the domestic sphere, taking care of children. Reflecting this tendency, a 2006 bill that received wide support would have, among other things, granted stay-at-home mothers a monthly allowance of 250 dinars (US$876). The proposed bill—containing 27 articles regarding women's social security, housing benefits, and work leave—was put on the agenda in the parliament, but it was later withdrawn following objections from women's rights organizations. Objections were raised specifically to articles that would have increased maternity leave from 40 days to 70 days and provided for six months of paid childcare leave with the option to extend it to three years at quarter pay. Women's rights advocates claimed that the prolonged leave would encourage women to stay at home, depriving the labor market of their productivity while discouraging the private sector from recruiting women due to the financial burden it would impose on employers.[15]

Women have unequal marriage rights under Kuwaiti law. A husband is allowed to have more than one wife under both Sunni and Shiite family law without the permission or even the knowledge of his first wife. A wife may not petition for divorce on the grounds that her husband has taken another wife. However, the personal status law bars the husband from bringing his second wife to live with the first unless the first wife agrees. Article 85 states that a husband must provide each wife with accommodation, although an aggrieved first wife does not always file a complaint in court. Furthermore, under Article 86, a husband cannot have adult male family members unrelated to his wife live in the same house with her.

Under the personal status law, a divorced woman retains custody of her children until her sons reach 15 years of age and her daughters are married. Shiite family law, however, grants a divorced mother custody of her daughter until the age of nine and the son until the age of two.[16] Child-support benefits offered by the state are allocated solely to men, even when a woman is awarded custody rights. In both schools of Islam, the mother forfeits her right to custody if she remarries. Should a husband divorce his wife on the grounds of her infidelity, he can receive custody of his young children, and the family courts are often willing to take issues of infidelity into account when judgments are made concerning child custody and maintenance.[17]

Kuwaiti women are provided with some protection against arbitrary divorce and mistreatment. A woman may receive financial compensation equal to one year of maintenance if her husband divorces her without her consent, but implementation of court verdicts is often irregular.[18] A woman has the right to seek a divorce if her husband fails to maintain her financially. In that case, the judge can grant the husband a period of time in which to pay maintenance, and if he fails to do so his wife may seek a divorce. She also has the right to seek a separation from her husband on the grounds of *darar* (physical or moral injury) or if he has deserted her, including if the husband is sentenced to a term of imprisonment. In such cases, however, proof of injury is required, which is often difficult to obtain because women are reluctant to file complaints with the police and do not report causes of injury to doctors. Unsupportive and untrained police and doctors who examine abuse cases also hinder the gathering of evidence.

Women do not have the legal right to choose their future marital partners freely and independently. By law, a Sunni woman cannot conclude a marriage contract without the presence and consent of her *wali* (marriage guardian). The wali is usually the woman's father or, in his absence, her brother, uncle, or other close male relative. The presence of the wali is required even in the case of divorcees, widows, and women who have reached the age of maturity, which is 25 years in Kuwait. Under Shiite family law, the participation of the guardian is not required; a woman who has reached the legal age for marriage may marry whomever she wishes, and the validity of the contract is not dependent on the presence of the guardian.[19]

A woman may refuse to marry altogether and remain single, but the social burden placed on aging single women is so high that most women prefer an unhappy marriage to the stigma associated with being a spinster. If a wali has refused the choice of husband of a woman over the age of 25, Sunni family law grants her the right to petition the family court to act as a surrogate wali. Regardless, she may not be forced into a marriage and must always agree with the final decision. Some women opt to marry outside Kuwait to circumvent the marriage restrictions, but these marriages are not legally recognized within the country, and the head of the bride's family has the right to ask the court to annul the marriage.

The minimum legal age for marriage is 15 for girls and 17 for boys. Within the urban community, it is rare for girls to be married at an early age or forced into marriage. However, arranged marriages between families of similar social standing are still the norm.

Kuwait's penal code prohibits all forms of slavery, torture, cruelty, or degrading punishments regardless of age, gender, religion, or nationality. No instances of slavery-like practices such as forced marriages and confinement to the home have been formally reported in recent years, but there are no specific protections against these practices either.

Kuwait's Labor Law (No. 38 of 1964) specifies that a working day should be restricted to eight hours. However, this law does not apply to domestic workers, the majority of whom are women working long hours at very low wages. Ministerial Decree (No. 60 of 2007) prohibits the increasingly common practice of employers withholding the passports of domestic workers.[20] Domestic workers may take legal action against their employers by filing complaints directly with the police, and all abused employees may complain to Kuwait's administrative courts.

In recent years Kuwait has made strides toward increasing protections for domestic workers. In 2005, the parliament's Human Rights Defense Committee set up the Expatriate Workers Affairs Committee to deal with individual complaints from foreigners living in the country. In addition, a shelter for runaway domestic workers has been created, and it operates closely with the Kuwait Union of Domestic Labor Offices (KUDLO). Licensed in 2003 for the protection of domestic workers, KUDLO provides a wide range of services for abused workers, including free legal counsel.[21]

Data and research on domestic violence in Kuwait continues to be sparse, making it difficult to assess the severity of the problem. No known NGO or government office works efficiently to collect such statistics. This scarcity of information is partly due to the societal belief that domestic violence is a family affair. Fear and shame often discourage victims of abuse from filing complaints with the police, and little effort has gone into providing assistance or protection to such victims. There are no laws against domestic violence, nor are there any shelters, support centers, or free legal services to aid female victims.

By contrast, gender-based violence such as rape and sexual assault that occurs outside the home tends to receive more scrutiny from the police and the press than incidents of domestic violence. Anyone found guilty of sexual violence may face a prison sentence or the death penalty, depending on the severity of the case. There have been reports of physical abuse of female detainees in police custody, but no monitoring mechanism is in place to record such violations systematically.

Family laws have been increasingly scrutinized in recent years by women's rights NGOs and activists. In 2007, the parliament's Women's Affairs Committee organized a conference on the status of women in national laws, during which calls were made to amend discriminatory provisions of divorce and marriage laws. In 2008 and 2009, the WCSS, in conjunction with Freedom House and the UN Development Fund for Women (UNIFEM), organized forums on women's rights and civil status law.[22] Despite these efforts, the government has been slow to introduce and implement changes in legislation regarding women's autonomy, security, and freedom of person.

Recommendations

❖ The government should amend the marriage contract rules under family law to allow all Kuwaiti women over age 18 to marry the partners of their choice.

❖ The government or private institutions should fund domestic violence centers to provide temporary shelter, legal assistance, and counseling for battered women.

❖ Government agency personnel responsible for law enforcement and health services should receive in-depth training on dealing with violence against women and children so that they are positioned to assist and protect victims of violence more effectively.

❖ The government should seek to protect migrant workers from abuse and exploitation—with special attention to female domestic workers—by introducing tougher penalties for employers who violate their rights and making it mandatory for all families to put the wages of their domestic workers in bank accounts, a rule that currently applies to workers in the public sector.

❖ The government or other bodies should create an independent women's rights research center tasked with compiling and publishing qualitative and quantitative data in a range of areas concerning women, such as domestic violence, social policies, employment, and women's health.

ECONOMIC RIGHTS AND EQUAL OPPORTUNITY

Women in Kuwait enjoy high literacy and employment rates, and their enrollment in postsecondary education and participation in the workforce have increased over the past decade. The government has invested efforts to create more employment opportunities for all Kuwaitis, men and women; however, the results have been mixed.[23]

Kuwaiti women are entitled to own and have full and independent use of their land, property, income, and assets. Nonetheless, their right to inheritance is unequal to that of men in accordance with the Koran, which stipulates that a woman's share is equal to half that of her brother. This reflects the Shari'a requirement that, while a woman may use her inheritance for her sole benefit, a male beneficiary must use his inheritance to support all the dependent female members of his family.

Kuwaiti women may enter freely into business and financial contracts and activities at all levels without the permission of a male family member. All Kuwaitis over 21 years of age may conduct any commercial activity in Kuwait provided that they are not affected by a personal legal restriction, such as a criminal record. In recent years, women have been increasingly willing to start their own businesses and gain economic independence.

According to Article 40 of the constitution, all Kuwaiti citizens are guaranteed free and equal access to the education system from primary school through university, and male and female students are provided with equal opportunities to study abroad. Women have made significant gains in education over the past three decades, and the percentage of young literate women in Kuwait is now equal to that of young literate men.

Women do not face any extraordinary obstacles in attending universities or enrolling in diverse courses of study, and they graduate at higher rates than men. At Kuwait University, however, female students are required to maintain significantly higher grade-point averages (GPAs) than men in order to be admitted into selected fields. For instance, female students must have a 3.3 GPA to be admitted to the engineering department, while male students need only a 2.8 GPA. As women comprise almost two-thirds of Kuwaiti university students, the disparity in admission requirements is officially justified as positive discrimination intended to increase the percentage of male students in certain academic fields.[24] Women outnumber men at the institutions of higher education in Kuwait largely because men often choose to pursue their degrees abroad.

A decade-old debate regarding segregation of postsecondary schools has recently resurfaced in the National Assembly. A 2000 law instituting gender segregation in private postsecondary schools remains unenforced, in part due to the inherently high costs associated with such an endeavor. However, in January 2008 the minister of higher education announced that the law would be implemented. This has left the National Assembly divided as liberal members call for the law to be rescinded or amended while conservative members push for its strict enforcement.[25] A similar law applicable to public postsecondary schools was enacted in 1996 and enforced in 2001, but because Kuwait University is the country's only public university, fewer logistical constraints existed to affect its implementation. In debating whether to segregate private universities, many have questioned whether men and women will receive equal educations and whether enforcing such measures will lead to greater segregation and conservatism throughout Kuwaiti society in general.[26]

Access to education has enabled women to become financially independent and pursue diverse careers. Women are now found in most professions including engineering, architecture, medicine, and law, as well as on executive boards of major banks and private companies. As of 2007, approximately 44 percent of working-age women were employed, with the majority working in the public sector.[27] The Ministry of the Interior has proposed a police academy for women to increase their participation in the police force, and in July 2008, the ministry began accepting applications from women seeking to join. Women still hold predominantly administrative and secretarial positions at the Ministry of Defense, however, and cannot join the army or work as judges in courts. Unemployment has risen recently among both men and women, with 7.5 percent of Kuwaiti female graduates unemployed in 2007, compared with 5.1 percent of Kuwaiti male graduates.[28] All citizens, women and men, are entitled to unemployment benefits equal to the minimum salary permitted in Kuwait.

Certain gender-based restrictions govern women's working hours and conditions. Article 23 of the labor law restricts female employees from working at night and, under Article 24, in jobs that may be hazardous to their well-being. Amendments to the law were passed in 2007 that specifically prohibit women from working between the hours of 8:00 p.m. and 7:00 a.m., but exempting those employed in medicine and a few other fields. Women are banned from working in positions that serve only men on the premise of protecting them from immoral exploitation. The amended law also includes a provision that gives the Ministry of Social Affairs and Labor (MOSAL) the authority to inspect employers, file reports, and arrest violators.[29]

Women and men performing the same type of work within the private sector must be paid equal wages under Article 27 of the labor law; similar protections exist in the public sector as well.[30] If a woman feels that she has been discriminated against, she may file a complaint directly with the administrative court or MOSAL. However, MOSAL lacks qualified staff to handle and investigate discrimination cases, and it has been swamped by a deluge of complaints that has rendered its work almost ineffectual. In 2007 alone, MOSAL received 14,840 complaints from expatriate workers, all related to unpaid wages and benefits. To date, 42 percent of these complaints remain unresolved.[31] Although the penal code generally addresses harassment, no laws specifically protect women from sexual harassment in the workplace despite the urgent need for such legislation, particularly among foreign women and domestic workers.

Gender-specific benefits such as the right to maternity leave and childcare exist in both the private and public sectors. Working women are entitled to 40 days of maternity leave after delivery and another four months' leave without pay if they certify that they are ill as a result of the pregnancy. Daycare facilities, both publicly and privately funded, are widely available and affordable in all parts of Kuwait for children aged three to six, although some complain that their hours of operation are not adequate for working women.

Women are entitled to pensions, but upon death their benefits are transferred to their dependent children and spouses only under specific conditions. Articles 64 and 65 of the social security law state that the pension of the deceased wife goes to the children if they are younger than 28 years old, and to the husband if he is unable to work due to a disability. If the children are employed or the only children are married daughters, the pension expires. If any other family members prove that they were dependent on the woman's income, they receive part of the pension.[32]

Women's rights organizations publicly protested the 2007 labor restrictions for fear that they could pave the way for further discrimination against women. The WCSS held a rally at its headquarters in June 2007 that drew many influential political figures and women's rights activists.[33] Despite this support, gender discrimination and stereotypes are likely to persist in light of the perceived threat of women's employment to men's job prospects and the dominance of conservative groups in the parliament.

Recommendations

✤ The government should enact laws that ensure equal employment opportunities and conduct public-awareness campaigns to eradicate the traditional gender stereotypes that inhibit women's participation in the workforce.

✤ The government should set gender-specific hiring targets for government jobs, with an emphasis on recruiting qualified women for expert and supervisory positions in all ministries.

✤ The government should establish and provide adequate resources for an independent complaint commission to investigate violations of workers' rights, including gender-based discrimination complaints filed by women against public or private actors and institutions.

✤ The government should amend its employment benefits and pension policies to ensure equal rights for men and women.

✤ The government should enact legislation that bans sexual harassment in the workplace, assigns penalties for employers who tolerate it, and provides for victim compensation.

POLITICAL RIGHTS AND CIVIC VOICE

The political rights of Kuwaiti women have sharply improved over the past five years. Today, women may vote in national and municipal elections, have been elected to parliament, and have been appointed to ministerial positions. Since 2004, new laws have been adopted that permit greater freedom of association and expression, but political parties remain banned.

Women have the right to peaceful assembly on par with men and may take part in organized protests and marches. In March 2005, a series of public demonstrations against the exclusion of women from the political process took place in front of parliament. Women were the dominant presence at these protests, although men sympathetic to the cause took part. There were no reports of harassment by the authorities taking place, and the protests were guarded by a heavy police presence. The attention created by these rallies increased pressure on parliament to address the issue, and two months later the election laws were amended to permit full political rights for women.[34]

The Public Gathering Law (No. 65 of 1979) previously required permission from authorities prior to public meetings or rallies, but it was amended in 2006 so that citizens must simply provide notice of organized public gatherings.[35] Neither notification nor permission is required to hold a *diwaniya*, an informal gathering in the home or a room adjacent to the home. Previously confined to the extended family and immediate local community, diwaniyas now bring together different groups of people, including politicians, and are important arenas for political activity. Only a few are open to both men and women, but during the recent election campaigns a number of women candidates visited diwaniyas, and some even held their own.[36]

In 2006, the parliament eased restrictions on freedom of expression by amending the Printing and Publications Law (No. 3 of 1961). The amended law prohibits the imprisonment of authors and journalists without a court verdict and gives citizens the right to appeal in court if their applications for newspaper licenses are rejected by the government. Incitement of religious hatred, criticism of the emir, and calls to overthrow the government, however, remain criminal acts punishable by up to one year in prison and fines.[37] Women's rights issues are discussed freely in the media, representing both conservative and more liberal points of view.

Women are not represented in Kuwait's judiciary. While they may hold positions as investigative judges, they are not permitted to serve as judges in court. Women account for 20 percent of the members of the Kuwait Bar Association.[38] Women's participation in the diplomatic corps is limited, and until recently only a few women were assigned to diplomatic positions.

Kuwaiti women gained access to local and national government structures in 2005 when two were appointed to the Municipal Council. The council, which controls the administration of public services, has 10 elected members and six members appointed by the emir. Within the national government, Massouma al-Mubarak became the first woman to hold a ministerial portfolio when she was appointed as minister of planning and minister of state for administrative development affairs in 2005. In 2007, Nuryia al-Subeih was appointed minister of education and higher studies, and in May 2008, Modhi al-Homoud was appointed minister for housing and administrative planning. Neither woman wore the hijab when they were sworn in to the new cabinet, and nine Islamist parliamentarians walked out to protest this perceived violation of the Shari'a dress code.[39] Following the cabinet restructuring accompanying the May 2009 parliamentary elections, Modhi al-Homoud was reassigned as the minister of education, becoming the sole woman in the 16-member cabinet.[40]

On May 16, 2005, the parliament amended the election law to allow Kuwaiti women to vote and hold elected office.[41] Due to pressure from Islamist parliamentarians, however, the law requires women, both voters and candidates, to "adhere" to the principles and rules of Shari'a. The implications that this provision may have for women's participation in political life are still difficult to gauge; wearing the hijab was not required for women to vote in local and national elections, but segregated polling stations were maintained. In October 2008, the National Assembly's legal and legislative committee has threatened Ms. al-Subeih and Ms. al-Homoud with dismissal after finding them in violation of the election law and the constitution for their refusal to wear a hijab, indicating that female voters and candidates may be required to do the same in the future.[42]

In the 2006 and 2008 parliamentary elections, 27 women ran as candidates, and in 2006 two women competed in a local by-election to fill a vacant seat in the Municipal Council.[43] None of the female candidates were elected, however, prompting women's rights advocates to call for the adoption of electoral quotas. Even without such a quota, four female candidates—Dr. Massouma al-Mubarak, Dr. Aseel al-Awadhi, Dr. Rola al-Dashti, and Dr. Salwa al-Jassar—were elected to the National Assembly in May 2009 for the first time in the country's history. Out of 210 parliamentary candidates, 16 were women. Notably, Dr. al-Mubarak finished first in her constituency and Dr. al-Awadi received the second highest number of votes in her district.[44] Furthermore, because cabinet members sit as ex officio members of parliament, Minister of Education Mohdi al-Homoud increases the number of female parliamentarians to five.[45]

Formal political parties remain banned in Kuwait, but their legalization has been repeatedly called for in recent years. There are a number of informal political groups, the most prominent of which are the National Democratic Alliance (liberal), the Islamic Constitutional Movement, and the Islamic Popular Alliance. These operate without government interference and campaign openly during the national elections. Hizb al-Umma, which has recruited women, is a more controversial Islamic political party that formed in 2005.[46] Kuwaiti women are involved in all major political groups and occasionally serve as founding members or contributing board members, with the exception of the Islamic organizations, in which women's participation is often confined to the women's committees.

Women's rights organizations face procedural obstacles to their creation and management. Requests to establish an NGO must be made directly to MOSAL, which has the authority to license, terminate, and, where fraudulent or criminal activities are involved, dissolve the elected boards of NGOs. Kuwait now has 70 NGOs, 22 of which were licensed between 2005 and the beginning of 2008.[47] Five women's rights NGOs currently operate in the country, all of which receive funding from the government. No new women's rights NGOs were created between 2005 and 2009 because the government rejects license applications if organizations with similar functions already exist. The women's rights groups that do exist are able to work with international and regional organizations and hold international conferences on women's rights.

Kuwaiti women experience only minor restrictions on their freedom of access to and use of information to empower themselves in both their civil and political lives. The Internet remains widely available at home, in offices, and in public cafes, but websites deemed immoral or politically radical are censored.[48] Nevertheless, the Internet continues to play an important role in women's lives and has enabled women's rights advocates to network with international organizations and share resources.

Recommendations

❖ Women's rights NGOs should initiate public education and advocacy campaigns on the importance of voting, aimed specifically at women, to increase turnout in the next election.

❖ The government and NGOs should initiate nonpartisan programs designed to support female candidates, teach them how to campaign and communicate their message effectively, and provide networking opportunities with other elected women leaders from the Arab world.

❖ By using Bahrain and the United Arab Emirates as examples of where such changes recently occurred, Kuwaiti NGOs should lobby the government to appoint qualified women as judges.

❖ The government should remove all obstacles to the registration and operation of NGOs.

SOCIAL AND CULTURAL RIGHTS

Kuwait has comprehensive social security and welfare schemes and offers modern health care services to all residents, including noncitizens and migrant workers. Citizens are free to participate in community life and non-Kuwaitis enjoy the right to form their own cultural associations openly.

Women are generally free to make independent decisions about their health and reproductive rights, although limitations to this right exist regarding abortion. Contraceptives are readily available and affordable through government health services, and private pharmacies offer birth-control pills without a prescription. Use of contraceptives is relatively high among educated Kuwaiti women and is the leading method for family planning in the country. As a result, the overall fertility rate decreased from 2.6 births per woman in 2000 to 2.3 births in 2006.[49]

Abortion is legal only if the pregnancy constitutes a serious threat to the health of the mother or if the child would be born with grave, unexpected, and incurable physical or mental defects.[50] Ministerial Decree (No. 55 of 1984) places strict procedural requirements on such abortions, including prior approval by the woman's husband or guardian. Even when permitted by law, doctors are reluctant to carry out the procedure due to the stiff penalties associated with abortion. Any woman who deliberately kills her newborn child to avoid dishonor, as well as any person who supplies a pregnant woman with drugs or other harmful substances, with or without her consent, may be sentenced to up to 10 years in prison.

Women have full and equal access to health care. Health care services at government-run clinics and hospitals are generally provided free of charge or at a low cost for all residents of Kuwait, including noncitizens. Since the mid-1990s, the government and women's groups have organized campaigns to raise women's awareness about female health issues like breast cancer and osteoporosis.

Although there are no reliable data available, women seem to be protected from harmful gender-based traditional practices such as virginity tests and female genital mutilation. Early marriage has grown uncommon, and cross-cousin marriages are no longer widely practiced.

Women are legally permitted to own their own housing, but unmarried men and women customarily live with their parents regardless of their age. Although the practice is not promoted by the government, landlords often choose to refuse to rent to Kuwaiti women without proof that they are married. No such restrictions are applied to single foreign-born female residents of Kuwait.

Housing is a serious problem for Kuwaiti women, particularly divorced women from low-income groups. The Housing Assistance Law (No. 47 of 1993) is structured around the traditional notion of a family headed by men and excludes women and unmarried men from the right to apply for government-subsidized housing. Moreover, women receive unequal benefits under the government's low-interest loan policy designed to encourage married men to build their own homes. For instance, a Kuwaiti man can apply for a loan up to 70,000 dinars (US$245,356) if he has been married for more than four years and has children. On the other hand, divorced or widowed Kuwaiti women with children from Kuwaiti husbands can apply for 45,000 dinars (US\$157,729), payable through monthly installments.[51] This disparity is commonly justified with the argument that it is the responsibility of men to support the family under Shari'a.

In 2005, amendments were made to Articles 14 and 15 of the housing law to allow disabled Kuwaiti women who are married to non-Kuwaitis and the families of slain war victims and prisoners of war the right to claim housing benefits. However, Kuwaiti women married to non-Kuwaiti men cannot bequeath state housing to their heirs. Article 32 states that in the event of the wife's death, the children (and, by association, their foreign-born fathers) have the right to stay in the house only until the daughters are married and the sons reach 26 years of age. In the case of the war victim's widow, the house is registered jointly in her and her sons' names even if she has daughters, as the daughters are expected to eventually marry.

The state does not provide for, or acknowledge, female-headed households as the main recipients of welfare benefits. The effects of this policy are exacerbated by the fact that there are no immediate penalties for men who do not financially support children in the custody of their divorced wives, even though such support is required by law. Low-income widows and divorced women with dependent children are entitled to monthly income supplements and rent subsidies, but only if they provide evidence that they have no one to support them and are unemployed.[52] In 2006, 7,087 divorced women and widows received welfare assistance.[53] However, there are no gender-disaggregated data regarding the economic status of women, which has prevented policymakers from implementing effective measures to protect women against economic hardship.

Kuwaiti women are involved in civic life and participate as both members and leaders of many types of NGOs, including mixed-gender professional associations, service-oriented organizations, human rights organizations, and religious groups. The Kuwaiti Human Rights Society, officially licensed in 2004, has two female board members. Women also have the right to join, vote, and hold office in unions and local cooperatives.

Women participate in and influence the media, holding jobs in both print and broadcast outlets as reporters, broadcasters, and producers. In 2008, Kuwait News Agency had 166 female employees, accounting for 38 percent of its total workforce.[54] Women in Kuwait use the media as a vehicle for bringing gender issues to the forefront of the public debate, and most newspapers devote considerable space to the activities of women's groups. Nevertheless, the media continue to stereotype women, often stressing the divisions between women's groups rather than presenting a more positive image of women's rights activists and female political candidates.

Women's rights groups have publicly addressed the economic and social challenges facing women and have lobbied parliament for policy changes. The National Assembly's Women's Affairs Committee and women's NGOs have held frequent meetings over the past three years to promote legislation that effectively protects women's social and cultural rights. Women's rights NGOs have also organized several conferences that highlight the plight of divorcees and female citizens married to noncitizen men. Despite these persistent efforts, the government and the parliament continue to delay the implementation of policies and legislation that would help to achieve gender equality.

Recommendations

❖ The government should commission an independent research institute to review the status of divorced women and female citizens married to noncitizen men. The institute should collect data on their economic situation, paying special attention to their housing rights. Such a project is necessary to assess the needs of these vulnerable groups better and tailor government policies based on the findings.

❖ The government should amend the laws that discriminate against women in determining the eligibility for welfare and housing benefits.

❖ Women's rights NGOs should adopt new information technology and Internet tools, such as online petitions or social networking sites, to mobilize support and advocate for reform.

❖ The government should promote positive representation and increased participation of women in the media, in part by sponsoring progressive programming and withholding support from counterproductive content in consultation with women's rights NGOs.

❖ NGOs should organize workshops to train journalists on gender sensitivity and how to cover women's issues in an effective and objective manner.

AUTHOR

Haya al-Mughni is a Kuwaiti sociologist and author of *Women in Kuwait: The Politics of Gender.*

NOTES

1   Youssef Ibrahim, "Mideast Tensions: A Kuwaiti Prince Sees Wider Rights," October 14, 1990, http://query.nytimes.com/gst/fullpage.html?res=9C0CE1DC153AF937A25753 C1A966958260&sec=&spon=&pagewanted=all.

2   Haila al-Mekaimi, "Kuwait Women's Tepid Political Awakening," *Arab Insight* 2, No. 1, (Winter 2008), 54.

3   "Blow for Kuwaiti Women's Rights," the BBC (London, UK), July 4, 2000, http://news .bbc.co.uk/2/hi/middle_east/818507.stm ; "Kuwaiti Court Rejects Vote for Women," the BBC (London, UK), January 16, 2001, http:/news.bbc.co.uk/2/hi/middle_east/11 19722.stm; Natasha Walter, "Electoral Shock," the *Guardian* (London, UK), September 29, 2003, http://www.guardian.co.uk/world/2003/sep/29/gender.uk.

4   "Women Protest for Right to Get Vote," the *Times* (UK), March 8, 2005, http://www .timesonline.co.uk/tol/news/world/article421890.ece.

5   "Kuwait: Majles Al-Ommah (National Assembly), Last Elections" Inter-Parliamentary Union, http://www.ipu.org/parline-e/reports/2171_E.htm.

6   Article 51 of the constitution provides that legislative powers are vested with both the Amir and the National Assembly.

7   B. Izzak, "Hijab-less Ministers Broke the Law," *Kuwait Times*, October 20, 2008, http:// www.kuwaittimes.net/read_news.php?newsid=MTM5NTAzMDUzMg==.

8   The bill allowing working mothers to retire after 15 years of service was passed in 1995; the gender-segregation bill was passed in 1996, ending three decades of coeducation at Kuwait University. In 2007, the penal code was amended to criminalize the act of imitating the opposite sex, with penalties of up to one year in prison. This resulted in the arrest and imprisonment of many young Kuwaiti men. For more details, see "Kuwait: Repressive Dress-Code Law Encourages Police Abuse" (Human Rights Watch [HRW], news release, January 16, 2008), http://hrw.org/english/docs/2008/01/17/ kuwait17800.htm.

9   In 2006, 638 marriages were contracted between Kuwaiti women and non-Kuwaiti men. Marriages between Kuwaiti women and foreign men represent roughly 5 percent of the total number of marriages contracted in a year, according to the newspaper *Al-Watan*, July 15, 2006, 60.

10 See Committee on the Elimination of Discrimination against Women (CEDAW), *Summary Record of the 634th Meeting* (New York: Office of the United Nations High Commissioner for Human Rights, January 27, 2004), http://www.iwraw-ap.org/ resources/pdf/SummaryRec_Kuwait1.pdf.

11 "Bail in Honour Killing," *Arab Times* (Kuwait), June 5, 2008, http://www.arabtimes online.com/kuwaitnews/pagesdetails.asp?nid=17977&ccid=22.

12 In 2006, Kuwait had 550 female prisoners, representing 14.9 percent of the total prison population. Roy Walmsley, *World Female Imprisonment List* (London: Kings College, International Centre for Prison Studies, April 2006), http://www.unodc.org/pdf/india/ womens_corner/women_prison_list_2006.pdf.

13 "Kuwait: Death Penalty: May Membriri Vecina (F)" (Amnesty International, news release, April 4, 2008), http://www.amnesty.org/en/library/info/MDE17/001/2008/en;

see also Agence France-Presse (AFP), "Kuwait's Emir Grants Clemency to Filipina Maid," Al-Arabiya News Channel, December 9, 2007, http://www.alarabiya.net/articles/ 2007/12/09/42715.html.

14 Law Firm of Labeed Abdal, "Family Law in Kuwait," Helplinelaw.com, http://www.help linelaw.com/law/kuwait/articles/labeed%20abdal/article3.php, accessed September 4, 2008.

15 "Housing, Paid Leave; Panel Nod to Major Benefits for Women," *Arab Times*, May 13, 2007; *Report on Gender Discussion with Women Activists in the State of Kuwait* (New York: UN Development Programme [UNDP], April 23, 2008), http://www.undp-kuwait. org/undpkuw/socialdev/Meeting%20with%20Dr%20Adel%20%20Alwugayn%20 -%20Proposed%20Gender%20Activities%2004-08.pdf.

16 Badria al-Awadhi, *Women's Legal Guide* (Kuwait: Dar Qortas Publication, 1994), 26, in Arabic.

17 Moamen al-Masri, "Litigant Wife Pays the Price," *Arab Times*, December 19, 2007, http:// www.arabtimesonline.com/kuwaitnews/pagesdetails.asp?nid=9581&ccid=22.

18 Interview with Talal al-Mutairi (Kuwaiti lawyer), *Al-Nahar*, May 27, 2008, http://www .annaharkw.com/annahar/Article.aspx?id=73256, in Arabic.

19 Kuwait Ministry of Justice, *Ministry's News*, September 12, 2006, http://www.moj.gov .kw/News/newsarchive1303.asp?id=1494&Year=2006&Month=9, in Arabic.

20 "Abuses in Saudi Arabia, Kuwait, Lebanon, and the United Arab Emirates," in *Exported and Exposed: Abuses Against Sri Lankan Domestic Workers in Saudi Arabia, Kuwait, Lebanon, and the United Arab Emirates* (HRW, November 2007), http://hrw.org/ reports/2007/srilanka1107/4.htm#_Toc181614231.

21 "International Best Practices," in *Trafficking in Persons Report 2006* (Washington, DC: U.S. Department of State, Office to Monitor and Combat Trafficking in Persons, June 5, 2006), http://www.state.gov/g/tip/rls/tiprpt/2006/65984.htm.

22 "Forum on Women's Rights, Civil Status Law Kicks Off in Kuwait," *Kuwait Times*, March 27, 2008, http://www.kuwaittimes.net/read_news.php?newsid=OTM2NDQ5MDEz.

23 The Kuwaiti government adopted a number of initiatives to create more employment opportunities for Kuwaitis. In 2000, it passed the national employment law to encourage Kuwaitis to work in the private sector. The law extends the government's social and child allowances to citizens in the private sector. In 2005, the National Manpower and Government Restructuring Program (GRP) was set up to provide training and facilitate recruitment in both the private and public sectors. By August 2007, GRP had received 11,792 job applications, 62 percent of them from women. Interview with Hind al-Sabeeh, *Al-Nahar*, October 18, 2007, http://www.annaharkw.com/annahar/ ArticlePrint.aspx?id=27245, in Arabic.

24 Ahmad al-Khaled, "Kuwaiti Women's Civil Rights at Issue," *Kuwait Times*, April 14, 2008, http://www.kuwaittimes.net/read_news.php?newsid=OTY1ODM2NzAw.

25 Ahmad Al-Khaled, "Segregation at the forefront," *Kuwait Times*, February 7, 2008, http://www.kuwaittimes.net/read_news.php?newsid=MTM0NTQ4MTUyMw==; Hussain Al-Qatari, "Liberals: 'No' to Segregation," *Kuwait Times*, http://www.kuwait times.net/read_news.php?newsid=MTA4NTI1MTQxMQ==.

26 Ahmad Al-Khaled, "Kuwaitis Divided Over Segregation," *Kuwait Times*, February 10, 2008, http://www.kuwaittimes.net/read_news.php?newsid=MTM3OTczMzA0Ng==.

27 World Bank, "GenderStats—Labor Force," http://go.worldbank.org/4PIIORQMS0 [accessed December 15, 2009].

28 *Kuwait Economic and Strategic Outlook* (Kuwait: Global Investment House KSSC, May 2008), http://www.globalinv.net/research/Kuwait-Economic-052008.pdf.

29 "Gender and Citizenship Initiative: Kuwait" (UNDP, Programme on Governance in the Arab Region [POGAR]), http://gender.pogar.org/countries/country.asp?cid=8, accessed June 25, 2008; Al-Sayed Al-Qassas, "Labor Inspectors Granted Right to Arrest Private Sector Violators," *Arab Times*, August 5, 2008, http://www.arabtimesonline.com/kuwait news/pagesdetails.asp?nid=16587&ccid=22.

30 The Labor Law (No. 38 of 1964) governs labor relations in the private sector, while the Civil Service Law (No. 15 of 1979) governs civil service employment in the public sector.

31 See "Social Affairs Received 15,000 Complaints from Expatriate Workers," *Al-Seyassah*, August 18, 2008

32 *Social Security Programs Throughout the World: Asia and the Pacific, 2004* (Washington, DC: U.S. Social Security Administration, Office of Research, Evaluation, and Statistics, March 2005), http://www.ssa.gov/policy/docs/progdesc/ssptw/2004-2005/asia/index .html.

33 "NGOs Hit Out at Assembly Law on Limiting Women's Work Hours; Ministry Works on Bylaws for 'Special Permissions,'" *Arab Times*, June 26, 2007, http://www.arabtimes online.com/client/pagesdetails.asp?nid=2066&ccid=9.

34 "Kuwait Hastens Women's Vote Bill," the BBC (London, UK), March 7, 2005, http:// news.bbc.co.uk/2/hi/middle_east/4325207.stm.

35 "Democratic Governance: Civil Society: Kuwait," UNDP-POGAR, http://www.pogar .org/countries/civil.asp?cid=8, accessed May 4, 2008.

36 Tamara Cofman Wittes, "Elections in the Arab World: Progress or Peril?" *Saban Center Middle East Memo* No. 11, February 12, 2007, http://www.brookings.edu/papers/2007/ 0212middleeast_wittes.aspx.

37 "Kuwait," *World Press Freedom Review, 2006* (Vienna: International Press Institute, 2007), http://www.freemedia.at/cms/ipi/freedom_detail.html?country=/KW0001/KW 0004/KW0096/&year=2006.

38 Note that not all lawyers are registered with the Kuwait Bar Association (KBA); registration is required only for lawyers working in the private sector. In 2008, the association had 1,500 members, of whom 300 were women. Author's interview with bar association officials, August 27, 2008.

39 Diana Elias, "Kuwait Hardliners Walk out of Parliament," Associated Press, June 1, 2008, http://www.usatoday.com/news/world/2008-06-01-2992318437_x.htm.

40 "Kuwait's Oil and Finance Ministers Return in New Cabinet," AP, *Gulf News*, May 29, 2009, http://gulfnews.com/news/gulf/kuwaitkuwait-s-oil-and-finance-ministers-return -in-new-cabinet-1.2083.

[41] The parliament's voting on the election law was as follows: 35 votes in favor, 23 votes against, and 1 abstention. See "Kuwaiti Women Get the Vote," *Times Online*, May 16, 2005, http://www.timesonline.co.uk/tol/news/world/middle_east/article523280.ece.

[42] "Kuwait Women Ministers Breach Law Over Hijab," *Al Arabiya News Channel*, October 21, 2008, http://www.alarabiya.net/articles/2008/10/21/58625.html.

[43] "Kuwait Parliamentary Elections: National Assembly" (UNDP-POGAR, May 17, 2008), http://www.undp-pogar.org/publications/elections/coverage/legislative/kuwait-2008-e.pdf; see also "Democratic Governance: Elections: Kuwait" (UNDP-POGAR), http://www.pogar.org/countries/elections.asp?cid=8#sub5, accessed June 25, 2008.

[44] Duraid al-Baik, "Kuwaiti Women Make History by Winning Seats," Arab Reform Initiative, May 18, 2009, http://arab-reform.net/spip.php?article2055.

[45] "Kuwait: Majles Al-Ommah (National Assembly), Last Elections," Inter-Parliamentary Union, http://www.ipu.org/parline-e/reports/2171_E.htm.

[46] The founders of Hizb al-Umma were arrested and charged with attempting to change the system of government, but they were later acquitted. See "Kuwait" in *Report 2007* (New York: Amnesty International, 2007), http://www.amnestyusa.org/annualreport.php?id=ar&yr=2007&c=KWT.

[47] Author's interview with officials in the Department of Public Welfare Organizations at the Ministry of Social Affairs and Labor, Kuwait, June 2008.

[48] For more details, see "Kuwait" in *Implacable Adversaries: Arab Governments and the Internet* (Cairo: Arab Network for Human Rights Information [ANHRI], 2006), http://www.openarab.net/en/node/360.

[49] World Development Indicators Database (Washington, DC: World Bank, September 2008).

[50] Law No. 25 of 1981; "Kuwait" in *Abortion Policies—A Global Review* (UN Department on Economic and Social Affairs, Population Division), http://www.un.org/esa/population/publications/abortion/profiles.htm. Abortion is banned under Articles 174 and 176 of the penal code (No. 16 of 1960). Article 175 of the same code legalizes abortion to preserve the mother's health.

[51] Kuwait lawyers' site, "Loans to Kuwaiti Women Married to Non-Kuwaitis Require New Legislation," *Al-Watan*, September 26, 2007, http://www.mohamoon-kw.com/default.aspx?action=DisplayNews&type=1&id=10883&Catid=58, in Arabic.

[52] Public Assistance Law (No. 22 of 1978).

[53] "Future Plans to Link Electronically the Social Care Units with the Ministry of Social Affairs" (Kuwait lawyers' site, July 4, 2006), http://www.mohamoon-kw.com/default.aspx?Action=DisplayNews&ID=7253, in Arabic.

[54] Author's interview with officials in Kuwait News Agency (KUNA), June 2008.

LEBANON

by Mona Chemali Khalaf

POPULATION: 3,876,000
GNI PER CAPITA: US$5,850

COUNTRY RATINGS	2004	2009
NONDISCRIMINATION AND ACCESS TO JUSTICE:	2.8	2.9
AUTONOMY, SECURITY, AND FREEDOM OF THE PERSON:	2.9	3.0
ECONOMIC RIGHTS AND EQUAL OPPORTUNITY:	2.8	3.0
POLITICAL RIGHTS AND CIVIC VOICE:	2.9	2.9
SOCIAL AND CULTURAL RIGHTS:	2.9	3.1

(COUNTRY RATINGS ARE BASED ON A SCALE OF 1 TO 5, WITH 1 REPRESENTING THE LOWEST AND 5 THE
HIGHEST LEVEL OF FREEDOM WOMEN HAVE TO EXERCISE THEIR RIGHTS)

INTRODUCTION

Lebanon's historical, geographic, and political characteristics have had a
significant impact on the status of women living within its borders. Though
it is one of the smallest Arab countries, it is nevertheless a major regional
center for culture, education, health, and finance. It contributed substantially to the preparation and formulation of the Universal Declaration of
Human Rights, but has since violated the agreement more than once in its
history of civil strife. Lebanon maintained a precarious democracy from
the time of its independence from France in 1943 until a 15-year civil war
broke out in 1975. While the war ended following a 1989 peace agreement, Syria maintained a military and intelligence presence that heavily
influenced domestic politics until the troops were withdrawn in 2005.

It is within this historical and political context that the Lebanese wom-
en's rights movement has emerged. The movement can be traced to the late
19th century, when a growing number of women began voicing demands
for greater rights. At the end of the century, many influential women
migrated with their families to Egypt, then the hub of Arab renaissance,
for either political or economic reasons. Once there, they started their own
magazines, focusing on women's issues and featuring articles in support
of education for women, their rights to work and earn a living, and their

249

freedom to choose whether to be veiled. Activists and scholars of this era insisted that Lebanese did not need to blindly imitate the West or deviate from their own culture and traditions.

The early decades of the 20th century brought an unprecedented increase in the number of female philanthropists, writers, educators, owners of women's journals, and political activists in Lebanon. Organizations founded and led by women offered access to education, health services, and vocational training to other women. Women also worked alongside men to liberate Lebanon from the Ottoman Empire. Such efforts paved the way for them to start making demands for greater civil and political rights. The French mandate authorities, in agreement with the Lebanese authorities, included equal civil and political rights for all Lebanese citizens in the 1926 constitution. However, the election law did not give women the right to vote, prompting new protests by women's rights activists.

With the emergence of the campaign for independence from the French mandate, women's suffrage lost its importance on the national front. Instead, women joined with men in organizing and taking part in demonstrations for independence across the country. After the independence was finally achieved in 1943, sectarian discord kept the women's movement from regaining its previous momentum. It was not until 1953 that the Lebanese Women's Council was officially established, and all Lebanese women received the right to vote and run in elections as candidates.[1] This achievement did not result in women's representation in the parliament until the early 1990s, apart from one exception in 1963.[2]

The women's movement was also derailed by the 1975–90 civil war, as activists shifted their focus to social and relief services, helping to fill the gap left by the shattered state. The movement was revived after the war, and newly created women's networks began to concentrate their efforts on the reform of discriminatory laws. Lebanon ratified the Convention on the Elimination of All Forms of Discrimination against Women (CEDAW) in 1997. The following year, the government formed the National Commission for Lebanese Women (NCLW) to oversee the implementation of the goals of CEDAW and the 1995 Fourth World Conference on Women in Beijing, and to develop national strategies and programs for the empowerment of women.[3]

The end of the Syrian occupation was precipitated by the February 2005 assassination of Rafic Hariri, who had overseen Lebanon's reconstruction while serving as prime minister for most of the postwar period.

He had broken publicly with the Syrians before his death, which triggered a mass anti-Syrian protest movement known as the Cedar Revolution and the eventual withdrawal of Syrian troops in April of that year. Lebanese women from various religious creeds and socioeconomic backgrounds participated in the movement in large numbers and were instrumental in its success. Women similarly became involved in relief operations during and after the 2006 war between Israel and Hezbollah, a Shiite Islamist militant group based in Lebanon. As in the previous instances of military strife, the campaign for women's rights became a secondary priority in the face of the immediate humanitarian crisis.

Progress on women's issues since the 2006 war has been minimal, and many Lebanese policies and laws remain discriminatory. For instance, Lebanese women are unable to pass their nationality to foreign husbands and their children, the definition of and punishment for adultery differs depending on whether the perpetrator is male or female, and men are given reduced sentences for committing so-called "honor killings," in which women are slain by male relatives for perceived moral transgressions. Systemic bias is also reflected in discriminatory provisions of the multiple personal status laws, which apply to citizens based on their religion. Under these laws, women are at a disadvantage in terms of marital rights, divorce proceedings, and child custody.

Women's rights groups have sought to correct these problems by lobbying for a new nationality law and amendments to the penal code. They have also launched media campaigns and conducted street demonstrations aimed at increasing public awareness regarding such issues and putting pressure on the government. However, the political unrest and security concerns that have prevailed in Lebanon for over three decades, coupled with an entrenched patriarchal system, have continued to hinder such efforts to date.

NONDISCRIMINATION AND ACCESS TO JUSTICE

In comparison with many other Arab states, the Lebanese legal system is fairly progressive with respect to women's rights, but the implementation of laws that assert gender equality has been uneven. Moreover, discriminatory provisions remain in the nationality law and penal code, and sectarian control over personal status law—reinforced by patriarchal social norms—generally puts women at a disadvantage. The country's many women's rights organizations have lobbied vigorously for legislative improvements, and the government has also taken steps to upgrade women's legal status, but major reforms have failed to win approval in the parliament in recent years.

Article 7 of the Lebanese constitution asserts the equality of rights and duties for all citizens, regardless of gender, and Article 8 stipulates that individual liberty will be guaranteed and protected by law.[4] Unlike in most other Arab states, Shari'a (Islamic law) is not held up as the main source of legislation. The preamble of the constitution declares that "Lebanon is committed to apply the Universal Declaration of Human Rights in all domains without exception," and that international treaties and their provisions have precedence over national laws and legislation.[5] In practice, however, gender-based discrimination persists in some laws, which have not been challenged as unconstitutional.

Certain provisions of the Lebanese Nationality Law (No. 15 of 1925) exemplify such discrimination. The foreign husbands of Lebanese women and their children have no right to obtain Lebanese nationality; even upon the father's death, the minor children may not adopt their mother's nationality. Article 2 provides that a Lebanese woman may pass on her nationality to her child only when the child's father is unknown. On the other hand, under Article 5, a foreign woman married to a Lebanese man may become a Lebanese citizen after one year of marriage. The children resulting from this union are automatically considered Lebanese under Article 1. A woman's inability to pass her Lebanese nationality to her foreign husband and children has serious repercussions on the entire family. Both the husband and children must continuously secure residency and work permits in order to live and work legally in Lebanon, which is a tedious and time-consuming process. As residents rather than citizens, the children also lack the same rights as nationals regarding access to education.

Defenders of this discrimination argue that it protects the fragile balance between the country's various religious sects, since the extension of citizenship to male Palestinian refugees married to Lebanese women, and to their children, would greatly increase the number of Sunni Muslim voters. Reflecting this concern, a draft nationality law that is currently being considered by the parliament would allow Lebanese women to pass their nationality to their foreign husbands and children, unless the husband is Palestinian. The nongovernmental organizations (NGOs) involved in the reform effort have objected to this draft, noting that discrimination against women is simply being replaced by discrimination against Palestinian men.

In 2003, the Directorate General of Public Security attempted to address this situation by adopting a measure that grants residency permits free of charge and for a period of three years to the children of a Lebanese mother, whatever the nationality of the husband.[6] While this offers some relief to the children involved, it does not alter the fundamental gender discrimination found in the existing law.

The penal code treats women and men differently in a number of sections, notably in provisions related to honor crimes, adultery, and rape. Article 562 condones violence against women in the name of honor by reducing the sentence of a man who kills or injures his wife or other female relative without premeditation if he can prove that he witnessed the victim engaging in illegal sexual intercourse. At one time the article allowed an acquittal in these circumstances, but it was amended in 1999 to offer only mitigation of the sentence.[7] Human rights NGOs continue to lobby for the total repeal of Article 562, and in August 2008 the respected Shiite cleric Sheikh Muhammad Hussein Fadlallah issued a *fatwa* (religious edict) against honor killings, describing them as "a repulsive act banned by Islamic law."[8]

The definition of adultery varies depending on whether the perpetrator is male or female. For a man, adultery requires that the act in question be committed in the marital home or that the adulterous relationship be made public. Conversely, a woman may be convicted of adultery if she commits an adulterous act anywhere and under any circumstances. Under Articles 487 and 488 of the penal code, sentencing options for men range from one month to one year in prison, while women may receive between three months and two years.[9] Notably, the partner of an adulteress is not subject to any punishment unless he too is married, whereas the female partner of an adulterer is subject to punishment regardless of her marital status. Women also have a greater evidentiary burden in attempting to prove their innocence. A man may be found innocent if there is a lack of material evidence, such as love letters, while an adulteress can be convicted through either factual evidence or witness testimony. Furthermore, charges are dropped against male adulterers who resume conjugal relations with their wives, while no such option exists for women.[10]

The penal code essentially treats rape as a crime against honor of the victim rather than a crime of violence, meaning it is not recognized within marriage. Under Article 503 of the penal code, the minimum punishment for rape is five years in prison with hard labor. If the victim is less than 15 years old, the minimum sentence is increased to seven years. However, if a legitimate marriage is subsequently contracted between the perpetrator and the victim, the conviction or pending charges will be voided.[11] Similarly, Article 504 allows a husband to go unpunished for rape or any kind of abuse when the victim is his wife.

Prostitution is technically legal in certain circumstances. The 1931 law on prostitution requires that brothels be licensed and that individuals working in them undergo medical testing regularly. Brothels may be opened only by women, female virgins may not work there, and employees, both male and female, must be over 18 years old. Since the late 1960s, the government has generally stopped issuing new licenses for brothels, meaning most of those operating today are unlicensed and therefore illegal. However, as a result of the civil war and the laxity of government institutions, the trade persists. Draft laws ordering the closure of all brothels have been submitted to the parliament over the years, but none has been adopted to date.[12]

Although discriminatory laws and policies exist, the government has expressed interest in reform. The first signs of a positive change emerged in 2000, when certain discriminatory provisions within the labor and social security codes were amended. Also that year, the Women and Children's Rights Commission was established to examine and amend existing laws that discriminate against women and children, and to propose new laws that safeguard their rights. Further progress was made in 2005, when for the first time in Lebanese history, a ministerial declaration explicitly addressed issues related to women and referenced the need to fulfill Lebanon's commitments at the 1995 Beijing conference.[13] While the latter moves have not so far produced effective actions or legal revisions, they suggest an ongoing shift—from indifference to active engagement—in the government's attitude on gender discrimination.[14]

Lebanon's judicial system consists of ordinary courts and special courts. Ordinary courts, divided into civil and criminal units, are hierarchical and include the courts of first instance, the courts of appeal, and the Court of Cassation, which has jurisdiction over final appeals and intercourt disputes. Special courts preside over specific areas of law and include juvenile courts, military courts, and labor courts. Religious courts for each sect hear cases pertaining to personal status and family law. Shari'a courts, for instance, are separated into Sunni and Shiite hearings, and ecclesiastical courts have jurisdiction over the personal status issues of the various

Christian denominations.[15] The court system is supervised by the Ministry of Justice and the State Consultative Council, the supreme administrative court of Lebanon.

All citizens, men and women, are guaranteed equal access to the judiciary under Article 7 of the code of civil procedure, which provides every Lebanese with the right to initiate proceedings and the right to defense. Article 427 of the same code stipulates that any Lebanese citizen may apply for legal aid if he or she is unable to pay the costs and fees of the proceedings.[16] However, women rarely claim these rights in practice, either because of legal illiteracy or because the prevailing patriarchal social system discourages them from asserting their rights in opposition to men. Similarly, noncitizen women have access to justice and are offered free legal assistance, but they rarely resort to courts due to ignorance of these services or the fear of becoming involved with an unfamiliar legal system.

Although women are not immune from cruel or degrading treatment by law enforcement agencies, they are considerably less likely than men to be subject to such practices. Torture and ill-treatment in detention have remained a problem in recent years.[17] Prisoners are usually detained in poorly ventilated cells and risk verbal and physical abuse at the hands of law enforcement personnel. In most cases female inmates in Lebanon are repeat offenders who have committed felonies and other crimes.

The number of women in the judiciary has increased substantially over the years. The first female law students graduated in the 1930s, but women were appointed as judges only in the 1960s. Despite this delay, women today hold 38 percent of the civil, commercial, and criminal court judgeships, or 192 out of the 507 available positions. They also make up 28 percent of judges in the administrative court, holding 21 out of 76 available positions.[18] Despite these and other remarkable achievements, no woman has ever been appointed to the Constitutional Council, the Higher Council of the Judiciary, or the Justice Council. Moreover, women are not permitted to serve as judges in the religious courts. Within the Sunni, Greek Orthodox, and Anglican courts, female lawyers may serve only in an advisory capacity, but their advice seems to influence the judges' verdicts.[19]

According to the code of civil procedure, the testimony of men and women are considered equal before civil courts, and male and female witnesses are subject to the same criteria for disqualification. Women may act as witnesses in the Property Register under Law No. 275 of 1993. Christian religious courts consider female witnesses and their testimony to be equal to that of men. However, within the Muslim religious courts, the testimony of two women is equal that of one man. Compensation owed to men and women is equal under Articles 122 and 234 of the Law of Contracts and Obligations, but a review of court judgments indicates that men are often awarded greater compensation than women in similar circumstances, reflecting the gender-role stereotype of men as the primary breadwinners.[20]

Lebanon ratified CEDAW in 1997 with reservations to Article 9(2), regarding nationality; several subparagraphs of Article 16(1), related to personal status laws; and Article 29(1), on the settlement of disputes. The reservations related to personal status are premised on the fact that Lebanon lacks a unified personal status law.[21] Establishing such a law and lifting these reservations is of primary importance if gender equality is to be secured.

In 2005, the NCLW established a CEDAW committee to prepare Lebanon's official report to the United Nations on the status of women and suggest ways in which Lebanon could implement the clauses of the CEDAW treaty. To this end, it organized a workshop entitled "On the Road to Applying CEDAW" that examined how state institutions and NGOs could work together to fully implement the convention.[22]

Women's rights NGOs have been instrumental in pushing to amend discriminatory laws, often working collectively within so-called women's networks. The networks secure funding through member organizations that are directly involved with a specific issue.

The right of Lebanese women to pass their citizenship to their husbands and children is an issue of particular concern to many activists. The Collective for Research and Training on Development–Action (CRTD-A) launched a 2002 campaign entitled "My Nationality Is a Right for Me and My Family." In early 2006, CRTD-A secured support for this initiative from leading politicians and members of the parliament's Women and Children's Rights Commission. The campaign continues to date and receives notable media coverage despite continuing political and security-related instability. In 2008, the UN Development Programme (UNDP) began a two-year citizenship project in coordination with the National Committee for the Follow-Up of Women's Issues.

Women's rights and human rights associations are also working hard to introduce amendments to the penal code, which has barely been modified since its promulgation in March 1943. The Lebanese Women's Democratic

Gathering, with the support of the Lebanese Women's Network, has launched a campaign that aims to remove all gender-based discriminatory provisions from the penal code. Moreover, the nonprofit organization KAFA ("Enough") Violence and Exploitation is committed to ending violence against women and children through outreach, advocacy, and awareness. KAFA considers current laws to be inadequate to fight family violence, and in cooperation with other NGOs and experts in the field, it has launched a campaign in support of a draft law that would protect women against domestic abuse.

Recommendations

+ Efforts should be made to fully implement Article 7 of the constitution, which establishes equality in the rights and duties of all citizens. Existing laws that promote equality should be fully enforced, new laws reinforcing equality should be promulgated, discriminatory laws should be repealed or amended, and steps should be taken to increase women's awareness about their legal rights.

+ The nationality law should be amended to allow Lebanese women to pass their nationality to foreign husbands and children. Specifically, Article 1 of Decree No. 15 of January 19, 1925, should be amended to read that any person born of a Lebanese father or mother shall be considered Lebanese.

+ The definition of adultery within the penal code should be made gender-neutral. Adulterous men should no longer be able to evade punishment by resuming sexual relations with their spouses unless the same opportunity is given to adulterous women.

+ Article 562 of the penal code, which offers reduced sentences to male perpetrators of "honor crimes," should be eliminated. Those convicted of killing or injuring a female relative for honor-related reasons should receive no special leniency from the courts.

+ Domestic and international NGOs should closely monitor the implementation of international conventions, which have legal precedence over national laws.

AUTONOMY, SECURITY, AND FREEDOM OF THE PERSON

Lebanon is one of the most diverse countries in the region and has 18 legally recognized religious groups.[23] Because of the great political sensitivity surrounding the relative size of each sectarian community, the state has not conducted a national census since 1932. However, the three largest groups are the Sunni Muslims, the Shiite Muslims, and the Maronite Christians. The smaller groups include a variety of other Christian sects as well as the Druze and a very small number of Jews.

Article 9 of the constitution guarantees freedom of conscience and religious practice, and asserts that the personal status interests of all sects will be respected. Each state-recognized religious group has the right to adhere to its own personal status laws, which regulate matters related to birth, marriage, divorce, and child custody. For example, the Muslim denominations alone are subject to four different personal status codes. The six Catholic denominations share a uniform personal status law, and some state-recognized denominations, such as the Ismailis, are no longer represented in Lebanon. Nonetheless, the personal status laws of all religious groups in some way discriminate against women and promote patriarchal stereotypes.

No laws restrict a woman's freedom of movement or her choice of place of residence. Lebanese women have had the right to travel without their husbands' authorization since 1974. According to both Sunni and Shiite religious courts, which adhere to interpretations of Shari'a, a wife cannot be compelled to reside in her husband's house through physical or mental coercion. However, the prevailing patriarchal social system prevents women from fully enjoying freedom of movement, particularly in rural areas where such norms are more strictly enforced. Conversely, urban women may have more opportunities to avoid conservative customs and traditions; some are even able to defy them, for instance by going out at night without a male chaperon or living on their own.

There have been several unsuccessful attempts to adopt a unified, civil personal status law over the years, beginning in 1974.[24] A bill that would create an optional civil law was proposed by President Elias Hrawi in 1998 and approved by the cabinet, but it met with strong opposition from all religious leaders, and the parliament eventually blocked it. In 2007, a group of students and young professionals used Facebook, the social-networking website, to launch a new initiative in support of civil marriage and a civil personal status law.[25] In February 2009, the group announced the completion of a new draft for an optional civil law, although it appears unlikely that the measure will be considered by the parliament in the near future. [26]

Most of the existing personal status laws stipulate a traditional division of roles within the family, placing the husband at its head and imposing upon the wife responsibility for domestic matters.[27] Under Muslim family laws, for example, a wife is required to obey her husband, while a husband has the duty to treat his wife well. Some positive amendments were introduced in the personal status law of the Catholic Churches of the East in 1990 to stipulate that spouses enjoy equality in their rights and duties.[28] Moreover, the Greek Orthodox Church issued a new personal status law in 2003 that contains no clauses related to the authority of the husband. Articles 11 and 25 emphasize that marriage entails mutual support between husband and wife and the sharing of household and child-rearing responsibilities. The new law also allows women from other Christian denominations to marry Greek Orthodox men without having to convert, and emphasizes that the wife's religion will not be used to discriminate against her in annulment or divorce proceedings. Nonetheless, due to widespread patriarchal attitudes, women of all faiths are traditionally expected to conform to their husband's demands.

Many Lebanese men and women choose to avoid the sectarian personal status codes by having a civil marriage abroad. Such marriages are recognized by law and are registered in the personal status offices. Disputes arising from civil marriage are regulated by the civil courts in Lebanon, which apply the civil law of the country where the marriage was contracted. For this purpose, bilateral agreements have been concluded between Lebanon and several countries, including the United States, Italy, and, recently, Switzerland. However, a newborn child is ascribed the religion of his or her father even if the parents had a civil marriage overseas.[29]

The ability of women to negotiate full and equal marriage rights is jeopardized by the discriminatory nature of the personal status codes. Furthermore, a woman's ability to enforce her rights often depends on her education, socioeconomic status, and whether she lives in a rural or urban area. The legal age of capacity for marriage varies by sect, but it is typically 18 for men and a somewhat younger age for women.[30] With the approval of a judge, Sunni and Shiite laws technically allow marriage for girls as young as nine, though this is no longer customary.[31]

Parents and occasionally the extended family of a prospective bride or groom heavily influence the young person's choice of spouse. Sometimes this influence is limited to whether the future spouse is from the same sect, although most are free to pick from among the various sects of their religion. It is an accepted practice in some social milieus, regardless of religious denomination, for a young man to ask his female family members to search for a prospective bride on his behalf, or for a young woman to be compelled to marry a person chosen by her family. However, such cases are becoming increasingly rare.

Interreligious marriages are increasingly common. Among Muslims, the marriage of a Muslim man to a woman of another monotheistic faith is acceptable—the bride is even permitted to retain her original faith. By contrast, a Muslim woman may not marry a non-Muslim man; should she choose to do so, her guardian has the right to annul the marriage, although that right is rarely exercised.[32] The Christian sects generally require prospective spouses of other faiths to convert, although some allow marriages between people of different Christian denominations.[33]

Divorce in Lebanon is most frequently a traumatic experience for family members, particularly women and children. While personal status codes regulate issues related to divorce, enforcement mechanisms are not strong enough to ensure that the rights of divorced women are upheld. Women often face fierce custody battles and serious financial problems if their husbands refuse to pay the alimony ordered by the court. The religious courts, generally headed and run by men, rarely consider the needs of women, and often decide and impose measures concerning children's care and nurturing without seeking out the opinion and consent of the mother. Furthermore, a divorce is always more taxing for foreign women married to Lebanese men because of their lack of awareness of the pertinent laws and, in many cases, because of a language barrier.

Among Muslims, a man can divorce his wife with relative ease through the practice known as *talaq*, or repudiation. The divorced woman is entitled to her dowry as well as financial maintenance throughout the *iddat*, the waiting period during which a husband may revoke his repudiation and reconcile with his wife, even if it is against her will. It is much more difficult for a woman to divorce her husband on her own initiative. Sunni women can argue their case in court by citing one or more of a defined set of reasons, such as the husband's failure to consummate the marriage, his illness or insanity, or his long-term absence or intermittent cohabitation.

Both the Sunni and Shiite family courts allow women to reserve the right to initiate divorce as part of their marriage contracts, making the process easier. Under Article 38 of the Sunni personal status law, women may also stipulate in the marital contract that the husband cannot take another wife. In addition, both Sunni and Shiite women can request *khula*, an Islamic practice wherein the wife forgoes financial maintenance and returns her dowry in exchange for divorce.[34]

The Greek Orthodox Church requires the husband, in case of desertion, to provide his wife and their children with a lawful domicile or an allowance. If he refuses, the court will order him to vacate the marital home so that his wife and children may reside there. Catholic sects continue to prohibit divorce but have recently increased the number of legitimate reasons for annulment.[35] All Catholics may invoke misrepresentation or fraud as the reason for annulment, for instance if one of the spouses does not tell the other about being a drug addict. Other valid reasons include polygamy or incest, violence and abuse, irresponsible behavior, mental incapacity as established by a medical doctor, and the inability or refusal of a partner to consummate the marriage.

Women face acute discrimination in matters of parental authority and child custody. In all denominations but the Armenian Orthodox, in which parents share authority equally, parental authority over the person and assets of minor children goes to the father first. Mothers rarely receive even secondary priority, which most denominations grant to the paternal grandfather or a trustee of the father's choosing.

Custody, or responsibility for the physical and mental upbringing of children, generally goes to mothers for a period of time, the length of which depends on the age and sex of the child and differs between religions. In 2005, the evangelical Christian denominations adopted a new personal status law that raised the age at which mothers lose custody from 7 to 12 years for both boys and girls.[36] Proposed amendments to the Sunni custody law would grant mothers custody over boys until they turn 13 and girls until they turn 15, up from 7 and 9, respectively. These amendments have been approved by the Sunni religious authorities, the Higher Council of the Judiciary, and the cabinet, but they have not yet been passed into law by the parliament.[37]

A mother does not necessarily lose custody of her children once the legal period of custody has expired. For instance, custody for Catholic mothers technically ends once the child is weaned, usually around the age of two. However, under Article 125 of the Catholic personal status law, courts may take into consideration the best interest of the minor in determining which parent will retain custody of the children. Muslim and other religious courts also often grant custody to the mother and resort to the assistance of social workers and psychologists to help the children in case of disputes. Either parent may lose custody if they change their religion or are responsible for the dissolution of a marriage, and Christian and Shiite mothers lose custody of their children upon remarrying.[38]

Women generally avoid the death penalty, but there are more women murdered in the name of honor than there are men sentenced to death in a given time period. Between 1995 and 1998, six men and no women were executed by order of the judiciary. In the same period, however, 36 women died in apparent honor killings.[39] Between 1999 and 2007, 66 court sessions related to the honor killings of 82 female victims took place.[40] However, these statistics are incomplete, as such murders often go unreported or are reported as suicides. In general, women in conservative environments, especially in remote areas, are more likely to be subject to honor killing than their counterparts in Beirut and other cities.

Domestic violence is not specifically prohibited by law. Draft legislation on the matter, backed by KAFA and other NGOs, was considered by the cabinet in June 2009, but it was referred to a ministerial committee for further review. There is currently no competent authority equipped to assist victims. Moreover, meddling in the private domestic matters of others is taboo, regardless of one's religion. Consequently, security forces are strictly forbidden from helping a known victim of abuse unless he or she submits a formal complaint to the police.[41]

Because of the lack of specific legislation, offenses related to domestic violence currently fall under Article 122 of the Law of Contracts and Obligations, which orders that restitution be paid to victims of illegal physical injuries. Restitution covers material damages, such as hospital bills, that result from violent acts perpetrated by the husband, as well as psychological and moral damages. The general provisions of the penal code that victims may rely on to prosecute their abusers do not take into consideration the private relationship between the perpetrator and the victim. Under the penal code, battery is punishable by a maximum of three years in prison. Nevertheless, some religious courts require battered wives to return to their homes, where they risk continued abuse by their husbands. In addition, many women are compelled to remain in abusive marriages because of social and family pressures, the possible loss of child custody, or a lack of financial means to support themselves.

Aside from a few tallies of complaints submitted to the police, no authoritative statistics exist regarding the extent or character of abuse committed against women by their male kin. The most reliable information comes from NGOs that work with and help battered women, which report that almost 80 percent of female victims of domestic violence are also victims of spousal rape.[42]

Women in Lebanon are often subjected to gender-based harassment outside the home, most often in the form of sexual harassment on the street and at work. Victims prefer to confide only in people close to them and are made to feel ashamed should they decide to report such incidents to the police, who often do not know how to deal with these issues. Verbal abuse in the forms of slander, defamation, and vilification are prohibited, but the punishment is usually reduced when such acts are not committed in public.

NGOs have initiated various projects in an effort to break the silence regarding domestic abuse. KAFA, the Lebanese Council to Resist Violence Against Women, and the Young Women's Christian Association (YWCA) have all established 24-hour hotlines that allow victims to report abuse and receive counseling. They have also launched awareness campaigns in an effort to focus the attention of the general public, the authorities, and experts on the plight of victims. Finally, they provide female victims with free legal advice, shelter, and access to social workers throughout their recovery process. As noted above, these organizations have drafted and lobbied the government to pass a law that would explicitly ban domestic violence. The Ministry of Social Affairs has been cooperating on the issue with a number of local NGOs for several years now, in some cases undertaking joint projects with the private groups.

Recommendations

❖ The parliament should enact an optional civil personal status law that would offer an alternative to the existing religious personal status laws, providing Lebanese citizens with freedom of choice without directly antagonizing religious leaders.

❖ The government should specifically outlaw domestic violence and spousal rape, create more accessible mechanisms through which victims can file complaints, and train police and other public employees on how to handle such cases.

❖ Custody laws that discriminate against the mother based on the child's gender and age should be amended to allow courts to determine the best interest of the child and the parents' custodial competency on a case-by-case basis.

✤ Temporary alimony should be provided to women for the duration of divorce proceedings in cases where the women were financially dependent on their husbands throughout marriage.

✤ In an effort to clarify the confusion caused by multiple personal status laws, a judicial monitoring body should be established to document and publicize new rulings by different courts on related issues.

ECONOMIC RIGHTS AND EQUAL OPPORTUNITIES

Political and civil unrest, including the 15-year civil war and the short but destructive war between Hezbollah and Israel in 2006, has taken its toll on Lebanon's economy. Although the gross domestic product (GDP) grew by an estimated eight percent in 2008, this trend is unlikely to continue considering the fact that the country has one of the highest debt-to-GDP ratios in the world, and in light of the international economic crisis that emerged in late 2008.[43] Female economic activity has grown considerably since the 1970s, but women remain grossly underrepresented in the labor force.

Article 215 of the Law of Contracts and Obligations stipulates that women have the same rights as men with respect to concluding contracts and owning and administering property. Married women and men hold and manage their property separately and dispose of it as they see fit, regardless of their religious affiliation. However, severe restrictions are placed on a woman's property if her husband declares bankruptcy. Articles 625 to 629 of the commercial code stipulate that property acquired by a woman during marriage is presumed to have been purchased with her husband's money—thus forming part of his assets—unless proven otherwise. These restrictions do not apply to the property of husbands and reflect the belief that wives are the dependents of their husbands.

Women have the legal right to full and independent use of their income and assets, but the prevailing patriarchal system and the stereotyped role assigned to women in the private sphere often prevents them from making such decisions on their own. A woman's husband, father, brothers, and sometimes more distant male relatives can heavily influence her financial choices, illustrating the predominance of social norms over legal rights. In rare instances, husbands or fathers have been known to completely control their wives' or daughters' income.

Inheritance laws differ between religious communities. Non-Muslims are subject to the 1959 Civil Law of Inheritance, which imposes complete equality between men and women, both in terms of the right to inherit and the share of inheritance. Muslims abide by the inheritance rules established under Shari'a provisions according to their respective sects. Under such rules, a man generally inherits twice as much as a woman. In addition, Muslims can only inherit from and bequeath to other Muslims, so that even the non-Muslim widow of a Muslim man cannot inherit part of his estate. Members of non-Muslim denominations are free to leave their estates to whomever they see fit, regardless of religion.[44] Although women are legally entitled to inherit land, they often cede their share to their brothers, as social norms dictate that land should be retained by the male line. In return, the brothers are expected to financially support their single sisters, although this trend is gradually subsiding as more women join the labor market.

No legal restrictions limit women's right to start their own business or get involved in income-generating activities. The number of enterprises owned by women is increasing among the middle and upper-middle income groups, while women in the lower income brackets often head small businesses and microenterprises.[45] However, female ownership does not necessarily mean female management. In the Middle East and North Africa region as a whole, only 54 percent of female business owners also act as managers for their enterprises, compared with 90 percent for male owners.[46]

The proportion of women who participate in the labor force has increased slowly over time, rising from about 21 percent in 1980 to 27 percent in 2007, although the figures remained largely static over the last five years.[47] The historical growth is partly attributable to governmental and societal investments in education. Women have enjoyed access to educational opportunities since the 19th century, and even older generations of Lebanese women are mostly literate. Of women aged 15 and older, 86 percent were literate as of 2007, compared with 93.4 percent of men from the same age group. This gender gap is markedly narrower than that of neighboring countries, and it entirely disappears among those aged 15 to 24 years old. In that group, 99.1 percent of women and 98.4 percent of men were literate as of 2007.[48] However, illiteracy is more common among rural women. Of women from Beirut, 5.6 percent are illiterate or not enrolled in school, compared with 8 percent of the women in the provinces of North Lebanon and 13.4 percent of the women in the Bekaa region.[49] More boys than girls are enrolled in primary school, but 83.3 percent of girls and only 79.8 percent of boys had completed their primary education as of 2007.[50] The gross enrollment rates in secondary and tertiary education were significantly higher for women than for men in 2007, and the gap has expanded over time.[51] This may be in part because boys are more likely to drop out of school to help support their families or to pursue their education abroad.

High literacy and enrollment rates among women have not translated into an equal place in the economy, however. In addition to being grossly underrepresented in the labor force, the overall female population earned on average about one-third the income of men.[52] While women are in principle free to choose their profession, societal attitudes tend to channel them into teaching, nursing, and administrative work at a rate that does not necessarily reflect the needs of the labor market.[53] These fields are often perceived as more compatible with women's nature and their primary role as homemakers and mothers. Textbooks used in all schools reinforce these stereotypes by portraying women in traditional gender roles while assigning leadership roles to men.

Professions that were previously reserved for men, including engineering and medicine, are beginning to open up to women. However, even female doctors tend to specialize in areas considered "natural" to them, such as pediatrics or obstetrics, rather than surgery or orthopedics. A woman's choice of profession is also influenced by the extent to which her job interferes with her reproductive and child-rearing roles, highlighting once more the primacy of these roles even among highly educated women.

Lebanon has ratified several International Labour Organization (ILO) conventions that promote equality,[54] and amended the labor code several times to remove discriminatory provisions. For instance, in 1987, both men and women became eligible for end-of-service indemnities at the age of 64, and in 1994, women were granted the right to undertake commercial activities without the prior approval of their husbands.[55] However, legal inequalities persist. Although men and women are officially entitled to the same minimum wage, women's net income is lower than that of men because married women's wages are taxed as if they were unmarried, while married men or male heads of households are granted a tax break.[56]

Women are entitled to maternity leave under Article 29 of the Employment Act, which was amended in 2000 to increase the period of maternity leave from 40 days to seven weeks with full pay. Nevertheless, Lebanon does not meet the standards dictated by ILO Convention 103, which grants mothers no less than 12 weeks of maternity leave. Paternity leave is not provided for under the Employment Act, and there are no effective requirements for employers to offer support services for working mothers, such as conveniently located childcare facilities. These deficiencies give rise to potential conflicts between women's professional and maternal responsibilities.[57] Lebanese law does not address the issue of sexual harassment in the workplace, despite the fact that its occurrence is increasingly recognized and openly discussed in the media and by NGO networks.

Female migrant workers, many of whom are employed as household help, are particularly vulnerable to labor exploitation. Since domestic workers are not covered by the labor law, they are denied a legal minimum wage, have no established maximum working hours per day, are not guaranteed time off or vacation, and are not entitled to accident and end-of-work compensation. Instead, their working environment is determined by a contract between them and their employer, and they are strictly forbidden from changing their employer unless the latter agrees to end the contract.[58] Some migrant women are also victims of human trafficking, tempted to immigrate to Lebanon by the promise of a decent job and then forced into prostitution once they arrive.

In response to pressures from international organizations, Lebanon created a committee in February 2006 to draft a model employment contract and to introduce an amendment to the labor law aimed at improving the status of domestic workers.[59] In October 2005 Lebanon signed and ratified international agreements that address the issue of trafficking,[60] and it has since begun implementing them. With assistance from the United Nations Office on Drugs and Crime, draft measures to prevent and combat trafficking in persons have been introduced.[61] Lebanon has not, however, ratified the UN Migrant Workers Convention, "which guarantees migrants' human rights and promises state protection against abuse by employers, agents and public officials."[62]

Palestinians are still considered to be resident foreigners despite their presence in Lebanon for over half a century. This status forces most Palestinian women to work in the informal sector, and their only support generally comes from women's NGOs and international organizations.

Civil society actors have fought for decades to amend the legal framework for women's economic rights and to educate women about these rights. In 1949, after a thorough examination of Lebanese legislation in light of international conventions and the legislation of other Arab countries, women's rights organizations established a plan of action for reform. Even then, activists were aware of the substantial influence that cultural norms and traditions have on society. Consequently, they adopted a policy of seeking gradual changes over time to alter deep-seated customs. This process continues today, and many NGOs focus entirely on women's economic rights and opportunities. The Working Women's League in Lebanon, for example, has lobbied for the amendment of discriminatory laws and the introduction of a new law penalizing sexual harassment in the workplace. The league also provides advice to working women regarding all employment issues and is currently negotiating with the private and public sectors to secure nurseries for the children of working women. The most pressing need, however, is for the proper enforcement of existing legal protections.

Recommendations

+ The government should partner with the NGO sector to support awareness campaigns promoting women's economic rights and potential as productive agents in Lebanon's economic development. A particular emphasis should be placed on outreach to rural women.

+ In an effort to increase women's workforce participation rates, educational and technical training should be structured to draw women into fields that meet market demands. NGOs should cooperate with business entities by providing occupational training for women in specializations and skills that are sought by the partner companies.

+ Employers in the public and private sectors should be required, both in law and in practice, to provide childcare facilities for their employees, making it easier for women to enter and remain in the workforce.

+ The government should provide technical and financial support to female-run enterprises in both the formal and informal sectors, regardless of the size of the enterprise.

+ Legislation designed to secure the fundamental economic and human rights of domestic workers, including noncitizens, should be enacted and fully enforced. This can be accomplished through a separate law or by extending the protections of the existing labor law to domestic workers.

POLITICAL RIGHTS AND CIVIC VOICE

Although women energetically fought for and achieved political rights over half a century ago, they have not been fully integrated into political life. A major factor behind this problem is the entrenched sectarian political system. Representation is apportioned on a sectarian basis, and powerful political families tend to retain the leadership of their respective communities, leaving women with only a token presence in the decision-making positions of the state and political parties. Prevailing patriarchal views on gender roles, reinforced by the blending of political and religious identity, discourage female political participation, and women have difficulty matching the financial resources of male incumbents during electoral campaigns.[63] Very little has changed regarding women's political rights in recent years, and repeated attempts to introduce a gender-based quota for women in parliamentary elections have been unsuccessful.

Lebanese women obtained the right to vote and run for seats in the National Assembly, the country's parliament, in 1953. The first Lebanese female member of parliament took office in 1963, having run unopposed to complete the term of her father, who had died without leaving a male heir. After her term ended, Lebanon did not have another female lawmaker until 1991, when one woman was appointed to replace her deceased husband. Three women were elected to the 128-seat parliament in 1992, and the number remained unchanged in the 1996 and 2000 elections, finally rising to six in 2005. In most of these instances, the successful candidates either belonged to traditional political families or were related to prominent male politicians.[64]

In the most recent elections, held on June 7, 2009, four women were elected to the National Assembly.[65] Once again, the typical female lawmaker was a close relative of a prominent male leader. The number of women in the parliament decreased in part because two of the incumbent female members, both widows of former presidents, stepped aside to allow their sons to contest the seats, although only one of the male heirs succeeded. Apart from the feudal political system, which equally impacts both male and female candidates, women are at a particular disadvantage due to their traditionally limited access to financial resources. Female challenges running in their own right often find themselves competing with well-financed, male-dominated political machines. They must also contend with cultural attitudes that resist female participation in the public sphere, resulting in the reluctance of various stakeholders within the society to be represented by a woman.

The parliament approved a new electoral law in September 2008, but important reforms proposed in the initial drafts were ultimately rejected. These included a measure backed by women's rights NGOs—such as the Lebanese Women's Council, the League of Lebanese Women's Rights, and the Lebanese Women's Democratic Gathering—that would have established a 30 percent quota for women's representation in the National Assembly.

The number of women running for and elected to local councils has increased in recent years, although the proportion of successful female candidates has remained the same. In the 2004 local elections, over 700 women ran for and 220 were elected to municipal councils, whereas in 1998, 139 of the more than 500 female candidates succeeded in their bid for local office. However, in both years, only 2.5 percent of the winning candidates overall were women, partly because additional municipal council seats were created in the interim. A total of 16 women were elected as mayors in 2004, but there are more than 1,600 such posts countrywide.[66]

Women also remain severely underrepresented in the national executive branch. In 2004, two women—Wafa Dika Hamzah and Leila el-Solh Hamadeh—became the first to be appointed to the cabinet, which in this case had 30 members, but they remained in office for only six months. Only one woman was appointed as a cabinet member in each of the subsequent two governments: Nayla Mouawad became minister of social affairs in 2005, and Bahia Hariri was appointed as minister of education in 2008. To date, no woman has become president of the republic, speaker of the parliament, or prime minister.

Furthermore, although the number of women appointed to serve in government departments and public institutions under the jurisdiction of the Civil Service Commission has increased over the years, women's representation in high-level positions remains significantly lower than that of men. No woman has ever been appointed as a governor, and only two are district presidents. Women are also underrepresented in delegations sent abroad by the Ministry for Foreign Affairs and Expatriates, though they are well represented in delegations concerned with women and children's affairs. According to a 2007 report by the World Bank on the progress of Arab women, only four out of the 53 ambassadors representing the Lebanese government abroad were women.[67]

While women are legally permitted to join political parties, their participation and representation remains low.[68] Those female members who are active in party affairs tend to work on committees focused on providing social services.

Freedoms of assembly and association are guaranteed under Article 13 of the constitution and a 1909 Ottoman law on associations. To establish a new organization, one need only inform the Ministry of Interior; no authorization from the state is required. Article 13 also guarantees freedom of expression and the press, although state and nonstate actors do not always respect this right in practice. Still, both male and female members of the media have risked their lives to push the boundaries of acceptable political discourse in recent years. In 2005, two male journalists, Samir Kassir and Jibran Tueni, were killed in separate car bombs, and prominent female news anchor May Chidiac survived an attempt on her life.

There are many women's rights organizations in Lebanon and they often take different forms. Important alliances of women's NGOs include the Lebanese Women's Council, the National Focal Point for the Elimination of All Forms of Discrimination against Women, and the Lebanese Women's Network. Other associations include NGOs that combat violence against women, women's committees in Lebanese political parties and trade unions, and NGOs concerned with culture, information, and communications.[69] However, these organizations are not equally distributed across Lebanon and are severely lacking in rural areas where they are needed most.

The involvement of female youth in civil society has significantly increased over the last 15 years. This can be attributed to a number of factors, the most important of which are the higher level of education of women, their increased participation in the labor force, and their genuine desire to take part in the political process.

Women of all ages engage in political protests and do not limit their activism to demonstrations alone. The 2006 war has apparently sparked civic and political activism among women, who are signing petitions in ever larger numbers.[70] Women actively organized and participated in sit-ins in downtown Beirut to protest the assassination of Rafic Hariri in 2005. And in the wave of activism that followed his death, women spearheaded a petition demanding liberation from Syrian occupation that collected more than 10,000 signatures and grew to over 500 meters in length.

The rise in civic activism has been aided by improved access to information. Satellite television is widely available, and the Internet has been expanding rapidly, with nearly a quarter of the population using the new medium by 2008.[71] However, because women remain underrepresented in both legislative and executive bodies, their lobbying efforts and awareness campaigns have had limited success in influencing national policies.

Recommendations

* The government, in conjunction with civil society actors, should counter the prevailing view, particularly among older generations, that politics is the domain of men. This could be achieved through national awareness campaigns focusing on the important role that women play in the public sphere, whether at the political, economic, or social level. In order to reach all Lebanese, even in the most remote areas of the country, such campaigns should utilize visual media, preferably television.

* Taking into consideration the historical reluctance of Lebanese voters to elect female politicians, the government must take steps to ensure that women have the opportunity to secure a substantial presence in the parliament. To this end, civil society actors should actively push for the temporary adoption of a gender-based quota within the electoral lists rather than parliament seats.

* The government, in cooperation with local NGOs, should offer training campaigns for potential female politicians that would guide them on how to properly conduct a campaign and convey their policy message to a wide audience.

* Women should be encouraged to join existing political parties and form new parties in which they would be accepted as equal partners. Moreover, they should create special networks, both within and across parties, to build alliances on the issues of female leadership and gender equality.

* Because municipal councils have the potential to affect the local community in a direct manner, increasing women's representation in the councils should be a high priority for the government. One way of achieving this would be to institute a quota on the electoral lists.

SOCIAL AND CULTURAL RIGHTS

Women's social and cultural rights have remained relatively unchanged in recent years, and what progress was made, such as improvements to the health sector, affected both sexes equally. The media continue to stereotype women, focusing primarily on their reproductive role or physical appearance. However, women are gaining a more substantive presence as talk-show hosts and political pundits.

Lebanese women are entitled to make decisions unilaterally regarding their reproductive rights and health, and the government has made efforts to provide adequate health care to its population. The country's commitment to this goal began with its 1972 ratification of the International Convention on Economic, Social, and Cultural Rights, which enshrines health care as a human right, and continued with its subsequent pledge to implement the Millennium Development Goals. Although Lebanon spends more on health care than any other Eastern Mediterranean country, this has not been accompanied by an efficient use of resources, as the country's performance on major health indicators is not significantly higher than that of its neighbors.[72] The system's shortcomings were temporarily compounded by the 2006 war, which hampered or destroyed health care facilities in the affected areas.[73]

Reproductive health services became a part of the primary health care system in 2003, making them more widely available throughout the country.[74] Women are able to obtain birth control without having to consult their husbands. Legal provisions that had criminalized the advertising, prescribing, or selling of contraceptives were abolished in 1983.[75]

Abortion is illegal under Articles 539 through 546 of the penal code, except to save the life of the mother.[76] A woman who induces an abortion on her own or allows another to administer an abortion is subject to between six months and seven years in prison. The person who administers the abortion for the woman is subject to the same punishment, unless the woman dies in the process, in which case the minimum sentence increases to four years in prison. When the abortion is performed in the name of preserving honor, both parties can receive a reduced penalty. Despite the ban, illegal abortions are widely available and are facilitated by underground medical and paramedical staff. The subject of abortion is still considered taboo at the familial, social, and religious levels.

The ability of citizens to access health care depends substantially on their economic status. Only 46.3 percent of women and 43.6 percent of men have health insurance, as the poverty gap in coverage is wider than the gender gap.[77] The lack of access to affordable health insurance and care has had a particularly negative effect on women. Within poorer families, the health of the main breadwinner—generally the husband—takes priority over women's health, and the health of male children is similarly valued due to their likelihood of joining the labor market at a relatively young age.

Decree 11802 of 2004 requires all workers in institutions that are subject to the provisions of the Employment Act—particularly pregnant women and mothers of infants—to undergo a periodic medical examination. Furthermore, it prohibits the employment of pregnant women and nursing mothers in "jobs involving exposure to gasoline or products containing gasoline."[78] While these measures indicate a concern for the reproductive health of women, the government does not provide information and support that could protect young women from the dangers of sexually transmitted diseases, unplanned pregnancy, and illegal abortion.[79] Female genital mutilation is not a common practice in Lebanon.

Women enjoy the right to own and use housing without discrimination, and several public institutions have been established to boost home ownership among women, one of the first being the Housing Bank established in 1977. Between 2000 and 2005, the Public Corporation for Housing, established in 1996, extended 30 percent of its total loans to single and married women to purchase houses individually or as a joint owner.[80] Ownership disputes arise during divorce proceedings if the house is jointly owned or is registered solely in the husband's name but the wife has contributed to its purchase. Social norms limit the housing rights of single women to the extent that they are expected to live with their parents until they get married. However, anecdotal evidence seems to indicate that this is changing gradually, particularly in Beirut and among young women who have either lived abroad on their own for some time or have moved to the city to pursue their studies or secure a job.

In the years since the women's rights movement truly took root, Lebanese women have generally been able to participate in and effectively influence their community. Women involved in NGOs and informal religious affiliations were particularly active during the 1975–90 civil war, taking on tasks traditionally reserved for the state, such as emergency relief, health care, and education for the needy.[81] Although women's representation in municipal councils remains far below the optimum level, it has increased in recent years, giving women an instrumental platform from which to shape local social development and policies.

Beginning with the establishment of their own journals and publishing houses in the late 1800s, Lebanese women have long been active in the media.[82] The number of female journalists increased during the 1960s, and women became hosts of talk shows on radio and television. By 2000, women such as Maggy Farah and May Chidiac had gained respect as hosts of political talk shows. This trend has continued in the last five years, and women such as Paula Yaacoubian, Chada Omar, and Najat Sharafeddine have become outspoken political pundits.

Despite this growth in women's visibility in the media, they hold few decision-making positions behind the scenes. A study entitled *Towards the Empowerment of Women in the Media* was carried out in 2008 by the Hariri Foundation for Sustainable Human Development, under the supervision of the Council for Development and Reconstruction and with financing from the World Bank. Its results clearly indicate that although women's presence in the media is increasing, their inability to reach decision-making positions hinders the introduction of fundamental changes regarding women's image at the content level. For example, the study finds that the morning shows, with their gender-stereotyped advertisements, are essentially geared toward housewives. Sets are made to look like the hosts' homes, reinforcing the idea that home, along with family care and children's education, are a woman's domain. Meanwhile, the production of entertainment programs is monopolized by men, and the resulting content often values women only for their physical beauty, as defined by the criteria of the prevailing consumer culture.[83]

Although no gender-disaggregated data exists regarding the poverty rates of individuals, there are reliable statistics related to the poverty levels of households. Women head 15 percent of households, which account for 10.3 percent of the population, and although poverty rates fluctuate between regions, female-headed households and male-headed households experience similar rates of poverty. Of the female heads of households, 71.4 percent are widows, and widow-headed households with more than three children have the highest poverty ratio and are the most vulnerable of all households. Their share among the poor is five times greater than their share of the population.[84]

Several factors have contributed to an increase in poverty in Lebanon, including the current global economic crisis, the 2006 war, and political unrest following the war. Civil society actors played a vital role in defusing the political tension, although many NGOs became politicized in the process, rendering their socioeconomic goals more difficult to achieve. However, women's rights associations and other civil society organizations, like the Family Planning Association, continue to conduct activities and training programs all over Lebanon in an effort to increase women's awareness regarding reproductive health, general health, participation in local politics, obtaining small loans, and public education programs related to women's rights issues.

Recommendations

❖ The government should adopt a unified health insurance scheme to which all Lebanese citizens, including the poor, would have equal access.

❖ The government should work with NGOs that are currently involved in alleviating poverty to design a new poverty-reduction program. The plan should address regional disparities and focus on education and job training without gender discrimination.

❖ In an effort to improve the image of women in the media, civil society should actively push for the promotion of women to decision-making positions within media organizations. To aid in these efforts, the government should solicit nominations from women's rights NGOs and appoint the best female candidates to senior positions in media regulatory bodies.

AUTHOR

Mona Chemali Khalaf is an economist and an independent consultant on gender and development issues. She is a former assistant professor of economics and former director of the Institute for Women's Studies in the Arab World at the Lebanese American University. She serves on the Advisory Board for the Gender Economic Research and Policy Analysis Initiative (GERPA), established by the World Bank and the Center for Arab Women Training and Research (CAWTAR) in 2006. Khalaf is also a member of the editorial board of *Al-Raida*, a quarterly magazine that addresses women's issues in the Arab world, and has authored several publications that focus on women's empowerment through education and work. She coordinated the World Bank's Gender Consultative Council in the Middle East and North Africa region, and was a member of the Lebanese NGO Commission for the Preparation of the 1995 Beijing World Conference on Women; the Lebanese National Commission for the Preparation of the 1995 Beijing World Conference on Women; the Lebanese National Commission for Women's Affairs; and the Board of Trustees of the United Nations International Research and Training Institute for the Advancement of Women (INSTRAW).

NOTES

1 In 1952, the parliament had granted only educated women the right to vote.

2 In this case, Myrna Boustani, the only child of lawmaker Emile Boustani, continued his term after his death. She ran for the vacant seat unopposed.

3 The National Committee for Lebanese Women was established through a ministerial decree in 1996 to monitor the implementation of the recommendations of the 1995 Beijing conference. In November 1998, this committee became the National Commission for Lebanese Women by virtue of Law No. 720.

4 An English translation of the constitution is available at http://www.servat.unibe.ch/icl/le00t___.html. See Alia Berti Zein, "Women's Civil Rights in Lebanon," *Al-Raida* 13, no. 111–112 (Fall/Winter 2005–06): 19, http://www.lau.edu.lb/centers-institutes/iwsaw/raida111-112/main.html.

5 Alia Berti Zein, "Women's Civil Rights in Lebanon," 19.

6 *Third Periodic Report of State Parties: Lebanon* (New York: UN Committee on the Elimination of Discrimination against Women, July 7, 2006), 31, http://www.un.org/womenwatch/daw/cedaw/reports.htm. See also statute 10955 of September 17, 2003.

7 *Initial Report of States Parties: Lebanon* (New York: UN Committee on the Elimination of Discrimination against Women, September 2, 2004), 29, http://www.un.org/womenwatch/daw/cedaw/reports.htm.

8 "Honor Killings Banned by Lebanon's Top Shiite Cleric," *Ya Libnan*, August 3, 2007, http://yalibnan.com/site/archives/2007/08/honor_killings_1.php.

9 *Third Periodic Report of States Parties: Lebanon.*

10 *Initial Report of States Parties: Lebanon*, 29.

11 Article 522 of the penal code.

12 Women's Right Monitor Project, *Report on the Convention on the Elimination of All Forms of Discrimination against Women (CEDAW), Draft of Initial Report* (Beirut: Lebanese NGO Forum, 2000), section IX(1), http://www.lnf.org.lb/windex/report.html.

13 *Third Periodic Report of States Parties: Lebanon*, 16. According to this declaration, "the Government will strive to focus on issues of woman as an essential and active partner in

public life by creating the appropriate legal environment to strengthen her role in various sectors, and will lay the foundations for the incorporation of the concept of gender in all fiscal, economic and social policies in line with new international thinking in this respect."

14   *Third Periodic Report of States Parties: Lebanon,* 29.

15   UN Programme on Governance in the Arab Region (POGAR), "Lebanon: Judiciary," UN Development Programme (UNDP), http://www.undp-pogar.org/countries/theme .aspx?t=9&cid=9.

16   *Third Periodic Report of States Parties: Lebanon,* 25.

17   Human Rights Watch, "Lebanon: Act Now on Steps to Prevent Torture," news release, November 5, 2008, http://www.hrw.org/en/news/2008/11/05/lebanon-act-now-steps-prevent-torture.

18   Moghaizel Law Offices, personal communication, February 2009; see also *Second Periodic Report of States Parties: Lebanon* (New York: UN Committee on the Elimination of Discrimination against Women, February 11, 2005), 48–49, http://www.un.org/womenwatch/daw/cedaw/reports.htm.

19   According to personal communication with lawyer Ikbal Doughan, president of the Family Rights Network, on March 14, 2009. However, the first woman judge was named public prosecutor at the Court of Cassation in November 2004, which entitled her to an ex officio place as vice president of the Higher Council of the Judiciary. See *Second Periodic Report of States Parties: Lebanon,* 48.

20   *Third Periodic Report of States Parties: Lebanon,* 84.

21   "Each Lebanese is subject to the laws, regulations and courts of his or her own religious community. This legislative and judicial pluralism . . . has a constitutional framework and roots associated with the establishment and stability of Lebanon as a political entity. Accordingly, this subject is extremely sensitive and linked to the broader political and social situation in the country." *Third Periodic Report of States Parties: Lebanon,* 11.

22   *Third Periodic Report of States Parties: Lebanon,* 17.

23   The officially recognized religious groups include 4 Muslim and 12 Christian denominations, in addition to the Druze and Jews.

24   Lebanese NGO Forum, "A Brief Review of the Current State of Violations of Women's Rights in Lebanon," http://www.lnf.org.lb/windex/brief1.html#a1.

25   The group, "All for Civil Marriage in Lebanon," has more than 8,000 members on its "Groups" page and more than 13,000 members on its "Causes" page as of November 2009. See the website of All for Civil Marriage in Lebanon on Facebook at http://www .facebook.com/Civil.Marriage.in.Lebanon.

26   This draft, in Arabic, can be found at http://www.civil-marriage-lebanon.com/Civil MarriageFeb09Proposal.pdf.

27   For example, Article 46 of the Armenian Orthodox law and Article 38 of the Assyrian Church of the East law state: "The man is the head of the family and its representative in law." The Armenian article also states: "It is the duty of the man to protect his wife and of the woman to obey her husband." A 1999 decision by the Supreme Druze Appeal Court found that "the wife who refuses to reside in the house of her husband shall be responsible for the consequences to her personal rights." *Third Periodic Report of States Parties: Lebanon,* 89–90.

28   The amended law states: "By marriage, rights and duties shall be equal between both spouses in matters relating to the communion of married life." It also holds that "the spouses must have a shared home or the likeness thereof," whereas the previous law commanded that "the wife keep the house of her husband." *Third Periodic Report of States Parties: Lebanon*, 89.

29   In February 2009, Minister of Interior Ziad Baroud succeeded in getting the government to agree that citizens are free to omit their religion on their *ikhraj qayd*, the family civil registry record. Stating one's religion on this document was previously mandatory.

30   The marriage age for Sunni and Druze women is 17; for Shi'a it is the age of puberty; for the Catholic denominations, Armenian Orthodox, and Syrian Orthodox it is 14; and for Greek Orthodox it is 18.

31   *Third Periodic Report of States Parties: Lebanon*, 87.

32   Article 58 of the Islamic personal status law permits Muslim men to marry women of any monotheistic faith while invalidating marriages between Muslim women and non-Muslim men. Article 47 allows a bride's guardian to annul a properly executed marriage if it is to an "unqualified" man.

33   *Third Periodic Report of States Parties: Lebanon*, 87.

34   *Third Periodic Report of States Parties: Lebanon*, 95.

35   *Third Periodic Report of States Parties: Lebanon*, 96, 98.

36   *Third Periodic Report of States Parties: Lebanon*, 94.

37   Ikbal Doughan, personal communication, 2009.

38   *Third Periodic Report of States Parties: Lebanon*, 94.

39   UNDP, *Lebanon National Human Development Report: Toward a Citizen's State* (Beirut: UNDP, 2009), 166, http://hdr.undp.org/en/reports/nationalreports/arabstates/lebanon/NHDR_Lebanon_20082009_En.pdf.

40   A. Charara-Baydoun, *Killing of Women and the Lebanese Judiciary System* (Beirut: KAFA [Enough] Violence and Exploitation, 2008), in Arabic.

41   *Second Periodic Report of States Parties: Lebanon*, 40.

42   Bureau of Democracy, Human Rights, and Labor, "Lebanon," in *2008 Country Reports on Human Rights Practices* (Washington, DC: U.S. Department of State, 2009), http://www.state.gov/g/drl/rls/hrrpt/2008/nea/119120.htm.

43   The 2008 GDP growth figures for Lebanon vary from 7 percent to 8.5 percent, depending on the source. The World Bank's estimate is 8 percent. World Bank Data Finder (Online Source), http://datafinder.worldbank.org. Also see International Monetary Fund, *Lebanon: Report on Performance Under the Program Supported by Emergency Post-Conflict Assistance* (Washington, DC: International Monetary Fund, July 2009), 1, 6, 9, http://www.imf.org/external/pubs/ft/scr/2009/cr09213.pdf.

44   *Third Periodic Report of States Parties: Lebanon*, 96, 97.

45   UNDP, *Lebanon National Human Development Report*, 136.

46   World Bank, *The Status and Progress of Women in the Middle East and North Africa* (Washington, DC: World Bank, 2007), 21, http://siteresources.worldbank.org/INTMENA/Resources/MENA_Gender_BW2007.pdf.

47   World Bank, "GenderStats—Create Your Own Table," http://go.worldbank.org/MRER20PME0 [accessed December 15, 2009].

48   World Bank, "GenderStats—Education," http://go.worldbank.org/RHEGN4QHU0 [accessed December 15, 2009].

49   UNDP, Lebanese Ministry of Social Affairs, and Lebanese Central Administration of Statistics, *Living Conditions of the Households of Lebanon* (Beirut: UNDP, 2006), 47, in English and Arabic, available at http://www.undp.org.lb/communication/publications/index.cfm.

50   World Bank, "GenderStats—Education," http://go.worldbank.org/RHEGN4QHU0 [accessed December 15, 2009].

51   World Bank, "GenderStats—Education." The secondary gross enrollment rate in 2007 was 85.6 percent for females, up from 78.7 in 2000, and 76.7 percent for males, up from 72.6 in 2000. The tertiary gross enrollment rate for 2007 was 56.3 percent for females, up from 34.7 in 2000, and 46.9 percent for males, up from 33.1 percent in 2000.

52   UNDP, *Lebanon National Human Development Report*, 55.

53   UNDP, *Lebanon National Human Development Report*, 142. "Two out of every three women work in administration or education, compared to one out of every four men."

54   Lebanon ratified ILO Conventions 100 and 111, on equal remuneration and discrimination in employment and occupation, respectively, in 1977. See ILO, "Ratifications of the Fundamental Human Rights Conventions by Country," http://www.ilo.org/ilolex/english/docs/declworld.htm.

55   Laure Moghaizel, *Houqouq al-Mar`a al-Insan fi Loubnan fi Daou` Ittifaqiyyat al-Qada` `ala Jami' Ashkal Attamyeez Ded al-Mar`a* (*Al-Lajna al-Wataniyya Li Shou`oun al-Mar`a*) [Women's Human Rights in Lebanon in Light of CEDAW] (Beirut: Mou`assasat Joseph wa Laure Moghaizel, 2000).

56   UNDP, *Lebanon National Human Development Report*, 60.

57   *Third Periodic Report of States Parties: Lebanon*, 59.

58   *Third Periodic Report of States Parties: Lebanon*, 62.

59   Human Rights Watch, "Middle East: Move Quickly on Labor Reforms for Migrant Women," news release, December 17, 2008, http://www.hrw.org/en/news/2008/12/17/middle-east-move-quickly-labor-reforms-migrant-women. This report indicates that every week, one of the nearly 200,000 domestic workers in Lebanon attempts or succeeds in committing suicide, and that Lebanon lags behind most other countries in the region in protecting migrant women's rights.

60   United Nations Convention Against Transnational Organized Crime (Law 680 of August 24, 2005); Protocol Against the Smuggling of Migrants by Land, Sea and Air, supplementing the United Nations Convention Against Transnational Organized Crime (Law 681 of August 24, 2005); Protocol to Prevent, Suppress and Punish Trafficking in Persons, Especially Women and Children, supplementing the United Nations Convention Against Transnational Organized Crime (Law 682 of August 24, 2005).

61   *Third Periodic Report of States Parties: Lebanon*, 43.

62   Human Rights Watch, "Middle East: Move Quickly on Labor Reforms for Migrant Women."

63   Marguerite Helou, "Women in the Lebanese Parliament 1992–1996," *Bahithat*, Fourth Issue (1997–1998): 170–202.

64   *Second Periodic Report of States Parties: Lebanon,* 44–45; *Third Period Report of States Parties: Lebanon,* 48.

65   Inter-Parliamentary Union, "Lebanon: Majlis Al-Nuwwab (National Assembly)," PARLINE, http://www.ipu.org/parline-e/reports/2179_E.htm.

66   *Second Periodic Report of States Parties: Lebanon,* 12, 46, 72.

67   World Bank, *The Status and Progress of Women in the Middle East and North Africa,* 54.

68   *Third Periodic Report of States Parties: Lebanon,* 50.

69   *Second Periodic Report of States Parties: Lebanon,* 22–23.

70   *Second Periodic Report of States Parties: Lebanon,* 51.

71   International Telecommunication Union, "Internet Indicators: Subscribers, Users and Broadband Subscribers, 2008," http://www.itu.int/ITU-D/icteye/Indicators/Indicators.aspx#.

72   UNDP, *Lebanon National Human Development Report,* 137.

73   World Health Organization, "Lebanon Health Facilities Have Suffered Considerable Damage," news release, September 6, 2006, http://www.who.int/mediacentre/news/releases/2006/pr48/en/index.html.

74   Decree 9814 of 2003. See *Third Periodic Report of States Parties: Lebanon,* 31. This amendment was made as part of the national reproductive health program that Lebanon launched based on the recommendations of the 1994 International Conference on Population and Development.

75   *Second Periodic Report of States Parties: Lebanon,* 68.

76   United Nations, "Lebanon," in *Abortion Policies—A Global Review* (New York: United Nations, 2002), http://www.un.org/esa/population/publications/abortion/profiles.htm.

77   UNDP, *Living Conditions of the Households of Lebanon,* 68.

78   *Second Periodic Report of States Parties: Lebanon,* 69.

79   *Third Periodic Report of States Parties: Lebanon,* 71.

80   *Third Periodic Report of States Parties: Lebanon,* 73.

81   Kareem Elbayar, "NGO Laws in Selected Arab States," *International Journal of Not-for-Profit Law 7,* no. 4 (September 2005): 3.

82   Hanifa al-Khatib, "Noshou` al-Haraka Annisa`ya fi Alloubnaniyya wa Fa'aliyyitiha fi Almoujtama' fi Marahel Tatawworiha," *Addiyar,* March 8, 1998. It is estimated that by 1940 the number of these journals reached 40.

83   Nahawand al-Kaderi Issa, *Towards the Empowerment of Women in the Media* (Beirut: Hariri Foundation for Sustainable Human Development, 2009), 15, http://www.hariri-foundation.org/admin/document/9.pdf.

84   UNDP, *Poverty, Growth and Income Distribution in Lebanon* (Beirut: UNDP, 2008), 68, http://www.undp.org.lb/communication/publications/index.cfm.

LIBYA

by Alison Pargeter

POPULATION:	6,283,000		
GNI PER CAPITA:	US$10,078		

COUNTRY RATINGS	2004	2009
NONDISCRIMINATION AND ACCESS TO JUSTICE:	2.4	2.4
AUTONOMY, SECURITY, AND FREEDOM OF THE PERSON:	2.6	2.6
ECONOMIC RIGHTS AND EQUAL OPPORTUNITY:	2.4	2.8
POLITICAL RIGHTS AND CIVIC VOICE:	1.8	1.8
SOCIAL AND CULTURAL RIGHTS:	2.4	2.5

(COUNTRY RATINGS ARE BASED ON A SCALE OF 1 TO 5, WITH 1 REPRESENTING THE LOWEST AND 5 THE HIGHEST LEVEL OF FREEDOM WOMEN HAVE TO EXERCISE THEIR RIGHTS)

INTRODUCTION

Libya has been ruled by Colonel Muammar al-Qadhafi since he came to power in a bloodless coup in 1969. He has organized the country's political landscape around his personal interpretations of Arab nationalism, socialism, and Islam, which are laid out in a treatise known as the *Green Book*. In March 1977, al-Qadhafi declared the establishment of the authority of the people and introduced a unique political system called the Jamahiriya (State of the Masses). Under this system, every Libyan citizen ostensibly participates in the ruling structure through membership in local congresses, the decisions of which are fed up into the General People's Congress (parliament). Al-Qadhafi himself has no formal position or title, preferring to refer to himself as "Brother Leader" or "Leader of the Revolution." In reality, however, he retains complete control of the state apparatus.

Libya spent much of the 1980s and 1990s in relative isolation, with United States and United Nations sanctions in place due to the country's involvement in a series of terrorist bombings. However, following the Libyan government's decision in April 1999 to hand over the two suspects in the 1988 bombing of a U.S. airliner over Lockerbie, Scotland, for trial in The Hague, Libya began to rebuild its relations with the international community. Its rehabilitation took a major leap forward in December 2003,

283

when the regime announced that it would abandon its nuclear, chemical, and biological weapons programs. The United States lifted most unilateral sanctions in 2004, and finally removed Libya from its State Sponsors of Terrorism list in 2006. Libya has since been working to fully reintegrate itself into the international community and to modernize and upgrade its national infrastructure, which had deteriorated during the years of sanctions. However, despite its achievements at the diplomatic level, Libya has made little progress in instituting genuine political or economic reform on the domestic front. The regime made certain promises of reform in the realms of human rights, personal freedoms, and economic liberalization, but Libya is still a highly centralized state in which al-Qadhafi's revolutionary ideology remains paramount.

As part of his bid to overhaul Libyan society, al-Qadhafi has sought to promote the status of women and to encourage them to participate in his Jamahiriya project. Some of his most progressive policies have directly challenged the prevailing conservatism in Libya, though his regime at times has struck a conciliatory tone with the Islamist political opposition and the conservative populace at the expense of women's rights. In his *Green Book* he asserts the equality between genders and strongly denounces discrimination. Paradoxically, the tome also makes note of the biological differences between men and women and declares that the two genders cannot be equal.[1]

Nevertheless, al-Qadhafi has pushed for women to become equal citizens and has introduced legislation aimed at reducing discrimination between the sexes. He has also sought to provide women with greater access to education and employment. As a result, women in Libya are now better able to participate in the country's political, economic, and social life.

These efforts by the state have run against Libya's extremely conservative patriarchal traditions and tribal culture, which continue to foster gender discrimination. Indeed, given the broader gap that exists between the regime and the population, there is a sense among many Libyans that the authorities are attempting to foist certain liberal values on the country without consent, and this has only strengthened societal adherence to conservatism and traditional religious principles. Such resistance has led the regime to cede ground on some gender issues in order to bolster its own legitimacy. For example, women still face unequal treatment in many aspects of family law.

An independent women's rights movement might be more successful in gaining credibility and sympathy among the public, but the authorities do not permit any genuinely independent organizations or political groups to exist. Membership in any group or organization that is not sanctioned by the state is punishable by death under Law No. 71 of 1972. There are a number of women's organizations in Libya that purport to be independent, but they are all in fact closely linked to the state. Consequently, their efforts to promote women's emancipation have yielded little progress.

Some positive developments in terms of women's rights have occurred in the past five years, such as the state's attempts to promote a greater awareness of domestic violence and the fact that more women are entering the workforce. However, women's rights have been at times threatened, as in the instance where the government temporarily restricted women from leaving the country without their male guardian, a step that the authorities later denied. Moreover, there has been no fundamental shift in societal attitudes or behavior in that time, and the gulf between the rhetoric of the regime and the reality on the ground remains as wide as ever.

NONDISCRIMINATION AND ACCESS TO JUSTICE

Although the government claims to have eliminated gender-based discrimination under Libyan legislation, women remain treated unequally in some aspects of the law, notably within provisions of family law that uphold the principles of Shari'a (Islamic law). Moreover, women face discrimination within the judiciary due to social attitudes and prevailing cultural values, and legislation designed to protect women is often not implemented in practice. Women are often treated as minors under the guardianship of their fathers or other male relatives, a cultural and in some cases legal reality that has remained unaltered in recent years.[2] Meanwhile, Libyan women who are married to non-Libyan men now face even greater disadvantage due to the new state-imposed fees for the schooling of their children.

Libya has no constitution, despite recent attempts by al-Qadhafi's son, Saif al-Islam, to develop one. Instead, the country's basic legal framework consists of a series of laws and key declarations, such as the 1977 Declaration of the Authority of the People and the 1988 Great Green Charter of Human Rights in the Age of the Masses (Great Green Charter).

These documents assert the equality of all citizens before the law. The Great Green Charter, for example, stipulates that men and women "are equal in everything which is human. The distinction between men and women is a flagrant injustice which nothing justifies."[3] However, portions of the Green Book seem to contradict this by stressing the biological differences between men and women, asserting, "man and woman cannot be equal."

In addition, Article 1 of Law No. 20 of 1991 asserts that the citizens of the Jamahiriya, both male and female, are free and equal in respect of their rights, and that these rights may not be violated.[4] The Charter on the Rights and Duties of Women in Jamahiriya Society—which was approved in 1997 and is considered one of the most important legislations that relates to women—includes provisions to guarantee the equal rights of men and women in areas such as national security duties, marriage, divorce, child custody, the right to work, social security, and financial independence.[5] It also guarantees women the right to participate in the country's governing institutions. These proclaimed rights, however, are undermined by specific laws that govern family life, such as the law that permits men to practice polygamy, which discriminate against women (see "Autonomy, Security, and Freedom of the Person").

Women have the right to full and equal status as citizens and enjoy the same rights as men regarding the right to acquire, change or retain their nationality, or replace it with another nationality. A Libyan woman forfeits her citizenship only if she wishes to adopt her foreign husband's nationality. However, unlike Libyan men, Libyan women do not have the right to transfer their nationality to their foreign-born spouses or the children of such unions. While the children of a Libyan father and foreign mother are granted Libyan nationality, children of a Libyan mother and foreign father are not and require visas to enter the country if they reside abroad.

In 2007 the government issued a decree ruling that children of Libyan mothers and non-Libyan fathers cannot attend public schools unless they pay a fee of 800 dinars (US$646). However, the General People's Committee, the executive arm of government, later ruled that fees may be waived for families that cannot afford them.[6] Families headed by Libyan mothers and foreign fathers are also discriminated against in that they are deprived of a family book (official documentation that permits access to certain state benefits such as subsidized food) and are not permitted to obtain loans. They are similarly excluded from state payments to families following the birth of a child.

Libya's judicial system consists of four types of courts: the summary courts, which are the courts of first instance; the primary courts; the courts of appeal; and the Supreme Court, which is the apex of the judicial structure and hears civil, commercial, criminal, administrative, and personal status cases. Al-Qadhafi merged civil and Shari'a courts shortly after coming to power, so these courts, all of which are civil in nature, have jurisdiction over family cases. There are also 10 special courts in Tripoli and Benghazi that deal only with personal status cases. The rationale for having these separate courts is to "respect women's special position and avoid women mixing with criminal elements."[7] In other words, they are intended to provide protection and a sense of security to women who bring legal cases on issues like divorce and child custody.

Although women and men have an equal right of recourse to the law and an equal right to pursue legal proceedings, and although an adult woman is generally recognized as a full person before the court, women continue to find themselves at a disadvantage due to cultural traditions. They typically consult with a male relative before taking legal action, and it is still accepted practice for a man to take legal action on a woman's behalf. A woman has the right to challenge discriminatory actions by the state and claim compensation should the courts rule in her favor. However, it is difficult to determine whether women actually file such claims, as court records are not easily accessible by the public.

Women have been eligible to become judges since 1981, although they remain underrepresented in the judiciary. The first female judge was appointed in 1991, and currently there are an estimated 50 female judges.[8] Women are free to work as lawyers, public prosecutors, and case administrators, and their representation in the legal profession is increasing. However, no female jurists have been appointed to the Supreme Court.

Libya has been developing a new draft penal code since 2003, but there has been little news of its progress; the General People's Congress must agree to the draft before it becomes law. Although the existing penal code applies equally to both men and women, they are treated differently in some cases such as adultery.[9] Both guilty partners face a possible penalty of 100 strokes of the whip, but Article 375 allows for a reduced punishment for a man who kills a female relative on account of her having committed adultery. Article 375 also asserts that if the man only inflicts bodily harm on the female relative, the prison sentence is limited to a maximum of two years, and a lesser beating or light injury should not be penalized at all.

Despite this leniency, so-called "honor killings," in which a male relative kills a woman for moral or sexual transgressions, are not common in Libya.

An adult woman is recognized as a full person before the court and is equal to a man throughout all stages of litigation and legal proceedings. However, in some instances, women are not considered to be as authentic witnesses as men. Common interpretations of Islamic principles assert that one male witness is equivalent to two females. Moreover, the testimony of a woman cannot be used to establish the crime of *zina* (extramarital sexual relations), illustrating at least one circumstance in which a woman's worth before the court is less than that of a man.[10]

Women suspected of engaging in oppositional political activity are subject to arbitrary arrest, detention, and exile. Although it is generally assumed that women do not engage to any significant extent in such activities, those suspected face the same penalties as men. However, women are subject to a form of gender-specific confinement in "social rehabilitation" homes for young women who have broken moral codes or who are "vulnerable to engaging in moral misconduct."[11] Women are transferred to these facilities by the public prosecutor and in some cases are detained there against their will. Others who have been raped or become pregnant out of wedlock enter the facilities voluntarily because they fear their families' reactions to their situations. Officially, these women are free to leave the rehabilitation homes when they turn 18 years old, when they consent to marriage, or when a male relative agrees to take them in. However, there is no limit on the length of time that the government can hold women in these facilities.[12]

Mohammed Youssef al-Mahatrash, the head of prosecutions in Tripoli, explained in 2005 that a resident of a rehabilitation home "can't leave when she wants. We don't let them go out in the street where there is no protection for them. It [the social rehabilitation facility] is a type of protection for them."[13] There is no mechanism for women to appeal their transfer into these facilities.

The women and girls in these centers also undergo other human rights abuses. For example, upon entering they are routinely tested for communicable diseases without their consent, and most are forced to endure invasive virginity examinations.[14] Although some of those sent to such facilities are school-age teenagers, they receive no education other than religious instruction aimed at "reforming" their moral character.

Libya acceded to the UN Convention on the Elimination of All Forms of Discrimination against Women (CEDAW) in 1989. At that time, it made reservations to Article 2 and Article 16, in relation to rights and responsibilities in marriage, divorce, and parenthood, on the grounds that these articles should be applied without prejudice to Shari'a. Libya made an additional general reservation in 1995, declaring that no aspect of accession can conflict with the laws of personal status derived from Shari'a.[15]

In June 2004, Libya became the first country in the Arab region to ratify the Optional Protocol to CEDAW.[16] The protocol allows Libyan groups and individuals to petition the UN CEDAW committee if they believe their rights under the convention have been violated.[17] However, because the committee can only issue nonbinding recommendations to states in response to these petitions, the practical effects of the protocol remain unclear.

There are no genuinely independent nongovernmental women's rights groups in Libya. Several women's organizations claim to be independent, such as Al-Wafa Association for Human Services, which seeks to improve the status of women and "to further women's education and social standing."[18] However, all such organizations have close ties to the authorities. The charity Al-Wattasimu, for example, organized an international conference on women's rights in Tripoli in April 2007. Participants sought to draft new concepts and principles on women's rights and "to realize a strategic support group project for African women."[19] Al-Wattasimu is run by Aisha al-Qadhafi, the daughter of Muammar al-Qadhafi.

Recommendations

❖ The government should amend Article 375 of the penal code to ensure that any man who kills or inflicts bodily harm on a female relative following alleged sexual transgressions does not receive a reduced punishment.

❖ The government should set up specialized support centers in all major cities that offer free legal advice to women.

❖ The government should implement a nationwide program to improve legal literacy among girls and women through media and leafleting campaigns.

❖ The government should close down the existing social rehabilitation centers and ensure that women are not sent to or held in any such facilities against their will. It should instead establish support networks and shelters that provide opportunities for education, childcare, and job training to women who have become pregnant outside of marriage or who have been ostracized by their families for "immoral" behavior.

✤ The state should permit the formation of truly independent nongovernmental organizations dedicated to advancing women's rights.

AUTONOMY, SECURITY, AND FREEDOM OF THE PERSON

The Libyan state has sought to promote women's autonomy and independence, and it has taken some steps to address violence against women. However, women's personal freedom and security remain limited in practice, and there has been little concrete progress on these issues in recent years. This is largely due to the traditional nature of Libyan society, which places huge social pressures on women to preserve their honor. Indeed, the honor of the entire family rests upon the extent to which its female members comply with social and moral norms. Women's security is also restricted in that domestic violence and rape are still considered taboo subjects that should be kept within the domain of the family. Elements within the government attempted to restrict freedom of movement for women in 2007, but they were soon forced to retract their position after an outcry in the official media and other parts of the regime.

Islam is the declared state religion, and Libya broadly follows the Maliki school of Sunni Islam. Women have the right to practice Islam freely, although the state does not tolerate any religious activity that is deemed to have a political dimension. The regime is deeply concerned about the threat of political Islam, especially that of a militant nature. Anyone suspected of having such tendencies—male or female—risks persecution. Although overt displays of religiosity, such as the *niqab* (veil that covers all but the wearer's eyes), may draw the attention of the authorities, they are not banned outright. In May 2008, the authorities of Gar Younis University in Benghazi posted a decision warning female students not to wear the niqab because it was being used as a disguise by "immoral women," namely prostitutes.[20] The decision also warned women not to wear makeup or mix with members of the opposite sex. However, this appears to have been a localized incident that reflects the arbitrary nature of Libyan governance.

The government is broadly tolerant of other faiths, and there is a small Christian community made up primarily of foreigners. However, the state is far less accepting of Muslims who convert to Christianity and has imprisoned a small number of such converts in recent years. Society is also uncomfortable with the idea of conversion, and any woman wishing to convert to Christianity would find it difficult to practice her new religion freely. A non-Libyan man must convert to Islam in order to marry a Muslim Libyan woman, while a non-Libyan woman is not required to convert if she marries a Muslim Libyan man. Atheism is generally not deemed acceptable by society.

Women have the right to freedom of movement and are not legally required to secure the permission of their husbands or male relatives to obtain passports.[21] Married women are able to travel with their children without the permission of their husbands. However, a Libyan husband may ask the authorities to prevent his wife from leaving the country with their children if there is a specific family dispute and the father fears that the mother may take the children away. In practice, many Libyan women travel only in the company of their husbands or male relatives due to the patriarchal nature of society. Those who are part of the social elite may have more freedom in this respect, but even they are expected to secure permission from a male relative to travel abroad. As a practical matter, women also face restrictions traveling inside Libya, as many hotels will not let rooms to unaccompanied women.

In March 2007, the state-owned newspaper *Al-Jamahiriya* reported that the authorities had introduced travel restrictions prohibiting women under the age of 40 from leaving the country without being accompanied by their husbands or a close male relative, prompting public outcry.[22] However, the government denied this act several days later, stating that the regulation had been an old and temporary remedy to address the problem of young girls traveling abroad.[23] The initial move seems to have been an isolated and arbitrary decision made by certain elements within the regime.

Social traditions also restrict women's day-to-day freedom of movement. For example, a woman walking in public after dark is expected to be accompanied by a male relative or another female. Without such escorts, she risks verbal harassment for what is considered the behavior of a "loose" woman. Unmarried women are generally expected to give their families the details of any excursion outside the home. Women also find it difficult to go to the beach and to swim on account of the male attention their presence would attract. There are a number of women-only beach resorts and swimming pools, and other facilities reserve certain days for women. These, however, tend to be the domain of the rich. Women from rural areas and small villages have far less freedom in this respect.

Family laws in Libya are, in part, based on the Maliki school of jurisprudence. The roles of men and women in marriage are established in Law No. 10 of 1984, which proscribes different rights based on gender. The husband is granted the right to his wife's "concern with his comfort and his psychological and sensory repose," and she is also tasked with the "supervision of the conjugal house and organization and maintenance of its affairs."[24] The wife is not granted reciprocity on these issues, but she is entitled to financial maintenance from her husband, control over her private wealth, and the right to be free from mental or physical violence.[25]

Women are legally empowered to negotiate their marriage rights, but their ability to do so in practice is often curtailed by cultural norms. Article 21 of the Great Green Charter prohibits forced marriage and describes marriage as "an equitable association between two equal partners." Article 8 of Law No. 10 of 1984 also states that a guardian "may not compel a young man or young woman to marry against his or her will."[26] The same article states that a guardian cannot prevent a prospective bride from marrying the prospective husband of her choice. If a guardian refuses permission without an acceptable legal reason, she may bring the matter to the court.

Nonetheless, tradition dictates that a woman should obtain the permission of her father or male guardian before she marries. Women who are of an appropriate age for marriage are generally put under "severe monitoring" by their families to ensure that they uphold their honor and, by extension, that of the entire family. Marriage is often deemed to be of greater importance than education or employment, as according to traditional norms, "marriage is the standard whereby the success of a woman can be measured."[27]

Most marriages in Libya, particularly outside of urban areas, are arranged through family and friends. Online dating, or at least chatting romantically, has become more common in recent years as Internet access has expanded somewhat. A minority of young people, most of whom live in Tripoli, are now more likely to date in public places such as cafes in shopping malls. However, this generally occurs without the knowledge of parents, given the social stigma attached to such behavior.

According to Article 6 of Law No. 10 of 1984, the minimum age of marriage is 20, although younger people can marry if a court and the woman's guardian grant permission.[28] Girls living in rural areas are particularly likely to marry young, but on the whole, Libyan women increasingly face the opposite problem. Low salaries and limited employment opportunities are compelling men to wait until they are older to marry, because they must be able to financially support a wife. Many men, especially those from low-income families, do not achieve the requisite level of financial stability until they are in their 30s, which forces women to wait longer to marry their fiancés. Although the trend toward later marriage is also attributable to the fact that some women have chosen to complete their education and enter the workforce before marrying, financial concerns remain the driving force behind this shift. Women over the age of 30 are generally considered to be past the acceptable age for marriage. Consequently, although the increase in late marriages affects both sexes, women tend to suffer more from the phenomenon.[29]

Article 3 of the 1984 law permits either prospective spouse to insert stipulations in the marital contract, so long as they do not contradict the purpose or aims of marriage. Such stipulations could theoretically include, for instance, the wife's right to work outside the home or complete her education, but in practice few women insist on special conditions in their marriage contracts.

Polygamy is permitted under Libyan law. A man may take a second wife if the existing wife agrees to the union in court, and if the court grants its permission. In some exceptional circumstances the court may authorize the second marriage in the absence of the existing wife's permission. However, polygamy is rare in practice in Libya, and al-Qadhafi has spoken out against it.

Law No. 70 of 1973 criminalizes fornication, and both men and women may be prosecuted for engaging in sexual relations outside of marriage, the punishment for which is flogging.[30] In October 2007, a Libyan government representative told the UN Human Rights Committee, which oversees the International Covenant on Civil and Political Rights, that Law No. 70 is based on the Koran and that the right to freedom of belief does not mean fornication should be practiced in society.[31] Although few people are punished for fornication, women who are discovered to have engaged in illicit sexual relations often find themselves shunned by society and their families, and are deemed to have violated the family's honor.

Unlike in most other Arab states, where a man can divorce his wife by declaring his intent three times before a witness, Libyan law holds that men must also petition the court in order for the divorce to be valid.[32] In keeping with Article 21 of the Great Green Charter, which requires mutual consent or a "fair judgment" for the execution of a divorce, the court will grant a divorce if both parties agree to it or if the petitioner is able to establish grounds for divorce based on certain legally defined reasons.[33] In cases where the parties cannot agree to a divorce, the court will first assign arbitrators (preferably from the two families) in an effort to reconcile the couple. If this fails, the court then has discretion to grant a divorce.

The legitimate reasons for which a woman may petition for divorce include the husband's inability to maintain her financially, absence without justification, or unjustified abandonment for a period of four months. Either party may petition for divorce if the other is unable to consummate the relationship. Under Article 48 of Law No. 10 of 1984, Libyan women also have the right to *khula*, a process that allows the wife to divorce her husband on other grounds, provided she is willing to give up financial rights including her dowry and maintenance.

If the court deems the woman to be the cause of the divorce, she forfeits her right to *sadaq* (deferred dowry payment) and custody of the couple's children. If the court deems the man to be at fault, he is obliged to pay his wife compensation as well as the sadaq agreed to at the time of marriage. After a divorce has been granted, the law imposes on the husband a duty to maintain his wife financially for a certain period, regardless of how wealthy she may be. Nonetheless, this rule is not often enforced in practice, and divorced women face acute difficulties if they have no family to rely on.

Although women are permitted to represent themselves before the court during divorce proceedings, in practice they are usually represented by a male family member. Divorce is still considered to be a family affair, meaning a woman's ability to secure a divorce is often dependent on the extent to which her family supports her decision. Moreover, it is generally easier for men to secure a divorce than women, and society is more accepting of divorced men than divorced women. However, as women have become more financially independent in recent years, they have grown more capable of pushing for divorce than they were in the past.

If a couple separates based on mutual agreement, the mother has custody of daughters until they marry and of sons until they reach puberty. If the mother is unable to exercise this right, custody transfers to her mother, then to the father, then to the father's mother, then to closely related females, and finally to closely related males. A father must provide financial support to his children unless they have private assets. Although the law favors granting custody to mothers, traditional norms favor the father; judges tend to use their discretion to enforce the latter, especially if the mother is not Libyan.[34]

Domestic violence is a problem in Libya. Article 17 of Law No. 10 of 1984 states that husbands should not cause physical or mental harm to their wives, but Article 63 of the penal code stipulates that evidence of injury is needed to prove assault.[35] As in most conservative societies, domestic violence remains a taboo issue, and its public airing is deemed to be something shameful that brings dishonor upon the victim as well as her entire family. At the official level, certain elements have been unwilling to acknowledge that violence against women exists. As the deputy of the Social Affairs Secretariat has stated, "We don't have violence against women . . . if there was violence, we would know."[36] Similarly, another Libyan official once explained to the UN Committee on the Rights of the Child that no organizations in Libya specifically defend the rights of women because "women did not suffer from discrimination and that kind of organization therefore served no purpose."[37] However, awareness regarding this issue has grown in recent years, and the state has made some efforts to educate the population. In March 2007, the charity Al-Wattasimu launched a cultural project in Tripoli on women's equality that included a number of forums and publications related to violence against women.

Despite these efforts, many women do not raise complaints about domestic violence due to the social stigma attached to the issue. Women generally fear that they will be rejected by their husbands and extended families should they come forward with accusations. One senior Libyan judicial official said that 99 percent of victims who filed domestic violence complaints eventually withdrew their cases.[38] There are no shelters for victims of violence in Libya. Spousal rape is not a crime, and like other forms of domestic abuse, such cases are considered private matters that carry a great deal of shame if publicly reported.

Gender-based violence that occurs outside the home is also deemed to be a matter of disgrace, and the female victim is often held responsible for the actions of the perpetrator. Only the most heinous of rapists are prosecuted, and rape victims themselves risk prosecution for extramarital sexual relations if they attempt to press charges.[39] A rapist is expected to marry his victim to "save her honor" as a "social remedy." The woman's consent is needed for such a marriage, but given the reality of social pressures, she effectively has no option but to marry the perpetrator. Most families prefer to conceal any violation of the woman's honor, and such matters are rarely discussed outside of the home. Moreover, the regime's denials regarding the existence of violence against women extend to crimes like rape. The deputy director of social affairs in the General People's Congress, Amal Safar, declared in 2005 that "violence and rape is very rare. You might find two cases [in Libya] from people belonging to non-Libyan cultures."[40]

There are no genuinely independent women's organizations working on the issues of women's autonomy and security, and no women's shelters exist aside from the social rehabilitation centers described above. Aisha al-Qadhafi's Al-Watassimu charity, which maintains close ties to the government, has worked to raise awareness of violence against women with limited success. The project it launched in March 2007 included promoting the issue in mosques, schools, and other public places.[41]

Recommendations

+ The government should introduce laws that specifically define and criminalize domestic violence and rape, including spousal rape.

+ The government should raise awareness of domestic violence through public campaigns using various media, including television soap operas, in a bid to dispel taboos surrounding the subject.

+ The Qadhafi Development Foundation should establish an association specifically designed to raise awareness about domestic violence and to reduce the taboos associated with it.

+ The country's religious authorities should initiate a public education campaign aimed at eliminating the perception that violence against women is religiously acceptable.

+ The police force should receive adequate training on how to deal with domestic violence and rape cases, and set up special units to handle these crimes.

+ The government should open well-resourced shelters for women who have been victims of domestic violence.

ECONOMIC RIGHTS AND EQUAL OPPORTUNITY

In recent decades, the government has encouraged women to participate in the workforce and to exercise their economic rights. They have increasingly done so, and some women, particularly among the elite, have been able to break into fields traditionally dominated by men, such as law, medicine, and business. Women have also made academic gains, attending universities in greater numbers. However, women remain underrepresented in the labor market, and those who are employed tend to work in fields traditionally associated with women, such as education. Society in general still considers women's primary role to be in the home. While more young women in Libya aspire to pursue professional careers, their working lives are often cut short when they marry. Moreover, husbands still tend to manage the family's financial affairs, though younger women are increasingly in control of their own salaries.[42]

Women in Libya have the same rights to own land and property as men, and they are free to buy and sell both. As mentioned above (see "Autonomy, Security, and Freedom of the Person"), women have the right to retain their private wealth upon marriage. However, given that men are usually responsible for land and property in accordance with dominant social traditions, only women of a higher social class tend to have control over their own financial affairs. Women are free to obtain bank loans and financial credit, and banks do not require the consent of the husband to issue a loan to a woman. In 2007 the Rural Bank granted 19,558 loans, of which 4,502 went to women.[43]

Women also have the right to full and independent use of their income and assets, but it is not uncommon for women to give their income to their husbands or other family members. According to one survey, out of 200 women questioned, only half kept their salaries.[44] The other half either handed over all their income to a male family member or gave up most of it after taking a cut for themselves.

The inheritance rights of women are not equal to those of men. Libya's inheritance laws are based on Islamic principles whereby a woman inherits only half of what is due to her brothers. In addition, it is not unusual for a woman to give her share of inheritance to her brothers, in part to ensure that the brothers will financially support her should she remain unmarried or find herself divorced or widowed.

Women are free to enter into business contracts and economic activities at all levels. They are increasingly participating in Libya's business sector, though it remains dominated by men. Most businesses that are owned by women are small, and many are private schools, sewing workshops, or import-export agencies.[45]

Libya has made women's education a key priority over the years. The state's decision to make education compulsory through the intermediate

level in the 1970s benefitted girls in particular, and female students currently tend to outperform male students. Within secondary education, the
enrollment ratio of girls to boys has gone up significantly in recent years,
from 106.1:100 in 2002 to 117.1:100 in 2006.[46] A significantly larger
number of girls than boys pursue higher education. For the 2007–08
academic year, 101,537 women were enrolled in a university, compared
with 59,179 men.[47] This represents a marked increase from the 2004–05
academic year, when 87,752 women and 62,419 men were enrolled in a
university.[48] Women are permitted to enter all fields of study, and admissions requirements are nondiscriminatory. Schools and universities are not
segregated by gender.

However, the entire public sector is currently undergoing a major
restructuring following a speech made by al-Qadhafi, and this has raised
concerns regarding the future of women's education in Libya. In the
March 2008 speech, he announced that the administration should be dismantled and that responsibility for public services, including education,
should be handed directly to the population. It is unclear what form this
restructuring will take, or indeed whether it will occur at all. The future
of the country's education system is particularly uncertain because al-
Qadhafi also announced that education would no longer be compulsory.
No related legal changes or attempts to pursue this policy shift have been
made to date, but should the proposal become a reality, it would likely
have a greater impact on girls than boys. Without the legal obligation to
educate their daughters, some families would revert to conservative social
practices and choose not to send their girls to school, particularly beyond
the primary level.

Women generally have the freedom to choose their profession, and
they are encouraged by the regime to join the workforce, although some
gender-based restrictions persist. The Resolution of the General People's
Committee of 1988 states that work is a duty for every woman who is
capable of working. The Consolidation of Freedoms Law (No. 20 of 1991)
stipulates that men and women are free to choose the work that suits them.
Al-Qadhafi has specifically encouraged Libyan women to work in the military, and there are special female police forces, bodyguards, and military
academies. Such roles are considered shameful because many Libyans
deem them to be contrary to cultural tradition. Women still require the
permission of their fathers to enter the women's police academy.[49]

Article 95 of the Labor Law (No. 58 of 1970) stipulates that women may not be employed in difficult or dangerous jobs. Under Article 96, Libyan women may not work more than 48 hours a week including overtime, nor can they work between 8 p.m. and 7 a.m. unless authorized by order of the Workforce, Training, and Employment Secretariat in the General People's Committee. As a result, some hospitals and clinics employ foreign women, to whom these provisions are not applicable.

According to the International Labour Organization, the female labor force participation rate was 27.3 percent in 2007, up from 25.6 percent in 2004 and 23.9 percent in 2000.[50] Despite the government's official stance on women's employment, which welcomes diversity in their choice of profession, women continue to work predominantly in fields that are traditionally associated with females, such as education, health services, and secretarial or cleaning work. Furthermore, Libyan men often prefer that their female family members work in jobs that do not entail mixing with the opposite sex.[51] They also prefer that women not work too far from the home, further limiting the options available to female professionals.

Under Section 31 of the Labor Law, men and women should receive equal pay if the nature and conditions of their work are the same.[52] However, in reality women are often paid less than men for doing the same job. It is still difficult for women to attain high-ranking positions in their professional life, and both men and women often exhibit resistance to the idea of women holding positions of authority over men. Even within fields that are traditionally associated with women, senior jobs tend to be awarded to men. In spite of the large numbers of women who work in the higher education sector, only a few attain the level of professor or lecturer. During the 2007–08 academic year at Sebha University, for example, there were 51 male and no female Libyan professors or associate professors, and 92 male but only 11 female lecturers.[53]

Professional women face many challenges both in the public and private sectors. As one female employee in a government investment company told the British Broadcasting Corporation (BBC), "Our society is very conservative and patriarchal. . . . It is unusual for a woman to live on her own and work in the public sector. I struggle all the time to overturn the stereotype of women working only as secretaries. . . . As a result my ability to do my job is often hindered and made difficult. I deal with bureaucratic and chauvinistic obstacles every day."[54] Within the private sector, which was banned until recently and is therefore generally underdeveloped, the status of women is far less clear.

No legislation exists to protect women from sexual harassment in the workplace. However, women have specific rights and protections related to maternity and childcare. A pregnant woman is entitled to one month's leave at full salary before the due date of her child, and under Article 43 of the Labor Law, women who have worked for the same employer for at least six months are entitled to what is known as "birth leave," during which they are paid 50 percent of their salary for 50 days.[55] In addition, under Article 25 of the Social Security Act (No. 13 of 1980), women are entitled to receive their full income during a three-month maternity leave.[56] Mothers who return to work are given two breastfeeding breaks of at least half an hour per day until the child is 18 months old. Any employer with 50 or more female workers at one site must provide a nursery. However, childcare is still generally considered to be the domain of the family.

The state provides an allowance of three dinars (US$2.46) a month to pregnant women from the third month of pregnancy until term, and a birth allowance of 100 dinars (US$82) per baby. If women leave work to marry or have their first baby, they are rewarded with half a month's pay for every year they have worked, up to the fifth year of employment. For every additional year of employment, they receive a full month's salary. However, both of these rewards are conditional and require the recipient to leave the job within six months of getting married or three months of giving birth.[57]

Although no true civil society actors are working to improve women's economic rights in Libya, a number of state organizations, such as the General Union of Women's Associations, are dedicated to addressing women's employment needs.

Recommendations

❖ The government should establish a nationwide program to encourage, train, and support women who wish to set up their own businesses. It should also encourage banks to provide preferential business loans for women.

❖ The government should introduce positive discrimination policies designed to promote qualified women in key areas, such as the university sector, to senior positions.

❖ The government should ensure that any administrative restructuring of the education system does not change the compulsory nature of school enrollment.

❖ The government should draft laws that protect women from sexual harassment in both public- and private-sector workplaces.

❖ To combat persistent negative stereotypes of women with respect to education and employment, the government should ensure that educational material and school textbooks present positive images of women as role models.

❖ The government should introduce women's studies or gender studies as a degree subject area in universities.

POLITICAL RIGHTS AND CIVIC VOICE

Libya's "State of the Masses" is a unique political system that was devised by al-Qadhafi and laid out in the *Green Book*. It consists of a complex hierarchy of congresses and committees, through which every member of society is supposed to participate in the decision-making process. Every Libyan citizen is expected to attend Basic People's Congresses (local assemblies) at which state policies are discussed. The decisions of these bodies are then fed up to the General People's Congress (parliament), which is made up of the secretaries (heads) of the Basic People's Congresses, among others. The executive arm of the General People's Congress is the General People's Committee (cabinet), and every Basic People's Congress also has its own People's Committee. Leaders are chosen through the system of *tasayeed*, in which people must raise their hands publicly to vote for those offering themselves as candidates. In theory this system enables all citizens to engage directly in the country's political life. However, the Basic People's Congresses are dominated by regime loyalists and are largely irrelevant in practice, since core decision making generally occurs outside the formal mechanisms of government. As a result, participation in these congresses is low.

In the official discourse of the state, women are encouraged to attend and participate in the Basic People's Congresses, and there are no formal restrictions preventing them from serving in leadership positions. However, Libyan women have made few inroads into what is still essentially a male-dominated political system. Their political rights and civic voice remain extremely limited on account of the nature of the regime and the fact that all political activity must be sanctioned by the authorities. Recent years have brought no real change in this respect, and women continue to play a marginal role in state institutions. For example, just 36 women gained seats in the 468-seat General People's Congress in the March 2009 indirect elections.[58]

Only a handful of women have secured positions in the executive structures of government. There are no women in the General People's Committee at present, and just three have ever been appointed to the body, serving as ministers of culture, media, and social affairs.[59] Between 1977 and 2006, only six women held positions in the Secretariat of the General People's Congress, and these posts were in women's affairs and social affairs.[60] One of these women, Huda Ben Amar, was appointed to the post of secretary for social affairs in March 2006.

Women are also largely absent from leadership positions in the *shabiyat*, the country's intermediate administrative divisions. A woman was appointed as secretary of the People's Congress of the Benghazi shabiya in 2004, but she lost the position in April 2006.[61] Women remain underrepresented in the judiciary, with none serving on the Supreme Court (see "Nondiscrimination and Access to Justice"), and there are few female ambassadors. One of these is Najat al-Hajaji, Libya's envoy to the United Nations in Geneva. In August 2008, she was appointed to chair a series of United Nations antiracism conferences. For all its discourse on women's rights, the regime clearly remains extremely reluctant to appoint women to senior positions.

At the local level, women are ostensibly free to contribute to debates and discussions in the Basic People's Congresses alongside their male counterparts, but social norms encourage women to remain out of the public eye, and far fewer women than men participate in practice. Women are even less likely to participate in the Basic People's Congresses in rural areas, and in some cases those who do attend choose to do so indirectly on account of conservative social attitudes. For example, they might attend special segregated sessions in private girls' schools or other public buildings.[62] Furthermore, some women participate only because, on some occasions, attendance is mandatory. Women have assumed leadership positions in the secretariats of the Basic People's Congresses, but they have generally been restricted to the position of secretary for social affairs, which replaced the post for women's affairs in the 1990s. Neither women nor men have the right to organize or participate in political parties, which are banned by the state.

The regime does not tolerate unauthorized peaceful assembly. Women, like men, are prohibited from engaging in any independent gatherings like strikes or demonstrations, which are banned under Law No. 45 of 1972. Freedom of expression is also limited, and anyone who airs critical views of al-Qadhafi, the government, or the Jamahiriya system risks arrest and mistreatment. There have been some improvements in this area since 2003, as the authorities have allowed a modicum of space for complaints—in the media or in some cases the courts—about issues like inefficiency, corruption, and the actions of the security forces. Consequently, women have a slightly greater degree of freedom in discussing women's rights and related issues like domestic violence, though it is clear that the state continues to dictate which topics are acceptable and which are forbidden.

Women have gained access to new sources of information in recent years, but the extent to which they can use this information to empower themselves in their civic and political lives remains limited by the general restrictions on independent political activity. It is still extremely difficult to purchase foreign newspapers or literature, and the local press is run by the state. However, a number of new newspapers and web-based publications have sprung up since 2003. Although established by al-Qadhafi's son, Saif al-Islam al-Qadhafi, these outlets are presented as independent media and are more informative than the traditional state media, which are little more than propaganda tools for the regime. Women increasingly use the Internet as a source of information, though satellite television, which is more accessible, is the most influential medium. Women are using online social-networking sites, and there is an increasing number of female Libyan bloggers, but these platforms have not been used as a means of connecting women's activists as such organizing would be deemed political and would not be tolerated.

Recommendations

❖ The government should appoint female judges to the Supreme Court.
❖ The government should ensure that women are promoted to senior positions within the executive branch and key political institutions such as the General People's Congress and the General People's Committee.

These appointments should expand women's roles beyond the traditional spheres of social affairs, culture, and women's affairs.

✤ The government should permit genuinely independent civil society groups to lobby the authorities on political and civic matters affecting women, and to form partnerships with international women's organizations.

✤ The Education Secretariat should work to develop new textbooks that promote positive images of women as political activists and leaders.

SOCIAL AND CULTURAL ATTITUDES

Despite state efforts to improve women's cultural and social rights, Libya remains a deeply conformist and traditional society that puts women at a distinct disadvantage. At the same time, social and cultural attitudes are being influenced by growing access to satellite television and the Internet, and by a partial opening in the domestic media, which has led to an increased awareness of women's issues and greater room for discussion. The expansion of mobile telephone access has also given women a greater degree of freedom, especially in dealings with the opposite sex.

Women have only a limited ability to make independent decisions related to their reproductive health, which is often considered a family affair. Contraceptives are available, but given the sensitivities surrounding sexuality, there is little information about birth control in the public domain; the same is true for information about sexually transmitted diseases, including HIV/AIDS. Under Article 18 of Law No. 17 of 1986, women must have permission from their husbands to obtain contraceptives, because they are only issued to a couple where there is mutual consent.[63] According to the most recent figures from the United Nations, in 1995, 45.1 percent of married women between the ages of 15 and 49 were using some form of contraception, although only 25.6 percent were using modern methods.[64] The overall fertility rate in Libya has declined from about 3.2 births per woman in 2000 to 2.7 in 2007.[65]

Abortion is a taboo subject in Libya, and the procedure is illegal unless it is necessary to preserve the mother's life. Under Article 390 of the penal code, whoever procures an abortion without the woman's consent faces up to three years in prison.[66] Under Articles 391 and 392, a woman who consents to or procures her own abortion, and anyone who procures an abortion with the woman's consent, is punished with a minimum sentence of six months in prison. Article 394 stipulates that if an abortion is carried out for the preservation of the honor of the offender, for instance in cases of pregnancy out of wedlock, the penalty is reduced by half. Some illegal abortions are carried out in Libya, although if they can afford it, women sometimes travel to Tunisia, where the service is more readily available.

Health care is free to all citizens, and Libyan women have the same access to health services as men. However, the health system as a whole is inadequate, prompting those with means to travel abroad for treatment, usually to Tunisia or Europe. Some efforts to improve health care have been made recently, including upgrades to hospitals. But the future of the entire sector has been called into question by al-Qadhafi's March 2008 speech, in which he declared that health services, along with other state functions, should be handed over directly to the population. Female genital mutilation is not known to be practiced in Libya, although some assert that it occurs within rural communities of migrants from sub-Saharan Africa.[67]

Given the nature of the Libyan state, any activities related to community and social development are managed by the authorities. The ability of women to influence community life revolves primarily around their role within the family. Traditionally, older women tend to be given more respect and are consulted about decisions that affect the family, such as marriage and other domestic affairs.

The Libyan media are also controlled by the government, and even the more "independent" press is in the hands of al-Qadhafi's son, Saif al-Islam. These new outlets have opened up opportunities for women, and there now appear to be more female journalists than there were five years ago. Several of them work for the new publications, such as the *Corina* newspaper, and the government-appointed head of the Tripoli Journalists' Union is also a woman, Salma al-Sha'ab. Nevertheless, given the ongoing state control, women's presence in the media has not resulted in an improved ability to influence content or portrayals of gender issues. The state media frequently promote the idea of women's rights and of their playing an active role in society, but this is largely propaganda designed to laud the achievements of the revolution.

Women are adversely affected by poverty due to their gender because the job types to which they are limited by tradition often fail to provide enough income for financial independence. Divorced and widowed women are particularly vulnerable to poverty as a result. Under the social security law, widows are entitled to welfare payments in the form of a percentage of their deceased husband's pension. However, in practice, due to bureaucratic inefficiencies, these payments appear to be difficult for women to collect.

Women who are divorced face particularly acute challenges. Although Libyan law calls for the man to leave the marital home to his wife and children upon divorce, tradition dictates otherwise. In reality, divorced women are expected to return to live with their families, as society does not tolerate the idea of a woman living alone and supporting herself.[68] Unmarried women are similarly expected to remain in the family home until marriage.

Recommendations

❖ The government should sponsor nationwide public information campaigns about reproductive health and modern methods of contraception.

❖ The government should run similar campaigns to raise awareness of HIV/AIDS and other sexually transmitted diseases.

❖ The government should introduce special shelters and support networks to provide temporary or group housing, as well as job training and other services, for divorced women or widows who have no family to support them.

AUTHOR

Alison Pargeter is a senior research associate in the Department of Politics and International Studies at the University of Cambridge. Her research focus is on North Africa, with a particular focus on Libya, and on issues related to political Islam and radicalization in the Middle East and North Africa region as well as in Europe. She has carried out numerous research projects on Libya that have included fieldwork in the country. She has also published widely on these topics, and her recent book—*The New Frontiers of Jihad: Radical Islam in Europe*—was published by I.B. Tauris in 2008.

NOTES

[1] Muammar al-Qadhafi, *The Green Book* (Tripoli: World Centre for the Study and Research of the Green Book, 1983).

[2] Human Rights Watch, *Libya: A Threat to Society? Arbitrary Detention of Women and Girls for "Social Rehabilitation"* (New York: Human Rights Watch, February 27, 2006), http://www.hrw.org/en/node/11468/section/1.

3 Principle 21 of the Great Green Charter of Human Rights of the Jamahiriyan Era, available at http://www.unhcr.org/refworld/type,LEGISLATION,,LBY,3dda540f4,0.html.

4 *Official Gazette* no. 22 (1991), cited in *Combined Second, Third, Fourth and Fifth Periodic Reports of States Parties: Libyan Arab Jamahiriya* (New York: UN Committee on the Elimination of Discrimination against Women, December 4, 2008), http://www2 .ohchr.org/english/bodies/cedaw/docs/AdvanceVersions/CEDAW.C.LBY.5.pdf.

5 UN Development Programme (UNDP), *Promotion of Opportunities for Women's Economic Empowerment* (New York: UNDP, September 2007), http://www.undp-libya.org/ gender/POWER.pdf.

6 "Al-Libyat al-Mutazowjat Min Ajanib Gharadna Khrij Serb" [Libyan Women Who Have Married Foreigners Sing as Lone Voices], *Al-Beit* (November 2007), http://albiytmag .com/details.php?&count=31&id_pages=2&id_subject=928&i=0.

7 *Combined Second, Third, Fourth and Fifth Periodic Reports of States Parties: Libyan Arab Jamahiriya.*

8 Amal Suleiman Mahmoud al-Obeidi, *Bawader al-Islah al-Siassi wa Atharau ala Siassat Temkeen al-Mara'a fi Libia: Dirasa Istiqshafia* [Signs of Political Reform and Their Impact on Women's Empowerment Policies in Libya: An Exploratory Study], Women Democracy Watch, October 29, 2006, http://www.womendw.org/nimages/doc12.doc.

9 Available in Arabic on the justice ministry website, http://www.aladel.gov.ly/main/ modules/sections/category.php?categoryid=17.

10 Protection Project, "Human Rights Reports: Libya," Johns Hopkins University School of Advanced International Studies, n.d., http://www.protectionproject.org/human _rights_reports.

11 Article 1, Internal Bylaw, Social Rehabilitation Home for Protecting Women [*Al-layha al-dahilaya lilbayt al-ijtima'I lihamayat al-mar'a*], cited in Human Rights Watch, *Libya: A Threat to Society? Arbitrary Detention of Women and Girls for "Social Rehabilitation"* (New York: Human Rights Watch, February 2006), http://www.hrw.org/reports/2006/ libya0206/index.htm.

12 Human Rights Watch, *Libya: A Threat to Society?*

13 Human Rights Watch, *Libya: A Threat to Society?*

14 Brian Whitaker, "Disgrace in the Desert," *Guardian*, February 28, 2006, http://www .guardian.co.uk/world/2006/feb/28/worlddispatch.libya.

15 See endnote 33 at UN Treaty Collection, "Status of Treaties: Convention on the Elimination of All Forms of Discrimination against Women," http://treaties.un.org/Pages/ ViewDetails.aspx?src=TREATY&mtdsg_no=IV-8&chapter=4&lang=en#33.

16 UN Treaty Collection, "Status of Treaties: Optional Protocol to the Convention on the Elimination of All Forms of Discrimination against Women," http://treaties.un.org/ Pages/ViewDetails.aspx?src=TREATY&mtdsg_no=IV-8-b&chapter=4&lang=en.

17 Articles 1–2, Optional Protocol, available at http://www.un.org/womenwatch/daw/ cedaw/protocol/text.htm.

18 Global Hand, "Al Wafa Association for Human Services," http://www.globalhand.org/ data/organisation.2006-01-04.8236084563/.

19 "Conference on Women's Rights Held in Libya," *Magharebia*, April 17, 2007, http:// www.magharebia.com/cocoon/awi/xhtml1/en_GB/features/awi/newsbriefs/general/ 2007/04/17/newsbrief-04.

[20] "Karar Libi Yemna al-Niqab Dahil al-Haram al-Jami Instissarun Lil Akhlak" [Libyan Decision to Ban the Niqab on University Campus for the Sake of Morality], Laha Online, May 24, 2008, http://www.mail.lahaonline.com/index.php?option=content&task=view&id=14062&sectionid=1.

[21] Article 20 of Law No. 2 of 1991 on the Consolidation of Freedom.

[22] "Paper Assails Ban on Women's Travel," *New York Times*, March 8, 2007, http://query.ny times.com/gst/fullpage.html?res=9A06E7DD1231F93BA35750C0A9619C8B63&ft a=y.

[23] "Libya Lifts Travel Ban on Women," *Namibian*, March 14, 2007, http://www.namibian .com.na/index.php?id=28&tx_ttnews%5Btt_news%5D=37957&no_cache=1.

[24] Article 18, Law No. 10 of 1984. The law is available in Arabic at http://www.aladel.gov.ly/ main/modules/sections/item.php?itemid=93.

[25] Article 17, Law No. 10 of 1984.

[26] *Combined Second, Third, Fourth and Fifth Periodic Reports of States Parties: Libyan Arab Jamahiriya*, 36.

[27] Mustafa Attir, *Al-Mara'a fi al-Jamahiriyat: Al-Musawat ma al-Iktilaf, Libia takrir al-tanmiat al-BaShari'at 2006* [Women in the Jamahiria: Equality with a Difference, Human Development Report No. 3, 2006] (Tripoli: National Organization for Information, Documentation and Communication, 2006).

[28] *Combined Second, Third, Fourth and Fifth Periodic Reports of States Parties: Libyan Arab Jamahiriya*, 39.

[29] Mustafa Attir, *Al-Mara'a fi al-Jamahiriyat*.

[30] Amnesty International, *Libya: Time to Make Human Rights a Reality* (London: Amnesty International, April 2004), http://www.amnesty.org/en/library/info/MDE19/ 002/2004.

[31] Mohammad Sharif, "In Geneva: Mutual Criticism Between Libya and the Committee on Civil and Political Rights," Swissinfo, October 20, 2007, http://www.swissinfo.ch/ara/ swissinfo.html?siteSect=43&sid=8330439 (in Arabic).

[32] Law No. 10 of 1984, Article 28.

[33] Articles 40, 42, and 43 of Law No. 10 of 1984.

[34] Reunite International, "Child Abduction and Custody Laws in the Muslim World: Summary Text for Libya," July 2005, http://www.reunite.org/edit/files/Islamic%20Re source/Libya%20Text.pdf.

[35] Abdel Salam Bashir al-Duwaiby, *Al Unf al-Ahili: Al Aba'at al-Silbiya wal Ijra'at al-Wikaiya (Al-Mustama al-Arabi al-Libi Kanamuthej)* [Family Violence: The Negative Dimension and Prevention and Treatment Procedures (Libyan Arab Society as a Sample)], AMAN, n.d., http://www.amanjordan.org/studies/sid=21.htm.

[36] Human Rights Watch, "Government Response to Violence Against Women," in *Libya: A Threat to Society?*

[37] UN Committee on the Rights of the Child, *Summary Record of the 433rd Meeting: Libyan Arab Jamahiriya* (Geneva: UN Committee on the Rights of the Child, January 8, 1998), http://www.unhchr.ch/tbs/doc.nsf/0/91efed20e26d8f5e802565a90034e809 ?Opendocument.

[38] Human Rights Watch, "Government Response to Violence Against Women," in *Libya: A Threat to Society?*

39 Human Rights Watch, "EU-Libya Relations: Human Rights Conditions Required," memorandum, January 4, 2008, http://hrw.org/english/docs/2008/01/04/libya17687 .htm.

40 Human Rights Watch, "Government Response to Violence Against Women," in *Libya: A Threat to Society?*

41 "Libya Launches Project Against Violence on Women," *Pana Press*, March 22, 2007, http://www.panapress.com/newslatf.asp?code=eng015668&dte=22/03/2007.

42 Mustafa Attir, *Al-Mara'a fi al-Jamahiriyat.*

43 *Combined Second, Third, Fourth and Fifth Periodic Reports of States Parties: Libyan Arab Jamahiriya.*

44 Mustafa Attir, *Al-Mara'a fi al-Jamahiriyat.*

45 Mustafa Attir, *Al-Mara'a fi al-Jamahiriyat.*

46 World Bank, "GenderStats—Create Your Own Table," http://go.worldbank.org/MRER 20PME0.

47 General Authority for Information, *Statistics Book 2007* (Benghazi: General Authority for Information, 2008), available in English and Arabic at http://www.gia.gov.ly/modules .php?name=Mygroups&file=articles&topicid=15&gid=21.

48 General Authority for Information, *Statistics Book 2005* (Benghazi: General Authority for Information, 2006).

49 Human Rights Watch, *Libya: A Threat to Society?*

50 World Bank, "GenderStats—Labor Force," http://go.worldbank.org/4PIIORQMS0.

51 Mustafa Attir, *Al-Mara'a fi al-Jamahiriyat.*

52 The law is available in Arabic on the justice ministry website, http://www.aladel.gov.ly/ main/modules/sections/category.php?categoryid=17.

53 General Authority for Information, *Statistics Book 2007.*

54 Rana Jawad, "Women's Lib Takes Off in Libya," British Broadcasting Corporation (BBC), April 29, 2008, http://news.bbc.co.uk/2/hi/africa/7360541.stm.

55 See the justice ministry website, in Arabic, http://www.aladel.gov.ly/main/modules/ sections/item.php?itemid=155.

56 The law is available in Arabic on the justice ministry website, http://www.aladel.gov.ly/ main/modules/sections/item.php?itemid=113.

57 Article 55 of Labor Law.

58 Inter-Parliamentary Union, "Libyan Arab Jamhiriya: Mutamar Al Chaab Al Aam (General People's Congress)," PARLINE database, http://www.ipu.org/parline-e/reports/2185 _A.htm.

59 Amal Suleiman Mahmoud al-Obeidi, *Bawader al-Islah al-Siassi.*

60 Amal Suleiman Mahmoud al-Obeidi, *Bawader al-Islah al-Siassi.*

61 Amal Suleiman Mahmoud al-Obeidi, *Bawader al-Islah al-Siassi.*

62 Amal Suleiman Mahmoud al-Obeidi, *Bawader al-Islah al-Siassi.*

63 The law is available in Arabic on the justice ministry website, http://www.aladel.gov.ly/ main/modules/sections/item.php?itemid=64.

64 UN Population Division, *World Contraceptive Use 2007* (New York: UN Department of Economic and Social Affairs, 2007), http://www.un.org/esa/population/publications/ contraceptive2007/contraceptive_2007_table.pdf.

[65] World Bank, "GenderStats—Health," http://go.worldbank.org/UJ0Q1KQKX0.

[66] The relevant excerpts from the penal code can be found in the *Annual Review of Population Law* database, hosted by Harvard University's School of Public Health, at http://www.hsph.harvard.edu/population/abortion/Libya.abo.htm.

[67] Bureau of Democracy, Human Rights, and Labor, "Libya," in *2008 Country Reports on Human Rights Practices* (Washington, DC: U.S. Department of State, 2009), http://www.state.gov/g/drl/rls/hrrpt/2008/nea/119121.htm.

[68] Mustafa Attir, *Al-Mara'a fi al-Jamahiriyat.*

MOROCCO

by Fatima Sadiqi

POPULATION:	31,495,000		
GNI PER CAPITA:	US$2,276		

COUNTRY RATINGS	2004	2009
NONDISCRIMINATION AND ACCESS TO JUSTICE:	3.0	3.1
AUTONOMY, SECURITY, AND FREEDOM OF THE PERSON:	3.1	3.2
ECONOMIC RIGHTS AND EQUAL OPPORTUNITY:	2.7	2.8
POLITICAL RIGHTS AND CIVIC VOICE:	3.0	3.1
SOCIAL AND CULTURAL RIGHTS:	2.9	2.9

(COUNTRY RATINGS ARE BASED ON A SCALE OF I TO 5, WITH I REPRESENTING THE LOWEST AND 5 THE HIGHEST LEVEL OF FREEDOM WOMEN HAVE TO EXERCISE THEIR RIGHTS)

INTRODUCTION

The Moroccan feminist movement can be traced back to 1946, when the Sisters of Purity Association publically issued a set of demands including the abolition of polygamy, full and equal political rights, and increased visibility of women in the public sphere. These demands were taken up by female journalists, academics, and civil society in the decades after Morocco gained independence from France in 1956. During this period, through journalistic and academic discourse, feminists started to question gender divisions, examine historical and ideological roots of gender inequality, and promote the recognition of women's labor. They depicted women's condition not as a "natural state," but as a state that stems from historical practices, and women's work, not as merely reproduction, but as production.

The women's movement was bitterly disappointed by the first Moudawana, or personal status code regulating all matters pertaining to family life, enacted in 1957. It was based on the Maliki school of Islamic jurisprudence, whereas other laws, such as the penal code and the constitution, were based on civil law.[1] Women obtained the right to vote in 1956 and had the right to a free education under the constitution, but even female cabinet members and entrepreneurs were considered the dependants of their husbands or fathers and treated like minors under the law. The fundamental principle of marriage required a wife's obedience to her husband in exchange for financial maintenance, and the husband retained the power to abandon his wife without a judge's authorization. Not surprisingly, the Moroccan feminist movement focused its efforts on the Moudawana, which was seen as the prime locus of legal and civil discrimination against women.

From the 1980s onward, the feminist movement also had to contend with growing support for Islamism.[2] The Islamists' ideology appealed particularly to young, unemployed males who were easily led to believe that women working outside the home robbed them of opportunities. In response, feminists also began to push for women's rights from a religious perspective.[3] They implemented new strategies, including a gradual downplaying of the "religious" role of the veil in their writings and practices; increased use of Arabic and references to the Koran and Hadith (the sayings of the prophet Muhammad); a gradual inclusion of children's rights within women's issues; and reinforcement of Islam as culture and spirituality.

These activists also endeavored to draw attention to the problems that women faced as a result of their lack of legal protection. They made excellent use of the media in depicting the misery of women and children who were victimized by divorce, thus reclaiming such social issues from the Islamists and reiterating the necessity of reforming the personal status law. Nonetheless, a package of reforms proposed by the government in 1999, including the abolition of polygamy, ultimately failed in the face of Islamist and conservative opposition. Despite this setback, feminists continued their campaign, increasingly concentrating on the "goals of Shari'a" rather than Shari'a itself.[4] They also forged an alliance with King Mohamed VI, who took the throne that year and did not welcome increased control by Islamists.

In April 2001, the king formed a commission to study the possibility of revising the Moudawana, but the final push for reform came after May 2003 terrorist attacks in Casablanca stoked widespread antifundamentalist sentiment. The king announced a draft family law in Parliament in October 2003. During the next few months, women's rights organizations, organized within the Spring of Equality network, analyzed the details of the draft legislation and organized workshops, roundtables, and discussion groups to prepare for renewed lobbying efforts in Parliament and to educate the public about the reforms.

The final text was adopted in January 2004. It secured several important rights for women, including the right to self-guardianship, the right to divorce, and the right to child custody. It also placed new restrictions on polygamy, raised the legal age of marriage from 15 to 18, and made sexual harassment punishable by law. However, it did not completely abolish polygamy, unilateral repudiation of the wife by the husband, separation by compensation (*khula*), or discrimination in inheritance rules. This was in part because such provisions are explicitly authorized by literal readings of the Koran.

Whereas the 1998–2003 period was characterized by a flurry of ideological and political debates about women and their rights in Morocco, the period extending from 2004 to 2009 was characterized by a calmer legal discussion over the gains and implementation of the new family law, the new labor code (promulgated in December 2003), and the revised nationality code (which took effect in April 2008).

The implementation of the family law in particular varies from region to region, but it has generally been met with resistance. It is still very poorly understood in rural and sometimes even urban areas, and many male judges are reluctant to apply it. Moreover, the ongoing societal influences of patriarchy, tradition, illiteracy, and ignorance may prevent women from invoking their rights or reporting crimes such as rape, child abuse, sexual exploitation, and domestic violence. Existing efforts to overcome this societal resistance, such as education campaigns conducted in the mother tongues (Berber and Moroccan Arabic), have proven insufficient. Many feminists argue that the new family law can be adequately implemented only in a democratic context, while some advocate a purely secular government system. Another issue is that the law does not adequately address the problems of single women and the non-Moroccan wives of Moroccan men.

Nevertheless, Moroccan women have achieved considerable progress in consolidating legal equality and access to justice in the last five years, and the autonomy, security, and personal freedom of women has also improved. Women now have more freedom to travel, obtain employment and education, greater equality at home, and more leeway to negotiate their marriage rights. They are spearheading business ventures and advancing to higher levels of education. Important progress has also been made in protecting women from domestic violence, and support networks are getting stronger despite restrictive social norms. Women are increasingly taking up national and local political posts and becoming more involved with the judiciary. Most recently, a 12 percent quota for women was applied to the June 2009 local elections, substantially increasing female political representation.

Women's rights groups and individual activists have collaborated with the government to improve the rights of all women, but true equality remains a distant goal. While the recent legal reforms have allowed the government to promote a modern and democratic image of Morocco at the international level, bringing certain benefits to society at large, more needs to be done to translate these changes into tangible gains for individual women in their daily lives.

NONDISCRIMINATION AND ACCESS TO JUSTICE

It is at the level of the law that Moroccan women's rights have achieved the most significant gains, and the last five years have been particularly rich in this regard. A revised nationality code passed in 2007 eased women's ability to pass citizenship to their children, the country lifted its reservations to CEDAW in 2008, and the Moudawana enacted in 2004 is now considered one of the most progressive legal texts in the Arab world. However, the implementation of that law is still problematic, and little headway is being made despite the sustained efforts of both women's rights activists and the government.

According to Article 5 of the 1996 constitution, "all Moroccan citizens shall be equal before the law."[5] Although the constitution does not specifically prohibit gender-based discrimination, as a practical matter Morocco's laws have become more attentive to the needs of female citizens in recent years. Even so, social and cultural constraints, as well as a certain reluctance to fully implement the laws, have yet to be overcome.

Thanks in part to the efforts of women's groups, particularly the Democratic Association of Moroccan Women, a new nationality code was passed in January 2007, thereby improving gender equality with respect to citizenship rights. Article 7 of the new law, which came into force in April 2008, enables women married to noncitizen men to pass their nationality to their children. However, the only children eligible for citizenship under this provision are those of a Moroccan woman and a Muslim noncitizen man who married in accordance with the Moudawana. In practical terms,

Moroccan women married to non-Muslim men and those married outside of the country and its laws are excluded by the code. Furthermore, while foreign wives may receive Moroccan citizenship within five years of marriage to a Moroccan man,[6] the foreign husbands of Moroccan women remain altogether ineligible for Moroccan citizenship. Although imperfect, the amendments to the code provide significant benefits for children with Moroccan mothers and noncitizen fathers who were previously excluded from receiving the free education and health care available to citizens.

Legal and societal barriers often obstruct women's access to the justice system, especially in rural areas. Although women enjoy equal testimony rights in most civil and criminal cases, the court gives their testimony half the weight of a man's when it comes to family matters. In addition, many women are reluctant to defend their rights in court, particularly if male family members are responsible for the violations or if it is perceived that their legal action could damage their family reputation. It is also customary for men to file court papers on behalf of women in rural areas, where illiteracy rates remain high. However, in some aspects, access to justice has improved in recent years. Family courts and the training of judges to staff these courts have served to create a friendlier environment for women. In addition, a fund has been established to guarantee payment of alimony and child support pursuant to an enforceable judgment.

Portions of the penal code remain discriminatory against women, and enforcement of amendments made in 2003 has proven difficult. Previously, under Article 418, only a man was given a reduced sentence for assaulting or murdering his wife or her partner if he caught them committing adultery. This leniency has now been extended to female defendants as well. In addition, under Article 491, the state can now prosecute an adulterous spouse in lieu of either wronged spouse if the latter is out the country; previously, the state would only stand in for an absent husband. Despite these improvements on the books, implementation has faced resistance from some judges and police, especially in rural areas, diminishing the real effect of the reforms.

Article 490 of the penal code criminalizes extramarital sex for women, calling for punishments ranging from one month to one year in jail. These cases are rarely taken to court, since a conviction depends on either eyewitness testimony or a confession by one of the perpetrators. An unmarried woman's pregnancy is proof of sexual relations and may lead to criminal prosecution, while the fault of her male partner is not established by law.

No laws specifically prohibit domestic violence, though general prohibitions against assault found within the penal code are theoretically applicable to such situations. Physical abuse is grounds for divorce, but the wife must be able to call on witnesses to support her claims.[7] If she is unable to prove her case, the authorities will return a woman to her abuser's home, leaving her in a worse situation than before she filed the complaint. Consequently, few women report domestic abuse.

Sexual assault and rape are both criminalized under the penal code, although spousal rape is not. The maximum sentence for each crime is five years in prison. Given prevailing societal concepts of personal and family honor, victims of sexual violence rarely come forward for fear of shaming their families.[8] "Honor killings," in which women are murdered by family members for perceived sexual or moral transgressions, do occur in Morocco but are rather rare compared with some other countries in the region. As with other forms of gender-based violence, honor killing is traditionally seen as a private issue, meaning police are rarely summoned and are hesitant to intervene.[9] Article 475 of the penal code stipulates that a kidnapper or seducer of a minor girl can be acquitted if he marries her.

Although prohibited under Article 184a and Article 184b of the penal code, prostitution is common, especially in urban centers. However, the government neither prosecutes nor protects women who have been coerced into providing sexual services. Trafficking in persons, particularly in child maids, is a problem.

In principle, women are protected from gender-based and discriminatory arrest, detention, and exile. Article 10 of the constitution formally protects all people from arbitrary arrest and detention.[10] In practice, however, women may be singled out for arrest when they are deemed to behave immodestly, particularly in rural communities.

In a move that bore both symbolic and substantive meaning for women in Morocco, the government announced on December 10, 2008, the 60th anniversary of the Universal Declaration of Human Rights, that it would lift all reservations to CEDAW.[11] When it ratified the convention in 1993, Morocco, like many other Arab and Muslim countries, made multiple reservations and declarations covering portions that were thought to conflict with Islamic or national law. The reservations include provisions such as Article 9, which relates to the transmission of nationality to children, and Article 16, regarding the equality of men and women's marital rights. The king declared that the reservations were "obsolete" in light of the progressive legislation adopted in recent years. The public proclamations regarding their removal created a stronger legal basis for additional progress on women's rights issues, and carried a political and universal message that was widely applauded by civil society.[12] The government and the media did not adequately explain the content of the convention or the implications of the decision to withdraw the reservations. However, the Moroccan Association of Human Rights and similar organizations are determined to ensure that CEDAW is fully implemented and that all discrimination against women is eradicated.

Women's rights groups and civil society actors work freely and effectively to promote gender equality and equal access to justice. Although they have gained momentum in recent years, their efforts are often challenged by cultural conservatism.[13] The Moroccan Association of Human Rights, established in 1979, is one of the greatest proponents of women's rights, and about one-third of the positions in the organization are held by women. The group is based on principles such as the universality of human rights, mass action, independence, progressive thinking, and democracy. It seeks Morocco's ratification of international conventions related to human rights, and the integration of these conventions into Moroccan legislation.

The removal of the reservations to CEDAW was the result of 14 years of hard work by Morocco's civil society organizations. The Democratic Association of Moroccan Women endeavored to help implement the changes, and other local nongovernmental organizations (NGOs) followed suit. Together, they have published booklets and released audiovisual materials explaining women's rights; even popular songs have captured the main themes of CEDAW. The group Global Rights released a booklet under the title *Model Marriage Contract*, and three human rights education sessions intended to raise awareness among women have been released in English, Arabic, and French. These efforts were very well received by the public.

Recommendations

- The constitution should be amended to specifically enshrine the principle of equality between men and women with respect to all rights and responsibilities.
- The government should abolish the prosecution of unmarried pregnant women and amend the penal code to criminalize spousal rape.
- The government should provide legal education to women and help illiterate women to learn about their rights. This may be achieved by

publishing booklets in all relevant languages and providing free and convenient classes on the new laws.

✤ Amendments should be made to the nationality code to provide women with the right to pass their citizenship to non-Moroccan husbands.

✤ The government should eliminate the clause in the penal code that allows the rapists of underage girls to escape punishment if they marry their victims.

AUTONOMY, SECURITY, AND FREEDOM OF THE PERSON

Autonomy, security, and freedom of the person are in principle guaranteed by law in Morocco, and much progress has been made in these domains over the last five years. In addition to the advances associated with the new family law, women have begun to serve as trained religious authorities, and the government is now tracking data on violence against women. However, social and cultural norms still prevent women from fully enjoying their legal rights or receiving adequate protection from domestic abuse.

Freedom of worship is guaranteed by Article 6 of the constitution.[14] Although most Moroccans are Sunni Muslims, the country is also home to small Christian and Jewish communities. Christian and Jewish women are subject to separate family laws, though they are generally similar to the family law for Muslims. A Muslim's conversion to another religion is socially stigmatized but not illegal. Under Article 39 of the family law, Muslim women may not marry non-Muslims, while Muslim men may marry women of Christian or Jewish faith. The logic behind this policy is that children usually follow the religion of their father, and the government would like to encourage an increased Muslim population.

Women are allowed to pray in mosques, lead women-only prayers, and practice their religious rites freely. They have been steadily increasing their religious freedom in recent years. In May 2006, the first cohort of 50 female *murchidat*, or Islamic guides, graduated from a government-backed program and were empowered to perform all of the same functions as male imams except leading the Friday prayers. The program was part of the government's drive to promote a more tolerant version of Islam.

The 2004 reforms to the family law improved Muslim women's freedom of movement. Women now have the legal right to travel freely both domestically and abroad,[15] but deeply ingrained social and cultural norms restricting women's ability to travel alone have hardly changed. In their implementation of the new family law, some judges tend to adhere to the traditional divisions between the male-dominated public space and the private space assigned to females.

Despite improvements, it remains difficult for women to negotiate their full and equal marriage rights. Article 19 of the 2004 family law fixes the minimum age for marriage at 18 for both men and women, in accordance with certain provisions of the Maliki school of Sunni jurisprudence. Women who have attained this age may contract their own marriages without the consent of their fathers.[16] However, judges are empowered to waive the minimum age rule, and as a practical matter they are very reluctant to uphold it. About 10 percent of marriages in Morocco involve underage girls, according to the Democratic League for the Rights of Women (LDDF), and such unions have increased in rural areas. The LDDF also warned against what it described as "too many exceptions" in the case of polygamy.[17] The family law (Articles 40–46) allows polygamy only when it is approved by a judge, who must verify that the husband can provide equally for each wife and their respective children. Women have the right to forbid polygamy as a condition in their marriage contracts. Moreover, the first wife must give her consent for a second marriage, and the prospective new wife must be informed of the husband's marital status. In practice, however, a first wife who lacks financial independence may feel compelled to agree to polygamy.

The 2004 family law gives women the right to file for divorce based on harmful behavior by the husband, such as abandonment or failure to provide financial support. Divorce due to irreconcilable differences, initiated by either spouse, is also possible, as is divorce by mutual consent.[18] The latter type of divorce can include khula, in which the woman obtains a divorce by providing the husband with financial compensation, traditionally by returning her dowry. Husbands can still initiate divorce through "repudiation," but the practice is now subject to more judicial oversight, and husbands can grant their wives the authority to use repudiation as well (Articles 78–93).

By law, all divorces go through a reconciliation period and should be finalized within six months, but in reality, divorce remains a tedious procedure that may drag on for many months. The results are often advantageous to the husbands due to bribery of the judge and the weight of tradition, which stigmatizes women's appearance in court. Existing social conditions also mean that the wife is sometimes unable to pay the court expenses because of poverty. Social norms encourage men to neglect to pay the *nafaqa*, or maintenance owed by a man to his ex-wife, and khula divorces are abused as an opportunity to extort money from women eager for a divorce. However, amendments to khula procedures under the 2004 law permit arbitration by a judge when the parties cannot agree to a final amount.

Under Article 171 of the family law, a mother is the first choice for custody of her child, followed by the father and then the maternal grandmother. In a change from previous rules, the father no longer automatically assumes custody of children whose divorced mothers remarry or move out of town. However, a divorced woman with children over the age of seven will lose custody at her ex-husband's request if she remarries. In such instances, the woman retains legal guardianship of her minor children only if their father is dead or incompetent. Both girls and boys are entitled to choose the mother or father as custodian when they reach the age of 15.

Generally, the biggest problem associated with the new family law is enforcing provisions that run contrary to traditional practices. The new provisions are virtually unknown in rural areas, and sometimes even urban areas.[19] In addition, many male judges resist the application of the law.

The new law also has a number of gaps. It concentrates on the rights of married Moroccan women, generally ignoring the needs of single women and foreign women married to Moroccan men. It also failed to abolish four institutions that perpetuate inequality: polygamy, repudiation, khula, and unequal inheritance rules. These institutions remain because activists considered the reforms contained in the new law to be radical enough; to push for more change would have jeopardized general support. Provisions related to inheritance are clearly outlined in the Koran, and many argue that polygamy is endorsed as well, meaning Muslims are generally unwilling to negotiate on these issues. The hope is that education will eventually succeed in conveying the inequality of such practices, and that polygamy, at least, will come to a natural end.

The institution of slavery was outlawed in the first half of the 20th century.[20] However, women, including noncitizen women, are not protected from slavery-like practices. Poor girls from rural areas are often employed as maids in cities, exposing them to exploitation by both their families and their employers. They are subject to severe restrictions on movement, physical or sexual abuse, nonpayment of wages, and threats. Poor girls and women are also trafficked abroad for commercial sex and involuntary servitude, though the government has been cracking down on human trafficking operations in recent years.[21] Several women's NGOs have demanded legal protection for exploited female trafficking victims, and their efforts have led the Ministry of Employment to announce that a bill addressing the issue is imminent.

Female victims of spousal violence are not well protected by the law or the society. Women often have difficulty providing evidence of domestic violence, as they usually lack witnesses and their word is not given much weight by the authorities. The Ministry of Social Development, Family, and Solidarity began publishing official data on violence against women in late 2007. In March 2008, the ministry responded to an upsurge in reported incidents by announcing an action plan to increase the number of support centers for victims and to prepare a draft bill that would specifically outlaw violence against women. According to the ministry, some 17,000 incidents of gender-based violence were reported in the first three months of 2008 alone, 78.8 percent of which were committed by the victims' husbands.[22] Violence against women instigated by men under the stain of financial difficulties is also on the rise.[23]

In February 2007, the Ministry of Social Development, Family, and Solidarity presented a draft bill offering a legal framework for protecting women's rights by providing safe spaces for female victims of violence. If a woman is a victim of violence perpetrated by her employer, she will be provided with a safe harbor in her workplace and, depending on her condition, reduced work hours or temporary cessation of work. Support networks and shelters for abused women started to appear in big cities like Casablanca, Rabat, and Fes in 2002.

On February 2, 2009, the Union for Women's Action and the Anaruz network launched an initiative to organize public forums aimed at sensitizing local communities to the plight of female victims of violence, set up "listening centers" where abused women are encouraged to speak about their traumatic experiences, and create a free telephone hotline to give legal help and counseling to women. A victim can either file a complaint with the court or, if she can afford it, hire a lawyer to handle the case.

The media play a role in raising awareness of violence toward women and showcasing the activities of civil society groups on the issue. There is debate in the media and within society about the creation of rehabilitation centers where violent men would be helped to control their behavior and psychological problems. Investigative reports and advertisements regarding violence against women are aired on television, and guests on talk shows are invited to discuss the topic.

Gender-based violence outside the home is still a reality. However, societal taboos prevent women from coming forward to report sexual violence, and the police and medical personnel are not trained to deal with such issues. Sexual harassment on the streets has decreased but is still a problem.

Women's rights groups and other civil society actors work freely and effectively to improve the status of women's personal autonomy and security. Their activities include national and international networking, tending directly to the victims of violence, and campaigns aimed at sensitizing the general public to the issues surrounding gender-based violence and implementation of the family law. The impact of these efforts has been tremendous, but they must be increased in rural and semi-urban areas.

Recommendations

❖ The implementation of the new family law requires training at all levels, including judges, psychiatrists, and policymakers, among others. This could be accomplished by creating pilot centers where experts would advise the authorities who promulgate and implement the laws on how best to enforce specific provisions.

❖ In addition to the laws that currently exist, additional punitive laws that specifically address domestic violence must be enacted.

❖ The government should establish a partnership with NGOs to provide aid for female victims of trafficking and violence. Legal counseling, social assistance, and relocation centers should be available in all cities and cater to rural areas as well.

❖ Proper implementation of the new family law requires the use of Berber and Moroccan Arabic (the mother tongues that the majority of women speak) in campaigns intended to explain the new provisions.

❖ The government should create centers where violent men can learn to control their behavior.

ECONOMIC RIGHTS AND EQUAL OPPORTUNITY

Since the mid-1970s, Moroccan women have increasingly worked outside their homes, thereby significantly raising the quality of life in Morocco and contributing to the economic transformation of the country. As of 2007, nearly 27 percent of women participated in the workforce,[24] compared with participation rates in the single digits in the 1970s. However, a combination of patriarchy, illiteracy, and discrimination in the workplace preclude women from fully enjoying their economic rights. More than five years after the enactment of the 2003 Labor Code, men still have better employment opportunities, make more money, and hold higher-level positions than women.

Article 15 of the constitution guarantees the right of private property. Moroccan women have the right to own and make full and independent use of their land and property, and various articles of the 2004 family law protect women's property rights within marriage. Article 29, for example, safeguards a woman's control over her dowry, while Article 34 protects the possessions she brings with her into the marriage. Article 49 allows couples to draw up a document separate from the marriage contract to govern the management of property acquired during the marriage. Without such an agreement, contribution to the family property is evaluated by judges according to the paperwork provided by each one of the parties. However, by encouraging women's financial dependence on men, social norms restrict women's property rights in practice, and it is not common for women to own land. Similarly, women have full legal access to their own income, but it is often the case that male family members manage their finances.

The 2004 family law made progressive changes to the rules of inheritance, although inequalities remain. As noted in the law's preamble, the children of a man's daughters as well as those of his sons may now inherit from him. Previously, only the grandchildren on the son's side were eligible for inheritance from their grandfather. However, women are still disadvantaged in a number of inheritance situations, with daughters typically receiving half the amount set aside for sons. Moreover, women, especially in rural areas, often give up their already unequal share of inheritance to male relatives.

The Moroccan commercial code was revised in 1995 to give a woman the right to enter into a contract of employment or initiate a business without her husband's authorization. While women are able to sign their own business contracts and obtain loans, high-level business contracts still usually go to men. In addition, social norms inhibit the interaction of male and female entrepreneurs, and women, especially in rural areas, face difficulty in securing loans because they often do not have bank accounts or assets in their names. Only about 1 percent of the total female workforce owns their own businesses, compared with 6 percent of the male workforce. A 2004 study by the Women Business Managers' Association of Morocco (AFEM) identified 2,283 companies that were run or managed by women.[25]

The main cause of the vulnerability of working women is a lack of education. According to the World Bank, 43.2 percent of adult women (age 15 and above) were literate as of 2007, an increase from 39.6 percent in 2004. For adult men, the literacy rate was 68.7 percent in 2007, up from 65.7 percent in 2004.[26] Women are legally free to access education at all levels and are protected from gender-based discrimination within the education system. No gender-based admissions requirements are in place, and men and women are able to attend the same classes and study the same subjects once enrolled. Yet girls continue to lag behind boys in enrollment rates, with 44.8 percent of girls attending secondary school and 10.7 percent pursuing higher education as of 2007, compared with 53.4 percent and 12 percent, respectively, for boys.[27] Social preferences tend to direct female students toward certain subjects, such as teaching and medicine, and a woman's family exercises a good deal of influence over her choice of field of study.

The combination of poor education and societal pressure to work in certain professions or industries has led most working women to take up low-paying jobs. For example, many women work in the textile industry (where they represent 71 percent of the workforce), the agricultural sector (which employed 61.4 percent of working women as of 2007), or as domestic servants. Morocco's failure to ratify the International Labor Organization's Convention 87 on freedom of association and collective bargaining has permitted a hostile environment for organized efforts to defend these workers' rights.[28] The 2003 labor code does not apply to domestic and agricultural workers, meaning they do not have the right to form unions. Furthermore, social norms discourage women from working at night, and to the extent that trade unions are able to operate and secure better working conditions and benefits, women are often excluded because union activities take place at night.

Decree No. 2-56-1019 of 1957 prohibits women from performing dangerous work, barring them from some occupations,[29] and construction and mechanical jobs are commonly reserved for men. However, some occupations that have traditionally been assigned to men are beginning to open to women, including law enforcement. Beyond such formal employment, large numbers of women are involved in informal economic activity that can be performed at home—like preparing food products for sale on the street—or in semiprivate spaces such as bathhouses.

Article 346 of the 2003 labor code mandates equal pay for work of equal value, but because women are often concentrated in lower-ranking positions in practice, their wages are significantly lower than those of men.[30] There is also a greater social tolerance for women's unemployment than for men's, as men are deemed to bear the responsibility for supporting their families financially.

Gender-based protections regarding maternity leave and other benefits provided by law, while essential for helping women balance their professional and private lives, often discourage private-sector employers from hiring or promoting women at the same rates as men. The cost of those benefits is not absorbed by the state through a social security program, but it is passed to individual employers. A woman is entitled to return to her job after giving birth without a penalty, and Act No. 20-94, promulgated by Decree No. 2-95-1 of January 24, 1995, extended maternity leave from 10 to 12 weeks with full pay. For one year after the birth of her child, a woman is granted daily one-hour breaks for the purpose of breastfeeding.

Women's rights NGOs, labor unions, and other groups have worked to bolster female education and improve access to employment for women. The National Institute of Solidarity with Women in Difficulty works on the socioeconomic integration and legal protection of two categories of vulnerable women: female domestic workers and single mothers. These two categories are interrelated, as domestic workers often become pregnant out of wedlock. They are subject to severe social stigma as well as ill-treatment at the hands of service providers, sexual abuse, infanticide, suicide, dangerous forms of employment, and forced confinement. The government is considering legislation to regulate the work of domestic servants in terms of working hours, health insurance, and other protections. Article 4 of the 2003 labor code called for a separate law covering domestic workers, but no such legislation had yet been enacted.[31]

Recommendations

❖ The government and NGOs should step up existing efforts to reduce illiteracy and encourage full school enrollment among women and girls, whether through public awareness campaigns, financial incentives, or adult education programs.

❖ The government should work in cooperation with women's NGOs to educate and inform women about their rights under existing inheritance laws, and provide women with legal assistance to defend those rights when necessary. Judges should be trained to more actively protect women's rights in inheritance and other property cases.

❖ The government, in consultation with women's NGOs, should revise education methods and materials to ensure that they incorporate concepts of gender equality and exclude negative stereotypes.

❖ The government should enact legislation to protect domestic servants by regulating working hours and conditions, guaranteeing health care, and allowing worker organization. Labor unions and NGOs should develop additional services for these workers, including personal-finance training, temporary shelters for abused women, and job-placement assistance for those in untenable working situations.

❖ Further efforts to extend maternity leave, provide childcare, and protect female employees from sexual harassment in the workplace should be accompanied by safeguards against gender-based discrimination in hiring and promotion. In addition to stricter laws on this issue, the government should provide effective complaint and adjudication mechanisms to encourage compliance.

❖ Women rights NGOs should develop grassroots projects that specifically address the needs of domestic and factory workers.

POLITICAL RIGHTS AND CIVIC VOICE

Moroccan women have come a long way in the field of politics. In the last decade, many have been appointed as cabinet ministers, diplomats, and judges, and thanks to implementation of a quota system, the number of women in the 325-seat lower house of Parliament rose from two in 1997 to 34 after the 2007 elections.[32] Another quota rule recently boosted women's representation in local government as well. However, more than five decades after independence, women's participation in political life is still hampered by sociocultural constraints, including the conservative notion that women's voices are *awrah* (not to be exposed in public, as with certain parts of the body). In addition, patriarchal and undemocratic structures within political parties tend to exclude women and youth, limiting their access to politics.[33]

Morocco is a constitutional monarchy with a royally appointed government, a popularly elected lower house of Parliament (the Chamber of Representatives), and an indirectly elected upper house (the Chamber of Counselors). Women have had the right to vote and compete for office since 1956, but the character of their engagement has been heavily influenced by traditionalist and Islamist political trends.[34] After their disillusionment with the 1957 family law, women's rights advocates generally aligned themselves with leftist parties. They later grew frustrated with the heavily patriarchal structure of political parties in general, choosing instead to organize within NGOs, first with connections to leftist parties and then as independent groups. Zouhour Chekkafi, elected to lead the Democratic Society Party in 2007, was the first woman to head a political party, but women today continue to participate more in NGOs than in political parties directly.

Political Islam emerged in earnest in the mid-1980s. Aware of the potential danger that extremist Islamist ideology presented to both feminist demands and the monarchy, women's rights activists began to coordinate their strategies with the government.[35] A new constitution was established in 1996, four women were appointed as ministers in 1997, the first socialist government was constituted in 1998, and a progressive new king took power in 1999. These events boosted women's presence in politics and civil society and led to the promulgation of the 2002 quota system, under which 30 of the 325 seats in the Chamber of Representatives are reserved for female candidates; 35 women were elected to the chamber that year, and 34 were elected in 2007.[36] However, women's presence in the 270-seat upper house—which is chosen by local councils, professional groups, and labor unions—has remained minimal, with just three female members elected in 2006.

The government formed in 2007 has the greatest number of women in Moroccan history: seven women head ministries, including the Health Ministry and the Ministry for Social Development, Family, and Solidarity. One woman acts as an adviser to the king, while three women serve as ambassadors and several others head executive departments. Moreover, women have increased their representation in the judiciary. One noteworthy change resulting from the 2004 family law is a growth in the number of female family court judges and a clear rejuvenation of the magistracy. As of 2006, women accounted for about 19 percent of all judges, and 16 percent of those on the Supreme Court.[37] Women make up a similar share of Morocco's lawyers.

Until very recently, women were not well represented in local politics: only 127 women won office in the 2003 local elections, giving them less than 1 percent of the contested posts.[38] However, women's NGOs and allied groups campaigned vigorously for a 12 percent quota system, and the measure was enacted in a package of December 2008 electoral reforms. As a result, more than 3,400 women secured positions in the June 2009 local elections.[39] Some 50 percent of the elected women are under 35 years old, 71 percent have secondary or tertiary education levels, and 98 percent were elected for the first time.[40]

Despite recent successes, women in decision-making positions frequently face various social challenges. Although they are generally seen as less corrupt than men, women leaders are forced to prove their credibility and accountability more than men. Women who do succeed as leaders within politics and the government, however, provide strong role models and help to dispel negative stereotypes.

Article 9 of the constitution guarantees freedom of opinion, freedom of expression in all its forms, freedom of assembly, and freedom to join any political organization. Although the authorities restrict critical coverage on a number of subjects, including Islam and the monarchy, there are no major constraints on discussion of women's rights, gender equality, domestic violence, and other such issues in the media. Similarly, demonstrations that directly challenge the government draw crackdowns from the security forces, but women's rights activists, who generally have maintained good relations with the state, are able to hold rallies.

Grassroots women's rights NGOs have been steadily proliferating in recent years. Although their ideological backgrounds sometimes conflict, they tend to share the goal of promoting women's dignity in and outside the home, and have had a beneficial overall effect on Moroccan society. The government and women's rights NGOs have collaborated to increase women's involvement in local civic life. In March 2009, the government allocated 10 million dirhams (US$1.28 million) to boost women's political participation.

In the last five years, women have increasingly gained access to information with the aim of empowering themselves in different spheres of life. Various associations, such as Tadros in Fes and Rabat, are offering computer training and instruction on how to protect oneself on the Internet.

They are also helping rural women artists and carpet weavers to sell their products online. Moreover, women in academia have been particularly instrumental in disseminating democratic ideas through the university system. Most current civil society leaders are university professors as well. Postgraduate programs in women's and gender studies are gaining some popularity, and the first cohorts of students have begun to receive advanced degrees in these areas.

Nevertheless, women generally, and rural women in particular, are frequently unaware of their political rights. There is a genuine communication problem in Morocco. Most literature regarding women's rights, political or otherwise, is written in Arabic and French, meaning it is inaccessible to large numbers of women. Some NGOs use Moroccan Arabic (Darija) and Berber in their outreach campaigns, but these efforts are insufficient, particularly in light of the high illiteracy rates among women.

The last five years constitute a turning-point for women's rights activists and the feminist movement. Hard-won gains have been realized, but there is a clear need to reassess priorities for the future. The generational tensions that inevitably accompany a renewal of leadership present a major obstacle. The youth's opinions regarding women's rights are complex, ranging from outright support of the gains the older generations have achieved to a sense of skepticism. The feminist movement will have to address this ambivalence and improve its ties with young people.

Up to now, illiteracy, socioeconomic exclusion, fundamentalist ideologies, and the use of women's issues by the state to combat radicalization have been highlighted as the main challenges for the Moroccan feminist movement.[41] However, urgent attention must be paid to educated, nonradicalized men and women who are politically savvy but cynical, and those who are university educated but unemployed. These groups are important because while they readily adhere to human rights and social justice principles, they do not appreciate the relevance of gender equity within the larger project of democratization. Fewer still see the many links between poverty and gender discrimination.

Recommendations

❖ Political parties and NGOs should actively recruit and train female politicians to help increase women's representation within party leadership structures.

❖ The government should promote the use of Moroccan Arabic and Berber in broadcast media to reach all segments of the female population and educate them about their civil and political rights.

❖ Women's rights NGOs should improve their ties with other groups working on the broader issues of social justice, economic development, and democratization, with the aim of highlighting their common goals and enlisting new supporters.

❖ The government should bolster public acceptance of its support for women's rights by renewing its practical commitment to human rights in general, including freedom of expression and freedom of assembly.

SOCIAL AND CULTURAL RIGHTS

In the past, women's rights activists argued that the laws were not designed to address real problems, but now that most relevant statutes have been reformed, reality has in many ways failed to catch up to the laws. While health and demographic statistics have improved in recent years, large disparities remain between urban and rural areas, and the media have helped to perpetuate harmful social and cultural attitudes toward women.

Morocco's medical infrastructure improved after independence, and free public health care has allowed most women to give birth in hospitals. The government's commitment to the health of women and their children has been reflected in statistical progress over the past two decades. Life expectancy for women had risen to 72.8 years by 2005, from 66.3 in 1990, and the mortality rate for children under five dropped dramatically over the same period, from 89 to 40 per 1,000 live births. In another sign of better access to medical care, including contraceptives, the fertility rate fell from 4 births per woman in 1990 to 2.4 in 2005.[42]

Women are generally able to make independent decisions about their health care needs, although poverty and economic dependence on men often weaken this freedom. Women may unilaterally decide to undergo surgery, whether it be necessary or elective. They can easily obtain birth control and legally seek out medical services without permission from their husbands or male guardians. Nonetheless, because women are often subject to a degree of traditional male control over their movements, they may need the consent of their husbands or male guardians to visit a doctor or go to the hospital. Similarly, a mother's permission is enough for her child to undergo medical procedures, but in practice cultural requirements oblige her to obtain the support of her husband.

Article 453 of the penal code was amended by Decree No. 181-66 in 1967 to legally sanction abortion if the life of the mother is in danger or if the fetus has fatal defects. Additionally, because of cultural concerns related to family honor, abortions of pregnancies resulting from rape are tolerated. However, factors such as poverty, the social stigma surrounding abortion and pregnancy out of wedlock, and the government's ambiguous attitude toward this issue have contributed to a situation in which many women die or suffer severe health consequences after undergoing illegal abortions.

In principle, women and men have equal access to health services. Nonetheless, various interrelated social variables divide Moroccan women and affect their access to health care. These variables include residence in urban versus rural communities, income levels, educational attainment, employment status, marital status, and linguistic ability.[43] Wealthy, urban, educated, working women tend to have better access than poor, rural, and illiterate women, in part because the health care infrastructure is deficient in rural areas.

Women are far less protected than men from gender-based harmful traditional practices. Although female genital mutilation is not practiced in Morocco, girls are culturally required to be virgins before marriage. As more girls engage in premarital sex, many resort to the surgical reconstruction of their hymens to make themselves more acceptable brides in the eyes of their own or the groom's family.

Women—usually urban and educated—can be found on school boards, in parent-teacher associations, and in neighborhood associations. In this capacity, they are able to participate in and influence local community life, policies, and social development. Although a trust in women's leadership abilities is growing among the youth, societal resistance to women as leaders, even at the community level, is still strong.

Part of this resistance comes from the rather passive and negative image of women that is presented in the Moroccan media, which constantly associate them with the home and the upbringing of children, and downplay their achievements in the public sphere. Female academics, journalists, filmmakers, and civil society activists have made various attempts to alleviate the harm caused by such portrayals. Although male broadcasters, talk-show hosts, and radio announcers outnumber their female counterparts, the latter are increasingly attracting attention from the public and are influential in opinion-making.[44]

The mainstream media do not reflect the real progress made by women, and rarely use gender-sensitive language. Although they have attempted to tackle issues such as sexual harassment, domestic violence, and gender roles, these efforts have been insufficient. There is a proliferation of magazines in Arabic and French that focus on women's interests, but they tend to be geared toward elite and educated women. Rural and semi-urban women are marginalized in the media generally due to poverty and illiteracy.

Poverty has a disproportionate effect on women. Although welfare is available to divorcees and widows, it is not offered to single mothers as such. Even in instances where they are entitled to welfare, poor or illiterate women often have difficulty maintaining the necessary paperwork and making frequent visits to the relevant offices.

Although women have the right to housing and the same legal opportunity to obtain housing as men, very few own their own residence in practice. The 2004 family law obliges a husband to house his wife during marriage and during the waiting period before a final divorce, either in the marital home or a suitable substitute. Article 53 of the family law states that if either spouse unjustifiably evicts the other spouse from the marital home, the public prosecutor will intervene on behalf of the evicted spouse and "shall take all necessary measures for his or her safety and protection." However, reports indicate that authorities are slow to implement this measure and that women are having difficulty proving that they were expelled from the house. Additionally, a father must provide financial maintenance, including housing, to his minor children, even if they are in the divorced mother's custody. However, there is no guarantee that the wife will retain the marital home after a divorce is finalized, and husbands often use personal connections and bribery to avoid a court ruling to that effect.

Women's rights NGOs have been very active in alleviating the plight of poor and illiterate women. Their work is encouraged by the government, and the positive effects are apparent. For example, groups like Feminine Solidarity and Bayti (My House) have been catering to women in financial distress and single mothers. Meanwhile, through investments in rural roads, other infrastructure, and social programs, the government is attempting to improve the life of the rural population as a whole, although these efforts are still very insufficient: paved roads, running water, and schools are still luxuries for most of the countryside of Morocco. The poverty rate in rural areas dropped from 36 percent in 2004 to 21 percent in 2007, according to the findings of a survey by the High Commissioner for Planning, but work to alleviate poverty is still sorely needed.[45]

Recommendations

✤ The government should allocate more funds to meet women's health needs, particularly by improving the health care infrastructure in rural and other underserved areas.

✤ The government should establish equitable welfare programs for single mothers and female heads of households, including those who have never married. NGOs should provide services that assist women in obtaining the state benefits for which they are eligible.

✤ Existing welfare payments should be supplemented by microcredit services, financial literacy training, and employment skills for women in impoverished rural and semi-urban areas.

✤ The government should sponsor media programs that fight negative stereotypes of women.

✤ The media sector should partner with women's rights NGOs to create content that would provide the youth with positive female role models, valorize women's impact on society, and lend credibility and stature to women's initiatives of all kinds.

AUTHOR

Fatima Sadiqi is Senior Professor of Linguistics and Gender Studies at the University of Fes and director of the Isis Centre for Women and Development. She is a former Fulbright scholar and recipient of a Harvard fellowship. Sadiqi has written extensively on Moroccan languages and Moroccan women's issues. She is the author of *Women, Gender, and Language in Morocco* (Brill, 2003), *Grammaire du Berbère* (L'Harmattan, 1997), *Images on Women in Abdullah Bashrahil's Poetry* (Beirut Institute, 2004). She has also edited and co-edited a number of volumes, including *Migration and Gender in Morocco* (Red Sea Press, 2008) and *Women Writing Africa: The Northern Region* (Feminist Press, 2009). Her co-edited volume *Women in the Middle East and North Africa: Agents of Change* will be published by Routledge in May 2010.

NOTES

[1]   For example, Moroccan laws related to banking interest and the sale of alcohol bypass very clear prohibitions in the Koran and Shari'a (Islamic law).

[2]   Islamism may be defined as a social movement or organization based on the exploitation of Islam for political aims, or the exercise of political power in the name of religion only. Moroccan Islamists do not constitute a homogeneous group; they represent a variety of conservative, moderate, and radical strains.

[3]   Indeed, it was the feminists who started to push for rights from a religious perspective. See Farida Bennani and Zineb Miadi, *Sélection des Textes Sacrés sur les Droits Humains de la Femme en Islam* (Rabat: Friedrich Ebert Stiftung, 2000).

[4]   Whereas Shari'a rules are based on a rigid and literal reading of the Koran and Hadith, the concept of "maqasid al-Shari'a" (goals of Shari'a) involves the contextualization of these rules in changing historical circumstances.

[5]   The text of the constitution is available in English at http://www.al-bab.com/maroc/gov/con96.htm.

[6]   See Article 10 of the nationality code, available (in French) at http://www.consulatdumaroc.ca/natma2007.pdf.

[7]   See Article 100 of the Moudawana.

[8]   See Fatima Sadiqi, *Women, Gender and Language in Morocco* (Boston: Brill, 2003).

[9]   See Stop Violence Against Women, "Morocco," Advocates for Human Rights, http://www.stopvaw.org/Morocco.html.

[10]   Article 10 states: "(1) No one can be arrested, detained, or punished except in the cases and forms provided by law. (2) The home is inviolable. There can be no searches or inspection except under the conditions and the forms provided by the law."

[11]   Democratic Association of Moroccan Women, "The Withdrawal of the Reservations to CEDAW by Morocco," news release, December 17, 2008, http://www.euromedrights.net/pages/556/news/focus/68402.

[12]   Sarah Touahri, "Morocco Retracts CEDAW Reservations," Magharebia, December 17, 2008, http://www.magharebia.com/cocoon/awi/xhtml1/en_GB/features/awi/features/2008/12/17/feature-02.

[13]   Sadiqi, *Women, Gender and Language in Morocco*.

[14]   Article 6 states: "Islam shall be the state religion. The state shall guarantee freedom of worship for all."

[15]   Note that Article 9 of the constitution guarantees all citizens the "freedom of movement and freedom to settle in any part of the Kingdom."

[16]   An English translation of the Moudawana by Global Rights is available at http://www.globalrights.org/site/DocServer/Moudawana-English_Translation.pdf?docID=3106.

[17]   Agence France-Presse (AFP), "Women in Morocco Progress But 'Could Do Better'—Activist," France 24, March 7, 2009, http://www.france24.com/20090307-women-morocco-progress-but-could-do-better-activist.

[18]   See Articles 94–114 of the Moudawana.

[19]   A recent (unpublished) study by Leadership Féminin, a local women's association, revealed that 87 percent of women in six rural areas in Morocco do not know anything about the new family law.

20   Mohamed Ennaji, *Serving the Master: Slavery and Society in Nineteenth Century Morocco*, translated from French by Seth Graebner (New York: St. Martin's Press, 1998).

21   Given its geographical location at the crossroads between the Maghrib, sub-Saharan Africa, and Europe, Morocco is at the same time a source, transit point, and destination for human trafficking. See *Combined Third and Fourth Periodic Report—Morocco* (New York: UN Committee on the Elimination of Discrimination against Women, 2006), 22, http://www.un.org/womenwatch/daw/cedaw/reports.htm#m.

22   Sarah Touahri, "Morocco Seeks to Criminalize Violence Against Women," Magharebia, April 1, 2008, http://www.magharebia.com/cocoon/awi/xhtml1/en_GB/features/awi/features/2008/04/01/feature-01.

23   Amina Barakat, "Renewed Efforts to End Violence against Women," Inter Press Service, March 17, 2009, http://ipsnews.net/africa/nota.asp?idnews=46150.

24   World Bank, "GenderStats—Labor Force," http://go.worldbank.org/4PIIORQMS0 [accessed December 15, 2009].

25   Gender Entrepreneurship Markets (GEM) Program, "Country Brief: Morocco 2005," International Finance Corporation, http://www.ifc.org/ifcext/gempepmena.nsf/Attach mentsByTitle/Morocco_Country_Brief_Oct05.pdf/$FILE/Morocco_Country_Brief _Oct05.pdf.

26   World Bank, "GenderStats—Education," http://go.worldbank.org/RHEGN4QHU0 [accessed December 15, 2009].

27   World Bank, "GenderStats—Education."

28   World Bank, "GenderStats—Labor Force"; International Trade Union Confederation (ITUC), *Internationally Recognized Core Labour Standards in Morocco* (Brussels, ITUC, 2009), http://www.ituc-csi.org/IMG/pdf/WTO_report_Morocco_Final_EN.pdf.

29   Bureau of International Labor Affairs, *Morocco Labor Rights Report* (Washington, DC: U.S. Department of Labor, July 2004), 26, http://www.dol.gov/ilab/media/reports/usfta/mlrr.pdf.

30   ITUC, *Internationally Recognized Core Labour Standards in Morocco*, 5.

31   Sarah Touahri, "New Law to Regulate Morocco's Domestic Services Industry," Magharebia, March 13, 2009, http://www.magharebia.com/cocoon/awi/xhtml1/en_GB/features/awi/features/2009/03/13/feature-03.

32   Inter-Parliamentary Union, "Women in National Parliaments: Statistical Archive," http://www.ipu.org/wmn-e/classif-arc.htm.

33   For a study on patriarchal and undemocratic structures within one of the leading socialist political parties, see Sassi, Mohammed, "Al-Azma Arahina Liddimoqratia Fi Al-Itihad Alishtirak," *Nawafid* 8 (2000): 26–52.

34   It should be noted that, of the 46 seats that the Islamist Justice and Development Party (PJD) holds in parliament, six are held by women, making it the party with the highest percent of female parliamentarians. One reason for this high level of involvement is because Islamist parties seem to more seriously engage in the implementation of the quota system and put women at the top of their party lists more often than other political parties. Inter-Parliamentary Union, Parline Database, Morocco, House of Representatives, Last Elections, http://www.ipu.org/parline-e/reports/2221_E.htm.

[35] Although NGOs do not have an official status that would allow them a high level of political influence, the government has gradually taken them more seriously.

[36] The 2002 quota system is not established by law; rather it is embodied in a charter among political parties that reserves 30 seats for women on a special National List.

[37] *Combined Third and Fourth Periodic Report—Morocco,* 26.

[38] *Combined Third and Fourth Periodic Report—Morocco,* 25.

[39] Amel Boubekeur, "Local Elections and National Democracy Opportunities in Morocco," France 24, June 29, 2009, http://www.france24.com/en/20090629-local-elections-national-democracy-opportunities-morocco-amel-boubekeur-carnegie-middle-east-centre-analysis.

[40] These statistics are taken from a speech by Nouzha Skalli, Minister of Social Development, Family, and Solidarity, delivered in Rabat on June 18, 2009, one week after the elections.

[41] See, for example, Moha Ennaji, *Multilingualism, Cultural Identity, and Education in Morocco* (Boston: Springer, 2005); Fatima Sadiqi, "Facing Challenges and Pioneering Feminist and Gender Studies: Women in Post-colonial and Today's Maghrib," *African and Asian Studies* 7, no. 4 (2008): 447–470; Sadiqi, "The Central Role of the Family Law in the Moroccan Feminist Movement," *British Journal of Middle Eastern Studies* 35, no. 3 (2008): 325–337; Sadiqi, "Language, Religion and Power in Morocco," in *Untangling Modernities: Gendering Religion and Politics,* ed. Anne Braude and Hannah Herzog (London: Palgrave, 2009).

[42] World Bank, "GenderStats—Create Your Own Table," http://go.worldbank.org/MRER 20PME0 [accessed December 15, 2009].

[43] See Sadiqi, *Women, Gender and Language in Morocco.*

[44] Fatema Mernissi, "Digital Scheherazade: The Rise of Women as Key Players in the Arab Gulf Communication Strategies," September 2005, http://www.mernissi.net/books/articles/digital_scheherazade.html.

[45] "Poverty Rate in Rural Areas Dropped to 21%, Minister," Morocco Newsline, July 16, 2008, http://www.morocconewsline.com/index.php?option=com_content&task=view&id=272&Itemid=1.

OMAN

by Rafiah al-Talei

POPULATION:	3,108,000		
GNI PER CAPITA:	US$14,768		

COUNTRY RATINGS	2004	2009
NONDISCRIMINATION AND ACCESS TO JUSTICE:	2.0	2.1
AUTONOMY, SECURITY, AND FREEDOM OF THE PERSON:	2.1	2.1
ECONOMIC RIGHTS AND EQUAL OPPORTUNITY:	2.7	2.9
POLITICAL RIGHTS AND CIVIC VOICE:	1.2	1.8
SOCIAL AND CULTURAL RIGHTS:	2.1	2.5

(COUNTRY RATINGS ARE BASED ON A SCALE OF 1 TO 5, WITH 1 REPRESENTING THE LOWEST AND 5 THE HIGHEST LEVEL OF FREEDOM WOMEN HAVE TO EXERCISE THEIR RIGHTS)

INTRODUCTION

Oman is a monarchy that has been independent since the expulsion of the Portuguese in 1650. Sultan Qaboos bin Said, who overthrew his father in a coup, has ruled the country by royal decree since 1970. After assuming power, Sultan Qaboos used oil revenues to institute ambitious plans to modernize the country and improve its infrastructure, health services, and educational system. Women took an active role in the process and were visible participants in various fields within the private and public sectors. However, Oman's relatively small job market became virtually saturated in the 1980s, leading to more starkly defined gender roles and setting back some of the progress previously achieved. As a result, women's representation in the labor force decreased from 17.1 percent in 1980 to 14.2 percent in 1990.[1]

In the mid-1990s, as government's efforts to reduce the number of foreign workers through the policy of "Omanization" came into full effect, national women along with men were recruited to fill jobs customarily held by the expatriates. This had a particularly positive effect on poor, less-educated women, who were increasingly able to obtain jobs as cleaners, hospital orderlies, and kitchen help, allowing them to support themselves in the face of hardship and giving them a new role in the community.[2] The number of female university graduates also increased during this period, acting as a catalyst for empowerment. By 2003, women's representation in the labor force resurged to 17.2 percent. Over the last five years, women have continued to enjoy higher levels of economic participation, and according to some sources they now represent 19.1 percent of Oman's workforce.[3]

Oman's patriarchal culture, in combination with conservative religious norms, continues to have a profound impact on women. Despite progress, women face discrimination in almost all areas of life, and men are traditionally and legally seen as heads of household. Women remain underrepresented in the judiciary and government structures, and do not have full freedom to make decisions about their health and reproductive rights. Moreover, they are afforded unequal rights under the personal status law, which governs inheritance, marriage, divorce, and child custody.

Attempts by the government to incorporate a more liberal interpretation of women's rights and duties into the country's laws and practices have had mixed success. Oman was one of the first Gulf countries to provide women with political rights and begin integrating them into government structures. Women have been allowed to vote and stand in elections for the *Majlis al-Shura* (Consultative Council), the lower house of parliament, since 1994, when only select individuals approved by government leaders could vote. Universal adult suffrage was offered for the first time in 2003. In November 2007, the sultan appointed 14 women to the 70-member *Majlis al-Dawla* (State Council), the upper house of parliament, doubling the number of female members from 2004. However, for the first time since they were permitted to run, female candidates failed to win any of the 84 seats contested in the 2007 elections to the Consultative Council. Despite the disappointing result, the traditional image of women is slowly changing as more women are becoming visible in their roles as political candidates, leaders, and decision makers.

One of the major challenges to women's rights advocacy in Oman is the overall denial of basic civil liberties. The rights of assembly and association are restricted for all citizens, men and women, and no meaningful organized political opposition exists. Public gatherings require official permission, and political parties are banned. While the government permits the formation of nongovernmental organizations (NGOs), no human rights or women's rights NGOs exist. Such restrictions impede the ability of women to organize independently and lobby effectively for the expansion of their rights. The Omani Women's Association (OWA), which is supervised by the Ministry of Social Development (MSD), does not address sensitive issues such as civil and political rights or women's autonomy and security. Moreover, freedom of expression and democratic debate are extremely limited. Media outlets are either governmental or under governmental supervision, impeding citizens' ability to start an open debate about their needs and issues. All media institutions, whether broadcast or print, must be licensed by the Ministry of Information.

Oman's ratification of the United Nations Convention on the Elimination of All Forms of Discrimination against Women (CEDAW) in February 2006 is viewed as progress toward the realization of women's rights and has encouraged women to fight for their legal rights.[4] However, implementation of the convention has proven difficult and slow.

NONDISCRIMINATION AND ACCESS TO JUSTICE

Omani women continue to face significant discrimination in domestic laws and difficulty accessing justice through the courts. However, the government instigated an important change by introducing a law in 2008 stipulating that men and women's legal testimonies are now considered equal, although it is unclear to what extent this will apply to personal status law cases. Additionally, over the past five years a growing number of educated women have advocated for greater awareness of laws and policies that women could use to empower themselves. In response, the Ministry of National Economy, in cooperation with international and national organizations, has started issuing booklets outlining laws of specific concern to women. However, the outreach to less-educated and rural women has been less successful, and overall, a lack of legal knowledge remains a significant problem.

Oman's legal system is founded upon the Shari'a (Islamic law) traditions of the Ibadi school of Islam, and its courts are organized into three tiers: courts of first instance, courts of appeal, and the Supreme Court. Rather than having a separate Shari'a court system, as many neighboring countries have, each level of the court system has a department of Shari'a within them that deals strictly with the personal status law. Although the 1996 Basic Law, which acts as Oman's constitution, states that the judiciary is independent, it remains subordinate to the sultan and the Ministry of Justice.

The Basic Law grants citizens limited civil liberties and Article 17 prohibits discrimination on the basis of "gender, origin, color, language, religion, sect, domicile, or social status."[5] Article 12 further guarantees justice, equality, and equal opportunity. The inclusion of protection from gender-based discrimination in the Basic Law is an important safeguard for women's rights, but because the Article 17 applies only to citizens, the country's large population of foreign guest workers, particularly female domestic servants, is left vulnerable to discrimination.

Despite constitutional guarantees, the laws and policies of Oman continue to subject women to gender-based discrimination. Men are heavily favored in personal status matters, and married women are legally required to secure their husband's permission before they may obtain passports.[6] Omani women may not transfer citizenship to their noncitizen spouses and children, who must obtain and renew their residency visas every two years, while Omani men may do so without restriction.[7] Noncitizen husbands are also not permitted to work without a sponsor.

Both men and women are entitled to equal access to justice by law, but access for Omani women is limited as a practical matter, in part because many women remain uninformed about laws and procedures that apply to them. Compounding this problem, women are severely underrepresented in the legal field. While no formal statistics exist regarding the male-to-female ratio among legal professionals, only five women serve as general prosecutors, and of the 117 lawyers permitted to appeal to the Omani high court, only two are women.[8] Moreover, although no law prohibits it, customs and traditions forbid women from acting as judges, a practice that neither governmental nor nongovernmental entities have challenged. That women constitute such a small percentage of legal professionals is detrimental for many women seeking justice, particularly those living in conservative rural areas who are generally reluctant to discuss their legal grievances with or be represented by male attorneys.

Rules of criminal procedure were established through royal decree in December 1999 to regulate evidentiary processes for criminal cases, measures for entering cases into the criminal system, and detailed provisions for a public trial. Despite those reforms, certain provisions of Oman's penal code continue to subject women to gender-based discrimination. Under Article 252 of the Penal Code (No. 7 of 1974), a man who commits a crime against his wife or a female relative immediately after having surprised her in an act of adultery may receive a reduced penalty or be exempted from penalty altogether. If such an act (e.g. murder) constitutes a felony punishable by life in prison or capital punishment, Article 109 permits the sentence to be reduced to "at least one year."[9] Additionally, when a gender-based violent crime such as rape is reported, it is often the female victim, in addition to the male perpetrator, whose actions are criminalized. The rape of a spouse is not considered a crime under Omani law.

Women and men are protected against arbitrary arrest and detention under Article 15 of the Basic Law by virtue of their citizenship, and Article 16 prohibits the state from deporting or exiling citizens or preventing their return to the country. Arbitrary arrests and detentions are believed to be rare for both men and women, but information on this topic is scarce as no human rights NGOs are available in Oman to monitor such issues. In 2005, several people were arrested for an alleged coup plot, although the sultan later pardoned them all. Taiba al-Mawali, a women's rights activist and former member of the elected Consultative Council, was arrested in September of 2005 for slander and sentenced to a six-month term as a political prisoner because of her support for the families of these detainees. In a June 2007 television interview with the American-funded Al-Hurra television channel, al-Mawali claimed that she had limited access to information regarding charges against her before and during her 2005 trial and that she had had only one week to prepare her defense.

Adult women may now be considered full persons before the law if recent amendments to the rules of evidence are fully enforced. Pursuant to Law No. 63 of 2008, the testimony of men and women is now deemed equal in court proceedings, although it is unclear whether this will be fully implemented throughout the legal system, particularly in family courts. For example, Oman's personal status law requires that marriage contracts be concluded with the witnessing and testimony of two men; a woman's testimony is not permitted in this instance. Adult women are entitled to file legal suit without permission from a male family member although, in practice, some judges request that women appear in court with their fathers or husbands.

Preliminary discussions regarding how to implement CEDAW are under way after its February 2006 ratification. The MSD, charged with supervising "women's issues," is the governmental body most responsible for CEDAW's implementation. It, along with the Ministry of Legal Affairs, the Ministry of National Economy, and the Ministry of Justice, is reviewing Oman's existing laws to determine whether they satisfy or contradict the convention. Oman has made a general reservation to "all provisions of the Convention" not in accordance with Shari'a law, and has specifically made reservations against Article 9, paragraph 2 (granting women rights equal to men in respect to deciding their children's nationality), Article 15, paragraph 4 (granting women equal freedom of movement and choice of domicile as men), Article 16, paragraph 1 (granting women equal rights regarding marriage and family life), and Article 29 (regarding arbitration of conflicts arising from the convention).[10]

Recommendations

✤ The government should bring its national laws into conformity with the equality clause in the Basic Law and the provisions of CEDAW to ensure that the laws do not discriminate against women.

✤ The government should provide professional training to women to increase their numbers in the judiciary at all levels and create educational programs for the public that will raise awareness about the importance of increasing the number of women in courts as officials, judges, and lawyers.

✤ The government should permit the formation of independent women's NGOs and allow them to work with international organizations without government interference.

✤ Once formed, NGOs should work to design programs that will educate women about their legal rights and the means by which to effectively exercise them.

AUTONOMY, SECURITY, AND FREEDOM OF THE PERSON

People of different faiths, languages, and cultures have lived in Oman together in relative peace in recent history. While Islam is the state religion, Article 28 of the Basic Law guarantees freedom of religion as long as it is practiced in a manner that does not "disrupt public order or conflict with accepted standards of behavior." The government generally respects this right and, overall, promotes religious tolerance. While non-Muslim residents are able to practice their religious rites, they are required to register with the Ministry of Endowments and Religious Affairs and may not proselytize or publish religious materials.[11]

Oman's Personal Status Law (Royal Decree No. 32 of 1997) is based on Shari'a, assigning men and women different rights and responsibilities.

Men are financially responsible for the family while women have no such economic obligation under law. The law does not require women to be completely obedient to men and it provides women with the explicit right to work outside the home. Moreover, if a woman refuses to breastfeed her children, her husband is legally obligated to find household help.[12] Article 282 of the personal status law allows non-Muslims to follow their own religious rules when it comes to family matters.

The personal status law tends to favor the rights of men over the rights of women in marriage, divorce, inheritance, and child custody. However, its interpretation by Oman's individual judges may vary. A woman may initiate divorce proceedings under certain limited circumstances, such as abandonment or a husband's failure to meet his financial obligations, and must file legal proceedings to make the divorce final. Otherwise, women may invoke their legal right to *khula*, the Islamic practice of unilateral divorce initiated by women if they return their *mahr* (dowry).[13] On the other hand, Omani men may divorce their wives for any reason by verbally announcing their intent to do so. Men generally retain custody of their children after a divorce except in special situations, such as if the mother is still breastfeeding the children. Regarding inheritance, Shari'a law mandates that women inherit half the amount men receive unless they are bequeathed more in a will.

Women in Oman are not entirely free to negotiate equal marriage rights. Muslim women are forbidden by law from marrying non-Muslim men, while Muslim men are free to marry outside the religion. Additionally, both men and women must seek the permission of the government to marry noncitizens, a process that may include long delays and ultimately end in a denial. Secret marriages are occasionally performed, but the spouse may be barred from the country or a child refused citizenship. Within these constraints, however, Omani women have the right to choose their husbands and are free to accept or refuse marriage partners suggested by their family, although they face societal pressures to accept their family's choice. Women may sign their own marriage contract without a guardian present, but a judge will ask the guardian to attend the marriage's registration. If the guardian refuses, the judge will complete the marriage process and the woman will sign the contract herself.

Currently, women are 25 years old on average at the time they marry, an increase from 17 years old in the 1980s and 21 years old in the 1990s.[14] The trend to postpone marriage is attributed to women's increased involvement in higher education and the workforce. Additionally, studies indicate that such a delay may also be because 45 percent of both boys and girls are afraid of becoming married and starting their own families, while 48 percent of youths are afraid of the opposite sex generally.[15]

Omani laws do not prohibit women from traveling abroad, and women in Oman are free to drive cars and share classes and workplaces with men. However, women must obtain written permission from their husbands before they may be issued a passport.

Slavery and slavery-like practices are prohibited under Article 12 of the Basic Law. This article protects a citizen's right to engage in the work of his or her choice "within the limits of the law." It also prohibits compulsory work except for fair compensation, in accordance with law, and for the public good. However, many women working in the private sector, both citizens and noncitizens, endure slavery-like conditions because Oman's labor laws do not regulate working conditions for domestic servants, temporary workers, or those with work contracts for less than three months. Some employers withhold wages or the passports of foreign workers so that they may more easily be forced to work. Female foreign domestic workers constitute a significant portion of noncitizen residents in Oman and are known victims of this practice. Although foreign workers have the right to file complaints with the Labor Welfare Board against their employers for illegal practices, most are either unaware of their rights or reluctant to report violations because they are fearful of losing their jobs or being deported.

The international community has recently raised concerns regarding human trafficking in Oman. In November 2006, an independent United Nations expert on human trafficking found that although some progress had been made, Oman was not adequately fulfilling its international obligations.[16] In the 2008 U.S. Department of State's *Trafficking in Persons Report*, Oman was placed in "Tier 3," the lowest possible ranking, due to the country's failure to meet the minimum standards for the elimination of trafficking. The government still does not provide shelter services, counseling, or legal aid to trafficking victims and lacks a systematic procedure for identifying trafficking victims among vulnerable groups like detained migrants and women arrested for prostitution.[17]

In November 2008, Oman issued its first major antitrafficking law.[18] The law, which came into force in December, prohibits all forms of trafficking; those who violate the law face 3 to 15 years of imprisonment and fines. Several workshops have been held in Oman that intended to educate officials about the legislation and the phenomenon of human trafficking. The most recent, a three-day workshop organized by the Ministry of Manpower in collaboration with the International Labor Organization (ILO), was held in October 2009.[19]

Article 20 of the Basic Law prohibits physical and psychological torture of any kind, as well as humiliating treatment. There have been no substantiated reports of torture or harsh and degrading punishments of either male or female Omanis in recent years. Although individual complaints have been made, prisons generally adhered to international standards for the treatment of prisoners. However, independent observers lack regular access to prisons, making it difficult to ascertain how female prisoners are treated.

Oman has no specific legislation that criminalizes domestic violence. While issues of domestic violence are not raised in the media or in public reports, such abuse exists in Omani society at various levels. Undisclosed government sources have indicated that the government conducted a study confirming that domestic violence is a problem that should be addressed, but this study has not been publicly released, and figures and facts are confidential. There is no way to document complaints from victims, no methods that permit women to report violence confidentially, and no facilities for women seeking refuge from violence.

Although the OWA offers temporary aid to victims of domestic abuse, it neither acts as a long-term shelter nor advocates on behalf of victims. Instead, societal pressures encourage battered women to seek assistance and protection from their families rather than from the police or the courts.[20] A number of recent cases, however, have been filed by female victims of domestic violence in Omani courts. Doctors do not have a legal responsibility to report spousal abuse to the police, but they may do so in especially serious instances.

Recommendations

✤ A campaign should be launched to educate women about their existing marriage and divorce rights under Islamic law, including the provisions they are permitted to make while negotiating the marriage contract.

✤ The government should specifically outlaw domestic violence and provide gender-sensitive training and guidance to medical, police, and judicial officials who handle cases of violence against women.

✤ In order to understand the full extent of the problem, Oman's academic community should conduct a quantitative survey of domestic violence, including a diverse sample of women from different geographical areas and backgrounds.

✤ The government should either create and maintain long-term domestic shelters or encourage and provide funding for civic organizations to do so.

✤ The government should remove all barriers that currently prevent women from making autonomous life choices, such as the requirement for a husband's permission to obtain a passport.

ECONOMIC RIGHTS AND EQUAL OPPORTUNITY

Despite widespread discrimination and traditional cultural attitudes, women play an increasingly influential role in Omani society due to their growing participation in the labor force. Approximately 25.8 percent of the adult female population were active in the workforce at the end of 2007, representing nearly a two percent increase from 2002.[21] Today, parents and husbands alike rely more heavily on the financial support provided by their daughters and wives, and divorced or widowed women actively seek out employment to support their families. Female participation in the workforce is expected to further increase as more women obtain education and delay marriage, but that will be contingent on whether society is able to address existing conservative concepts of appropriate gender roles.

A woman's right to own and use her property independently is protected under Article 11 of the Basic Law, which permits all persons to dispose of their property as they so choose. In practice, though, authorities rarely intervene when men exert control of the property of female family members because these situations are considered by society to be private matters. Choices regarding how a woman can dispose of her income and assets are usually decided by the head of the household, traditionally a man. However, women are gaining more decision-making power within the family due to their increased economic participation and corresponding ability to contribute financially to the family.

While women are legally entitled to enter into business contracts and activities at all levels, the decision to do so is traditionally made within the family and almost never individually. Men are legally required to financially support their families, including all female family members, and courts may judicially enforce this obligation. In case of divorce, however, the amount of maintenance owed to a woman by her ex-husband is generally insufficient to meet her needs.

Article 13 of the Basic Law reaffirms that education is "a fundamental element for the progress of society which the state fosters and endeavors to make available to all." However, women face gender-based discrimination when seeking access to postsecondary education. Women's enrollment in universities increased from 20.7 percent in 2004 to 36 percent in 2006, but a gender-based quota system limits the number of women in disciplines such as agriculture, medicine, and engineering. Disparities also exist in the grades necessary to enroll in universities. Some female college applicants with relatively high grades choose to repeat their final year of high school to increase their chances of being admitted, while boys with lower grades are often accepted immediately.

Notably, Omani women who leave school because of marriage or family issues often return to school after establishing their social life. Women fill 97 percent of literacy classes and 32 percent of adult education classes.[22] Domestic and international stakeholders recognize education as a key measure of the status of women's autonomy, and it is commonly assumed that education will lead to increased autonomy for women in Oman.[23] Reflecting this, a royal grant was established in October 2009 to fund 500 annual scholarships for female high school graduates who meet the merit- and needs-based criteria.[24]

Women are legally entitled to choose their careers under Article 12 of the Basic Law. This decision, however, is usually made in consultation and negotiation with a woman's father, brothers, and/or husband, and women may face social obstacles if their choices are not supported by their male family members. The government does not interfere in family disputes concerning a woman's career choice, meaning that women are often forced to accede to the decisions of the family patriarch.

Article 12 of the Basic Law specifically prohibits gender-based discrimination in the labor sector and emphasizes justice and equality as pillars of Omani society. By law, men and women should receive equal pay for the same work, although it is legally permissible to provide women with work benefits that are not equal to those of men. No studies have been conducted to examine whether wage disparities exist among men and women who possess the same professional qualifications. The government has made efforts to hire public sector employees in a nondiscriminatory manner, and over one-third of government employees in Oman are women, but only a few occupy high-level posts.

Article 81 of the Oman Labor Law (No. 35 of 2003) prohibits women from working between 7:00 p.m. and 8:00 a.m. without permission from the minister of labor, although exceptions are made in certain instances, such as for health care professionals who need to work overnight. However, women are often forced to work beyond these hours by their employers without additional pay, particularly those working in the private sector. Employers are required to display the entire labor law in the workplace but often fail to do so,[25] and this, combined with women's generally low level of legal literacy, prevents them from knowing and demanding their labor rights.

Some gender-specific protections exist for female employees, but women often face discrimination within employment contracts and regarding labor benefits. Women are entitled to 45 days of maternity leave according to the Civil Service Law (No. 8 of 1980) and Article 83 of the labor law. However, while most employers provide insurance benefits to the families of deceased male employees, equal benefits are not provided to the families of deceased female employees, in part because women are not considered heads of households. Additionally, Oman does not have a law against sexual harassment in the workplace. Female employees are discouraged from reporting sexual harassment, not only for fear of losing their jobs but also because social pressures place the responsibility for "proper moral behavior" on them.

In 2006, Sultan Qaboos issued a law that allowed the formation of labor and trade unions and founded the General Labor Union, which was followed by the establishment of smaller labor and workers' unions. Omani workers now have the right to organize strikes and complain about working conditions, and those who participate in union activities are protected from retribution by their employers.[26] No unions, however, currently address women's issues.

Women participate in the workforce at a notably lower rate than men in all age categories. There are 18 women for every 100 men in the Omani workforce. Of the female workforce, 39.7 percent are employed in the education sector, 14.2 percent are in the social and health sectors, and 14.8 percent contribute in the public administration sectors and related jobs.[27] As of March 2008, women make up 38.3 percent of government employees and only 17.1 percent of private sector workers.[28] This disparity is attributed to the fact that society is more comfortable with women working the shorter hours associated with public sector jobs. To minimize the gender gap that exists in the workforce, more opportunities for women must be provided in both the public and private sector.[29]

Most women cite the traditional attitudes of men as the single greatest obstacle to their advancement in the workplace. These attitudes range from disapproval of women working outside the home to lack of acceptance of women holding senior positions. Further complicating matters, tradition encourages women to have a poor self-image and lack confidence, attitudes that in turn negatively impact their work performance and affect their motivation to pursue work opportunities. In addition to discrimination and lack of viable employment opportunities, these cultural issues must be addressed if women are to be fully integrated into the formal workforce.

Ideally, unions and women's rights organizations should form to address these inequalities, but this is not possible under the current Law on Nongovernmental Societies (No. 14 of 2000—NGO Law). In recent years, however, several organized events have focused on increasing women's economic participation. "Women in Focus," Oman's first business forum for professional women, was organized by a loose affiliation of businesswomen in Muscat in April and June 2004. It aimed to provide networking opportunities for female professionals and presented a variety of keynote speakers from the region. When the businesswomen who organized it attempted to register as an NGO, their application was denied and all further meetings were prohibited as illegal gatherings. In March 2008, the "Women in Business Conference" provided businesswomen with the opportunity to share their success stories and exchange experiences in an effort to encourage young women to become more active in Oman's economy.[30]

Recommendations

❖ The government should work with the OWA to provide skills training and create centers that offer career counseling and opportunities for networking between working women.

❖ The OWA should organize classes in both rural and urban areas that provide instruction on how to start small or home-based businesses, as well as community courses on basic accounting and management.

❖ The government should enact laws criminalizing sexual harassment in the workplace and should establish programs to provide information and support to female victims of sexual harassment.

❖ The government should eliminate gender discrimination in the education sector and provide women with equal resources, funding, and access to higher and technical education facilities.

❖ The government should ensure that all jobs are open to women by establishing affirmative action programs in both the public and private sectors.

POLITICAL RIGHTS AND CIVIC VOICE

Omani men and women do not have the right to change their government democratically, and have only limited rights to peaceful assembly and freedom of speech. All organized activities require prior government approval, political parties continue to be banned, and all opposition to the government is prohibited. Nevertheless, the Omani political field is liberalizing gradually as women are beginning to play more important roles in the upper level of government, are registering to vote in larger numbers, and are increasingly running as candidates in parliamentary elections. Universal suffrage was offered for the first time to both women and men in the 2003 elections, although selected groups of citizens of both genders had been voting since 1994. Recently, civic associations have been established in a variety of fields, and in November 2004, the Oman Journalists Association was approved three years after submitting its application.

Oman has a bicameral advisory parliament consisting of the appointed State Council and the elected Consultative Council, neither of which has legislative powers. Elections for the Consultative Council most recently occurred in October 2007, drawing approximately 63 percent of the more than 388,000 registered voters. The number of female candidates increased from 15 in the 2003 election to 21 in the 2007 election, but for the first time since they were permitted to run as candidates in 1994, no women were elected.[31] Some analysts blamed this on widespread vote-buying, while others contended that there were no qualified female candidates that could capture widespread support. Meanwhile, many women argue that they need extraordinary skills to compete with ordinary men if they are to overcome the bias against women leaders that continues to pervade Oman's increasingly conservative society.

Women occupy only 5.15 percent of the leadership and decision-making positions in government and are not allowed to serve as judges in Omani courts, despite constituting approximately half the population.[32] They also hold few positions within the upper level of the government: 14 women were appointed by the sultan in a royal decree issued in November 2007 to serve in the 70-member State Council, and there are currently only four female ministers. In 2003, Aisha al-Siyabia was appointed head of the Public Authority for Craft Industries, giving her the rank of minister. The remaining three are ministers with portfolio. The first, Dr. Rawiyah al-Busaidiyah, was appointed as minister of higher education in March 2004, making her first female minister with portfolio in the Gulf Cooperation Council states. Later in 2004, Rajiha bint Abdulamir became minister of tourism and Sharifa al-Yahya was appointed minister of social development. Of the four women appointed as undersecretaries in 2003, only one remained as of June 2008. In 1999, the country's first female ambassador was appointed to the Netherlands, and in 2005, a second was appointed as ambassador to the United States.

Women and men both have the right to participate in civic life and influence decision making under Article 34 of the Basic Law, which states that citizens may "address the public authorities on personal matters or on matters related to public affairs." In practice, however, men fill the majority of policymaking positions in the executive, legislative, and judiciary branches of government, thereby limiting the influence women may have on shaping and enforcing policy.

Restrictions to freedom of expression and the press are applied equally to both men and women in Oman. In theory, the Basic Law protects all forms of free expression under Article 29, but because it is illegal to criticize the sultan in any manner, journalists practice self-censorship to avoid criminal prosecution. The Oman Journalists Association is prohibited from demanding more freedoms for its members and all of its activities must be reported to the government. Women's rights issues are not frequently covered in the media and public discourse on the subject seems to be discouraged by the government.

Women are generally free to access and use information to empower themselves, as well as to share their experiences regionally. The Internet and new media have played a significant role in encouraging new generations of young women to become involved in civic work. Women are increasingly using the Internet as a means to gain and exchange information.

Few NGOs are active in Oman, and those that exist are predominantly concerned with charitable causes. Although Article 33 of the Basic Law grants citizens freedom of assembly, it limits such association to "legitimate objectives" that do not conflict with the aims of the Basic Law. Article 4 of the NGO Law limits the scope of NGOs to charitable social work or any other area approved by the minister of social development.[33] Article 5 forbids organizations from engaging in politics and interfering with religious matters; prohibits association with tribal or sectarian groupings; bans groups from associating with, participating in, or joining a foreign association without prior government approval; and requires government approval before NGOs may organize any "public ceremony, festivals or public lectures," send delegations outside the country, or host a foreign delegation.

The MSD supervises the activities of the OWA, which was established by a group of educated, elite Omani women in 1971. It is considered to be the first women's organization in Oman and now has 47 branches and an estimated membership of more than 3,550 women. It promotes traditional Omani customs and values but does not address sensitive issues such as civil and political rights or women's autonomy and security. The OWA satellite branches offer services such as informational lectures on health practices, childcare, crafts training, and support for women seeking legal action or subjected to domestic abuse or forced marriages.

In 2005, newly appointed OWA board members sought government approval to address a more diverse set of issues concerning women. While programs such as computer skills and legal education were accepted by the government, the OWA was unable to secure approval for voter education courses or issues related to politics. No international women's rights NGOs operate in Oman, and it is very difficult for international or foreign organizations to gain permission to research or conduct studies about human or women's rights.

Recommendations

* The government should appoint women to policymaking positions and the State Council at a rate that is representative of their proportion of the population.
* The government should allow independent political associations to operate freely so that they may encourage and support women's issues through their agendas and empower female party members.

❖ The government should allow independent civil society organizations to operate freely so that women's rights NGOs may address issues that directly affect women, as well as compile and distribute information about their social and economic standing.

❖ The OWA should organize girls' debate clubs to encourage women to develop oratory and persuasion skills, which are often necessary for successful political careers.

SOCIAL AND CULTURAL RIGHTS

Omani women face significant obstacles in their efforts to establish social and cultural equality with men. Although women are respected and appreciated in community life, there is a clear cultural preference for males. When the growing rights of women threaten the traditional privileges of men, society tends to err on the side of men.

Women are not entirely free to make decisions about their health and reproductive rights. The written consent of a male relative is necessary before a woman may have surgery of any kind, and a husband's permission is necessary before birth control may be made available to a woman. Also, abortion continues to be illegal except to save the life of the mother.[34] Beyond those limitations, women are entitled to equal access to health services, which is free in public hospitals and wildly available, even in rural areas. Family planning is practiced in Oman, and a birth-spacing program was initiated by the government in 1994 in an effort to educate married couples about the benefits of family planning. Unattended births and the maternal mortality rate have decreased; the number of children per mother has also declined to 3.1 in 2007 from 6.6 in 1990 to 4.4 in 2004.[35]

The Omani government has neither formally prohibited female genital mutilation (FGM) nor initiated any public education campaigns regarding its dangers. FGM is not common in Oman, but it is still performed in some small communities in the Dhofar and Al-Batinah regions, although the practice seems to be declining. This is hard to determine because no formal statistics exist. Like domestic violence, FGM is considered to be a private matter about which society is reluctant to talk. However, in 2008 the Ministry of Health assured the CEDAW committee that the practice is considered a crime because it is the intentional infliction of bodily injury. Additionally, the ministry launched an aware-ness campaign the same year that is intended to educate people about the negative effects of FGM.

A woman who is not the head of her household has traditionally faced significant challenges to her right to property and ability to secure loans. Previously, Oman's housing benefits were granted only to heads of house-holds, a status that women could achieve only if they are widowed or divorced. However, the government land entitlement system was amended in November 2008. Men and women may now apply for residential plots of land subject to the same criteria: all applicants must be over the age of 23 if single or 21 if married.[36] Additionally, the government issued instruc-tions that all loans from the public housing bank be distributed equally to men and women who are over the age of 21 and own a plot of land.[37]

In general, older, illiterate women have difficulty owning property or participating in economic activities in the modern sector of the economy. The MSD has increasingly taken into account the housing needs of indi-viduals, particularly women who are widowed and/or poor, by either providing free housing, collecting housing payments in low monthly in-stallments, or sharing expenses depending on the financial condition of the person or the family.

Omani women are active participants in community life and help to implement social development policies, which are generally formulated at the national level. Local elected offices do not exist, but women often belong to their local associations, which combat poverty and educate women regarding pressing health issues. Local Al-Wafa centers that help children with disabilities also attract female volunteers.

Women can influence and participate in the national media, but free-dom of expression is very limited in Oman (see "Political Rights and Civic Voice"). While prohibited from accusing the government or sultan of any wrongdoing, male and female members of the media are generally permitted to discuss social and cultural issues. Whether a woman may discuss political issues depends more on her social status than on govern-ment restrictions, and her family or husband may forbid her to appear on television or talk to the press. Despite these social constraints, many women work in the media, especially television and radio, and hold some supervisory positions within the state-run media outlets. All higher-level positions, however, are held by males.

The poor in Oman are entitled to financial assistance from the MSD, but it is not enough to meet their basic needs. As women in Oman typically rely on male relatives for financial maintenance, divorced and widowed women often lack the means to support themselves and their children. Recognizing that single women are the most vulnerable to poverty, the Social Security Act was amended in 2008 to increase monetary support for widows, divorcees, abandoned women, unmarried girls, and women with a family member in prison. This increase, however, does not adequately correspond to the recent sharp rise in the cost of living felt throughout the world, and these women remain vulnerable to poverty.

The government has designed programs that provide support services and income-generating training programs in an effort to aid those deemed susceptible to poverty, particularly widows and unemployed women. The Sanad Project, or support project, for example, helps young men and women start their own businesses and provides vocational training for women in industries such as tailoring and childcare. Additionally, in November 2009, Sultan Qaboos established a fund of 7 million Omani rials (approximately US$18.2 million dollars) for women involved in agriculture.[38]

Organizations are limited in their ability to advocate freely for the promotion and protection of women's rights in Oman. The OWA and the local organizations it controls work to provide vocational training, health care, and literacy campaigns for women, but these groups do not have the authority to address more sensitive issues regarding women's rights and lack the proper training and knowledge necessary to do so. Although there seems to be a lack of general awareness regarding the importance of volunteer work, many Omanis volunteer for the civic organizations that do exist. To encourage volunteerism, a royal directive was issued on October 19, 2008, that offers a permanent headquarters for all OWA-affiliated associations that currently lack facilities and increased funding to the OWA.[39]

Omani women often do not exercise their existing rights because of societal pressures and a lack of legal knowledge. When they do, they are faced with additional barriers such as unsympathetic government officials, prejudiced judges, and disapproval by family and society. Thus, even though there are laws that protect women, greater effort must be made to create a supportive, gender-sensitive environment that addresses the legal rights of women in the implementation of such laws.[40]

Recommendations

❖ The government should encourage the Ministry of Social Development to develop programs that directly address societal perceptions about women.

❖ The government should establish a 10-year strategy to address gender discrimination in its various forms. The strategy should include short-term goals that establish gender-sensitive education curriculum and encourage the media to address gender inequalities and biases.

❖ The government should issue a law that bans female genital mutilation and expand its public education campaigns against this harmful practice.

AUTHOR

Rafiah al-Talei is a seasoned Arab journalist who specializes in civil rights, women's issues, and political developments in the Middle East and North Africa (MENA). She is currently a freelance columnist at the *Alshabiba* daily newspaper in Muscat, as well as a frequent writer for the *Arab Reform Bulletin* (Carnegie Endowment for International Peace, Washington, DC) and *Araa* magazine (Gulf Research Center, UAE). She has held various positions in the Omani press, including editor in chief of the only bilingual women's magazine in Oman. She was a candidate for Oman's Consultative Council in 2003 and is a frequent spokesperson on media rights and women's empowerment in the MENA region.

NOTES

[1] *World Development Indicators,* Online Database (Washington, DC: World Bank, 2009), http://web.worldbank.org/WBSITE/EXTERNAL/DATASTATISTICS/0,,content MDK:20523397~isCURL:Y~pagePK:64133150~piPK:64133175~theSitePK:23 9419,00.html (subscription required). Last accessed on December 15, 2009.

[2] Dawn Chatty, "Women Working in Oman: Individual Choice and Cultural Constraints," *International Journal of Middle East Studies* (Cambridge University Press) 32 (2000), 241–254, 242, www.jstor.org/stable/259593.

[3] *World Development Indicators,* Online Database (World Bank, 2009). Last accessed on December 15, 2009.

[4] "States Parties," Convention on the Elimination of All Forms of Discrimination against Women (CEDAW) (New York: United Nations, 2007), www.un.org/womenwatch/ daw/cedaw/states.htm.

5   The White Book: The Basic Law of the Sultanate of Oman (Muscat: Sultanate of Oman, Ministry of Information, 1996), Article 17, www.omanet.om/english/government/basic law/overview.asp?cat=gov&subcat=blaw.

6   Omani Passport Law (No. 69 of 1997), Chapter 2, Article 2, www.mola.gov.om/marasee mno.htm, in Arabic.

7   Oman Citizenship Law (No. 3 of 1983), Articles 1–2, www.mola.gov.om/maraseemno .htm, in Arabic.

8   *The Man and the Woman in the Sultanate of Oman: Statistics Image* (Muscat: Ministry of National Economics, National Population Committee, 2007).

9   Oman Penal Law (No. 7 of 1974), Article 8; Penal Process Law (No. 97 of 1999), Chapter 4 and Article 293; "Women's Situation in the Legislation of the Sultanate of Oman" (Muscat: UNICEF and Ministry of National Economics, National Population Committee, December 2005).

10   "Reservations to CEDAW," CEDAW (UN, UN Doc. CEDAW/SP/2006/2, April 10, 2006), www.un.org/womenwatch/daw/cedaw/reservations.htm.

11   *International Religious Freedom Report – 2007: Oman* (Washington, DC: U.S. Department of State, Bureau of Democracy, Human Rights, and Labor, September 14, 2007), www.state.gov/g/drl/rls/irf/2007/90218.htm.

12   The Personal Status Law (No. 32 of 1997), Chapter 3: Couples' Rights, Article 36, www .mola.gov.om/legals/ala7wal_alshkhseiah/leg.pdf, in Arabic.

13   The Personal Status Law (No. 32 of 1997), Articles 94–97 (on the practice of khula) and Articles 98–114 (on instances in which a judge can order divorce despite a husband's unwillingness).

14   *Special Issue: Omani Woman* (Oman: National Population Committee, International Women's Day, March 2007).

15   *To Better Understand the Youth* (Oman: Ministry of Health, 2001).

16   "UN Expert on Human Trafficking Calls on Oman to Do More to Help Victims," UN News Centre, November 8, 2006, www.un.org/apps/news/story.asp?NewsID=20537& Cr=human&Cr1=traffic.

17   *Trafficking in Persons Report—2007* (U.S. Department of State, June 2008), www.state .gov/documents/organization/105501.pdf.

18   Royal Decree No. 126 of 2008, available in Arabic at: www.mola.gov.om/legals.htm.

19   "Oman Urges Joint-Efforts to Tackle Human-Trafficking," *Khaleej Times*, October 6, 2009, http://www.khaleejtimes.com/DisplayArticle08.asp?xfile=data/middleeast/2009/ October/middleeast_October120.xml&section=middleeast.

20   *The Man and the Woman in the Sultanate of Oman* (Oman: National Population Committee, 2007).

21   *World Development Indicators,* Online Database (World Bank, 2009). Last accessed on December 15, 2009.

22   *Facts and Figures 2006* (Oman: Ministry of National Economy, May 2007).

23   "Beyond 2003: Situation Analysis of Children and Women in Oman" (UNICEF and Ministry of National Economy, 2006), 96.

24   "Women's Groups Get Royal Support," *Gulf News*, October 21, 2009, http://gulfnews .com/news/gulf/oman/women-s-groups-get-royal-support-1.517131.

[25]   Oman Labor Law (No. 35 of 2003), Articles 80–84.

[26]   Oman Labor Law (No. 74 of 2006), Articles 108–110, www.mola.gov.om/legals/al3amal/amd1.pdf, in Arabic.

[27]   *Special Issue: Omani Woman* (March 2008).

[28]   *Special Issue: Omani Woman* (March 2008); see also "Recommendation for Funding from Other Resources Without a Recommendation for Funding from Regular Resources: Oman" (UN, UNICEF Executive Board, UN Doc. EICEF/2006/P/L.22, para. 4), www.unicef.org/about/execboard/files/06-PL22_Oman_ODS.pdf.

[29]   *Special Issue: Omani Woman* (March 2008).

[30]   Women in Business Conference, March 15–16, 2008, http://womeninbusiness-oman.org/program.html.

[31]   Associated Press, "Women Fail to Win Any Seats in Omani Elections for Consultative Council," *International Herald Tribune*, October 28, 2007, www.iht.com/articles/ap/2007/10/28/africa/ME-GEN-Oman-Elections.php; see also "Democratic Elections, Governance, Oman" (Beirut: United Nations Development Programme [UNDP], Programme on Governance in the Arab Region [POGAR]), www.pogar.org/countries/elections.asp?cid=13.

[32]   *Facts and Figures 2006* (Ministry of National Economy, May 2007).

[33]   Law on Nongovernmental Societies (No. 14 of 2000), Oman, www.ngoregnet.org/country_information_by_region/Middle_East_and_North_Africa/Oman.asp, in English, or www.mola.gov.om/maraseemno.htm, in Arabic.

[34]   "World Abortion Policies 2007" (UN Department of Economic and Social Affairs, Population Division), www.un.org/esa/population/publications/2007_Abortion_Policies_Chart/2007AbortionPolicies_wallchart.htm.

[35]   WHO Statistical Information System (World Health Organization, 2008), http://www.who.int/whosis/en/.

[36]   Royal Decree No. 125 of 2008; "Applications for Residential Plots," *Times of Oman*, December 1, 2008, http://www.timesofoman.com/innercat.asp?cat=1&detail=21125.

[37]   Ministry of Information, "Thirty Housing Loans During the First Six Months of This Year," in Arabic, Oman News Agency, October 31, 2009, http://www.omanet.om/arabic/news/local.asp?cat=news; Ministry of Housing, "Social Housing and Housing Loans," in Arabic, http://www.housing.gov.om/pages_ar.php?pageid=7.

[38]   "HM Orders Special Fund for Farm Sector," *Times of Oman*, November 4, 2007, http://www.timesofoman.com/innercat.asp?cat=1&detail=31555.

[39]   Maryam Khalfan, "Royal Grants in Favor of OWA, Scholarships for Girls," *Oman Observer*, October 20, 2009, http://www.omanobserver.com/20/index.htm.

[40]   "Beyond 2003: Situation Analysis of Children and Women in Oman" (UNICEF and Ministry of National Economy, 2006), 95–96.

PALESTINE
PALESTINIAN AUTHORITY AND
ISRAELI-OCCUPIED TERRITORIES

by Suheir Azzouni

POPULATION: 3,933,000
GNI PER CAPITA: US$1,519

COUNTRY RATINGS	2004	2009
NONDISCRIMINATION AND ACCESS TO JUSTICE:	2.6	2.6
AUTONOMY, SECURITY, AND FREEDOM OF THE PERSON:	2.7	2.4
ECONOMIC RIGHTS AND EQUAL OPPORTUNITY:	2.8	2.9
POLITICAL RIGHTS AND CIVIC VOICE:	2.6	2.7
SOCIAL AND CULTURAL RIGHTS:	2.9	2.6

(COUNTRY RATINGS ARE BASED ON A SCALE OF 1 TO 5, WITH 1 REPRESENTING THE LOWEST AND 5 THE
HIGHEST LEVEL OF FREEDOM WOMEN HAVE TO EXERCISE THEIR RIGHTS)

INTRODUCTION

Palestinian women have been socially active since the beginning of the
20th century, forming charitable associations, participating in the nationalist struggle, and working for the welfare of their community. Originally
established in Jerusalem in 1921, the General Union of Palestinian Women
organized women under occupation and in the Palestinian diaspora so that
they could sustain communities and hold families together.

The character of women's involvement shifted in the late 1970s, as
young, politically oriented women became active in the fight against Israeli
occupation, as well as in the establishment of cooperatives, training centers, and kindergartens. They formed activist women's committees, which
were able to attract members from different spheres of life and create alliances with international feminist organizations. Women also played an
active role in the first intifada, or uprising, against Israeli occupation in
1987, further elevating their status in the society.

Soon after the beginning of peace negotiations between the Palestinians
and Israelis in 1991, which resulted in the 1993 Oslo Accord, women's
organizations formed a coalition called the Women's Affairs Technical
Committee (WATC) to advocate for the equal rights of women. By this time,
women throughout Palestine had started to push against discriminatory

359

aspects of the society and work together on gender-empowerment strategies. They began advocating for a future Palestinian entity with a culture of human rights that mainstreams gender concerns in all spheres of life, leading to the creation of specialized women's organizations and research centers that focus on gender-equality issues.[1]

The Palestinian Authority (PA) was established in 1994 to exercise limited governmental authority over the Palestinian population living in the Israeli-occupied territories, which include the West Bank, the Gaza Strip, and East Jerusalem.[2] After the establishment of the Palestinian Legislative Council (PLC), the PA's legislative body, women's groups and coalitions intensified their lobbying efforts for equal rights, publicly protesting discriminatory legislation and regulations.[3] However, political unrest hindered the establishment of a Palestinian state and the resumption of negotiations between Palestinians and Israel, which in turn distracted the women's rights movement from issues related to equality.

Palestinian women currently face two major types of obstacles to their rights: those arising from within their own culture and society, and those imposed as the result of occupation, war, and civil unrest. On the domestic front, women are subjected to restrictive personal status laws, which retain discriminatory provisions related to marriage, divorce, and child custody. Domestic abuse remains a significant problem, and violence against women has increased in recent years. Discriminatory laws and traditions also affect women's inheritance, alimony, and employment opportunities, thereby reducing their economic autonomy and making them more vulnerable to poverty than men. Furthermore, some segments of society seem to be growing more conservative and returning to traditional values.

Nonetheless, all discussions about Palestine's constitution, its laws, and their impact on women must also address the limitations imposed by the Israeli occupation, which heavily influences the ways in which the PA conducts its affairs, how Palestinians conduct their daily lives, and the personal security of all Palestinians. The areas under PA rule are not contiguous, but are separated by numerous checkpoints, roadblocks, and other physical and administrative barriers erected by the Israeli authorities. These barriers have significantly curtailed Palestinians' freedom of movement, and combined with a general lack of security, they have had a devastating effect on the local economy.

The increased number of checkpoints over the last five years and the construction of a West Bank separation wall,[4] which is over 50 percent complete, have worsened social and economic conditions for all Palestinians. In particular, women now experience further separation from their families, farmlands, water resources, schools, and hospitals. When the wall is completed, it will stand eight to nine meters tall and stretch more than 700 kilometers, adversely affecting the lives of an estimated one-third of the Palestinian population in the West Bank.[5]

Women's lives have also been dramatically affected by the international and domestic fallout from the January 2006 PLC elections, in which the Islamist group Hamas defeated PA president Mahmoud Abbas's more moderate Fatah party. In response to Hamas's victory, the Israeli government froze the transfer of customs revenues, which it collects on behalf of the PA, and key international donors also froze aid to the territories, leading to significant deterioration of humanitarian conditions. Although Abbas and Fatah were hostile to Hamas, the parties attempted to form a unity government on March 17, 2007. However, Hamas attacked and took over government and security positions in the Gaza Strip in June, and Abbas formed a new government based in the West Bank, declaring Hamas's control over Gaza to be illegal.[6] Since then, the two territories have been governed by two different authorities.

The new, more conservative social order imposed by Hamas has led to greater restrictions on women's rights in Gaza. For example, reports have started surfacing of women being warned against immodesty,[7] lawyers being forced to wear the veil in courts, female students being forced to wear the veil in schools, and Hamas targeting women's rights activists.[8] Under media and civil society pressure, Hamas has denied its involvement in these incidents.[9] Women in the West Bank, by contrast, have continued to enjoy a more liberal environment.[10]

In addition to the effects of the freezing of international aid, Gaza suffered from an interruption in electricity and water supplies after its power plant was bombarded by Israel in mid-2006. Border crossings out of Gaza have only been opened sporadically since the Hamas takeover, leaving residents with little access to basic resources and severely damaging the quality of life for women. The territory's problems were sharply exacerbated by an Israeli military assault that began in late December 2008. It left some 1,400 people dead, including many women and children, and thousands more injured or homeless.[11]

Ongoing political tensions between Fatah and Hamas—coupled with Israeli restrictions and incursions—have seriously affected women's health, employment opportunities, access to education, and political and civil liberties throughout the Palestinian territories.[12] In addition to presenting challenges in women's day-to-day lives, these factors have consistently drawn attention away from calls for gender equality at the societal and political levels. Nonetheless, women's rights activists and organizations are determined to persevere in their efforts to reform discriminatory laws and practices, as they have many times during Palestine's tremulous history.

NONDISCRIMINATION AND ACCESS TO JUSTICE

The instability of Palestine's domestic and international political situation has prevented revisions or even parliamentary discussions of many pivotal laws that affect women's lives, including the citizenship law and the penal code. In addition, with peace negotiations between Israel and the Palestinians stalled, the status of Palestinians in East Jerusalem remains unresolved, subjecting them to discriminatory Israeli laws on residence and citizenship. Gender-based discrimination and insufficient access to justice persist, and civil society lacks the necessary legal tools and financial resources to combat such treatment.

The supreme law of Palestine is the Basic Law, ratified in 2002 and amended in 2003 and 2005.[13] It acts as a temporary constitution until the establishment of a Palestinian state,[14] after which the latest draft constitution will take force.[15] Under Article 9 of the Basic Law, Palestinians are "equal before the law and the judiciary, without distinction based upon race, sex, color, religion, political views or disability." Article 11 describes personal freedom as "a natural right" that "shall be guaranteed and may not be violated." Article 4, however, stipulates that Shari'a (Islamic law) is a main source of legislation, opening the door to discriminatory provisions based on conservative interpretations of Islamic principles.

Despite the Basic Law's guarantees, many laws currently in force do not penalize gender discrimination, while those that do are difficult to enforce due to weak institutional mechanisms for handling such cases. Four different sets of laws control the lives of Palestinians: those of the PA, Israel, Egypt, and Jordan.[16] This creates confusion and makes it more difficult for women's rights activists to focus their advocacy efforts. A unified court system created in 2002 was designed to alleviate some of this uncertainty and was seen as a step toward the unification of the legal system itself.

Some of the laws drafted in recent years are more sensitive to gender issues, often specifying that gender-neutral terms refer to both men and women. For instance, unlike the Basic Law, Article 19 of the draft constitution declares that the terms "Palestinian" and "citizen," as used in that document, refer to both men and women. Certain laws, like the labor law (No. 7 of 2000), contain provisions that clearly render discrimination illegal. Nonetheless, to be truly effective, Article 11 of the Basic Law should guarantee gender equality in the law, within each piece of legislation and its provisions, rather than merely before the law, as in equal treatment in a courtroom.[17] If adopted, the draft constitution would retain the phrase "equal before the law" in Article 19, but it would also guarantee women's rights under Article 22 by declaring that women "shall have the same rights, liberties, and duties as men."

Palestinian women's rights activists are actively engaged in dialogue with the PLC, which serves as the PA's parliament, in an effort to reform discriminatory laws. Debates have covered discriminatory provisions related to labor rights, the civil service, and higher education.[18] Despite these initiatives, few reforms that directly improve the status of women have been enacted over the past five years. In particular, the PLC has avoided addressing issues related to the personal status law, focusing instead on administrative, regulatory, commercial, and financial matters; issues pertaining to land and services, including health and education; and political issues, including elections and transference of powers.[19]

Palestinian women do not have the same citizenship rights as men. Citizenship rights are still governed by the laws and regulations in effect before the 1967 Israeli occupation: the Jordanian nationality code (No. 6 of 1945) and its amendments are applied in the West Bank, while the Egyptian nationality code applies in Gaza. Both codes allow only men, not women, to pass their nationality to their spouses or children. In addition, a woman loses her nationality if she marries a non-Palestinian, unless she submits a written application to the minister of interior within one year following her marriage. In practice, however, women married to non-Palestinians are not always asked by the Ministry of Interior to give up their Palestinian nationality.

Palestinian women and men from the West Bank and Gaza who marry Palestinians with Israeli citizenship face difficulty in transferring citizenship to their family members. Although the 1952 Israeli nationality law provided citizenship rights to Palestinians residing in Israel at that time, it did not entitle Palestinian citizens of Israel to family reunification with foreign spouses and children.[20] In July 2003, the Israeli government enacted the Citizenship and Entry into Israel Law (Temporary Order) following a May 2002 freeze on applications for family reunification between Israeli citizens and Palestinians from the West Bank and Gaza.[21] The law prohibits Palestinians from the occupied territories who are married to Israeli citizens or permanent residents (such as Palestinian residents of East Jerusalem) from receiving Israeli citizenship or residency. This measure affected 21,000 families as of 2004, and applies to even more today, forcing spouses as well as parents and children to live apart.[22] On May 15, 2005, the Israeli cabinet endorsed a continuation of the law with limited exceptions depending on the age and sex of the Palestinian spouse.[23]

Under both the Jordanian and Egyptian laws that were in effect prior to 1967, a woman has the right to keep her maiden name after marriage. The decision on whether to adopt the husband's last name is left up to the individual woman. In practice, Palestinian women's family names are automatically changed at marriage on both the Palestinian passport and the Israeli identity card that all Palestinians under occupation and in the PA-administered areas are obliged to carry.

As noted above, a unified Palestinian court system was established in 2002, ending the previous system of separate judicial authorities in Gaza and the West Bank. Ordinary civil and criminal disputes are adjudicated by magistrates' courts, with possible appeals to courts of first instance, courts of appeal, and finally the Supreme Court. Personal status cases are handled by a separate system of Shari'a courts for Muslims and other religious courts for Christians. There are also special courts for military cases and other limited functions.[24] In the aftermath of its Gaza takeover, Hamas began creating new administrative structures and appointing judges to replace those who refused to cooperate with its rule. While it did not jettison the existing legal system, its parallel institutions opened a new rift in the Palestinian judiciary.[25]

As a practical matter, access to justice is limited for Palestinian men and women, particularly since the start of the second intifada against Israeli occupation in 2000. Women face unique challenges in light of the male-dominated and sometimes discriminatory law enforcement structure, which further weakens the already inadequate legal framework for women's rights. At a basic level, women are not recognized as full persons before the Shari'a courts, where the testimony of two women is equal to the testimony of one man in matters related to marriage, divorce, and custody of children. However, in all other matters, the testimonies of men and women are regarded as equal. Women are sometimes reluctant to seek help from courts or law enforcement agencies, in part because the overwhelming majority of lawyers and judges are men,[26] and women are only marginally represented among police officers. Moreover, Israel's actions, combined with the volatile political situation, have often undermined the efficacy and credibility of PA institutions. In response, there has been a resurgence of informal justice through tribal and customary laws that are often biased against women, and marital and family disputes are left to the meddling of elders or the intervention of local notables. So-called "honor killings," which typically involve the murder of women by relatives as punishment for extramarital sex, have also escalated.

The treatment of women within the penal code varies depending on which portion of the Palestinian territories a woman lives in. The code is derived from Egyptian and Jordanian law, but has not necessarily been updated in tandem with the laws of those countries. Article 340 of the Jordanian penal code, applicable to residents of the West Bank, and Article 17 of the Egyptian penal code, applicable to residents of Gaza, both offer reduced sentences for honor killings.[27] The leniency in the Jordanian code applies to a man who kills his wife or female relative and her sexual partner immediately upon catching them committing adultery. The provision in the Egyptian code applies only to husbands who have murdered their wives and their wives' lovers. Both penal codes reduce the prison sentence to as little as six months; neither offers such reduced sentences for similarly situated women. A coalition of several civil society organizations and governmental bodies has challenged these provisions and submitted proposed revisions to the president, who has yet to approve them.[28]

Separately, Hamas drafted a "unified penal code" in 2008 that would incorporate *hudud*, a seventh-century Islamic penal code featuring punishments such as amputation, whipping, and stoning. Persons found to have committed adultery would be subject to execution by stoning under this system. The third reading of the law has not passed, and women's organizations in Gaza believe that the issue has been put to rest.[29] However, even the consideration of such a legal regime indicates a trend of growing conservatism in Gaza that may seriously affect women in the future.

President Abbas signed the United Nations Convention on the Elimination of All Forms of Discrimination against Women (CEDAW) in March

2009, but it is unclear what effect this move will have on Palestinian laws, and whether it is legally valid given the PA's lack of full statehood and other impediments.[30] Nevertheless, women's rights organizations continue to push for equality to the extent that they are able in the current political disorder. Under Article 26 of the Basic Law, Palestinians may establish and participate in organizations and associations in accordance with the law. Multiple women's rights organizations have been established for the purpose of combating gender discrimination. However, the continued Israeli occupation and the lack of a unified legal structure has made effective advocacy extremely difficult.[31]

The urgent political and economic problems stemming from the second intifada and the Fatah-Hamas rift have overshadowed issues related to patriarchy and discrimination. The uphill battle faced by women's rights activists is evident in the legislative record of recent years. The PLC elected in 1996, in which women held only 5.7 percent of the seats, was able to enact far more gender-sensitive legislation than the troubled legislature elected in 2006, in which women held 12.9 percent of the seats.

Recommendations

- ❖ The PA should enact a penal code that would apply to all parts of the occupied Palestinian territories. It should offer women protection from all forms of violence, embody internationally recognized human rights standards, and include accepted punitive measures to safeguard women's rights.

- ❖ The penal code should specifically be amended to prohibit honor killings and impose sentences equal to those for ordinary murder.

- ❖ The future Palestinian nationality law should grant women the right to pass their nationality to their husbands and children without discrimination and retain their maiden names on their passports.

- ❖ The PA should appoint more women as judges and prosecutors. Legal education should be made more accessible to girls through affirmative-action methods, including scholarships.

- ❖ Court and police officials should be obligated to attend training seminars regarding gender issues and women's rights. Courts and police stations should be made more accessible to women, in part through the hiring of more female personnel.

- ❖ The Ministry of Women's Affairs, the government entity charged with empowering women, should take a more active role in ensuring that the principles of gender equality are reflected in all legislation. It should review proposed and existing laws, consult with regional and international experts, and advocate for its recommended changes in the public sphere, including the news media.

❖ In keeping with President Abbas's recent endorsement of CEDAW, the PA and women's rights groups should develop a national plan to ensure the integration of the convention's provisions into local laws.

AUTONOMY, SECURITY, AND FREEDOM OF THE PERSON

The autonomy, security, and freedom of Palestinian women have been regularly threatened in recent years. The personal status laws discriminate against women in their freedom of movement and their rights in marriage, divorce, and child custody. Their situation is worsened by Israeli barriers and the West Bank separation wall. At a basic legal level, women's security is poorly protected by the penal code, and domestic violence is not outlawed. Violence against women has escalated in the past five years, and this trend has included a rise in the number of unpunished honor crimes.

Article 18 of the Basic Law, like Article 5 of the third draft constitution, guarantees freedom of belief, worship, and religious practice for all Palestinians. Both documents declare Shari'a to be a key source for legislation and Islam to be the official religion, while protecting all other "divine" or "monotheistic" religions.[32] The vast majority of Palestinian residents are Sunni Muslims, although some are Christians. Jewish Israeli settlers continue to live in the West Bank and Jerusalem but are not under Palestinian jurisdiction. Access to Muslim and Christian religious sites in Jerusalem is restricted for residents of the West Bank and Gaza due to border barriers and checkpoints.

Although Article 20 of the Basic Law guarantees freedom of residence and movement within the limits of the law, there are legal and practical restrictions on women's freedom of movement. The principle of "house of obedience," an archaic provision derived from Egyptian and Jordanian family laws, enables husbands to force their wives to return to the marital home, although it is rarely invoked or enforced in courts. The same principle entitles men to bar their wives from leaving the country with a court order. In addition, government officials often demand proof that a male "guardian" has given his permission to a woman before she can obtain a passport. This requirement was legally abolished in 1996, thanks to lobbying by the WATC, but the political disorder of subsequent years allowed the practice to return without consequences.[33]

Israeli checkpoints and barriers, including the separation wall, also restrict freedom of movement. The separation wall in particular has made women the "most isolated social group" in Palestine, as families prefer to let men rather than women request travel permits to work on the opposite side of the wall.[34] The number of roadblocks and obstacles in the West Bank increased to 580 in February 2008,[35] and the three crossings out of the Gaza Strip (Rafah, Karni, and Erez) have been closed for most purposes since June 2007.[36] Such restrictions on free movement have prevented some women from reaching hospitals and health care centers in time to give birth; as a result, several have died in transit at checkpoints.[37]

Most Palestinians living in Jerusalem under Israeli rule hold Israeli identity cards and are recognized by Israel as noncitizen residents of the city. The identity cards serve as residency permits and enable Palestinians to travel, work, and attend school. Many women—and some men—holding Jerusalem identity cards and married to Palestinians from the West Bank and Gaza cannot obtain Jerusalem identity cards for their spouses, meaning the spouses are not allowed to live in Jerusalem. It is also difficult for children to live or attend school in Jerusalem if only their mother holds a Jerusalem identity card. Palestinians from Jerusalem risk losing their residency status if they are unable to present documents demonstrating continuous residence for the past seven years and proving that their "center of life" is in Jerusalem. Those who lose their status are effectively barred from returning to their native city.[38]

Both Christian and Muslim women are discriminated against in matters of personal status, particularly in marriage, divorce, and child custody. Muslim women in the West Bank are subject to the Jordanian personal status law of 1976, which is based on the Hanafi school of Islamic jurisprudence, while those in the Gaza Strip are subject to the unmodified Egyptian family law of 1954. Although Jordan, Egypt, and other neighboring countries have made certain progressive changes to their personal status laws in recent decades, the laws applied in Palestine remain essentially unaltered.[39]

Palestinian women lack the freedom to negotiate their equal marital rights. According to the concept of *qawama*, women of all ages must obtain the consent of their closest relative from their father's side. A woman's male guardian, or *wali*, executes the marriage contract on her behalf, while men are free to act independently. In the absence of a wali, a judge may act as the guardian. To be valid, a marriage contract must have at least one male witness or two female witnesses.[40] The local interpretation of Shari'a allows women to make stipulations within their marital contracts, such as the right to finish their education or work outside the home. However, as a practical matter, prevailing customs discourage women from taking advantage of this right. For instance, men are reluctant to marry a woman who has the right to divorce, and families discourage women from adding conditions that may drive away potential husbands.

The age of legal capacity for marriage in the West Bank is 15 for girls and 16 for boys, according to Article 5 of the 1976 Jordanian personal status law. In Gaza it is 17 years for girls and 18 for boys, as stipulated in Article 6 of the 1954 Egyptian law and relevant judicial rulings. Some 48 percent of females between the ages of 15 and 19 were married as of 2000.[41] As of 2008, the median age at first marriage was 19.5 for women and 24.8 for men.[42] The gender gap reflects the social perception that males are the breadwinners of families and must therefore be more economically independent when they get married.

Other social factors influencing women's choice of marriage partners include religion and the effects of the separation wall. Marriages between Christian and Muslim Palestinians are uncommon, although they do occur. They are generally frowned upon, and Christian women have been killed under the pretext of protecting family honor as a result of such marriages.[43] Christian men must convert to Islam if they wish to marry Muslim women. While Christian women marrying Muslim men are not obliged to convert, law prevents Christian wives from inheriting from their husbands. The fragmentation of the Palestinian territories and the restriction of Palestinian travel and movement have heavily influenced marriage patterns. A 2006 survey indicated the emergence of a tendency to choose a spouse from one's own side of the separation wall or from nearby villages to avoid family separation.[44] Polygamy is legal for Muslims but rarely practiced; although men may take up to four wives at one time, less than 4 percent exercise this right.[45]

Men and women have grossly unequal divorce rights. A Muslim husband may unilaterally divorce his wife without judicial certification by declaring "I divorce you" three times, a practice known as *talaq*. By contrast, a Muslim woman can only divorce under Jordanian law if she is able to establish harm based on authorized grounds: impiety; incurable skin or sexual disease; mental disease; desertion for more than one year; inability to pay the *mahr*, or dowry; inability to provide financial maintenance; or inability of the wife to live with the husband.[46] Articles 103 to 107 provide for a mechanism known as *khula* whereby a couple agrees to divorce and the woman surrenders her dowry and any claim to financial maintenance. However, unlike the current, reformed laws in Egypt and Jordan, the laws applicable in Palestine offer no option that allows women to undergo khula when their husbands do not consent.[47] Divorced women are entitled to custody over their children until girls reach the age of 12 and boys reach the age of 10. However, with a judicial decree, she may retain custody until the boy turns 18 or until the girl gets married. A divorced mother loses custody of her children upon remarriage.

In 2008, a more progressive personal status law was drafted by the National Campaign for the Family Law. If approved, it would raise the age of marriage to 18 for both men and women and place restrictions on polygamy, requiring the approval of the first wife for a second marriage. However, the draft has not been discussed in the PLC to date. Until the council members currently incarcerated by Israel are released and the rift between Gaza and the West Bank is repaired, the PLC will remain relatively ineffective and many personal status rights will continue to be regulated by legislation enacted prior to the 1967 occupation.

Palestinian Christian women are governed by the laws established by their respective churches. In general, the Orthodox Church permits divorce if a woman is found to be unfaithful, refrains from getting pregnant, is found not to be a virgin upon marriage, or refuses to obey her husband in a dispute for a period of three years after being instructed to do so by the Church.[48] The Catholic Church and its ecclesiastical courts offer no possibility for divorce, but annulment is possible if the marriage was contracted with legal flaws; men and women enjoy exactly the same rights in this respect.[49] Because the Catholic Church allows only a separation when spouses have an irreconcilable dispute, whereas the Orthodox Church has granted divorces in such cases, some Catholics have converted to Orthodoxy to obtain a divorce. Protestant church law allows a divorce if one of the spouses is found to be adulterous and the husband and wife do not engage in sex after the adultery is revealed. Other possible grounds include abandonment for two years, eloping with another, or attempted murder. When a marriage is ended in this way, either of the spouses is able to marry again.[50]

Domestic violence is not prohibited by law. In 2006, the Palestinian Central Bureau of Statistics (PCBS) reported that among unmarried women over the age of 18, some 25 percent had been physically abused and 52.7 percent had been psychologically abused.[51] Among married women, psychological abuse affected 61.7 percent, physical abuse affected 23.3 percent, and sexual abuse affected 10.9 percent.[52] Women are theoretically able to press ordinary assault and battery charges against their abusers, but several factors keep domestic violence victims from doing so. Social norms shame women who report abuse to the police and encourage them to remain silent for the sake of their children. Moreover, women often have no alternative place to live. There is a lack of private or government-sponsored shelters, with only three shelters operating in the West Bank and none in Gaza.[53] Women who are reluctant or unable to file domestic violence or sexual violence complaints on their own have little recourse, since the law allows only close relatives to file such complaints on their behalf, and most of these crimes are perpetrated by close relatives.

Violence against women reflects the broader violence and lack of rule of law in the Palestinian territories, and it has become more common over the last five years. Honor killings remain a problem, though the true toll is uncertain, as a number may go unreported. A coalition of women's organizations, Al-Muntada, published a report in 2007 that found 32 cases of honor killings in Palestine between 2004 and 2006.[54] Seventeen of those murders occurred in 2006 alone—12 in the Gaza Strip and 5 in the West Bank.[55] The PCBS reported that at least 10 women were victims of honor killings in 2007.[56] In response to the violence, seven women's rights and human rights organizations submitted a memorandum to President Abbas, urging the issuance of a presidential decree treating honor killings as murders.[57] However, no such decree had been issued as of October 2009.

In a front-page article published in 2008, the Birzeit University newspaper *Al-Hal* reported that 19 more women had been killed that year, and that a woman in the Palestinian territories is killed each week "under the pretext of honor killing" and "under the protection of the law."[58] Some were killed for merely demanding their legal share of inheritance. The article claimed that political parties have not addressed the issue of amending the penal code to eliminate tolerance of honor killings for fear of losing their support among men. By offering a weak legal framework and poor enforcement mechanisms, the PA has failed to uphold its duty to protect women from violence and has left them without redress or justice.

The broader violence and absence of the rule of law has also motivated families to restrict the movements of their daughters, for fear that they could be killed in military clashes or other acts of violence outside the home. The organization Miftah (the Palestinian Initiative for the Promotion of Global Dialogue and Democracy) noted in a recent report that 475 people were killed by illegal weapons in 2005 and 2006, including many women and children.[59] Women's organizations, such as the WATC and the Women's Centre for Legal Aid and Counseling (WCLAC), freely express their views about women's autonomy and security and the difficulties women face because of Palestine's discriminatory laws. There are also a number of women's organizations in Jerusalem, the West Bank, and Gaza that offer services ranging from lobbying and advocacy work to training and psychological counseling. Four years of work by lawyers and rights activists has focused on proposed laws to combat domestic violence, but such measures have yet to be considered by the president and the PLC.[60]

Recommendations

❖ The PA should enact a more progressive, unified personal status law that ensures equal rights in marriage, divorce, and custody of children. To stem the negative effects of early marriage, the law should include a minimum marriage age of 18 for both sexes as proposed by the National Campaign for the Family Law.

❖ Civil society and political parties should escalate their advocacy efforts for a new personal status law through a clear strategic plan targeting all decision-makers. They should base their proposals on CEDAW, international human rights documents, and the reform proposed by the National Campaign. Islamic women's organizations should look into the experiences of other countries that have adopted a more progressive interpretation of Shari'a, such as Morocco.

❖ The court system should adopt technological upgrades that enable easy access to court decisions and documents, allowing women to verify whether their husbands have taken second wives or are already married.

❖ The PA should eliminate the "house of obedience" concept from its legal system, ensuring autonomy and freedom of movement for married women.

❖ The PLC should introduce new laws to protect women from all forms of physical, psychological, and verbal violence at home and in public places, and create special police units to handle cases of family violence.

❖ To ensure the security and personal freedoms of women living under Israeli jurisdiction, the responsible authorities should guarantee the rights of such women to an identity card, residency, freedom of movement, and access to their chosen place of employment.

❖ Customs and passport officials who require women to obtain written permission from a male guardian before they can receive a passport should be reprimanded or prosecuted for their violation of the law.

ECONOMIC RIGHTS AND EQUAL OPPORTUNITY

The rights of Palestine's female workforce are governed by one of the most advanced labor laws in the region. While economic participation among women remains low due to socioeconomic, cultural, and political factors, the rate of participation increased from 2005 to 2007, particularly in the West Bank. In addition, the PA's new scholastic curriculum, introduced in 2002, reflects a greater degree of gender equality, and a growing number of young women are enrolling in colleges and universities. As with other rights, a more politically stable situation and open borders will be crucial to advancing women's economic and academic rights in the future.

The property rights of Palestinians are controlled by Jordanian laws in the West Bank and Egypt's Law No.1 of 1965 in the Gaza Strip, with the latter discussing the application of Shari'a to *miri*, or state-owned property. Although women have the legal right to own and exercise control over their land and other assets, only 5 percent of women own land and 7.7 percent own a home or other real estate.[61] This inequity reflects the impact of custom, which encourages married men to retain property individually rather than jointly with their wives. There are no legal restrictions on women's ability to access credit, but because men own most property, they tend to have the collateral necessary to secure loans.[62]

Women often lack control over their income and rarely enter into business contracts and activities. This is mainly due to the customary belief that men, as the traditional family breadwinners, are in charge of financial decisions, even those involving the income and assets of their female family members.

Jordanian inheritance laws apply in the Palestinian territories and are derived directly from the Koran. Although women have legally enforceable inheritance rights, they are entitled to half the share of their male counterparts.[63] This arrangement is based on the man's duty under Shari'a to provide for his female relatives; his failure to do so is considered socially reprehensible and can have legal consequences. Moreover, prevailing traditions and customs encourage women to give up their share of inheritance to male family members.[64] As previously noted (see "Autonomy, Security, and Freedom of the Person"), women who assert their inheritance rights sometimes risk physical harm.

Article 24 of the Basic Law mandates that public education be free to all citizens and compulsory through the basic level (up to the age of 12 or 13). As a practical matter, access to education for all Palestinians is restricted by the ongoing armed conflict and by the construction of the separation wall. The wall has negatively affected access to education for 48.4 percent of households located on its eastern side.[65]

The literacy rate among women reached 89.8 percent in 2006, a nearly six-point increase from 2000, though a gender gap still exists. The literacy rate among men increased from 94.4 percent to 97.1 percent during the same period.[66] The more rapid growth in female literacy is a result of the efforts of the Ministry of Education and civil society organizations to advocate females' right to education, as well as an increased societal awareness of the importance of female education. Men now prefer educated wives who are able to help them earn a living, especially in light of the worsening economic situation. Boys drop out twice as often as girls during primary education, possibly to enter the workforce as manual laborers. However, at the secondary level, girls drop out slightly more often than their male counterparts, in part because girls are more likely than boys to marry at this stage.[67] Significantly more women than men attend the 20 universities and colleges that offer undergraduate degrees in the Palestinian territories;[68] families with means tend to send their male children abroad for higher education.[69] In fact, the ratio of women to men in local colleges and universities increased from 103.6:100 in 2004 to 122.3:100 in 2007.[70]

Article 24 of the Basic Law grants the PA the authority to establish curriculums for public and private educational institutions. The Ministry of Education's official 1998 curriculum plan stated that equality and equal learning opportunities "must be ensured without discrimination on grounds of race, religion, color, or sex."[71] And during the drafting of the new curriculum in 2001, the ministry declared that it intended "to avoid all forms of stereotyping on the basis of race, gender, disability or religion."[72] A 2006 study by UNESCO reported that the Palestinian curriculum portrayed nonstereotypical gender roles in several subjects, and reflected gender equality using a moderate, liberal-humanist approach.[73] However, it also noted that gender-segregated Islamic religion courses used textbooks that employed only masculine pronouns and included illustrations of covered women. Vocational education provided to women generally directs them toward stereotypically female roles, and even when courses for male-dominated vocations are open to girls, social norms render it difficult for girls to enroll.

Women are legally free to choose their profession, but they face social pressure, particularly from their family, to pursue work that is related to their future roles as mothers and caretakers. The Palestinian security forces have recently started to recruit women, but their numbers remain low.[74] Of the female Palestinian labor force, 46.2 percent worked in the service sector as of 2007, 36 percent worked in agriculture, 9.5 percent worked in mining or manufacturing, and 7.7 percent worked in restaurants, hotels, and commerce.[75] However, a 2004 survey classified 267,000 workers—male and female—as employers, self-employed, or unpaid family members, representing 45.7 percent of the workforce.[76] Although the statistics are not segregated by gender, most of the unpaid family members are thought to be female, especially in agricultural and home-based enterprises.[77]

According to the PCBS, Palestinian women's overall labor force participation rate rose from 13.4 percent in 2005 to 15.7 percent in 2007, with consistently higher rates in the West Bank than in Gaza.[78] The overall rate remains one of the lowest in the world and the Arab region. The increase in recent years may be due to the fact that more women are now educated and eager to work, while husbands feel unable to make ends meet on their own. More women have also been compelled to work because their male partners have been imprisoned, exiled, or killed. At 45.6 percent in 2007, the overall labor force participation rate for both men and women is low. The unemployment rate in Gaza is 35.2 percent; this is higher than the 24.5 percent rate in the West Bank because of Israeli restrictions and the boycott by major donors in protest of Hamas's legislative victory.[79]

Gender-based discrimination within employment is specifically prohibited under Article 100 of the Palestinian Labor Law (No. 7 of 2000).[80] Article 25 of the Basic Law guarantees all citizens the right to work, allows for the creation of labor unions, and grants the right to conduct strikes within the limits of the law. Despite these guarantees, the comparatively progressive labor law retains discriminatory provisions. For example, it does not cover domestic, agricultural, and informal labor, all of which feature higher proportions of female workers. The law also excludes places of work with fewer than five employees, and few means of proper enforcement are available. A gender-based wage gap persists, though it shrunk during the second intifada as men lost their relatively high-paying jobs in Israel and women kept their jobs in governmental and UN institutions located in the Palestinian territories.[81]

In addition to legal inequality, female workers deal with challenges in their personal lives that men do not face. Many Palestinian women are forced to take on increased family responsibilities after male family members are exiled, migrated, or are imprisoned in Israeli jails. Women's traditional role as family caretaker has also magnified the effects of Israeli measures like curfews, movement restrictions, demolitions, and land appropriations, making it even more difficult for female workers to carry out both economic activities and domestic duties.[82]

The labor law provides a variety of gender-based protections for women, though cultural norms and delays in the establishment of planned labor courts restrict their practical benefits. For example, Article 103 grants 10 weeks of maternity leave to any woman employed for more than 180 consecutive days by the same employer. Article 103 also prohibits the dismissal of a woman on maternity leave unless it can be proven that she has worked somewhere else. For a year after giving birth, female employees are entitled to a one-hour nursing break during the workday. Under Article 105, women are eligible for an undefined period of leave without pay to care for their child or accompany their husbands abroad. However, some employers, particularly small businesses, selectively implement the laws or avoid hiring married women in an effort to evade these regulations. Although labor offices in various governorates send representatives to hear complaints and try to settle disputes amicably, enforcement suffers because of the ongoing lack of special labor courts.[83]

There are no specific legal protections from sexual harassment in the workplace, despite calls for such a law by women's rights organizations like the Palestinian Working Woman Society for Development (PWWSD) and the WCLAC. Accusations of sexual harassment are seldom made public because female victims are often stigmatized as a result.

While there are several organizations that lobby for women's political, social, and economic rights, no organizations are specifically dedicated to improving women's access to education. Nevertheless, there are several initiatives among women's organizations to assist female university students with their expenses.[84] A number of organizations, both Islamist and secular, attempt to provide women with income-generating opportunities, though these are usually traditional in nature. Since 1967, In'ash al-Usra in Al-Bireh has provided training in stereotypically feminine economic activities like tailoring, knitting, cooking, catering, and hairdressing.[85]

Recommendations

✤ The government should ensure that all women have access to their full and equal inheritance rights. It should launch media campaigns that encourage women to demand their inheritance rights, and strict penalties should be imposed on those who force women to give up their share. Specialized female lawyers should be made available to women seeking assistance.

✤ The PLC should enact and provide for the enforcement of laws that ensure gender equality in labor rights and benefits. These may include stiff penalties for employers who avoid hiring or retaining married women, and tax incentives for employers who establish daycare facilities for their workers' children.

✤ The Ministry of Education should encourage girls to receive vocational training, for example by opening up vocational facilities to girls that were previously accessible only to males, and opening new facilities that utilize advanced industrial machinery, electronics, and information technology, including computer design software.

✤ In recognition of the fact that many women work in the agricultural sector, vocational training that concentrates on agricultural studies should be made accessible to women, especially those largely invisible female workers who work in family-owned enterprises.

✤ The PLC should draft and enforce laws that protect women against all forms of discrimination and harassment in the workplace. Perpetrators should be harshly penalized, and victims' identities should be protected.

Effective enforcement requires the PA to create labor courts and institute female-friendly policies therein.

❖ Labor unions should encourage a strong female presence, in part through a quota system setting aside 30 percent of seats in decision-making bodies, and advocate on behalf of labor issues that affect women specifically.

POLITICAL RIGHTS AND CIVIC VOICE

Women's access to and full enjoyment of civil liberties and political rights are affected by the economic, social, and cultural restraints placed on their lives within Palestinian society. Despite this, women continue to enjoy the freedoms of expression and assembly to a moderate degree. Progress in recent years has included the establishment of limited gender-based quota systems for legislative and municipal council elections. As a result, women's political participation has increased significantly, particularly at the local level. However, the political impact of women is muted by security issues, which often take precedence over women's demands for equal rights.

Equal voting rights are guaranteed under Article 26(3) of the Basic Law, which establishes universal suffrage and states that all Palestinians may vote, nominate candidates, and run for elections. Women living under the PA first exercised these rights in 1996, when the first PLC elections were held. Five female candidates were elected that year.

In preparation for the second PLC elections in 2006, a new electoral law (No. 9 of 2005) was adopted to expand the legislature from 88 to 132 seats.[86] Article 3 of the law established a mixed electoral system whereby 66 seats were filled through nationwide, party-list proportional representation and the other 66 through contests between individual candidates in multimember districts. On election day, each voter received two ballots: the first contained 11 nationwide party lists, and the second listed candidates in the voter's local constituency.[87] Article 4 of the electoral law required each party list to include at least one woman among the first three names, at least one woman among the next four names, and at least one woman in every five names thereafter.

Eight women from Fatah, six from Hamas, and one each from three smaller parties were elected in this way, and one female Fatah candidate won in the district races, raising women's overall representation in the PLC from 5.7 percent in 1996 to 13.6 percent in 2006.[88] Since 1994, women's organizations, and especially the WATC, have been demanding a quota that would set aside 30 percent of the seats for women. The inclusion of the more limited party-list quota in the 2005 election law was the result of lobbying efforts by both women's rights organizations and the Ministry of Women's Affairs.

The mixed voting system was the key to Hamas's victory in the 2006 elections. After a unity government between Hamas and Fatah fell apart in 2007, President Abbas of Fatah appointed his own government and issued a decree nullifying the 2005 electoral law. This September 2007 decree—viewed by some as legally invalid[89]—is in many ways similar to the 2005 law, including the provisions related to women's representation. However, under the new rules, all 132 PLC seats would be filled through the nationwide, party-list system.[90]

The WATC, the women's committees it represents, and Miftah were very active in training candidates and drafting election guides for women, as well as in helping female candidates hold events in cities and villages to meet with potential voters. According to one account, a total of 12 women's organizations were actively involved in increasing women's representation.[91] It is important to note that these civil society organizations may find it difficult to enter communities where Hamas is popular and conservatism is on the rise. Nevertheless, since the party-list quota system was established, it has become more acceptable for female politicians to meet with voters of both sexes and promote their candidacies.

Women's presence within the PA executive branch is minimal, and they hold few decision-making positions. A female activist—Samiha Khalil, founder of In'ash al-Usra—ran for president in the 1996 election, but longtime Palestinian leader Yasir Arafat won an overwhelming majority. No women ran in the only other presidential election held to date, which Abbas won in 2005. Currently, five women act as cabinet ministers. Their portfolios are education, culture, women's affairs, tourism, and social affairs.[92] The Palestinian ambassadors to France, Belgium, Chile, Brazil, the Netherlands, and Portugal are also women; all were appointed in late 2005.

After the 1996 elections, a gender unit was established at the Ministry of Planning to coordinate the work of gender units in other ministries, with the objective of mainstreaming gender issues in PA institutions. The Ministry of Women's Affairs was established in 2003 after the WATC lobbied for its creation for nearly a decade. Its purpose is to address the gender gap found at all levels of society, amend existing laws, and introduce new legislation that would improve the status of women. However, existing political conditions have made it impossible for the ministry to fulfill its mission. Since the Hamas electoral victory in 2006, four different ministers have led the Ministry of Women's Affairs,[93] and it has not been publicly active.[94] Its strategic plan of 2006 remains to be implemented, and aside from holding a conference on violence against women and participating with women's organizations in proposing legislative amendments, the ministry has registered few accomplishments.

Local elections were held in the Palestinian territories between 2004 and 2005, marking the first such voting since 1976 and improving women's ability to participate in civic issues and influence local policies. The election process began in December 2004 and was intended to continue, region by region, through five rounds. On December 1, 2004, after tireless lobbying by women's rights organizations, the PLC passed a quota law that reserved two seats for women in every municipal or village council. Following the quota's adoption, the number of female candidates jumped from 56 to 152 in a matter of days,[95] and 73 seats (roughly 17 percent of the total) were won by women in the first round, held in December 2004 and January 2005.[96] The second round was held in May 2005, and women gained 165 of 917 seats (18 percent); 103 of those women won outright and 62 won thanks to the quota.[97] Many of these candidates were trained by women's organizations on campaigning and advocacy skills.

Adding to this momentum, the Local Councils Election Law (No. 10 of 2005) was adopted on August 13, 2005, even though the election rounds had already begun.[98] Article 17 of the law established another gender-based quota system, reserving the minimum of two seats for women in local councils with up to 13 members, and requiring one female candidate to be placed among the first five names and a second among the following five names on party lists. For larger councils, party lists had to include a woman among the next five names as well. The third and fourth rounds of local elections were held in September and December 2005,[99] but plans for the fifth and final round were interrupted by the strife that broke out after Hamas's PLC victory. Nevertheless, by this time women had made their mark.

Women and men are generally free to assemble peacefully within the PA-administered areas, so long as they avoid Israeli checkpoints. Article 26(5) of the Basic Law guarantees the right to conduct public meetings, processions, and assemblies within the limits of law. Women are also entitled to free expression under Article 19 of the Basic Law, while

Article 27 guarantees freedom of all forms of media as well as for individual members of the media sector. Under Article 25 of the Jordanian Press and Publication Law (No. 16 of 1967), which remains in effect,[100] authorities have the right to close newspapers that are proven to be "harmful" to "general conduct" or "national feeling." In order to march or demonstrate, groups must obtain permission from the PA, which is usually granted without difficulty. Conversely, Palestinian women who assemble in Jerusalem or near Israeli checkpoints to protest the human rights violations are often attacked, beaten, imprisoned, and occasionally shot at by the Israeli army and police.[101] Women are free to access information via the Internet, though mostly through home connections; young men tend to predominate in public Internet cafes, especially the smaller facilities.

The tense domestic political situation and the rift between the West Bank and Gaza have focused the priorities of activists on national unity, peace, and security, meaning demonstrations regarding gender equality are deemed less important. Equality is regarded as an issue that can wait, whereas the ongoing violence and suffering associated with the Fatah-Hamas schism and the Israeli occupation have spurred women to mobilize and protest.[102] Even the worsening economic situation has drawn attention away from fundamental women's rights issues, raising concerns, for instance, about whether the government will be able to pay its employees. Nevertheless, women's rights organizations continue to work on multiple fronts, linking their programs on gender equality with the situation on the ground. They emphasize the view that the realization of gender equality is a prerequisite for national liberation, and document the impact of Israeli human rights violations on women in particular. Palestinian women's groups periodically present reports on the latter issue to various international bodies.

Palestinian women have been visible and effective in politics for decades, even if their representation has been low within formal political parties. In the most recent party elections in August 2009, however, no women were elected to Fatah's Central Council, its main governing body, while 11 women were elected to the Revolutionary Council, Fatah's 120-member legislative body. Women's rights organizations have long insisted on a formal quota of 30 percent within all decision-making party bodies.[103]

The WATC and Miftah continue to provide training for female candidates and young leaders on advocacy, communication skills, working with the media, preparation of a campaign, and presenting an argument to voters. The political parties sometimes offer similar training, as do youth organizations like Taawon and Sharek.

Recommendations

❖ In accordance with the demands of the Palestinian women's movement, a 30 percent quota for female representatives should be established in the PLC and in all branches of government, including ministers, deputy ministers, general directors, and heads of units in ministries, offices, and diplomatic missions.

❖ The PA should support a training program designed to improve the leadership skills of women who already hold government positions, thereby preparing them for promotion to more senior posts.

❖ Women's organizations should hone their ability to influence women's votes, monitor the efficacy of elected female candidates, and hold them accountable for their performance in light of their campaign promises.

❖ Women's organizations should develop programs to provide financial support for the campaigns of female candidates, enabling them to compete on an equal footing with male opponents, including incumbents.

❖ Political parties, which remain primary vehicles for women's political engagement, should ensure that they present their male and female candidates in an equitable manner.

SOCIAL AND CULTURAL RIGHTS

Palestinian women continue to face challenges to their social and cultural rights. Problems including a high—though declining—fertility rate, early marriages, and poverty persist in society, particularly in Gaza. Women's health is affected by the lack of adequate local facilities and limited access to health care across the Israeli border. The health status of women is further compromised by continuing Israeli incursions and prevailing laws and customs that restrict women's ability to make free decisions regarding their reproductive rights.

Decisions regarding a woman's health and reproductive rights are subject to social and cultural pressures from her family and husband. Together, the West Bank and Gaza have the second-highest fertility rate in the Middle East, with 4.6 births per woman registered in 2007. Even this rate represents a drop from 2000, when there were 5.1 births per woman.[104]

Only 50.2 percent of married women between the ages of 15 and 49 used contraceptive methods as of 2006.[105]

Sociopolitical, cultural, and economic factors encourage women to bear multiple children. The pressure to get pregnant—preferably with male children—begins as soon as women get married. Multiple births are valued as a means of compensating for deaths related to armed conflict, and more children are traditionally perceived as bringing strength to the family. They are also seen as a means of discouraging polygamy.[106] The relatively young age at which women marry,[107] combined with their low labor force participation rate (see "Economic Rights and Equal Opportunity"), contribute to the high fertility rate and women's increased dependence on men.

Abortion is not allowed in the Palestinian territories and is considered a crime unless the physical health of the mother is threatened by the pregnancy itself, as opposed to the circumstances surrounding the pregnancy. Consequently, abortions in instances of rape or incest—which put the pregnant woman at risk of becoming the victim of an honor killing—are impermissible.[108] Nevertheless, women's organizations that assist victims of rape and incest have established a support network among physicians and gynecologists, who help the victims end unwanted pregnancies.

Beyond the limitations to their reproductive rights, women are generally able to make their own decisions regarding health care. Although they do not need permission from a husband or guardian to undergo medical procedures, economic factors limit their access to health care as a practical matter. The high cost of medical exams to detect osteoporosis, as well as breast and cervical cancers, lead women to postpone preventative exams until acute symptoms strike. As of 2004, only 20.4 percent of those aged 20 to 54 in the West Bank and 27.1 percent in Gaza had pap smear testing at least once every three years.[109] However, some health rights organizations have sporadically offered free screenings and exams in certain areas.

Access to health care is a problem for all Palestinians, male and female, and is worse in Gaza than in the West Bank due to Israeli military incursions, continued border blockades, and electricity cuts. The border closures in particular pose serious problems for the Palestinian health system and its ability to deliver care at appropriate levels. Of 124 people who have died in recent years because border blockades prevented them from receiving medication that was unavailable in Gaza, 43 were women and 24 were children.[110] In 2007, the infant mortality rate in the Palestinian territories was 23.9 per 1,000 births, down slightly from 24.4 in 2005.[111] According to the Ministry of Health, since September 2000, women in the West Bank who are about to give birth have needed between two and four hours to reach a hospital, whereas prior to the creation of the separation wall, the same trip would have taken them between 15 and 30 minutes.[112] Although 98.9 percent of births are attended by a skilled medical professional,[113] the Palestinian Independent Commission for Citizens' Rights reported that 68 women had to give birth at checkpoints, and 34 infants and 4 women died, from September 2000 to July 2006.[114] A study conducted by the UN Relief and Works Agency found that 34.3 percent of children in the West Bank and 54.7 percent of children in the Gaza Strip were anemic, as were 29.95 percent of mothers in the West Bank and 45.7 percent of mothers in Gaza.[115] Female genital mutilation is not common in Palestine.[116]

The right to adequate housing is assured to all Palestinians under Article 23 of the Basic Law. However, most houses are registered in the name of the man, even if husband and wife worked together to purchase or build it. Recently, as a growing number of women move into cities to seek greater income-generating opportunities, more houses and apartments have been purchased or rented by single, divorced, or widowed women, and it has become more socially acceptable for such women to live on their own. However, social norms that favor male ownership of housing and female habitation with husbands or male relatives still prevail. Male ownership perpetuates women's economic dependence, since it is more difficult to obtain loans without property as collateral.

Women are able to participate in the media and influence portrayals of gender issues, particularly through written publications. A number of women occupy senior positions in media outlets. The editors in chief of Birzeit University's progressive newspaper, *Al-Hal*, and the newspaper *Al-Bayader al-Siyasi* are women,[117] as is the deputy director of the Palestinian Broadcasting Corporation. Women's organizations have their own newspapers, such as *Sawt al-Nissa'* (The Voice of Women), published by the WATC in Ramallah; *Al-Ghaida'* (Beautiful Woman), published by the Women's Affairs Center in Gaza;[118] and *Yanabee*, published by the PWWSD. The WATC also broadcasts a weekly radio program, *Did al-Samt* (Against Silence), on the official Palestinian radio channel, while the PWWSD runs a radio program entitled *Through the Eyes of Women*.

The WCLAC has established a Media Forum, which gives male and female journalists training on issues such as violence against women, gender and the media, and gender and law, so as to raise their consciousness regarding women's rights and present a more constructive discourse on women's issues. Female members of the media freely express their views, but seldom touch on issues related to sexuality. The one exception is the issue of honor crimes, which they oppose strongly and publicly.

Despite these achievements, many media outlets continue to discriminate against women and promote traditional gender roles. *Al-Quds*, the most widely circulated newspaper in the Palestinian territories, portrays women in a stereotypical way and publishes religious articles on how women should behave.

Women affiliated with Hamas have their own newsletters but not proper media outlets. Hamas has one newspaper, *Ar-Risala*, and one television station, *Al-Aqsa*. Although women under Hamas rule experience no official form of censorship, they tend to self-censor, expressing what is "appropriate under the prevailing economic and political situation" in an effort to avoid antagonizing the group.[119] In the aftermath of Hamas's 2006 electoral victory,[120] many women have chosen to act and behave in an "appropriate" manner given the facts on the ground, and women's media outlets have consequently avoided a debate on the veil or on women's control over their own sexuality.[121] In addition, Hamas has reportedly forced some girls and women to wear the veil, a practice they later denied. Women in the West Bank continue to have a greater degree of freedom than those in Gaza.[122]

The rampant poverty present throughout the Palestinian territories especially affects the lives of women. In 2007, the poverty rate was 19.1 percent in the West Bank and 51.8 percent in Gaza. If only household income is counted, excluding remittances and food aid, the rate rises to 45.7 percent in the West Bank and 79.4 percent in Gaza.[123] However, 73 percent of female-headed households are likely to be so impoverished that they are unable to satisfy the basic needs of the household, as compared with 63 percent of similarly situated male-headed households.[124]

Poverty affects more women than men in part because of discriminatory laws and traditions that limit women's access to employment, property through inheritance, and financial compensation upon divorce.[125] Women must deal with a labor market and legal system that favor men and are often unable to afford the childcare that would allow them to pursue careers. Women also suffer greater health effects from poverty in households headed by men, as the health of the male breadwinner and the children takes precedence over that of the financially dependent mother.

Palestinian women's rights organizations in general tend not to tackle issues involving veiling and women's sexuality,[126] and are more vocal when addressing discrimination in economic or political rights. Nevertheless, secular women's rights activists continue to demand that the PA respect international conventions on gender-equality issues, which address the full range of women's social and cultural rights.

Recommendations

+ The PA should increase its budget allocations and services for women's health programs, with a special focus on rural women.
+ The international donor community should finance modern and adequate health services for women, concentrating on illnesses that are currently not treatable inside the Palestinian territories, such as osteoporosis and breast and cervical cancer.
+ The Ministry of Health, in cooperation with Palestinian nongovernmental organizations, should ensure that mothers are provided with adequate prenatal and postnatal care, that women are educated about family planning, and that society is aware of the negative effects of early marriage on the health of women and girls.
+ The Israeli government should ensure that Palestinian women have access to hospitals through checkpoints, lifting closures of Gaza's borders if necessary.
+ The Ministry of Education and civil society organizations should cooperate to offer lectures and workshops that raise women's awareness of their social, health, and reproductive rights.

AUTHOR

Suheir Azzouni is a Palestinian expert on gender and human rights. She established the offices of the Women's Affairs Technical Committee (WATC) in the Palestinian territories, serving as general director from 1994 to 2001. Ms. Azzouni worked as freelance trainer and researcher with several international organizations, training hundreds of men and women in 20 countries. She prepared a manual on gender and education for UNESCO in 2004, and worked as adviser and as chief of the Centre for Women with the United Nations in Beirut from November 2005 to June 2008. She holds a master's degree in gender, law, and development from Birzeit University.

NOTES

1 Suheir Azzouni Mahshi, "A Free Palestinian, a Free Woman," *Palestine-Israel Journal of Politics, Economics and Culture* 2, no. 3 (1995).

2 Israel claims sovereignty over East Jerusalem, though it is not internationally recognized.

3 Several marches for women took place in a number of Palestinian cities in 1994, calling for a quota of 30 percent in all decision-making bodies and the abolition of regulations requiring women to obtain the written consent of their guardians in order to obtain passports.

4 Ostensibly designed to prevent infiltration by Palestinian militants, the barrier extends roughly along the Palestinian side of the 1949 armistice line separating the West Bank from Israel. It sometimes veers deep into the West Bank to incorporate Jewish settlements.

5 B'Tselem, "Separation Barrier: Statistics," http://www.btselem.org/english/Separation _Barrier/Statistics.asp.

6 World Bank, "West Bank & Gaza: Country Brief," September 2008, http://go.worldbank .org/Q8OGMLXI40.

7 Khaled Abu Toameh, "Gaza Women Warned of Immodesty," *Jerusalem Post*, December 2, 2006, http://www.jpost.com/servlet/Satellite?cid=1164881802888&pagename=JPo st%2FJPArticle%2FShowFull.

8 Hannah Wright, "Listen to the Women of Palestine," Guardian.co.uk, August 13, 2009, http://www.guardian.co.uk/commentisfree/2009/aug/13/palestinian-women-fatah.

9 Diaa Hadid, "Hamas 'Virtue Campaign' Aims to Make Gaza More Islamic," *Huffington Post*, July 28, 2009, http://www.huffingtopost.com/2009/07/28/hamas-virtue-campai gn-aim_n_246046.html.

10 Brenda Gazzar, "Palestinians Debate Women's Future Under Hamas," WeNews, April 23, 2006, http://www.womensenews.org/article.cfm/dyn/aid/2714/.

11 Amnesty International, *Operation 'Cast Lead': 22 Days of Death and Destruction* (London: Amnesty International, July 2009), http://www.amnesty.org/en/library/info/ MDE15/015/2009/en; "Half of Gaza Dead, Women, Children and Elderly," RIA Novosti, January 11, 2009, http://en.rian.ru/world/20090111/119414133.html.

12 According to the Palestinian Central Bureau of Statistics (PCBS), a total of 5,901 Palestinians were killed between the years 2000 and 2008, and 332 of those were women. For more information see PCBS, "Killed Palestinians (Martyrs) in Al-Aqsa Uprising (Intifada), by District of Residence, Age Group and Sex, September 29, 2000–December 31, 2008," http://www.pcbs.gov.ps/Portals/_pcbs/intifada/9a4af320-4ea9-4fb9-9dc6-a 0e9eafe5bc8.htm.

13 The amended Basic Law of 2003 is available in English at http://www.palestinianbasiclaw .org/2003-amended-basic-law. For the 2005 amendments, see http://www.palestinian basiclaw.org/2005-amendments.

[14] Article 115, Basic Law.

[15] See Article 193 of the third draft of the Constitution of the State of Palestine (March 7, 2003, revised March 25, 2003), http://www.jmcc.org/documents/palestineconstitution-eng.pdf. The process of drafting a constitution in preparation for statehood began in 1999 under the instruction of the Palestinian Liberation Organization (PLO) Executive Committee. The first draft was completed in February 2001, just as negotiations with Israel collapsed. See Asem Khalil, *Which Constitution for the Palestinian Legal System?* (Rome: Pontificia Universita' Lateranense, 2003), 98–100, http://www.profpito.com/Th_se_Lateran_Compl_te.pdf.

[16] Between 1949 and 1967, Egypt governed the Gaza Strip and Jordan governed the West Bank, leaving legal legacies that have persisted as the territories' status remains unresolved.

[17] A presidential decree in 1993 established the Palestinian Independent Commission for Citizens' Rights (PICCR), with a mandate to ensure respect for citizens' rights in Palestine. For more information, see the commission's website, http://www.piccr.org/about/about.html.

[18] Camilia El-Solh and Nadia Hijab, *Women's Economic Rights in the South Mediterranean Region: A Comparative Analysis of Laws, Regulations and Practice* (Egypt: Euromed, 2008), 35, http://www.roleofwomenineconomiclife.net/downloads/EcoRightsAcomparative legalEnglish.pdf.

[19] Birzeit University Institute of Law, "Legal Status in Palestine," http://lawcenter.birzeit.edu/iol/en/index.php?action_id=210&PHPSESSID=9fc28f3ca00d37ef6aa59d52935 9dc7cab042885.

[20] Nationality Law, Israel, 5712–1952, http://www.geocities.com/savepalestinenow/israel laws/fulltext/nationalitylaw.htm; Entry into Israel Law, Israel, http://www.geocities .com/savepalestinenow/israellaws/fulltext/entryintoisraellaw.htm.

[21] Nationality and Entry into Israel Law (Temporary Order), 5763–2003, July 2003, http://www.hamoked.org.il/items/1140_eng.pdf.

[22] Anna Seifert, *Separated Families* (Jerusalem: Quaker Peace and Social Witness, 2005), 3, available at http://www.jcdhr.ps/eng/reports-studies/2.html.

[23] The current law permits Palestinian women over the age of 25 and Palestinian men over the age of 35 to apply for temporary visitor permits to be with their Israeli spouses. See Human Rights Watch, "Israel: Family Reunification Ruling Is Discriminatory," news release, May 17, 2006, http://www.hrw.org/en/news/2006/05/17/israel-family-reunification-ruling-discriminatory.

[24] International Commission of Jurists, "Palestine," in *Attacks on Justice 2005* (Geneva: International Commission of Jurists, 2008), 13, http://www.icj.org/IMG/PALESTINE. pdf; Programme on Governance in the Arab Region (POGAR), "Judiciary: Occupied Palestinian Territories," UN Development Programme, http://www.pogar.org/countries/theme.aspx?t=9&cid=14.

[25] Nour Odeh, "Hamas Stamps Its Authority on Gaza," Al-Jazeera, October 7, 2007, http://english.aljazeera.net/news/middleeast/2007/10/2008525183358414169.html; Amira Hass, "Hamas Builds Separate Courts in Gaza," *Haaretz*, December 12, 2007, http://www.haaretz.com/hasen/spages/933191.html.

[26] As of 2006, women accounted for 16.9 percent of lawyers, 12.1 percent of prosecutors, and 11.2 percent of judges. PCBS, "Gender Statistics—Decision Making and Political

Life: Occupation and Specialization," http://www.pcbs.gov.ps/DesktopDefault.aspx?tab
ID=4113&lang=en.

27 For adultery cases in the West Bank, the code states: "He who surprises his wife, or one
of his [female] Mahrams committing adultery with somebody [*in flagrante delicto*], and
kills, wounds, or injures one or both of them, shall be exempt from liability." It also
stipulates: "He who surprises his wife, or one of his female ascendants or descendants or
sisters with another in an unlawful bed, and he kills or wounds or injures one or both
of them, shall be liable to a lesser penalty." Lynn Welchman, "Extracted Provisions from
the Penal Codes of Arab States Relevant to 'Crimes of Honour,'" School of Oriental
and Asian Studies, University of London, http://www.soas.ac.uk/honourcrimes/Mat
_ArabLaws.htm.

28 The organizations involved are the Women's Affairs Technical Committee (WATC), the
General Union of Palestinian Women (GUPW), the Women's Centre for Legal Aid and
Counseling (WCLAC), the Palestinian Working Women's Society for Development
(PWWSD), Al-Haq, the Women's Study Center, and the Ministry of Women's Affairs.

29 Interview with lawyer Amal Siam from the Women's Affairs Center in Gaza, April 12,
2008.

30 Rose Shomali, "CEDAW and the 8th of March," *Voice of Women* 305 (March 12, 2009),
http://www.watcpal.org/english/display.asp?DocID=276.

31 Jennifer Plyler, interview with Hanadi Loubani, "Occupation, Patriarchy, and the
Palestinian Women's Movement," Mediterranean Women, November 10, 2003, http://
www.mediterraneas.org/article.php3?id_article=48.

32 Article 4 of the Basic Law; Article 5 of the third draft constitution.

33 Interview with Palestinian women activists in Ramallah, January 2008; see also Social
Institutions and Gender Index, "West Bank and Gaza," Organization for Economic
Cooperation and Development (OECD) Development Centre, http://genderindex
.org/country/west-bank-and-gaza.

34 Eileen Kuttab, *Social and Economic Situation of Palestinian Women, 2000–2006* (Birzeit:
Economic and Social Commission for Western Asia, January 2007), 7, http://www.escwa
.un.org/information/publications/edit/upload/ecw-07-tp1-e.pdf.

35 United Nations Office for the Coordination of Humanitarian Affairs (OCHA), *The
Humanitarian Impact on Palestinians of Israeli Settlements and Other Infrastructure in the
West Bank* (Jerusalem: OCHA, July 2007), 46, http://www.ochaopt.org/documents/
TheHumanitarianImpactOfIsraeliInfrastructureTheWestBank_full.pdf.

36 Palestinian Authority (PA), *Progress Report on the Implementation of the Palestinian
Reform and Development Plan 2008–2010: Report to the Meeting for the Ad-Hoc Liaison
Committee* (London: PA, May 8, 2008).

37 Amnesty International, *Israel and the Occupied Territories: Conflict, Occupation, and
Patriarchy: Women Carry the Burden* (London, Amnesty International, March 2005), 11,
http://www.amnesty.org/en/library/asset/MDE15/016/2005/en/623916bd-f791-11d
d-8fd7-f57af21896e1/mde150162005en.pdf.

38 Jerusalem Center for Social and Economic Rights (JCSER), "Residency Rights," April
23, 2009, http://www.jcser.org/index.php?option=com_content&view=article&id=12
&Itemid=15.

[39] Women's Centre for Legal Aid and Counseling (WCLAC), *The Legal and Social Status of Palestinian Women: A Gap Analysis Report Using CEDAW as Reference* (Ramallah: WCLAC, 2005), available at http://www.mediterraneas.org/article.php3?id_article=278.

[40] Adrien K. Wing, "The Impact of Custom and Islamic Heritage on Women's Rights," in *Democracy, Constitutionalism and the Future State of Palestine, with a Case Study on Women's Rights* (Jerusalem: Palestinian Acadmic Society for the Study of Interational Affairs, July 1994), http://www.passia.org/.

[41] Eileen Kuttab, *Social and Economic Situation of Palestinian Women*, 15.

[42] PCBS, "Median Age at First Marriage by Sex and Governorate—2008," http://www.pcbs.gov.ps/Portals/_pcbs/populati/c8ed432f-717c-4b52-a798-32ca2fb93943.htm.

[43] Chris McGreal, "Murdered in Name of Family Honour," *Guardian*, June 23, 2005, http://www.guardian.co.uk/world/2005/jun/23/israel.

[44] Eileen Kuttab, *Social and Economic Situation of Palestinian Women*, 7.

[45] Social Institutions and Gender Index, "West Bank and Gaza."

[46] "Divorce starts as a revocable event and later becomes permanent. Husbands can divorce a wife three times without fully terminating the marriage, just by the oral announcement, 'I divorce you.' The wife must wait a three month period (*idda*) before she can remarry, but if the husband changes his mind within the three months, she must resume the marriage. The divorce is final only if he divorces her three times on three separate occasions. Each time a husband [divorces] a wife, she has to leave the house since it belongs only to him. The wife is entitled to alimony to meet minimal needs." Adrien K. Wing, "The Impact of Custom and Islamic Heritage on Women's Rights."

[47] Interview with lawyer Khadija Hussein Zahran from Al-Haq, previously the head of the Legal Department at the Ministry of Women's Affairs, October 14, 2009.

[48] WCLAC, *The Legal and Social Status of Palestinian Women*.

[49] These cases are dealt with in the Catholic Church's Code of Canon Law, Cnn. 1055–1165, and also according to the judicial process mentioned in Book VII of the Code of Canon Law, Cnn 1400–1752. According to an e-mail response from Bishop Kamal Bathish of the Latin Patriarchate in East Jerusalem, a marriage can be annulled if it was based on deception, for example if information related to mental or physical sickness or homosexuality was not revealed before marriage. Infidelity is not a valid reason for divorce or separation according to the Catholic Church.

[50] Palestinian Legal and Judicial System Al-Muqtafi, "Personal Status Laws for Christians—Evangelical Lutheran Church Law of 1954, Articles 31 and 32," Birzeit University Institute of Law, http://muqtafi2.birzeit.edu/Legislation/GetLegFT.aspx?LegPath=1954&MID=14956&lnk=2#A14956_30 (accessed October 13, 2009).

[51] PCBS, *Domestic Violence Survey December 2005–January 2006: Main Findings* (Ramallah: PCBS, June 2006), http://www.pcbs.gov.ps/Portals/_PCBS/Downloads/book1258.pdf (in Arabic).

[52] PCBS, "Percentage of Ever Married Women Exposed to Any Violence by Husband at Least Once, by Region, Type of Locality, and Types of Violence, During the Year 2005," http://www.pcbs.gov.ps/Portals/_pcbs/gender/vio1.htm.

[53] "Few Legal Options for Abused Palestinian Women, Say Activists," Integrated Regional Information Networks (IRIN), October 3, 2007, http://www.irinnews.org/

Report.aspx?ReportId=74610; "Gazan Women Face Rise in Abuse," British Broadcasting Corporation (BBC), March 30, 2009, http://news.bbc.co.uk/2/hi/middle_east/7968421.stm.

54 Emma Hansson, *Women Under Siege: A Review of Violence Against Women in Palestine and Its Extreme Expression in the Form of 'Honor' Killings* (Jerusalem: Palestinian Human Rights Monitoring Group, April 2008), 7, http://www.phrmg.org/Women%20Under%20Siege%20honor%20killings%204-2008.pdf.

55 Kandy Rinder, "Palestinian Women Subject to 'Honour' Killing," *BBS News*, March 7, 2007, http://bbsnews.net/article.php/2007030719462242.

56 PCBS, news release on the occasion of "Palestinian Children's Day," April 5, 2007, http://www.pcbs.gov.ps/Portals/_pcbs/PressRelease/CHILD07E.pdf.

57 Rose Shomali Musleh, "People Behind Walls, Women Behind Walls: Reading Violence Against Women in Palestine," in *Violence and Gender in the Globalized World: The Intimate and the Extimate*, eds. Sanja Bahun-Radunovic and V.G. Julie Rajan (London: Ashgate, 2008), 68.

58 The article, in Arabic, can be found on the following website: http://home.birzeit.edu/media/production/hal-43.pdf

59 Nazzal Kattaneh, *Palestinian Women and Resolution 1325* (Ramallah: Miftah, 2009), http://www.miftah.org/Publications/Books/Palestinian_Women_and_Resolution1325.pdf.

60 Interview with one of the lawyers working on the proposed legislation, October 7, 2009.

61 The PCBS reported in a 1999 survey that only 7.7 percent of women in the Palestinian territories owned or shared a home or other real estate (5.7 percent in the West Bank and 11.1 percent in Gaza). The survey also showed that 5 percent of women owned or shared a piece of land (5.4 percent in the West Bank and 4.3 percent in the Gaza Strip), and only 1 percent owned a private car (1.3 percent in the West Bank and 0.4 percent in Gaza). PCBS, *Ownership and Access to Resources Survey* (Ramallah: PCBS, August 1999), Table 17-B, http://www.pcbs.gov.ps/Portals/_PCBS/Downloads/book418.pdf.

62 To address this problem, some nongovernmental and women's organizations have provided greater access to microcredit. It is worth noting, however, that social norms and the restricted freedom of movement make it more difficult for women to engage in entrepreneurial activities.

63 Gihane Tabet, *Women in Personal Status Laws: Iraq, Jordan, Lebanon, Palestine, Syria*, Social and Human Sciences Papers in Women's Studies/Gender Research No. 4 (Paris: UNESCO, July 2005), 24, http://portal.unesco.org/shs/fr/files/8090/11313662721Women_in_Personal_Status_Laws.pdf/Women_in_Personal_Status_Laws.pdf.

64 "The historical problem with women's inheritance rights to land in Palestine was primarily due to the problem of land fragmentation. No rule of primogeniture existed in Palestinian society, thus inheritance among a number of sons over generations led to land being broken down into ever smaller, economically unviable units. In this context, women's inheritance rights were viewed not only as a luxury, but more so as a threat to their brothers' ability to inherit enough land to form an economic base for a whole family. The generalized social compromise that took place on this issue was

that peasant women exchanged their rightful share of land inheritance for the guarantee of economic and social support from their brothers." Marianne Heiberg, Geir Øvensen, et al., "Women, Property and Access to Economic Resources," in *Palestinian Society in Gaza, West Bank and Arab Jerusalem: A Survey of Living Conditions* (Oslo: Forskningsstiftelsen Fafo, 1993), http://almashriq.hiof.no/general/300/320/327/fafo/reports/FAFO151/10_4.html.

[65] According to the nongovernmental organization Badil, 48.4 percent of households on the eastern side of the wall and 8.7 percent on the western side said that the wall has negatively affected their access to education. Of the students in the Jerusalem governorate aged 5 and above, 43.9 percent have attended school; 24.7 percent began school but dropped out; 24.6 percent attended and have graduated; and 6.8 percent have never attended school. Nonattendance (12.3 percent) and the dropout rate (28.8 percent) were higher among Palestinians east of the wall than among those in the west. The Badil study also found that 32.9 percent of Jerusalemites have changed their last place of residence since the wall was built. Of these, 20 percent have done so involuntarily; and of these, 83.3 percent have been forcibly displaced once, 9.3 percent twice, and 7.4 percent three times or more. Karine Mac Allister and Ingrid Gassner Jaradat, *Displaced by the Wall: Pilot Study on Forced Displacement Caused by the Construction of the West Bank Wall and Its Associated Regime in the Occupied Palestinian Territories* (Bethlehem and Geneva: BADIL Resource Center for Palestinian Residency and Refugee Rights and the Norwegian Refugee Council/Internal Displacement Monitoring Centre, September 2006), 29, 35, http://www.unhcr.org/refworld/country,,IDMC,,PSE,4562d8cf2,4550a17f2,0.html.

[66] PCBS, *Women and Men in Palestine: Issues and Statistics, 2007* (Ramallah: PCBS, August 2007), http://www.pcbs.gov.ps/Portals/_PCBS/Downloads/book1379.pdf; for a graphic depiction of literacy by age group as of 2006, see PCBS, *Palestine in Figures 2006* (Ramallah: PCBS, May 2007), 34, http://www.pcbs.gov.ps/Portals/_PCBS/Downloads/book1342.pdf.

[67] As of 2006–07, the dropout rate at the basic education level was 0.5 percent for girls and 1.3 percent for boys. At the secondary level it was 3.8 percent for girls and 3.0 percent for boys. PCBS, *Palestine in Figures 2007* (Ramallah: PCBS, May 2008), 25, http://www.pcbs.gov.ps/Portals/_PCBS/Downloads/book1432.pdf; Palestinian Ministry of Education, *The Phenomenon of Dropping Out from School: The Reasons, the Curative and Preventative Measures* (Ramallah: Ministry of Education, August 2005), 8, http://www.moehe.gov.ps/publications/index.html (in Arabic).

[68] The Educational Institutions Census of 2006/2007 found that 86,098 women and 72,034 men were enrolled in universities. PCBS, "Education—Current Main Indicators," http://www.pcbs.pna.org/DesktopModules/Articles/ArticlesView.aspx?tabID=0&lang=en&ItemID=256&mid=10967.

[69] PCBS, *Palestine in Figures 2006*, 28–29. This may also explain why more men attend less costly community colleges: 6,319 male students were registered in community colleges in 2006–07, as opposed to 4,922 female students. PCBS, "Education—Current Main Indicators."

[70] World Bank, "GenderStats—Education," http://go.worldbank.org/AETRQ5QAC0.

[71] Palestinian Ministry of Education, *First Palestinian Curriculum Plan* (Ramallah: Palestinian Ministry of Education, May 1998), http://www.pcdc.edu.ps/first_curriculum _plan.pdf.

[72] Palestinian Ministry of Education, "The Palestinian Curriculum and Textbooks: A Clarification from the Ministry of Education—Palestine," online statement, May 12, 2001, http://www.pcdc.edu.ps/moe_clarification.htm.

[73] David Webb, Maher Hashweh, and Roger Avenstrup, *Studies on Palestinian Curriculum and Textbooks* (Ramallah: UNESCO, 2006), http://unesdoc.unesco.org/images/0015/ 001515/151551e.pdf.

[74] Ilene R. Prusher, "Palestinian Security Gets a Feminine Touch," *Christian Science Monitor*, November 21, 2008, http://www.csmonitor.com/2008/1121/p01s02-wogn.html.

[75] PCBS, "Labor Statistics: Percentage Distribution of Employed Persons in the Palestinian Territory by Economic Activity and Sex, 1995–2007," http://www.pcbs.gov.ps/ Portals/_PCBS/Documents/lab14.htm.

[76] PCBS, *Work Conditions Survey: Main Findings, May–June 2004* (Ramallah: PCBS, December 2004), 23, http://www.pcbs.gov.ps/_pcbs/labor/WorkCondition_E.pdf.

[77] Female unpaid family members, while counted as employed in national statistics, do not enjoy financial independence or benefits like health insurance, and they are vulnerable to exploitation. Their economic work is usually an addition to their domestic chores.

[78] The regional breakdown is 18.3 percent in the West Bank and 11 percent in Gaza in 2007, and 15.8 percent in the West Bank and 9 percent in Gaza in 2005. See PCBS, *Labour Force Survey Annual Report: 2007* (Ramallah: PCBS, April 2008), 64, 72–73, http://www.pcbs.gov.ps/Portals/_PCBS/Downloads/book1423.pdf.

[79] PCBS, *Palestine in Figures 2007*, 18.

[80] The law is available in Arabic at http://www.pogar.org/publications/other/laws/labor/ laborlaw-pal-00-a.pdf.

[81] Eileen Kuttab, *Social and Economic Situation of Palestinian Women*, 22, 45.

[82] World Bank, *The Impact of Israeli Mobility Restrictions and Violence on Gender Relations in Palestinian Society: 2002–2007* (Washington, DC: World Bank, September 2008), 79.

[83] Rabab Abu Sarah, *Violations of the Rights of Working Women* (Jerusalem: Arab Thought Forum [Al-Mutaqa], 2004), 4, http://www.multaqa.org/pdfs/Media-WomenLabor Rights.pdf.

[84] One of them is Birzeit University's master of arts program on gender law and development, which offers a few scholarships for girls. Another is run by the WCLAC, whose staff collectively donate a day's pay each year to a university female student. They also financially adopted a previous victim of domestic violence for four years of her studies. A more stable program within the Women's Studies Center also supports students in need.

[85] See the vocational training section on the organization's website, http://www.inash.org/ accomplishments/vocation.html.

[86] Palestinian Electoral Law (No. 9 of 2005), Article 2(3), available at http://www.elections .ps/pdf/Elections_Law_No_9_of_2005_EN.pdf; see also POGAR, "Elections: Oc-

cupied Palestinian Territories," UNDP, http://www.pogar.org/countries/theme.aspx?t=3 &cid=14.

[87] To win representation via the party list system, a party needed to win more than 2 percent of the national vote. Meanwhile, the seats in each multimember district went to the top vote-earners in that constituency. If a district's population meant that it was allocated six seats, for example, the six top vote earners in that district would win. See European Union Electoral Observation Mission, *West Bank and Gaza Strip: Palestinian Legislative Council Elections* (Brussels: European Union, 2006), 35–36, http://ec.europa.eu/external_relations/human_rights/election_observation/westbank/legislative/final_report_en.pdf.

[88] European Union Electoral Observation Mission, *West Bank and Gaza Strip: Palestinian Legislative Council Elections*, 37.

[89] Arab Election Watch, "Palestine and the Amendment of the Electoral Law to Introduce the Principle of Full Proportionate Representation," October 24, 2007, http://www.intekhabat.org/look/en-article.tpl?IdLanguage=1&IdPublication=1&NrArticle=3884&NrIssue=2&NrSection=3.

[90] Presidential Decree (September 2, 2007), Article 4(1), http://www.elections.ps/pdf/Election_Law_(2007-Sept_02)-EN.pdf.

[91] Women's Campaign International, *Preliminary Program Ideas Report: Palestine* (Philadelphia: Women's Campaign International, 2008), http://www.womenscampaigninternational.org/wp-content/uploads-wci/2008/11/palestine-assessment-report-2006.pdf.

[92] These are Lamis Alami for education, Siham Barghouti for culture, Khuloud Deibes for tourism, Rabha Diab for women's affairs, and Majida al-Masri for social affairs.

[93] These are Zahira Kamal, Maryam Saleh, Amal Siam, and Khulud Deibes.

[94] Eileen Kuttab, *Social and Economic Situation of Palestinian Women*, 19.

[95] Atef Saad, "Municipal Elections Stir Democratic Bones," *Palestine Report* 11, no. 26 (December 2004), http://www.palestinereport.ps/article.php?article=614.

[96] National Democratic Institute for International Affairs (NDI), *Report on Palestinian Elections for Local Councils: Round One* (Washington, DC: NDI, 2005), 19, http://www.ndi.org/files/1816_palestinianelectionreportrd1_033105.pdf..

[97] NDI, *Report on Palestinian Elections for Local Councils: Round Two* (Washington, DC: NDI, 2005), 5, http://www.ndi.org/files/1913_wegz_localcouncil_092905.pdf.

[98] Local Councils Electoral Law (No. 10 of 2005), http://www.elections.ps/pdf/lOCAL_ELECTIONS_LAW-EDIT-EN.pdf. The first two rounds of voting were carried out under the rules established prior to this law, while the next two were carried out under the new law; see Central Elections Commission—Palestine, "Electoral System—Local Elections," http://www.elections.ps/template.aspx?id=333.

[99] For the results in detail, see Central Elections Commission—Palestine, "Local Elections: Statistics and Results," http://www.elections.ps/template.aspx?id=351&sndx=5.

[100] See the Birzeit University Institute of Law database at http://muqtafi2.birzeit.edu/en/Legislation/LegCard.aspx?id=6196.

[101] See for example Palestinian Centre for Human Rights (PCHR), "Israeli Occupation Forces (IOF) Continue Systematic Attacks Against Palestinian Civilians and Property in the Occupied Palestinian Territory (OPT) and a Serious Humanitarian Crisis in

the Gaza Strip Due to the Closure of Its Border Crossings," *Weekly Report: On Israeli Human Rights Violations in the Occupied Palestinian Territory*, November 20–26, 2008, http://www.pchrgaza.org/files/W_report/English/2008/27-11-2008.htm; Mel Frykberg, "Israel Under Pressure over Divided Jerusalem," Inter Press Service, March 23, 2009, http://www.ipsnews.net/news.asp?idnews=46250.

[102] Shatha Odeh, "Long Live the Eighth of March . . . Long Live the Struggle of the Palestinian Woman," Health Work Committees, March 8, 2008, http://www.hwc-pal.org/ar/display_news_details.php?id=152.

[103] WATC, "Women in Political Parties: Between Discrimination and Ambition," *Sawt al-Nissa'*, February 10, 2000.

[104] World Bank, "GenderStats—Middle East and North Africa," http://go.worldbank.org/AETRQ5QAC0.

[105] Of married women aged 15–49, 45.9 percent in the West Bank and 41.7 percent in Gaza used family planning methods as of 2006. According to 18.6 percent of women, the final decision on the issue rested with the husband; 70.8 percent said it was a collective decision, and 9.4 percent said the final decision was up to them. Among women aged 15–49 who did not use family planning methods, 45.6 percent explained that they wanted to have more children. The remainder said the main reason was fear of side effects (8.3 percent), menopause (7.7 percent), discomfort with available methods (7.2 percent), or the husband's refusal (4.9 percent), among other explanations. Just 0.3 percent said the main reason was that it contradicted their religious beliefs, and nearly all of those were in the Gaza Strip. The husband's refusal was cited by 6.3 percent of those in the Gaza Strip and 3.8 percent of those in the West Bank. PCBS, *Palestinian Family Health Survey 2006: Final Report* (Ramallah: PCBS, 2007), 72, 75, http://www.pcbs.gov.ps/Portals/_PCBS/Downloads/book1416.pdf.

[106] According to a 1997 survey, the reasons for having many children included "family strength" (38 percent); the fact that they simply liked having many children (22 percent); preventing the husband's marriage to a second wife (10 percent); the desire for children to provide care for their families (4 percent); and the idea of children as a source of income (3 percent). PCBS, *Palestinian Maternal and Child Health: A Qualitative National Study* (Ramallah: PCBS, July 2000), http://www.pcbs.gov.ps/Portals/_PCBS/Downloads/book597.pdf.

[107] The median age of marriage for women was 19.5 as of 2008, compared with 24.8 for men. PCBS, "Median Age at First Marriage by Sex and Governorate—2008," http://www.pcbs.gov.ps/Portals/_pcbs/populati/c8ed432f-717c-4b52-a798-32ca2fb93943.htm.

[108] Randa Siniora, "The Right to Be Protected Against Violence," in *The Legal and Social Status of Palestinian Women: A Gap Analysis Report Using CEDAW as Reference*.

[109] PCBS, "Socio-Health Status of Palestinian Women 2006," poster, http://www.pcbs.gov.ps/Portals/_PCBS/posters/pal_mother.htm.

[110] Palestinian Working Women Society for Development (PWWSD), "Women and Occupation: Statistics and Numbers," May 24, 2008, http://www.pwwsd.org/index.php?option=com_content&task=view&id=64&Itemid=75.

[111] World Bank, "GenderStats—Health," http://go.worldbank.org/UJ0Q1KQKX0.

[112] PWWSD, "Women and Occupation: Statistics and Numbers."

[113] World Bank, "GenderStats—Health," http://go.worldbank.org/UJ0Q1KQKX0.

[114] Saed Bannoura, "Report: 68 Women Gave Birth on Checkpoints, 33 Infants and 4 Women Died," International Middle East Media Center (IMEMC), April 11, 2007, http://www.imemc.org/index.php?obj_id=53&story_id=47767.

[115] *Report of the Secretary General: Situation of and Assistance to Palestinian Women* (New York: UN Commission on the Status of Women, December 2007), http://www.unhcr .org/refworld/country,,,COUNTRYREP,PSE,4562d8cf2,478491e32,0.html.

[116] E-mail exchange with Rita Giacaman, Research and Program Coordinator, Institute of Community and Public Health, Birzeit University.

[117] Arabic Media Internet Network (AMIN), "On the International Women's Day, AMIN Launches the 'Annual Palestinian Media Woman Award,'" news release, March 8, 2009, http://www.amin.org/Print.php?t=ENews&id=2840.

[118] Women's Affairs Center—Gaza, *Annual Narrative Report* (Gaza: Women's Affairs Center, April 2007), http://www.wac.org.ps/annual_reports/finnal%20annual%20report%202 0060.pdf.

[119] Personal interview with journalists working in major women's newspapers in Ramallah and Gaza, April 2009.

[120] Donald MacIntyre, "Women of Gaza Fear for Their Freedoms Under New Religious Regime," *Independent,* January 30, 2006, http://www.independent.co.uk/news/world/ middle-east/women-of-gaza-fear-for-their-freedoms-under-new-religious-regime- 525149.html.

[121] Interview with women activists in Gaza and Ramallah, April 2009.

[122] Brenda Gazzar, "Palestinians Debate Women's Future Under Hamas," WeNews, April 23, 2006, http://www.womensenews.org/article.cfm/dyn/aid/2714/.

[123] World Bank, "West Bank & Gaza: Country Brief," September 2008, http://go.world bank.org/Q8OGMLXI40.

[124] Eileen Kuttab, *Social and Economic Situation of Palestinian Women*, 22.

[125] Eileen Kuttab, *Social and Economic Situation of Palestinian Women*, 22.

[126] Interview with Palestinian women activists in Ramallah, February 2009.

QATAR

*by Julia Breslin and Toby Jones**

POPULATION:	1,409,000	
GNI PER CAPITA:	US$72,795	

COUNTRY RATINGS	2004	2009
NONDISCRIMINATION AND ACCESS TO JUSTICE:	1.8	2.1
AUTONOMY, SECURITY, AND FREEDOM OF THE PERSON:	2.0	2.3
ECONOMIC RIGHTS AND EQUAL OPPORTUNITY:	2.7	2.9
POLITICAL RIGHTS AND CIVIC VOICE:	1.7	1.8
SOCIAL AND CULTURAL RIGHTS:	2.4	2.5

(COUNTRY RATINGS ARE BASED ON A SCALE OF I TO 5, WITH I REPRESENTING THE LOWEST AND 5 THE
HIGHEST LEVEL OF FREEDOM WOMEN HAVE TO EXERCISE THEIR RIGHTS)

INTRODUCTION

With major reforms beginning as early as 1995, Qatar has taken several
steps in recent years toward promoting equality and addressing cultural
and social traditions that discriminate against women. The 2004 enactment of a new constitution provides hope that equality will be achieved
both in law and in practice, but to accomplish this, existing laws must be
brought into accord with the nondiscrimination clause in the constitution and women need to be educated about their new rights. These efforts
on the part of the government are necessary in light of the challenges to
gender equality presented by strict cultural norms, as well as sheer demo-
graphics. As in many other oil-rich nations that depend on foreign guest
workers to fuel their national economy, women in Qatar are outnumbered
by men nearly two to one, creating a society saturated by men. This, in
turn, inherently influences women's economic participation and involvement in all aspects of Qatari society.

Women's sense of security, enjoyment of personal freedoms, and ability
to make autonomous life decisions has improved with the enactment of the
country's first codified family law in 2006. Previously, cases dealing with

---

* Sanja Kelly and Tyler Roylance also contributed to this report.

personal status issues—such as marriage, divorce, child custody, and inheritance—were decided by judges based on their interpretations of Shari'a (Islamic law), the process which was often arbitrary and detrimental to women's rights. While the new law is perceived as a notable improvement over the old system, women remain disadvantaged in comparison to men. In addition, the Supreme Council for Family Affairs (SCFA), the government entity charged with protecting and supporting the family unit, now formally recognizes that domestic violence is an issue and has openly initiated a social dialogue on this previously taboo subject.

Women remain underrepresented in the workforce, predominantly as a result of cultural and social, rather than legal norms. Nonetheless, the female labor participation has been on the rise, as more women graduate from universities and seek employment. Citizens are entitled to free education through secondary school, and today, more women are literate than men. A woman's ability to choose her profession remains legally and socially restricted to fields that offer "acceptable" roles for women, and in practice, most women are employed as health care or education professionals or fill clerical jobs. Very few women work in the private sector, and even fewer hold top-level positions, but the government has established the Qatari Business Women Forum to encourage female leadership in private businesses.

Political rights for all Qataris remain limited despite provisions within the new constitution that promised an elected parliament, and women remain underrepresented at various levels of government. In 2007, only one woman succeeded in her bid for a seat in the citizen-elected Central Municipal Council, an advisory body for the minister of municipal affairs. Freedoms of assembly, expression, and the press are also restricted for all Qataris, although women are now employed as media and press professionals in greater numbers than before. Government posts have been filled by women more often in recent years, but not at a rate representative of their proportion of society, and men continue to hold the primary positions of power. For women to have an opportunity to effect change in their lives, the political rights of all Qataris must be improved and society must address the cultural biases that currently prevent women from being viewed as suitable leaders.

Several governmental and quasi-governmental organizations have been created to analyze and address human rights concerns. The National Human Rights Committee (NHRC) is an often bold quasi-governmental organization established in 2002 for the purpose of monitoring the rights of all residents of Qatar. In an effort to ensure greater personal safety, the government established a shelter for women and children in 2003. Other centers and forums have been founded to develop women's roles in society, such as the Center for Girls' Creativity, the aforementioned Qatari Business Women's Forum, and a committee concerning women's sports. Government institutions have made efforts to adopt, either formally or informally, policies that increase participation by women in their activities.

Despite many legal changes, however, traditional gender roles continue to persist. Women are conditioned from an early age to avoid direct confrontation with their male counterparts, relying instead on dialogue and gradual persuasion as means through which to achieve their goals. While this allows women to exercise some rights without causing friction within their families, adhering to customs that retain women's traditional role within family and society often inhibits the overall improvement of women's rights. It is not enough to have laws and organizations that support women if the social value system and the stereotypical image of women remain unchanged. As such, it is important to alter the content of educational material, the media, and the socialization of children to reduce gender bias and create a new image of a Qatari woman.

NONDISCRIMINATION AND ACCESS TO JUSTICE

Although the principles of equality and nondiscrimination are enshrined in Qatar's constitution, de jure and de facto gender discrimination continue to exist. Noncitizen husbands of Qatari women and their children are greatly disadvantaged in their ability to obtain Qatari citizenship, particularly as compared to the noncitizen wives of Qatari men and their children. The government—especially the SCFA and the Qatar Foundation for the Protection of Women and Children (Qatar Foundation)—has made efforts to inform women of their legal rights and provide them with social and legal services. However, the 2004 law governing private associations is so restrictive that independent women's rights NGOs remain nonexistent, thereby limiting civil society's influence on related legal and policy issues.

Qatar's constitution explicitly prohibits gender-based discrimination under Article 35, which reads: "[A]ll people are equal before the law. There shall be no discrimination on account of sex, origin, language or religion." Article 34 also provides that all citizens have equal rights and duties, thereby providing female citizens with additional legal protection against discrimination. Women who feel they have been the victims of gender-based discrimination may complain to the police, appeal through the judicial system, or approach the NHRC, although not many use these complaint mechanisms. Any individual who has been affected by a discriminatory administrative decision may file a claim with the Administrative Court under Law No. 7 of 2007, or, if the complaint is labor-related, the affected woman can file a case with the labor court or complain to the Ministry of Labor. Most rights in the constitution (among them, rights related to employment and property ownership) apply only to Qatari citizens, which is significant in a country where the majority of residents are noncitizens.

Qatari women have the limited ability to pass their nationality to their non-Qatari husbands and children. The Qatari Citizenship Act (No. 38 of 2005) replaced its 1961 predecessor, a notoriously exclusive law that previously limited citizenship to descendants of those persons living in Qatar before 1930. The new law provides several avenues by which citizenship may be obtained, but it retains preferential treatment for native as opposed to naturalized citizens and continues to discriminate against Qatari women. For instance, Article 8 grants citizenship to the foreign wives of Qatari men after five years of marriage and upon notification to the Ministry of the Interior, but the noncitizen husbands of Qatari women face far more onerous preconditions for obtaining citizenship under Article 2.

Article 2 permits any person—including noncitizen husbands and children—to seek Qatari citizenship subject to extensive restrictions. The applicant must have maintained 25 successive years of residence in Qatar; traveled abroad for less than two months each year; maintained legal employment; established a good reputation and maintained good behavior; and learned to communicate adequately in Arabic. As noted by the NCHR, the 25-year residency requirement limits this law's value because children's needs for the benefits conferred by citizenship, such as health care and education, are most acute while they are still young.[1] On the other hand, children of native-born Qatari fathers gain full citizenship rights upon birth.

Qatar's judicial system is comprised of the Supreme Court, the court of appeals, and courts of first instance. The Shari'a courts that existed prior to 2003 were abolished and any matters pending before them were assimilated into the new court system. The courts of first instance are divided into criminal, administrative, and civil courts. The appeals court is divided into circuits and hears both civil and criminal matters. Most recently, a Constitutional Court was created in October 2008 as a division of the Supreme Court under Law No. 6 of 2008, the purpose of which is to settle disputes between opposing lower courts and determine the constitutionality of laws and regulations.[2] This added layer of independent oversight regarding judicial decisions, legislation, and regulations could help to ensure enforcement of legal protections for women and eliminate discriminatory provisions that currently exist.

The new courts still apply Shari'a principles when dealing with family and probate issues between Muslim couples. In at least some instances within family law a woman's testimony or worth as a witness is unequal to that of a man's. For example, under Article 36 of the newly codified Family Law (No. 22 of 2006), two men must witness a marital contract and may testify to its validity before a court of law while women are excluded from acting as witnesses in such cases. Additionally, when determining the identity of a child's father, Articles 93 through 95 of the same law require either two men or one man and two women as witnesses. No such gender-based testimony or witness preferences exist within the criminal and civil code.

Women usually attend court proceedings in which they are involved and may either represent themselves or, increasingly, be represented by an attorney. There are no female judges in Qatar, the result of social rather than legal norms. Many, including legal professionals, deem women too emotional or inconsistent to be competent judges, although this opinion may change with the increasing number of women in the legal profession.[3] After the first woman, Haifa al-Bakr, was granted a license to practice law in 2000, the number of female lawyers in private practice has increased sharply, and there are now more female than male students in Qatar University's college of law.[4] However, women remain underrepresented within the legal profession, although they are permitted to be professors in the Shari'a law faculty at Qatar University.

Most foreign female laborers in Qatar are domestic workers and have only moderate access to justice, both because many are illiterate and consequently face difficulties in learning their legal rights and because inadequate efforts have been made to enforce existing laws and inform such workers of their rights. All forms of compulsory labor are prohibited under Emiri Decree (No. 74 of 2006), which amends in part the Labor Law (No.

14 of 2004).[5] Domestic workers are protected under a different decree issued in 2008, which stipulates that domestic workers are to work only in conditions agreed upon by both parties and should not be forced to work in a way that would insult them either mentally or physically. The sponsor must provide them with suitable accommodation and health care and pay the agreed-to salary into the worker's bank account at the end of every month or three days after. If the worker has no bank account there should be a proof that the salary was paid in full.

Despite legal protections, domestic workers who do face physical, mental, and sexual abuse are often reluctant to seek court protection due to fears of job loss and deportation. It is thus too early to tell how effective the new laws will be, particularly without significantly strengthened enforcement mechanisms and public education about their existence.

Both the Penal Code (No. 11 of 2004) and the Code of Criminal Procedure (No. 23 of 2004) treat men and women equally. Accused criminals are presumed innocent until proven guilty in a court of law and are entitled to all "necessary legal assistance" under Article 39 of the constitution. Although Shari'a prohibits all forms of physical violence, the Qatari legal system often treats leniently those men who commit acts of violence against women who, in their view, behave immodestly.[6] In January 2007, the sentence of a Jordanian teenager convicted of murdering his sister was reduced by an appeals court from three years' imprisonment to a one-year suspended sentence. The sentence was reduced because the court found there to be insufficient evidence to establish premeditated murder. This ruling overturned the lower court, which had held that it was a premeditated murder based on the suspect's admitted displeasure that the sister had been having a "telephone affair" with one of his friends. The lower court, however, stopped short of calling it an honor killing because the autopsy proved that the sister was still a virgin.[7]

Article 36 of the constitution protects all persons from arbitrary arrest and detention, and Article 38 protects citizens from exile. In practice, unjustified gender-based imprisonment and detention are rare. Prisons generally meet international standards, with overcrowding as the main concern, and women are held separately from men. At the end of 2004, women constituted only 1.1 percent of convicted prisoners, down significantly from 11.8 percent in 2000.[8] Detention centers for noncitizens awaiting deportation, however, have been roundly criticized by both the NHRC and international bodies as failing to satisfy detainees' basic rights to personal freedom and safety. Those awaiting deportation are generally simple laborers who often spend six months to two years in the detention centers, with extreme cases ranging up to four years or more, as they await final adjudication on labor disputes or a paid flight home from their former employers. In 2006, out of the approximate 1,500 detainees in such centers only 250 were women, reflecting the lower number of female compared to male migrant workers in Qatar.

In April 2009, Qatar became the final Arab country to ratify the Convention on the Elimination of All Forms of Discrimination against Women (CEDAW) following a strong push by domestic activists and governmental officials, particularly from the NHRC.[9] However, the government placed reservations on Article 2(a), regarding gender equality in domestic laws and policies; Article 9, paragraph 2, regarding the right of women to pass their citizenship to their children; Article 15, paragraphs 1 and 4, regarding equality before the law, freedom of movement, and freedom to choose one's own domicile; Article 16, paragraph 1(a), (c), and (f), regarding marital, parental, and divorce rights; and Article 29, paragraph 2 regarding dispute resolution. Qatar has also indicated interest in ratifying the International Convention on Civil and Political Rights in the near future.[10]

Women's rights organizations continue to be predominantly state-run, mainly because of the strict regulations placed on nongovernmental associations. The Associations and Private Institutions Law (No. 12 of 2004) was passed in 2004 and, as a practical matter, originally allowed only for professional associations and trade unions.[11] Civil society organizations such as the Migrant Workers Protection Society have since formed, but their finances and activities are heavily monitored.[12] Organizations are prohibited from participating in undefined "political issues" under Article 35(3) and existing NGOs do not generally have goals that push the bounds of culturally accepted topics.[13] NGOs are also not free to affiliate with foreign organizations. Article 31 initially prohibited domestic organizations from partnering with foreign NGOs at all, although a 2006 amendment now permits such affiliations upon approval by the Ministry of Civil Services and Housing.[14] Although the association law is a step in the right direction, it is too restrictive to permit the existence of an effective civil society.

As a result, it falls upon governmental and quasi-governmental organizations to advocate for equality in Qatar. In particular, the Qatar Foundation provides women with legal aid, advocates for policy reforms that would better protect women, and raises awareness of women's issues.[15] The SCFA has, among other things, compiled gender statistics and has issued reports on Qatar's implementation of the Beijing Declaration, the World Millennium Challenge, and the UNDP *Human Development Report.* In 2005 and 2006, the NCHR issued frank, critical, and relatively thorough human rights reports that outlined legal provisions related to equality and nondiscrimination and highlighted the plight of vulnerable populations such as women, children, and migrant workers.[16] Finally, a variety of charitable associations, including the Qatar Red Crescent Society, focus on the welfare of Qatar's residents and in so doing sometimes address gender issues.[17]

Despite the progress made by these governmental entities, most Qatari women remain unaware of their impact or even their existence. According to one survey, 53 percent of female respondents had not heard of the Qatar Foundation.[18] Traditional cultural norms hold a family's honor above all other considerations, preventing many women from approaching these organizations for fear of bringing shame to their families. For the government entities to be truly effective, these social norms must be addressed and women must be made aware of the nature of the organizations so that they feel comfortable asking for help.

Recommendations

✤ The government should ensure that all laws are consistent with constitutional guarantees of gender equality and train judicial personnel to enforce them effectively.

✤ Article 8 of the citizenship act should be made gender neutral, thereby permitting all noncitizen spouses of Qatari nationals to be become naturalized citizens after maintaining five years of residence in Qatar.

✤ The SCFA should publish brochures containing information about women's legal rights, and the channels through which to uphold them, and distribute them to the most vulnerable portions of society, with a special emphasis on impoverished women and foreign female guest workers.

✤ Adjudication of deportation should occur at a much swifter pace, and the number of detainees in deportation centers must be reduced. To increase the number of cases being heard at any given time, the government should allocate resources toward training deportation judges, lawyers, and ancillary personnel (courthouse clerks, legal aids) to increase the number of cases heard.

✤ To encourage women's rights organizations to form without fear of undue influence by the government, the Associations and Private Institutions Law (No. 12 of 2004) should be amended to ease registration requirements for new societies. Additionally, the government's ability to monitor the activities and finances of organizations should be limited to instances where fraud or criminal activity is reasonably suspected.

✤ The government should remove the reservations to CEDAW and fully implement the convention within domestic law.

AUTONOMY, SECURITY, AND FREEDOM OF THE PERSON

Qatar has taken notable measures to ensure freedoms for women in recent years, but it remains a patriarchal society in which men are the primary decision makers of the family. Activism by the SCFA pushed the government to codify a new family law in 2006, and although the new law succeeded in instituting some improvements, women continue to be treated unequally. The government has recognized that violence against women is an issue but has not yet specifically outlawed domestic violence. Despite increased legal protections, noncitizen women continue to be subject to harsh treatment and exploitation, particularly at the hands of their employers.

The state religion of Qatar is Islam, and women of all faiths are largely free to practice their religion and beliefs. Article 50 of the constitution formally guarantees freedom of worship to all. Although the national population is overwhelmingly Sunni, there is also a significant Shiite minority, and the expatriate population includes practitioners of many other religions. In March 2008, Qatar's first Christian church, St. Mary's Roman Catholic Church, opened in Doha on land donated by the emir, and five additional churches are under construction. A 2004 law criminalizes the possession of non-Muslim missionary materials and proselytizing, with penalties of up to 10 years in prison, and it is illegal for Muslims to convert to other religions. While Muslim men may marry non-Muslim women of monotheistic faiths, Muslim women are not permitted to marry men of other faiths.

Qatari women face certain restrictions in their freedom of movement. While foreign women may obtain a driver's license, Qatari women are required to have the permission of their male guardian.[19] Social norms restrict interactions between unrelated men and women, and some areas of the public sphere such as workplaces and public schools are largely segregated. Law No. 5 of 2007 permits adult women to obtain a passport without the permission of a male guardian and they are not legally required to have a male guardian's approval to travel abroad, but few women travel alone. Men can prevent female relatives from leaving the country by giving their names to immigration officers at departure ports, but women in this situation may appeal to the NHRC to intervene on their behalf.

Employers often restrict the freedom of movement of noncitizen women, particularly domestic workers, and their ability to travel abroad.[20] Employers must give consent before exit permits are issued to foreign workers wishing to leave the country.[21] The NHRC reported in 2006 that more than 200 non-Qatari women were detained in deportation centers in unhealthy conditions. While some of the women have been detained to provide them shelter, others are kept in detention at the request of their sponsors.[22]

Largely as a result of the advocacy of the SCWA, Qatar ratified the new family law in 2006 that regulates engagements, marriage contracts, separation and divorce, child custody, guardianship, and inheritance, among other things. Where the law makes no specific proscriptions, it allows judges to draw upon any of the four main Islamic legal schools in rendering decisions when appropriate. For non-Muslims the law stipulates that their cases be determined by "the respective laws of the groups concerned."[23] Women are now granted custody of boys up to the age of 13 and girls up to the age of 15; previously, mothers lost custody once boys turned seven and girls hit puberty.[24] Fathers, however, retain the guardianship and the right to gain custody of older children should they so desire.

Women have the legal right to negotiate a marriage contract, which may grant them greater rights than those guaranteed by law, but they do not have full and equal freedom to choose their marriage partner. While a woman's consent is necessary for a marriage contract to be legal, Article 28 of the family law stipulates that her guardian carries out the contract on her behalf, ultimately subjecting her choice of husband to the guardian's approval. If the guardian is not present, a prospective bride can ask the judge to carry out the contract instead. Both husband and wife may include conditions in the marriage contract and both are legally required to uphold such conditions.

The high profile case of Hamda Fahad Jassem al-Thani, a member of the ruling family, illustrates an extreme example of the extent to which a

woman's freedom of movement and freedom to choose her marriage partner may be inhibited by her family. Al-Thani married an Egyptian national
in November 2002 in Egypt without her family's permission; nine days
later she was kidnapped and returned to Qatar. After being detained by
security forces for several months she was transferred to her family's home
in October 2003 where she remained under house arrest until October
2006, when she was hospitalized following an escape attempt. At that
point, the NHRC, the Ministry of the Interior, and other officials stepped
in to protect her and secure travel documents so that al-Thani could return
to her husband in Egypt.[25]

Men in Qatar have the right to divorce by verbally announcing their
intent to do so three times, a common Islamic practice found throughout
the region. Options for women are far more limited. They may seek a judicial divorce by citing injury caused by the husband, or they may invoke
khula, a practice that permits women to obtain a divorce unilaterally upon
satisfaction of certain conditions. The first option requires that a woman
go before a court and satisfy one of several codified reasons for a divorce.
These relate to the husband's failure to uphold his marital duties, and
many are difficult or embarrassing to prove. They include, for example,
his inability to provide adequate fiscal support, an absence lasting longer
than a year, and his contraction of a contagious disease. The second option
for divorce, khula, is codified in Article 122 of the family law. A rapid
resolution requires the husband's consent, but if he does not agree to the
divorce, a mandatory six-month period of arbitration and reconciliation is
necessary. If the spouses still cannot be reconciled, the court may order the
divorce, though this obliges the woman to give up any right to financial
support and return her *mahr* (dowry).

The codification of khula, despite its restrictions, is considered a boon
to women's rights in that it provides the opportunity to escape unhealthy
marriages. However, it is rarely invoked. The divorce rate in Qatar is high,
with one in three marriages ending in divorce in 2007.[26] The vast majority
of these were initiated by men, and of the 971 registered divorces, only
41 were khula divorces.[27] Divorce stigmatizes women more than men,
both socially and psychologically, leaving them less desirable to potential
future husbands, potentially limiting their ability to remarry. In a society
in which women are often dependent upon their spouses for financial support, khula carries high risks for those who do not have extended families
on which to rely.

The terms and conditions of polygamy are outlined in Article 14 of the personal status law. Polygamy is an accepted tradition but has become less widespread due to changing social and economic realities that place a heavy fiscal burden on the husband.

An update to the penal code in 2004 formally criminalized slavery, bondage, and forced labor. Violations can result in prison terms of up to seven years.[28] Yet, despite measures taken by the government, including the creation of the National Organization for the Combating of Human Trafficking (NOCHT) in 2005, Qatar remains a destination country for women who are trafficked and placed in situations of coerced labor.[29] In its 2006 annual report the NHRC reported that trafficking in foreign women was on the rise.[30] Although Qatar codified expanded protections for foreign workers, domestic workers, particularly from Asia, often labor under conditions approaching involuntary servitude (long hours, withheld pay, restricted movement), and some are sexually exploited.[31] The government has put in place punishments for violators of the labor laws, and those found guilty of withholding pay for forced labor are subject to prison terms of up to six months and fines of up to 3,000 riyals (US$825).[32] Nevertheless, the laws are not consistently enforced, particularly for domestic workers, many of whom are unwilling to report abuses.[33] Foreign embassies occasionally provide shelter for their citizens who have left employers due to abuse or for other reasons.[34]

Women are generally free from torture and cruel, inhuman, and degrading punishment, and violence against women outside the home is rare. Pursuant to Article 279 of the penal code, the maximum penalty for rape in Qatar is death, although no specific law protects women from domestic violence.[35] Article 57 of the 2006 family law, however, states that a woman's marital rights include the right to be free from physical and mental harm at the hands of her husband. The Qatari Foundation reported 107 instances of domestic abuse in 2007.[36] Additionally, according to a 2006 survey carried out by the SCFA, nearly 20 percent of the 2,787 female Qatar University students questioned had been subjected to childhood violence.[37] In an effort to further understand the role of violence in Qatari society, the SCFA is currently conducting a survey of violence against married women.[38] The Qatar Foundation has established a family consultation center and a hotline for women and children to report abuse and continues its efforts to educate women on their legal rights and advocate on their behalf.[39]

Violence against women has been officially recognized by government officials as an important issue in need of attention. During a two-day seminar held in November 2008, a representative of the SCFA called upon the country to address violence against women openly and without shame. The event, which followed another held in November 2006, gathered women's rights leaders from around the world, including the UN special rapporteur on violence against women, to discuss how to prevent violence from occurring, protect victims, and effectively prosecute perpetrators.[40] Some protection from domestic violence is provided by social networks rather than by law. Notably the tendency toward family endogamy (a cultural preference for marriage between cousins) offers some protection to women because an abuser married to his cousin would have to answer to his wife's parents, who are members of the same clan and may come to her defense. As family standing is critical to economic and social access and success in Qatar, this pressure can be formidable.

There are few, if any, independent, nongovernmental women's rights groups working on domestic violence or immigrant women's rights issues in Qatar, and no organizations of female lawyers or independent legal aid groups operate in the country.

Recommendations

❖ The government should criminalize domestic violence and take effective measures to prosecute offenders and protect victims by, among other things, increasing police and medical training to recognize and intervene where abuse is evident, continuing to conduct workshops and seminar series intended to help society overcome its reluctance to address the issue, and providing shelter and economic aid to victims of domestic abuse and their dependent children.

❖ The government should rescind the law requiring a male guardian's permission for a woman to obtain a driver's license and abolish rules that may prohibit women from travelling freely.

❖ The government should deepen its commitment to fighting human trafficking by establishing more severe punishments for violators and by more strictly enforcing existing labor laws.

❖ To further understand the extent to which trafficking is an issue and how to allocate its resources better, the government should collect gender-disaggregated data regarding how many people are trafficked each year, their countries of origin, and their intended role and alleged treatment while residing in Qatar.

❖ Child custody should not be allocated based on the age and sex of the children. Instead, each case should be decided based on the best interests of the children in light of the individual parent's ability to provide care for them.

ECONOMIC RIGHTS AND EQUAL OPPORTUNITY

Despite fluctuating oil prices, Qatar has experienced unprecedented economic growth since the discovery of oil in the 1940s and has become per capita one of the wealthiest countries in the world. Women's economic rights and academic opportunities have also increased in recent years as more women pursue university education and seek employment outside the home. The education system is undergoing extensive reform, and courses are being offered for women that reflect the actual market demands for labor. As a result, women are increasingly encouraged to enter fields traditionally deemed inappropriate for them. Despite progress, women in Qatar remain underrepresented in the workforce, particularly in leadership positions, and are subjected to strong cultural and familial pressures when making career and academic choices.

Women in Qatar have property rights similar to those of men. Law No. 40 of 2004 provides Qatari men and women with the same rights of guardianship over their individual incomes, and no legal restrictions exist on women's right to own and have independent use of their land and property. Noncitizens, however, are not permitted to own property, and cultural norms tend to inhibit the ability of all women to exercise these rights fully.

In Qatar, as in many neighboring states, Muslim women do not have equal inheritance rights, and they inherit half what a similarly situated male relative would receive. The common rationale behind this tenet is that Shari'a and cultural traditions require men to bear the financial burden for their entire families, including all female family members, while women may retain their inheritance and any other assets for their own personal use.

A woman has the right to enter into business and economic contracts and activities without the permission of her husband or legal guardian. A woman's participation in business activities that require close contact with unrelated men, however, will typically face family opposition. Several mechanisms exist to support the participation of women in the sector, including the Women's Investment Company of Qatar and the Businesswomen's Club, a division of the Qatar Chamber of Commerce and Industry. Although only a small fraction of women engage in investment activities, anecdotal evidence shows that those numbers have increased recently, particularly with the advent of online banking. Internet-based investment tools appeal to women because they allow transactions to be conducted from home without requiring interaction with financial advisers, most of whom are male.

The government emphasizes the importance of education for the continued economic growth of Qatar, and beginning in 2001, the Supreme Education Council spearheaded intense reform efforts for the primary, secondary, and postsecondary education systems. On the outskirts of Doha, Education City now houses campuses for more than half a dozen foreign universities, including Northwestern University and Georgetown University. The entire public education system in Qatar is segregated by gender, and Qatar University has separate campuses for men and women. However, foreign universities within Education City are not required to be gender-segregated.

Article 49 of the constitution grants the right to free and compulsory education up to the secondary level to all citizens. Women are slightly more likely to be literate than men,[41] and women constituted 50 percent of students enrolled in secondary education and 68 percent of all graduates from postsecondary education in 2007.[42] Women's outstanding achievements in academia indicate that society has put credence in the idea that education will eventually lead to gender equality. Promoting education among women, however, is not enough if they are unable to find positions of power in their chosen professions or if they are not accepted by society as adequate leaders. In late 2008, women were accepted into the electrical engineering program at Qatar University for the first time in the hope of cutting back Qatar's dependence on foreign workers for research and development jobs. The university also recently permitted women to study architecture and chemical engineering for the first time.

Employed women tend to be highly educated compared to their male counterparts, with 66.6 percent of female citizen laborers and 35.1 percent of female noncitizen laborers holding degrees.[43] Despite this, they remain underrepresented in the workforce, constituting only 14 percent of the total adult workforce, a statistic tempered only by the fact that there are half as many women as men in Qatar to begin with.[44] Nonetheless, more women hold jobs or seek employment now than ever before. Approximately 42 percent of adult women participated in the labor force as of 2007, compared to 38 percent in 2002.[45]

Although women's academic choices are increasing, long-standing cultural ideals regarding proper professions for women persist. Article 94 of the labor law prohibits women from undertaking dangerous or arduous work, or that which could be deemed detrimental to their health or morals, while Article 95 permits the minister of labor to determine suitable work hours for women. Both of these provisions treat women as minors who are unable to make decisions regarding their own safety. Additionally, Qatari women remain excluded from the diplomatic service.[46] In practice, women are employed almost entirely in the health care, education, and clerical professions,[47] fields that are predominantly gender segregated and do not challenge traditional female gender roles. Qatari men, meanwhile, are distributed relatively evenly across most professions except education, where they are significantly underrepresented.[48]

Qatari nationals generally, and women in particular, exhibit reluctance to work in the private sector, an additional limitation for women. Instead, 9 out of 10 Qatari citizens are public employees, and women make up 33.6 percent of the total government workforce.[49] A recent government-sanctioned study analyzed the reasons behind Qataris' prejudices against the private sector. Of the women surveyed, 76 percent cited concerns over a mixed-gender work environment, 53 percent felt it conferred a low social status, and 18 percent cited low wages. Conversely, the men surveyed cited low wages as their top concern, followed by poor working hours and low social status. Based on these findings, societal restrictions regarding what constitutes a proper work environment for women play heavily into women's occupational choices, while men tend to have other concerns.[50]

As academic choices for women are slowly growing, so too are occupational choices, and a small percentage of women are now doctors, lawyers, and police officers.[51] Nevertheless, social opinions still affect the nature of women's employment, and this will continue for years to come if the situation remains unaddressed. Formal statistics indicate that very few upper management positions are occupied by women, regardless of the fact that they have the necessary skills. In 2005, only 8.1 percent of all management and senior positions were held by women.[52]

The government has also encouraged female leadership within the private sector by establishing the Qatari Business Women Forum, which has more than 500 registered members. According to the Qatar Chamber of Commerce, women were issued approximately 1,360 business licenses between 2003 and 2005. Moreover, approximately 17 percent of all entrepreneurs in 2005 were women.[53]

In accordance with the government's goal of preserving the family unit, female employees are eligible for maternity benefits. Under Article 96 of the labor law, if a woman has worked for her current employer for at least a year, she is entitled to 50 days of maternity leave, at least 35 days of which must be used after the baby is delivered. If the birth renders a woman unable to return to work, she has 60 days (continuous or interrupted) of unpaid leave pending medical certification of such need. Additionally, Article 97 provides new mothers with an hour per day to breast feed in addition to normal rest periods required by law. Sexual harassment is punishable by imprisonment and fines under Article 294 of the penal code, which the public prosecutor has invoked against men who harass women with obscene gestures or phone calls. In 2006, there were eight reported cases of sexual harassment, five of which ended in convictions.[54]

Article 93 of the labor law mandates equal pay for men and women if they perform the same work, as well as equal opportunity for training and promotion. The NHRC found that employers consistently violate the principle of equal pay for equal work. In particular, the NHRC noted that this form of discrimination tended to manifest itself in benefits provided by the employer, such as "residence allowances, or senior official loans or allocation of land."[55]

Several governmental and quasi-governmental organizations monitor women's economic rights. The Women's Affairs Department was established by the Council of Ministers in 1996 for the purpose of "finding work opportunities compatible with the Qatari women's nature and role in society."[56] The Women's Affairs Committee of the SCFA proposes "policies, plans and programs" that it deems necessary for the improvement of women's cultural, economic, and political standing.[57] Although the NHRC does not focus solely on women's issues, portions of its annual reports are dedicated to analyzing violations of women's rights, including their economic rights. Additionally, the Social Development Center is a nonprofit organization established by Her Highness Sheikha Moza bint Nasser al-Missned, the emir's wife, that attempts to empower low-income families and women with the goal of creating self-sufficiency. These entities have stridently advocated on behalf of women, albeit within the traditional social and cultural constraints.

Recommendations

* ✤ The government should encourage women's participation in the private sector by directly addressing and, where possible, remedying the cultural stigmas associated with such work.
* ✤ The government should continue to tailor academic opportunities for women to the actual market needs of Qatar in an effort to diversify future job options for women. Additionally, high schools and universities should coordinate with local businesses to create internship programs that involve female students in fields in which women are underrepresented.
* ✤ The government should amend Articles 94 and 95 of the labor law, which treat women as minors who are unable to make informed decisions when choosing their professions, and should permit women to act as representatives of Qatar abroad by allowing them to participate in the Foreign Service.
* ✤ The government should actively recruit qualified female jurists to serve in all levels of the judiciary, thereby expanding professional opportunities for women and encouraging more women to study law.
* ✤ The work of the SCFA should be expanded to prepare women for professional careers outside the home and should include training programs that encourage women to work in sectors traditionally dominated by men such as banking, science, and technology.

POLITICAL RIGHTS AND CIVIC VOICE

Qatari women remain underrepresented in political life even within the limited field of activity allowed by the emir, who appoints the government and rules without an elected parliament. Although the 2004 constitution has the potential to increase male and female citizens' participation in public affairs, promised legislative elections have been delayed, and there has been little progress in easing legal constraints on political activity.

Qatari women began participating in a form of electoral politics in 1996, when elections were established for the country's commercial and industrial chambers. Female candidates have since been nominated for membership many times, but none have won. Women's electoral participation expanded after Law No. 12 of 1998 created the Central Municipal Council (CMC), a 29-member body tasked with advising the minister of municipal affairs and agriculture on issues including trash collection, street repair, and other public works.

The emir granted women suffrage in a 1999 decree. In the first CMC elections that year, women accounted for about 45 percent of the 13,656 voters who took part. However, none of the 6 women in the field of 230 candidates were successful. The sole female candidate in the 2003 elections won a seat, but only after her male opponent withdrew. In the 2007 election the percentage of female voters rose to 46.6, but there were just 3 female candidates facing 118 men. Sheikha Yusuf al-Jifairi, an incumbent and the only one of the three women to win, was reelected to her seat with 96 percent of her constituency's votes.[58] The role of women in CMC elections is noteworthy, but the body has no power to make policy, and the eligible electorate consists of only about 28,000 people. This leaves hundreds of thousands of male and female residents entirely out of the process. Of those eligible to vote, about 51 percent turned out in 2007, up from 32 percent in 2003.[59]

Article 77 of the new constitution intended to convert the country's appointed 35-member Consultative Council into a 45-seat body with 30 elected members, offering female voters and candidates a more substantial role in national politics. The envisioned legislature would have the power to approve the government's proposed budget, draft legislation and pass it with a two-thirds majority (although the emir's approval would be required for a bill to become law), and scrutinize cabinet ministers through questioning and confidence votes.[60] The first elections for the new council were repeatedly postponed, however, after the constitution took effect, and they have not taken place to date. In the meantime, Qatari women have prepared for the promised elections by attending training courses organized by the Elections Committee and monitoring elections in neighboring countries.

As with the few available elective positions, women are not adequately represented in appointive government offices, although their numbers have increased in recent years. As previously mentioned (see "Nondiscrimination and Access to Justice"), the emir, who appoints judges, has chosen no females for the positions. However, women now head the Ministry of Health and the Ministry of Education and have been appointed as president of the Supreme Council for Information and Communication Technology, president of Qatar University, manager of NOCHT, president of the Elections Committee, executive director of the Family Consultation Center, and executive director of the Social Development Center. Despite these advances, women fail to hold positions of power such as ambassadorships or as police commissioners, or any positions within the security systems and planning fields. On the other hand, women dominate leadership positions in education.

Political parties are banned in Qatar, meaning the country's limited political and electoral activity is generally based on family and local ties. While the constitution does guarantee freedom of association within the confines of the law, the relevant legislation imposes a number of bureaucratic obstacles to the formation and operation of civil society groups. Licensed groups are barred from straying beyond their approved missions and into politics or other sensitive areas.[61] Government-affiliated organizations like the NHRC, however, have advocated improvements in women's rights, including political and associational rights.

The constitution guarantees the right of assembly "in accordance with the provisions of the law" under Article 44, but this right is severely restricted for both men and women.[62] The few demonstrations that have been allowed in recent years are typically aimed at supporting foreign policy positions favored by the government. For instance, an officially sanctioned rally in March 2007 expressed support for Iraqi unity and the Palestinian cause.[63]

Similarly, the constitutionally guaranteed freedoms of expression and the press are curtailed rather than protected by the law.[64] The country's only broadcasters—Qatar TV, the satellite television station Al-Jazeera, and the Qatar Broadcasting Service radio network—are either run by or financially dependent upon the state. Al-Jazeera's international programming has highlighted women's issues on occasion, however, and local newspapers have highlighted the plight of women evicted from their homes for failure to pay rent.

While the media environment on the whole is restrictive, women have increased their participation as professionals in the press and broadcast media in recent years. Female writers work in various fields, in many cases displaying courage in the issues they discuss. Some women, such as Miriam al-Saad, have gained significant recognition through their writing.

Women's participation in civic affairs is further limited by social conventions that hold certain fields to be unfit for female involvement. It is acceptable for women to engage in charitable activities, for example, but it is not as readily accepted for women to take on political or leadership roles. Nevertheless, in the past three years, women have started to break into more public activities within the small civil society sector, expanding beyond charitable and humanitarian fields.

In a 2007 study that investigated political attitudes, 55 percent of the survey sample supported women's political participation.[65] However, when the respondents were asked whether they would elect a male or female candidate, approximately 62 percent said they would choose the male. Interestingly, this figure was the same for both male and female respondents. Although the existing laws and government policies officially aim to raise the status of Qatari women and increase their involvement in political life to some extent, the social and cultural structure is unlikely to change radically in the near term.

Recommendations

❖ The legislative body envisaged by Article 77 of the constitution should be fully realized.

❖ In keeping with the current positive trend, women should be progressively appointed to leadership roles within diverse areas of the government and should be given positions of power at a rate on par with their proportion of the citizen population.

❖ Female candidates for municipal elections should receive training on how to effectively communicate their message and campaign for public office.

❖ Existing laws on peaceful assembly should be reformed to meet international standards, and demonstration permit denials should be subject to appeal in the courts, thereby permitting all legal protesters, including women, to fully realize their right to assembly.

❖ Annual conventions should be held for high-school girls that show distinct leadership qualities that provide them with the opportunity meet with female politicians, activists, and government officials from the region. Speakers should discuss obstacles that they faced as women and offer the girls advice on how to avoid or address such obstacles.

SOCIAL AND CULTURAL RIGHTS

As the Qatari government takes a mostly hands-off approach in addressing women's social and cultural issues, tradition and custom continue to control the extent of women's activities at home and in the community. The government, however, has taken some measures to improve the lives of divorced and widowed Qatari women who lack families that can provide them with support by providing housing programs. In recent years activism on behalf of women has been directed from government leaders, and few grassroots organizations have been established to help address the concerns or interests of citizen and noncitizen women alike.

Family dominates the social lives of Qatari men and women. Little meaningful social, economic, or political life takes place outside the family. In the home, women organize the daily routine and holiday family gatherings and play a central role in arranging marriages. While women are able to participate in all matters related to the family (marriage, children's education, health care, housing), tradition holds that men have the final word regarding many key decisions, particularly with regard to finances. Public life is customarily segregated by gender; many public places have separate times or spaces for men and for "families" (women and children). Although they are not compulsory, most women wear the hair-covering *hijab* and the black cloak-like *abaya* in public.

Qatar nationals have free access to a government-supported health care system while noncitizens must generally pay for services. The labor law stipulates that employers must provide health care for their workers and improves care for expatriates, although these relatively new regulations are not often carried out in practice.[66] Qatar's health care system covers a range of health issues, including mental, dental, and complete maternity care programs.[67] Women have significant freedom to make independent decisions about their health, and the vast majority of women receive professional pre- and postnatal care.

Women's reproductive rights are rarely discussed in public, although birth control is widely available; issues such as rape and non-marital sex are seldom addressed. Based on laws passed in 1971 and 1983, abortion is permitted in the first trimester if a physician determines that the pregnancy would cause harm to the mother's health or if the fetus has a serious, incurable physical or mental defect. Both husband and wife must consent to the abortion, and it must be carried out in a government hospital. Qatari society traditionally values large families, and women are typically pressured by their families to have children. Abortions are not legal in cases of rape or incest.[68]

While it is not formally prohibited, few Qatari women or men live alone. Young women are likely to face opposition from their families and possibly male harassment if they try to live on their own. The man is considered the head of household in Qatar and is therefore responsible for providing housing for his wife and the family. In 2007 the government passed a new law expanding opportunities for Qatari and non-Qatari women to take advantage of government housing programs. Qatari women married to foreign nationals are eligible for government housing, as are widows and divorced women with children who did not inherit homes from their husbands. Unmarried women over 35 who support members of their family are also eligible for state housing assistance.

Women work in both print and broadcast media in Qatar, employed as journalists, reporters, broadcasters, and producers, but their numbers in the field are modest. Among the obstacles to women's participation in the media are the social customs that restrict women's work to a narrow field of careers. The media tend to portray women in stereotypical roles and rarely cover the problems of and restrictions on women's lives.

Although little research has been conducted on the problem of poverty in Qatar, local observers note that small numbers of Qatari nationals struggle to make ends meet. Widows, divorced women, and deserted wives make up a significant proportion of the ranks of the Qatari poor.[69] Information on the economic, social, and cultural problems of non-Qatari women is scarce, partly due to the lack of independent groups to investigate these issues.

While the government has undertaken important steps toward improving the lives of women in recent years, the future of these reforms continues to remain uncertain. The reforms that have provided women with important rights have come about not through democratic mechanisms but through decrees from the top, with many reforms the result of the activism of Her Highness Sheikha Moza. For progressive reforms such as these to endure beyond the current heads of state, they must be institutionalized through democratic means. Moreover, in a society where cultural norms are the source of most restrictions on women's lives, and where laws are often unknown to people and inconsistently enforced, legal reforms alone will be of limited consequence.

Recommendations

* The government should implement improvements to and ensure enforcement of health insurance and health care for non-Qatari women.
* The government should allow and encourage the creation and institutionalization of nongovernmental organizations serving women and addressing women's concerns.
* The media should examine the impact of increased economic participation on women's role in society and consistently report on violations of women's rights, paying particular attention to the plight of impoverished women.
* Foreign embassies should make efforts to provide basic computer literacy courses to their citizens residing in Qatar and offer online and printed materials that inform these individuals about their employment, housing, and health care rights and the means by which to invoke them in the Qatari legal system.

AUTHORS

Julia Breslin is a human rights lawyer, having earned her law degree from Florida State University and her LL.M. in human rights law from Lund University, Sweden. She is a research and editorial associate at Freedom House, authored the Iran chapter of Freedom House's 2009 *Freedom in the World,* and is a contributing author to the Max Planck Institute's Encyclopedia of Public International Law.

Toby Jones is an assistant professor of history at Rutgers University, with a research interest in the Middle East. He earned his PhD from Stanford University and his M.A. and B.A. from Auburn University. In 2003, he was awarded a Fulbright-Hays scholarship to conduct research in Saudi Arabia, Bahrain, and Jordan. He is also the author of the Gulf country reports for Freedom House's 2009 *Freedom in the World.*

NOTES

1   *Annual Report on the Situation of Human Rights in Qatar* (Qatar: State of Qatar, National Human Rights Committee [NHRC], 2006), 11, http://www.nhrc-qa.org/en/files/downloads/NHRC-AnnualReport-2006.pdf.

2   "Judicial Foundation and Legal Codification," in *Democratic Governance —Qatar* (New York and Beirut: United Nations Development Programme [UNDP] and Programme on Governance in the Arab Region [POGAR]), http://www.pogar.org/countries/theme.asp?th=9&cid=15.

3   Mohammed Saeed, "Men's Verdict: No Women Judges," *The Peninsula* (Qatar), January 1, 2008, http://www.thepeninsulaqatar.com/Display_news.asp?section=local_news&month=january2008&file=local_news2008010822652.xml.

4   "Woman in Qatar Gets the Right to Be Lawyer for the First Time," ArabicNews.com, February 17, 2000, http://www.arabicnews.com/ansub/Daily/Day/000217/2000021706.html.

5   Sigma Huda, Special Rapporteur on Trafficking of Persons Report to the UN Human Rights Council, *Mission to Bahrain, Oman and Qatar* (New York: United Nations, Human Rights Council, UN Doc A/HRC/4/23/Add.2, April 2007), 13.

6   *Country Reports on Human Rights Practices—2007—Qatar* (Washington, DC: U.S. Dept. of State, March 11, 2008), http://www.state.gov/g/drl/rls/hrrpt/2007/100604.htm.

7   Nour Abuzant, "Sentence of Teen Who Killed Sister Is Commuted," *Gulf Times* (Doha), January 15, 2007, http://www.gulftimes.com/site/topics/article.asp?cu_no=2&item_no=127490&version=1&template_id=36&parent_id=16; see also *Country Reports on Human Rights Practices—2007—Qatar* (U.S. Dept. of State, March 11, 2008).

8   "Prison Brief for Qatar" in *World Prison Brief* (London: King's College London, International Centre for Prison Studies, 2008), http://www.kcl.ac.uk/depsta/law/research/icps/worldbrief/wpb_country.php?country=182.

9   United Nations Office of the High Commission for Human Rights, "Status of Ratification, Reservations, and Declarations: Convention on the Elimination of Discrimination against Women, Qatar," http://treaties.un.org/Pages/ViewDetails.aspx?src=TREATY&mtdsg_no=IV-8&chapter=4&lang=en#EndDec.

10 Sigma Huda, *Mission to Bahrain, Oman and Qatar*, 7, fn. 5.

11 *Annual Report on Human Rights & the Activities of the Committee* (NHRC, 2005), 38, http://www.nhrc-qa.org/en/files/downloads/NHRC%20Annual%20Report%20-%202005.pdf.

12 Associations and Private Institutions Law (No. 12 of 2004), chapter 4, "The Finances of the Association and Supervision of Its Activities" and chapter 5, "Dissolution of the Association" (Washington, DC: International Center for Not-for-Profit Law, 2005), http://www.icnl.org/knowledge/library/searchResults.php?s=800&np=53&txtSearch=&subCategory=&sort=countrydesc (password protected).

[13] For a non-exhaustive list of NGOs, see *Directory of Nongovernmental Organizations* at Explore Qatar, http://www.explore-qatar.com/directory/Society-and-Culture/52/Non-Governmental-Organizations/.

[14] Law No. 8 of 2006; *The Situation of Human Rights in Qatar* (NHRC, 2006), 38.

[15] *Qatar Foundation for Child and Women Protection* (Qatar Government Online, Ministries and Authorities), http://www.gov.qa/wps/portal/!ut/p/c0/04_SB8K8xLLM9M SSzPy8xBz9CP0os3gjAwsDA39311CvIENXAyMfC18_S39jQwMDA_2CbEdFAN 2NVzg!/?WCM_PORTLET=PC_7_20800OGEUJR1E02L8MN9O31003_WCM &WCM_GLOBAL_CONTEXT=/wps/wcm/connect/cnt/en/1_home/14_mini stries_and_authorities/qfcwp_en/qfcwp_min.

[16] It is unclear why annual reports are no longer issued, although the work of the NHRC continues. Existing reports available at: *Human Rights* (NHRC, 2005), 38; *The Situation of Human Rights in Qatar* (NHRC, 2006), 11.

[17] For a list of charitable associations see Qatar Authority for Charitable Activities, http://www.qaca.gov.qa/English/Association/Pages/default.aspx.

[18] Zahra Hassan, "Hitting Home," *The Peninsula*, November 26, 2007, http://www.thepeninsulaqatar.com/Display_news.asp?section=Local_News&subsection=Qatar +News&month=November2007&file=Local_News200711262446.xml.

[19] "Qatar," *Country Profiles* (Beirut: United Nations Economic and Social Commission for Western Asia [ESCWA], 2002), http://www.escwa.un.org/index.asp.

[20] *The Situation of Human Rights in Qatar* (NHRC, 2006), 12.

[21] *Country Reports on Human Rights Practices—2007—Qatar* (U.S. Dept. of State, March 11, 2008).

[22] *The Situation of Human Rights in Qatar* (NHRC, 2006), 32.

[23] *The Situation of Human Rights in Qatar* (NHRC, 2006), 13–14.

[24] *Country Reports on Human Rights Practices—2007—Qatar* (U.S. Dept. of State, March 11, 2008).

[25] Amnesty International, "Qatar: Further Information on Fear for Safety: Hamda Fahad Jassem al-Thani," October 20, 2007, http://www.amnesty.org/en/library/asset/ MDE22/003/2006/en/ccca433d-d3e2-11dd-8743-d305bea2b2c7/mde220032006en .html.

[26] "Divorce Rate High in Qatar," *The Peninsula*, December 6, 2008, http://thepeninsula qatar.com/Display_news.asp?section=Local_News&month=December2008&file =Local_News200812064135.xml.

[27] *Vital Statistics Annual Bulletin* (Marriages and Divorces 2007) (Qatar: Qatar Statistic Authority, 2008), Table 21, http://www.qsa.gov.qa/Eng/publication/other_ publications/marriage_divorce/Marriages_divorces2007.pdf.

[28] *The Situation of Human Rights in Qatar* (NHRC, 2006), 33–35.

[29] "Trafficking in Persons Report" (Washington, DC: U.S. Dept. of State, June 4, 2008).

[30] *The Situation of Human Rights in Qatar* (NHRC, 2006), 28. There are more than 500,000 foreign workers in Qatar, around 70 percent of the total population.

[31] Sigma Huda, *Mission to Bahrain, Oman and Qatar*, 13–14.

[32] Sigma Huda, *Mission to Bahrain, Oman and Qatar*, 16.

33   Sigma Huda, *Mission to Bahrain, Oman and Qatar*, 18.

34   "Reply by the State of Qatar to the Questionnaire to Governments on Implementation of the Beijing Platform for Action (1995) and the Outcome of the Twenty-third Session of the General Assembly (2000)" (Supreme Council for Family Affairs, 2004), 16, http://www.un.org/womenwatch/daw/Review/responses/QATAR-English.pdf; see also "The Qatari Foundation for the Protection of Women and Children" (SCFA, 2005), http://www.scfa.gov.qa/foundation_women_children.asp.

35   "Report to U.N. Committee Against Torture" (Geneva: UN, Committee Against Torture, May 1–19, 2006).

36   *Country Reports on Human Rights Practices—2007—Qatar* (U.S. Dept. of State, March 11, 2008).

37   "Focus on Violence Against Women," *The Peninsula*, November 20, 2008, http://www.thepeninsulaqatar.com/Display_news.asp?section=local_news&month=november2008&file=local_news2008112051314.xml.

38   "Focus on Violence Against Women," *The Peninsula*, November 20, 2008.

39   "Reply . . . to the Questionnaire to Governments . . ." (SCFA, 2004), 16; see also "The Qatari Foundation for the Protection of Women and Children" (SCFA, 2005).

40   "Focus on Violence Against Women," *The Peninsula*, November 20, 2008.

41   Custom table: "Qatar, literacy, 2005–2007" (Montreal: UNESCO Institute for Statistics), http://www.uis.unesco.org [accessed December 15, 2009]. As of 2007, the female youth (15 to 24) literacy rate was 99 percent and the adult literacy rate was 90.4 percent. The male youth literacy rate was 99.1 and the adult literacy rate was 93.8.

42   Custom table: "Qatar, Education, 2007," (Montreal: UNESCO Institute for Statistics) http://www.uis.unesco.org [accessed December 15, 2009].

43   *Qatar's Labour Force: Trends and Patterns* (Qatar: Qatar Planning Council, General Secretariat for Development Planning, September 2008), 1, http://www.gsdp.gov.qa/portal/page/portal/GSDP_Vision_Root/GSDP_EN/GSDP_News/GSDP%20News%20Files/SHD-QLF.pdf. Only 30.6 percent of male citizen laborers and 25.1 percent of male noncitizen laborers held degrees.

44   Statistics and Indicators on Women and Men (United Nations Statistics Division 2006) http://unstats.un.org/unsd/demographic/products/indwm/tab5a.htm.

45   World Bank, "GenderStats—Labor Force" (Washington, DC: World Bank), http://go.worldbank.org/4PIIORQMS0 [accessed December 15, 2009]. Working-age persons include those ages 15 to 64.

46   Dell Felder and Mirka Vuollo, *Qatari Women in the Workforce* (Santa Monica, CA: Rand-Qatar Policy Institute, August 2008), 15, http://www.rand.org/pubs/working_papers/2008/RAND_WR612.pdf.

47   *Qatar's Labor Force: Trends and Patterns* (Qatar: General Secretariat for Development Planning, Social Affairs Department, Social and Human Development Profile No. 1, September 12, 2008), 4, http://www.gsdp.gov.qa/portal/page/portal/GSDP_Vision_Root/GSDP_EN/GSDP_News/GSDP%20News%20Files/SHD-QLF.pdf.

48   Felder and Vuollo, *Qatari Women in the Workforce* (Rand-Qatari Policy Institute), 15.

49   *Qatar's Labor Force* (General Secretariat for Development Planning), 6.

50   Cathleen Stasz, Eric Eide, and Francisco Martorell, *Post-Secondary Education in Qatar:*

Employer Demands, Student Choice, and Options for Policy (Rand-Qatar Policy Institute 2007), 21, http://www.rand.org/pubs/monographs/2007/RAND_MG644.pdf.

51 Felder and Vuollo, *Qatari Women in the Workforce* (Rand-Qatar Policy Institute), 16.

52 *Human Development Report 2007* (Qatar: The State of Qatar Planning Council), 20, http://www.planning.gov.qa/PDF_Files/Human_development_Report_2007/Human _development_Report_2007.pdf.

53 Felder and Vuollo, *Qatari Women in the Workforce* (Rand-Qatari Policy Institute), 11 (citing Ibtehaj al-Ahmadi, 2005, Board Member of the Qatar Chamber of Commerce).

54 *Country Reports on Human Rights Practices—2006—Qatar* (Washington, DC: U.S. Department of State, March 6, 2007), http://www.state.gov/g/drl/rls/hrrpt/2006/ 78861.htm.

55 *Human Rights* (NHRC, 2005), 50; *The Situation of Human Rights in Qatar* (NHRC, 2006), 28.

56 "Qatari Women" (Washington, DC: The Embassy of Qatar, 2005), http://www.qatar embassy.net/women.asp.

57 "Qatari Women" (The Embassy of Qatar, 2005).

58 "Woman Candidate Creates History in Polls . . . Once Again," *Gulf Times*, April 2, 2007, http://www.gulf-times.com/site/topics/article.asp?cu_no=2&item_no=141515 &version=1&template_id=36&parent_id=16.

59 "Municipal Elections," *Arab Reform Bulletin*, April 2007, http://www.carnegieendow ment.org/arb/?fa=show&article=20977.

60 "Parliamentary Elections Announced," *Arab Reform Bulletin*, April 2006, http://www .carnegieendowment.org/arb/?fa=show&article=20934.

61 *The Situation of Human Rights in Qatar* (NHRC, 2006).

62 Constitution of the State of Qatar, Art. 44, http://english.mofa.gov.qa/details.cfm ?id=80.

63 "Qataris Join Rally for Palestinians, Iraqis," *Gulf Times*, March 29, 2007, http://www .gulf-times.com/site/topics/article.asp?cu_no=2&item_no=140830&version=1&tem plate_id=36&parent_id=16.

64 Constitution of the State of Qatar, Art. 47 (freedom of expression) and Art. 48 (free-dom of the press), http://english.mofa.gov.qa/details.cfm?id=80.

65 "Qatari Attitude Towards Political Participation—Constraints and Ways [of] Em-powerment" (Qatar: The State of Qatar, Standing Committee for the Elections, 2007).

66 *The Situation of Human Rights in Qatar* (NHRC, 2006), 25–27.

67 "Reply . . . to the Questionnaire to Governments . . ." SCFA, 2004).

68 *Abortion Policies: A Global Review* (New York: UN Population Division, Department of Economic and Social Affairs, 2002), http://www.un.org/esa/population/publications/ abortion/doc/qatar.doc.

69 *Situation of Human Rights in Qatar* (NHRC, 2006), 24.

SAUDI ARABIA

by Eleanor Abdella Doumato

| POPULATION: | 28,687,000 |
| GNI PER CAPITA: | US$15,339 |

COUNTRY RATINGS	2004	2009
NONDISCRIMINATION AND ACCESS TO JUSTICE:	1.2	1.4
AUTONOMY, SECURITY, AND FREEDOM OF THE PERSON:	1.1	1.3
ECONOMIC RIGHTS AND EQUAL OPPORTUNITY:	1.4	1.7
POLITICAL RIGHTS AND CIVIC VOICE:	1.0	1.2
SOCIAL AND CULTURAL RIGHTS:	1.6	1.6

(COUNTRY RATINGS ARE BASED ON A SCALE OF 1 TO 5, WITH 1 REPRESENTING THE LOWEST AND 5 THE HIGHEST LEVEL OF FREEDOM WOMEN HAVE TO EXERCISE THEIR RIGHTS)

INTRODUCTION

The Basic Law of the Kingdom of Saudi Arabia does not guarantee gender equality. To the contrary, gender inequality is built into Saudi Arabia's governmental and social structures, and is integral to the country's state-supported interpretation of Islam, which is derived from a literal reading of the Koran and Sunna.[1] In issuing religious opinions, state-funded *ulema* (religious scholars) generally avoid consideration of judicial precedent and evolving social contexts, so that their official posture resists pressure for change, especially when it comes to controlling women's behavior.

A healthy majority of Saudi citizens agree with the social agenda of the ulema, and would not view the inequalities between men and women as discrimination, but as equivalence—a balance between the rights and duties of men and women as prescribed in Islam and necessary to uphold honor and family values.[2] A vigorous progressive movement, however, is pushing to improve women's bargaining power in Islamic family law courts and to create parity with men in terms of civil rights, including the right to vote, drive, work, and obtain better access to health care and educational opportunities. Progressive spokespersons are hampered by the kingdom's limits on political activism and by opposition to legal reforms by religious leaders, but King Abdullah ibn Abd al-Aziz al-Saud has shown himself to be an ally in the liberal-feminist struggle, and positive changes are occurring.

For example, while women are still at a significant disadvantage when it comes to family law—men are allowed four wives, the right to divorce at will, and custody of children—yet-to-be-implemented court reforms call for specialized family courts staffed by judges educated in family welfare as well as in family law, and by women with law degrees who can act as advocates for women litigants. Due to an enforced separation between men and women in public, the opportunities for women's employment remain limited, with the vast majority of working women employed in the kingdom's single-sex education bureaucracy or in health care. At the same time, new opportunities have opened up in women-only manufacturing and shopping malls, the hospitality industry, and government commissions that cater to women's needs. Furthermore, some courses of study that were previously closed to women, such as engineering and law, are now available to them on the premise that work in these fields will become more widely available to women in the future. Higher education, in fact, is one area in which women have significantly out-performed men in terms of PhD degrees earned.

Women's lack of mobility remains a salient point of contention in the kingdom, as they still are not allowed to drive a car. They are not allowed to travel abroad by airplane without the express permission of a male guardian, and their right to travel internally without a guardian's permission is subject to the arbitrary approval of airport personnel. When it comes to civil rights, women were not permitted to vote in Saudi Arabia's first elections for municipal councils, yet a number of women put their names forward as candidates and expectations are high for women's inclusion in future elections. In addition, while a 2007 reform in Saudi citizenship laws allows non-national women who have been divorced by Saudi husbands to apply for Saudi citizenship, Saudi women nationals married to non-Saudi husbands remain unable to pass their citizenship on to their children or spouses. However, their sons, but not their daughters, may apply for citizenship at the age of 18.[3]

NONDISCRIMINATION AND ACCESS TO JUSTICE

The manner in which Islam is incorporated into the Saudi judicial system and governance has a profound impact on gender relations and access to justice for both men and women, with particularly discriminatory effects on women. In recent years, however, there have been improvements, or the promise of improvements, in women's access to courts and their rights as citizens.

Article 8 of the Basic Law requires that the government be premised on justice, consultation, and equality in accordance with Shari'a, or Islamic law. However, Shari'a in Saudi Arabia does not offer equality to women, particularly regarding family law. Instead, women are considered legal minors under the control of their *mahram* (closest male relative) and are subject to legal restrictions on their personal behavior that do not apply to men. The religious police, known as the Committee for the Promotion of Virtue and Prevention of Vice (*al-hay'at al-amr bil ma'ruf wa al-nahia 'an al-munkar*), are concerned with overseeing public moral behavior, including proper dress and the interaction between men and women.[4]

Saudi Arabia's laws and policies do not generally protect women from gender-based discrimination. Numerous enforcement authorities, including the regular, religious, and *mubahith* (secret police), have the power to accuse and detain suspects, and each may apply the laws of the country arbitrarily. Saudi Arabia has a hierarchical society that provides privileges to men over women and the elite over the common people. These biases are reflected in the kingdom's laws, in the latitude afforded to well-connected Saudi citizens by the judicial system, and in the differential treatment of workers based upon their country of origin.

In 2004 a royal decree affirmed the principle of equality between men and women in all matters relating to Saudi nationality,[5] but women remain unable to pass their Saudi citizenship automatically to their noncitizen spouses and children. However, amendments to the law in October 2005 allow non-Saudis, including foreign-born husbands of Saudi women, to apply for citizenship if they have lived in the kingdom for at least 10 years and have professional qualifications deemed desirable by the interior ministry. A new amendment in 2007 allows the sons of citizen mothers and noncitizen fathers to apply for Saudi citizenship once they reach age 18. Similarly situated daughters, however, may obtain citizenship only through marriage to a Saudi male citizen.

Additionally, Article 16 of the citizenship law was amended in 2007 to grant Saudi citizenship to noncitizen women married to or widowed by Saudi men on the condition that they relinquish any other citizenship.[6] An additional amendment grants the government the discretion to revoke a foreign-born woman's Saudi citizenship upon divorce if she has retained her original citizenship. These two amendments benefit women by letting them remain in the country to be near their children after being divorced or widowed, but they also limit their future options for residence in their home countries by requiring renunciation of their original citizenship.[7]

In 2002, women were allowed to apply for their own individual civil status (ID) card rather than, as in the past, having a legal identity only as a dependent on their guardian's identity card. The Executive Regulation for the Travel Documents Law states that at 15 years of age all persons must obtain a civil status card, with the approval of their guardian. In 2008, according to the Saudi National Society for Human Rights, women for the first time were allowed to receive their civil status cards without their guardian's permission.[8]

In practice, women in Saudi Arabia lack equal access to courts because they must rely on a male relative or lawyer to represent them. Many judges arbitrarily require that before a woman may represent herself in court, a guardian must be present to verify her identity and grant her permission to do so. Identification by a guardian is necessary because women's faces must be covered and judges do not accept the ID card as proof of a woman's identity. This is particularly detrimental in divorce and child custody cases in which the guardian is also likely to be the husband, who is also the woman's legal adversary. Women are at a further disadvantage in the courts in that the testimony of one man is taken to be equal to that of two women, and for the purpose of compensation for accidental death or injury, a woman's worth is calculated at half that of a man.

Access to justice for women, however, may soon improve. In 2004, a National Dialogue Conference on Women, initiated by then-Crown Prince Abdullah, recommended that women be allowed to sit as judges in family court and that family law be standardized so that decisions are not left to the arbitrary opinions of individual male judges.[9] That conference has sparked change in the judicial system, and as of 2007, three Saudi Arabian educational institutions now permit women to study law. While women are currently not allowed to be judges or act as lawyers on behalf of clients in court, the Ministry of Justice announced in 2007 that it will allow women to act as legal consultants to other women.[10] The justice minister, Dr. Abdullah bin Muhammad al-Ash-Shaikh, declared in March 2008 that courts would soon have reception centers for women staffed by female law graduates.[11]

Saudi Arabia lacks a written penal code. Men and women are subject to arbitrary arrest and detention, and convicted persons are punished in accordance with Shari'a as interpreted by individual judges. In the absence of a written penal code, judges may determine punishments arbitrarily for crimes both real and imaginary, a practice to which non-Saudis and marginal persons are particularly vulnerable. For example, in 2007 an Egyptian man named Mustafa Ibrahim was executed for sorcery in Riyadh, and in April 2006 a Jordanian woman named Fawza Falih was sentenced to death for witchcraft.[12] Sorcery, witchcraft, magic tricks, and wearing amulets are forbidden practices that are discussed in Saudi public school textbooks, and are punishable crimes under Islamic law as interpreted by Saudi ulema.

One crime for which women are especially targeted is *khulwa* (the illegal mixing of unrelated men and women), which can occur whether men and women are dining together in a restaurant, riding in a taxi, or meeting for business. In February 2008, a 37-year-old American businesswoman and mother of three was arrested by the Riyadh religious police for sitting at a table in public with a male colleague, who was also arrested. The police took her to Malaz prison, where she was strip-searched and forced to remove her clothes, which were wiped over the floor of a wet, filthy bathroom. She was then told to put her clothes back on and taken before a judge, who berated her for her behavior, telling her that filthy clothes were appropriate for the filthy person that she was. After signing a confession, she was released to the custody of her husband.[13] Additionally, in March 2009 a 75-year-old Syrian woman was convicted of khulwa and sentenced to 40 lashings, four months in jail, and deportation after the religious police found her alone with two young men—reportedly her nephew and his friend bringing her loaves of bread.[14]

The religious police are notorious for their abuses. When two people died in their custody in 2007, instead of punishing the individuals responsible, the Committee on Vice and Virtue created a Department of Rules and Regulations for future guidance of religious policemen. Meanwhile, in response to these deaths, the Ministry of the Interior issued a decree requiring that the committee surrender detained persons promptly to the regular police and to have no involvement with them from that point forward.[15] This decree has not been enforced, however, and detainees continue to be abused at the hands of the religious police. The extent to which the religious police are insulated from governmental oversight is illustrated by an event that occurred in 2002, when members of the religious police refused to allow fleeing schoolgirls out of a burning building without their *abayas* (the cloak worn over clothing), and 15 girls subsequently died. Despite local and international protests, no one from the religious police force was punished.

Saudi Arabia ratified the UN Convention on the Elimination of All Forms of Discrimination against Women (CEDAW) in 2000, with reservations stating that the kingdom is under no obligation to observe terms of the treaty that contradict Islamic law. One such contradiction, noted by the CEDAW Committee that reviewed Saudi Arabia's compliance with the treaty, involves the provision for equal citizenship rights between men and women, which goes against the presumed Shari'a requirement permitting citizenship to be passed to children exclusively through fathers.[16] The committee's 2008 report was critical of Saudi Arabia's compliance with the convention and called for Saudi Arabia "to enact a gender equality law." Dr. Musfir al-Qahtani, deputy chairman of the Saudi National Society for Human Rights, responded by saying that laws related to marriage, inheritance, and women's testimony—examples cited by the committee as discriminatory—are fixed by religious law, and are, by implication, non-negotiable.[17]

Recommendations

❖ The government should review all laws and policies and amend the Basic Law to ensure gender equality and to explicitly prohibit discrimination.

❖ The government should implement the court reforms that were approved by King Abdullah in 2004 by creating separate family courts, codifying family law, and allowing women to act as lawyers and judges in family courts.

❖ The private sector should partner with universities to create legal internship programs in order to encourage more women to enter the profession and to provide them with practical training.

❖ Women should be allowed to represent themselves in court without a male guardian and as citizens with full rights.

❖ Women should be awarded equal citizenship rights as men and be able to pass citizenship to their spouses and children.

❖ The Interior Ministry should enforce its decree preventing the Committee for the Promotion of Virtue and Prevention of Vice from detaining apprehended individuals, including women.

AUTONOMY, SECURITY, AND FREEDOM OF THE PERSON

Autonomy, security, and freedom of the person are areas much in need of improvement for all Saudi residents, especially for women, and most especially for foreign women who come to the kingdom as domestic workers. Whether the issue is religious freedom, freedom to choose one's marriage partner, lack of access to public accommodations, lack of freedom of movement, or gender-based violence, a rising public awareness has yet to produce legal protections.

Freedom of religion is highly restricted in Saudi Arabia for both men and women. Saudi public schools, religious spokespersons, and media present Islam as one monolithic faith to which all citizens must adhere. All variant Muslim schools of thought, ritual practices, and sectarian differences are ignored or openly disparaged and considered illicit, while in the textbooks of public schools Shiite and Sufi practices are singled out as signals of apostasy. The public practice or preaching of religions other than Islam is forbidden and subject to punishment, and Saudi citizens who disagree with the official version of Islam lack a safe way to express their dissent or advocate for alternative interpretations. Despite the pivotal role of women historically in the foundations of Islam, women are excluded from leadership positions within the country's religious institutions and are encouraged to pray at home even though prayer, as described in Saudi school books and standard prayer manuals, is considered best when performed in congregation in the mosque.

Freedom of movement for women in Saudi Arabia is limited by overlapping legal constraints and social controls, and as a result women may not drive cars, travel on airplanes, work, or be outside their own home without a guardian's permission.[18] In 2007 and 2008, renewed pressure mounted to allow women to drive, and an ad hoc Committee for Women's Right to Drive organized a petition addressed to the king.[19] In January 2008, days after Saudi Arabia faced criticism by the CEDAW committee for restricting "virtually every aspect of a woman's life,"[20] the government announced that a royal decree allowing women to drive would be issued "at the end of the year."[21] In March, the Consultative Council recommended that women be allowed to drive during the daylight hours of weekdays if they get permission from their guardians, undergo drivers' education, wear modest dress, and carry a cell phone. To allay concerns about women's safety, the council added the imposition of a sentence and a fine on any male in another car talking to or sexually harassing a female driver.[22]

As of October 2009 these goals had not been implemented, but government approval for the idea of women's driving is a milestone for the kingdom. Only three years earlier, Consultative Council members threatened to expel another member for merely suggesting that the council discuss the same issue. A regulatory change that offers promise for future driving rights for women occurred in the fall of 2009, with the opening of the new King Abdullah University for Science and Technology, an institution designed to be coeducational where women are to be allowed to drive within the campus grounds.

At the end of 2007, the long-standing bans on women checking into hotels alone and renting apartments for themselves were lifted by royal decree, and a women-only hotel opened in 2008 in Riyadh.[23] Despite these improvements, limitations continue on women's freedom of movement. Women are prohibited from most ministry buildings and discouraged from walking along public streets or attending mosques except at pilgrimage. Where separate accommodations are available to both men and women, such as hospital waiting areas, dining areas in restaurants, government office buildings, and prayer rooms in public facilities, the men's accommodations are always of a quality superior to those of women. The public spaces in Saudi Arabia that are intended for the enjoyment of the general public, such as parks, zoos, libraries, museums, and the national Jinadriyah Festival of Folklore and Culture, are also segregated by hours of access, with men allocated the greater number and most convenient time slots.

Foreign women, especially those from developing countries, are particularly affected by restrictions to their freedom of movement. Saudi employers routinely take their employees' passports on arrival, thereby preventing foreign female workers from traveling outside their town of residence or leaving the country of their own volition. Some employers use the requirement of a guardian to justify locking women employees in at night. Prohibited from driving themselves, unable to afford private taxis or cars, and faced with a lack of accessible public transportation, working women are often forced to walk on the streets, where they may be apprehended by the religious police on accusations of soliciting sex.

The personal status laws of Saudi Arabia are determined by the Shari'a and favor men in matters of marriage, divorce, child custody, and inheritance. A marriage contract is executed by the prospective husband and the guardian of the intended bride. Today, it is a simple form that asks for the amount of the *mahr* (dowry) and permits stipulations to be made by the contracting parties, such as the prospective husband's pledge to grant his wife a divorce if he should take a second wife. The contract requires the intended bride to specify whether she is a virgin, widow, or divorcee but does not require the same information of the man. The formal contract excludes the bride as a signatory and is merely the legal confirmation of decisions taken jointly by two families or, increasingly, by the prospective husband and wife.

The degree to which a woman participates in decisions regarding her own marriage depends on her family's predilections and her own professional or social situation and age. In May 2009, an eight-year-old girl made headlines by securing a divorce from her 50-year-old husband, a marriage brokered by her father to settle old debts.[24] The incident sparked a public debate regarding whether to establish a minimum age for marriage.[25]

Technology, however, has opened new avenues for single Saudis searching for suitable marriage partners. Two satellite television channels that broadcast in Arabic are devoted entirely to marriage advertisements. There are no photographs, but Saudi men and women describe their physical characteristics, what they are looking for in a spouse, their ages, their professions, and their finances. These singles appear to be searching for partners who are outside the circle of family alliances within which marriages are traditionally arranged.[26]

Saudi women are marrying foreign men on a rapidly increasing basis, with approximately 20,000 such marriages carried out in the past five years. Both men and women must obtain permission from the Interior Ministry to marry a non-national under Article 6 of the Saudi intermarriage bylaw. The ministry requires proof that the intended spouse is Muslim and has an "acceptable character, nationality, and religion."[27] Men's applications on behalf of foreign-born wives are routinely accepted without undue delay, while the intended spouses of Saudi women must provide the ministry with medical records, a passport, a formal petition for marriage, and other supporting documents. Even then, a positive response is not guaranteed and is often based on the woman applicant's age and her perceived ability or inability to find a Saudi husband.[28]

A Saudi woman may initiate and obtain a divorce if her husband had granted her the right to divorce at the time of signing the marriage contract, although there is a likelihood that stipulations in marriage contracts deemed contrary to Shari'a will be invalidated by judges when presented for enforcement before the courts. Otherwise, a woman may petition for divorce in a court if she can show that her husband has deserted her, is impotent, or has a loathsome disease, which is humiliating and a logistically difficult claim to present before a court of male judges. Alternatively, she may also buy her way out of her marriage by forgoing her maintenance rights and mahr, a practice known as *khula*. By contrast, a Saudi husband is entitled to a divorce without explanation simply by registering his intent to divorce with a court and repeating his intent three times. A man is obligated to provide maintenance for his wife for a period after divorce, but a gap exists between legal obligation and its enforcement.

In some sectors of Saudi society, the family group retains a legal interest in individual marriages, even consummated marriages of long standing, and a legal guardian may initiate divorce proceedings on behalf of a woman without her approval. In 2005, a 34-year-old woman named Fatima Azzaz was legally divorced from her husband, Mansour al-Timani, after her half-brothers claimed that al-Timani had misrepresented his tribal affiliation when he asked his wife's now-deceased father for her hand. The brothers successfully argued that al-Timani's lineage was beneath that of their own family and the marriage was detrimental to their family's reputation. Azzaz refused to return to the home of her half-brothers, where she had previously experienced physical violence, but could not remain with her husband because of the divorce. In desire of a safe place to live, she and her children were held in a detention center administered by the Ministry of Social Affairs. In 2007 the divorce decision was upheld by a Riyadh Court of Appeals.[29]

Women rarely receive custody of their children upon divorce, although the age at which a child is surrendered to his father in Saudi Arabia is seven if a boy, but not until puberty if a girl. For some Saudi women, family connections may be sufficient to influence court negotiations or the husband's decision regarding his claim for custody, and some judges may grant custody to the mother if a father is found unfit. In the absence of codified law, however, decisions regarding custody are left to judges who lack training in social and family welfare. Cases exist in which patently unfit fathers have been awarded custody or judges recognize paternal grandparents' claim to the child over the mother's.

A royal decree in 2007 announced a comprehensive overhaul of the judicial system. The system is currently comprised mainly of religious courts headed by judges with wide discretion to issue rulings according to their own interpretation of Shari'a. Proposed changes establish a supreme court that will, among other tasks, take over the functions of the high judicial council, which currently is composed of ulema, to review capital sentences and oversee the implementation of Shari'a and royal decrees. Under the new system, disputes related to divorce and other personal status issues are to be adjudicated in specialized personal status courts,[30] one of the recommendations from the 2004 National Dialogue Conference on Women.[31] Another positive initiative, which is receiving some government support, is a web-based grassroots movement (www.saudidivorce.org) whose purpose is to effect change in divorce laws.

Slavery in Saudi Arabia was outlawed in 1962, but, like all the other countries in the Gulf Cooperation Council, the kingdom continues to be a known destination for persons trafficked for the purpose of involuntary servitude. The U.S. State Department's 2008 *Trafficking in Persons Report* indicates that Saudi Arabia has not taken corrective measures to end the practice. Some people who are voluntarily recruited as domestic workers continue to be routinely forced by their employers to remain in the country as unpaid workers.[32] In its report on compliance with specific articles of CEDAW, Saudi Arabia denied that such practices exist to any significant degree.[33] Yet particularly vulnerable to this form of abuse are women from developing countries. Although there are approximately 1.5 million domestic workers in Saudi Arabia, they are specifically excluded from the protections afforded to foreign workers in the current Saudi labor law.[34] In July 2009, a bill was passed by the Consultative Council that would, if accepted by the cabinet and the king, require employers to provide domestic workers with adequate rest and accommodations and would limit their workday to nine hours.[35]

Domestic workers rarely complain to police about sexual exploitation or other abuses at the hands of their employers for fear they may face criminal charges for making false allegations. For instance, Nour Miyati, an Indonesian domestic worker, claimed that she was forced to work long hours without rest or pay and was beaten daily by her employers, resulting in a lost tooth and damaged eye. When she tried to escape, she was locked up and denied adequate food. At the time of her first hospitalization in 2005, she was suffering from malnutrition and gangrene that required the amputation of her toes and fingers. Despite the severity of her injuries, Miyati was convicted of making false accusations against her employers and sentenced to 79 lashes, although the ruling was overturned in April 2006.[36] Meanwhile her employers were exonerated from any wrongdoing after a Riyadh appeals court reversed the guilty verdict of a lower court in 2008.

A new level of awareness may be emerging in Saudi Arabia regarding the mistreatment of domestic workers. In May 2008, an employer was forced to pay seven months' back wages and a return flight to an Indian female domestic worker who had been physically abused. In this instance, the Indian Embassy and the local Indian community supported the domestic worker after she came forward with accusations, and the police took her to the hospital so that her injuries could be treated.[37]

There are no reports of female Saudi citizens living in involuntary servitude. Within the framework of marriage and family, however, women can be trapped in similar conditions due to poverty, illiteracy, physical isolation, or dependence upon their guardian. The potential for entrapment is exacerbated by the idea that a woman must always be obedient to her husband, an Islamic legal principle taken literally by the Saudis and culturally reinforced for girls in the national religious curriculum.[38]

Domestic violence became the subject of public discussion in 2004 when a well-known television personality broke a Saudi taboo by allowing photos of her battered face to be published after she had been savagely beaten by her husband. Open and honest public discussions regarding domestic violence are made difficult by Saudi political culture, which promotes the Muslim family as "the fundamental building block of society" that allocates rights and duties to each family member according to age and sex.

The privacy of women, which involves their anonymity and chastity, is fused with ideals of family "honor," so society cannot talk about the reality of domestic violence without challenging public myths about themselves. Women in particular cannot talk about their personal situation without damaging their family's honor and their own reputation. Guardianship laws make it very difficult for battered wives to find a safe haven, there are few government support services and shelters for victims of domestic violence, and women die because police are not willing to intervene in domestic situations. In one case, when one of five daughters being sexually molested by their father sought police protection, she was turned away and told to bring her father in to file the complaint.[39]

Women have no legal protections against gender-based violence outside the home. Women who report sexual abuse or rape are unlikely to find sympathetic judicial authorities, and instead of receiving protection, they are often accused of having had illicit sex. In rape cases, the burden of proof lies with the victim, and the offense may only be proven through the perpetrator's confession or the testimony of four witnesses.

The presumption on the part of police, judicial authorities, and society in general is that if something untoward happens to a woman, it happened because she asked for it. In October 2006, a young woman from Qatif was sentenced to 90 lashes for khulwa after being kidnapped and gang-raped. Allegedly, the woman had met in a car with a former male acquaintance to retrieve a photo that she had given him before she was married, at which point they were both abducted and raped by a group of seven men. The rapists as well as the victims were all found guilty and punished. Only after the woman received her sentence of 90 lashes did she learn that she had been indicted, and she was never directly presented with charges.

When she appealed the case, the conviction was upheld and the sentence increased to six months in prison and 200 lashes. In November 2007, the Ministry of Justice issued a statement explaining that the woman was being punished because she was a married woman who admitted to having an illegal affair and to meeting with the other victim alone, both of which are religiously prohibited crimes.[40] The following month King Abdullah pardoned the woman so that the punishment would not be carried out but did not nullify the verdict.[41]

Recommendations

- ❖ The government should continue to eliminate guardianship requirements and clarify rules regarding when a guardian's permission is required so that there will be consistency and uniformity in their application.
- ❖ The government should institute the minimum age requirement for marriage to prevent young girls from being married before they are emotionally and physically ready.
- ❖ The government should enforce existing criminal and civil laws—such as those against rape, physical abuse, forced confinement, and those mandating payment of wages—that are directed toward employers who abuse foreign workers.
- ❖ The government should enact both antitrafficking laws and laws that protect trafficking victims.
- ❖ The government should implement the criminal procedure code that was adopted in 2002, which prohibits torture or other harmful treatment of detainees (Article 2) and forced confessions (Article 102),

ensures the right to counsel, and requires a public trial and public announcement of the verdict (Article 182).

ECONOMIC RIGHTS AND EQUAL OPPORTUNITY

In Saudi Arabia, obstacles to women's economic independence and work opportunities have not been adequately addressed, especially as women continue to graduate with university degrees in greater numbers than their male counterparts and seek professional employment. Government efforts to support women's legal right to work are in reality ambiguous, giving comfort to those who believe that women should stay at home as well as to those who demand the right to pursue economic independence.

Islamic law provides women with the right to own and manage their property and other assets, including real estate, the mahr, inheritance, investments, and earned income. The distribution of inheritance is fixed according to Shari'a, and women are generally entitled to half the amount allocated to a male relative who is equally distant in relationship to the deceased. In practice, women's ability to manage their own assets and to earn an income are restricted by a combination of social customs and religious values that have been incorporated into the kingdom's commercial regulations, codes of public conduct, and the minds of the bureaucrats who administer them. Gender segregation in the workplace, government ministries and offices, retail establishments, hotels, restaurants, recreational facilities, and banks greatly affects women's ability to manage and make use of their own assets. Until 2005 a woman could not legally obtain a commercial license for a business without proving first that she had hired a male manager, and she needed permission from her guardian to go into business or take out a bank loan.[42]

The female employment rate in Saudi Arabia is among the lowest in the world and, specifically, the Middle East. Statistics on women's economic activity vary somewhat depending on the source. According to the Ministry of Economy and Planning, women constituted only 5.4 percent of the total Saudi workforce in 2005, a figure that was expected to rise to 14.2 percent by the end of the 2005–09 five-year development plan.[43] Government-sponsored projects aimed to increase women's economic opportunities have repeatedly failed to reach targets in the past. The five-year development plan anticipates tripling the rate of women's employment within the plan period by increasing occupational training for women and "eliminating obstacles" to their participation.[44]

Two such obstacles include the prohibition of mixing the sexes in the workplace and the requirement that a woman's guardian give permission for her to work. A new labor law enacted in 2005 does not include either requirement and appears to support women's right to work; as Article 3 states, "work is the right of every citizen" and "all citizens are equal in the right to work." Article 4 of the new law, however, requires that all workers and employers adhere to the provisions of Shari'a when implementing this law, implying that gender segregation remains in force. Article 149 says that women shall work in all fields "suitable to their nature," excluding jobs "deemed detrimental to health" and "likely to expose women to specific risks."[45] In effect, this new law offers an ambiguity that can be used by those arguing either for or against women's increased participation in the workforce. Those in favor can cite the equality and right to work clauses and can also argue that Shari'a law and the terms "women's nature" and "risk" are subject to interpretation. However, those against women in the work force except in jobs stereotypically suitable for women's nature can use Articles 4 and 149 to legally deny employment to women in most fields.[46]

Softening legal restrictions on women's employment does not mean the public will embrace these changes, as evidenced by the outcome of the government's attempt to permit women to work as sales clerks in stores that cater to women's needs. In response to women's complaints of feeling embarrassed to have to buy intimate items from men, the government ordered all shops selling women's undergarments to hire all-female sales staff by July 2006; the policy was extended to stores selling dresses and abayas by 2007 as well.[47] The labor ministry organized training courses to prepare women for these jobs and also produced a list of conditions under which saleswomen would be allowed to work.[48] However, an outcry against this policy emanated from conservative ulema, including the Grand Mufti, who did not think women should be working in retail under any conditions and personally criticized Dr. Ghazi al-Ghosaibi, the minister of labor who originally promoted the policy. Some women shoppers did not like the policy either, complaining of the potential discomfort and humiliation that would arise from buying underwear in a place where windows had to be papered over and doors kept locked just because everyone inside was a woman.[49] The issue was put on hold for a year, and in 2008, women were being employed as sales clerks, but only in segregated areas of shopping malls.

The Council of Ministers, the appointed body that controls most aspects of government, promulgated a directive that requires all ministries to open positions for women. In 2007, the Ministry of Foreign Affairs provided positions for women in several departments, including those that address political rights, economic rights, and women's rights. The Ministry of Education has placed women in some senior positions, including five deanships. The Ministry of Labor is seeking to provide 200,000 jobs for women in different sectors of the economy and has initiated technical training programs to help women become cashiers and receptionists.[50] The question remains, however, how these jobs will be created and in what sectors of the economy, as well as what kind of logistic accommodations will be devised so that sex-segregation on the job can be maintained.

A Saudi woman's freedom to choose her profession is limited more by social than by legal norms. The vast majority of working women are employed in the public sector, and of these 84.1 percent work in education. Additionally, 40 percent of the kingdom's doctors with Saudi citizenship are women.[51] In spite of the social forces militating against women in the private sector, Saudi businesswomen own nearly 20,000 companies, and women's investments amount to about 21 percent of the total volume of private sector investment in the kingdom.[52] In 2006, the National Commercial Bank reported that Saudi women owned 40 percent of the kingdom's real estate assets, 20 percent of stocks, and over 18 percent of then-current bank accounts. In Jeddah, women have taken out more than 3,000 commercial licenses in their own names, and even more are reported in Riyadh.[53] Enterprising women have set up a number of women-only light manufacturing plants, and in Jizan, an underdeveloped region on the western coast of Saudi Arabia, women's response to the prospect of employment at a planned women-only shrimp-processing factory was overwhelming positive.

With 121,000 female students graduating from secondary schools and 44,000 from universities every year, the government must do much more to facilitate job creation.[54] Lack of transportation options for women further limits their participation in the work force by creating a potential burden for employers. Most women who are assigned jobs as teachers in remote towns have to carpool long distances over rough roads, and fatal accidents happen. During the 2007–2008 school year, 21 female teachers were reported killed and 38 others injured while commuting to their teaching jobs.[55]

The 2005 labor law provides women with substantial maternity and childcare benefits. Unfortunately, these benefits discourage private employers from hiring women because they are so costly. Women are guaranteed maternity leave four weeks prior to and six weeks after delivery at full pay if employed for at least three years and at half pay otherwise.[56] The employer is responsible for the woman's medical care during pregnancy and delivery and must provide paid rest-periods for nursing once the woman returns to work. In addition, a woman's employment cannot be terminated while on maternity leave. A business that hires at least 50 women must provide babysitters and a suitable place for childcare, while those hiring 100 women or more may be required to set up a daycare facility or contract with an existing professional daycare facility in the vicinity.[57]

There are no legal protections for women against sexual harassment, but as of June 2008, sexual harassment policies for women in education and in the workplace are under consideration in the Consultative Council.

Public education in Saudi Arabia is free at all levels, and in 2004 primary education became compulsory for both boys and girls aged 6 through 15.[58] The enrollment rate for girls equaled that for boys around 2000, and since 2004 the Ministry of Education has aimed to expand school availability so that secondary education can also be made compulsory for everyone. Girls' secondary education is now within the domain of the Ministry of Education, which until 2002 oversaw only boys' education.[59] The kingdom's current 10-year plan for the development of public education makes no distinction between boys and girls in goals, funding allocation, or curriculum except to expand girls' course options to include information technology and vocational training.[60] In practice, girls continue to be denied access to sports programs in schools, although a 2004 ministerial decree called for the creation of sports and cultural centers exclusively for women.[61] Reports of all-female basketball games in Jeddah surfaced by May 2008, and in July 2009 several high-level religious scholars opined that Shari'a does not prohibit women from participating in sports.[62]

Secondary education is currently undergoing an extensive reform effort which is experiencing both successes and set-backs. The greatest beneficiaries of these reforms are private schools, which now are able to run

International Baccalaureate and American Diploma programs. Dropping the National Secondary Exam also was a boon to private schools which can now focus their teaching on more rigorous, creative, and gender-inclusive materials, but is less helpful to public schools which do not have personnel trained to take advantage of reform opportunities.

In 2004, 79 percent of all PhD degrees awarded in the kingdom went to women, and if the 102 all-women's colleges for teachers are included, about 75 percent of all students are women.[63] However, according to the Minister of Education, women constituted only one-third of students at public universities.[64] Not all universities have women's sections, and where they do, women's facilities are often inadequate and inconveniently located, libraries are open to women's use only at limited times, and fewer courses are offered to women.[65] Some professors simply refuse to admit females to their programs regardless of the policies of the university or Ministry of Education. At the King Fahd Teaching Hospital in Al-Khobar, for example, women have not been admitted to programs in general surgery, orthopedic surgery, or pediatrics due to faculty resistance.[66]

Course options in higher education are to some extent keyed to the job market. Since women are not expected to be employed in mechanical or civil engineering, for instance, these programs were not available to women in public education in the past. However, these courses, as well as interior design and law, have recently opened for women, prompting expectations that more women will be able to obtain jobs in those fields in the future. Furthermore, study abroad offers a wider range of educational options for women.[67] Women are entitled to apply for government scholarships that will pay tuition, living stipend, medical insurance, and school fees for any accompanying children, as well as financial accommodations for a spouse.[68] To qualify for a scholarship to study abroad, a woman should be accompanied by her legal guardian the whole time she is abroad, but in practice this requirement is not enforced.

Two new institutions with Western curricula have opened recently, both of which are designed to accommodate a coeducational environment. King Abdullah University of Science and Technology, located near a Red Sea fishing village 50 miles from Jeddah, opened in September 2009 and offers courses for both men and women. Although only 15 percent of the student body is comprised of Saudi nationals, the university met with harsh criticism from at least one prominent hard line cleric who was later removed from his post within the Council of Senior Islamic Clerics.[69] Another institution, Al-Faisal University in Riyadh, welcomed its inaugural class in the fall of 2008. The university's classroom buildings are designed for men and women to attend classes together, although they would be segregated in transit by separate corridors and entrances, and in the classroom by different floor levels and glass partitions. Due to opposition to and logistics associated with coeducation, however, women have not yet been admitted, and no date has been set to admit them.

In the past decade, a number of private colleges for women have been founded. Dar Al-Hekma College and Effat College, both in Jeddah, offer an American curriculum in English that includes engineering and nursing, as well as work/study internships and exchange programs with American universities. The Prince Sultan University College for Women in Riyadh also teaches in English and offers among other subjects a bachelor's degree in law.[70]

Women's access to education is affected by guardianship laws even though the government has moved to void some of them. Some universities require that women have their guardian's approval before they are permitted to register for classes and then have permission for each individual class they choose to take.[71] In January 2008, the College of Education at the University of Riyadh permitted women students to register using only their civil status cards instead of by their guardian's consent. In this instance, it was the students rather than the administration who complained that the state was breaking the rules of religion by not asking for a guardian's permission. Others accused the Ministry of Education of voyeurism because male employees in the ministry would be able to view the photographs on women's civil status cards.[72]

Recommendations

❖ The government should reform the religion curriculum in public schools, especially in areas that teach women to be obedient to men and equate their invisibility with religious piety.

❖ Women should be permitted to drive or, at a minimum, should be provided with safe public transportation that would adequately meet their employment needs.

❖ Women's sections of chambers of commerce must be empowered and given opportunity to shape polices that better serve the needs of the female business community.

❖ Educational opportunities for women in public educational institutions should not be decided by the goodwill of faculty members but by clearly stated and implemented educational policies.

❖ The government should introduce athletic programs for girls at every level of education.

POLITICAL RIGHTS AND CIVIC VOICE

Saudi Arabia remains a country without the basic freedoms necessary for civil society to take root. Political parties are prohibited, there are no constitutionally guaranteed rights to free speech, press, religion, or assembly in the Basic Law of the Kingdom, and forming trade unions, striking, and engaging in collective bargaining are forbidden. Article 39 of the Basic Law prohibits unspecified "acts leading to disorder and division," rendering anyone who engages in political activity, including human rights advocacy, vulnerable to prosecution. While Article 36 of the Basic Law prohibits arbitrary arrest and detention, Saudi laws are applied to individual cases arbitrarily by judges trained in religion in a manner that fails to guarantee due process.

The Kingdom of Saudi Arabia is a monarchy ruled by the al-Saud family. When King Abdullah took the throne in 2005, he established the Bay'ah Commission the following year. This entity may accept or reject the king's chosen nominee for succession and declare the reigning monarch unfit to rule.[73] There are no elected legislative institutions, but the king appoints the Council of Ministers, responsible for all aspects of government administration, and the 150-seat Consultative Council, which offers advice to the king and, as of 2004, initiates legislation and amends existing laws.

The sole public means of direct access to the government is through the weekly majlis held by the king and by each governor in the provinces which citizens may attend and petition for redress of grievances or personal favors. Although the majlis is "open to all citizens and to anyone who has a complaint or a plea against an injustice," women are not admitted and instead must send a written petition to be delivered by a male relative.[74]

Women were prohibited from voting or running as candidates for municipal councils during Saudi Arabia's first elections for public office in February 2005.[75] The question of whether women have the right to vote in Saudi Arabia, however, remains unresolved. When the Consultative Council announced in October 2003 that municipal council elections would be held, no criteria for voters or candidates were mentioned, and a few women put themselves forward as candidates. The justice ministry supported full voting rights for women,[76] but objections came primarily from conservative ulema.[77] Eventually, Interior Minister Prince Naif bin Abd al-Aziz announced that women would not be voting because polling places and the municipal meetings themselves would have to be sex-segregated for women to take part. By citing logistic rather than religious reasons against women's participation, he left the door open for women to take part in future elections.[78] Although municipal elections were slated to be held in late 2009, officials announced in May that elections would be postponed for an additional two years to consider, among other things, whether women should be permitted to vote.[79]

Women have not been appointed to the Consultative Council, but the king selected three women to serve as advisers to the council on women's issues. These appointments are either a first step toward council membership or a dead end, as the appointees' duties were unspecified and they have not been invited to sit in on council deliberations. In July 2006, six more women were appointed advisers to the council with portfolios as nebulous as that of the first group.[80]

However, women are now more able to participate in civic life than ever before as high-profile women have recently been appointed to elite ministry posts, university deanships, and directorships in quasi-governmental civic organizations. Female physicians were appointed for the first time as Deputy Director of Health Affairs for the Mecca region and head of the General Directorate of Nursing in the Ministry of Health.[81] A member of the royal family, Princess al-Jawhara Fahad bin Mohammed bin Abdel Rahman al-Saud, was appointed as undersecretary of the Ministry of Education. And in a step that garnered international attention, Nora bint Abdullah al-Fayez was named the deputy minister of education in charge of girls' education in February 2009, marking the highest appointed post achieved by a woman in Saudi Arabia's history.[82]

The opening of a women's department in the law faculty at King Saud University in Riyadh raises the possibility of appointments to judgeships for women in the future, however distant. Additionally, a National Organization for Human Rights was established in Saudi Arabia in 2004, and 10 of the 41 members appointed were women with a mandate to monitor women's rights.[83] Women have also run for election in the Jeddah and Riyadh Chambers of Commerce and Industry, organizations normally dominated by men.[84] Finally, in 2005 Nadia Bakhurji was elected to the board of the Saudi Engineers Council, an organization with only 20 women among its 5,000 members.[85] As women emerge into spaces that were previously considered the exclusive domain of men, systemic changes in society may take place. On the other hand, the electoral successes and high-profile appointments of women may turn out to be empty gestures, with elected and appointed women finding themselves in powerless and nonparticipatory positions.

Advocating for political reforms outside of the framework of government-approved organizations presents activists with risks. In recent years, numerous prominent political activists have been fired from their jobs or detained without a clear statement of charges or fair trial.[86] Lawyers who have advocated for feminist causes have been detained, admonished, and threatened with loss of their license to practice.[87] The lawyer who appealed on behalf of the Qatif girl sentenced to 90 lashes after being kidnapped and raped (see "Autonomy, Security, and Freedom of the Person") had his law license suspended by the Qatif court for having undermined Saudi Arabia's reputation by bringing the case to the attention of the international media. Wajeha al-Huwaider, a human rights campaigner, was taken from her home in 2006, interrogated, and forced to sign an agreement to stop engaging in women's rights protests.

The Internet has played a major role in political activism in Saudi Arabia by helping to bring human rights abuses to international attention. One example of such influence occurred in 2006 when a Mecca government committee proposed that women be prohibited from praying in view of television cameras near the Kaaba and instead be removed to a reserved area off to one side of the mosque. A well-reasoned letter of protest written by King Saud University professor and historian Hatun al-Fasi was widely circulated on the webpage of Muslim, women's, and human rights groups. This letter provoked enough international attention and letters of support that the order to remove women from Islam's holiest site was rescinded. However, in practice women continue to be intimidated by religious police and forced to remove themselves to an area distant from the Kaaba.

Recommendations

✤ The government should allow women to vote and run for office in the 2012 municipal elections and allow the candidates to use public media in their campaigns.

✤ Women should be appointed to the consultative council as members with full rights, and not only in advisory capacities for select issues.

✤ The government should appoint a greater number of qualified women to high-profile positions so that the public will become accustomed to the idea of women in leadership roles.

✤ The government should amend Article 39 of the Basic Law to allow for lawful civil dissent so that those who sign petitions or engage in peaceful protest demonstrations on behalf of women's rights need not fear arrest and punishment.

SOCIAL AND CULTURAL RIGHTS

The social and cultural rights of women are circumscribed by the same sex-segregation values that limit the expression of all other forms of women's activities. Tolerance for women in public life, however, is changing, as women's presence in public life has expanded, with women appointed to high-profile positions, elected to office in mixed-sex business organizations, and filling indispensable roles on the staff of public hospitals. The determination of women's rights activists not to tolerate discrimination and violence against women has also grown, which in turn gives impetus to the movement for increased social, cultural, and other rights for women. The Ministry of Social Affairs is engaged in implementing a social awareness campaign on domestic violence, working with professional counselors, physicians, judges, and police officers who are trained in recognizing and dealing with cases of domestic violence.[88]

Women's access to health care and freedom to make independent decisions regarding their health and reproductive rights are curtailed by hospitals that require their guardians' permission before they may be treated. Although no law requires this, hospitals in Saudi Arabia consistently exercise the discretion to refuse treatment without guardian consent, thereby creating life-threatening challenges to women and ill children with absentee fathers.[89] Hospitals are not consistent in this practice, however, and some do permit women to consent to their own treatment. Urban centers offer free, state-of-the-art, government-funded medical care for Saudi citizens, and Saudi Arabia ranks high in the UNDP's human development index for its commitment to health care. Remarkable improvements have been made to health care over the last quarter century, and indicators for

women's health do not show an imbalance in allocation of health care resources between men and women. All clinics and hospitals offer reproductive health services, and methods of contraception are readily available at
public and private pharmacies.[90]

Life expectancy increased by more than 17 years between 1975 and
2000, and women are living about four years longer than men according
to the 2008 Human Development Report.[91] Among married women aged
15 to 49, 32 percent use contraception, a low figure that is reflected in
Saudi Arabia's high birth rate of 3.89 births per woman.[92] The vast majority of births (91 percent) take place attended by skilled health personnel,[93]
but the maternal mortality rate is 18 per 100,000 live births (compared
with 11 in the United States, 7 in Canada, 4 in Israel, and 130 in Syria).[94]
The infant mortality rate also needs to improve, as there are 21 deaths per
1,000 live births (compared to 6 in the United States).[95] The mortality
rate for children under age five is 26 per 1,000 live births, which is very
high compared to almost all other countries in the "High Human Development" category but marks a huge improvement since 1970, when
children in Saudi Arabia under five died at the rate of 185 out of 1,000.
While there is no evidence that women receive less medical care than men
do, the rates of death for infants and children raise questions about the quality of childcare, prenatal care, and parents' access to doctors and hospitals.

Female genital mutilation (FGM) is not a common practice in Saudi
Arabia, although anecdotal evidence suggests that the custom exists in
some Shiite communities in the Eastern Province. FMG was also documented earlier in the 20th century among some Bedouin communities.
No Saudi religious scholars endorse FMG, however, and interviews with
nurses at the Saudi Arabian National Guard hospital in 2002 produced
evidence of only one case.[96]

The extent to which women are free to participate in and influence
community life, policies, and social development depends on their family's
support for such activities, their family connections, their education, and
their personal abilities. Family networks are the easiest route to communicating with the broader community for Saudi men and women alike. Saudi
women influence policies and social development in their roles as teachers,
doctors, social workers, journalists, university professors, investors, and
religious scholars engaging in public debates on the role of women. If they
have the connections they can also communicate their objectives directly
to members of the royal elite.

While women do participate in and influence media content, their impact is limited by self-censorship. Women are employed as journalists, television presenters, producers, bloggers, and newspaper columnists, and they are members of research and advocacy groups that disseminate information to the media. The content of their messages and how they appear on television, however, are tempered by the political realities of the moment, which are constantly shifting.

Women in Saudi Arabia are disproportionately affected by poverty due to their gender because they have limited options for employment, access to justice, access to transportation, and ability to act as independent entrepreneurs as compared to men. They are under the legal control of their closest male relative and often lack choices regarding fundamental life decisions such as marriage, childbearing, and whether to work outside the home. Additionally, if a woman enters into a marriage as the second or third wife, she may lack a sense of proprietorship in her own home and a stake in its economic value. Together, these factors greatly affect the economic well-being of women and prevent those women facing economic hardship from taking care of themselves.

Women's rights activists who advocate for change outside government-sponsored channels, particularly in the area of human rights and political reform, face sanctions regularly. However, several women's organizations do operate, including the women's welfare associations supported by the royal family that exist in all major cities. Additionally, the Khadija bint Khuwailed Center for Businesswomen in Jeddah, a research institute operating under the auspices of the Jeddah Chamber of Commerce, advocates for increased participation by women in education, business, and employment.

Recommendations

❖ The government should require medical staff to treat all adult patients at their own request and allow women to approve medical care for themselves and their children.

❖ The government should provide adequate public transportation and an ambulance system so that mothers and other female caregivers can have access to emergency medical assistance for themselves, their children, and others in their care.

❖ The government should permit human rights and democracy advocates, including women's rights groups, to operate without threat of arrest and detention.

✤ Media restrictions should be relaxed so that images of women in all walks of life may appear, with the goal of raising public consciousness of women as citizens, as individuals, and as people with contributions to make to society.

✤ Saudi universities should initiate research and data collection projects that examine issues related to women, including the prevalence of domestic violence, treatment of women under the law, and economic activities, among others.

AUTHOR

Eleanor Abdella Doumato writes on gender, Islamic education, and the Gulf region. Her most recent book, *Teaching Islam: Religion and Textbooks in the Middle East* (edited with Gregory Starrett), is the product of a collaborative research project designed to determine what kind of Islam is being taught in state schools in the Middle East, including Iran, Turkey, Palestine, and Israel. Dr. Doumato is currently a Visiting Fellow at the Watson Institute for International Studies at Brown University and a past president of the Association for Middle East Women's Studies. She serves on the boards of *Hawwa* and the *Journal of Middle East Women's Studies*, and is a frequent consultant for government agencies.

NOTES

1 The Koran is the holy book of Muslims, and Sunna is the tradition of the Prophet Muhammad.

2 The concept of gender equivalence is commonly held in Muslim-majority countries. According to this view, the roles of men and women complement each other but are not equal, and this complementarity is thought to work in women's favor. For example, while men are required to provide for their families, women are expected to manage the household and care for children and elderly parents; daughters inherit half of what sons inherit, but women retain ownership of their property after marriage and have no obligation to spend their wealth on household expenses as married men must.

3 Hassna'a Mokhtar, "Saudi Women Demand Equal Citizenship Rights," *Arab News* (Jeddah), March 7, 2007, www.arabnews.com/?page=1&section=0&article=93232&d =7&m=3&y=2007. Daughters of Saudi women married to foreigners have not always been so disadvantaged when it comes to obtaining Saudi nationality: the 1954 Law of the Saudi Arabian Nationality, issued by Royal Decree 8/20/5604 (Umm Al-Qura, No. 1539, 16/3/1374H) makes no distinction between sons and daughters in their right to Saudi citizenship. A non-Saudi widow of a Saudi could also apply for citizenship

according to the 1954 law. The issue of women nationals' inability to pass citizenship to their children is common region-wide. More information on this subject is available through The Women's Learning Partnership, a women's rights organization based in Washington, D.C., which has been leading a campaign on behalf of women's citizenship rights in Muslim countries. See the organization's web publication, "Claiming Equal Citizenship: The Campaign for Arab Women's Right to Nationality," www.learning partnership.org/citizenship/category/countries/.

4   Members of the religious/moral police force are known as *mutawwa'in* (literally "obedience causers").

5   Royal Decree no. M/54 (29 Shawwal 1425 AH). "Consideration of Reports Submitted by States Parties Under Article 18 of the Convention, Combined Initial and Second Periodic Reports of States Parties: Saudi Arabia" (United Nations, Committee on the Elimination of Discrimination against Women, CEDAW/C/SAU/2, 07-29667 [E] 120507 230507, March 29, 2007), 16, http://daccessdds.un.org/doc/UNDOC/GEN/ N07/296/67/PDF/N0729667.pdf?OpenElement.

6   Maha Akeel, "New Law May Help Non-Saudi Wife," *Arab News,* June 25, 2007.

7   Sarah Abdullah, "Foreign-Born Women Married to Saudis Concerned Over New Citizenship Rule," *Arab News,* June 18, 2007.

8   Awad al-Maliki, "Saudi Women Can Obtain ID Cards Without Guardian's Permission," *Al-Madinah,* March 4, 2008, in Arabic.

9   Abd al-Raheem Ali, "Saudi Family Courts, Female Judges Recommended," islamonline .net (Doha, Qatar), June 14, 2004, www.islamonline.net/English/News/2004-06/14/ article03.shtml.

10 Hamid al-Shahri, "Saudi Justice Minister Says Female Lawyers Permitted Only to Provide Legal Advice," *Al-Watan,* GMP20070201614006, February 1, 2007, in Arabic.

11 "Women to Work in Saudi Courts," *Arab News,* March 31, 2008. Dr. Al Ash-Shaikh noted that in his view women have the right to practice the legal profession. Mariam al-Hakeem, "Saudi Women 'Have Right to Practise Law,'" *Gulf News,* October 25, 2007.

12 "Saudi Arabia: Halt Woman's Execution for 'Witchcraft': Fawza Falih's Case Reveals Deep Flaws in Saudi Justice System" (New York: Human Rights Watch [HRW], February 14, 2008).

13 "Religious Police in Saudi Arabia Arrest Mother for Sitting with a Man," TimesOnLine, February 7, 2008, www.timesonline.co.uk/tol/news/world/middle_east/article3321637 .ece.

14 "75-Year-Old Widow to Be Flogged," *The Independent,* March 10, 2009, http://www .independent.co.uk/news/world/middle-east/75yearold-widow-to-be-flogged-1641548.html.

15 "Saudi Arabia: Morality Police Under Pressure," in "News and Views," *Arab Reform Bulletin* (Carnegie Endowment) 5, no. 5 (June 2007).

16 For the text of the hearing on the report, see "Summary Record of the 815th Meeting Held January 17, 2008, Consideration of Reports Submitted by States Parties Under Article 18 of the Convention" (United Nations, Convention on the Elimination of Discrimination against Women, Committee on the Elimination of Discrimination against Women, Fortieth session, CEDAW/C/SR.815, February 18, 2008), www2

.ohchr.org/english/bodies/cedaw/docs/CEDAWSR815.pdf. For discussion of the Saudi reaction to the committee report, see Muwaffaq al-Nuwaysir, "Saudi Official Explains Reservation on 2 Clauses in Agreement on Women," *Al-Sharq al-Awsat* (London), August 23, 2000, 4.

17 Mustafa al-Anssari, "Riyadh Jurists Consider UN Report on Saudi Women as Contrary to Reality," *Al-Hayat* (Beirut), February 2, 2008.

18 The mahram's permission is legally required for women to travel internationally, and in practice, it is also required for them to travel domestically despite there being no such official requirement. According to Human Rights Watch, women who do not present proof of their mahram's permission may be prevented from boarding domestic flights as well. See "Perpetual Minors: Human Rights Abuses Stemming from Male Guardianship and Sex Segregation in Saudi Arabia" (HRW, April 2008), section II, www.hrw.org/reports/2008/saudiarabia0408/.

19 "Saudi Arabia: Succession Law; Judicial Reforms; Women Driving Campaign," *Arab Reform Bulletin* 5, no. 8 (October 2007).

20 Reuters, "Saudi Restrictions on Women Questioned," *Los Angeles Times*, January 18, 2008.

21 Damien McElroy, "Saudi Arabia to Lift Ban on Women Drivers," *The Telegraph* (London), January 21, 2008.

22 "Saudi Shura Council Recommends Allowing Saudi Women to Drive with Limitations" (Middle East Media Research Institute [MEMRI], Special Dispatch Series No. 1875, March 18, 2008), www.memri.org/bin/latestnews.cgi?ID=SD187508; this "special dispatch" cites *Alarabiya.net* (Dubai), March 17, 2008, as its source.

23 "Saudi Arabia Opens Its First Women-Only Hotel," Chinadaily.com.cn, March 20, 2008.

24 "8-Year-Old Saudi Girl Divorces 50-Year-Old Husband," *Khaleej Times*, May 1, 2008, http://www.khaleejtimes.com/DisplayArticleNew.asp?section=middleeast&xfile =data/middleeast/2009/may/middleeast_may2.xml.

25 "Saudi Arabia Mulls Marriage Ban for Girls Under 18," *Khaleej Times*, May 2, 2009, http://www.khaleejtimes.com/DisplayArticleNew.asp?section=middleeast&xfile=data/middleeast/2009/may/middleeast_may20.xml.

26 Louay Bahry, "Marriage Advertisements in Saudi Arabia," Middle East Institute *Encounter* no. 7 (March 2008).

27 Interior Ministry, Law of Marriage of Saudi Citizen with a Non-Saudi, Number 874, 12/20/1422 H, in Arabic.

28 Najah Alosaimi, "Saudi Women Marrying Foreigners on Rise," *Arab News*, September 14, 2007.

29 "Perpetual Minors" (HRW, April 2008), 30–31, www.hrw.org/reports/2008/saudiara bia0408/.

30 "Saudi Arabia: Succession Law; Judicial Reforms; Women Driving Campaign," *Arab Reform Bulletin* (October 2007), www.carnegieendowment.orgarb/?fa=show&article =20823.

31 "Saudi to Get Supreme Court, Other Tribunals," IslamOnline.net, June 14, 2004.

32 "Trafficking in Persons Report 2008" (Washington, DC: U.S. Department of State, Office to Monitor and Combat Trafficking in Persons, June 4, 2008), www.state.gov/g/tip/rls/tiprpt/2008/105386.htm.

33 "Consideration of Reports Submitted by States Parties Under Article 18 of the Con-
    vention, Combined Initial and Second Periodic Reports of States Parties: Saudi Arabia"
    (United Nations, Committee on the Elimination of Discrimination against Women,
    CEDAW/C/SAU/2, 07-29667 [E] 120507 230507, March 29, 2007), 22 (hereafter
    cited as CEDAW/C/SAU/2), http://daccessdds.un.org/doc/UNDOC/GEN/N07/296/
    67/PDF/N0729667.pdf?OpenElement. Article 6 of the convention requires that
    "States Parties shall take all appropriate measures, including legislation, to suppress all
    forms of traffic in women and exploitation of prostitution of women." In addressing
    this issue, the Saudis indicate there is no such problem in the kingdom: "In view of the
    fact that the Kingdom applies the Islamic Shariah, which exhorts to virtue and forbids
    vice, fornication and immorality, as well as the fact that these conflict with tradition
    and custom, traffic in women and exploitation of prostitution of women are practices
    unknown to Saudi society. . . . The Kingdom has been able to take practical measures
    to close all the loopholes through which unlawful sexual practices might establish a
    presence in the country. . . . These efforts have achieved notable success, reflecting the
    State's sincere desire to combat such unlawful practices. It should be stated that these
    practices are limited and almost negligible, and are contained by the authorities. . . ."

34 Labor Law, Royal Decree M/51, 27 September 2005, 1st ed. (English), 2006, Part I,
    Chapter 2, Article 7. Article 7 also includes a directive to the Labor Ministry to "draft
    regulations for domestic helpers and the like to govern their relations with their employ-
    ers and specify the rights and duties of each party. . . ."

35 Katie Mattern, "Saudi Arabia: New Bill Fails to Protect Domestic Workers, HRW Says,"
    IPS News, July 10, 2009, http://ipsnews.net/news.asp?idnews=47621.

36 "Saudi Arabia: Nour Miyati Denied Justice for Torture, Judge Ignores Evidence in Case
    of Extreme Abuse Against Indonesian Domestic Worker" (HRW, May 21, 2008).

37 Shabna Aziz, "Dammam Police Helps Maid Get Her Rights," Saudi Gazette, May
    25, 2008, http://www.saudigazette.com.sa/index.cfm?method=home.regcon&content
    ID=200805257407.

38 Hadith for the 12th Grade (Riyadh: General Presidency for Girls' Education, 2000), in
    Arabic.

39 "Perpetual Minors" (HRW), 22. Sexual abuse within families is historically a problem
    in the sex-segregated societies of the Gulf. American physicians running hospitals in
    Kuwait and Bahrain from about 1912 documented cases of "honor killings" that were
    meant to hide incest. For more on this topic, see Eleanor Doumato, Getting God's Ear
    (New York: Columbia University Press, 2000).

40 "New Explanatory Statement by the Ministry of Justice on Qatif Girl," Saudi Press
    Agency (Riyadh), November 24, 2007, www.spa.gov.sa/English/details.php?id=502890.

41 Ebtihal Mubarak, "Pardoned Rape Victim Subjected to 'Brutal Crime'—Saudi King,"
    BBC Monitoring, Arab News website, December 20, 2007. For more analysis of
    the legal reasoning behind the judicial decisions and the king's pardon in the "Qatif
    girl" case, see "Precarious Justice: Arbitrary Detention and Unfair Trials in the Deficient
    Criminal Justice System of Saudi Arabia" (HRW, March 24, 2008), http://hrw.org/
    reports/2008/saudijustice0308/.

42 Resolution no. 120 (12 Rabi II 1425 AH) says that "government bodies which issue
    licenses to practice economic activities receive applications from women for such licenses,

which are granted and issued accordingly," http://daccessdds.un.org/doc/UNDOC/ GEN/N07/296/67/PDF/N0729667.pdf?OpenElement. Cabinet Decree no. 187 (17 Rajab 1426 AH) allows "private enterprises to open sections employing women without a licence being required."

[43] Khalid al-Gosaibi, Minister of Economy and Planning, "Plan Aims to Triple the Number of Saudi Women in the Workforce by 2009" (Washington, DC: Royal Embassy of Saudi Arabia, November 4, 2007), http://www.saudiembassy.net/archive/2007/news/ page531.aspx.

[44] Khalid al-Gosaibi, op cit.

[45] Kingdom of Saudi Arabia, Labor Law, Royal Decree Number M/51, 23 Shaaban 1426, September 27, 2005, 1st ed., 2006.

[46] A summary discussion of the obstacles to women's employment in the private sector was prepared by Noura Alturki, "Gender Analysis of the Eighth National Development Plan, 2005–09" (Jeddah: Khadijah bint Khuwailid Businesswomen Center, unpublished manuscript, August 27, 2007). These obstacles are more fully detailed in a report issued by the Khadija bint Khuwailid Center for Businesswomen, located in Jeddah, available on the Jeddah Chamber of Commerce website, www.jcci.org.sa/JCCI/AR/ Specialized+Centers/Khadija+Bint+Khuwailid+Center/, in Arabic.

[47] Women's complaints were mainly about feeling humiliated at having to endure snide sexual remarks from the clerks. See, for example, Arifa Akbar, "Hello Boys: Lingerie Leads the Fight for Saudi Women's Rights," *Independent News*, April 27, 2006.

[48] "Hiring of Foreign Women in Lingerie Shops Ruled Out," *Gulf News*, April 11, 2006.

[49] Anton La Guardia, "Muslim Clerics' Anger Delays Saudi Plan to Let Women Sell Lingerie," *The Telegraph*, May 16, 2006.

[50] "Foreign Ministry to Appoint Women in Various Departments" (Washington, DC: Royal Embassy of Saudi Arabia, February 27, 2005), http://208.246.28.149/2005News/ News/RigDetail.asp?cIndex=5088.

[51] "Saudi UN Representative Hails 'Growing Role' of Women," Saudi News Agency, SPA, March 8, 2007.

[52] "Saudi UN Representative Hails 'Growing Role' of Women," Saudi News Agency.

[53] "Women Said to Own 40 % of Saudi Real Estate Assets," *Arab News* website, April 27, 2006.

[54] In the 1990s, 80 percent of all working Saudis were employed in the public sector. "Public Sector Employment as a Share of Total Employment in MENA Countries," in *The Road Not Traveled: Education Reform in the Middle East and North Africa* (World Bank, 2008), Fig. 2.2, 53.

[55] Donna Abu-Nasr, "Female Teachers Dying on the Roads in Saudi Arabia," Associated Press, April 29, 2008.

[56] Kingdom of Saudi Arabia, Labor Law, Articles 151–152.

[57] Kingdom of Saudi Arabia, Labor Law, Articles 153–159.

[58] Royal Decree no. 22646/R (22 June 2004), CEDAW/C/SAU/2, 16.

[59] Girls' education was consigned to the ulema-controlled General Presidency for Girls Education, a measure put in place to mitigate conservative opposition to opening

schools for girls. It was for this reason that the education policy for the kingdom incorporated language limiting the purpose of girls' education to helping them become good wives and mothers, and to work only in fields that are considered to suit their nature, such as childcare and teaching.

60 "Executive Summary of the Ministry of Education Ten-Year Development Plan (2004–2014)," 2nd ed. (Riyadh: Kingdom of Saudi Arabia, Ministry of Education, General Directorate for Planning, 2005).

61 Deputy Prime Ministerial Order no. 8110 (11 Safar 1425 AH, 2004 CE).

62 Donna Abu-Nassr, "Underground Sports: Saudi Women Shed Veils to Play Basketball," *USA Today*, May 8, 2008, http://www.usatoday.com/news/world/2008-05-08-saudi-sports_N.htm; "No Bar on Women's Sports Activity in Shariah, says Saudi Scholar," *Khaleej Times*, July 27, 2009, http://www.khaleejtimes.com/DisplayArticleNew.asp?section=middleeast&xfile=data/middleeast/2009/july/middleeast_july358.xml.

63 "Saudi Education Minister on Universities and Curricula," *Al Hayat*, April 23, 2004.

64 "Saudi Education Minister on Universities and Curricula," *Al Hayat*, April 23, 2004.

65 "Perpetual Minors" (HRW), 16. For instance, at King Saud University in Riyadh 14 languages are offered for male students but only two for females.

66 "Perpetual Minors" (HRW), 16.

67 Royal Order no. 651/M (8 Jumada II 1422 AH) requires that scholarship grants for overseas study be made available for "medical and health-related specializations and other fields in which women work and where the demands of work require qualification through overseas study, in response to a pressing need which cannot be fulfilled by the programs of study available at Saudi universities."

68 "Saudi Education Minister on Universities and Curricula," *Al Hayat*, April 23, 2004.

69 "Saudi King Dismisses Cleric After Criticism," CBS News, October 5, 2009, http://www.cbsnews.com/stories/2009/10/05/ap/middleeast/main5363169.shtml.

70 For issues arising from the attempt to found new universities on American models see Zvika Krieger, "Saudi Arabia: Reforms in Higher Education Raise Questions," *Arab Reform Bulletin* 5, no. 10 (December 2007). See also Beth McMurthie, "New University Seeks to Help Saudi Arabia Broaden Its Economy," *Chronicle of Higher Education* 53, no. 30 (March 30, 2007): 41.

71 "Perpetual Minors" (HRW), 16–17.

72 Haya al-Manie, "Paranoia in Society," *Al Riyadh*, reprinted in *Arab News*, January 9, 2008.

73 Text of the Allegiance Institution Law of October 20, 2006, http://www.saudi-us-relations.org/fact-book/documents/2006/061106-allegiance-law.html; Hugh Miles, "Saudi King Loses Power to Choose His Successor," *The Daily Telegraph*, February 10, 2007; Text of Law of the Provinces, http://www.saudiembassy.net/about/country-information/laws/The_Law_of_The_Provinces.aspx.

74 Basic Law, Article 43.

75 The prohibition on government employees' political activism is broad. In September 2004, the Council of Ministers announced that public employees are forbidden to challenge government policies by "participating, directly or indirectly, in the preparation of

any document, speech or petition, engaging in dialogue with local and foreign media, or participating in any meetings intended to oppose the state's policies," *Arab Reform Bulletin* 2, no. 9 (October 2004).

76 As reported in a Saudi newspaper, a ministry spokesman said that "there is no reason to stop them from participating in the elections. Trends coming from the West which are beneficial and do not contradict our laws and religion should not be banned." *Okaz*, December 4, 2004, www.aljazeera.com.

77 Nawaf Obaid, "Clerical Hurdles to Saudi Reform," *Washington Post*, March 9, 2004.

78 "Women Shut Out of Upcoming Saudi Vote," Associated Press, October 12, 2004.

79 Abdul-Ramad Shaheen, "Saudi Analysts Hail Postponement of Elections," *Gulf News*, May 20, 2009, http://gulfnews.com/newsgulf/saudi-arabia/saudi-analysts-hail-postpone ment-of-elections-1.2032; Michael Slackman, "Saudis' Local Elections Delayed Two Years," *New York Times*, May 19, 2009, http://www.nytimes.com/2009/05/20/world/ middleeast/20saudi.html?_r=2&partner=rss&emc=rss.

80 Maha Akeel, "More Women Consultants Join Shura," *Arab News*, June 29, 2006. Hatoon al-Fassi, an associate professor at King Sa'ud University and one of the women appointed, commented that "if the committee is to be as described, there is no need for it and I object to being included. This is not a first step; it is very much the same as what we have now. Women are asked as consultants with no right to make decisions, no authority and their opinions are not taken."

81 Maha Akeel, "Woman Appointed to Top Health Post in Jeddah," *Arab News*, July 12, 2004.

82 Julia Borger, "Saudi Arabia Appoints First Female Minister," *Guardian*, February 16, 2009, http://www.guardian.co.uk/world/2009/feb/16/saudi-cabinet-woman-minister.

83 Khalid al-Dakhil, "2003: Saudi Arabia's Year of Reform," *Arab Reform Bulletin* 2, no. 3 (March 2004); Abdul Ghafour, "First Independent Human Rights Organization Established," *Arab News*, March 3, 2004.

84 Maha Akeel, "Women in JCCI Poll Fray," *Arab News*, October 3, 2005.

85 Somaya Jabarti, "Engineers Council Poll: One More Step for Saudi Women," *Arab News*, December 28, 2005.

86 See, for example, "Saudi Arabia: Free Detained Advocates of Reform," "Secret Police Arrest 7 Prominent Reformers in Replay of Events in 2004" (HRW, February 8, 2007).

87 See, for example, "Teachers Silenced on Blasphemy Charges" (HRW, November 16, 2005), http://hrw.org/english/docs/2005/11/16/saudia12049.htm; "Saudi Arabia: Lift Travel Ban on Government Critics" (HRW, February 13, 2007), http://hrw.org/english/ docs/2007/02/14/saudia15335.htm.

88 Royal Order no. A/14 (April 2, 2005) established the program on domestic violence.

89 "Perpetual Minors" (HRW), 20. The HRW report contains a copy of a surgical procedure consent form for King Fahd hospital in al-Khobar, which asks for the agreement to accept the risk of surgery of both the patient and her guardian. The form is dated 1985.

90 Saudi Arabia CEDAW report, op cit., 40, http://daccessdds.un.org/doc/UNDOC/ GEN/N07/296/67/PDF/N0729667.pdf?OpenElement.

91 *Human Development Report 2007–2008* (New York: UNDP, 2008), Table 10, Survival: Progress and Setbacks, http://hdr.undp.org/en/media/HDR_20072008_EN_Complete

.pdf; "Mortality Country Fact Sheet 2006" (World Health Organization), indicates that in 2004, women on average lived six years longer than men.

92 *Human Development Report 2007–2008*, UNDP.

93 *Human Development Report 2007–2008*, UNDP, Table 6, Commitment to Health: Resources, Access and Services, 248. For comparison, 75 percent of women in Canada use contraception, and 98 percent are attended by skilled health personnel.

94 *Human Development Report 2007–2008*, UNDP, Table 10, Survival: Progress and Setbacks, 263–264. "Mortality Country Fact Sheet 2006" gives the maternal mortality rate in 2000 at 23 per 1,000 live births.

95 *The CIA World Factbook* for 2008 gives a much lower figure for infant mortality, at 12.01 deaths per 1,000, double that of the United States. www.cia.gov/library/publications/the-world-factbook/geos/sa.html#People.

96 Interviews conducted by author in Riyadh at the National Guard Hospital, Riyadh, January 2002.

SYRIA

		2004	2009
POPULATION:	21,906,000		
GNI PER CAPITA:	US$1,730		

COUNTRY RATINGS	2004	2009
NONDISCRIMINATION AND ACCESS TO JUSTICE:	2.7	2.7
AUTONOMY, SECURITY, AND FREEDOM OF THE PERSON:	2.2	2.3
ECONOMIC RIGHTS AND EQUAL OPPORTUNITY:	2.8	2.9
POLITICAL RIGHTS AND CIVIC VOICE:	2.2	2.2
SOCIAL AND CULTURAL RIGHTS:	2.3	2.5

(COUNTRY RATINGS ARE BASED ON A SCALE OF I TO 5, WITH I REPRESENTING THE LOWEST AND 5 THE HIGHEST LEVEL OF FREEDOM WOMEN HAVE TO EXERCISE THEIR RIGHTS)

INTRODUCTION

Women in Syria have a relatively long history of emancipation, and the country is one of the more advanced in the Arab world when it comes to women's rights. Women obtained the right to vote in 1949, and their involvement in politics dates to the struggle for independence from the Ottoman Empire at the beginning of the last century. However, the effects of their participation have been stifled by the realities of the repressive political climate. The Ba'ath Party, a pan-Arab nationalist group, seized power in a 1963 coup and imposed a state of emergency that indefinitely suspended many provisions and protections of the legal system.[1] In particular, freedoms of expression and association have been severely curtailed.

Over the years, the Ba'ath regime has invested some efforts to improve the rights of women. The 1973 constitution, for example, calls for equality among all citizens and includes an article that obliges the state to remove all obstacles to women's advancement. Government policies have also encouraged women's education and participation in the workforce. Reflecting these measures, women's literacy increased from 37 percent in 1981 to 76 percent in 2007, while women's labor participation rates grew from 12 percent to 31 percent during the same period.[2]

Nevertheless, legal reforms necessary to ensure equality between genders have been very limited, and women lack channels through which they may challenge discriminatory laws and practices. Although women's representation in the national parliament is higher than in most neighboring countries, they have a limited presence in the executive and judiciary, reducing their potential role in developing, implementing, and enforcing policy decisions. The restrictions on freedom of association force many women's rights organizations to operate illegally. Consequently, change is typically imposed by the national leadership or through government-affiliated organizations, rather than arising through civil society activism.

Syria ratified the Convention on the Elimination of All Forms of Discrimination against Women (CEDAW) in 2003, sparking a flurry of activity among the existing women's rights groups. However, the country filed several reservations affecting key provisions of the covenant. Although officials have indicated their willingness to revisit these reservations and more thoroughly implement the convention, few concrete changes have been instituted to date. The nationality law continues to prohibit women from passing on their citizenship to their children, while placing no such restrictions on men. This particularly affects the assimilation of the Palestinian population of about half a million and the more recent influx of about 1.5 million Iraqi refugees. Several discriminatory provisions of the penal code also remain unchanged. For instance, the definition of and evidentiary burden for adultery is different depending on the gender of the perpetrator, and women face higher minimum sentences than men.

Patriarchal values in society and the authoritarian political system leave women vulnerable to gender-based violence, both inside and outside the home. Recent studies have shown that domestic violence is common throughout Syria, but such abuse is not specifically outlawed; spousal rape is excluded as a punishable offense under the legal definition of rape. Under the existing personal status law, women also lack full control over issues related to marriage, divorce, custody, and other family matters.[3] A woman's husband can forbid her from working outside the home or from leaving the country if accompanied by her children. Although the penal code was amended in 2009 to increase the penalty for so-called honor killings, honor remains a mitigating factor in sentencing. However, the government has begun to draft new legislation that would directly address human trafficking, and the first shelter for trafficking victims was opened in Damascus in 2009.

Many women, particularly those living in rural areas, do not fully understand their legal rights and cede what rights they do have in response to social or family pressure. This is particularly evident with respect to property rights. The unequal inheritance rights mandated by Shari'a-based laws are commonly justified by the requirement that men provide for the women in their family, but women often turn over the entirety of their inheritance to their brothers to keep it in the family. Such practices greatly exacerbate women's financial dependence on men.

Opposition to increased women's rights comes from Islamic fundamentalist groups as well as from conservative customs that relegate women to a secondary position in society and continue to hold greater sway than formal law for many Syrians. Society expects women to shoulder domestic responsibilities, and it imposes on them the burden of upholding the family's honor. Failure to conform to social norms draws sharp pressure from within the family and from society at large, culminating in murder in some cases. The government often appeases such sentiments on women's rights for broader political purposes.[4]

The lack of a free public sphere makes it difficult for activists to operate, whether by lobbying the government for changes in the law or working within society to raise awareness and change public attitudes. Access to the Internet, however, is changing this reality. When a retrogressive draft personal status was leaked to the public in early 2009, civil society actors led a successful protest against its adoption, causing the government to cancel the draft. Despite this success, negative social attitudes, which are held by both men and women, play a considerable role in discouraging women from taking advantage of what opportunities exist.

NONDISCRIMINATION AND ACCESS TO JUSTICE

Although there have been efforts to reform discriminatory legislation and promulgate new laws that would protect women from discrimination, very few practical changes have been made in recent years. The government took a major step forward by ratifying CEDAW in 2003, which has increased the amount of attention paid to women's rights issues. However, the reservations Syria filed upon ratification eviscerated much of the purpose of the treaty. Access to justice for all Syrians remains limited, and the penal code contains multiple provisions that discriminate against women with respect to the definition, evidentiary requirements, or sentencing for certain crimes.

Article 25 of the constitution stipulates that "citizens are equal before the law in regard to their rights and obligations."[5] Moreover, Article 45 states that women are guaranteed "all the opportunities that enable them to participate fully and effectively in political, social, cultural, and economic life. The state works to remove the restrictions that prevent women's development and their participation in building socialist Arab society." The emergency law enacted in 1963, however, has eclipsed many of the legal protections offered by the constitution.

No legislation specifically prohibits gender-based discrimination, and no complaint mechanisms are available to women who have been denied the aforementioned rights and opportunities.[6] While progress has been made at the official level in recognizing problems related to honor killings and trafficking in persons, little has been done to actually outlaw these practices, and the penal code and personal status law retain discriminatory provisions. Non-Muslim communities are permitted to have their own personal status laws, although these too discriminate against women. For example, Jewish women are required to be obedient to men, and a man may take more than one wife in some cases. The personal status law for Orthodox Christians discriminates against women in terms of child custody.

Article 3 of the nationality law permits only men to pass their nationality onto their children.[7] Women married to noncitizen men may retain their Syrian citizenship but cannot transfer it to their husbands. Children of such marriages lack the rights of Syrian citizens, meaning they cannot inherit property, lack access to free education and health care, and have difficulty obtaining employment generally. Additionally, they are not able to start a private business because non-Syrians are ineligible to buy or lease property. By contrast, Syrian men may confer their citizenship onto their spouse and children by the virtue of their marriage and blood relationship. The Syrian Women's League, which has led a national campaign to amend the law, in October 2004 presented a bill to the government calling for equal nationality rights for men and women. As of October 2009, nonetheless, the nationality law remained unchanged.

The judiciary is not independent, and corruption in the judicial system is rife, negatively affecting access to justice for all. Judges are appointed by the Supreme Judicial Council, which is headed by the justice minister. The judicial system is divided into civil, criminal, and religious courts. The religious courts hear personal status cases, such as those related to family relationships and inheritance, and they exercise personal jurisdiction over those who practice the faith of the court. There is no option to have such cases heard in a civil court.

Women were admitted to practice law in 1975, but their representation within the judiciary remains low even today. Women constitute 13 percent of judges and public prosecutors, and these are concentrated overwhelmingly in Damascus, where their representation is about double the national average.[8] This male dominance makes women less trustful of the judicial system and less likely to turn to the courts for justice.

Certain provisions of the penal code discriminate against women. In instances of adultery, for example, women and men receive disparate treatment under Articles 239 through 242 and Article 548.[9] To prove his case, a man may present any form of evidence before the judge, while a woman may submit written evidence only, such as a written confession by the husband. A woman may be prosecuted for committing adultery anywhere, while a man can only be brought to court for committing adultery inside the family home. And if convicted, a man faces sentences ranging from one month to one year in prison, while a woman faces three months to two years.

Article 33 of the constitution prohibits exile and protects free movement within the country, but all citizens—particularly those who are politically active—are subject to arbitrary arrest and detention. The emergency laws allow a state security court to hear cases related to "national security," which is commonly invoked against political activists to justify their imprisonment.[10]

The evidentiary worth of a woman's testimony depends on which system of courts is hearing her case. Women are treated as full persons before the civil and criminal courts, which are secular and come under the umbrella of the Ministry of Justice. Similarly, the civil and commercial codes grant women the same legal capacity as men.[11] In Shari'a courts, however, a woman's testimony is worth only half that of a man.

When Syria ratified CEDAW in 2003, it made reservations to many key articles, citing their incompatibility with national law and Shari'a. Reservations made to Article 2 were particularly unwelcome for other parties to the convention, as this article establishes the purpose of the convention and commits the signatory state to make efforts to end discrimination against women. Syria also filed reservations to Article 9(2), concerning the mother's right to pass on her nationality to her children; Article 15(4), regarding freedom of movement and choice of domicile; Article 16(1), mandating equal rights and responsibilities during marriage and upon its dissolution with regard to guardianship, kinship, maintenance, and adoption; Article 16(2), regarding the legal effect of the betrothal and marriage of a child; and Article 29(1), regarding arbitration between countries in the event of a dispute.[12] Syria's grand mufti recommended removing some of the reservations because he found the relevant articles to be compatible with Shari'a.[13] The government has also endorsed removing some reservations, especially to Article 2, but the final decision remains pending.[14]

Although the government's ninth five-year plan aims to raise the participation of women in public life and in decision-making positions to 30 percent, civil society actors are limited in their ability to lobby against discriminatory laws and policies.[15] The only legal women's organization is the General Union of Syrian Women (GWU), an affiliate of the Ba'ath Party that receives state funding. According to party philosophy, the GWU represents all Syrian women, obviating the need for independent women's groups. In practice, this monopoly excludes dissenting views on government policies and delays action on specific problems, since initiatives and complaints have to filter up through the unwieldy, multilayered administrative structure of the Ba'ath Party.

Despite their illegal status, independent groups do operate in varying degrees of secrecy. The Syrian Women's League, for instance, has carried on its work continuously since 1948. However, this precarious existence has made it difficult for such groups to function. Unregistered groups have problems raising funds, particularly in light of a ban on accepting grants from abroad. They also face significant obstacles in attracting members and mobilizing women to claim their rights.

Recommendations

* ❖ The government should reform the judicial system to improve accessibility and fairness for female litigants, for instance by increasing the percentage of women judges and appointing female police officers to serve in courthouses.
* ❖ The government should reform or eliminate the discriminatory provisions in the personal status law, the penal code, and the nationality law.
* ❖ Government policies should integrate gender awareness plans in all sectors and allocate a budget for gender awareness and development.
* ❖ The government should remove all CEDAW reservations and pursue its full and effective implementation.

✤ The government should revoke the state of emergency and uphold all constitutional rights, including those granted to women under Article 45.

AUTONOMY, SECURITY, AND FREEDOM OF THE PERSON

The single greatest legal obstacle to gender equality remains the personal status law, which limits women's autonomy in matters such as marriage and divorce. The prevalence of domestic violence in Syrian society, and the permissive attitude toward so-called honor killings in some areas, mean that women also face threats to their physical security. The government has begun to acknowledge the need to amend the laws and alter deep-rooted societal attitudes toward these issues, and in 2009 it took steps to stiffen the penalties for honor killings, but women have yet to feel change in their day-to-day lives.

Syria does not have an official religion, and freedom of worship is protected under Article 35 of the constitution. However, Article 3 stipulates that all legislation derives from Shari'a and that the president must practice Islam. The population is predominantly Sunni Muslim, but there are large communities of Alawites (a minority Muslim sect), Christians, and Druze, as well as a small number of Jews. The personal status and family issues of religious minorities are governed by their own sectarian laws. Muslim women are prohibited from marrying non-Muslim men under Article 48(2) of the personal status law, while Muslim men face no such restriction.

Women's ability to travel and move freely is subject to legal and social restrictions. Although Article 33 of the constitution protects freedom of movement within Syria for all citizens, it is silent regarding international travel. Consequently, husbands may prevent their wives from leaving the country with their children, though women on their own are able to obtain a passport and leave without their husbands' permission.[16] In addition, the state often imposes international travel bans on political and human rights activists in an effort to silence expressions of dissent overseas. Women constituted 10 percent of more than 400 activists under travel bans as of May 2009.[17] Married women face other restrictions on their freedom of movement under the personal status law. Specifically, a disobedient wife is not entitled to financial support from her husband for the duration of her disobedience, which can be broadly defined to include leaving the conjugal home for reasons that contravene Shari'a or preventing the husband from entering their home before petitioning to be moved to another residence.[18]

The Syrian government, in a 2005 submission to the UN committee overseeing CEDAW, acknowledged that the personal status law is "largely discriminatory."[19] It governs the private lives of Muslims, including marriage, divorce, custody, and guardianship, as well as wills and inheritance rights. Article 307 establishes certain rules that apply to the Druze community, such as the prohibition of polygamy, and increases the discretionary powers of religious judges over marriages and divorces. Article 308 entitles each Christian sect to adopt its own personal status law. For all Christian sects, a husband is legally required to provide financial maintenance for his wife, and if they are divorced, for his ex-wife for a limited period, unless they separate for reasons attributable to her.

The government drafted a new personal status law in 2009 that, if adopted, would have upheld the most oppressive of the existing provisions while adopting new, retrogressive measures. For instance, Article 21 of the draft law would have established a legal body entitled to unilaterally divorce a couple, regardless of their will, should one of the parties renounce their Muslim faith. Civil society actors unleashed a firestorm of criticism after the draft was leaked to the public, with activists utilizing social networking and electronic communication devices in a campaign against its adoption. Efforts concentrated on online outreach and successfully compelled the government to cancel the draft law.[20]

Muslim women are not free to marry without the permission of their *wali*, or male marriage guardian, who is generally the father or a *mahram*, a close male relative.[21] The marriage contract cannot be executed without the signature of a wali and two witnesses. However, according to Article 20 of the personal status law, a judge has the discretion to override objections by a wali if the objection "is not worthy of consideration." Under Article 27, if a marriage is contracted without the permission of the wali, he may request that it be dissolved only if the husband is deemed incompatible. Men reach the age of capacity for marriage at 18 and women at 17, but judges retain the discretion to marry girls as young as 13 and boys as young as 15 upon determination that the underage party has reached puberty.[22] Many marriages continue to be arranged between families rather than between the bride and groom. While the phenomenon is difficult to quantify, women may be placed under pressure to consent to a marriage they are not completely comfortable with, either for economic reasons or because their family desires the match.[23]

Although women are legally entitled to negotiate their rights within the marriage contract, social constraints limit their ability to do so. Article 14 of the personal status law permits a woman to make stipulations in the marriage contract that guarantee her right to work outside the marital home, continue her education after marriage, or obtain a divorce. Most stipulations are valid so long as they do not violate the word or intent of Shari'a. However, as a practical matter, many women—particularly those who are poor or illiterate—are not aware of these possibilities, and social customs pressure women not to demand too much.

Polygamy is legal, and the consent of the first wife is not a necessary precondition for a valid second marriage.[24] Article 17 of the personal status law requires a man who wishes to take a second wife to prove before a judge that he has the financial means to support her, as well as a legal justification, such as the first wife's inability to bear children.[25] In practice, these conditions do not present a significant obstacle to polygamous marriages. According to a 2005 survey, approximately 9 percent of urban and 16.3 percent of rural men have at least two wives.[26]

Men and women have unequal divorce rights. Men enjoy the right to *talaq*, or unilateral repudiation, which can be revocable or irrevocable and requires only that the man inform the authorities of his decision.[27] By comparison, women's access to divorce is time consuming and arduous. One option is *khula*, or a consensual divorce in which the wife returns her dowry to her husband and forfeits her right to financial maintenance. Alternatively, women may initiate divorce proceedings in the courts by showing injury, invoking a justification such as "dissension, prejudice, lack of affinity, absence, or ailments."[28] Women's rights within marriage, including grounds for divorce, are governed less by law and more by each couple's marriage contract. In the case of a divorce by the husband, women are entitled to continued financial support for a period of four months only.

Upon divorce, the mother is the primary custodian of children until boys reach 13 and girls reach 15, unless she remarries, in which case she automatically loses custody to the father.[29] Should a divorced mother be unfit or unable to fulfill her custodial role, the paternal grandmother is next in the succession, followed by other female relatives. While married women are prohibited from traveling with their children without permission from the children's guardian, typically the father, divorced mothers who hold custody of their children need no such permission. If a mother holds custody of the children, the father or other guardian must secure her permission before traveling with the children.[30]

In 2006, a personal status law was adopted for Syria's Catholic community. Under its provisions, women enjoy inheritance rights on par with men, parents have equal guardianship rights over children during marriage (although upon divorce, guardianship is offered to a father first and the mother second), and individual property acquired prior to marriage belongs solely to the original owner upon the dissolution of a marriage.[31] Although Catholic women represent only a small fraction of the population and it is unclear the extent to which these provisions have been enforced, this law represents an improvement to women's rights at the legislative level.

Women are generally protected against slavery and gender-based slavery-like practices, and Syria is not a major destination or transit country for human trafficking. However, trafficking of women for sexual exploitation does occur, and the war in Iraq has increased the influx of trafficked women and children; many female Iraqi refugees who lack other sources of income have turned to prostitution. The first shelter for trafficked women was opened in Damascus in December 2008. It is operated by a local nongovernmental organization (NGO) with support from the International Organization for Migration and the Ministry of Social Affairs and Labor, and provides psychological and medical services as well as legal assistance.[32]

Articles 509 through 516 of the penal code prohibit prostitution, harshly punishing the prostitutes while treating their clients merely as civil witnesses.[33] Pressuring or tricking women into prostitution is prohibited, as is the trade in women generally,[34] but Syria lacks specific antitrafficking legislation that would treat trafficked persons as victims. Instead, trafficking is only addressed through antiprostitution legislation.[35] A committee was established in 2005 to draft an antitrafficking law, but the legislation has yet to be enacted.

Article 28(3) of the constitution flatly prohibits torture, and Article 391 of the penal code outlaws the use of torture or "physical or mental pressure" to obtain a confession. Syria ratified the UN Convention Against Torture in 2004.[36] Despite these protections, it is widely recognized that torture and indefinite arrest are routinely used to silence critics.[37] In addition to opposition parties, the regime targets independent human and civil rights organizations, journalists, and religious activists.[38] The mistreatment of detainees has included cases of rape and violence against female inmates.[39]

No laws prohibit domestic violence, and a 2005 survey of 1,891 rural and urban families indicated that it is a prevalent practice throughout Syria. Of the women surveyed, 67 percent said they had been "punished" in front of their families, either through verbal insults, revocation of pocket money, or, in 87 percent of these cases, physical beatings.[40] In the same survey, 21.8 percent of women claimed to have been "exposed to violence." Of those who had been beaten, family members—particularly husbands and fathers—were the perpetrators 80.4 percent of the time.[41] Women have little redress in such situations, as police tend to be unsympathetic to victims of domestic violence and there are few public shelters.[42] Families tend to discourage women from making formal complaints so as to avoid public attention,[43] though they may confront the perpetrator behind closed doors. When the police do become involved, they generally attempt to reconcile the husband and wife, and only very rarely do women press criminal charges against men.

Women are also vulnerable to honor killings, or murders by close male relatives as retribution for actions that they see as damaging to the reputation of the family. Although such killings are most often prompted by real or perceived illicit sexual activities, they have also been used to punish marriage outside the family's religion. The premeditated honor killing of 16-year-old Zahra Ezzo by her brother in 2007 elicited public debate over the issue and drew condemnation of the practice from prominent religious leaders in Syria.[44] At that time, Article 548 of the penal code permitted the complete exoneration of a man who kills or injures his wife, sister, or other close female relative, along with her lover, if they are caught in an illicit sexual act. Additionally, Article 192 permits a large measure of discretion for judges in sentencing those convicted of any crime associated with restoring family honor. While Article 548 was amended in 2009 to replace the maximum one-year prison sentence with a minimum two-year sentence, Article 192 remains unchanged. An estimated 200 women are killed each year in honor-crime cases.[45]

Women lack protection against gender-based violence that occurs outside the home, such as rape. Article 489 of the penal code provides a minimum sentence of five years of hard labor for rapists and 21 years in prison if the victim was less than 15 years old. However, under Article 508 of the penal code, the perpetrator can avoid punishment by marrying his victim, and the code's definition of rape specifically excludes the rape of a spouse.[46]

The Syrian Commission for Family Affairs, a governmental body, has been at the forefront of the women's equality movement. Although it was only established in 2003, it lobbied heavily and successfully for the ratification of CEDAW and authored Syria's initial report to the CEDAW committee.

Recommendations

✤ The government should enact and enforce legislation that prohibits violence against women, including domestic violence. Victims of violence should have immediate access to means of redress and protection through the judicial system.

✤ The government should establish secure shelters across the country that provide services for female victims of violence and have adequately trained staff.

✤ Legislation should be adopted that fully addresses trafficking in persons and distinguishes properly between offenders and victims.

✤ Police forces should undergo training to improve their handling of gender-based violence, including domestic violence. Treatment of victims in police stations and in the field should be safeguarded by clear and rigorous procedures.

✤ The government should establish easily accessible mechanisms that allow women to file complaints of domestic violence.

✤ The government should reform the personal status law to ensure that women and men have equal rights in marriage, divorce, and child custody, and that polygamy and child marriages are prohibited.

✤ The government should raise awareness regarding gender issues among religious figures who can instill greater sensitivity in the public.

ECONOMIC RIGHTS AND EQUAL OPPORTUNITY

Women's labor participation rates have grown considerably in recent decades, but they still remain low in comparison to men's. The public sector is the main source of jobs, employing around 73 percent of the workforce. Agriculture continues to employ 19 percent of the workforce, while exports and government income are dominated by the oil sector, which is the largest single export earner despite being rather small by regional standards.[47] The majority of women are housewives, and those who work outside the home are generally employed in sectors like education and agriculture.

Women enjoy the right to own property, manage businesses independently, control their own income and assets, and initiate legal proceedings on an equal footing with men.[48] However, family pressure and a lack of confidence or expertise sometimes lead women to hand day-to-day control over these matters to male relatives. A husband may legally prohibit his wife from working outside the home, and can withhold financial maintenance if she does so without his permission. However, no laws prevent single women or married women with permission from their husbands from freely entering into economic contracts and activities. As noted above (see "Autonomy, Security, and Freedom of the Person"), women can also stipulate the right to work outside the home in their marriage contracts.

Women's inheritance rights are limited by law as well as in practice. In accordance with Shari'a, a woman receives only half of her brother's share of the parental estate. Male relatives from another branch of the family may compete for a share with the deceased's daughters if there is no direct male heir. These practices are based on the idea that men are culturally and legally responsible for the financial maintenance of the women in their family. Muslim women who are predeceased by their husbands receive their deferred dowry, followed by their legal share of the estate under Shari'a. However, non-Muslim women do not inherit from their Muslim husbands.[49] As a practical matter, even the limited inheritance rights granted to women are frequently violated, particularly when it comes to inherited land, as women are pressured to cede their inheritance to male family members.[50] The Muslim inheritance laws apply to followers of all religions except Catholics. Under the 2006 Catholic personal status law, Catholic men and women now enjoy equal inheritance rights.

State-funded education is free under Article 37 of the constitution, but attendance is only mandatory through the primary level, and dropout rates for both boys and girls are particularly high at the secondary level. This is partly because children who would otherwise enter secondary school are pressured to begin earning money or working in the home or on the family farm. Still, net secondary school enrollment has improved considerably in recent years, rising from 38.1 percent in 2000 to 66.7 percent in 2007 for boys, and from 35.3 percent in 2000 to 64.7 percent in 2007 for girls. Literacy rates remain fairly low, with only 76.5 percent of adult women and 89.7 percent of adult men literate as of 2007. However, this represents a steady improvement from 1981, when only 37.1 percent of adult women and 73.6 percent of adult men were literate. The gender gap narrows among those aged 15 to 24, with literacy rates at 92 percent for women and 95.4 percent for men as of 2007.[51]

School curriculums and textbooks have long reinforced gender stereotypes, though the Ministry of Education has been developing CEDAW-compatible materials for grade schools and universities in recent years.[52] Perceptions of women's roles with respect to education and employment have also been changing at the societal level, especially as worsening economic conditions encourage some conservative families to allow their daughters to pursue degrees and jobs in the formal sector.

Women now represent about 46 percent of university students,[53] though they continue to be concentrated in fields associated with their traditional gender roles, such as education and literature. They remain underrepresented in subjects such as mechanical engineering, medicine, economics, and political science.

Moreover, the employment options available to women are limited by overlapping legal restrictions and cultural norms. For example, not only must a woman ask her husband for permission to work outside the home, but Articles 131 and 132 of the labor law (Employment Act, No. 91 of 1959) prohibit women from working at night or in fields that are injurious to their health or morals. This rules out jobs in heavy industry, but there are exceptions to the night-work rule for jobs in fields like medicine, entertainment, and air travel.[54] Around 64 percent of women are housewives, according to 2006 estimates,[55] although the labor force participation rate of women aged 15 to 64 has grown from 12.6 percent in 1980 to 21.9 percent in 2007.[56] Despite these gains, women's participation lags far behind that of men, which stood at 80.4 percent for those aged 15 to 64 in 2007.[57]

Syria is still a largely agrarian society, and an estimated 49.1 percent of the female labor force worked in agriculture as of 2004, compared with 22.6 percent of the male labor force.[58] Women constitute 24.1 percent of public employees and tend to be relegated to clerical and administrative positions.[59] Within the stereotypically female-dominated teaching profession, women account for 64.5 percent of primary school teachers, 43 percent of secondary school teachers, and only 15 percent of university professors.[60] Women are also heavily represented in certain types of industrial work, particularly in the textile sector, where wages tend to be low and working conditions poor. In the private sector, especially in small businesses, workers are hired on a daily basis, which allows the employer to circumvent the labor law.

Rural women are particularly marginalized. Over 70 percent of rural women work more than 15 hours a day, yet their participation in marketing is only 3 percent, and their ownership of lands and machinery is also 3 percent.[61] Because most of this labor is unpaid and informal, female rural workers are unable to access the benefits available to white-collar employees. The pressure on girls to provide unpaid domestic and agricultural labor, as noted above, leads to higher school drop-out rates in rural areas, though the government has operated special programs to educate young female drop-outs in the rural north and east of the country.[62] The greater lack of schooling means rural women are less likely to be aware of their legal rights. Custom, as opposed to law, tends to be strongest in rural areas, compounding women's disadvantages with respect to marriage, inheritance, and other matters.

Financial institutions are reluctant to grant loans to rural women. Seventy-eight percent of rural women are interested in obtaining credit, according to a 2002 UNIFEM report, and half of those women would use it to start a business or expand their farming activities.[63] However, both state-owned and private banks generally focus on funding large-scale projects and require substantial assets as collateral.[64] A lack of training programs and awareness about credit opportunities puts would-be female entrepreneurs at a disadvantage. The practice of offering microfinancing, an approach utilized in other countries to benefit rural women, is still in its infancy in Syria. The first microcredit lending institution was established only in 2008.

The country's labor law, as stipulated in Article 130, treats men and women working in the same job equally, though it excludes women from certain types of employment, as noted above. Nevertheless, there is a large gender-based income gap, with women earning US$1,549 per capita in 2002, while men earned US$5,496 per capita.[65] It should be noted that such statistics fail to take into account the value of unpaid work performed by women in the home, obscuring women's true contributions. Much of the income disparity stems from lower levels of education among women and the high numbers of women working outside the formal economy.

Women employed in the formal sector enjoy gender-specific protections including 120 days of paid maternity leave for the first child, 90 for the second, and 75 for the third.[66] In addition, women may not be fired for taking maternity leave; unless they take more than six months' leave, they must be permitted to resume work with their employer.[67] However, few women are employed in the formal sector, reducing the positive impact of these measures, and women with temporary employment contracts do not have access to maternity benefits.[68] In jobs with pension benefits, women have the option of retiring five years before men; widows and widowers have equal rights to the pensions of their deceased spouses.[69]

Articles 505 and 517 of the penal code outlaw sexual harassment, including in the workplace, but there are no special provisions for the offense in the labor law. In the public sector, harassment is grounds for internal disciplinary procedures, while in the private sector such cases must be pursued through the courts as criminal matters. In practice, women usually attempt to resolve harassment problems informally rather than appealing to the authorities,[70] in part because they fear reprisals or dismissal by their employer.[71]

There are some organizations devoted to the economic empowerment of women. For example, MAWRED (Modernizing and Activating Women's Role in Economic Development) is an NGO founded in 2003 with the support of Syria's first lady. It aims to improve Syrian women's participation in economic and social development by training and providing assistance to female entrepreneurs.[72] In addition, the government cooperates with international organizations on a variety of rural antipoverty programs, with special provisions to benefit rural women.[73] However, labor organizations do not play a major role in promoting the role of women in the economy. Partly because of their smaller presence in the formal workforce, women constitute only around 20 percent of trade union members.[74] Women make up a similar proportion of the membership in professional associations, and an even smaller proportion of the officeholders. No women has held office in the Damascus branch of the Bar Association, though some have held leadership positions in provincial branches.[75]

Recommendations

✤ Labor unions should become more heavily involved in ensuring equal rights for women, preventing gender discrimination in the workplace, and improving women's access to economic resources and occupational training.

❖ Public and private lenders should take special measures to ensure equal access to savings and credit services for women.

❖ The government should step up its rural development schemes to ensure that rural women enjoy adequate living conditions, especially in relation to housing, sanitation, electricity, water supply, transportation, and communications.

❖ The government should incorporate sexual harassment provisions into the labor law that protect victims of harassment from retaliation and establish efficient procedures for filing and adjudicating civil complaints.

❖ School curriculums and materials should be thoroughly amended to remove gender stereotypes and introduce discussions of gender equality.

❖ NGOs and civil society activists should work to raise awareness and change cultural values that prevent women from obtaining formal employment and higher education.

POLITICAL RIGHTS AND CIVIC VOICE

The single biggest obstacle to participation in political and civic affairs is not specific to women, but arises from the nature of the regime and the restrictions it imposes on the whole of society. The political rights of all citizens have been curtailed under the state of emergency maintained since 1963. The government uses a dense network of intelligence agents to keep tabs on its population, and continues to restrict the activities of independent groups. While women have long played a role in public life, the repressive political environment prevents women's rights advocates from operating freely, constraining their ability to improve the status of all Syrian women.

Women obtained the right to vote in 1949, and in 1953 they gained the right to stand for elections, though the closed political system diminishes the practical value of both rights. Women have enjoyed a relatively large presence in Syria's unicameral parliament, the *Majlis al-Chaab*, or People's Assembly. In the national elections of April 22, 2007, women accounted for 1,004 of the 9,770 candidates running for the parliament's 250 seats. Thirty-one women were elected, representing 12.4 percent of the chamber.[76] Female politicians have had less success at the local level. On August 26 and 27, 2007, a total of 32,058 candidates competed for

9,687 council seats. Only 319 female candidates were elected to office, making up 3.2 percent of local council members.[77] Women are often hesitant to run for local council seats, partly because of societal norms that discourage female leadership in public life,[78] but also because citizens have little confidence in the local councils' integrity or effectiveness.

Men dominate the national political scene and hold the majority of decision-making positions within the executive branch, which has a history of military influence. The powerful presidency has been monopolized by the Assad family since 1970, when General Hafez al-Assad took office. Power was passed to his son, current president Bashar al-Assad, after his death in 2000. Under the constitution, the president is nominated by the Ba'ath Party and confirmed in office for seven-year terms through uncontested referendums. Women first made inroads in the executive branch in 1976, when a female culture minister was appointed to the cabinet. The government's ninth five-year plan set the goal of increasing the proportion of women holding decision-making positions in all branches of the government to 30 percent by 2010,[79] but few high-level positions are currently held by women.[80] They occupy 10 percent of ministerial positions, 11 percent of diplomatic posts, and 13 percent of judgeships, and a woman has served as state attorney since 1998. One woman has been a member of the Ba'ath Party's leadership body since 2005.[81]

Although women are involved in political parties, they continue to make up only a small proportion of the membership and tend not to be the driving force behind policy formation. Women seem to be best represented within the Communist Party, making up 20 percent of the membership.[82] However, all legal parties belong to an umbrella organization, the National Progressive Front (NPF), of which the ruling Ba'ath Party is the dominant component. Two-thirds of the parliament seats are reserved for the NPF, with the remainder going to independent candidates who are in practice vetted by and allied with the regime. Parties and other political groupings operating outside these parameters are not legally recognized and face severe constraints on their activities. As a result, they tend to focus on the broader questions of political freedom, as well as Syria's urgent economic problems, pushing women's issues to a back burner.

Although the unrecognized political groups opposing Ba'ath Party rule have failed to attract women in large numbers, many Syrian women have played important leadership roles in the fight for democracy and human rights. One example is Fida al-Hourani, a leader of a broad coalition known as the Damascus Declaration for Democratic National Change (DDDNC). The group unites liberal, Islamist, and Kurdish activists around a 2005 manifesto calling for peaceful democratic reforms. Al-Hourani and 11 other DDDNC activists were sentenced to 30 months in prison in October 2008. Another example is Suheir al-Atassi of the Jamal al-Atassi Forum for National Dialogue. She was arrested along with other Forum leaders in May 2005, and although she was released the following month, the authorities continued to persecute the group.

Both of these women are the daughters of notable Syrian political figures, but they have earned their own credentials through civic activism. By contrast, other women hold superficial positions within mainstream politics by virtue of their husband's or their family's names. A prime example of this phenomenon is First Lady Asma al-Assad, who since 2000 has established five charitable associations focusing on women and children, in addition to assuming a high-profile role in cultural activities and promoting Syria's image abroad. The fact that no woman has attained such prominence in her own right reflects the weak standing of female politicians, both within their parties and with the public at large.

All charitable organizations in Syria require official patronage, which often renders them mere extensions of the government rather than independent entities. The same is true of women's organizations generally. Under the Private Associations and Institutions Act (No. 93 of 1958), an association's charter and purpose must be approved by the Ministry of Social Affairs and Labor, and it cannot stray from its original mission. Article 2 of the law states that any group "established for an illicit reason or purpose, or which contravenes the law or the moral code, or the purpose of which is to prejudice the integrity or form of the republican government, shall be null and void." Similarly, all public meetings or demonstrations except religious services must be approved in advance by the authorities, and can be prohibited if they are deemed to threaten "public safety, national security, public order, the rights of others, public health or public morals."[83]

The GWU, which is affiliated with the Ba'ath Party, is the only legally recognized women's organization in Syria. While independent groups do operate, their work is often obstructed because they lack legal status. For example, the Syrian Women's League, founded in 1948, has been active in conducting studies on gender and development and training journalists on gender issues, but it faces close scrutiny by the government, limiting its ability to raise funds and hold events. Decades of political repression have stunted independent civic activism in general, as most citizens are unwilling to risk angering the authorities by participating.

The conditions described above leave women with little political influence, either as a voting bloc or as individual candidates and activists. Women have a degree of influence within economic organizations, accounting for around a fifth of the membership of trade unions and professional associations,[84] though all unions must belong to the Ba'ath-controlled General Federation of Trade Unions. Women's representation in leadership positions within unions has increased to 16.3 percent in recent years, with 16 women in executive offices in the provinces and one woman leading an association of trade unions. A number of the professional associations— such as the lawyers' syndicate, the engineers' syndicate, and the civil servants' syndicate—have established special committees for women, but these tend to be merely advisory or educational in nature, guiding the work of the larger organization and raising awareness of women's legal rights.[85]

The government's controls on political and civic discourse extend to the news media, which are subject to routine censorship. Journalists who criticize or offend the government face arrest and imprisonment, and media outlets practice self-censorship to avoid punishment. The state or allies of the government own most print and broadcast outlets, while private radio stations cannot carry news or political content. However, satellite television is widely available, giving viewers access to uncensored foreign broadcasts. The government is relatively tolerant regarding coverage of domestic violence and other women's rights issues, though religious groups occasionally exert pressure in an effort to suppress discussion of such topics.

As with satellite television, the expansion of the Internet has provided new sources of information on matters of significance to women's political and civic lives, although the government sometimes blocks websites that it deems politically sensitive and jails critical bloggers or website administrators. There are now over 3.5 million Internet users in Syria by some estimates,[86] and they are producing an array of blogs and other sites featuring news and commentary.[87] Those focusing on women's issues include Nesaa Souria (or Syrian Women Observatory, http://www.nesasy.org), Thara (http://www.thara-sy.com), and Ishtar (http://www.ishtar-sy.com). The social-networking site Facebook has been an important platform for women's rights campaigns, including a recent online campaign against a regressive draft personal status law.

Recommendations

❖ The government should allow civil society organizations and women's rights groups in particular to operate independently, in part by removing existing restrictions on registration and on the holding of meetings and demonstrations.

❖ The government should set aside public funds to support the campaigns of independent female candidates, with the aim of increasing women's representation in the national parliament and local councils.

❖ Political parties should phase in quotas for women in the rank and file as well as in leadership positions, using training programs and other incentives to attract new members.

❖ The government should fulfill existing goals with respect to female representation in the judiciary and executive branch entities, and raise its targets to match women's presence in the general population.

❖ The government should enact legislation that specifically protects free online expression as well as unrestricted access to the Internet and other new information technologies. It should devote additional resources to the improvement of the telecommunications infrastructure.

SOCIAL AND CULTURAL RIGHTS

Customary practices and attitudes dominate women's lives in Syria, often at the expense of the law of the land.[88] Women are treated as subordinate to men in the highly patriarchal culture, and social customs place gender-based restrictions on their rights. It is widely believed that the most appropriate sphere for women is the home and the family, while the wider world and the sphere of public interaction is reserved for men. However, there are signs that this is changing as women gain more access to education, participate in the workforce in larger numbers, and make important contributions to the family income amid difficult economic conditions.

While women are expected by society to exhibit a traditionally "feminine" personality, which includes submissiveness and adherence to patriarchal customs, older women often enjoy considerable influence over male family members within the household and in private settings. For example, a mother can pressure her sons to get married, and can choose their brides for them. There are no formal restrictions on women's dress, but women from conservative families may be obliged to wear *hijab* (head covering).

Health care is available free of charge in Syria, and men and women receive treatment on an equal basis. There are no societal restrictions on women's access to health care, though there may be economic pressures on the system that affect men and women alike. Women's ability to make decisions about their sexual and reproductive health has improved since the 1980s, when the government began promoting access to and use of contraceptives as part of its family planning program. Despite the fact that contraceptives technically remain illegal,[89] the government pays for 40 percent of the country's reproductive health tools and services, while the private sector accounts for the remainder. The Syrian Commission for Family Affairs operates a birth-control program through its 19 medical centers spread across the country, as well as a mobile clinic. The Syrian Women's League also plays an important role in raising awareness on birth control and family planning,[90] and information and family planning services are similarly available at government health centers and clinics run by the GWU and the Syrian Family Planning Association. An estimated 93 percent of women give birth in the presence of trained medical staff.[91]

The population growth rate has declined from 3.30 percent in 1993 to 2.45 percent in 2004.[92] More recently, the birth rate fell to 3.1 children per woman in 2007, from 3.7 in 2000.[93] Birth rates have fallen the fastest among urban women, due in part to the increase in the cost of living in the cities and the easier access to birth control. In rural areas, birth rates are kept higher by a culture of preference for sons and the need for unpaid agricultural labor by family members.

Abortion is a criminal offense and carries a prison sentence of at least six months for the woman and at least a year for anyone who assists her, with harsher penalties depending on the circumstances.[94] Despite these restrictions, it is possible to find doctors who will perform the operation, though often for a fee that is out of reach for many women, and in unsanitary conditions. In wealthier families, unmarried girls who become pregnant are pressured to have an abortion to maintain the appearance of family honor.[95]

Harmful gender-based traditional practices like female genital mutilation are rare in Syria, but early marriage remains fairly common. The practice has negative effects on the psychological and personal growth of young women and prevents them from developing themselves professionally or educationally, as they shoulder the brunt of domestic responsibilities and have little time for study. Yet for women without education or connections, marriage represents the primary means of obtaining economic security, and many families consider it desirable to have their daughters married off expeditiously.[96] A 2005 study found that 38 percent of women had married between the ages of 15 and 19.[97] Another survey found that 85 percent of rural women had married under the age of 20.[98] However, notions of early marriage have changed drastically over time, in part because society has come to appreciate the value of female education and employment. With larger numbers of both men and women postponing wedlock for various reasons, the average age of marriage is believed to have risen to the mid-20s for women and about 30 for men in recent years.[99]

Women are socially stigmatized by divorce,[100] and because they tend to work informally, at home, or in low-paying jobs, they have difficulty supporting themselves without their husband's financial maintenance. This problem is compounded by the fact that divorcees have no legal right to live in the marital home. Instead, a divorced woman must return to the home of her parents or a male relative. Although women have the legal right to rent or own houses and to live on their own, it is relatively rare for either married or single women to do so even when they have the means, as it has traditionally been considered unsafe or improper. Still, the number of young women living on their own is slowly increasing, mainly in urban areas.

Women's influence in community life and social development at the local level is very limited, especially in rural areas, due to the societal norms described above that discourage their participation in the public sphere. Moreover, there are few local organizations in Syria that could serve as a forum for such independent, apolitical community involvement.

Due to the expansion of private media and particularly of new technologies like the Internet, women are becoming more involved in the media and exerting a greater influence over public perceptions of gender. A woman was recently chosen to be the first female editor in chief of *Tishreen*, one of the most important newspapers in Syria.[101] Women comprise about 38 percent of the membership in the Journalists' Union.[102] Magazines produced by the GWU and the Syrian Women's League are devoted to women's rights and development specifically, though their circulation is small.

Recommendations

❖ The government should sponsor training programs for journalists and other news media workers to instill sensitivity to gender stereotypes, emphasize the importance of women's rights issues, and increase women's representation on the staff of state-owned outlets.

❖ The government should develop a package of financial incentives and career-track education programs to encourage families to postpone their daughters' marriages until after the teenage years.

❖ The government should work with international and domestic women's groups to develop engaging media content, including television programming, that deals with the challenges faced by Syrian women and aims to reshape public perceptions of women's role in society.

NOTES

1 Military Order, Law No. 2, March 8, 1963.
2 World Development Indicators (World Bank 2009), http://go.worldbank.org/U0FSM 7AQ40 (subscription required)
3 Personal Status Act (No. 59 of 1953).
4 OECD Development Centre, "Syrian Arab Republic," in *Social Institutions & Gender Index 2009* (Paris: OECD Development Centre, 2009), http://genderindex.org/country/ syrian-arab-republic.
5 *Initial Report of States Parties: Syria* (New York: Committee on the Elimination of Discrimination against Women [CEDAW], August 2005), 30, http://www.un.org/women watch/daw/cedaw/reports.htm#s.
6 *NGOs Report on the Initial Report of the Syrian Arab Republic on the CEDAW* (New York: CEDAW, 2007), 3, http://www.arabhumanrights.org/en/countries/shadow.asp?cid=19.
7 Law No. 276 of 1969.
8 Monique Cardinal, "Women and the Judiciary in Syria," *International Journal of the Legal Profession* 15, no. 1–2 (March–July 2008): 6.
9 Naser al-Ghazali and Khaoula Dunia, *Syrian Women: Between Reality and Ambition* (Damascus: Damascus Centre for Theoretical and Civil Rights Studies, 2007), http:// www.dctcrs.org/rep.nesasy.htm (in Arabic).
10 Syrian Human Rights Committee (SHRC), *Eighth Annual Report on Human Rights Status in Syria* (London: SHRC, January 2009), http://www.shrc.org/data/pdf/ANNUAL REPORT2009.pdf.
11 Article 46 of the civil code, Article 15 of the Commercial Law (No. 149 of 1949).
12 *Initial Report of States Parties: Syria*, 10.
13 Tomader Fateh, "Female Muftis in Damascus and Aleppo Soon: Syria's Grand Mufti Speaks," *Breaking Barriers* 14, no. 130 (April 2008), http://www.sabrang.com/cc/archive/ 2008/april08/bbarrier2.html.
14 Zafer Ahmad, "The Dilemma of Syrian Reservations to CEDAW," *Maan* no. 64.
15 *Initial Report of States Parties: Syria*, 33.
16 George Jabbour, "Syrian Women and Human Rights," paper presented at Damascus University, June 25–26, 2006, 4, http://www.fafo.no/ais/middeast/syria/syrianwomen/ SW-Jabbour.pdf.

[17] Front Line, the International Foundation for the Protection of Human Rights Defenders, *Travel Ban on Activists in Syria* (Dublin: Front Line, May 2009), http://www.frontlinedefenders.org/files/en/Travel%20Ban%20on%20Activists%20in%20Syria%20Final.pdf.

[18] Articles 74 and 75 of the Personal Status Act.

[19] *Initial Report of States Parties: Syria*, 15.

[20] Fay Ferguson and Nadia Muhanna, "Personal Status Matters," *Syria Today*, August 2009, http://www.syria-today.com/index.php/august-2009/377-society/2443-personal-status-matters.

[21] Article 21 of the Personal Status Act.

[22] Articles 15(1), 16, and 18 of the Personal Status Act.

[23] George Jabbour, "Syrian Women and Human Rights," 5.

[24] The personal status law is silent on this issue.

[25] Personal Status Act, Article 17.

[26] UN Development Fund for Women (UNIFEM), "Violence Against Women Study: Syria 2005," June 8, 2006, available at http://www.unifem.org/news_events/story_detail.php?StoryID=462.

[27] Personal Status Act, Article 91.

[28] Personal Status Act, Articles 105–12.

[29] *Initial Report of States Parties: Syria*, 95; Articles 139 (establishing hierarchy for custodianship) and 146 (setting the age for the end of custody) of the Personal Status Act.

[30] Articles 148–50 of the Personal Status Act.

[31] Items owned jointly, however, will go to the man upon dissolution of marriage unless "special circumstances are proved." "Laws Concerning Personal Status for Catholics in Syria," *Thara*, http://www.thara-sy.com/TharaEnglish/modules/news/articlephp?storyid=23.

[32] "Syria: First Shelter for Trafficked People Opens in Damascus," Integrated Regional Information Networks (IRIN), February 2, 2009, http://www.irinnews.org/Report.aspx?ReportId=82686.

[33] *Initial Report of States Parties: Syria*, 36.

[34] Suppression of Prostitution Act, No. 10 of 1961. Articles 1, 2, 3, 4, 6, and 7 prohibit trade in women.

[35] *NGOs Report on the Initial Report of the Syrian Arab Republic*, 4.

[36] George Jabbour, "Syrian Women and Human Rights."

[37] UN Human Rights Committee, *Concluding Observations: Syrian Arab Republic* (Geneva: UN Human Rights Committee, August 2005), http://www.unhcr.org/refworld/docid/43f2ff770.html.

[38] Human Rights Watch, *No Room to Breathe: State Repression of Human Rights Activism in Syria* (New York: Human Rights Watch, October 2007), http://www.hrw.org/sites/default/files/reports/syria1007.pdf.

[39] Interview with human rights activist (anonymous), June 9, 2009.

[40] UNIFEM, "Violence Against Women Study."

[41] UNIFEM, "Violence Against Women Study."

[42] Aside from the shelter for trafficking victims described above, there are at least two women's shelters in Damascus. One is administered by the Sisters of the Good Shepherd, and

the other is not equipped to handle a large number of women; neither is well known among the public. Interview with women's rights activist (anonymous).

43 Mousa Daad, "Discrimination Against Women in Syrian Penal Code," Conference on Women and Traditions, Damascus, November 13–15, 2005, http://www.thara-sy.com/thara/modules/tinycontent/print.php?id=23 (in Arabic).

44 Katherine Zoepf, "A Dishonorable Affair," *New York Times*, September 23, 2007, http://www.nytimes.com/2007/09/23/magazine/23wwln-syria-t.html; Rasha Elass, "'Honor' Killing Spurs Outcry in Syria," *Christian Science Monitor*, February 14, 2007, http://www.csmonitor.com/2007/0214/p07s02-wome.html.

45 "Syria Amends Honour Killing Law," British Broadcasting Corporation (BBC), July 2, 2009, http://news.bbc.co.uk/2/hi/middle_east/8130639.stm; Human Rights Watch, "Syria: No Exceptions for 'Honor Killings,'" news release, July 28, 2009, http://www.hrw.org/en/news/2009/07/28/syria-no-exceptions-honor-killings.

46 Article 489(1) states: "Anyone who uses violence or threat to force a person *other than his spouse* to engage in sexual intercourse shall be punished with a minimum of five years of hard labor." *Initial Report of States Parties: Syria*, 37 (emphasis added).

47 *Initial Report of States Parties: Syria*, 7.

48 Civil code, Articles 40 and 46; Commercial Law (No. 149 of 1949), Article 15. See also "Syrian Arab Republic," in *Member States Responses to the Questionnaire on Implementation of the Beijing Platform for Action (1995) and the Outcome of the Twenty-Third Special Session of the General Assembly (2000)* (New York: UN Division for the Advancement of Women, 2004), 11, http://www.un.org/womenwatch/daw/Review/responses.htm.

49 *Initial Report of States Parties: Syria*, 89.

50 "Women Miss Out on Property Rights in Syria," *Turkish Weekly*, October 18, 2008, http://www.turkishweekly.net/news/60305/women-miss-out-on-property-rights-in-syria.html.

51 World Bank, "GenderStats—Create Your Own Table," http://go.worldbank.org/MRER20PME0.

52 *Initial Report of States Parties: Syria*, 51.

53 Samira Soubh, *Women Empowerment in Syria: Policies & Related Institutions*, Working Paper No. 34 (Damascus: National Agricultural Policy Center, March 2008), 22–23, http://www.napcsyr.org/dwnld-files/working_papers/en/34_women-empower_ss_en.pdf,

54 *Initial Report of States Parties: Syria*, 51, 55.

55 Samira Soubh, *Women's Role in Agriculture and Gender Issues in Syria*, Policy Brief no. 10 (Damascus: National Agriculture Policy Center, March 2006), 1, http://www.napcsyr.org/dwnld-files/divisions/rdd/pubs/pol_brf/en/10_women_role.pdf.

56 World Bank, "GenderStats—Create Your Own Table," http://go.worldbank.org/MRER20PME0.

57 World Bank, "GenderStats—Labor Force," http://go.worldbank.org/4PIIORQMS0.

58 World Bank, "GenderStats—Labor Force."

59 "Syrian Arab Republic," in *Member States Responses*, 74.

60 *Initial Report of States Parties: Syria*, 49.

61 Hazzaa Assaf, "Women in Rural Development," *Thawra*, January 1, 2005 (in Arabic).

62 Samira Soubh, *Women Empowerment in Syria*, 19.

63 Rana Shanawani, *National Gender-Sensitive Programming Guidelines for Small and Micro Enterprises in Syria: The Regional Technical Resource Network for Women's Small and Micro Enterprises in the Arab States, Jordan, Lebanon, Syria and the Gaza Strip, September 2002* (Amman: UNIFEM, 2002), 24, http://www.unifem.org.jo/Attachments/307/bc6ea68f-2969-4ca6-ad6d-258c804b0126.pdf.

64 Rana Shanawani, *National Gender-Sensitive Programming Guidelines*, 13.

65 UN Development Programme (UNDP), *Gender Mainstreaming in Trade and Economy: The Case in Syria* (New York: UNDP, 2006), 5, http://www.undp.org.sy/files/Gender.pdf.

66 Article 133 of the labor law. See *Initial Report of States Parties: Syria*, 34.

67 Article 135. In addition, under Articles 133 and 137, working women who are breast-feeding are afforded breaks for that purpose for up to 18 months after giving birth, and the labor law provides for the establishment of childcare facilities, though these remain inadequate. See *Initial Report of States Parties: Syria*, 11, 34, 54.

68 Under Article 134, a woman is only entitled to these benefits if she has worked for her employer for at least seven months, thus excluding women working on temporary contracts.

69 *Initial Report of States Parties: Syria*, 13, 53.

70 *Initial Report of States Parties: Syria*, 55.

71 *NGOs Report on the Initial Report of the Syrian Arab Republic*, 3.

72 Samira Soubh, *Women Empowerment in Syria*, 15.

73 *Initial Report of States Parties: Syria*, 78.

74 *Initial Report of States Parties: Syria*, 11.

75 Issam Khoury, "Syrian Arab Republic—Gender Equity," 3.

76 Inter-Parliamentary Union, "Syrian Arab Republic: Majlis al-Chaab (People's Assembly)—Last Elections," PARLINE, http://www.ipu.org/parline-e/reports/2307_E.htm.

77 Program on Governance in the Arab Region (POGAR), "Country Theme: Local Government, Syria," UNDP, http://www.pogar.org/countries/theme.aspx?t=6&cid=19.

78 Interview with women's rights advocate (anonymous), June 11, 2009.

79 *Initial Report of States Parties: Syria*, 41.

80 Sawah Wael, "Women's Organizations and Societies in Syria," Nesaa Souria, May 7, 2009, http://nesasy.org/content/view/7247/257/ (in Arabic).

81 Samira Soubh, *Women Empowerment in Syria*, 21. http://www.napcsyr.org/dwnld-files/working_papers/en/34_women-empower_ss_en.pdf.

82 Interview with Communist Party member (anonymous), June 17, 2009.

83 *Third Periodic Report: Syria* (New York: UN Human Rights Committee, October 2004), 80, 88, http://www.arabhumanrights.org/publications/countries/syria/ccpr/ccpr-c-syr-2004-3-04e.pdf.

84 Issam Khoury, "Syrian Arab Republic—Gender Equity," 3.

85 Interview with women's rights advocate (anonymous), June 11, 2009.

86 International Telecommunication Union, "Internet Indicators: Subscribers, Users and Broadband Subscribers, 2008," http://www.itu.int/ITU-D/icteye/Indicators/Indicators.aspx#.

[87] Guy Taylor, "After the Damascus Spring: Syrians Search for Freedom Online," *Reason* (February 2007), http://www.reason.com/news/show/118380.html.

[88] *Initial Report of States Parties: Syria*, 35.

[89] Articles 523 and 524 of the penal code ban the advertising, promoting, selling, obtaining, or facilitation of contraceptive use.

[90] Yahya Aous, "Family Planning in Syria," *Al-Mizan* (December 2008), http://www.almizanmag.com/modules/news/article.php?storyid=31 (in Arabic).

[91] World Bank, "GenderStats—Health," http://go.worldbank.org/UJ0Q1KQKX0.

[92] Yahya Aous, "Family Planning in Syria."

[93] World Bank, "GenderStats—Health."

[94] Syrian law recognizes the fetus as a full person with rights of its own. The penalties for abortion are set out in Articles 527–29 of the penal code. See *Initial Report of States Parties: Syria*, 63; *Third Periodic Report: Syria* , 67.

[95] Ruba Shadoud, "The Black Market of Abortion," *Forward* (March 2009), http://www.fw-magazine.com/content/black-market-abortion.

[96] Muna Ghanem, Samuel Abboud, Sbaah al-Hallaq, and Sawsan Zakzak, *Women and the People's Assembly in the Syrian Arab Republic* (Amman: UNIFEM, March 2006), 8, http://www.unifem.org.jo/pages/articledetails.aspx?aid=743.

[97] UNIFEM, "Violence Against Women Study," 2.

[98] *Initial Report of States Parties: Syria*, 69–70.

[99] AMAN Jordan, "Rights of Syrian Women in Personal Status Law," August 2005, http://www.amanjordan.org/aman_studies/wmview.php?ArtID=921 (in Arabic); UNIFEM, *Evaluating the Status of Women* (Amman: UNIFEM, 2003), 24.

[100] Anna Jozwik, "Breaking the Bonds That Bind," *Syria Today* (January 2009), http://www.syria-today.com/index.phpjanuary-2009/105-society/368-breaking-the-bonds-that-bind-.

[101] "Women Advance in Media Battle in Syria," *Syrian Economic*, July 21, 2009, http://www.syrianeconomic.com/?page=show_det&select_page=39&id=816 (in Arabic).

[102] Naser al-Ghazali and Khaoula Dunia, *Syrian Women: Between Reality and Ambition.*

TUNISIA

Lilia Ben Salem

POPULATION: 10,429,000
GNI PER CAPITA: US$3,195

COUNTRY RATINGS	2004	2009
NONDISCRIMINATION AND ACCESS TO JUSTICE:	3.6	3.6
AUTONOMY, SECURITY, AND FREEDOM OF THE PERSON:	3.4	3.4
ECONOMIC RIGHTS AND EQUAL OPPORTUNITY:	3.1	3.2
POLITICAL RIGHTS AND CIVIC VOICE:	2.8	3.1
SOCIAL AND CULTURAL RIGHTS:	3.3	3.3

(COUNTRY RATINGS ARE BASED ON A SCALE OF 1 TO 5, WITH 1 REPRESENTING THE LOWEST AND 5 THE HIGHEST LEVEL OF FREEDOM WOMEN HAVE TO EXERCISE THEIR RIGHTS)

INTRODUCTION

Some 98 percent of Tunisia's roughly 10.4 million inhabitants are Muslim.[1] Tunisian society, as with all societies in the Arab world, was long characterized by clear differences between the roles of men and women, a distinction that was sanctified by religious texts and beliefs. Education, for both women and men, has been the main driver of social change. In the early 20th century, some urban families began to educate their daughters, and this trend gained a forceful momentum after independence. Today, the younger generations of women are as educated as their male counterparts and equally capable of participating in the economic life of the country as well as in decision making in all domains. Despite considerable progress, however, a cultural tendency to consider boys superior to girls and men superior to women largely persists within the social landscape.

Tunisia obtained its independence from France in 1956 and has been a republic since 1957. During the colonial period, women were marginalized and secluded: there was little access to education, economic activity was largely confined to the household, wearing of the veil was widespread, and there was no female participation in public life. These conditions were interpreted as the expression of Islamic identity and Tunisian culture. In the 1920s and 1930s, as the struggle for independence intensified, voices

487

were raised for greater equality between the sexes. A few women publicly denounced women's confinement, illiteracy, subservient position within the family, and imposed marriages, though their pleas for change went unanswered. The first women's association, the Tunisian Women's Islamic Union, was created in 1936.[2] Women went on to participate in the fight for independence, and slowly affirmed their place in society. By 1956, nationalist leader Habib Bourguiba's speeches were emphasizing that the development of the country depended upon the participation of everyone, women and men alike.

The code of personal status, promulgated in 1956 and amended several times since, most notably in 1993, created conditions that would permit women to fulfill their role in society in many aspects. The abolition of polygamy and repudiation, the legal right for women to ask for divorce, the establishment of a minimum age for marriage, and the required consent of both spouses to marriage have all further strengthened the freedom and social status of women. A 1958 reform introduced the idea of generalized and free education from ages 6 to 14 for all, creating conditions for the massive schooling of girls. In 1957, women became citizens with the right to vote, and by virtue of the 1959 constitution both men and women were enabled to seek elected office.[3] The constitution also enshrines the principle of equality, which has been incorporated through time into other legal texts, including the electoral code, the labor code, and the code of nationality. As a result, women have obtained the right to work, to move freely, to open a bank account, and to establish a business, all without the permission of their father or husband.

In recent years, women in Tunisia have continued the positive trajectory in terms of education and economic empowerment. The comprehensive 1991 reform of the educational system made attendance for both girls and boys compulsory from ages 6 to 16, resulting in a dramatic increase in the enrollment rates to secondary schools. Today, more university students are female, and women constituted 27.9 percent of the labor force in 2007.[4] They hold diverse positions in most sectors, including those traditionally closed to women, such as the judiciary, the army, engineering, and medicine. Yet inequity persists, particularly in rural settings, where women rarely own land and are overwhelmed by having to balance both farm and domestic work. Additionally, women are promoted to managerial positions less often and earn less than men on average, particularly in the private sector.

Together, the Ministry of Women, Family, Childhood, and the Elderly (MAFFEPA), the National Board for Family and Population Affairs, approximately 20 women's organizations, and women's committees within the political parties actively contribute to the consolidation of women's rights and the reduction of gender-based inequality in all areas. Furthermore, researchers in social sciences are frequently solicited to study women's issues. Their findings and work, as well as the innovative behavior of women themselves, often meet with resistance by supporters of a conservative form of Islam.

NONDISCRIMINATION AND ACCESS TO JUSTICE

Since the year 2000, very few new laws that favor women have been adopted. The bulk of the juridical corpus seems to be in place, and the remaining legal issues, such as inequality with regard to inheritance, have not prompted fresh reforms. Conflicts within the judiciary continue between those who—referring to the first article of the constitution, which states that the religion of Tunisian society is Islam—tend to support Islamic law, and those who favor application of substantive law, personal status code, and international conventions ratified by Tunisia. An oscillation persists between traditional values and a spirit of innovation as the tendency toward the principles of equality, nondiscrimination, and liberty continues to be in competition with the dominant conservative values.[5]

Tunisia's primary legal texts were promulgated during the colonial period (1881–1955) and were largely inspired by French law, but personal status issues remained under the jurisdiction of religious law. After independence, the personal status code and a unified civil court system replaced the existing Shari'a and rabbinical tribunals. The Tunisian constitution, drafted by the National Constituent Assembly and promulgated on June 1, 1959, was conceived "to guarantee a stable political system." The Constitutional Council, created in December 1987, did not have the power to rule on the constitutionality of laws—its role was primarily advisory in nature.[6] However, amendments introduced since 1990 require that all projects concerning organic law and those pertaining to individual rights and freedoms must be in accordance with the constitution.[7]

Article 6 of the constitution guarantees the equal rights of all citizens, men and women alike. The preamble affirms that the Tunisian people should "consolidate national unity and remain faithful to human values which constitute the common heritage of peoples attached to human dignity, justice, and liberty." Constitutional amendments made in 1997 consolidated the principle of equality among citizens, while a 2002 amendment stressed the guarantee of fundamental freedoms and human rights, pluralism, human dignity, and the free exercise of beliefs (Article 5). It also enshrined the inviolability of the home, the secrecy of correspondence, and the protection of personal data (Article 9).

Despite these guarantees, the nationality law contains discriminatory provisions regarding the right of female citizens to pass their nationality to their noncitizen spouses. The noncitizen wife of a Tunisian man automatically adopts Tunisian citizenship upon marriage, often forfeiting her original nationality in so doing. Even if she retains her previous citizenship, she can acquire Tunisian nationality by simply declaring domicile in Tunisia.[8] However, the noncitizen husband of a Tunisian woman can acquire Tunisian nationality only by decree and only if he is a Muslim who resides in Tunisia and has sufficient knowledge of the Arabic language. Even those who fulfill the conditions of naturalization often have difficulties obtaining Tunisian citizenship. A 2002 amendment to the nationality law permits Tunisian women married to noncitizens to transmit their nationality to their child, even if the child is born abroad, provided that the father consents.[9]

Most women have equal access to justice, due in large part to Tunisia's long history of women in the judiciary and the state's executive-level commitment to women's rights. The first woman judge was appointed in 1968, and today an estimated 27 percent of judges and 31 percent of lawyers are women. Additionally, the principle of equality of men and women before the law is affirmed in many of Tunisia's legal codes. With regard to the right to work, the equality of men and women is established both within the civil service and Article 5 of the 1993 labor code, which emphasizes the legislators' intent to "repeal all forms of work-related discrimination between the sexes." An adult woman's legal capacity is affirmed by the 1956 Law of Obligations and Contracts, and a woman's testimony carries the same weight as a man's before the court. Nonetheless, discrimination persists, most often in policies grounded in religious interpretations, such as those related to family life including a women's right to choose her husband and her right to inheritance. The existence of these religion-based disparities within Tunisian legislation and the popular support for such provisions explains the reluctance of the state to embrace certain international standards, such as those found in the Convention on the Elimination of All Forms of Discrimination against Women (CEDAW) and established during the Beijing Fourth World Conference on Women.

Following the 1993 amendments to the personal status code, the penal code was amended to criminalize domestic violence and remove gender-discriminatory language that had allowed for a reduction in sentencing for a man who committed acts of violence against his spouse.[10] The amended law now treats this crime as subject to the penalty applicable for manslaughter, namely life imprisonment.[11] Additional amendments to the penal code consider domestic violence as more serious than typical assault and battery; one amendment provides that the person who commits the assault is actually liable for a heavier punishment if the victim is his spouse.[12] The impact of this amendment, however, is often weakened by the provision which stipulates that "withdrawal of the complaint by a victim who is an ascendant or spouse shall terminate any proceedings, trial or enforcement of penalty."[13]

Prostitution is illegal under a 1942 decree, and is punished as incitement to immoral behavior under Article 231 of the penal code.[14] Additionally, Article 234 imposes heavier sentences in the case of "corruption of minors." Soliciting a prostitute for sex is similarly punished under Articles 232 and 233 of the penal code.

Tunisia signed CEDAW in 1980 and ratified it in 1985, while issuing a general declaration statement positing that Tunisia "shall not take any organizational or legislative decision in conformity with the requirements of this Convention where such a decision would conflict with the provisions of Chapter I of the Tunisian Constitution" (referring to the identification of Islam as the state religion). Reservations were also made to Article 9(2), regarding the right of a woman to pass her nationality to her children; Article 15(4), regarding the right of the woman to choose her own domicile; several paragraphs of Article 16 related to marriage and divorce; and Article 29, regarding arbitration of disputes arising from the convention. In September 2008, Tunisia became only the second Arab country after Libya to ratify the Optional Protocol to CEDAW. By ratifying this document, Tunisia has recognized the competence of the CEDAW Committee to hear complaints from individuals and groups of individuals who believe their rights under the convention have been violated by the state. However, because the committee is only able to issue nonbinding opinions, the impact of the protocol is as yet unclear.

The fundamental purpose of the women's affairs ministry, MAFFEPA, is to ensure the equality of the sexes. It coordinates the activities of various government institutions in an effort to promote the status of women and the family, and to encourage women to assume a major role in the development process. Women's rights are part of the concerns of organizations such as the National Union of Tunisian Women (UNFT), the Tunisian Association of Democratic Women (ATFD), and more than 20 other women's groups. The Women and Development Committee, founded in June 1991, examines different development plans through their various stages to ensure that gender equality is respected.

The National Council of Women and Family, established in 1992, was strengthened in 1997 with the creation of three commissions—the Commission on the Image of Women in the Media, the Commission on the Promotion of Equal Opportunities for All and for the Application of the Law, and the Commission of National and International Deadlines Pertaining to Women and the Family. The Center for Research, Documentation, and Information on Women (CREDIF), the Association of Tunisian Women for Research and Development (AFTURD), as well as the National Office of the Family and Population Affairs—which primarily acts to watch over the health and reproductive rights of women—have all undertaken a number of studies on conditions for women. The Center for Arab Women Training and Research (CAWTAR), based in Tunis, carries out comparative studies among Arab nations and promotes gender equality through advocacy and workshops.

Recommendations

* The government should ensure that the laws, in particular those concerned with the protection of the individual, are properly enforced in a nondiscriminatory manner.
* The government should amend the Code of Nationality to allow Tunisian women to transfer their nationality to their non-Tunisian husbands.
* The government should withdraw Tunisia's reservations to CEDAW and ensure its implementation by bringing national laws in conformity with the convention.

AUTONOMY, SECURITY, AND FREEDOM OF THE PERSON

Tunisian citizens, whether male or female, generally enjoy freedom of movement, religious belief, and other individual freedoms under the law. However, societal attitudes continue to perpetuate inequity in practice. Pressure by Islamists cropped up in the late 1980s and again in 2004, with a campaign intending to "safeguard tradition" by promoting regressive measures regarding women's rights. These efforts were rapidly quelled following public protests by women's groups, but a state of tension persists between the notion of gender equality and a sense of religious identity that promotes the traditional division of gender roles. Over the last five years, several progressive measures were undertaken that have a potential to improve women's lives in the time to come. In particular, the minimum age for marriage has been raised to 18 for both men and women and the government has begun tackling the issue of domestic violence more aggressively.

Although the Tunisian constitution guarantees freedom of belief, the state tends to restrict what it perceives to be manifestations of religious fundamentalism. In recent years, the government has increased pressure on residents to refrain from wearing traditional religious clothing, applicable to both men and women. In 1981, a law was passed banning the wearing of the *hijab* (traditional Islamic veil) by women in public offices, and decree 108 of 1985 bans hijabs in educational establishments. Enforcement of these rules revived in the beginning of the 1990s and intensified again in 2006. Despite these measures, the wearing of the hijab has become more widespread, especially among young working women and students, many of whom claim the right to wear a hijab as a form of freedom. In 2008, lawyer Saida Akremi won a lawsuit on behalf of a schoolteacher who contested her inability to wear the veil at work, but the effects of the case have been limited because of the resistance to implement the decision throughout the country due to its divisive nature.[15]

No laws limit freedom of movement for women. However, they continue to face restrictions on the societal level, and it is within the family that gender inequality is the most apparent. Although women do not require an authorization from their fathers or husbands to travel, family honor tends to dictate movement of women and girls in public, ostensibly for their own protection. The men of the family—father, brothers, husbands—often intervene to restrict and control the physical space of their daughters, sisters, and wives.

A woman's ability to negotiate her marital rights is influenced by social pressure more than law. Young people are free to choose their marriage partners, and while they are respectful of their family's wishes, they can no longer be forced into marriage. A Muslim man may marry a woman outside his faith, but a Muslim woman is prohibited from marrying a non-Muslim. Should a Muslim Tunisian woman and a non-Muslim man attempt to circumvent this law by marrying outside the country, the marriage would not be recognized in Tunisia.

Both prospective spouses have the right to include stipulations within the marital contract, which may include provisions related to the division of property upon divorce or the right of either spouse to complete his or her education.[16] Amendments made to the personal status code in 2008 establish 18 as the minimum age for marriage for both men and women. Previously, the minimum age was 17 for women and 20 for men. The age of legal majority, previously 20, was also set at 18 in 2008.

Amendments made in 1993 to Article 23 of the personal status code established the equality of spouses with regard to reciprocal family obligations, cooperation in household management, and assistance in childcare. Both husband and wife are expected to treat each other well and refrain from injuring one another; both are expected to fulfill their "conjugal duties"; and both are expected to cooperate in running the family affairs. The wife does not have the duty to obey, but the husband is still considered the "head of the family" with the responsibility to financially support his wife and children. However, the wife also has the duty to contribute to maintaining the family, if she has the means to do so, a rather unique provision as compared to the personal status laws of neighboring countries.

Recent studies have shown a persistent imbalance in how family members budget their time on a daily basis; such inequality is especially prevalent in rural areas, but is also apparent in urban environments.[17] The data show that gender roles are deeply entrenched, and that while men divide their time between work and leisure, women spend most of their time doing household work.[18] One study also indicated that women's total daily workload, including paid labor, family care-giving, and domestic work, is on average two hours longer than that of men, and that "whatever their professional situation, women always have a greater workload than men."[19]

The workload of rural women is particularly heavy. The same study found that while men spend on average 36 percent of their time outside the home in a public or professional environment, women spend only 14 percent of their time outside the home.

Another study was conducted in 2007 on the extent to which men and women adhere to "egalitarian values," using a representative sample of 1,320 men and women living in an urban setting with their families.[20] It showed that even though a majority of men and even more women favor the principle of sharing duties equally, most uphold the traditional division of domestic chores. The organization of the family unit is increasingly open to negotiation, and women participate more in family decision making. However, the belief that a wife has a duty to obey her husband is held by 82 percent of men and 68 percent of women.[21] Also, while 50.3 percent of women and 36.6 percent of men surveyed agreed that men and women should be equal and have the same authority within the family, 32 percent of men and 20 percent of women absolutely opposed this principle of equality.[22]

Unless they choose otherwise, Article 24 of the personal status law mandates a separation of goods between spouses in conformity with the principle of equality, a provision that is confirmed by Islamic law.[23] In 1998, amendments were made to the personal status law that introduced a sense of community within the institution of marriage. As such, couples may opt for marriages with a communal estate comprised only of property acquired after marriage, except goods transferred specifically "to one of the two spouses by inheritance, gift or legacy."[24]

Divorce may be secured in three different manners. First, the two spouses may mutually consent to divorce. Second, one of the spouses may establish injury as the basis of divorce, giving rise to damages by the offending spouse. Article 53bis of the personal status code (as amended by law No. 74 of 1993) envisages penalties for husbands who default on their debts to their wives. Finally, divorce may be granted based on the request of either spouse. Law No. 65 of 1993 established a fund for alimony and divorce annuity that ensures the payment of pensions and annuities, as established by a court, when the husband refuses to pay them to divorced women and their children. In an effort to strengthen enforcement of laws related to divorce, the position of "family judge" was created in 1993.[25] This type of judge intervenes primarily in divorce cases, and the position was strengthened with the 1995 Code for the Protection of Children to further protect children at risk.

Under Article 58 of the personal status code, judges have the discretion to grant custody to either parent based on the best interest and welfare of the child, so long as the parent is over 21 years old, is able to support the child, is free from contagious disease, and is of sound mind. The same article stipulates that if the father is awarded custody, he must demonstrate that there is a woman in his life to help him shoulder the responsibility. On the other hand, the female custodian must not be married except in certain circumstances.

Fathers are automatically granted guardianship—the right to make life decisions—over their children in the event of a divorce, even if the mother retains physical custody.[26] Amendments made in 1993 increased the guardianship rights of a custodial mother, giving them a say in decisions related to their children. Additionally a judge may grant guardianship to a mother if the father proves unable to fulfill his duties, if he abandons his child, or for any other reason deemed to be in the best interest of the child. In the case of the father's death, children are now placed with their mothers rather than the husband's closest relative.

Child support is routinely awarded to custodial mothers, who also receive the state family allowance.[27] On February 19, 2008, the Chamber of Deputies passed a bill that ensures the right to housing for mothers with children in their custody. As of 1993, both the maternal and paternal grandparents with custody over their grandchildren are entitled to a family allowance, an advantage formerly enjoyed only by the paternal grandparents. Under Law No. 200-51 of 2003, a mother can give her name to children born out of wedlock.

Acts of gender-based violence, including incidents that occur within the family, are criminal offenses. The bond of marriage is considered an aggravating circumstance when violence has been committed against a woman.[28] However, legislation only punishes physical violence, and while rape is harshly punished under Article 227 of the penal code, marital rape is not a crime. In practice, many cases of violence are not reported by victims or their families, in part because it is difficult to secure effective inquiries into such claims. Police officers often lack the training and resources necessary to conduct objective investigations or protect victims.

The issue of domestic violence is rarely acknowledged at a social level. Although 60.4 percent of men feel that a husband must not be violent toward his wife, 38.5 percent feel that they may beat their wife in certain circumstances. Such circumstances include disobedience or when the wife does not fulfill what her husband considers to be "women's obligations." One study found that one-quarter of women and girls have experienced some form of gender-based violence within the family, and over a quarter of men admitted to having been violent toward their wives, sisters, or daughters.[29] In response to findings such as these, the government in cooperation with women's groups launched a campaign against domestic violence in 2007, holding workshops and engaging religious scholars, policemen, judges, and social workers to raise awareness of the issue.

Women's rights organizations have increasingly invested efforts to combat gender-based violence. The ATFD has been interested in this issue since it was founded in 1989, and it established a center in Tunis for counseling and legal assistance for female victims in 1993. Also in the early 1990s, the UNFT sponsored the first study evaluating the problem.[30] One of its recommendations was to create a Welcome Center, opened in 2003, to shelter women who are mentally or physically abused.

Today, violence toward women is a concern not only of women's groups with international ties, but also of numerous local groups and governmental ministries, including the ministries responsible for public health, women and the family, social affairs, education and training, and higher education. A national strategy against violent behavior within the family and in society was initiated in January 2009.[31] Since 2000, numerous doctoral and master's theses in sociology and medicine have focused on gender-based violence.[32] AFTURD undertook two studies in recent years in which the question of violence toward women was examined.[33] The National Office of the Family and Population Affairs and CAWTAR are working together on a joint research project on the same issue.

Recommendations

✤ The government should ensure that the culture of gender equality is promoted in schools and through the media by establishing educational programs and civic awareness campaigns.

✤ All forms of violence and harassment of women should be penalized, including verbal and psychological violence, as well as marital rape.

✤ The question of violence, in particular gender-based violence, should be the focus of a print and broadcast media campaign intended to make different social groups more sensitive to the issue.

✤ Women's shelters and centers should be established throughout the country to receive victims of violence. They should be able to accommodate women, young girls, and teenagers, as well as mothers with their children who have suffered abuse.

✤ Qualified personnel in various fields, including social workers, police, judges, psychologists, sociologists, and doctors, should receive in-depth training on how to deal with victims of gender-based violence.

ECONOMIC RIGHTS AND EQUAL OPPORTUNITY

Under current legislation, women benefit from the same rights as men concerning economic matters. They have the right to own property,[34] and once they reach adulthood at the age of 18, they can open a bank account, take out a loan, and enter freely into business and financial contracts and transactions. In practice, however, women remain underrepresented in the workforce and face gender-based salary inequity and obstacles in career advancement, notably in the private sector. Nonetheless, the economic role of women has improved in recent years. Women are increasingly rising to managerial positions or taking the initiative to establish their own businesses, despite considerable social resistance.[35] They have the same legal access as men to education and continue to outperform men academically while instilling hope that gender equality at the workplace is not a distant goal.

Although both Tunisian law and Islam recognize women's right to own property, including land, women rarely exercise this right in practice. The existing secular tradition transfers the ownership of land and real estate from father to son in a patrilineal manner. Until recently, women could not own land except when it was inherited, and even then, rural women traditionally renounced their inheritance in keeping with the idea that land was an expression of familial honor and could not in any circumstance be transferred to another family. Thus women inherited only when they married a paternal cousin, allowing property to be retained by the patrilineal group.[36]

Today, land and real estate are rarely registered in the woman's name, and rental contracts for family residences are usually under a man's name as well. In the study on egalitarian values mentioned above, the majority of single people surveyed said their dwelling (whether rented or owned) was registered in their father's name, while a very small percentage listed their mothers.[37] Married men usually declared the registration under their own name and only rarely under the wife's name or jointly as a couple.[38] Some young couples opt for a marriage in which all goods acquired after marriage are divided equally, in accordance with the law of November 9, 1998.

With regard to inheritance, the personal status code and Shari'a as traditionally practiced in Tunisia generally recognize the preeminence of patrilineal relatives and men over women.[39] Article 143bis of the code was amended in 1959 to permit girls to receive the full inheritance of their father or mother when there were no male heirs.[40] Nonetheless, in practice, if paternal relatives make a claim to inheritance, the wives, sisters, and daughters will often inherit half the share of male heirs with equal family ties. One of the most glaring examples of gender-based discrimination is the law that prohibits a non-Muslim wife from inheriting from her Muslim husband or their children, who are Muslim through agnatic filiation. In February 2009, however, the Supreme Court of Appeals issued a judgment that a non-Muslim woman had the right to inherit from her husband under the constitutional provision that guarantees freedom of worship.[41] It is unclear what impact this ruling will have on the existing law.

Inequality in the inheritance rights of men and women has been frequently challenged by women's organizations. AFTURD sponsored a research paper on the question of inheritance,[42] and two law professors advocating for equality in inheritance describe their work as "a plea for the establishment of egalitarian inheritance rights to put an end to the discrimination women still face."[43]

Some studies indicate that the unequal inheritance laws can be circumvented, either by the equal sharing of estates or the distribution of gifts by still-living parents to their daughters or by husbands to their non-Muslim wives. Legislation has facilitated these strategies by granting tax exemptions, lowering the registration fee of gifts and succession to 5 percent between siblings and to 2.5 percent for exchanges made between spouses, ascendants, and descendants.[44]

Primary education became widely available after independence, and in 1991, education became compulsory until the age of 16. These factors, in addition to the high value placed on education by society, have permitted both women and men to increase their educational attainment. Education reform instituted by Law No. 65 of 1991 stipulates that "the primary goal of the education system is to prepare students for a life that leaves no room for any discrimination or segregation based on sex, social class, race or religion." In the 1956 census, 84.7 percent of the Tunisian population over 10 years old was illiterate—74.5 percent of men and 96 percent of women. As of the 2004 census, the illiteracy rate for adults had dropped to 22.9 percent—14.8 percent of men and 31.1 percent of women.[45] By 2007, the literacy rate for youths ages 15 to 24 had improved to 94.3 percent for girls and 97 percent for boys.[46] The National Program of Adult Education makes basic courses available to uneducated adults, and attendance by women from both rural and urban areas is particularly high.

As of 2007, 96.7 percent of school-age girls and 95.5 percent of boys were enrolled in full-time primary education.[47] After primary schools, women tend to achieve higher levels of education than boys, outnumbering boys at universities by a large margin. During the 2007–2008 academic year, 59.5 percent of students registered in higher education institutions in Tunisia were female. Students display gender bias in their choice of discipline, however. Whereas women constitute the majority of students in the arts, social sciences, and medicine, men dominate engineering and technical vocations. According to Ministry of Higher Education enrollment figures for the 2002–2003 academic year, women made up 68.7 percent of students registered in the arts and social science departments, 63 percent in medicine and paramedical disciplines, and 57.5 percent in law, economics, and management. They accounted for just 29.7 percent of those registered in engineering schools or preparatory courses.[48]

The right to work is legally recognized for women as well as men. The labor code calls for the repeal of "all forms of discrimination between the sexes with regard to work,"[49] and Article 234 of the labor code mandates a penalty for all violations of this basic right. In 1993, the requirement that a woman must secure her husband's authorization to work was struck from the Law of Obligations and Contracts. A woman's right to work is further developed in Article 64 of the labor code, regarding maternity leave and nursing mothers. Articles 66 and 68 prohibit women from working between 10 p.m. and 6 a.m. except in certain circumstances. Although women make up 59.5 percent of postsecondary graduates, however, female degree-holders have more trouble finding work than their male counterparts. Of those degree holders in search of work, 51.6 percent of men are successful, compared with 38.3 percent of women.[50]

According to the World Bank estimates, women represented 26.7 percent of Tunisia's working population in 2007, a slight increase from the 2003 figures, when women's share stood at 25.9 percent.[51] Women's access to higher levels of education has helped them enter the workforce in greater numbers and obtain promotions to managerial positions that were once the exclusive domain of men.[52] That said, women are concentrated in certain sectors, particularly in agriculture, even if the statistics do not yet reflect this reality.[53] Numerous farms rely heavily on female workers,[54] even though official data show that only 16.7 percent of agricultural enterprises are headed by women. More often, they are household help or seasonal employees.[55]

Some 23.9 percent of the active female workforce is employed in the agricultural and fishing sector, 37.7 percent in the service industry, and 38.3 percent in manufacturing, mostly in the textile industry. Women form 39 percent of the staff in the civil service, and 24.3 percent of women bureaucrats hold managerial positions. Many women work in the education sector, constituting 51 percent of primary school teachers, 48 percent of secondary school teachers, and 40 percent of higher education professors. Within the health field, women make up 42 percent of doctors, 72 percent of pharmacists, and 57 percent of dental surgeons. In recent years, women have been establishing their own businesses in larger numbers, and in the informal sector they show initiative in ensuring their self-employment. Training sessions given by the MAFFEPA encourage women to develop their competencies and to adopt an entrepreneurial spirit. At a January 2009 press conference, the ministry stated that by the end of 2009, at least 30 percent of managerial positions would be held by women.[56]

Law No. 30 of 1968 instituted salary parity and equality between men and women in the civil service and broader public sector. However in the private sector there is a noticeable gender difference in earnings.[57] General revenue studies indicate that far more women than men earn a monthly salary of less than 200 dinars (US$152). When earnings are between 200 and 400 dinars (US$152 to US$303), there is little difference between men and women, but as salaries increase, inequity becomes more apparent.[58]

Professional women, particularly those with demanding careers, experience difficulties in balancing their professional and familial duties. Studies of female managers and engineers show they lack time and are subject to fatigue and stress. Men rarely participate in housework or share childcare responsibilities, instead retaining their traditional gender roles. Adding to the pressure, women in modern Tunisian society have less opportunity to benefit from the traditional support of their mothers, mothers-in-law, or sisters, in part because they may have their own careers or live some distance away. Social services are grossly insufficient substitutes for these family members. As a result, women who are strongly attached to their traditional domestic role suffer career setbacks, and those who concentrate on their career either utilize family and social support or rely on paid domestic help.[59] Furthermore, women in managerial positions increasingly opt to remain single. Women who start their own businesses have difficulties securing loans and are frequently pressured to turn over the management and benefits to male family members.

The 2004 census shows unemployment figures at 13.9 percent (12.9 percent for men and 16.7 percent for women). During the last five years, 600 businesses in the textile industry have closed. Because 29 percent of working women are employed in that industry, the closures have led to layoffs for over 35,000 women. Most had not availed themselves of the services of the commission that oversees layoffs and are consequently not protected by the labor code.[60]

Women in the workforce enjoy some gender-based benefits. Those in the civil service may take two months of maternity leave at full pay. In the private sector, maternity leave technically lasts only 30 days, but it can be extended for 15-day periods for medical reasons for up to 12 weeks. Mothers are also entitled to a half-hour break twice a day for one year to breastfeed infants. Since 2006, in the public sector, the law has permitted mothers with children under 16 or with a handicapped child to work part-time while receiving two-thirds of their salary for a period of three years, twice renewable.[61] However, these measures have the unfortunate effect of consolidating the inequity between men and women in their representation in various social institutions, and of accentuating the differences between the public and private sectors.

The MAFFEPA recently mandated new requirements with regard to the provision of nurseries and daycare facilities, and between 2004 and 2008 the number of childcare centers increased from 11 to 186.[62] As of July 2004, Article 226ter of the penal code now criminalizes sexual harassment, punishable by up to one year in prison and a fine of 3,000 dinars (US$2,274).[63] If the victim is a minor, the punishment is doubled. Studies have shown that women frequently experience discrimination in their interactions with men at work.[64] They do file sexual harassment complaints, even if, as with domestic violence, it is still difficult to secure effective inquiries.

Women have become more involved in professional organizations in the past two decades. Such organizations include the National Association of Women Business Leaders, founded in 1990 under the framework of UTICA (Tunisian Union of Industry, Commerce, and Handicrafts); the National Federation of Women in Agriculture, established in 1990; UTAP (Tunisian Union of Agriculture and Fishery); and the Committee of Women Workers, which has been a part of the UGTT (General Union of Tunisian Workers) since 1991. Although their numbers are increasing, however, very few women are presently board members of these organizations. While 25 percent of the membership of UGTT are women (an accurate reflection of the proportion of employed women within the general population), only 9.3 percent hold union posts. At the UGTT congress in 2002, only 27 of the 457 delegates were women, and none of the four female candidates for the union executive board were elected.[65]

Recommendations

❖ The government should initiate workshops to educate women about their inheritance rights and enforce strict penalties against those individuals who force women to give up their share.

❖ The inheritance provision within the personal status code should be amended to treat all heirs equally, regardless of their gender.

❖ The government and NGOs should institute special programs to promote education and vocation training of women in rural areas, in efforts to increase these women's employment opportunities.

❖ The government, in cooperation with NGOs, should institute targeted efforts to inform women about their rights in the workplace and promote the mechanisms through which the existing laws can be effectively enforced.

❖ Professional organizations and unions should invest efforts to recruit women, both as members and as leaders.

POLITICAL RIGHTS AND CIVIC VOICE

Tunisian politics remain dominated by men, but women are venturing into the fray more often. In recent years, women have been appointed to high-level positions within the executive branch in greater numbers and their representation within parliament has increased. However, while more women are working in government at the local and regional level than ever before, they are still underrepresented in political and community life.[66]

Tunisia is a republic with a strong presidential system. Since independence, the country has had only two presidents. The first, Habib Bourguiba, was the principal architect of Tunisia's independence and ruled from 1956 to 1987. Current president Zine el-Abidine Ben Ali, who overthrew Bourguiba in November 1987, won his fifth five-year term as president on October 25, 2009. He plays a central role in the political life of Tunisia,[67] and is responsible for appointing the prime minister and other members of the cabinet. He is also president of the ruling political party, the Democratic Constitutional Rally (RCD), whose members hold 161 of the 214 seats in the elected Chamber of Deputies (the lower house of parliament). The 126-seat Chamber of Advisors (upper house), which is also dominated by the RCD, was created by a 2002 constitutional amendment and first convened in 2005. The dominance of the RCD grants it important prerogatives, allowing little room for dissent, but other political parties are represented in both houses of parliament; six opposition parties hold 53 seats in the Chamber of Deputies.

Women have made small gains in parliamentary elections in recent years and hold more parliamentary seats than their counterparts in neighboring countries. Eighty-five seats for the Chamber of Advisors are filled indirectly by an electoral college that consists of municipal councilors and regional council members. The remaining 41 seats are appointed by the president. To date, only 112 of the available seats are filled because UGTT has boycotted the elections, refusing to fill the 14 seats allotted to it. In 2005, eight women were voted into office and seven more were appointed by the president, giving women 13.4 percent of the chamber's occupied seats. In August 2008, renewal elections were held for half of the chamber, with four women winning seats. At the same time, the president appointed 20 new councilors, including five women. These nine women joined the eight existing female councilors, bringing women's representation up to 15.2 percent.[68]

Renewal elections for the Chamber of Deputies were held in October 2009 and were characterized by increased women's presence. Women now hold 27.6 percent of the seats, an increase from 22.8 percent after the last elections in 2004.[69] Notably, both houses of parliament have a female vice-president. Before the elections, the RCD and the opposition parties agreed to introduce measures to increase women's participation. The RCD specifically instituted a 30 percent minimum quota for women among its nominated candidates.

Women have held positions within the executive for decades, with the first female minister appointed in 1983. Although their appointments have tended to relate to women's affairs or social affairs, their roles have diversified in recent years. Currently, there is only one female minister, and she has headed MAFFEPA since 2007, and the Ministry of Equipment, Housing, and Territorial Planning was headed by a woman from 2004 until 2008. In addition, five female secretaries of state are responsible for: American and Asian affairs with the Foreign Ministry; hospitals within the Health Ministry; children and the elderly within the MAFFEPA; computer technology, the Internet, and software development within the Technology and Communications Ministry; and social development within the Social Affairs Ministry. The current president of the Court of Accounts is a woman, and several have been named to ministerial posts within the Ministries of Health, of Employment and Training, of the Environment, of Public Works, and of Housing.

Among other state bodies that are directly or indirectly controlled by the executive, women account for 25 percent of the Constitutional Council, 13.3 percent of the Higher Council of the Judiciary, and 20 percent of the Economic and Social Council. Although the first woman judge was only appointed in 1968, as of 2008, 27 percent of judges and 31 percent of lawyers were women, and all judges receive specific training in the field of women's rights.[70] Women also make up 24 percent of the diplomatic corps.[71]

Women are active at the regional and local levels, but rarely in positions of power. In 2004, Ben Ali appointed Tunisia's first female governor to the governorate of Zaghouan. Women represent 32 percent of the members of regional councils, and although only a few have been elected as mayors in their communities, they are a growing presence in municipal councils. According to news reports, women won 26.7 percent of available seats in the May 2005 municipal elections. This indicates a marked increase from 2000 and 1995 when women won 20.9 percent and 17.3 percent of municipal seats, respectively.[72]

Freedoms of speech and of the press are limited for both men and women, and emphasis is placed on consensus, national unity, and order, characteristics that are part of the national motto. That said, a degree of freedom of expression exists within the structure of the different political parties, national associations, and numerous nongovernmental organizations. The National Syndicate of Tunisian Journalists was created in January 2008 with a mandate to improve the work conditions of journalists and to further promote freedom of the press. Gender equality is frequently discussed in newspapers, on the radio, and on television. The media does not shy away from portraying the difficulties that women experience in their domestic life, in their workplace, and in the public sphere.

Women's governmental and nongovernmental organizations (NGOs) appear to be working effectively to promote the status of women throughout the country, but as most Tunisian civil society actors, they face certain constraints on their associational rights. Under the country's laws of association, persons wishing to form an association must submit an application to the Ministry of Interior that includes: a declaration mentioning the name, objectives, and the physical location of the association; a list of founding members and any directors or administrative staff, along with an address, date of birth, and profession for each; and the statutes of the association. Some types of organizations repeatedly face obstructions in trying to become legally established; the government refuses to legalize most independent human rights organizations. Despite these constraints, however, women's groups and Tunisian feminists continue to push for greater rights, and their numbers have been on the rise.

Recommendations

✤ Participation by women in politics should be encouraged at all levels of government and decision making, especially at a local level.
✤ Political parties should institute more proactive efforts to recruit women. Female party members should form special subcommittees and internal networks so they would be able to influence the parties' agenda more successfully.
✤ The government should institute better protections for freedom of association and freedom of the press so that all issues pertinent to women's political rights and civil liberties are openly discussed.
✤ The government and the NGO sector should organize special leadership camps for girls and train them in public speaking, networking, and other skills necessary for success in politics.

SOCIAL AND CULTURAL RIGHTS

Since independence, Tunisian society has undergone numerous important changes, and the pace of change has increased of late. In particular,
there has been a continuous rise in the standard of living, and 80 percent
of households are now considered middle class.[73] Some 68.7 percent of
the population lives in an urban environment, and poverty has decreased,
with only 3.8 percent of the population now living below the poverty
line.[74] Women's prominence in society has continued to rise as they achieve
scholarly success, increased presence in the workplace, access to managerial positions, business initiatives, and presence in intellectual and artistic
venues. However, inequality between men and women persists in cultural
practices. This is a legacy of the "traditional" society, wherein the public
and private spheres are distinct entities, with men essentially dominating
the public sphere and the private sphere being "reserved for women."

Advances in public health policies and family planning have enabled
women to strengthen their liberty. With a reasonably easy access to contraception, more women are able to limit family size and increase the intervals
between births, allowing them to attain "autonomy of personal status."[75]
Additionally, under Article 214 of the penal code, abortions performed in
the first trimester are legal.[76] As pointed out by Jacques Vallin and Thérèse
Locoh in their 2001 analysis of the evolution of the country's fertility
index, "moving in the space of 30 years from 7.5 children per woman to
2.2, Tunisia has changed planets. And this change is irreversible."[77] Due
to the government's rather successful family planning program, the fertility
rate was 2.0 children per mother in 2007, among the lowest in the developing world, a decrease from 2.1 in 2000 and 3.5 in 1990.[78]

The government has spearheaded multiple health-related social policies, including the legalization of the import and sale of contraception;
the limitation of family allowances to the first three children to encourage
smaller families; the legalization of regulated abortion in 1973; the creation of an agency for the protection of mother and child by the Ministry
of Public Health; and the creation of the National Office for the Family
and Population. Women are able to access medical care in much the same
way as men, in part because a widow and her young children now enjoy
medical benefits that were previously provided to her husband and is entitled to 70 percent of his pension. Additionally, an increasingly large

portion of the population receives social security benefits, up from 54.6 percent in 1987 to 93.3 percent in 2008.[79] Thanks to such policies, which allow women to care for their own health and the health of their children, the overall well-being of the nation is improving. According to the 2004 census, the average life expectancy is 73.9 years: 71.8 for men and 76 for women.[80] There are no documented cases of female genital mutilation or similar forms of gender-based harmful traditional practices.

The state financial aid for buying or constructing new homes has also positively impacted the lives of everyday women. Homeownership has a significant social value for Tunisians, and in recent decades an increase in new housing construction has surpassed the demographic rise. The housing expansion has coincided with a societal shift from large extended families toward the nuclear family and the emergence of the married couple as a family unit. This in turn reflects the growing autonomy of young, married couples, and the increasing liberation of women from dependence on their in-laws and the authority of their mothers-in-law.[81] Nonetheless, social norms restrict women's ability to own and use housing. Most single individuals live in homes registered in their father's name, while married couples tend to register their dwellings in the husband's name.

Social development indicators have improved dramatically over the years, particularly those that affect what are generally perceived as "women's chores." In 2007, 84.8 percent of dwellings had drinking water, eliminating the need to fetch water that had long been one of the duties of women and young girls. In addition, 99.5 percent of households now have electricity, which allows 81.7 percent of households to have refrigerators and 34.8 percent to have washing machines. Widespread use of modern technology permits women to enjoy more free time, which in turn allows them to devote more time to participation in public life. Additionally, television is found in 90.2 percent of homes and is considered an essential form of entertainment for families that is especially enjoyed by women.[82]

The gap between the poorest 20 percent and the richest 10 percent of the population is relatively small in Tunisia.[83] However, important imbalances still exist between rural and urban areas, between coastal and interior regions, between social classes, and between men and women.[84] In needy areas, women have shown potential and a marked sense of initiative when they are able to access financial support, which permits them to fight poverty. As for social programs, intervention by the Ministry of Social

Affairs, Solidarity, and Tunisians Abroad has increased benefits to rural women by 55 percent.[85] Social policies and a national solidarity policy have played an active role in eradicating poverty and diminishing the disparities, and 20 percent of the GDP is earmarked for this purpose. The effort focuses on developing infrastructure, providing housing aid, improving public health and social aid, and promoting the widespread general education of boys and girls.

Different legal mechanisms and institutions have been set up to help the populations most vulnerable to poverty.[86] These entities promote socioeconomic progress and permit women and men to participate in the economy, even in rural areas. In 2001, a government action plan was established to evaluate the productive aptitudes of women in rural areas and protect them against all forms of discrimination. However, few figures are available as to the distribution of funds by gender. A quarter of beneficiaries of microcredit loans in urban areas allocated by the Tunisian Solidarity Bank were women.[87] The president of the UNFT called for microcredit institutions to further support women's initiatives during a meeting of the sixth session of the Higher Council of Population in March 2009.[88]

The MAFFEPA, the National Office of the Family and Population Affairs, and feminist groups, including those integrated with political parties and professional associations, encourage the government to create conditions that improve women's status and eliminate all forms of gender-based discrimination. The Higher Committee for Human Rights and Fundamental Freedoms, established in 1991, and the Higher Communication Council demonstrate in their various reports that they are attentive to women's rights and aware of the gender inequalities that persist.[89]

Recommendations

❖ The government should initiate development programs at the local level and encourage women to participate, so as to reduce the inequalities between rural and urban areas and between men and women.

❖ The government and nongovernmental agencies should provide adequate training to needy women and young girls, taking into consideration their particular circumstances and the local needs.

❖ The government should encourage the founding of social clubs that support women and give them a place to discuss their problems with regard to the family and society, so that they become empowered to find solutions to the problems that directly affect them.

✤ Universities and research centers should initiate more projects investigating population issues, as well as the condition of women, their role
in economic and social development, and their participation in decision making in all aspects of life.

AUTHOR

Lilia Ben Salem earned her PhD from the Université de Paris V (la
Sorbonne) and is a researcher and professor at the Faculty of Social Sciences
at the University of Tunis. Her work focuses on major social changes
within Tunisian society. Her publications concern educational sociology,
managerial training, and the rural environment, as well as the family and
its recent transformations.

NOTES

[1] National Statistics Institute, July 1, 2008, evaluation.

[2] For more details, see Ilhem Marzouki, *Le mouvement des femmes en Tunisie au XXème
siècle* [The Women's Movement in Tunisia in the 20th Century] (Tunis: Cérès production, 1993).

[3] Article 20 of the constitution guarantees the right to vote for all citizens holding
Tunisian nationality for at least five years.

[4] World Bank, "GenderStats—Labor Force," 2007, http://go.worldbank.org/4PIIORQ
MS0. According to the 2004 census in Tunisia, women represent 26.6 percent of the
active working population.

[5] Sana Ben Achour, "Femme et droit en Islam" [Women and Law Under Islam], *Université
de tous les savoirs,* October 2007.

[6] Mohamed Charfi, *Introduction à l'Étude du Droit* [Introduction to Law Studies]
(Tunis: Centre d'Études et de Recherches et de Publications de l'Université de Droit,
d'Économie et de Gestion [Center of Study, Research, and Publication at the University
of Law, Economy, and Management], 1990).

[7] *Constitution de la République Tunisienne* [Constitution of the Tunisian Republic], Article
72(1) (Tunis: Publications de l'Imprimerie Officielle de la République Tunisienne
[Tunisian Official Press Publications], 2004).

[8] Articles 13 and 14 of the nationality code.

[9] A decree from June 19, 1914, regulating the attribution of Tunisian nationality had
made it nearly an exclusive right of the father (only children of a Tunisian mother with
an unknown father could take the mother's nationality). The code of nationality, promulgated in 1957, had extended this prerogative to a child born in Tunisia to a Tunisian
mother and a foreign father, but not to children born abroad to a non-Tunisian father.
Alya Cherif Chamari, *La Femme et la Loi en Tunisie* [Women and the Law in Tunisia]
(Rabat: Editions le Fennec, 1991).

[10] Article 207 of the penal code had permitted the reduction of a sentence to a simple misdemeanor for a man convicted of an "honor crime"—a crime in which a man murders or injures his wife and/or her partner who are caught *in flagrante delicto* in the act of adultery.

[11] "Consideration of Reports Submitted by States Parties Under Article 18 of the Convention on the Elimination of All Forms of Discrimination against Women. Combined Third and Fourth Periodic Reports of States Parties. Tunisia" (New York: UN Committee on the Elimination of Discrimination against Women [CEDAW], CEDAW/C/TUN/ 1-2, 2 August 2000), 14.

[12] Article 207 of the penal code, which established a five-year maximum prison sentence for men who murdered their adulterous wives, was struck from the penal code, and Law No. 93-92 considers marriage to be an aggravating circumstance in instances of violence.

[13] Tunisia, CEDAW Committee, 14.

[14] Article 231 of the penal code states that "women who, by gestures or words, offer themselves to passers-by or engage in prostitution, even on an occasional basis, are punishable by six months to two years imprisonment and a fine of 20 to 200 dinars. Any person who has had sexual relations with one of these women is considered an accomplice and subject to the same punishment."

[15] Daniel Williams, "Tunisia Veil Case Threatens 'Odious Rag' Struggle," January 3, 2008, http://www.bloomberg.com/apps/news?pid=20601085&sid=aVnYog.7H.yI&refer =europe.

[16] Article 11 of the personal status code.

[17] Souad Triki, *Le budget-temps des ménages ruraux et travail des femmes rurales en Tunisie* [Time-Budgets of Rural Households and the Work of Rural Women in Tunisia] (Tunis: CREDIF, 2000); Dorra Mahfoudh-Draoui, Hafedh Zaafrane, Ahmed Khouadja, and Habib Fourati, *Enquête budget-temps des femmes et des hommes en Tunisie 2005* [The 2005 Time-Budget Study of Women and Men in Tunisia] (Tunis: Ministry of Women and Family Affairs, 2007).

[18] Mahfoudh-Draoui et al., *Enquête budget-temps*, 44.

[19] Mahfoudh-Draoui et al., *Enquête budget-temps*, 73.

[20] Collective 95 Maghreb Equality and the Association of Tunisian Women for Research and Development (AFTURD), with support from the United Nations Development Fund for Women (UNIFEM) and the Tunisian General Labor Union (UGTT), *Degré d'adhésion aux valeurs égalitaires dans la population tunisienne* [Degree of Adhesion to Egalitarian Values in the Tunisian Population], unpublished text, Tunis, 2007. A brochure presenting the major findings of this study was published in Tunis in March 2008.

[21] Collective 95, *Degré d'adhésion*, 38 et seq.

[22] Collective 95, *Degré d'adhésion*, 44.

[23] Article 24: "The husband has no administrative power over his wife's goods."

[24] Law No. 94 of 1998, relating to the regime of community of goods between spouses.

[25] Article 32 of the CPS, modified by Law No. 74 of 1993. The family law judge is named by the president of the Court of First Instance.

[26] Article 67 of the personal status code. Mothers do, however, gain guardianship over their children in the event of the father's death.

[27] Amendment to the CPS, April 5, 1996.

[28] Article 207 of the penal code, which had prescribed a five-year prison sentence for husbands who murder their adulterous wives but did not similarly reduce the sentence for wives killing their husbands in such circumstances, has been eliminated. Law No. 92 of 1993 considers marriage to be an aggravating circumstance in instances of violence.

[29] Collective 95, *Degré d'adhésion*.

[30] Cabinet de Prospective Sociale (Social Prospective Cabinet) and National Union of Tunisian Women, *La violence conjugale en Tunisie: Composantes sociologiques, culturelles, juridiques et institutionnelles* [Conjugal Violence in Tunisia: Sociological, Cultural, Legal and Institutional Components], 1992.

[31] "Press Conference: Ministry of Women, Family, Children and the Elderly," *La Presse*, January 29, 2009.

[32] For more information, see Public Health Ministry, National Office of the Family and Population, *La violence fondée sur le genre en Tunisie: Etat des lieux* [Gender-Based Violence: State of Affairs] (Tunis: ONFP, 2007).

[33] AFTURD, *Divorce, violence et droits des femmes* [Divorce, Violence and Women's Rights], 2001; and Collective 95, *Degré d'adhésion*.

[34] Article 14 of the constitution states: "The right to property is guaranteed. It is exercised within the limits established by the law."

[35] Collective 95, *Degré d'adhésion*.

[36] The *habous* system, which was repealed by law upon independence in 1957, long permitted girls to be disinherited to the advantage of male descendants. Habous is a sort of trust that permits its founder to render his property inalienable and devote it to religious work or some other usage. The enjoyment of the property can be effective immediately or upon the extinction of the descendants of the founder. The managers of the habous are named in the founding document, and are generally, but not always, the descendants of male lineage. They benefit from the revenues of the trust in a very strict and precise manner. See Sophie Ferchiou et al., *hasab wa nasab, Parenté, Alliance et Patrimoine en Tunisie* [hasab wa nasab, Kinship, Alliance and Patrimony] (Paris: National Center of Scientific Research, 1992).

[37] In the sample, 43 percent were unmarried people; 37 percent of those declared that the property or rental contract of their residence was in their father's name, and 3 percent said it was in their mother's name. Among married respondents, 38 percent of men declared the contract in their name, while only 8 percent of women did the same. And 41 percent of women stated that it was in their husband's name, whereas only 4 percent of men said it was in their wife's name. Only 4 percent of couples declared co-ownership. Collective 95, *Degré d'adhésion*, 106.

[38] A law enacted on April 5, 1996, gave couples the right to take out a joint loan for housing.

[39] See Book Nine of the CPS, Articles 85 to 170.

[40] According to Shari'a, in the absence of a direct male heir, a part of the inheritance is distributed to the male collaterals.

[41] Case No. 31115, February 3, 2009.

[42] AFTURD, *Egalité dans l'héritage, Pour une citoyenneté pleine et entière* [Equality in Inheritance, for an Equal and Full Citizenship] (Tunis: AFTURD, 2006).

[43] Ali Mezghani and Kalthoum Meziou-Douraï, *L'égalité entre hommes et femmes en droit successoral* [Equality Between Men and Women in Succession Rights] (Tunis: Sud Editions, 2006), 6.

[44] Article 20 of the Law of Obligations and Contracts.

[45] National Statistics Institute, 2004.

[46] World Bank, "GenderStats—Education," http://go.worldbank.org/RHEGN4QHU0.

[47] World Bank, "GenderStats—Education."

[48] When considering higher education, studies show that young women take into account their role within the family, and particularly the education of their own children. This said, more young women are choosing technical and science disciplines.

[49] Article 5bis, 1993, of the labor code: "There can be no discrimination between men and women in the application of the present code and related texts."

[50] Ministry of Employment and Professional Integration of Youth, in collaboration with the World Bank, *Dynamique de l'emploi et adéquation de la formation parmi les diplômés universitaires* [Work Dynamics and Adequate Training Among University Graduates], 2005.

[51] World Bank Development Indicators 2009 (World Bank, Washington DC). Online Database (subscription required) http://publications.worldbank.org/ecommerce/catalog/product-detail?product_id=631625&. Last accessed on December 22, 2009.

[52] It permits them to "potentially obtain work, develop a career and be promoted to managerial positions in an equal and equitable manner." Karima Bouzguenda, *Gestion des carrières et phénomène du glass ceiling en Tunisie: Le cas des femmes cadres en Tunisie* [Career Management and the Glass Ceiling Phenomenon in Tunisia: The Case of Women Executives in Tunisia], doctorial thesis in management, University of Sfax, Faculty of Economics, Business, and Management, 2004–05.

[53] Women are not recorded as economically active if their labor falls under domestic work.

[54] A. Gana and M. Picouët, "Population et environnement" [Population and Environment], in *Population et Développement en Tunisie: La métamorphose* [Population and Development in Tunisia: The Metamorphosis], ed. J. Vallin and T. Locoh (Tunis: Cérès Editions, 2001), 513–529.

[55] Gana and Picouët, "Population et environnement," 525.

[56] *La Presse*, January 29, 2009.

[57] Chamari, *La Femme et la Loi.*

[58] National Statistics Institute, 2005; Collective 95, *Degré d'adhésion.*

[59] Bouzguenda, *Gestion des carrièrs.*

[60] Dorra Mahfoudh Draoui, "Crise du chômage, crise d'identité: Le cas des ouvrières du textile en Tunisie" [Crisis of Unemployment, Identity Crisis: The Case of Women Textile Workers in Tunisia], in *Genre et politiques néo-libérales* [Gender and Neoliberal Policies] (AFARD/Dawn/Fennec, 2006), 177–183.

[61] A 1985 law had authorized women civil servants to opt for part-time work at only half their salary.

[62]   *La Presse,* January 29, 2009.

[63]   Article 226 of the penal code now states: "Whosoever commits sexual harassment is punishable by 1 year of imprisonment and a fine of 3,000 dinars. Sexual harassment is defined as all unwanted persistent behavior that is disturbing to another by repeated acts, verbal or physical conduct of a sexual nature that is unwanted and undermines a person's dignity and sense of modesty. And this, for the purpose of sexual advances, for themselves or for another, or for pressure to weaken resistance to such advances."

[64]   Collective 95, *Degré d'adhésion,* 70 et seq.

[65]   UGTT, *Diagnostic de l'UGTT par ses cadres* [Diagnosis of UGTT by Its Managers], 2007.

[66]   Collective 95, *Degré d'adhésion.*

[67]   "La galaxie Ben Ali" [The Ben Ali Galaxy], *Jeune Afrique* [Young Africa] no. 2488 (September 14–20, 2008).

[68]   InterParliamentary Union, PARLINE Database, Tunisia, Chamber of Councilors, http://www.ipu.org/parline-e/reports/2322_A.htm.

[69]   InterParliamentary Union, PARLINE Database, Tunisia, Chamber of Deputies, http://www.ipu.org/parline-e/reports/2321_A.htm.

[70]   Sfeir, *Tunisie, terre des paradoxes,* 134.

[71]   Bouzguenda, *Gestion des carriers.*

[72]   "Women, Opposition, Gain Ground as Result of Municipal Elections in Tunisia," TunisiaOnline.com, May 10, 2005, http://www.tunisiaonline.com/municipales2005/n_1_10.html.

[73]   Sfeir, *Tunisie, terre des paradoxes,* 134.

[74]   National Statistics Institute, *Enquête Nationale sur les revenus, la consommation et les niveaux de vei* [National Survey of Revenues, Consumption and Lifestyle] (Tunis: National Statistics Institute, 2005), 23. The rate of poverty was 22 percent in 1975, 12.9 percent in 1980, 6.2 percent in 1995, and 4.2 percent in 2004.

[75]   This is a reference to the anthropologist Françoise Héritier's remark that "contraception is the pet peeve of states that do not want women to attain autonomy of personal status," interview with Cl. Laroche, "Regard et anthropologie" [Outlooks and Anthropology], Communications no. 75 (2004).

[76]   Past the first trimester, abortions are permissible only for the mental well-being of a woman or if the fetus would be born with a serious disease or infirmity.

[77]   J. Vallin and T. Locoh, "Les leçons de l'expérience tunisienne" [Lessons of the Tunisian Experience], in *Population et Développement en Tunisie: La métamorphose* [Population and Development in Tunisia: The Metamorphosis], ed. J. Vallin and T. Locoh (Tunis: Cérès Editions, 2001), 577.

[78]   World Bank, "GenderStats—Create Your Own Table," http://go.worldbank.org/MRER 20PME0.

[79]   Ministry of Social Affairs, Solidarity and Tunisians in Foreign Countries.

[80]   National Statistics Institute, July 1, 2008, evaluation. Life expectancy was 51.1 years in 1966, 67.5 years in 1987, and 70.6 years in 1991 (68.8 for men, 72.3 for women).

[81]   Lilia Ben Salem, *Familles et changements sociaux en Tunisie* [Families and Social Changes in Tunisia] (Tunis: University Publication Center, 2009).

82 National Statistics Institute, 2004 census.

83 André Wilmots, *De Bourguiba à Ben Ali: L'étonnant parcours économique de la Tunisie* (1960–2000) [From Bourguiba to Ben Ali: Tunisia's Surprising Economic Voyage] (Paris: L'Harmattan, 2003), 73.

84 National Statistics Institute, *Enquête Nationale*.

85 Report of the sixth session of the Conseil Supérieur de la Population [Higher Council of Population], *La Presse*, March 2009.

86 Such organizations include the Tunisian Solidarity Bank, the National Fund for Promotion of Handicraft and Small Business, the Working Capital of the National Office of Artisans, the Fund for the Promotion and Decentralization of Industry, the Rural Development Programs, and the National Program of Productive Families.

87 Mahfoudh Draoui, "Crise du chômage, crise d'identité."

88 Report of the sixth session of the Conseil Supérieur de la Population.

89 Decrees No. 2846 of November 8, 2006, and No. 886 of April 10, 2007, consolidated the prerogatives of the committee, which in the future will monitor Tunisia's compliance with international treaties that it has ratified.

UNITED ARAB EMIRATES

by Serra Kirdar

POPULATION: 5,066,000
GNI PER CAPITA: US$41,031

COUNTRY RATINGS	2004	2009
NONDISCRIMINATION AND ACCESS TO JUSTICE:	1.7	2.0
AUTONOMY, SECURITY, AND FREEDOM OF THE PERSON:	2.1	2.3
ECONOMIC RIGHTS AND EQUAL OPPORTUNITY:	2.8	3.1
POLITICAL RIGHTS AND CIVIC VOICE:	1.2	2.0
SOCIAL AND CULTURAL RIGHTS:	2.3	2.5

(COUNTRY RATINGS ARE BASED ON A SCALE OF 1 TO 5, WITH 1 REPRESENTING THE LOWEST AND 5 THE HIGHEST LEVEL OF FREEDOM WOMEN HAVE TO EXERCISE THEIR RIGHTS)

INTRODUCTION

The United Arab Emirates (UAE) is quickly transforming its formerly tribal Bedouin society into an emerging economy that is catching the eye of the world. Dubai, one of the seven emirates, has established itself as a financial hub that has attracted expatriate workers and investors from around the world. Over the past decade, it has become a sprawling metropolis sporting an array of ambitious real-estate projects. However, the billions of dollars of debt incurred by Dubai-based investors during this period left the emirate particularly vulnerable to the global economic downturn that emerged in late 2008. Abu Dhabi, the largest of the seven emirates and home to the federal capital, has also driven the UAE's economic growth. It is the top oil producer in the federation, controlling more than 85 percent of the country's total output capacity and over 90 percent of its crude reserves.[1] As of mid-2009, Emirati citizens comprised only 20 percent of the country's five million inhabitants.

Emirati women are undergoing a transition as their society, exposed to foreign influences, adapts to changing identities while protecting cultural and religious traditions. The government has worked to improve several aspects of women's rights over the last five years, though some reforms have been slow to take effect. Certain steps in the right direction are obvious:

women are entering new professional fields such as engineering and information technology; there has been a rapid expansion in higher education for women; the ratio of females to males in the workforce is increasing; and women have been appointed to high-profile positions within the government and the business world. Nevertheless, restrictions still apply to some professions, and support for advancements in women's rights varies among the emirates. Moreover, societal and familial perceptions of a woman's proper role continue to pose a significant barrier to advancement.

Women have experienced little change since 2004 in their ability to access justice through the courts and combat discrimination, although they are now able to serve as judges and prosecutors. However, their personal autonomy and economic rights have improved. Furthermore, women have experienced gains in political, social, and cultural aspects of their lives, as the government has recognized both the need to support women's participation in these areas and the significance of such participation as a measure of success in national development. Although legal changes have been made to acknowledge women's pivotal role, there remains considerable resistance to change in practice. The UAE must carry out reforms at both the governmental and societal levels for any lasting development to take root.

NONDISCRIMINATION AND ACCESS TO JUSTICE

Women in the UAE are informally divided in several categories based on their standing in the society: UAE citizens, foreign professional women temporarily residing on an employment contract, foreign women employed in the informal sector such as domestic work, and the wives of temporary foreign workers. This division is particularly evident in the ability of women to access justice through courts and exercise their rights. Female domestic workers are the most vulnerable group, as they are often denied basic protections under the law. Despite some modest improvements over the last five years, many noncitizen women remain uninformed of the rights and legal protections available to them.

The UAE is governed both by Shari'a (Islamic law) and civil law. Some criminal activities as well as personal status and family issues are subject to Shari'a, while the codified criminal, civil, and commercial law apply to select issues such as traffic rules, immigration, fraud, and the trafficking of illegal substances. The extent to which Shari'a-derived legislation applies varies from emirate to emirate. Shari'a rules on marriage only apply to Muslim marriages and where a Muslim man marries a Christian or Jewish wife.

Article 25 of the constitution provides for equality among Emirati citizens, "without distinction between citizens of the Union in regard to race, nationality, religious belief, or social status."[2] Although the law states that all people are equal, there is no mention of gender equality, nor are there any laws or policies designed to eliminate existing gender-based discrimination. Additionally, the constitution controls personal status in two separate articles. Article 15 states that the family is the basis of society, while Article 16 requires that welfare and social security legislation be promulgated to protect "childhood and motherhood," as well as those who are unable to look after themselves. As a result, laws and policies tend to reinforce traditional roles for women rather than encourage true equality between the genders.

Gender discrimination is built into the laws governing citizenship in several ways. First, an Emirati woman loses her citizenship upon marriage to a foreign man in the absence of a special dispensation from the Naturalization and Residence Directorate of the emirate in which the wife lives. Even with such a dispensation, she may not transfer her citizenship to her foreign husband unless the couple was granted permission from the Presidential Court prior to marrying. Conversely, in the case of a marriage between a national man and a non-national woman, the man need only submit a copy of his wife's passport, a copy of the marriage contract, and proof of his nationality, at which time a family book is issued within 24 hours as proof that their marriage is sanctioned by the state. Second, only fathers can pass their nationality to their children. The children of an Emirati mother and noncitizen father have no claim to UAE citizenship. On the other hand, the children of an Emirati father, whether he is dead or divorced from their mother, automatically receive his nationality. These children, even if they are minors, can sponsor their non-national mother's residency in the UAE.[3] Related to this, foreign women continue to be unable to sponsor their children's residence permits in the UAE, unlike their male counterparts.

The extent to which women are treated equally under criminal law has not changed much over the past five years. Apart from immigration cases and prostitution by noncitizens, crimes committed by women in the UAE receive very little publicity and little material is published about the subject. Due to the lack of data, it is difficult to determine a specific rule regarding the treatment of women accused of crimes. Instead, several factors affect the outcome of each individual case, including the woman's identity, family name and influential standing, the identity of the victim, the location, the severity of the crime, and the level of publicity that the crime received. Discussions with legal sources confirm that often, to avoid bringing shame on an arrested woman's family by sending her to prison, police officers "allow women to pay a penalty" instead of facing prosecution, but the issue is left to the discretion of the local police station and arresting officer.

All articles in the Federal Penal Code (No. 3 of 1987) are addressed to both men and women equally. Although citizens and noncitizens are generally subject to the same crimes, except those related to immigration, the penal code is often applied to them in a discriminatory manner, particularly if the offender is female. One journalist has noted that the "punishment for drug offences is severe, although the severity of your sentence is likely to depend upon your nationality." She cites a case in which a Pakistani woman was sentenced to death by Fujairah's Shari'a court after having been found guilty of possessing cannabis with intent to supply. Conversely, a male UAE national convicted of the same offense had his sentence reduced from 12 to 8 years upon appeal.[4] There are numerous cases in which the severity of sentences appears to correlate closely to one's ethnic background and status within the society.[5]

Article 26 of the constitution guarantees personal liberty to all citizens and prohibits arbitrary arrest, searches, detainment, and imprisonment, as well as torture and other degrading treatment. Article 28 protects criminal defendants by stipulating a presumption of innocence, guaranteeing the right to appoint one's own legal counsel, providing for publicly funded defense counsel in certain circumstances, and prohibiting physical and "moral" abuse of accused persons. The Criminal Procedure Law (No. 35 of 1992) permits public prosecutors to hold a suspect for up to 21 days without charge, which may be extended by the judge and court. No reports indicate that women are particularly subject to arbitrary arrest or harassment by the police.

Women are not considered full persons before the law in all instances. According to the Hanbali school of Shari'a, a woman's testimony in criminal matters is equal to only half of a man's, although their testimony is considered to be equal in some civil matters.[6] A woman may seek legal counsel and representation without a guardian at the age of 18 and, with the exception of cases involving marriage contracts, no cases were reported in which a woman was required to appear in court with her husband or father. Such a request would be in violation of Article 41 of the constitution, which grants all persons the right to submit claims before competent authorities concerning abuse of or infringements upon their constitutional rights.

No specific provisions or allowances guarantee gender equality with respect to access to justice at all levels. In practice, social mores discourage women from seeking legal protection because it involves recourse to the male-dominated public sphere. As such, family-related problems are typically dealt with in private. Women are similarly discouraged from entering the legal profession, even if they studied law at university, because it would entail mixing with men in courts and police stations, and with male clients and lawyers.

The UAE ratified the Convention on the Elimination of All Forms of Discrimination against Women (CEDAW) in October 2004, but has reserved the right to implement Articles 2(6) (inheritance), 9 (discrimination in granting nationality to children), 15(2) (testimony and right to conclude contracts), 16 (discrimination in marriage and family relations), and 29(1) (jurisdiction) in a manner compatible with Shari'a.[7] Several cases that have occurred since then—most notably a case in which a 14 year-old girl was sentenced to 60 lashes for engaging in illicit sex while the male involved was sentenced to six months' imprisonment—have led human rights organizations to claim that the UAE is in contravention of CEDAW's prohibition of gender-based violence.[8] Such cases serve to highlight the fundamental inequality and injustice of mandating different sentences for the same "crime," irrespective of which punishment is considered to be worse.

Significant restrictions are placed on the formation and effectiveness of independent women's rights groups. In 1975, the UAE Women's Federation was established by Sheikha Fatima bint Mubarak, the wife of the former president. It now serves as an umbrella group for women's organizations in the country and covers such topics as religious affairs, mother care, both pre- and postnatal care and childcare, social affairs, cultural affairs, arts, and sports.[9] In essence, it serves to reinforce the accepted female gender roles as perceived by Emirati society.

The Women's Federation also provides access to legal counsel for women who cannot afford their own lawyer, but this is rarely used, either out of shame, concerns about confidentiality, or lack of knowledge about the service.[10] It does not deal with the promotion of women's freedoms, nor does it address, aside from the occasional press conference, the issues of human trafficking, domestic and public violence against women, discrimination, or other controversial problems that hinder women's rights. Some governmental and charitable organizations such as the Red Crescent and the Dubai Foundation for Women and Children attempt to address such issues, but few NGOs are able to do the same. Activists and philanthropists have run up against bureaucracy that has made it nearly impossible to gain the necessary approvals to operate legally as a NGO in the traditional sense seen in the West.

Recommendations

+ The nationality law should be amended to permit Emirati women to transfer citizenship to their husbands and children.
+ The Women's Federation should publish a legal resource guide for women that clearly defines their political and legal rights and provides them with practical tips on how to better exercise such rights.
+ The government should encourage women to participate more at every level of the judiciary, particularly as lawyers, by offering scholarships and awards to female law students and introducing a gender-based quota system at the Ministry of Justice.
+ The government should fully adhere to CEDAW by removing its reservations and prohibiting all forms of gender-based violence.
+ The government should remove the obstacles that currently exist to the formation of independent women's rights NGOs. Instead, such NGOs should be encouraged to develop in recognition of their importance for a healthy civil society that adequately addresses the needs of Emirati women.

AUTONOMY, SECURITY, AND FREEDOM OF THE PERSON

The Personal Status Law (No. 28 of 2005), enacted in November 2005, is the first of its kind for the UAE. Previously, personal status issues were decided by individual judges' interpretations of Shari'a. The codification of such issues is viewed by many as a positive development for women's rights as it guarantees Emirati women certain rights, including greater personal freedom regarding marriages. Most notably, it legally recognizes *khula* (divorce that may be initiated by a woman in exchange for her dowry) and permits women to make stipulations within marriage contracts. The extent to which these measures have in fact improved women's autonomy, however, is subject to debate, and other provisions of the personal status law simply codify pre-existing inequalities.

Under Article 32 of the constitution, women enjoy the right to practice their religion and follow their religious beliefs in a manner "consistent with public order and with public morals," while Article 7 establishes Islam as the state religion. All mosques, including those in Dubai, are accountable to the federal Ministry of Islamic Affairs and Awqaf for the content of their sermons, whether they are publicly or privately funded, Sunni or Shiite. The ministry releases weekly lists of approved topics and follows up on individual imams to ensure compliance.[11] In recent years, various emirates have individually authorized increases in non-Muslim houses of worship.[12] Women are permitted to serve as religious teachers, both in schools and for adults through the Ministry of Islamic Affairs and Awqaf. Moreover, women, like men, may convene private religious discussion groups and study sessions, but they are subject to government restrictions if they intend to publish anything discussed.

Article 29 of the constitution guarantees all UAE citizens, men and women, freedom of movement and residence within the limits of law. However, in practice, some restrictions on freedom of movement for both Emirati and foreign women still exist. Women who are citizens may be restricted from leaving the country if they lack permission from their husbands or guardians. According to custom, a man may prevent his wife, children, and adult unmarried daughters from traveling abroad by confiscating their passports, and government institutions will not challenge a husband's right to do so. In addition, the courts have restricted freedom of movement for a small number of women who have left their husbands by ordering them to return to the marital home.[13] Foreign women are not protected by Article 29, an oversight that employers often exploit by illegally confiscating their passports, thereby restricting their ability to leave the country or run away and forcing some to live in involuntary servitude.[14]

The new personal status law codifies many of the common Shari'a provisions that previously controlled the UAE's family courts, interpretations of which were left to individual judges. Some, such as the Article 56 requirement that a husband has the right to obedience from his wife "in accordance with custom," sanction and encourage the perpetuation of traditional gender roles and stereotypes. Others potentially provide safeguards for women, assuming they are properly enforced. For instance, Article 110 codifies the Shari'a practice of khula, which allows women to request a divorce from their husbands if they return their *mahr* (dowry).[15] This is a welcome alternative to their other option, a cumbersome judicial procedure that only allows women to petition for divorce based on extremely limited circumstances.

Additionally, Article 20 permits women to include stipulations regarding education and work in the marriage contract, another significant assurance of women's rights. This has precedents in all four Sunni schools of jurisprudence, and some women made such stipulations prior to the law's codification, but the status of the practice was ambiguous. Now women are officially permitted to include terms in a marriage contract specifying that, among other things, they have the right to work or finish a master's degree. However, because the vast majority of Emirati nationals are not aware of these new amendments, they are not often used in practice.

The ability of women to negotiate an equal marriage remains limited. Under Article 39 of the personal status law, a woman's guardian and prospective husband are the parties to the marital contract, although its validity is contingent upon her approval and signature. The guardian's signature is necessary except where the woman was previously married, is over a specific age, or, in certain circumstances, where she has asked the court to serve as her marriage guardian. The justifications given for requiring a guardian vary, but in general, it is regarded as protection for the bride.[16]

Muslim women, unlike men, are prohibited from marrying outside their faith. Moreover, men are legally permitted to have up to four wives, as long as they obtain permission from their existing wives. The khula reform has been applauded as a step in the right direction, but it still requires women to give up all their financial rights from the marriage (namely, the mahr) for the sake of their freedom. By contrast, Muslim men are permitted to divorce their wives simply by verbally proclaiming their wish to do so. In such cases, the women keep the mahr if the marriage has been consummated.

If a woman is granted a divorce, she receives custody of female children until they reach the age of 13 and male children until they reach the age of 10. According the UAE government, once the children reach these predetermined ages, the family courts reassess custody.[17] If a woman chooses to remarry, she forfeits her rights to custody of her children from the previous marriage.[18]

The UAE remains a destination country for trafficked men and women, but the government has invested certain efforts to combat the problem in recent years.[19] While men tend to be trafficked for the purpose of forced labor in the construction industry, women of a variety of nationalities tend to be trafficked either into the sex industry or as domestic workers, where their passports are often removed and they are forced to work without pay. To combat forced labor, employers are now required to pay foreign workers via an electronic system monitored by the government.[20] Additionally, Federal Law (No. 39 of 2006) lays the framework for bilateral cooperation with countries that supply labor to the UAE. Enacted months later, Federal Law (No. 51 of 2006) defines human trafficking as an element of organized crime and sets stiff penalties for convicted traffickers, ranging from one year to life in prison, as well as civil fines of between 20,000 and 1 million dirham (approximately US$5,500 to US$270,000).

These new antitrafficking laws appear to be the result of the government's effort to improve the country's human rights reputation. The UAE ratified the UN Transnational Organized Crime Convention in May 2007, which calls for international cooperation in efforts to combat human trafficking. In January 2008, the Red Crescent Society in Abu Dhabi announced the establishment of the first shelter exclusively for victims of human trafficking,[21] but despite these gains, victims continue to be prosecuted for prostitution if they turn to the police for assistance.

Domestic laws regarding torture and degrading forms of punishment have not changed in recent years. Despite the prohibition against torture under Article 26 of the constitution, Amnesty International reports that flogging sentences continue to be carried out, most commonly as punishment for adultery. In June 2006, in the emirate of Fujairah, a Shari'a court sentenced a Bangladeshi national to death by stoning for adultery with a migrant domestic worker. Although the death sentence was revoked, he was imprisoned for one year and subsequently deported.[22] What became of the female domestic worker, who was sentenced to 100 lashes and imprisonment for one year, is unknown. In October 2005 it was reported that Shari'a courts in the emirate of Ras al-Khaimah sentenced a female domestic worker to 150 lashes for becoming pregnant outside marriage.[23] Other such cases of cruel and inhumane punishments are not uncommon in the

UAE.[24] Furthermore, the UAE still has not ratified the United Nations Convention against Torture and Other Cruel, Inhuman, or Degrading Treatment or Punishment (UN Convention against Torture).

Physical abuse is prohibited under the law, but many women are subjected to domestic violence by their male family members. Women remain at the mercy of their husbands because the police are reluctant to get involved in the private affairs of married couples and do not afford them appropriate security.[25] No formal studies have been conducted or authorized by the government to document domestic violence, so the available figures on women abused at home are rough estimates. However, Dubai now has two safe houses where women may seek shelter from domestic abuse.[26] One, City of Hope, is privately run, while the other, the Dubai Foundation for Women and Children, is public.

Men who harass women on the street or in public places such as shopping malls are subject to legal penalty. Pictures of men caught harassing women appear weekly in newspapers, a source of shame for the men's families. However, these legal and social punitive measures have not eradicated the problem.

Rape is a serious criminal offence punishable by death under Article 354 of the penal code, but many victims remain reluctant to report the crime for fear that they will be accused of adultery, shamed before society, and disowned by their families. For this reason, many offenders are left unpunished. For example, when a French woman reported that she was gang-raped in Dubai in 2002, she was taken to jail under allegation of having "adulterous sexual relations." A similar incident occurred in 2008 when an Australian woman was jailed for eight months on charges of "illicit sexual relations" after reporting to the police that she had been drugged and gang-raped.[27] Furthermore, a significant number of noncitizen victims of abuse have been reluctant to report rapes, assaults, and other crimes, fearing that they could jeopardize their residency status and risk deportation.[28] The lack of official data on this matter exacerbates the problem because the government feels no need to implement countermeasures.

As previously noted (see "Nondiscrimination and Access to Justice"), the only established entity specifically designed to address women's rights is the state-sponsored UAE Women's Federation. All other civil initiatives working to promote women's freedoms are still in their nascent phases. Some receive funding and support from the U.S. Middle East Partnership

Initiative, but no legal framework currently exists to accommodate civil society organizations outside the state's sphere of influence.[29]

Recommendations

- ❖ The government should launch an educational public-awareness campaign that portrays domestic violence as being intolerable, illegal, and socially unacceptable, and the police should strictly enforce laws that prohibit physical abuse.
- ❖ Enslaved human trafficking victims should be protected from prosecution, encouraged to testify against their captors, and provided with resettlement assistance.
- ❖ The UAE should ratify the UN Convention against Torture, and the penal code should be brought into compliance with the agreement.
- ❖ Recent changes to the personal status law should be widely publicized in mediums that will reach all segments of the community, particularly those who are traditionally vulnerable to abuse such as the poor and those with less education. A radio and television campaign should be launched that depicts the practical repercussions of the changes, and the print media should feature articles that detail the changes and their affects.
- ❖ Additional reforms to the personal status law should be enacted that ensure freedom of movement for adult women, regardless of their marital status.
- ❖ Foreign women should be provided with the legal means to resist— and the practical means to report—exploitation or confinement by employers.

ECONOMIC RIGHTS AND EQUAL OPPORTUNITY

Educational awareness campaigns, scholarships, and Emiratization laws, described below, have allowed women to make steady inroads into universities and public and private sectors jobs in recent years. The proportion of working adult women has grown from 25 percent (in 1990) to 35 percent (in 2000) to 40 percent (in 2007).[30] Nevertheless, women in the UAE are significantly underrepresented in upper level positions both in governmental institutions and particularly in the private sector. Moreover, the Labor Law (No. 8 of 1980) continues to place certain restrictions on women's employment options and rights based on gender stereotypes.

Women in the UAE exercise the right to own land and have full, independent use of their property from the age of 18. A married woman need not share her assets with her husband, who has no legal claim to her property whether they are married or divorced. Article 21 of the constitution guarantees the protection of private property, which states that deprivation of private property is only permissible in "circumstances dictated by the public benefit in accordance with the provisions of the law and on payment of a just compensation."

The concept of joint property arising through marriage does not exist, and property is only regarded as jointly owned where both husband and wife contributed financially to its purchase during the course of marriage. Upon divorce, the property would be divided according to each party's contribution, so where a husband purchased the family home using his salary alone, he is regarded as the sole owner. Additionally, while female citizens are not entitled to government housing benefits, male citizens are given either a house or a piece of land and money with which to build a house. The premise for this disparity is the presumption that it is a legal obligation under Shari'a for the husband to financially support his wife. According to a law adopted in April 2009, Emirati women married to non-nationals may receive government housing benefits if their husband is unable to provide housing to them.[31]

The right to inheritance for Muslims in the UAE is governed by Shari'a, which controls how estates are divided. Under Shari'a, women inherit one-third of the assets while men inherit two-thirds. As with their wives, men bear the responsibility of caring for their unmarried sisters and all other female members of their family, although there are no effective complaint mechanisms in place that would hold men accountable if they do not fulfill this role.

Under Shari'a, any gift given to a woman by her fiancé before marriage is her property, and the husband has no legal right to it after marriage. At the time of marriage, a Muslim woman receives mahr, often in the form of money that is her property. Even if the woman is independently wealthy, she is not responsible both legally and culturally for expenses relating to her clothing, health care, household needs, food, and recreation. Any income or profits a wife earns is hers alone. In the event of divorce, any unpaid part of the agreed-upon mahr is owed to the woman immediately, and the husband is responsible for maintaining her financially until she is remarried.[32]

Emirati women are permitted to license, own, and head their own businesses. Their actual economic involvement spans across many sectors, including trade, real estate, restaurants, hotels, and retail. Though women are free to enter into businesses of their choice, some municipalities have created barriers that prevent women from applying for licenses without the signature of a male guardian.[33] Some of these barriers are not always as apparent at first glance. In the case of the Sheikh Mohammed Establishment for Young Leaders, business capital is provided for residents of any emirate provided that the business itself is based in Dubai. This presents a challenge to women who live with their families outside of Dubai. While they are technically eligible for such grants, they face social challenges if they were to move away from home to pursue a business.

No legal or policy changes regarding women's access to education have been made since 2005. Education in the UAE is free for all nationals and compulsory for both boys and girls up to the age of 11. With exception of a few private universities, most academic institutions are gender segregated, and curriculums and textbooks are provided by the government. As of 2004, 65 percent of all university students were women, the majority of whom choose to study social sciences and humanities. Although these are the most recent government-published statistics, individual university figures show that women are filling an ever-increasing percentage of university slots every year.

The disparity in numbers between men and women at Emirati universities is substantial and is not simply because more men study abroad or join the military. One common explanation is that women are not expected to earn an income, and when they do, what they earn is often considered to be disposable income. Free from the pressure to earn a living, women enjoy greater space to complete degrees and pursue further studies and are more likely to graduate than men. For instance, at the University of Sharjah in 2006, 50 percent of the students admitted and 71 percent of graduates were women.[34] Unpublished statistics from the class of 2007 at UAE University indicate that 74 percent of those admitted and 79 percent of graduates were women.[35]

Nevertheless, social mores and gender biases play a large part in subject choices, and the long-term result has been the "feminization" of certain fields of study.[36] Girls are particularly discouraged to study science in the emirates outside of Dubai and Abu Dhabi. Some evidence suggests that this process has resulted in employers' devaluation of degrees in traditionally "female" subjects, such as humanities or social sciences. This trend has been well documented internationally, but published research on the issue in the Arab world is scarce. Regardless of the rationale behind it, upon graduation women are more likely to earn less than men by virtue of the positions they tend to assume in addition to gender discrimination they may encounter.

Women's economic rights in the UAE have remained largely unaltered in recent years, although a draft labor law is currently under consideration. Article 34 of the constitution provides every Emirati citizen with the right to freely choose his or her own occupation, trade, or profession within the limits of the law and subject to regulations on that profession or trade. However, Article 29 prohibits the recruitment of women for "hazardous, arduous, or physically or morally harmful work" or other forms of work to be decided by the Ministry of Labor.[37]

Article 27 of the labor law states that "no woman shall be required to work at night," which is defined as "a period of no less than 11 successive hours between 10 p.m. and 7 a.m." This has generally been interpreted by international organizations as a ban on women working at night. However, the plain language of the article is unclear and seems only to prohibit employers from mandating that their female employees work at night, instead leaving it to the discretion of each woman. Exceptions to this prohibition exist under Article 28 for instances in which a woman's nighttime work is necessitated by force majeure, is executive, administrative or technical in nature, is in the health services, or does not involve manual labor as decided by the minister of labor and social affairs.

These provisions hinder a woman's right to freely choose her profession, treating women as if they are incapable of making independent decisions regarding the best interest of their health and safety. Additionally, Article 34 holds a woman's guardian responsible if he has consented to employment that violates these provisions. In so doing, women are treated as minors whom guardians have a responsibility to protect. By fostering the concept of a dependent female, this provision opens the door for guardians to have further control over the occupational choices of their female charges.

The proposed draft labor law, released for public review in February 2007 and currently under consideration by the government, would retain these discriminatory provisions while simultaneously bolstering protection against discrimination in other areas. Article 3 of the draft labor law would, for the first time, specifically prohibit any form of discrimination between people with equal qualifications and experience levels. It also protects the rights of all persons to enjoy equal opportunities to find and remain in their jobs and enjoy full employment rights and benefits. Under this same provision, rules promoting increased participation by UAE nationals in the workforce do not constitute discrimination. Additionally, the draft labor law would amend current Article 32, which requires equal pay for equal work among male and female employees, to also prohibit discrimination against women in regards to their job security. In particular, the amended article would prohibit termination of employment on the basis of marital status, pregnancy, delivery, or maternity.

Article 3 of the draft labor law directly addresses "Emiratization," a nationalization program introduced by the government to promote employment in the private sector in an effort to reduce the UAE's dependence on foreign labor. One aspect of the program is a quota system that requires companies in fields such as finance and insurance to increase the number of nationals they employ by 4 to 5 percent annually.[38] As a result, private-sector companies have started to aggressively recruit young Emirati women to fill these quotas, and the Ministry of Labor no longer allows work permits for foreigners working as secretaries, public relations officers, and human resource personnel, effectively limiting all new hires for these positions to nationals.[39] Often, the perception is that the women are hired strictly to satisfy the regulations, and many Emirati women have complained of difficulty in advancing beyond entry-level positions. In effect, the program has resulted in a "'sticky floor' for young and ambitious UAE national women."[40]

In reality, cultural rather than legal barriers are what constrain women from entering certain professions. In many instances, familial conflicts are cited as the cause of both resignations by and termination of employment for many women. Women, particularly nationals, are inclined to join the public sector rather than the private sector because it is deemed more respectable by society, requires shorter working hours, and shows commitment to the country. Generally, women still have few opportunities for professional development and promotion, and local men often show more respect in the workplace for foreign than for Emirati women, since the former are free from the traditional cultural stigma placed on working women. As stipulated in the personal status code, sexual harassment is prohibited and can be reported at any police station, though no such reports have ever been made.

The labor law provides gender-specific benefits and protections in the workplace. Article 30 entitles all female employees to a 45-day paid maternity leave if they have completed at least one year of service to their employer. Women who have not met that requirement are entitled to half-pay leave. An additional 100-day unpaid continuous or discontinuous leave is available if the mother is unable to resume work at the end of her paid leave as a result of an illness linked to pregnancy or delivery. Article 31 entitles all breastfeeding women to two half-hour rest periods daily during the 18 months following delivery, in addition to their regular rest break. If enacted, the draft labor law would increase maternity leave to 100 days; the first 45 days would be at full pay and the remaining 55 days would be at half-pay. Those who have been employed with their current company for less than a year would only be entitled to half pay for the first 45 days; subsequent time off for illness related to birth would be reduced to 45 days of unpaid leave.

The chambers of commerce and industry for both Dubai and Abu Dhabi established women's business councils in 2002 as a means of encouraging Emirati women to participate in the economy. The Dubai Business Women Council partnered with the private company Naseba Group to organize the Women in Leadership Forum in Dubai. This three-day conference was an opportunity for hundreds of female leaders and entrepreneurs from around the world to network and learn from one another's experiences.[41] The UAE Women's Federation is also involved in promoting women's economic participation through a number of ongoing programs.[42] However, these initiatives neither lobby for change nor challenge government policies.

Recommendations

❖ The government should amend the draft labor law so that it removes all gender-based barriers to employment and guarantees women access to the same professional and vocational opportunities as men.

❖ The government should withdraw provisions of the draft labor law that fail to recognize women as autonomous adults with legal rights equal to those of men, including rules requiring a husband or guardian's permission for a woman to seek employment.

❖ In an effort to avoid the "sticky floor" syndrome created by setting
  hiring quotas for nationals, the government should make the private
  sector responsible for developing and training women for professional
  advancement.

❖ Municipal-level obstacles that prevent women from starting or operating businesses without the permission of male relatives should be
  eliminated.

❖ Local chambers of commerce should create programs specifically tai-
  lored to empower women in business and launch nationwide campaigns
  in which they partner with local universities and private companies to
  encourage more women to pursue careers in the private sector.

POLITICAL RIGHTS AND CIVIC VOICE

Women in the UAE have made significant inroads into high level government positions in recent years. With the introduction of elections for the
Federal National Council, one woman successfully ran as a candidate,
joining eight other women appointed to their positions in this advisory
body. Additionally, amendments to federal judicial law paved the way for
the appointment of female federal judges and prosecutors. However, it
remains to be seen to what extent these high-level appointments will permit greater women's representation in middle management and leadership
positions in the realm of public policy.

The UAE is not an electoral democracy. All decisions about political
leadership rest with the hereditary rulers of the seven emirates, who form
the Federal Supreme Council, the highest executive and legislative body
in the country. In 2006, the UAE became the final Gulf state to introduce
elections into its political system, albeit to a very limited extent for both
men and women. Previously, the 40-member Federal National Council
(FNC), an advisory body that lacks legislative powers, was appointed by
the seven rulers in numbers proportionate to each emirate's population.[43]
Under the new arrangement, the seven rulers appoint members to electoral
colleges, each of which consists of at least 100 times more members than
the emirate has FNC members. These electoral colleges choose half of the
FNC members for their emirates, while the remaining half continues to be
appointed by the rulers. Only those appointed to the electoral colleges are
entitled to vote or stand for office, meaning just 6,595 people—less than
1 percent of the total population—voted in 2006. This also represents

a tiny fraction of the country's 825,000 citizens, more than 300,000 of whom are over the age of 18.

Of the 6,595 electoral college members, 1,163 were women, as were 63 of the 438 who stood for office. Amal Abdullah al-Kubaissi, a female architect, was elected to the FNC, marking the only time that a woman has won an election during the first national vote in any of the Gulf states.[44] Eight other women were appointed to the FNC by the emirate rulers. At 22.5 percent, this level of representation indicates the expanding participation of Emirati women in government and politics.

Although far from ideal, the introduction of indirect elections is seen as a first step in enhancing the political role played by the FNC. There are also plans to expand the number of FNC members, to strengthen the body's legislative powers, and to develop more effective channels of coordination between the FNC and the executive authorities, namely the cabinet. Discussions regarding the introduction of local elections have also been initiated, although no dates have been set for this.

Significant breakthroughs regarding women's participation in the judiciary occurred in early 2008. UAE law was amended to allow women to serve as federal prosecutors and judges, and in March, Kholoud al-Dhahiri was appointed as the first female judge in the Abu Dhabi Justice Department. Meanwhile, two women were hired as the first female prosecutors that same year.[45] In March 2009, Ebtisam al-Bedwawi became the second female judge and the first to be appointed to the Dubai court system.[46] Sultan Saeed al-Badi, undersecretary of the Abu Dhabi Justice Department, said that the appointment reflects government efforts to increase participation by women in the UAE's development.[47] At present, however, women's representation in the judiciary remains limited, which has negatively affected women seeking legal counsel to uphold their rights.

Women are also increasingly represented in cabinet positions. In 2004, Lubna al-Qassimi was appointed as minister of the economy and planning, and in 2008 she became the minister for external trade. Her groundbreaking appointment in 2004 marked the first time a woman had been appointed to the Council of Ministers. As of February 2008, there were four female ministers.[48] Additionally, the first female ambassadors were appointed in September 2008, with Shaikha Najla Mohammad al-Qasimi appointed to Sweden and Dr. Hussa al-Otaiba appointed to Spain.[49] Aside from high-profile appointments, however, evidence suggests that women are failing to achieve promotions at a rate comparable to that of men in management positions within the executive branch. In March 2008, the UAE's permanent representative to the United Nations, Ahmad Abdul Rahman al-Jarman, noted that women constituted 66 percent of public-sector employees, but only 30 percent of those held "leadership and decision-making posts."[50] Political parties continue to be banned in the UAE.

Some analysts have cynically argued that the government's recent campaign to increase participation by women in civil and political arenas is simply "state-sponsored feminism," and it does not present a meaningful change on the societal level.[51] Women have received numerous high-profile appointments, but most were to institutions with no real power. The FNC has no legislative authority, and of the four women serving on the Council of Ministers, one serves "without portfolio" and the other leads the Ministry of Social Affairs. Moreover, mid-level management positions are still occupied disproportionately by men. Taken together, the evidence shows that although women are making inroads into the public sphere in the UAE, they still lack influence over policy decisions.[52]

Neither men nor women in the UAE enjoy true freedom of assembly, association, or expression. Article 33 of the constitution guarantees freedoms of assembly and association "within the limits of law." In practice, labor unions are banned and all public gatherings require government permits; the government has only granted one such permit for a pro-Palestinian demonstration in 2006, and women were free to participate.[53] Freedom of expression, whether oral or written, is guaranteed under Article 30 of the constitution within the limits of the law. However, there are both de jure and de facto limitations on this right. Most important, Articles 372 and 373 of the penal code criminalize speech and writing that causes "moral harm" or defamation to a third party. The Court of Cassation has defined both terms liberally. As a result, journalists are forced to exercise self-censorship or face punishment. Although Sheikh Mohammed issued an announcement banning the imprisonment of journalists who express their opinions, many journalists still exercise a degree of self-censorship due to high fines and penalties that newspapers may incur. [54]

Recommendations

❖ The government should grant universal adult suffrage and convert the FNC into a fully elected legislature with functioning political parties that has the capacity to draft, recommend, and reject legislation rather than acting solely in an advisory capacity.

❖ Women should be trained and promoted into positions of leadership within the government at a proportion that truly reflects equality between men and women rather than nominal representation.

❖ The government should permit and encourage free debate regarding women's rights in the press. Journalists should receive special training on how to avoid gender stereotyping in news stories and television programming.

❖ The government should lift restrictions on the freedoms of assembly and association, allowing the formation of labor unions and other independent groups that can champion women's interests as workers and citizens.

❖ A program should exist that encourages cooperation between potential and existing female members of the FNC and female politicians abroad, both in the Arab world and beyond, so that Emirati women can learn innovative strategies to help them campaign more effectively in the future and, once elected or appointed, retain the confidence of their constituents.

SOCIAL AND CULTURAL RIGHTS

Although the UAE is comprised of many nationalities, the country still remains segregated, not only in terms of gender but also by ethnicity. Schools, mosques, and hospitals are segregated by gender, and the large expatriate population also tends to self-segregate, forming separate communities and attending their own schools and hospitals.

There have been few significant changes to women's freedom with respect to health and reproductive rights since 2004. Women in the UAE are free to make decisions regarding their own medical care except in regard to cosmetic procedures intended to "restore" their virginity, which requires a guardian's permission. However, such permission is not required for procedures related to child birth, such as cesarean sections.[55] Birth-control pills are widely available, and women are free to purchase them without a prescription or permission from a spouse. Abortion is still prohibited under the penal code, but Federal Law (No. 7 of 1975) permits the Ministry of Health to grant applications for abortions when there is a threat to the life of the mother.[56] The Ministry is currently working with the religious and legal experts on a draft law that would permit termination of pregnancy within the first 120 days of pregnancy for the life of the mother or if the fetus would have serious congenital defects; after the first 120 days, abortions would only be granted to save the life of the mother.[57] However, abortions for financial reasons or due to concerns over family size remain illegal.[58] As a result of the abortion ban, there is some extralegal use of labor-inducing drugs purchased on the black market, although the extent of this practice is unknown.[59]

All citizens have free access to publicly funded health services. Due to substantial government investment, major improvements have been made to the national health system, and the UAE now ranks 39th out of 177 industrialized and developing countries of the Human Development Index and Gender-Related Development Index in the latest United Nations Development Programme *Human Development Report*.[60] According to the Ministry of Health, there are nine specialized centers, 95 clinics, four specialized maternity hospitals, and 14 general hospitals that provide medical services to women and children. Over 97 percent of births now take place in hospitals, and infant mortality rates have dropped to one per 100,000 births, approximately equal to rates in developed countries.[61] Ninety-five percent of pregnant women receive professional prenatal care.

Policies vary between the emirates on the question of health care for foreign nationals. The Abu Dhabi government enacted a new Code of Regulations of the Health Insurance Policy in July of 2007 that requires all employers to purchase health insurance for their employees. To the extent the employees are informed about this regulation, they can lodge a complaint with the Ministry of Labor if their employer fails to respect the code. Dubai is expected to eventually follow suit. Foreign nationals without a residency visa, however, are entitled only to free emergency medical care and must pay for all other care. Female genital mutilation is not widely practiced in the UAE.

Women are subjected to gender-based discrimination regarding their right to own and use housing. Traditionally, Emirati women live either with their husband or, if unmarried, their parents, and there is a powerful social stigma associated with women living away from their families. In the event that they wish to acquire property for investment or other purposes, they are free to do so. With respect to foreign nationals, there has been a growing movement in the last three years to segregate housing for married and single people. Single residents have been banned from Dubai villas and limited to housing in nonresidential zones in Sharjah, and there are a number of proposals for the construction of separate "bachelor housing" in Abu Dhabi.[62]

Unmarried couples may not live together legally, but this is not generally enforced for foreigners. However, in some areas, foreign women who have children out of wedlock may be imprisoned and deported if they are found living with a man to whom they are not married.

Women are increasingly participating in business, medicine, arts, politics, and education.[63] However, there is a disparity between women's progress as measured in literature published by the UAE and as measured in international sources. With the exception of a few high-profile women from the social elite who hold important positions, women's overall influence in the UAE remains limited.[64] As noted above (see "Political Rights and Civic Voice"), there is talk of conducting local elections in the same manner as the FNC elections, which would increase women's voice in society, but no changes have been made to date. Currently, women's ability to influence policies at the emirate level is minimal, both formally, as members of each ruler's advisory council, and informally.

The Emirati media provides little opportunity for women to shape its content, and they remain underrepresented in the media both as employees and subjects. The General Women's Union (GWU), led by Sheikha Fatima bint Mubarak, recently held a workshop intended to improve the image of women in Arab media.[65] Under the auspices of the GWU, the Arab Women's Organization has planned a series of initiatives, conferences, and workshops to encourage women in the field, though progress has been slow.

A number of women who have achieved high-profile status on television use their fame as a platform to discuss women's issues in the emirates and the Arab world in general. While there are no legal obstacles to women's participation in the media, social stigmas related to what is acceptable for women must be fully challenged and addressed if there are to be significant changes. One successful initiative started four years ago with Kalam Nawaem, a talk show hosted by four Arab women that remains one of the top-rated programs across the Arab world.[66] It is aired by a Saudi-owned company headquartered in the UAE.

Women are not required by law to cover themselves, but women nationals often wear a *sheila*—a traditional black scarf that covers some, or all, of a woman's hair—and an *abaya*—an article of clothing that covers the entire body from the shoulder to the ankles. Those inclined to dress differently are not likely to face verbal and physical abuse from male family members or restrictions that might be imposed on their freedom to leave home. Rather, many women wear sheila and abaya by choice as a sign of religious and national pride.

The UAE affords its citizens generous social welfare benefits, but there is little research on how poverty affects foreign-national women in particular. The Ministry of Social Affairs pays unemployment benefits to men and women equally, provided that they meet certain minimum requirements such as actively seeking work. Furthermore, the Beit Al-Khair society pays a type of social security to those who are unable to work, including divorcees, widows, the disabled, and the elderly. These payments are usually reserved for nationals. Moreover, Marriage Fund payments are still made exclusively to national men to encourage marriages among Emirati citizens. Begun in 1992, these grants are intended to help new Emirati families set up a home, and only national men who marry national women qualify. A common justification is that men are traditionally expected to pay for wedding-related expenses, including the mahr.

Limited progress has been made regarding the ability of women's rights organizations to freely advocate for social and cultural rights. In 2006, the Ministry of Social Affairs granted a license to the first and only human rights NGO, the UAE Human Rights Association (UAE/HRA), according to the criteria laid down in Federal Law (No. 6 of 1974). However, the UAE/HRA has thus far failed to effectively pursue sensitive women's issues, and instead has opted to act as an ombudsman and liaison between social-welfare bodies and the public. No other human rights organizations are authorized to operate in the country.

Recommendations

✤ The government should launch a campaign to positively influence the image of women in the media. An award should be granted to the best female Emirati journalist each year, enticing more women to participate in and influence the press and its content.

✤ Media outlets should spearhead serious programs that address critical social issues in an effort to educate the public about the challenges and successes of Arab women in the UAE.

✤ A writing competition should be sponsored for high school and university-aged women that calls for essays analyzing the societal and cultural realities of women in the UAE. By highlighting the experiences of average women, the project will encourage a social dialogue regarding the pros and cons of the cultural status quo.

❖ The Women's Federation should work with local universities to establish gender studies programs in an effort to raise awareness of women's rights and the challenges that women face in their daily lives.

AUTHOR

Serra Kirdar is the founder and director of the Muthabara Foundation in Dubai, which aims to maximize the potential of Arab women to achieve managerial and professional roles in the private sector. She earned her B.A. in the Middle Eastern Studies at the University of Oxford, where she also completed her M.Sc. in Comparative and International Education. Dr. Kirdar received her D.Phil. at St. Anthony's College, Oxford, in 2004, with a dissertation *Gender and Cross-Cultural Experience with Reference to Elite Arab Women*. A founding member of the New Leaders Group for the Institute for International Education, she also established the Initiative for Innovative Teaching, which works to develop locally geared professional training programs for public sector teachers in the Arab world.

NOTES

[1] Ibrahim al-Abed, and others, eds., *UAE Yearbook 2008* (London: Trident Press, 2008), http://www.uaeyearbook.com/default.asp.

[2] *Constitution of the United Arab Emirates* (drafted in 1971 and made permanent in 1996), http://www.helplinelaw.com/law/uae/constitution/constitution01.php.

[3] Citizenship information, http://www.abudhabi.ae/egovPoolPortal_WAR/appmanager/ADeGP/Citizen?_nfpb=true&_portlet.async=false&_pageLabel=p16246&lang=en, in Arabic.

[4] Pippa Sanderson, *Working and Living in Dubai* (Pyjama Publishing, August 2006), http://www.justlanded.com/english/Dubai/Tools/Articles/Moving/Home-Life.

[5] Fuad Ali, "Fujairah Court Rules in Cannabis Case," *Gulf News,* May 15, 2005.

[6] Eugene Cotran and Chibli Mallat, *Yearbook of Islamic and Middle Eastern Law* 4 (The Hague: Kluwer Law International, 1998).

[7] *Declarations, Reservations, and Objections to CEDAW*, Convention on the Elimination of All Forms of Discrimination against Women, http://www.un.org/womenwatch/daw/cedaw/reservations-country.htm.

[8] "UAE: Flogging: 'R.A.,' teen girl" (Amnesty International, ed., June 28, 2007), http://asiapacific.amnesty.org/library/Index/ENGMDE250022007?open&of=ENG-ARE.

[9] *Fatima Bint Mubarak: Women Associations*, http://www.uaezayed.com/zayed8/25.htm.

[10] Sara Sayed, *Women, Politics, and Development in the United Arab Emirates* (thesis, Zayed University, 2004), 27–29.

11 *Country Profile: United Arab Emirates* (Washington, DC: Library of Congress, 2007).

12 Tad Stahnke and Robert C. Blitt, "The Religion-State Relationship and the Right to Freedom of Religion or Belief: A Comparative Textual Analysis of the Constitutions of Predominantly Muslim Countries," *Georgetown Journal of International Law* 26 (2005).

13 Adel Arafah, "Wife's Petition to Leave Hubby Is Rejected," *Khaleej Times,* December 11, 2006, http://www.khaleejtimes.com/DisplayArticleNew.asp?xfile=data/theuae/2006/December/theuae_December301.xml&section=theuae&col>&section=theuae&col.

14 Hassan M. Fattah, "Workers' Protest Spurs Arab Emirates to Act," *New York Times,* September 11, 2005, http://www.nytimes.com/2005/09/25/international/middleeast/25dubai.html.

15 *Personal Status Law,* United Arab Emirates, http://www.gcc-legal.org/MojPortalPublic/BrowseLawOption.aspx?LawID=3128&country=2> &country=2, in Arabic; "New Divorce Rule Gives UAE Women Big Boost," *UAE Interact,* July 16, 2005, http://uae interact.com/docs/New_divorce_rule_gives_UAE_women_big_boost/17020.htm.

16 Altaf Hussein, "The Wisdom Behind Having a Mahram," May 17, 2007, http://www.islamonline.net/servlet/Satellite?c=Article_C&cid=1178724264796&pagename=Zone-English-Youth%2FYTELayout.

17 "Women in the United Arab Emirates: A Portrait of Progress," UAE Ministry of State for Federal National Council Affairs (2008), 3, http://lib.ohchr.org/HRBodies/UPR/Documents/Session3/AE/UPR_UAE_ANNEX3_E.pdf.

18 *International Parental Child Abduction: The United Arab Emirates* (Washington DC: U.S. Department of State), http://travel.state.gov/family/abduction/country/country_532.html.

19 *Trafficking in Persons Report,* UAE Country Narrative (Washington DC: U.S. Department of State, June 4, 2008), http://www.state.gov/g/tip/rls/tiprpt/2008/105389.htm.

20 *Trafficking in Persons Report,* http://www.state.gov/g/tip/rls/tiprpt/2008/105389.htm.

21 "Red Crescent Society Opens Shelter Home for Women and Children," *UAE Interact,* http://uaeinteract.com/docs/RCA_opens_shelter_home_for_women_and_children/28177.htm.

22 "Further Information on Death by Flogging/Stoning" (London: Amnesty International, ed., July 2, 2006), http://www.amnesty.org/en/library/info/MDE25/006/2006/en.

23 *UAE: Flogging* (London: Amnesty International), http://asiapacific.amnesty.org/library/Index/ENGMDE250062005?open&of=ENG-ARE> &of=ENG-ARE.

24 See "United Arab Emirates" in *Report 2008* (London: Amnesty International, 2008), http://thereport.amnesty.org/en/regions/middle-east-north-africa/uae.

25 Robert F. Worth, "Advocate for Abused Women in Dubai Has Enemies in Emirates," *International Herald Tribune,* March 23, 2008, http://www.iht.com/articles/2008/03/23/mideast/dubai.php?page=2.

26 Worth, "Advocate for Abused Women."

27 Lisa Mahoy, "I Was Gang Raped Then Jailed in Dubai," *Daily Telegraph,* June 14, 2009, http://www.dailytelegraph.com.au/news/world/i-was-gang-raped-then-jailed-in-dubai/story-e6frev00-1225734459965.

[28] Discussion with U.S. Fulbright Fellow conducting fieldwork in social work at Zayed University, May 2008.

[29] *Strengthening the UAE's Nascent Civil Society* (Abu Dhabi: Middle East Partnership Initiative, ed., 2008), http://www.abudhabi.mepi.state.gov/eeg.html.

[30] World Development Indicators Database, Female Labor Participation Rate (World Bank 2009), http://web.worldbank.org/WBSITE/EXTERNAL/DATASTATISTICS/0,,con tentMDK:21725423~pagePK:64133150~piPK:64133175~theSitePK:239419,00 .html (last accessed on December 15, 2009).

[31] Najla al-Awadhi, "A Small Step for Women's Rights in UAE," *Gulf News*, April 2, 2009, http://gulfnews.com/opinions/columnists/a-small-step-for-women-s-rights-in-uae- 1.62214.

[32] *Inheritance Law in the UAE* (Dubai: Al-Tamimi & Company, 2005).

[33] Sayed, *Women, Politics, and Development* (2004).

[34] *Facts and Figures,* University of Sharjah, http://www.sharjah.ac.ae/English/About_UOS/ Pages/FactsFigures.aspx.

[35] Unpublished statistics from: UAE University Facts and Figures Report (2008).

[36] John Willoughby, "Segmented Feminization and the Decline of Neopatriarchy in G.C.C. Countries of the Persian Gulf," *Comparative Studies of South Asia, Africa, and the Middle East* 28, no. 1 (2008).

[37] The law actually refers to the Ministry of Labor and Social Affairs, which was bifurcated into the Ministry of Labor and the Ministry of Social Affairs in 2006.

[38] Abbas al-Lawati and Wafa Issa, "Finding Jobs for UAE Nationals," *Gulf News*, August 12, 2006, http://archive.gulfnews.com/indepth/labour/Emiritisation/10059252.html.

[39] Samir Salama, "New Emiritisation Drive," *Gulf News,* April 8, 2008, http://archive. gulfnews.com/indepth/labour/Emiritisation/10049370.html.

[40] Aisha Bilkhair, *Global Perspective: Political Reforms for Access and Equity: Women's Education in the United Arab Emirates,* Association of American Colleges and Universities, http:// www.aacu.org/OCWW/volume36_3/global.cfm?printer_friendly=1.

[41] Women in Leadership website, http://www.wilforum.com/EventContent/Home.aspx?id =59&new=1; "Naseba, Dubai Business Women Council Partner for Women in Leadership Forum," AME Info, September 13, 2009, http://www.ameinfo.com/209360 .html.

[42] *Fatima Bint Mubarak: Women Associations,* http://www.uaezayed.com/zayed8/25.htm.

[43] "About FNC," *United Arab Emirates: Federal National Council* (2007), http://www.majles -uae.com/English/subject_details.aspx?parent_no=2&cat_no=2.

[44] "Sole Woman Elected in UAE Maiden Polls," *Middle East Online,* December 21, 2006, http://www.middle-east-online.com/english/?id=18884.

[45] Eman Mohammed, "UAE's First Female Judge Says Not Afraid of New Role," *Gulf News,* April 1, 2008, http://www.gulfnews.com/nation/Society/10201944.html.

[46] Bassam Za'za', "Dubai Names Ebtisam al-Bedwawi as First Woman Judge," *Gulf News,* March 27, 2009, http://gulfnews.com/news/gulf/uae/government/dubai-names- ebtisam-al-bedwawi-as-first-woman-judge-1.59637.

[47] Lin Noueihed, "UAE Appoints First Female Judge," *Reuters UK,* March 27, 2008, http://uk.reuters.com/article/worldNews/idUKL2714342720080327.

48 "Women Ministers Doubled as UAE Shuffles Cabinet," *Arab News,* February 18, 2008, http://www.arabnews.com/?page=4&section=0&article=106891&d=18&m=2&y=2008.

49 "UAE Names Female Envoys," *Gulf News,* September 16, 2008, http://www.gulfnews.com/Nation/Government/10245659.html.

50 Dana el-Baltaji, "The Gender Issue," *Kipp Report,* 2008, http://www.kippreport.com/article.php?articleid=1153.

51 Peyman Pejman, "Rights–UAE: Sporadic 'State-Sanctioned Feminism' Is Not Enough," *Interpress Service,* March 28, 2007, http://www.accessmylibrary.com/coms2/summary_0286-30170516_ITM.

52 Pejman, "Rights–UAE," http://www.accessmylibrary.com/coms2/summary_0286-301 70516_ITM.

53 *Country Reports on Human Rights Practices: United Arab Emirates* (Washington, DC: United States Department of State, 2002), http://www.state.gov/g/drl/rls/hrrpt/2002/18291.htm.

54 "UAE Upholds Press Freedom," *Gulf News,* September 25, 2007, http://archive.gulfnews.com/articles/07/09/25/10156138.html.

55 "UAE Upholds Press Freedom," *Gulf News,* http://archive.gulfnews.com/articles/07/01/29/10100179.html.

56 Nina Muslim, "UAE Authorities Study Legalising Therapeutic Abortion," *Gulf News,* May 3, 2007, http://archive.gulfnews.com/articles/07/05/03/10122596.html.

57 Asma Ali Zain, "New Medical Law Follows Islamic Code of Ethics," *Khajeel Times,* January 1, 2008, http://www.khaleejtimes.com/DisplayArticleNew.asp?section=theuae&xfile=data/theuae/2008/january/theuae_january23.xml.

58 Nada S. Mussallam, "Abortion Only on Valid Reasons," *Khaleej Times,* September 6, 2006, http://www.khaleejtimes.ae/DisplayArticle.asp?xfile=data/theuae/2006/September/theuae_September140.xml&section=theuae.

59 Jonathan Sheikh-Miller, "Abortion Drugs Risks Health in UAE," *AME Info,* June 17, 2006, http://www.ameinfo.com/89027.html.

60 *United Nations Human Development Report* (New York: United Nations Development Programme, 2007/2008), http://hdr.undp.org/en/statistics/.

61 *Health Services,* Ministry of Finance and Industry, http://www.fedfin.gov.ae/Government/health.htm#Maternity%20and%20Child%20Care.

62 Samir Salama, "Bachelors Unhappy with Segregated Housing Plans," *Gulf News,* May 14, 2007, http://archive.gulfnews.com/articles/07/05/14/10125176.html.

63 Hamida Ghafour, "Women of Influence," *The National,* April 20, 2008, http://www.thenational.ae/article/20080420/ONLINESPECIAL/992306773.

64 Ola Galal, "Women Directors Few and Far Between in Gulf Firms," *Reuters,* May 19, 2008, http://www.reuters.com/article/lifestyleMolt/idUSL1966031220080519.

65 "Experts Discuss Strategy to Train Arab Women in the Media—UAE," *Khaleej Times,* May 13, 2008, http://www.menafn.com/qn_news_story_s.asp?storyid=1093196505.

66 Note that the show has been MBC's highest rated show for the last three years. See: Mona Abu Sleiman, "Tough Talk in a Soft Voice," *MEB Journal,* http://www.mebjournal.com/component/option,com_magazine/func,show_article/id,194/.

YEMEN

by Elham Manea

POPULATION: 22,880,000
GNI PER CAPITA: US$864

COUNTRY RATINGS	2004	2009
NONDISCRIMINATION AND ACCESS TO JUSTICE:	1.9	1.9
AUTONOMY, SECURITY, AND FREEDOM OF THE PERSON:	2.0	1.9
ECONOMIC RIGHTS AND EQUAL OPPORTUNITY:	1.8	1.9
POLITICAL RIGHTS AND CIVIC VOICE:	2.1	2.0
SOCIAL AND CULTURAL RIGHTS:	2.1	2.0

(COUNTRY RATINGS ARE BASED ON A SCALE OF 1 TO 5, WITH 1 REPRESENTING THE LOWEST AND 5 THE HIGHEST LEVEL OF FREEDOM WOMEN HAVE TO EXERCISE THEIR RIGHTS)

INTRODUCTION

The Yemen Arab Republic (North Yemen) and the People's Democratic Republic of Yemen (South Yemen) united on May 22, 1990, to form the present-day Republic of Yemen. North Yemen had been established as a tribal-military polity in 1962 after the overthrow of the theocratic Zaydi Shiite imamate. By contrast, South Yemen, which gained its independence from Britain in 1967, was the only Marxist regime in the Arab world. The two countries' attempts to unify were long hindered by political differences, including two wars, but the process was accelerated in part by the end of the Cold War. A 1994 civil war between northern and southern factions ended with the victory of the close circle of tribal, sectarian, and military groups led by Ali Abdallah Salih, who had ruled North Yemen since 1978 and remains united Yemen's president to date.

Yemen has a vibrant civil society and media that do not shy away from criticizing the government. However, its political system is increasingly dominated by one party, the General People's Congress (GPC), despite a competitive presidential election in 2006. In February 2009, the parliament approved a two-year postponement of that year's legislative elections, perpetuating the GPC's control. The Salih regime is facing an increasingly vocal southern movement against alleged northern hegemony, and a

Zaydi Shiite rebellion in the northern region of Sa'ada. After four years of fighting, the president declared the end of that conflict in 2008, but the security situation in Sa'ada remains unstable.

The lives of Yemeni women have been greatly affected by all of these political developments. The 1990 unification led to the codification of a family law that was considered a setback for southern women, who had previously enjoyed legal equality in family affairs. The end of the civil war led to new modifications of the constitution and the family law, marking a clear regression toward more conservative and gender-biased provisions. As the political situation has deteriorated, women's rights activists have increasingly faced harassment by security forces, and immediate political needs have absorbed resources that might otherwise have been used to improve the status of women and tackle the serious economic and social challenges facing the country today. Adding to these strains have been the diverse waves of migrants seeking refuge from war and persecution in the Horn of Africa, or transit to economic opportunities in the Gulf states and beyond.

Yemen is a tribal and traditional country where prevailing cultural attitudes, patriarchal structures, and Islamic fundamentalism accord women low status in the family and community and limit their participation in society. Women are subjected to various forms of violence and discrimination, including domestic abuse, deprivation of education, early or forced marriage, restrictions on freedom of movement, exclusion from decision-making roles and processes, denial of inheritance, deprivation of health services, and female genital mutilation (FGM).

The past five years have been marked by both positive and negative developments for women's status in Yemen. On the positive side, Yemeni nongovernmental organizations (NGOs) and activists have been vigorously advocating for gender equality, fostering awareness of gender-based violence, and demanding a change in Yemeni laws, especially family laws, which are heavily biased against women. The 2008 court case of a 10-year-old girl who demanded a divorce from her adult husband caused a public debate that culminated in the parliament considering a minimum marriage age of 17. Some educational and executive institutions have allowed women to enroll in their ranks for the first time, and the Islamist party Islah undertook internal changes that led to the first election of women to its higher decision-making bodies.

However, Yemeni laws still discriminate against women, treating them as inferiors or minors who need perpetual guardianship. Major political parties, including the ruling GPC, refrained from supporting female candidates during the 2006 local elections, and women's representation in the executive and legislative bodies remains very low. Finally, the country's economic and political crises have drawn resources away from the education and health sectors, undercutting attempts to narrow the gender gap and improve conditions for women and girls. The primacy of rule of law is largely absent, and it is particularly challenging for women and the poor to access their rights and benefits.

NONDISCRIMINATION AND ACCESS TO JUSTICE

Patriarchal social norms continue to hinder women's access to the judicial system, and legal provisions still give them an inferior status. The government has made no apparent progress on legal reforms that would allow women to pass on their citizenship to their children. Minorities continue to face discrimination and limited access to state health and educational services.

Article 3 of the 1994 constitution identifies Shari'a (Islamic law) as the source of all legislation. This provision has shaped the legal framework regulating women's lives and led to officially sanctioned gender discrimination. Although Article 40 declares that "citizens are all equal in rights and duties," this is clearly undermined by Article 31, which states that "women are the sisters of men. They have rights and duties, which are guaranteed and assigned by Shari'a and stipulated by law." In the cultural context, being sisters of men indicates a status where women are protected by their brothers, but are weaker and lesser in worth. Consequently, laws such as the Personal Status Law (Family Law), the penal code, the Citizenship Law, the Evidence Law, and the Labor Law systematically discriminate against women.

The 1994 constitution stands in contrast to the clear language used in the Unification Constitution of 1991, which stipulated that "all citizens are equal before the law. They are equal in public rights and duties. There shall be no discrimination between them based on sex, color, ethnic origin, language, occupation, social status, or religion." The new constitution, drafted after the end of the civil war, was greatly influenced by conservative political elements. President Salih's victory in the war depended in part on the support of the Islamist party Islah and the Hashid tribal confederation. Both of these factions were hostile toward women's rights, and as a result, the 1991 constitution was modified to eliminate antidiscrimination provisions.

Yemen's judicial system has three levels of courts: first instance, appeals, and the Supreme Court. The higher courts are divided into specialized sections: civil, criminal, commercial, and personal status. According to Yemen's application of Shari'a, an adult woman is not recognized as a full person before the court. Article 45 of the Evidence Law (No. 21 of 1992) posits that a woman's testimony is not accepted in cases of adultery and retribution, or in cases where corporal punishment is a possible penalty. Also under Article 45, a woman's testimony is given half the weight of a man's in financial cases. A woman's testimony is accepted in instances where only women are involved, or when the act in question occurred in their segregated places (Article 30).

Women face additional difficulties obtaining justice because police stations and courts—which are always crowded with men—are commonly considered to be inappropriate places for "respected women."[1] Moreover, the lack of female judges, prosecutors, and lawyers discourage women from turning to the courts. Given the social discrimination experienced by women, they hesitate to approach male legal consultants, particularly for issues such as abuse or rape. Instead, women often rely on male relatives to go to court in their place, or turn to them to solve their problem rather than taking the matter to the judiciary.[2]

Under Yemen's laws, women do not enjoy the same citizenship rights as men. The children of male Yemeni citizens automatically receive their father's citizenship, regardless of whether their mother is Yemeni.[3] The foreign-born wife of a Yemeni man has the right to apply for citizenship after four years of marriage, although her husband may object to this application. On the other hand, Yemeni women married to foreign citizens are unable to pass on their citizenship to their children. The government has taken steps to amend some of the discriminatory aspects of the law, but the new legislation fails from guaranteeing equality. Specifically, Law No. 24 of 2003 added Article 10 to the Nationality Law (No. 6 of 1991), allowing Yemeni women to transfer their citizenship to their children only if they are divorced, widowed, or abandoned by their non-Yemeni husbands. This amendment, while representing a step forward, failed to provide women with the unconditional right to pass on their citizenship currently enjoyed by Yemeni men. In March 2008, Article 3 of the nationality law was amended to allow a Yemeni woman to transfer her citizenship to her child if the father is unknown or if he has no nationality.

Several NGOs have played an active role in calling for equal citizenship rights. The Women's Forum for Research and Training, a Yemeni NGO dedicated to women's rights, highlighted the issue in the context of CEDAW. Moreover, the Sisters' Arab Forum for Human Rights (SAF) in March 2008 organized the fourth Democratic Forum, which discussed the legal challenges that hinder women's political participation, including those concerning their citizenship rights.[4]

Women are also treated unequally in the Crimes and Penal Code (No. 12 of 1994). According to Article 42, the financial compensation (*diyya*, or blood money) owed to the family of a murdered or wrongfully killed woman is half that owed to the family of a male victim. The same article mandates that *aroush*, the compensation owed to a person if they have been permanently injured, is three times larger for an injured man than for an injured woman. Article 232 stipulates that a husband who kills his wife and her adulterous partner upon witnessing them in the act of adultery is subject to fines or up to one year in prison. This very lenient punishment also covers murders committed by men who find a female relative in an adulterous situation. Women who are beaten by their male relatives upon suspicion of extramarital sex are often left without any legal protection. According to police officers cited in a study on such "honor crimes" in Yemen, women who turn to the police for help are typically brought back to their male relatives.[5]

Article 273 of the penal code criminalizes "shameful" or "immoral" acts, loosely defined as "any act that violates public discipline or public decency," including nudity or exposing oneself. Violations are punishable by fines of up to 1,000 riyals or as much as one year in prison. The terms "public discipline" and "public decency" are left to the interpretation of police officers and judges, subject to each region's customs and traditions. Consequently, some women have been detained simply for being alone with men who are not their relatives.[6] Poor women or those who are members of marginalized groups, such as the Akhdam or Somali and Ethiopian refugees, are more likely to be detained or arbitrarily arrested on such grounds.

Political motives have also led to the arbitrary arrests of female human rights activists. For example, Hanan al-Wada'ai, an officer for the Child's

Rights Program in the Swedish organization Save the Children–Sana'a, was snatched from the street by security personnel on March 17, 2007. She was detained without due process and accused of entering the Iranian embassy, only to be released after two hours.[7] This tactic is used against both men and women who are politically active or involved in the defense of human rights.

Minorities including Jews, refugees, and the so-called *Akhdam* (servants)—Yemenis who are popularly believed to be descendants of East African invaders from the sixth century and who languish at the bottom of Yemen's social ladder[8]—are theoretically equal before the law. However, in practice they face denial of state services, verbal harassment, and attacks on their property and persons. Female members of these groups face a double burden of discrimination, and hesitate to report gender-based violence for fear of being abused by policemen. Women who belong to the Akhdam minority often face different forms of sexual harassment and abuse, and in cases where a child or a woman dies as a result, police forces frequently fail to investigate. Girls are most affected by the denial of education rights, and women are more likely to be turned away by hospitals.

The government of the People's Democratic Republic of Yemen (South Yemen), which signed CEDAW in 1984, made one reservation, declaring that it did not consider itself bound by Article 29, paragraph 1, relating to the settlement of disputes which may arise concerning the application or interpretation of the convention. South Yemen's treaty obligations were transferred to the unified Republic of Yemen in 1990, but CEDAW has not yet been fully implemented and incorporated into the country's legislative and institutional framework, as indicated by the laws described above.

Women's rights groups and civil society actors face constant obstacles in their attempts to combat gender discrimination because women's rights issues are extremely controversial within Yemen's conservative society. Activists are routinely intimidated and subjected to harassment and detention without justification by security forces. A'afraa al-Hariri, the head of Relief Center for the Care of Women in Aden, has been targeted since 2006 for her work in support of female juveniles who are former prisoners and victims of gender-based violence and child marriage.[9] Religious sheikhs, supported by semi-official newspapers, also target women's rights activists with damaging smear campaigns. One well-known case was that of Amal al-Basha, the director of the SAF. In 2006, because of her public call for changes to the Personal Status Law, she was vilified in the mosques during Friday sermons. She also received death threats, and semi-official newspapers participated actively in inflaming the public against her.[10]

Women's NGOs like SAF and the National Organization for Defending Rights and Freedoms have worked in cooperation with the National Committee on Women, a governmental body for women's affairs established in 1996, to advocate for amendments to the penal code. For example, they have submitted a proposal to the government that would amend Article 42, which stipulates that the blood money for a slain woman is half that for a man. However, their recommendations have yet to be addressed.

Recommendations

* The government should revise Articles 3 and 31 of the constitution so as to embrace without reservation—religious or otherwise—the concept of gender equality.
* The government should fulfill its international obligations and fully integrate the provisions of CEDAW into its national laws and constitution.
* The government should take specific measures to allow women non-discriminatory access to justice at all levels. These measures should include educating women on their rights and providing training to law enforcement officers and members of the judiciary regarding women's rights.
* The government should amend the penal code, striking down all articles that are biased against women and formally integrating the concept of gender equality into its provisions.
* The government should establish a mechanism that allows women's rights activists to report and obtain justice for harassment they face at the hands of security forces. Such a mechanism may include the establishment of a legal department dedicated to dealing with these cases.

AUTONOMY, SECURITY, AND FREEDOM OF THE PERSON

The cultural attitudes prevalent in Yemen's tribal and traditional society have accorded women a low status in the family and the community. As a result, women are subject to mental and physical abuse within the family, deprived of their freedom of movement, and excluded from private decision-making processes. Women and girls among Yemeni Jews, Akhdam, and African refugees often face the worst discrimination. Studies conducted by local and international NGOs have highlighted the social prejudice exercised against women and minorities in the name of tradition, customs, or religion. No progress has been reported on the implementation of CEDAW, women's access to identity and travel documents continues to depend on the permission of male guardians, and the Personal Status Law remains discriminatory in its unequal treatment of husband and wife in their family relations. The highly publicized case of a child divorce in 2008 led to a proposed law that would set the age of marriage at 17, but it is unclear whether Islamist and conservative members of parliament will allow the measure to take effect.

Freedom of religion or belief is not guaranteed by the constitution. Although Article 41 stipulates that "the state shall guarantee freedom of thought and expression of opinion in speech," the charter does not specifically mention freedom of religion as a basic right of Yemeni citizens. This omission is not incidental. Article 259 of the penal code criminalizes conversion from Islam to another religion, with violators subject to the death penalty. This punishment is mandated by Shari'a, and is based on a saying attributed to the prophet Muhammad. Christian immigrants are allowed to practice their religion publicly, for instance in the churches of Aden, but they observe a degree of self-restraint out of fear of Islamic fundamentalists. By the same token, Yemeni Jews, both men and women, have been targeted by Islamic fundamentalists and public anti-Semitism. Muslim women are not allowed to work as religious preachers or imams, although they are often recruited to disseminate Islamists' ideology as activists.

Freedom of movement for Yemeni women is restricted. A woman is unable to obtain a personal identity card or passport without the consent of her guardian, who is her closest male relative.[11] This is not based on any valid law but is the customary practice of the authorities. A personal identity card is essential for a woman seeking to enter the workforce or access various state services. In a demonstration of the restrictions on foreign travel, female activists with the SAF were denied their passports at the Migration and Passport Department on June 1, 2008, because they were not accompanied by their male guardians.[12] It was unclear whether the decision was motivated by the SAF's role in defending human rights. However, these restrictions are systematically implemented, and women can only bypass them if they are well connected socially.

The Personal Status Law (No. 20 of 1992) and the amendments enacted through Law No. 27 of 1998 and Law No. 24 of 1999 discriminate against women in matters concerning marriage, divorce, and child custody, and treat women as inferior members of the family. Discriminatory provisions include the requirement that a male guardian approve of a marriage before the contract can be completed, and rules that allow a man to marry up to four women (Articles 16 and 12, respectively). Article 40 mandates that a wife must obey her husband by deferring to his choice for their place of residence, following his orders and undertaking her domestic chores, not leaving her marriage residence without his permission, and fulfilling his sexual desires. This final provision flagrantly legitimizes sexual violence and rape within marriage.

Moreover, the husband has the right to *talaq*, a form of unilateral divorce without justification in which he has only to pronounce the sentence "I repudiate you" three times. Article 58 of the Personal Status Law does not specify whether the husband should say the sentence to his wife directly, nor does it require a witness or notification of a court. It simply states that the divorce becomes valid once the husband utters the sentence with the intention of divorcing his wife.

A woman has the right to ask for a divorce if she can prove that her husband has caused her harm. According to Articles 47 through 55, "harm" includes the husband's mental sickness or alcoholism, his inability to provide for his family or his wife financially, his absence in an unknown place or outside the country for more than one year, his imprisonment for more than three years, or the basic reason that the wife hates him. Alternatively, she may seek out a *khula* divorce, in which she ends the marriage in exchange for her financial rights. A husband's consent is necessary for khula to take effect. Nevertheless, this alternative is often used by women of greater economic means, who can afford its financial sacrifice. Khula is not a viable option for women who are entirely financially dependent on their husbands, namely the majority of Yemeni women. In addition to the general difficulties, noted above, that women face when attempting to access the judicial system, their chances of securing a divorce often depends on the judge's sympathy—an arbitrary factor that cannot be guaranteed in every case.

Women's ability to negotiate their full and equal marriage rights is severely limited by both social customs and the Personal Status Law. According to Article 15, the permission and signature of a woman's male guardian is required for a marriage contract to be valid. Although the law states in Article 10 that any marriage contracted by force is void and requires in Article 23 the bride's consent to marry, Article 7 does not require the presence of the bride to seal a marriage contract. Only the presence of her guardian and the prospective groom is required, leading to cases in which women are married without ever having been informed and must either accept the marriage or face intimidation or violence from their male guardians and families. Those who dare to marry without permission face legal punishment. According to the findings of Oxfam's Legal Protection and Advocacy Program, women who married without their guardians' consent or who escaped to marry men of their choice have been charged with adultery or shameful acts.[13] Adultery is punishable by up to 100 lashes if committed by unmarried men or women, a sentence that is frequently carried out.

Article 15 of the amended Personal Status Law of 1999 permits child marriage if there is "an interest" in such a union. The law is ambiguous in its wording and does not indicate what it means by an "interest," nor does it specify whose interest should be taken into account. In practice, both girls and boys are subjected to child marriage, especially in rural areas. However, due to economic factors, girls are more likely to be married off to adult men in exchange for dowries.

The recent case of Nojoud, an eight-year-old girl who was married to a 32-year-old neighbor against her will, caused local as well as international uproar and illustrates the limited extent to which a child can negotiate her full and equal marriage rights.[14] Although Nojoud repeatedly rejected the marriage, she was forced to consent under pressure. Her husband immediately consummated the marriage. Traumatized by this sexual abuse, the child went to a court alone in 2008 and, at the age of 10, demanded a divorce. Thanks to the combined support of her lawyer, Shatha Nasr, and the judge handling her case, Mohammed al-Kadi, Nojoud was able to get an annulment. The resulting public debate led to the introduction of a draft law by women's rights activists that would set an age limit for marriage at 17. Although the parliament initially approved the draft in February 2009, opposition from Islamist factions led to a postponement of its enactment "for further deliberation."

Yemeni girls and female noncitizens are the two populations most likely to suffer from gender-based, slavery-like conditions. The number of female refugees arriving in Yemen increased substantially beginning in June 30, 2008, although a half of the new arrivals intend to move to Saudi Arabia.[15] Fleeing war and persecution in the Horn of Africa and desperately seeking protection or economic opportunities in the Gulf and beyond, these women often fall prey to human traffickers and are more likely to end up in slavery-like conditions. With 42 percent of the population living under the poverty line, some Yemeni families are forced to sell their young daughters to rich men from the Gulf as a source of income. The young brides of these unions, referred to as "tourist marriages," are sexually exploited for several months and then divorced and left traumatized.[16]

The 1994 constitution specifically omitted Article 33 of the 1991 constitution, which forbade the use of cruel or degrading forms of punishment and declared that "no laws permitting such means may be enacted." Reflecting this omission, cruel, inhuman, and degrading punishments are integrated into the penal code today. For instance, Article 38 sanctions execution by stoning, amputation of body parts, and crucifixion as means of punishment. Several cases arose in 2006 and 2007 in which women of poor economic means were convicted of adultery and sentenced to death by stoning. Although these cases have since been successfully appealed, they suggest that such punishments are more than theoretical, particularly when it comes to impoverished women.[17]

Domestic violence is not penalized, and there is little reliable data on the prevalence of the phenomenon.[18] There are no shelters in Yemen for the victims of domestic abuse. The problem is compounded by the reluctance of abused women to turn to the police for help, the fear of social stigma, police officers' lack of sensitivity toward such cases, and the absence of female social workers and officers who are qualified to deal with women's cases.[19] Studies have suggested that women accept some forms of violence as legitimate on religious grounds.[20] Sura IV, Verse 34 of the Koran lays out the "disciplinary" steps that a husband can follow in the case of his wife's *noshouz*, or disobedience, the last of which is beating her. This verse has been used by some religious preachers to justify the beating of women.

Domestic violence in cases related to honor is a concealed phenomenon in Yemen. Normally such cases are handled discreetly within the family and rarely reach police records. If the parties to the problem are not relatives, it is often resolved amicably through tribal mechanisms. Cases of honor-related homicide perpetrated against women are usually not reported, and no health certificate is required for a burial, particularly in rural areas. As a result, such deaths are often attributed to natural causes.[21]

Rape, sexual abuse and exploitation, sexual harassment, human trafficking, and forced prostitution are all crimes under Yemeni law. However, refugee women and girls face high incidences of such sexual and gender-based violence both inside and outside their homes, according to the Office of the UN High Commissioner for Refugees (UNHCR) and Yemeni authorities. The UNHCR estimated the number of refugees as of February 4, 2009, to be 140,148, a third of whom were women.[22] Refugee women, usually employed as domestic workers in urban areas, are at risk of serious exploitation, including poor working conditions, relatively low pay, and sexual abuse. Moreover, some refugee women resort to prostitution and survival sex to support themselves and their dependents. "Survival sex" is a term used by UNHCR to describe a situation in which female refugees are forced to sell themselves to survive.

Women's rights groups and civil society actors working to improve the status of women have often faced harassment, obstacles, and hostile social attitudes. Shatha Mohammad Nasr, a prominent women's rights activist and lawyer, met with insults and accusations that she was trying to disturb social customs when she represented Nojoud, the child bride in the 2008 divorce case. Family members of her client launched such verbal attacks even within the courthouse.[23]

Yemeni NGOs have been active in fostering awareness of and combating violence against women. As a consequence of the Nojoud case, the Yemeni Network for Combating Violence against Women, known as SHIMA, collaborated with the Higher Council for Motherhood and Childhood to organize a two-day workshop in the Yemeni parliament in May 2009. The workshop, which was attended by Yemeni lawmakers, covered issues including FGM and the minimum age of marriage, and called for the amendment of laws that did not provide protection to children. On another front, the SAF commissioned a study on honor crimes and organized in May 2005 a panel discussion on the issue. The results of this effort were published in a document entitled *Crimes of Honor in Yemen.*[24]

Recommendations

❖ The government should reform the Personal Status Law to bring it into compliance with CEDAW; this should include amendments to Articles 12, 15, 16, 40, and 58.

❖ The parliament should approve the draft law setting the minimum age of marriage at 17, and the government should take appropriate measures to ensure that the law is properly implemented, especially in rural areas.

❖ The government should outlaw domestic violence and establish a safe and secure mechanism that helps women to file complaints against their abusers. It should build shelters for abused women, establish a telephone hotline for victims of violence, take serious steps to hire and train female police officers to deal with women's cases, and provide training courses for policemen on this issue.

❖ The government should take active measures to protect minorities and ensure their safety. It should establish a legal department to deal with complaints from minorities and create a task force that monitors their access to education and health services.

❖ Yemeni NGOs should coordinate their work in highlighting the gender discrimination sanctioned by the Personal Status Law, and join together in their efforts to foster awareness regarding minorities' rights, honor crimes, and domestic violence.

ECONOMIC RIGHTS AND EQUAL OPPORTUNITY

Women's economic rights and opportunities in Yemen are undermined by social barriers as well as deficiencies in the state's ability to implement and coordinate its economic development efforts. These obstacles have led to a wide gap between officially announced plans and actual conditions.

Women's financial dependence on their male relatives or husbands continues due to a combination of cultural and economic factors, and the gender gap in education remains as large as ever. The government has taken some positive steps in recent years to protect women from gender-based employment discrimination, but they were restricted to Yemenis and did not extend to noncitizen residents. Women were allowed to enroll in the High Judicial Institute for the first time in 2007, and the Central Security Agency has started to accept female applicants. Despite requirements mentioned in Yemeni laws, no daycare facilities exist in any public institutions or private companies.

No laws prohibit women from owning or having full and independent use of their land and property, and women technically have full and independent use of their income and assets. However, patriarchal tribal customs, widespread illiteracy, and women's ignorance of their economic rights have prevented them from exercising these rights in practice. Instead, they often hand over the administration of their property and income to their male relatives.

Women have limited inheritance rights, which are further undermined by tribal customs. Article 23 of the 1994 constitution provides that "the right of inheritance is guaranteed in accordance with Islamic tenets (Shari'a)." Shari'a holds that among beneficiaries who have the same degree of familial proximity to the deceased (such as brothers and sisters), men are generally entitled to twice as much as women. In practice, even this inferior share is often withheld from women by male relatives, particularly in rural areas.[25] In an effort to keep property within a family, some women are forced to marry relatives. Despite documentation of these violations, the government has yet to suggest policies that would enable women to obtain their full inheritance rights.

With respect to economic activity, there is a divergence between what is legally possible for women and what is actually put into practice. The laws permit women to freely enter into business contracts and activities at all levels. However, according to the *Annual Report on the State of Women 2007* published by the National Committee on Women, only a limited number of women are able to exercise these rights. Dominant social norms, which reject gender equality in the household and pressure women to stay home, have made it difficult for them to engage in innovative entrepreneurial activities.[26] Women with backgrounds in the upper-middle or upper classes are more likely to break away from traditional social constraints than those with a lower socioeconomic status. Equality of opportunity among women is therefore not guaranteed.

The constitution and other national laws emphasize education as a right for all citizens, regardless of sex. The government has paid great attention to girls' education and considers education to be a cornerstone of economic development. This conviction is reflected in general education policies and short-term plans. Important measures that have been implemented since 2007 aim to encourage impoverished households to send their girls to school in exchange for food rations provided by the UN World Food Programme.[27]

However, these policies have so far failed to produce the expected results. Enrollment levels remain unchanged compared with four years ago. The literacy rate among Yemeni women—40.5 percent in 2007, compared with 77 percent for men—is still one of the lowest in the Middle East and North Africa (MENA) region.[28] The dropout rate among girls in elementary school is 15 percent, compared with 13 percent for boys.[29] And the general education gap between females and males remains significant, as Table 1 demonstrates:

Education Indicators	Male	Female
Primary Enrollment	85.1%	64.9%
Secondary Enrollment	48.5%	25.8%
Primary Completion Rate	73.9%	46.2%
Expected Years of Schooling	10.6 years	6.6 years

Table 1. Education Gender Indicators According to Education Level (World Bank Gender Statistics, 2007)

Article 54 of the constitution maintains that education is compulsory and free, but in practice it is neither, and there are no monitoring mechanisms to ensure that parents send their children to school. The fact that many parents in rural areas do not register the birth of their daughters complicates the matter further. The law does not penalize parents who deprive their children of an education. On the matter of cost, Article 8 of the Law on Education (No. 45 of 1992) holds that education is free at all levels and guaranteed by the state to its citizens. Nevertheless, fees are required to register pupils in schools, and parents are asked to buy educational materials for their children. Prior to the presidential and local council elections in 2006, the education minister issued a resolution exempting male students from school fees until grade three, and female students until grade six. The move was interpreted as a political maneuver aimed at securing more votes for the president and his party, and the decree was never fully applied.[30]

Widespread poverty has negatively affected both male and female pupils' ability to attain a decent education. Children are often removed from school by their parents to work and contribute to the household income. Girls are more likely to remain illiterate as a result of their family's poverty. In fact, in rural areas, 43.5 percent of girls aged 10 to 14 are illiterate, compared with 13.3 percent of boys. The rate increases with age: 57.4 percent of girls aged 15 to 17 are illiterate, compared with 12.1 percent of boys. The trend is less obvious in urban areas, where 11.9 percent of girls aged 10 to 14 and 18.2 percent of girls aged 15 to 17 are illiterate, compared with 4.7 percent and 6.7 percent of boys, respectively.[31]

Access to higher education remains limited for both men and women. According to World Bank data for 2007, the gross school enrollment rate at the tertiary level was 5 percent for women and 13.5 percent for men.[32] There are no formal restrictions on the subjects women can study at university, but they are often expected to focus on the social rather than the natural sciences. Most universities are not segregated by gender, although one private Islamist university, Al-Iman, does impose segregation between male and female students.

According to the Labor Law (No. 5 of 1995) and the Civil Service Law (No. 19 of 1991), women have the same right as men to work and occupy public office. Yet the patriarchal nature of Yemeni society often restricts women's freedom to choose their profession. Women's male relatives often interfere with their decisions on such matters, and social norms dictate that certain professions, such as teaching, public administration, and medicine, are more appropriate for a woman. These norms also emphasize that society most favors women's reproductive role. Yemen's 2007 report to the UN CEDAW committee noted that the economic participation rate is 22.8 percent for women and 69.2 percent for men. Women's participation is generally limited to traditional activities such as agriculture and handicrafts, and most women work in the informal sector. High illiteracy rates, a lack of skills, and inadequate training contribute to women's limited participation in the workforce.[33]

The government has taken some positive measures to protect women from discrimination in employment. Decree No. 191 of 2007 dictates the abolition of such discrimination, though it is restricted to Yemenis and does not improve conditions for noncitizen residents. Also in 2007, women were allowed to enroll in the High Judicial Institute for the first time. A certificate from the institute is a prerequisite for a career as a judge. Prior to this change, all female Yemeni judges came from the former South Yemen, whose socialist policies fostered women's emancipation. In a more recent development, the previously closed male domain of the Central Security Agency, which has responsibilities ranging from ensuring the safety of property and persons to border security and counterterrorism, announced in March 2009 that it would begin accepting female applicants to be trained as part of women's police units.

Some professions, such as the army, are still limited to men, and social customs prevent women from becoming taxi drivers, construction workers, or car mechanics. Systemic nepotism and corruption limits the opportunity for qualified men and women to be hired by an employer with whom they lack a previous relationship.

Yemeni laws do not include provisions penalizing sexual harassment in the workplace, and only 17 complaints of such harassment were registered in police records during 2007.[34] There are few valid statistics on this issue, but several cases were documented through a hotline provided by the Yemeni Society for Psychological Health in Aden.[35] Somali refugees or Ethiopian, Eritrean, and Southeast Asian female expatriates working as domestic servants expressed unwillingness to file official complaints, fearing social stigma or the loss of their jobs.[36] Yemeni women are no different, often declining to report sexual harassment due to social prejudice that often blames them rather than the perpetrators.

Gender-based employment benefits are offered to women on a limited basis. Women are entitled to 60 days of maternity leave, according to Article 59 of the Civil Service Law. This short period is not sufficient to meet the intensive demands of childrearing at this early stage, and should be increased to at least three months. Men are denied a parental leave under this law. Article 45 of the Labor Law requires Yemeni entities that employ more than 50 women to provide daycare facilities; Article 106 of the Child Rights Law (No. 45 of 2002) repeats this mandate but lowers the requisite number of female employees to 20. Despite these legal provisions, no daycare facilities exist in any public institutions or private companies.[37]

Yemeni NGOs, local organizations, news portals,[38] and women's activists that promote economic rights and equal opportunity for women have successfully raised awareness in Yemeni society of some of the major topics involved. They are credited with breaking taboos surrounding certain issues, such as sexual harassment, and have pushed for relevant changes in Yemeni laws. These efforts culminated in 2008 in a Dutch-funded project that aims to provide better protection for women and children exposed to violence and sexual abuse. The SAF will implement the four-year project in all 21 governorates of Yemen; it will include training courses, capacity-building activities, and a review of current laws, in addition to a telephone hotline for complaints from women and children exposed to sexual harassment.

On another front, the Federation of the Yemeni Chambers of Commerce and Industry, the Yemen General Federation of Workers' Trade Unions, and the Ministry of Social Affairs and Labour (MOSAL) joined forces to implement a technical cooperation project entitled "Promoting Decent Work and Gender Equality in Yemen" (2004–08), with financial support from the government of the Netherlands. The project focused on enhancing the capacities of MOSAL and other institutions in coordinating the implementation of the national strategy on women's employment. It encouraged positive perceptions of female employees among policymakers, employers, workers, media, and other stakeholders.[39]

Recommendations

❖ The government should establish a mechanism that would allow women to file complaints regarding denial of their inheritance. It should establish a section in the court system that specifically deals with female inheritance denials and provide it with the necessary resources to remedy this problem.

❖ NGOs should conduct awareness campaigns in rural areas on women's inheritance rights and establish voluntary legal advice centers that can advise women on how to fully realize their inheritance rights.

❖ Maternity leave should be increased to a minimum of three months at full pay.

❖ The government should enforce the requirement that public and private sectors provide daycare for young children in their facilities. It should allocate the necessary financial resources in its yearly budget to such facilities in the public sector, and impose financial penalties on private institutions that fail to comply with the law.

❖ The government should promulgate laws that criminalize sexual harassment and discrimination, and establish a mechanism, such as a legal department or a telephone hotline, that will allow women to file gender-based discrimination and sexual harassment complaints.

❖ The government should implement its education and antipoverty policies and take active measures to eliminate the gap between men and women in these areas.

POLITICAL RIGHTS AND CIVIC VOICE

Yemeni women have enjoyed political rights to varying degrees for several decades. Those from South Yemen gained full political rights under the 1970 constitution, while those from North Yemen were able to vote and run for office in the country's first local elections in 1983.[40] In 2006, for the first time in Yemeni history, women were nominated in a presidential election, although none of the three female candidates made it through the entire nomination process in the bicameral parliament. And for the first time in the history of Islah, the main Islamist opposition party, pressure by its female activists has led to the election of women to its higher decision-making councils. However, the party continues to oppose women's candidacy in elections for public office. Political maneuvering and opportunism by both the GPC and opposition parties generally prevented the nomination of women in the 2006 elections, and the rate of political participation by women remains as low as ever.

Official and social biases have led to comprehensive exclusion of women from Yemeni political life, despite constitutional and legislative provisions that guarantee their political equality with men. Article 41 of the constitution guarantees a citizen's right to "participate in the political, economic, social and cultural life of the country" and "the freedom of thought and expression of opinion in speech, writing, and photography." Similarly, Article 42 provides all citizens with the right to be elected or nominated as a candidate in an election and the right to participate in referendums. Finally, Article 57 grants citizens the right to "organize themselves along political, professional, and union lines." Neither the constitution nor the Election Law (No. 13 of 2001) set restrictions on women's voting and nomination rights. From a legal perspective, therefore, Yemeni women have the right to peaceful assembly, to freedom of expression, and to participate in competitive and democratic elections with full and equal suffrage. However, these rights are often violated on various levels in practice.

Women face continued discrimination within politics and are unable to compete in elections on an equal footing with men. Since the country's 1990 unification, three elections (1993, 1997, 2003) have been held for the lower house of parliament, the House of Representatives, but women have never held more than two of the 301 seats. Similarly, few women have been appointed to executive posts or the 111-member upper house, the Consultative Council, since its creation in 2001.

The results of the 2006 local council elections illustrated the gap that exists between what officials have promised and what has been delivered. During the 2006 campaign, President Salih publicly called on women to nominate themselves, pledging to support independent candidates from the state budget. He appealed to male candidates to withdraw in favor of their female colleagues, and said that 15 percent of the candidates nominated by the GPC would be women.[41] Women responded to the call, and their numbers among the candidates reportedly increased. However, there is no evidence that independent candidates received state funding or that male GPC candidates withdrew from the election. On the contrary, women were apparently harassed and verbally intimidated by the GPC on a large scale, and the GPC did not meet its goal of 15 percent female candidates.[42]

These elections also demonstrated the practical difficulties—both social and fiscal—faced by female candidates. Women generally ran as independents and lacked the benefit of institutional support that many of their male counterparts enjoyed. Women were also restricted in their ability to canvass publicly or show their faces on campaign posters for fear of allegations against their morality. In addition, there were credible reports that female candidates experienced discrimination during the registration process, including instances in which applications were arbitrarily refused by the main electoral district committees.[43] Nevertheless, the generally negative treatment of female voters and candidates seemed to have no effect on the final voting patterns among women, suggesting that they tend to cast their ballots based on tribal or familial loyalties rather than their own free choice or interests.[44]

Ultimately, only 131 women competed with 28,498 men in the 2006 local elections, which filled councils for the 21 governorates and 333 districts. Just 37 of these female candidates, or 0.5 percent of over 7,000 successful candidates, were elected, and all but four of these were with the GPC. The results echoed the 2003 parliamentary vote, in which only 11 women competed against 1,385 men for the 301-seat lower house, and just one woman succeeded.[45] The Yemeni government's lack of support was also evident, as only two women were appointed to the 111-seat Consultative Council. Table 2 gives an overview of female representation in the legislative and local councils:[46]

Type of Council	Women	Men	Female Share
House of Representatives	1	300	0.3%
Consultative Council	2	109	1.8%
Local Councils	37	7,000	0.5%
Total	40	7,409	0.5%

Table 2. Female Representation in the Legislative and Local Councils

Although Yemeni political parties claim to support women as full party members with equal rights and duties, women are separated into distinct units and premises by most of the political parties, and generally occupy few leadership positions.[47] The Islah party underwent an internal transformation in 2006 after its female members demanded to be fully integrated into leadership positions. That year, women were elected for the first time to Islah's General Secretariat and Shura Council. They now represent 38.1 percent of the General Secretariat, the top leadership body in the party. In March 2009, the 5,000-member assembly of Islah unanimously voted against a Salafi fatwa, or religious edict, that had denied women the right to political participation in these decision-making bodies.

Despite an agreement between the ruling and opposition parties in 2006 that called for all to support women's legal rights, half of the parties did not nominate any female candidates. Chief among them was Islah, which adhered staunchly to its public rejection of female candidacy despite its acceptance of women in the internal party hierarchy. Due to Islah's stance against women's nomination, the five leading opposition parties that had formed a coalition with Islah were hesitant to name female candidates for fear of undermining their own electoral chances.[48] The Yemeni Socialist Party (YSP) was the only party that offered additional support to its female candidates.[49]

In general, women's ability to participate in the political arena and influence decision making is consistently and severely compromised by widespread negative attitudes toward their involvement. This problem is rooted in the belief—shared by many women as well as men—that women inherently lack the capacity to fully engage in public life. Moreover, Islamic fundamentalists have targeted the few gains made in women's political rights in recent years on religious grounds. In June 2008, a group of Salafist sheikhs issued a small handbook that petitions against quotas for women's political participation, arguing that "opening the door for women to leave their houses and mix with men will lead to sexual chaos."[50]

Women remain significantly underrepresented in the judiciary and the executive branch, although some positive developments have occurred in recent years. The first female judge was appointed to the Supreme Court in September 2006. Also that year, women ran for president for the first time in Yemeni history: three women were among 49 potential candidates in the run-up to the September presidential election. According to Article 66 of the Elections Law (No. 13 of 2001), the application of a potential candidate for the presidency must be approved by at least 5 percent of all members of the bicameral parliament who attend the session. None of the female applicants secured the required endorsement, and only five male candidates were approved.[51] Table 3 provides more detail on female representation in the judicial and executive branches:[52]

Position	Women	Men	Female Share
Minister	31	2	6.1%
Ambassador	116	2	1.7%
Deputy Minister	214	2	0.9%
General Manager	4,971	186	3.6%
Judge	953	85	8.2%

Table 3. Female Representation in Judiciary and Government (2007)

In recent years, security forces have implemented heavy-handed polices toward opposition groups and journalists who criticize the government. Men have been targeted more than women. Citizens of both gender were allowed to demonstrate and express their anger over the Danish cartoons of the prophet Muhammad in 2006 and the war in Gaza in 2008, but when demonstrations were held to express social and political grievances, security forces used violent and oppressive measures to break them up. Such was the case with the 2007 demonstrations by retirees in several southern regions who were protesting their forced retirement and dire economic situation, and with follow-up protests that occurred in April 2008.

If Yemeni authorities consider a female journalist to be independent or part of the opposition, she is bound to face obstacles in the conduct of her work. Tawakol Abd al-Salam Karman, president of Women Journalists Without Chains (WJWC), a domestic NGO that monitors and documents abuses related to freedom of expression, was forcibly stopped from covering a political opposition strike in November 2008. Security personnel surrounded her and forcibly expelled her from the area.[53] The same organization was denied the right to publish a newspaper in 2007. The Ministry of Information has often politicized decisions on newspaper closures, violating the clear guidelines provided by the Law of Press and Publications (No. 25 of 1990).[54] These sorts of denials highlight the control the government exercises over the media and its growing attempts to silence critical coverage.

Women have limited freedom to access and use information to empower themselves in all areas of their civic and political lives. The 2006 local elections demonstrated that high levels of illiteracy among women severely constrained their exposure to information about the elections and their wider civil and political rights. The broadcast media are controlled by the government, and even among literate women, the Internet is a practical means of communication for a small, well-educated minority. Many of the voter-education initiatives specifically aimed at women were inadequate in reaching their target audience. Civil society organizations representing women demonstrated enthusiasm in their efforts to support women in the elections, but they suffered from a lack of coordination, partisanship among key figures, and a dearth of positive female role models.[55]

Recommendations

✤ The government should amend its laws to establish a reasonable minimum quota for women in all legislative, executive, and judicial structures.

✤ The government and NGOs should combine their efforts and launch public-awareness campaigns, using television and radio advertisements that highlight the importance of women's participation in political and civic life.

✤ Civil society organizations should create a body during election periods to foster cooperation in their efforts to promote women's political participation.

✤ The NGOs and private sector should establish a permanent center that specializes in providing training for young women aspiring to enter political life.

SOCIAL AND CULTURAL RIGHTS

Yemen is ranked 140 out of 182 countries in the UN Development Programme's 2009 Human Development Index. Its gross national income per capita was just US$864 (2007 estimate), although that represented an improvement from US$491 in 2000. The recent drop in oil prices has struck at the main source of national income and will no doubt affect the implementation of Yemen's development plans. The country's meager resources and dire economic situation have left it unable to fulfill its obligations in providing health and education services to its citizens. Yemen's maternal mortality rate remains one of the highest in the MENA region. In rural areas especially, male relatives deny women what legal rights they have with respect to health care and maternity. NGOs and female journalists have been active in promoting women's social and cultural rights, but some have consequently faced smear campaigns aimed at intimidating them.

Articles 54 and 55 of the constitution state that all citizens have the right to health care and that the government has the responsibility to provide free health services by establishing hospitals and other medical institutions. Yemen's 2007 country report to the UN CEDAW committee places a special emphasis on women's health, particularly with respect to pregnancy, childbirth, postnatal care, care for working mothers, and nutrition for the child and mother.[56] The objectives of the Population Action Plan of 2001–05 included providing health care to 60 percent of pregnant women, increasing attended births to 40 percent, and providing postnatal care to 15 percent of women. As of 2007, however, only 35.7 percent of all births were attended by skilled health staff. There are no updated figures on the share of pregnant women receiving prenatal care, which was 41.4 percent in 2003.[57] The government's stated goals are quite difficult to achieve, especially if only a small portion of the budget is allocated to the health sector.[58] In addition, the government announced in 2008 that it would cut its budget allocations for ministries and institutions by 50 percent, which is bound to make the health goals even harder to attain.[59]

Yemeni women generally lack the freedom to make independent decisions about their health and reproductive rights. On a social level, they are absent from most such decision making within their families, and are often unaware of their rights to use contraception and determine the number of children they wish to bear. On a legal and official level, women must get permission from their husbands before they can undergo an operation on the uterus—including a hysterectomy or a cesarean section—or obtain contraceptives.[60]

The maternal mortality rate is one of the highest in the MENA region, at 430 per 100,000 live births.[61] Several factors contribute to this, including early marriage and teenage pregnancy, short birth intervals, high fertility rates (5.5 births per woman as of 2007), malnutrition, and anemia. The lack of access to and availability of skilled care during pregnancy is also a serious problem. Even where the medical infrastructure exists, the lack of female health workers inhibits women's access because they are reluctant to consult male doctors. Weak logistics and supervision systems are chronic shortcomings that lead to unreliable services.[62]

Yemeni women are not protected from harmful, gender-based traditional practices. Early and forced marriages, as well as female genital mutilation (FGM), are seen as part of Yemeni culture. FGM is also widespread among the refugee communities, especially the Somalis. It is often practiced among Yemeni Sunni Muslims living in the coastal and southern areas of the country, but is not practiced at all among Yemen's Zaydi and Ismaili Shiites. While national figures hide regional variations, the 1997 Demographic Health Survey reported that FGM prevalence among newborn girls was as high as 97.3 percent in Hodeida, 96.6 percent in Hadramout, 96.5 percent in Al-Mahra, 82.2 percent in Aden, and 45.5 percent in the capital, Sana'a.

There is no law against FGM, although a ministerial decree that took effect on January 9, 2001, did prohibit the practice in both government and private health facilities.[63] According to the UN news agency, the first public discussion of FGM in Yemen took place in 2001, at a seminar on women's health issues sponsored by the Ministry of Public Health and funded by the U.S.-based MacArthur Foundation. Campaigns to eliminate the practice have since been carried out across the country. Some of the largest public and private NGOs devoted to women's issues have shaken off their previous hesitance to tackle this issue and run public-awareness campaigns on television, radio, and in community gatherings to discourage the practice. For example, the Girls' Health Project, conducted by the National Committee on Women in Aden and International Health and Development Associates (IHDA), sponsored 12 local organizations to carry out awareness campaigns across the Aden governorate between 2001 and 2003.[64] The Yemeni government, supported by UN agencies, has also started in the last two years to target refugee communities with awareness campaigns against FGM.

Yemeni civil society is active and vibrant despite increased reports of official harassment of NGOs working in the field of human and woman's rights. It is widely accepted that around 2,900 NGOs are registered and working in Yemen.[65] However, no reliable records exist regarding the number of women's NGOs participating in and influencing community life, public policies, and social development at local levels. Despite this lack of documentation, it is worth mentioning that some of these NGOs, such as the SAF, have gained local as well as international recognition for their contributions to civic life. The SAF has been at the forefront in creating awareness and fostering debates on women's issues and rights. In 2008, the government of the Netherlands chose it to implement a US$700,000 project that aims to provide better protection for women and children exposed to violence and sexual abuse.

Women remain underrepresented in the media, limiting their ability to influence content and shape public perceptions on gender issues. Only 703 women were employed in the media across all sectors, compared with 4,302 men. In particular, women's representation in senior positions within the media remains very low, and the appointment of a woman to such positions is considered exceptional. The only female deputy minister of information has left her post to serve in United Nations.[66]

While the media generally portray women in stereotyped roles as mothers and housewives, new forms of press harassment have started to target women activists. Quasi-official newspapers, such as *Addastour, Al-Bilad,* and *Akhbar al-Yum,* have published slanderous articles about female journalists or civil society activists that provoked traditional segments of the community against them. Victims of such verbal assaults include Rashida al-Qaili, Samia al-Aghbari, Mahasin al-Hawati, Rahma Hugira, and Amal Basha.[67] These tactics aim to intimidate women activists and journalists into silence, adding yet another obstacle to their participation in Yemeni civic life.

As the poverty gap in Yemen is widening, women represent the vast majority of the poor. The *Annual Report on the State of Women 2007* found that of the families living below the poverty line, 17.5 percent are headed by women, an increase of 4.5 percent compared with four years ago. In addition, the average income of a family headed by a woman is one-third less than that of families headed by men. Poverty leads to a higher school dropout rate and affects girls more than boys, especially in the rural areas. Due to women's lower status in society and the preferential treatment boys receive within the family, women, including pregnant women, are more likely to suffer from malnutrition in poor households. In a country where 42 percent of the population lives under the poverty line, the effects of this deficiency on future generations are serious. The combination of poverty, lack of health services, and illiteracy has contributed to the country's high infant mortality rate, which stands at 69 per 1,000 live births.[68]

Women have a legal right to own and use housing as individuals, but they face discrimination in the case of divorce. Unlike the 1974 family law of South Yemen, which allocated the marital house to the wife if she maintained custody of children, the current Personal Status Law denies her these benefits. Hence, unless she owns the marital house, she is required to leave it with her children after a divorce.

Yemeni women have begun to challenge more conservative Islamic interpretations regarding the proper role for women in society and actively campaign against gender-based violence practiced in the name of tradition and custom. However, they face continuous attacks by Islamic fundamentalists who attempt to smear their reputations, accusing them of undermining Islamic teachings and social morals. They have also increasingly become a target of harassment by security forces, which systematically suppress human rights activism in general. Combined with negative public attitudes regarding women's participation in public life, these factors present daunting obstacles to women's rights activists. Yet their determination to continue their efforts and exercise their rights despite such adversity is a reason for optimism.

Recommendations

❖ The government should increase its budget allocations for the health sector so as to fully implement its policies on improving women's access to health services.

❖ The government should take active measures to increase women's participation in the media. This may include special recruitment initiatives targeting women, scholarships in journalism in Yemen and abroad, and setting a hiring quota for women in senior positions of all state-owned media outlets.

❖ The government should issue a law prohibiting and penalizing the practice of female genital mutilation. The law should be complemented with community awareness campaigns that aim to eliminate public tolerance and acceptance of this type of violence.

❖ The government, in cooperation with Yemeni NGOs, should conduct awareness campaigns in the media and schools to promote the concept of women's right to make independent choices regarding birth control and health in general.

❖ The government should provide incentives for the private sector to establish a sustainable program of small credits (loans) to help women start or expand their own businesses.

❖ The government should take concrete steps to protect female journalists and rights activists from smear campaigns and government-sanctioned harassment. It should amend its laws and procedures to penalize such practices.

AUTHOR

Elham Manea holds dual nationalities, Yemeni and Swiss. She is a writer, human rights activist, and political scientist focused on the Middle East. She is a Fulbright scholar and holds a doctorate in political science from the University of Zurich, a master's degree in comparative politics from the American University in Washington, D.C., and a bachelor's degree in political science from Kuwait University. She has published academic and nonfiction books in English, German, and Arabic, in addition to two novels in Arabic. She works as a lecturer at the University of Zurich's Political Science Institute and a consultant for Swiss government agencies.

NOTES

[1] Shadow Report prepared by Yemeni NGOs on the CEDAW implementation, initiated and coordinated by the Sisters' Arab Forum for Human Rights (SAF) in 2007, 9, available at http://www2.ohchr.org/english/bodies/cedaw/docs/ngos/SAFHRYemen41.pdf.

[2] SAF, Shadow Report.

[3] See Yemen's sixth periodic report to the UN Committee on the Elimination of Discrimination against Women (CEDAW), March 13, 2007, 7–8, available at http://www.un.org/womenwatch/daw/cedaw/reports.htm; see also SAF, Shadow Report.

[4] See Women's Forum for Research and Training, "Series of Questions and Answers 7: The Convention on the Elimination of All Discrimination against Women, Civil Rights," in Arabic, http://www.wfrt.org/dtls.php?ContentID=191; Rasha Jarhum, "Discriminative Legislation Hinders Women's Political Participation," *Yemen Times*, March 3–5, 2008, http://www.yementimes.com/article.shtml?i=1134&p=local&a=2.

[5] SAF, *Crimes of Honor in Yemen* (Sana'a: SAF, May 2005), 31, in Arabic, http://saf-yemen.org/saf_books.asp?myid=30&safbok=79.

[6] SAF, Shadow Report, 6.

[7] N. M., "The Democratic School Condemn the Kidnapping of the Human Rights Activist Hanan al-Wada'ai by Security Members," *Sahwa Net*, March 18, 2007, in Arabic, http://www.alsahwa-yemen.net/view_news.asp?sub_no=3_2007_03_18_55243.

[8] Robert F. Worth, "Languishing at the Bottom of Yemen's Ladder," *New York Times*, February 27, 2008, http://www.nytimes.com/2008/02/27/world/middleeast/27yemen.html. For more information, see Huda Seif, "The Accursed Minority: The Ethno-Cultural Persecution of Al-Akhdam in the Republic of Yemen: A Documentary & Advocacy Project," *Muslim World Journal of Human Rights* 2, issue 1 (2005).

9 Elham Manea, "The Shame of Yemen," *Al-Nedaa*, April 12, 2007, in Arabic.

10 For example, on March 17, 2007, the newspaper *Akhbar al-Yum* published a quota-tion from an official working for the Sunni Salafi Islamist Al-Iman University accusing al-Basha of infidelity and apostasy against Islam. See also SAF, Shadow Report; Elham Manea, *The Arab State and Women's Rights: The Trap of the Transitional State*, postdoc-toral thesis, 2009, 11.

11 SAF, Shadow Report, 8.

12 SAF statement, July 5, 2008, in Arabic, http://saf-yemen.org/details.asp?field=issue _news&id=1586&page_no=1.

13 SAF, Shadow Report, 6.

14 See for instance Rachid Sekkai, "Yemeni Child Bride Gets Annulment," BBC, April 16, 2008, http://news.bbc.co.uk/2/hi/middle_east/7351336.stm; Delphine Minoui, "Nojoud, 10 ans, divorcée au Yémen," *Le Figaro International*, June 24, 2008, in French, http://www.lefigaro.fr/international/2008/06/21/01003-20080621ARTFIG00036-nojoud-ans-divorcee-au-yemen.php; Annette Langer, "Achtjährige trennt sich von Ehemann und bangt um ihr Leben," *Spiegel Online*, April 15, 2008, in German, http://www.spiegel.de/panorama/gesellschaft/0,1518,547398,00.html.

15 Office of the UN High Commissioner for Refugees (UNHCR), *Women New Arrivals Survey* (Sana'a: UNHCR, September 2008).

16 See Fouad al-Shibami, "Social Consequences of Tourist Marriage in Yemen," *Al-Motamer Net*, June 1, 2005, in Arabic, http://www.almotamar.net/news/22140.htm.

17 See for instance Claudia Bandet, "Rescue Amina," *Yemen Times*, September 29–October 2, 2005, http://www.yementimes.com/article.shtml?i=881&p=letters&a=1.

18 The *Annual Report on the State of Women 2007*, published by the National Committee on Women, cited a 2003 health survey suggesting that 5 percent of married women or those who were previously married (aged 15 to 49 years) were beaten. Of those, 56.4 percent were beaten by their husbands, 21 percent claimed that the beating was unprovoked, 10 percent were beaten for perceived disobedience, and 17 percent needed medical treatment. These numbers are not reliable and do not reflect the actual inci-dence of domestic violence in the country. The report did not indicate where the sur-vey was done, by whom, or how many people participated. See National Committee on Women, *Annual Report on the State of Women 2007*, 129, in Arabic, http://www .yemen-women.org/reports/wmenreport.pdf.

19 National Committee on Women, *Annual Report*, 129–131.

20 SAF, Shadow Report, 20.

21 SAF, Shadow Report, 20.

22 UNHCR, *Asylum and Migration: Fact Sheet* (Sana'a: UNHCR, January 2009).

23 "The Lawyer Shatha Nasr in an Interview with Sayyidati: The Child Nojoud Is Still in Need of Help and Care," republished online in Aman—The Arabic Centre for Sources and Information on Violence against Women, July 29, 2008, in Arabic, http://www .amanjordan.org/a-news/wmview.php?ArtID=23511&page=2.

24 Kawkab al-Thaibani, "MPs Say: No to Genital Mutilation, 18 Is Minimum Marriage Age, Juveniles Cannot Be Punished as Adults," *Yemen Times*, June 26–29, 2008, http:// yementimes.com/article.shtml?i=1167&p=local&a=1; SAF, *Crimes of Honor in Yemen*, 31.

[25] SAF, Shadow Report, 20.

[26] National Committee on Women, *Annual Report*.

[27] World Food Programme, "Over One Million Yemenis to Benefit from New WFP Project," news release, March 14, 2007, http://www.wfp.org/node/416.

[28] World Bank, "Genderstats: Middle East and North Africa," http://go.worldbank.org/AETRQ5QAC0.

[29] Estimate based on the 2004 statistics cited in SAF, Shadow Report, 11.

[30] SAF, Shadow Report, 11.

[31] National Committee on Women, *Annual Report*, 74.

[32] World Bank, "GenderStats: Education," http://go.worldbank.org/RHEGN4QHU0.

[33] Yemen's sixth periodic report to CEDAW, 15.

[34] National Committee on Women, *Annual Report*, 130.

[35] SAF, Shadow Report, 23.

[36] SAF, Shadow Report, 23.

[37] SAF, Shadow Report, 8.

[38] See for instance Nazar Khuthair al-Abaddi, "Sexual Harassment of Working Women in Yemen: The Struggle Between Will and the Inherited [Traditions]," Nabanews, May 10, 2006, in Arabic, http://www.nabanews.net/2009/3106.html.

[39] Kandy Ringer, "Sisters Arab Forum Implements Project in Yemen to Protect Women and Children," BBSNews, October 2, 2008, http://bbsnews.net/article.php/20081002160621254; International Labour Organization, *Country Brief 3: Promoting Decent Work and Gender Equality in Yemen* (Beirut: Regional Office for Arab States, October 2008), http://www.ilo.org/wcmsp5/groups/public/---dgreports/---gender/documents/publication/wcms_100282.pdf.

[40] South Yemeni women first utilized their political rights in the 1977 local elections. The political rights of women from North Yemen were never clearly established under the constitution, Article 19, which used the masculine form of "All Yemeni are equal in rights and duties." Taking advantage of the vagueness of this article, Islamic elements were able to limit women's political rights during the 1988 parliamentary elections by only allowing them to vote—not run as candidates.

[41] See for instance "He Called on the Congress to Withdraw Its Male Nominees in the Districts Where Women Are Nominated," *26 September* (newspaper), August 20, 2006, in Arabic, http://www.26sep.net/news_details.php?lng=arabic&sid=17812.

[42] *Yemen—Final Report: Presidential and Local Council Elections* (EU Election Observation Mission, September 20, 2006), 27, http://ec.europa.eu/external_relations/human_rights/election_observation/yemen/final_report_en.pdf.

[43] *Yemen—Final Report: Presidential and Local Council Elections*, 27–28.

[44] *Yemen—Final Report: Presidential and Local Council Elections*, 28.

[45] *Yemen—Final Report: Presidential and Local Council Elections*, Yemen's sixth periodic report to CEDAW, 19–20.

[46] National Committee on Women, *Annual Report*, 115.

[47] SAF, Shadow Report, 18–19.

[48] In an attempt to unify their challenge to the ruling GPC, the six leading opposition parties established a combined platform in 2004 called the Joint Meeting Parties (JMP).

The JMP includes the Islah; the YSP, which formerly ruled South Yemen; the Nasserite Unionist Party (NUP); the Al-Haq Party; the Ba'ath Party; and the Popular Forces Union Party.

49 Elham Manea, *The Arab State and Women's Rights*, 164–165.

50 A Message from Yemeni U'lama regarding Women's Quota, June 2008.

51 SAF, Shadow Report, 17.

52 National Committee on Women, *Annual Report*, 113, 122, 123.

53 Women Journalists Without Chains, *Fourth Annual Report on Press Freedom in Yemen in 2008*, in Arabic, 21, http://www.womenpress.net/articles.php?id=166.

54 Strikers for the Right to Own Media, Freedom of Expression, and the Right to Receive and Disseminate Information, news release, May 29, 2007, http://www.hoodonline.org/det.php?sid=982.

55 *Yemen—Final Report: Presidential and Local Council Elections*, 28.

56 Yemen's sixth periodic report to CEDAW, 46.

57 World Bank, "GenderStats: Create Your Own Table," http://go.worldbank.org/MRER 20PME0.

58 In the 2003–04 fiscal year, only 4 percent of the budget was used for health care.

59 See Decree No. 467 of 2008.

60 SAF, Shadow Report, 24–25.

61 World Bank, "GenderStats: Middle East and North Africa," http://go.worldbank.org/AETRQ5QAC0.

62 UNDP, *United Nations Common Country Assessment for the Republic of Yemen, 2005*, 18–19, in Arabic, http://www.undg.org/docs/8080/Yemen%20CCA%20Arabic.pdf; Ricardo Hausmann, Laura D. Tyson, and Saadia Zahidi, *Global Gender Gap Report 2007* (Geneva: World Economic Forum, 2007), 158, http://www.weforum.org/pdf/gendergap/report2007.pdf .

63 Country Assessment on Violence against Women, Yemen, 2007, 9, UNICEF, *Situation Analysis on Female Genital Mutilation/Cutting (FGM/C) in Yemen* (Sana'a: UNICEF, June 2008), 8.

64 "YEMEN: Eradicating FGM Will Be a Slow Process, Experts Say," Integrated Regional Information Networks (IRIN), November 14, 2005, http://www.irinnews.org/Report.aspx?ReportId=25685.

65 Mohammed bin Sallam, "More NGO Accountability Needed," *Yemen Times*, October 25–27, 2004, http://www.yementimes.com/article.shtml?i=784&p=community&a=2.

66 National Committee on Women, *Annual Report*, 140–142.

67 SAF, Shadow Report, 21–22.

68 SAF, Shadow Report, 24–25; National Committee on Women, *Annual Report*, 69–71; Hausmann, Tyson, and Zahidi, *Global Gender Gap Report 2007*.

METHODOLOGY

INTRODUCTION

Women's Rights in the Middle East and North Africa provides a cross-regional comparative analysis of women's freedom to exercise their human rights. It is an important tool for scholars, activists, journalists, and government officials in the Middle East and North Africa (MENA) and worldwide. The study's methodology is based largely on the Universal Declaration of Human Rights (UDHR), which has long guided Freedom House in its continuous evaluation of the state of freedom, political rights, and civil liberties throughout the world. Each country report takes into account both the de jure and the de facto status of women's rights. The methodology is organized within the context of the following key areas:

    I. Nondiscrimination and Access to Justice

   II. Autonomy, Security, and Freedom of the Person

 III. Economic Rights and Equal Opportunity

 IV. Political Rights and Civic Voice

  V. Social and Cultural Rights

The first edition of this project was published in 2005. The new edition takes a fresh look at the same set of issues and provides an opportunity for analysis of the extent to which each country has backslid, stalled, or improved over the last five years. The project covers events through October 31, 2009.

EVALUATION PROCESS

The methodology for this project was drafted by Freedom House staff and experts, and was reviewed and approved by a committee of senior academic specialists.

Analytical Country Reports and Scores

The core of the study consists of analytical reports for each of the 17 countries and one territory under study. The writers have been drawn from a broad pool of country and regional specialists, all possessing expertise in women's rights, the history and politics of the Middle East, democracy issues, and international human rights standards.

The reports are based on a checklist of questions that address the most critical issues of women's rights and freedoms in the region. Each author received guidelines developed by the methodology committee for interpreting the questions. These guidelines were expanded for the 2010 edition to ensure a higher degree of scoring consistency. Consequently, the 2005 country scores were modified in several instances to correspond to the adapted interpretive guidelines and ensure year-on-year compatibility.

The narrative reports, each approximately 10,000 words long, reflect the content of the questions and are accompanied by scores that rate each country's performance in the five key areas. While writing the chapters, each author conducted interviews with a range of in-country stakeholders, and used other primary and secondary sources including legal texts, statistics, government documents, newspaper articles, and current literature, studies, and reports on the topic.

Based on the list of questions provided to the authors, each country's performance is evaluated on a scale of 1 to 5, with 1 representing the lowest and 5 the highest degree of freedom women have to exercise their rights The checklist questions are scored individually, culminating in an average score for each of the five key areas that the survey has identified as crucial to women's freedom. Based on the use of identical benchmarks for both the narrative and the ratings, the two indicators become mutually reinforcing. The final result is a system of well-defined comparative ratings, accompanied by a narrative that objectively reflects the legal and judicial, civil and political, economic, and social and cultural conditions in a country, and the degree to which these conditions facilitate or obstruct a woman's freedom to exercise her basic rights.

Together, the scores and the narratives assess the performance of each state by taking into account a variety of factors: the state's actions and omissions; the legal system and its impact on women's rights; the overall political environment of the country; and the actual implementation of laws and official policies. The role of non-state actors who have an impact on the strengthening or weakening of women's rights is also examined, as is the treatment of both citizen and noncitizen women. The narratives highlight both major obstacles to women's rights and the consistent achievements and forward-looking strategies made possible by either the state or the efforts of non-state actors. Finally, the survey presents a human rights and democracy–oriented review of women's needs and priorities defined by women in the region, obstacles and challenges to their freedom, and recommendations for effective promotion and protection of women's rights.

Review by Regional Experts

Upon completion of the country reports by the writers, each narrative and its corresponding proposed ratings were reviewed and critiqued by senior advisors. Most of the experts live in the countries they reviewed, giving them particular insight into the nuances and factual realities of the country. They are all renowned scholars and activists who specialize in women's rights, law, democracy issues, gender studies, and sociology.

Ratings Review Meetings and Consultations in the Region

Freedom House convened two regional review meetings attended by the senior project advisors. The first was held in September 2008 in the United Arab Emirates (UAE), and the second was held in October 2009 in Jordan. During these meetings, country scores were scrutinized and debated in a group setting, thereby promoting cross-regional coherence within the scoring process. Moreover, Freedom House staff traveled to Bahrain, Egypt, Kuwait, the UAE, and Jordan to conduct in-depth consultations with women's rights activists and advocates, civil society leaders, scholars, and government officials. These on-the-ground consultations focused on the particular issues assessed in the survey narratives, and the results were used to hone the country narratives and final report recommendations.

RESULTS AND RECOMMENDATIONS

The writers were asked to draft concrete recommendations for the improvement of women's rights within the five key areas under review. These recommendations focus on urgent issues and address national governments, international policymaking institutions, and domestic and international women's rights organizations.

The publication will be widely disseminated in Arabic and English throughout the MENA region and the world. Target audiences for the survey include women's rights advocates, civil society organizations, the media, and policymakers in the countries under review. Freedom House will also make the publication easily accessible to international institutions, NGOs, educational institutions, and global media through its website.

CHECKLIST QUESTIONS

INTERPRETIVE GUIDELINES

Authors were requested to consider the following as conceptual factors while examining and addressing each survey question, both in the narrative and in the scoring process.

De jure and de facto status

For each question, please try to examine both the *de jure* and *de facto* dimensions of the situation under study in order to assess the following:

❖ Existence (or lack) of domestic or internationally recognized laws, policies, and legal protection mechanisms that women can use to advance and secure their rights, including legal institutions, funds, public services, special seats allocated to women, etc.

❖ Actual practices within a society—consider acts and omissions of both state and/or non-state actors to negate or ensure women's de jure rights and freedoms in a country. This survey aims at measuring the *actual* freedom a woman has in a country to exercise her human rights during all stages of her life. Please try to assess the level of *implementation* of laws and policies supporting women's freedom and the obstacles to the practice and realization of these freedoms.

State and Non-State Actors

Please examine each question by measuring the impact of state and non-state actors in facilitating or denying women's freedom. For example, consider the performance of state agents such as prison guards, police, or military who might prevent women from successfully accessing and/or exercising their rights. Also consider acts by non-state actors, such as religious groups who might issue statements to condemn women who take part in politics, or tribe or family members who stop a female family member from benefiting from legal rights accorded to her by domestic law or international human rights standards ratified by the state.

Status of All Groups of Women in a Country

Your report should attempt to review the freedoms of *all* women within a society to exercise their human rights. In your analysis, please consider all ethnic groups, religious groups, cultural groups (including language identity), economic and social classes, urban and rural dwellers, and citizens and noncitizens (including female migrants).

Nondiscrimination and Rights of Women in Comparison with Men

One of the core initiatives of this survey is to examine a woman's right to be free from gender-based discrimination, in all situations, and during all stages of her life. While the overall context of human rights in a country will be noted (e.g. freedom of speech is limited for all persons in Tunisia), the fact that women face restrictions to their free speech rights is still a denial of a universally accepted right. The status of women's freedom does not always need to be determined in comparison to men. In some cases, women have different and special needs, such as maternity leave or protection from gender-based violence, that need to be taken into account and assessed separately. Finally, the aim of our survey is to show the status of women's freedom in light of universally accepted human rights standards that may or may not be present for the men in a country under review, but nonetheless still remain important in their assurance of full and equal rights for women as human beings.

CHECKLIST QUESTIONS FOR THE FIVE KEY AREAS

Section I: Nondiscrimination and Access to Justice

1. To what extent does the national constitution ensure equal rights for men and women as citizens?
2. To what extent do the country's laws and policies provide protection to all women from gender-based discrimination?
3. To what extent do women have the right to full and equal status as citizens (nationals)?
4. To what extent do women have nondiscriminatory access to justice in the country at all levels?

5. To what extent are women treated equally in the penal code and under the criminal laws?

6. To what extent are women protected from gender-based and discriminatory arbitrary arrest, detention, and exile?

7. To what extent is an adult woman recognized as a full person before the court?

8. Has the government ratified CEDAW, and if so, to what extent is the government compliant with implementing the stipulations of CEDAW?

9. To what extent are women's rights groups and/or civil society actors working freely and effectively to promote the status of women's freedoms addressed in this section?

Section II: Autonomy, Security, and Freedom of the Person

1. To what extent do women have the right to freely practice their religion or belief?

2. To what extent do women have the freedom of movement?

3. To what extent are women treated equally in the Personal Status Code (Family Law)?

4. To what extent can women negotiate their full and equal marriage rights?

5. To what extent are women protected from slavery or gender-based slavery-like practices?

6. To what extent are women free from torture, and cruel, inhuman, or degrading punishment?

7. To what extent do women have protection from domestic violence?

8. To what extent are women protected from gender-based violence outside the home?

9. To what extent are women's rights groups and/or civil society actors working freely and effectively to promote the status of women's freedoms addressed in this section?

Section III: Economic Rights and Equal Opportunity

1. To what extent do women have the right to own and have full and independent use of their land and property?

2. To what extent do women have the freedom to have full and independent use of their income and assets?

3. To what extent do women have the right to inheritance?
4. To what extent can women freely enter into business and economic-related contracts and activities at all levels?
5. To what extent are women free to access education at all levels and to be protected from gender-based discrimination within the education system?
6. To what extent do women have the freedom to choose their profession?
7. To what extent are women protected from gender-based discrimination in the area of employment?
8. To what extent do women have gender-specific protections in the workplace, including maternity leave, protections from sexual harassment, and child-care?
9. To what extent are women's rights groups and/or civil society actors working freely and effectively to promote the status of women's freedoms addressed in this section?

Section IV: Political Rights and Civic Voice

1. To what extent do women have the right to peaceful assembly?
2. To what extent do women have the right to freedom of expression?
3. To what extent are women guaranteed the right to participate in competitive and democratic elections with full and equal suffrage?
4. To what extent are women represented in the judiciary?
5. To what extent are women represented in national government (executive) structures?
6. To what extent do women have the right to participate in local assemblies and the national parliament?
7. To what extent can women organize and participate in political parties and processes at all levels?
8. To what extent do women have the freedom to full and equal participation in civic life issues to influence policies and decision making?
9. To what extent do women have the freedom to access and use information to empower themselves in all areas of their civic and political lives?

Section V: Social and Cultural Rights

1. To what extent do women have the freedom to make independent decisions about their health and reproductive rights?
2. To what extent do women have full and equal access to health services?

3. To what extent do women have the freedom to be protected from gender-based harmful traditional practices?
4. To what extent are women protected from gender-based discrimination in their right to own and use housing?
5. To what extent are women free to participate in and influence community life, policies, and social development at local levels?
6. To what extent are women able to participate in and influence media content, including the shaping of women's images in the media?
7. To what extent are women disproportionately affected by poverty due to their gender?
8. To what extent are women and/or women's rights activists free to advocate openly about the promotion and protection of women's human rights in the country?

SCORING SYSTEM

The survey is comprised of 18 narrative country reports and a set of corresponding ratings for each of the five key areas for the country under study. The ratings should not be taken as absolute indicators of all women's freedom in a country, but as a general assessment of the degree of freedom women have within that country to exercise their human rights. While the opinions expressed in each report are those of the report writer, the ratings and scores reflect the consensus of Freedom House, the regional advisors and experts, and the report writers. Each country or territory's key area ratings are presented in the statistics section that precedes the narrative report. These ratings are meant to help in assessing where, in a country, the most immediate attention should focus to improve women's rights. The ratings also serve to measure whether women's rights have experienced setbacks or made progress in a given country since the previous scores were published.

STEPS IN THE RATING PROCESS

The writers have been assigned a checklist of questions for each of the five key areas examined in the survey. Each question from the checklist was awarded a raw score of 1 to 5; the total raw scores from each key area's questions is calculated and averaged. This averaged score reflects a total rating of 1 to 5 for each of the five key areas, demonstrating the degree to which state and non-state actors affect women's freedom within each of the five key areas for that country.

> **A rating of 1** represents a country where women's freedom to exercise their human rights is almost entirely restricted by the actions of state and/or non-state actors. Women have almost no adequate human rights protections and face systematic gender-based discrimination.

A rating of 2 characterizes a country where women's freedom to exercise their human rights is mostly restricted by the actions of state and/or non-state actors. Women have very few adequate human rights protections and they often face gender-based discrimination.

A rating of 3 represents a country where women's freedom to exercise their human rights is sometimes restricted by the actions of state and/or non-state actors. Women have some adequate human rights protections but they are poorly implemented. Women occasionally face gender-based discrimination.

A rating of 4 characterizes a country where women's freedom to exercise their human rights is rarely restricted by the actions of state and/or non-state actors. Women have adequate human rights protections that are mostly implemented. Women rarely face gender-based discrimination.

A rating of 5 represents a country where women's freedom to exercise their human rights is almost never restricted by the actions of state and/or non-state actors. Women have adequate human rights protections that are fully implemented. Women almost never face gender-based discrimination.

ABOUT FREEDOM HOUSE

Freedom House, an independent nongovernmental organization, supports the expansion of freedom in the world. Freedom is possible only in democratic political systems in which the governments are accountable to their own people; the rule of law prevails; and freedoms of expression, association, and belief, as well as respect for the rights of minorities and women, are guaranteed.

Freedom ultimately depends on the actions of committed and courageous men and women. We support nonviolent civic initiatives in societies where freedom is denied or under threat and we stand in opposition to ideas and forces that challenge the right of all people to be free. Freedom House functions as a catalyst for freedom, democracy, and the rule of law through its analysis, advocacy, and action.

❖ **Analysis.** Freedom House's rigorous research methodology has earned the organization a reputation as the leading source of information on the state of freedom around the globe. Since 1972, Freedom House has published *Freedom in the World*, an annual survey of political rights and civil liberties experienced in every country of the world. The survey is complemented by an annual review of press freedom, an analysis of transitions in the post-Communist world, and other publications.

❖ **Advocacy.** Freedom House seeks to encourage American policy-makers, as well as other governments and international institutions, to adopt policies that advance human rights and democracy around the world. Freedom House has been instrumental in the founding of the worldwide Community of Democracies, has actively campaigned for a reformed Human Rights Council at the United Nations, and presses the Millennium Challenge Corporation to adhere to high standards of eligibility for recipient countries.

♣ **Action.** Through exchanges, grants, and technical assistance, Freedom House provides training and support to human rights defenders, civil society organizations, and members of the media in order to strengthen indigenous reform efforts in countries around the globe.

Founded in 1941 by Eleanor Roosevelt, Wendell Willkie, and other Americans concerned with mounting threats to peace and democracy, Freedom House has long been a vigorous proponent of democratic values and a steadfast opponent of dictatorships of the far left and the far right. The organization's diverse Board of Trustees is composed of a bipartisan mix of business and labor leaders, former senior government officials, scholars, and journalists who agree that the promotion of democracy and human rights abroad is vital to America's interests abroad.